THE
INTERNATIONAL ENCYCLOPÆDIC DICTIONARY

of

PHILATELICS

R. SCOTT CARLTON

Published by

**krause
publications**

700 E. State Street • Iola, WI 54990-0001
Telephone: 715/445-2214

Please call or write for our free catalog.
Our toll-free number to place an order or obtain a free catalog is 800-258-0929
or please use our regular business telephone 715-445-2214
for editorial comment and further information.

Library of Congress Catalog Number: 96-076695
ISBN: 0-87341-448-9

Printed in the United States of America

769.56
CAR

Gratefully Dedicated
to my Friends and Colleagues
at the
American Philatelic Society
for the
generous technical assistance
and constant encouragement
they have given me.

Appreciation is also expressed to
R. J. Sutton, Kenneth A. Wood,
Stewart T. Bailey, John W. Scott,
and the other philatelic scholars,
past and present,
whose efforts paved the way
for this present work.

.... *R. Scott Carlton*

British Guiana One Cent Magenta

[Photo courtesy of the American Philatelic Society]

Table of Contents

Encyclopædic Dictionary

The purpose of the Encyclopædic Dictionary is to provide definitions and relevant information on a wide range of philatelic topics and to give accurate and concise English translations of foreign philatelic terminology. The translations and many of the encyclopædic articles, including a collection of scholarly essays on selected topics, were supplied by some of the world's top philatelic and linguistic experts. The articles cover the entire gamut of stamp collecting from pre-adhesive covers to present-day postage stamps, revenues, cinderellas, booklets, and all other relevant areas of philately. Also included are biographies of key people whose faces grace our stamps.

Roman Alphabet

The Roman Alphabet section includes words in English, most European languages, Tagalog, and Turkish, plus romanized transliterations of non-Roman languages (Chinese, Hebrew, Greek, etc.). When transliterations are used, either the official versions have been chosen (such as the Pinyin system of Chinese) or the spellings most likely to be seen in English documents are included.

Alphabetization

This dictionary is arranged in strict English alphabetical order, meaning that diacritical marks, punctuation, spaces between words in multi-word entries, and capitalization are ignored. The alphabetizing does not take into account unusual letter combinations or configurations found in many other languages. For example, *ch* is one single letter of the Spanish alphabet (*a, b, c, ch, d, e,* etc.); *chelín* would follow *colección* in a normal Spanish dictionary, but in the present work *chelín* precedes *colección*. Also, the Turkish alphabet has both a dotted "I" (*İ* and *i*) and an undotted "I" (*I* and *ı*). Because there is no equivalent in English, these differences are ignored here. Foreign letters which do not resemble English letters are alphabetized as logically as possible, such as the German *ß* which is positioned as "ss."

Capitalization

In the Roman, Greek, and Cyrillic sections, entry words are only capitalized if they are *always* capitalized in normal use, such as proper names, accepted names of certain stamps and types (e.g., Allegorical Group Type), all German nouns, etc.

Definitions

Many of the entries have non-philatelic as well as philatelic meanings, but the only definitions listed here are those with philatelic application. Every effort has been made to provide accurate and up-to-date definitions. Some archaic words and non-current definitions are included (and listed as such) because they are still found in English texts.

Abbreviations

The following abbreviations are used throughout this encyclopædic dictionary:

Ar.	Arabic	*Ger.*	German	*Pol.*	Polish
Bul.	Bulgarian	*Grk.*	Greek	*Port.*	Portuguese
Bur.	Burmese	*Heb.*	Hebrew	*Rom.*	Romanian
Cher.	Cherokee	*Hin.*	Hindi	*Russ.*	Russian
Chin.	Chinese[1]	*Hun.*	Hungarian	*Serb.*	Serbian
Cr.	Croatian	*Ice.*	Icelandic	*Srb.-Cr.*	Serbo-Croatian
Cz.	Czech	*Indo.*	Indonesian	*Slov.*	Slovak
Cz.-Sl.	Czech-Slovak	*Ire.*	Irish	*Span.*	Spanish
Dan.	Danish	*Ital.*	Italian	*Swed.*	Swedish
Dut.	Dutch	*Jpn.*	Japanese	*Tag.*	Tagalog
Eng.	English	*Kor.*	Korean	*Turk.*	Turkish
Finn.	Finnish	*Lat.*	Latin	*Viet.*	Vietnamese
Fr.	French	*Nor.*	Norwegian	*Wel.*	Welsh

Mid.	Middle	*c.*	noun, common	*m.-c.*	masculine-common[2]
abbr.	abbreviation	*f.*	noun, feminine		
q.v.	*quod vide* (cross-reference notation)	*f.adj.*	feminine adjective	*n.*	noun, neuter
		f.-c.	feminine-common[2]	*n.adj.*	neuter adjective
		m.	noun, masculine	*pl.*	plural
adj.	adjective	*m.adj.*	masculine adjective	*r.*	reale[3]
adv.	adverb			*v.*	verb

[1]Chinese transliterations appear either in the nineteenth-century Wade-Giles (*w.g.*) version which spells the name of the Chinese capital as *Peking,* or in the more recent Pinyin (*p.y.*) style in which that city is written *Beijing.* Similarly, words printed in Chinese characters can either be the traditional Complex Character (*c.c.*) still used in Taiwan, or in the updated Simplified Character (*s.c.*) developed in the P.R.C.

[2]Some parts of the Dutch-speaking world still retain the masculine and feminine genders of nouns, while other areas have adopted the concept of common gender. Dutch nouns that fall into these categories are designated *m.-c.* and *f.-c.* in this dictionary.

[3]Reale is a form of neuter which corresponds somewhat to the common gender. It is found only in the Swedish language.

A a

a. [*abbr.*] about; almost.

A 1. [*abbr.*] avo (unit of currency of Macao and Timor).

2. [*o/p*] AVIANCA (overprint authorizes use of Colombian postage stamps by that country's national airline in the early 1950s); indication of departmental use by the Government Architect on stamps of South Australia.

AA [*Fr.*] *Armée Autrichienne* (Austrian Army). Abbreviation used as a pre-adhesive postmark.

aanschaffing (*f.-c.*) [*Dut.*] acquisition.

AB Army Bag. Abbreviation used as a pre-adhesive postmark.

Abart (*f.*) [*Ger.*] variety.

abbreviazione (*f.*) [*Ital.*] abbreviation.

Abduction of Europa See *Europa and the Bull.*

Abierta por la Censura [*Span.*] Opened by the Censor. A censor mark from Spanish-speaking countries. See *censored mail.*

Abkürzung (*f.*) [*Ger.*] abbreviation.

ablösen (*v.*) [*Ger.*] to peel.

abonament kasowany (*m.*) [*Pol.*] precancel.

abreviatura (*f.*) [*Span., Port.*] abbreviation.

abril [*Span., Port.*] April.

abstempeln (*v.*) [*Ger.*] to cancel.

Abstempelung (*f.*) [*Ger.*] cancellation.

Abwertung (*f.*) [*Ger.*] devaluation.

Académie de Philatélie, l' Academy of Philately, a prestigious French organization founded in 1928. Membership is limited to forty. Foreigners are eligible only as Corresponding Members. The Academy publishes a scholarly journal, *Documents Philatéliques*, introduced in 1959.

accolated [also known as *conjoined* or *jugate.*] Postage stamp design showing two or more heads or busts which face in the same direction and overlap. See *conjoined* for additional information and illustrations.

accolé [*Fr.*] accolated, conjoined[*q.v.*], jugate.

accompte est requis, un [*Fr.*] deposit required.

A.C.C.P. [*abbr.*] Azerbaijan Soviet Socialist Republic. [These are actually Cyrillic letters that resemble Roman letters.]

accumulation Unsorted and usually unclassified and unattributed mixture of stamps or covers. The term is often used to describe cancelled stamps offered in bulk which are not first sorted as to country of origin, denomination, or whatever, and are sold on an as-is basis.

aceitam-se cartões de crédito [*Port.*] credit cards accepted.

acélba vésés [*Hun.*] steel engraving.

A Censurar en Destino [*Span.*] Pending censorship on arrival. A censor mark from Spanish-speaking countries. Also sometimes written as *Pendiente de Censura.* See *censored mail* for additional information.

acheter (*v.*) [*Fr.*] to buy.

acheteur (*m.*) [*Fr.*] buyer.

à cheval (Canada)

à cheval [*Fr.*] on horseback. The term refers either to an "action" scene or a stationary position.

achiziție (*f.*) [*Rom.*] acquisition.

acht [*Ger., Dut.*] eight.

achtzig [*Ger.*] eighty.

acid paper Some philatelists are fearful that their collections are literally disintegrating because many rare stamps were printed on acid paper. The problem is legitimate and needs to be addressed, yet there may be no viable solution.

Paper is made of cellulose fibers. In the early days of paper making, the fibers came from cotton or linen rags pulped to separate the fibers. Those seventeenth and eighteenth century papers have stood the test of time very well.

For philatelists, the problem began in the late nineteenth century when it was found that cellulose in wood could be separated from lignins by treating wood chips with solutions of sulfite. This paper was much cheaper to produce than rag paper, and many books, pamphlets, and other material of the late nineteenth century and the first half of the twentieth century were produced from such pulp.

These papers contained residues of the sulfur compounds which were or became acidic. Sizings such as aluminum sulfate (alum) which were added to decrease the absorption of inks made the problem worse. The acid acts as a catalyst for the hydrolysis of the cellulose, breaking down the fibers and making the paper brittle. As a catalyst, tiny amounts can cause the reaction of a large amount of reactant (the cellulose) without themselves being consumed. Therefore, the catalyst is not consumed and continues to create damage. To sum this up in layman's terms, acidic paper disintegrates by destroying itself from within.

Three approaches can be used to attack the problem of acid paper, but none is ideal for stamps: 1. Treating the paper with solutions of magnesium or calcium hydrogen carbonate (bicarbonate). This is time consuming and necessitates getting the material wet. 2. Treating the paper with a gaseous base such as ammonia or an organic amine. This does not last, as the ammonium ions formed eventually break down, releasing the base and leaving the acidic compound to continue to do its damage. 3. Treating the paper with diethyl zinc, which decomposes to form zinc oxide which remains in the paper and permanently neutralizes the acid. Diethyl zinc is a volatile compound which ignites spontaneously in air. The procedure can be carried out only using vacuum chambers. The Library of Congress has built chambers to handle thousands of books at one time.

But treating books is not the same as treating rare stamps. The Library of Congress is concerned about preserving its books because it wants to save the knowledge contained within them. Stamps, on the other hand, are treasured for the medium as well as for the message. A rare stamp can be destroyed even if its paper is preserved. The treatment methods mentioned above can alter or destroy gum, fade or change colors, and do other types of permanent damage to rare stamps. The third treatment, the use of diethyl zinc, can turn a stamp into dust in seconds if the method is not applied correctly.

Mercifully, many fine postage stamps have *not* been printed on disintegrating paper, so the problem is not universal. Yet many of today's philatelic treasures will not be around for future generations of collectors to enjoy unless satisfactory treatment methods are found.

[Contributed by Halbert Carmichael.]

acolado [*Span., Port.*] accolated, conjoined[q.v.], jugate.

acolat; acostat [*Rom.*] accolated, jugate, conjoined[q.v.].

à condition [*Fr.*] on approval.

acquisto (*m.*) [*Ital.*] acquisition.

across-the-lines mail Mail carried by express companies as a special postal route starting June 1, 1861, when mail was suspended between the North and the South during the U.S. Civil War (1861-1865). The Adams Company and the American Express Company carried such mail for a 25 cent fee until President Abraham Lincoln suspended all communication between the Union (the North) and the Confederacy (the South) on August 16, 1861.

[Contributed by Richard Corwin. Lawrence L. Shenfield, *Confederate States of America: The Special Routes*, pp. 16-31; *Dietz Confederate State Catalog*, p. 193.]

U.S. domestic "additive" stamp

additive stamp Unusual provisional[q.v.] stamp issued by the United States in conjunction with its emission of the "F" domestic stamp. The "additive" stamp is an undenominated stamp which was ultimately valued at four cents and was intended to be used with a 25c stamp (the postal rate prior to the increase) to equal the new postal rate, whatever it might be. The values of the "F" stamp and of the "additive" stamp were unknown when the stamps were printed, because the exact rate of increase had not yet been determined. See *domestic stamp*.

A.E.F. [*Fr. abbr.*] *Afrique Equatoriale Française* (French Equatorial Africa).

adhesive 1. A chemical substance such as glue, paste, or gum which will cause one object to adhere to another.

2. Philatelic term for any postage, fiscal, postage due, newspaper, military, revenue, or other stamp printed on a gummed label. This is in contrast to imprinted stamps which are found on postal stationery.

Adler (*m.*) [*Ger.*] eagle.

Admirals: Canada, Rhodesia, and New Zealand

Admiral 1. Series of Canadian stamps issued from 1911 to 1925 portraying King George V in a naval uniform. Eleven denominations were represented in this series ranging from one cent to one dollar.

2. New Zealand stamps of 2 and 3 shillings which show George V in his Admiral's uniform. These 1926 stamps exhibit a design different from that of the Canadian *Admirals* described above.

3. Southern Rhodesian's first stamps (1924-30) are also referred to as *Admirals*. They were printed in thirteen denominations from one-half penny to 5 shillings. Again, the design is not the same as those of Canada and New Zealand.

[Michael Madesker, "The *Admiral* Booklets of Canada," Part 1, *Canadian Philatelist*, March-April 1985, pp. 108-124; et al.]

adó [*Hun.*] tax.

a due colori [*Ital.*] bicolored, bicoloured.

adviesprijs (*m.-c.*) [*Dut.*] suggested bid.

æblegrøn [*Dan.*] apple green.

A.E.D. [*Fr.*] *Affranchie a l'Étranger jusqu'a Destination*. Pre-adhesive postmark, usually seen in the form of an oval postmark with a code number indicating the post office at the border. It was used after 1827 on mail from the Kingdom of Sardinia to France where the postal rate had been prepaid by the sender.

Three of the 1912 Dodecanese overprints

Aegean Islands *Dodecanese* is the Greek word for "Twelve Islands"; the term was used in ancient times for a group of islands in the Aegean Sea and was revived at the beginning of the 20th century. The twelve islands in question are Casos, Karpathos, Kharki, Tilos, Symi, Nisiros, Atypalaia (Stampalia), Kos, Kalimnos, Leros, Lipsos, and Patmos.

Italian interest in the region began to surface with the blockade of Crete (1897), followed by the opening of an Italian post office at Canea in 1900. During the Italo-Turkish conflict in Libya (1911), it became apparent that in order to win the war the Italians had to engage the Turks on the sea. Although the islands occupied by the Italians during the Italo-Turkish war in Libya were originally thirteen (the twelve named above plus Rhodes), and later became fourteen when Italy acquired Castellorizo from the French (January 1921), the name Dodecanese remained unchanged. Some special circumstances favored the Italian acquisition of the islands. In 1909, Ottoman rule became unpopular as compulsory military service was introduced and enforced. This triggered massive emigration to Egypt, Australia, and the Americas.

In 1911 the islanders formed an underground committee for the liberation of the Dodecanese from Turkish rule. On May 5, 1912, an Italian fleet of 42 vessels occupied the archipelago, and in due course all the Turkish garrisons on the various islands capitulated. On May 21, three stamps depicting the Sun God Apollo and inscribed "Community of Leaders" were issued by a committee of the chiefs of the islands who had assembled in Calymnos. These stamps had been lithographed by the Aspiotis Brothers Press of Corfu. By mid-June Italian stamps were available at local post offices, and the self-rule stamps issued earlier by the independentists were confiscated bringing to an end any dream of autonomy.

EGEO overprint

In September 1912 a decree issued by the Commissioner for Civilian Affairs attached to the occupying forces authorized the over-printing of two Italian definitive stamps (25c and 50c) with the inscription "EGEO." The overprint was locally executed by the Military Printing Works of the Sixth Division. Italian supremacy in the Dodecanese was sanctioned by the Lausanne-Ouchy Treaty on October 18, 1912. Accordingly, Italians agreed to return the islands to Turkey after the Turkish evacuated Libya.

On December 1, 1912, a set of seven definitive stamps overprinted with the name of each individual island was issued for the thirteen Aegean Islands. The overprints were typographically executed by the Governmental Printing Works at Turin, Italy. However, and irrespective of the overprints, all these new stamps were valid for use throughout the Aegean area. It must be pointed out that a Russian post office had been in operation in Rhodes since the 1860s. After the First World War, on August 10, 1920, the Treaty of Sevres awarded Rhodes and Castellorizo to Italy. The Dodecanese islands, however, were to be handed over to Greece. But through pro-crastination Italy evaded this clause of the agreement. The stamps with the names of the thirteen islands were gradually phased out and substituted by current Italian definitive stamps.

On March 1, 1921, Castellorizo was handed over to Italy and on July 11, 1922, Italian stamps overprinted "CASTELROSSO" were issued. In 1923, and with British mediation, Italy signed the Treaty of Lausanne with Kemalist Turkey confirming the acquisition of the Aegean Islands. Disillusioned islanders continued to emigrate, while the Italians carried out massive structural and agricultural developments.

The issue of special stamps for the Aegean Islands was resumed on May 19, 1929, and a set of nine definitive stamps inscribed "RODI" was issued. The same designation was used later for airmail, express, postage due, and parcel post stamps. The use of Italian definitive stamps was supposed to be discontinued but in reality was widely tolerated.

On October 20, 1930, the official name of the possession "ISOLE ITALIANE DELL'EGEO"

(Italian Islands of the Aegean) was used for the first time to overprint three airmail values of the Ferrucci set issued on the same date. The Ferrucci (1930) and Garibaldi (1932) sets were also overprinted with the names of each of the fourteen islands in the archipelago. During the Second World War the airfields of Rhodes, Kos, and Leros became the main Axis bases for air raids against British forces in Egypt. In April 1941 Greece capitulated; the following month Italian forces completed the occupation of the Cyclades Islands.

The ousting of Mussolini during the summer of 1943 was followed by Italy's signing of an armistice with the Allies. On September 8, Germans began to take over Rhodes; the operation was completed in a matter of days and the Italian governor, Admiral Inigo Campioni, was sent to Germany as a prisoner of war and was later executed. The Aegean under German military rule was, however, administratively run by Italian civilians. Between November 1943 and February 1945 several colonial stamps were issued despite the takeover. These stamps were mostly definitive stamps overprinted with surcharges in aid of refugees and victims of war. In the meantime, Italian soldiers had been held in eight internment camps on Rhodes and were gradually sent to Germany.

Greek stamp overprinted Σ Δ Δ

German forces evacuated Greece in October 1944. Their counterparts in the Aegean were cut off from sea-route supplies and mail. Only air links were possible, thus impacting severely the influx of mail to and from German soldiers in the area. As a result, rationed concessionary stamps for Field Post overprinted "INSELPOST"

(Island Post) were issued. On December 22, Italian postal authorities made available quantities of the 5c Rhodes definitive stamps to the Germans who overprinted them with the inscription "WEIHNACHTEN 1944" (Christmas 1944).

In May 1945 the German capitulation in the Aegean was formally ratified in Berlin and a British Military Administration was established in Rhodes. British stamps overprinted M.E.F. (Middle East Forces) were placed in use. On March 31, 1947, British Military Administration ended and the Aegean was handed over to Greece. The following day a Greek stamp overprinted with the Greek initials Σ.Δ.Δ. (*Stratiotiki Dioikisis Dodecanissou*— Military Administration of the Dodecanese Islands) was issued. Seven denominations with the same overprint were added on September 21. On November 20, these overprints were withdrawn and replaced by ordinary Greek stamps beginning with the "Restoration of the Dodecanese" definitive series. On March 7, 1948, the Aegean Islands were officially annexed to the Kingdom of Greece.

[Contributed by Giorgio Migliavacca.]

ægte [*Dan.*] authentic, genuine.

ægthedsbevis (*n.*) [*Dan.*] authentication mark.

A.E.J.F. [*Fr.*] *Affranchie a l'Étranger Jusqu'a la Frontiere.* Pre-adhesive postmark on prepaid letters transiting in France.

ændre (*v.*) [*Dan.*] to alter.

aerofilatelia (*f.*) [*Span.*] aerophilately.

aërofilatelie (*f./c.*) [*Dut.*] aerophilately.

aerofilatelistyka (*f.*) [*Pol.*] aerophilately.

aërogram (*n.*) [*Dut.*] aerogramme, air letter.

aerograma (*m.*) [*Span., Ital., Port.*] aerogramme, air letter.

aerogramma (*m.*) [*Ital.*] aerogramme, air letter.

aérogramme (*m.*) [*Fr.*] aerogramme. See *air letter.*

aeronaute (*m.*); **aerostier** (*m.*) [*Fr.*] Names given to crew members who operated the Balloon Post[q.v.] service of Paris in 1870-71 during the Siege of Paris in the Franco-Prussian War.

aérophilatélie (*f.*) [*Fr.*] aerophilately.

aerophilately The study and collecting of airmail stamps and covers. Included is the examination of related materials such as Zeppelin stamps, etiquettes, aerogrammes, Lindbergh overprints[q.q.v.], and anything else associated with the shipping of mail by air.

Flying in the 1910s and 1920s was regarded by the general public as a great adventure, and the first pilots were viewed almost as legendary figures. Many early airmail stamps featured well-known flyers or airplanes, so the stamps themselves added something to the mystique of flying. Shortly after his historic one-man flight to Paris in 1927, Charles Lindbergh's plane, the "Spirit of St. Louis," was featured on a U.S. airmail stamp. The following year, Cuba overprinted its airmail stamps with a tribute to Lindbergh.

Willingly or not, aerophilately includes the study of errors, because some of America's most famous and desirable stamps are error versions of an airmail issue. The Jenny[q.v.] invert, a 1918 24c airmail stamp showing a Curtis Jenny flying upside-down, is regarded by many collectors as the most popular and interesting stamp in U.S. history. A lesser-known version of that same stamp is one in which the plane is right-side up, but poor registration of the red and blue plates caused the plane to be printed so low on the stamp that it is sitting on top of the word *CENTS*. This stamp is appropriately known as the "grounded plane" variety.

Also see *airmail*.

aetos αετός (*m.*) [*Grk.*] eagle.

affrancare (*v.*) [*Ital.*] to frank.

affranchir (*v.*) [*Fr.*] to frank.

affranchissement (*m.*) [*Fr.*] postage.

A.F.I.S. Abbreviation for postwar Italian Somaliland: *Amministrazione Fiduciaria Italiana della Somalia* (Italian Trusteeship of Somalia).

On November 21, 1949, the former Italian colony of Somalia was placed under United Nations Trusteeship when the General Assembly voted that Somalia be given her independence after a transition period of ten years (1950-1960). At the time, Italy was not yet a member of the United Nations. Preparations for independence were set in motion during the 1950s, both in British

Somaliland and in the former Somalia Italiana. Full independence was given to the British colony on June 26, 1960; on July 1st, it joined with the former Italian part to create the independent Somali Republic.

A.F.I.S. stamp for Italian Somaliland

During the transition of the 1950s, A.F.I.S. issued 151 stamps and one souvenir sheet. Many stamps issued during this decade tend to convey the message that Italy was doing a good job with her former colony. The various Mogadishu Trade Fairs, anti-TB, and anti-leprosy campaigns were philatelically publicized by Somali stamps that reflected the rapid progress, under Italian tutelage, towards independence. Most of the postwar stamps continued to be printed in Italy in photogravure by the State Printing Institute (Istituto Poligrafico di Stato, recently renamed I.P.Z.S.: Italian Government Mint and State Printing Works).

[Contributed by Giorgio Migliavacca.]

afkorting (*f.-c.*) [*Dut.*] abbreviation.

África del Sur [*Span.*]; **África do Sul** [*Port.*] South Africa. [Note: the accent mark over the capital "A" is usually omitted.]

Africa Orientale Italiana [*Ital.*] Italian East Africa[q.v.]. An amalgamation of Ethiopia, Eritrea, and Somalia created by Italy on June 1, 1936.

Afrique du Sud [*Fr.*] South Africa.

Afryka Południowa [*Pol.*] South Africa.

afskilning (*c.*) [*Dan.*] separation.

afstempelen (*v.*) [*Dut.*] to cancel.

afstempeling (*f./c.*) [*Dut.*] cancellation; obliteration.

folded air letter (South Africa)

afstempeling op bestelling (*f./c.*) [*Dut.*] cancelled to order.

aftokratoras αυτοκράτορας (*m.*) [*Grk.*] emperor.

afwijking (*f./c.*) [*Dut.*] variety.

A.G. [*o/p*] Attorney General's Department. Seen on official stamps of South Australia.

AGDP [*Ital.*] *Amministrazione Generale Delle Poste* (General Administration of the Posts). Pre-adhesive postmark in the Kingdom of Two Sicilies.

agol עָגֹל [*Heb.*] round.

agosto [*Port., Ital., Span.*] August.

águila (*f.*) [*Span.*] eagle.

agujero (*m.*) [*Span.*] hole.

Ağustos [*Turk.*] August.

A.H.PD. [*o/p*] Angra, Horta, and Ponta Delgada. Overprint on 1906-1910 stamps of Portugal for use in the Azores.

AIDS [Acquired Immune Deficiency Syndrome.] AIDS is a devasting disease that seemed to come out of nowhere in the late 1970s and quickly became the greatest plague of the twentieth century. Its primary mode of transmission is through unprotected sex.

AIDS Awareness stamp (U.S.)

The AIDS stamp in the illustration features a red ribbon, an object which has become associated with AIDS awareness. The U.S. Postal Service came under fire from religious conservatives who claimed that AIDS was God's punishment of homosexuals, and that the Postal Service had no right to issue such a stamp. Protest covers[q.v.] were prepared and sent through the mail.

But many medical experts defended the stamp by pointing out that AIDS is a virus which can be caught by anyone, proof of which lies in the fact that the vast majority of people worldwide who have contracted the disease are heterosexual.

The stamp has become very popular among AIDS activists. Many of these stamps have been encased in plastic holders with a pin on the back and are intended to be worn in lieu of an actual red ribbon. They are sold at a premium with the profits going towards AIDS research and other AIDS-related causes.

[Contributed by James Oliver.]

A.I.F. [*abbr.*] Australian Imperial Forces.

aihe- [*Finn.*] topical; thematic.

aigle (*f.*) [*Fr.*] eagle.

air letter; aérogramme [*Fr.*] Thin sheet of writing paper with gummed flaps and an imprinted postage stamp. After the message is written on the sheet, the paper is folded and sealed to form a type of envelope. This lightweight, self-contained letter goes by airmail at a reduced cost. Enclosures are not permitted. (See previous page for illustration).

airlift stamp (U.S.)

airlift stamp U.S. $1 stamp used for shipping parcels to servicemen and women stationed overseas or in Alaska, Hawaii, or Puerto Rico. They were first issued in 1968 and were prompted by postal needs arising from the Vietnam War.

At first, they were valid for all regular postage. But in April 1969, the regulation was changed making them valid only for paying the postage or fees for special services on airmail articles.

airmail stamp (Nicaragua) with surcharge

airmail; air mail; air post Airmail service started not with planes but with balloons. The first documented attempt at air delivery was by a professor, John Wise, on August 17, 1859. He attempted to transport mail in his balloon *Jupiter* from Lafayette, Indiana, to New York. Unfortunately, his balloon came down shortly after takeoff, landing in Crawfordsville, Indiana.

The Siege of Paris in the Franco-Prussian War prompted another attempt at airmail transport. The Balloon Post of Paris[q.v.] was the world's first official airmail service. It operated from September 23, 1870, to January 28, 1871. Mail leaving Paris went by balloon, and mail coming in arrived by pigeon. Out-going covers were marked *Par Ballon Monté* ("By piloted balloon") and are highly prized by collectors today.

It has never been established for certain who carried the first airmail by motorized aircraft, but there are several good candidates. A flight was apparently made in August 1908 from Paris to St. Nazaire, France. Another possibility is Hans Grad, who is said to have carried mail in an airplane in 1909 on behalf of the Chamber of Commerce of the town of Bork in Germany. Claude Graham White carried mail on a flight from Blackpool to Southport, England, in 1910.

The progress of airmail was quite amazing, if we remember that the first flight of any kind in a heavier-than-air mechanized craft had only taken place just a few years earlier in 1903 by the Wright Brothers. Within a decade of that first flight, many different organizations, some private-based and some government-sponsored, were experimenting to determine the best methods of carrying the mail using this new technology.

The first government-sponsored airmail delivery by motorized aircraft took place between Allahabad and Naini, India, on February 8, 1911. Henri Pequet, the pilot, is believed to have carried 6,500 pieces of mail on that flight. The first airmail flown on a regular basis took place in September 1911 between London and Windsor, England. This service was known as "Coronation Airmail" because of its tie-in with the coronation of King George V. Approximately 130,000 letters and postcards were transported between the two cities. They were postmarked *First United Kingdom Aerial Post*.

The first international airmail deliveries took place between Austria and Ukraine in 1918. By 1919 airmail service was available between London and Paris. Within a very few years, airmail service connected much of the world.

The United States put out some semi-official "Balloon Postage" stamps in 1877 in conjunction with balloon flights performed by Samuel Archer King. Only two on-cover specimens are known to survive. Nevertheless, Italy is credited with having issued the first true airmail stamps, some existing express stamps overprinted to accommodate an experimental service between Rome and Turin. Austria was another early provider of airmail stamps. That nation issued special stamps on March 30, 1918, to serve the above-mentioned international deliveries between itself and Ukraine.

Over the next half-century, virtually all nations issued airmail stamps. As a rule, these stamps were put out specifically for that purpose and were not valid for surface mail. By the 1980s, that rule was not always enforced. In the latter decades of the twentieth century, airmail stamps have lost much of their importance simply because a great deal of mail is shipped by air whether it is specified that way or not. The United States, for example, no longer has domestic airmail service. Current U.S. airmail stamps are used exclusively for overseas air deliveries.

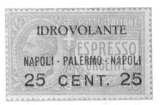

one of the first true airmail stamps: Italy, 1917

Carrying mail by air without extra charge is not a new idea. The Empire Air Mail Scheme, commonly known as *All-Up Service*, was initiated in Great Britain in 1937. Its purpose was to air ship all first-class mail between Britain and the various Commonwealth members. The service was discontinued at the outbreak of World War II.

The study and collecting of airmail stamps and covers is called *aerophilately[q.v.]*. This field also includes the study of specific related materials such as Zeppelin stamps, etiquettes, aerogrammes, Lindbergh overprints[q.q.v.], and anything else associated with the shipping of mail by air.

[R. J. Sutton, *The Stamp Collector's Encyclopædia*, p. 14-15; Kenneth A. Wood, *This Is Philately*, Vol. I, pp. 11-12.]

aito [*Finn.*] authentic, genuine.

aitousmerkki [*Finn.*] authentication mark.

ajánlani (*v.*) [*Hun.*] to offer.

ajánlat [*Hun.*] an offer.

ajánlott ár [*Hun.*] suggested bid.

akirosis kopis ακύρωση κοπής (*f.*) [*Grk.*] cut cancellation.

akkvisisjon (*m.*) [*Nor.*] acquisition.

äkta [*Swed.*] genuine.

aláírás [*Hun.*] signature.

Alankomaat [*Finn.*] Holland; The Netherlands.

alaosa [*Finn.*] bottom.

alăturat [*Rom.*] accolated, conjoined[q.v.], jugate.

alb [*Rom.*] white.

Albania [World War II occupations] The 1913 Treaty of London gave independence to

Albania. The stamps of the new country depicting Skander-Beg (also known as Gjergji Kastrioti) were printed in Italy.

Following a period of anarchy and unrest during World War I and with the help of Italy, the country stabilized itself. The cordial relationship with Rome improved as years went by, and quite a few pre-war stamp issues of Albania were printed by the Italian Government Printing Works.

The situation deteriorated in 1939, when King Zog refused to align Albania with the Axis. Mussolini, who would not take no for an answer, occupied the country in a matter of days. On April 12, 1939, Victor Emmanuel III became King of Albania. To mark the event, Albanian stamps were overprinted to indicate the change. This was to be followed by definitives depicting the Italian monarch. The definitive series blended the image of Victor Emmanuel with local pictorial elements and featured Albanian inscriptions and currency. Although the fasces was also a design element, later issues featured the Albanian coat of arms, included to circumvent local criticism. Metropolitan postal rates were adopted and the use of Italian definitives was tolerated for about twelve months.

In June 1941, Albania expanded its boundaries at the expense of Yugoslavia. As a result, some fifteen post offices in the Kossovo and Metohija regions became part of the Albanian postal network. Covers with stamps of Albania under Italian rule cancelled by postmarks of these post offices exist but are quite elusive.

Mbledhja Kushtetuëse 12-IV-1939 XVII overprint

Only the first issue of definitive stamps and airmail stamps (Scott 299-309 and C43-45) issued on April 12, 1939, was overprinted *Mbledhja/ Kushtetuëse/ 12-IV-1939/ XVII* by

the Tirana-based Luarasi Press utilizing Albanian stamps. The inscription served as a reminder of the decision taken by a "puppet" Constituent Assembly which had met in April of that year to offer the Albanian crown to King Victor Emmanuel III. The roman numerals shown at the bottom of the overprint referred to the year of the fascist era.

Not listed in Scott is a set of four 1929 *Imperiale* stamps of Italy overprinted with a bilingual inscription reading *REGNO D'ITALIA/ MBRETNIJA SHQIPTARE.* Some 50,000 sets were printed in 1940 and sent to Albania aboard an Italian vessel that was sunk en route by enemy action; only about 200 sets are said to have survived. Some of these stamps are known to have forged postmarks or forged overprints.

man in national attire: King Zog?

The 1939-40 definitive had better luck and saw a great degree of acceptance from the occupied country. The 1 qindar in particular was exceedingly popular with Albanians and stock were quickly depleted, leaving Italian authorities rather perplexed. It was soon discovered that the stamp featured a man in national attire that Albanians had somehow identified as King Zog. When Italian authorities examined the stamp, they found more than a coincidental resemblance to the king, so the sale of 1 qindar stamps was terminated.

Albania became a springboard for the invasion of Greece, and on October 28, 1940, Italian troops moved into that country. But an adverse terrain and heavy snowfalls impeded any significant penetration. By November 22, Greece was counter-attacking, and Korytsa, the historical capital of northern Epirus, with a strong Greek ethnic presence, was occupied by

Greek troops. To mark what the Greeks regarded as the liberation of southern Albania, on December 10, 1940, Greece overprinted seventeen definitive stamps with the Greek inscription ΕΛΛΗΝΙΚΗ ΔΙΟΙΚΗΣΙΣ meaning "Greek Administration." At the same time, three charity stamps and five postage dues were similarly overprinted. On March 1, 1941, the set of Greek Youth Organization stamps and its airmail appendage were overprinted, this time in red, with the same words.

Greek stamp overprinted ΕΛΛΗΝΙΚΗ ΔΙΟΙΚΗΣΙΣ
("Greek Administration")

On July 25, 1943, Mussolini was toppled and Italy signed an armistice with the Allies which was made public on September 8, plunging Albania into civil war. German troops flooded Albania and a truce with the partisans was negotiated. Thirteen definitive stamps (1939-40) and the 25 qindar special delivery stamp of Italian Albania were overprinted *14/ Shtator/ 1943* in red, marking the date of the German takeover. The ink used for this overprint was carmine red for all denominations except for the 15 qindar stamp (gray-lilac) and the special delivery stamp (carmine-brown). On September 22, 1944, a set of seven stamps in aid of war refugees was issued by Albania under German occupation; the 25 q. + 10 q. is known imperforate, and imperforate horizontally.

In mid-1944, with the U.S.S.R. army breaking through as far as Yugoslavia, the Germans began a swift evacuation of the area leaving a small force to hold the fort. General Hoxha was then able to free the country, and on October 22 he proclaimed Albania a democratic republic. With communist and Yugoslav help, the Albanian communists were able to win victories over the various partisan factions, and by July 1945 Hoxha was firmly in charge of the situation. On January 4, 1945 (although some catalogues say October 1944), selected denominations of the 1939-40 definitives of the Italian regime were overprinted with the inscription *QEVERIJA/ DEMOKRAT./ W SHQIPERISE/ 22-X-1944* to celebrate the liberation of the country.

[Contributed by Giorgio Migliavacca.]

Albert I King of the Belgians. Born 1875; died in 1934 from a fall while mountain climbing.

King Albert was perhaps the most popular Belgian king in history. He was well-educated and well-traveled, and he was a staunch believer in democracy. His greatest challenge came in 1913 when he was informed of Germany's plans for war by Kaiser Wilhelm II. He immediately warned France. The next year he notified Wilhelm that Belgium would remain neutral, but the Kaiser ignored Albert's letter and proceeded to invade Belgium. Albert personally took command of the Belgian army and conducted a successful delaying action against the invading Germans. Throughout the war, he remained with his troops.

In 1919, he made a successful plea to the Allies to abolish the Treaty of London which made Belgium neutral ground, vulnerable to foreign invasion. Because of his actions, Belgian neutrality was not incorporated into the Treaty of Versailles.

Albert was killed in a mountain climbing accident in 1934. His son, Leopold III, succeeded to the throne. But when faced with invading German armies in World War II, Leopold's troops were surrounded and quickly surrendered. Leopold was accused of treason and ultimately lost his throne.

The most notable stamps featuring Albert I is the set known as *Tin Hat*[q.v.], a 1919 series picturing him wearing a World War I-style trench hat. It symbolizes his courage and leadership.

albino Error usually caused by an uninked impression made by a printing plate. Most known examples are on postal stationery. Albino adhesives do exist, but they are quite scarce. Albinos can also occur if two pieces of paper go through the press at the same time. The top piece receives the ink, but the bottom piece receives only the impression.

aldrig hængslet [*Dan.*] never hinged.

Alemanha [*Port.*] Germany.

Alemanha Ocidental [*Port.*] W. Germany (B.R.D.).

Alemanha Oriental [*Port.*] E. Germany (D.D.R.).

Alemania [*Span.*] Germany.

Alemania Occidental [*Span.*] West Germany (B.R.D.). [Official name in Spanish: *República Federal de Alemania.*]

Alemania Oriental [*Span.*] East Germany (D.D.R.). [Official name in Spanish: *República Democrática de Alemania.*]

alheña [*Span.*] henna (color).

alıcı [*Turk.*] buyer.

alkuperäinen [*Finn.*] original.

alkuperäinen liima [*Finn.*] original gum.

Allegorical Group Type [also known simply as *Group Type.*] A common design issued for French colonies from 1892 until about 1910. Prior to 1892, France had issued general "French Colonies" stamps for us in all colonies. The new uniform design, with space for each colony's name to be printed in a cartouche at the bottom, was issued to prevent speculators from buying stamps in one colony and selling them in another where the currency exchange value was different.

The allegorical figures in the design represent Navigation and Commerce, not to be confused with France's own "Peace and Commerce" allegorical design. The two figures are apparently seated on the prow of a ship putting out to sea under the French flag.

The design was created by Alphée Dubois and the master die by engraver M. E. Mouchon. The stamps were printed by typography in Paris, produced in full sheets of 300 clichés, divided into two groups of 150 (known as *post office sheets*), made up of panes of twenty-five (five by five)— two panes across and three deep. In the vertical gutter between each pair of panes, single digit numbers representing the last digit of the year of printing (known by the French term *millésime*) were almost always printed. These are found only in the second row. The colony names were printed afterward, by typography, from a separate plate of 150 subjects. The stamps were perforated 13.5 to 13.75 by 13, comb type. A few imperforate varieties exist, but whether they were proofs, errors, or printer's waste is not clear.

Stamps of the Allegorical Group Type were issued for twenty-four colonies; given name changes that occurred during the period, twenty-nine different names appear. The stamps finally represented as many as seventeen different values, although just thirteen values were first issued. The original colors did not conform to the Universal Postal Union code, so— in preparation for the 1900 Paris Exposition— four or five values (depending on the colony) were reissued in different colors to conform.

The history of the stamps includes many printings of from two to fifteen values in any year through 1910. A special printing (apparently for the archives) of the original thirteen values was made in 1900 on bristol card, imperforate, with a few sets overprinted with sepia-colored, imitation "simili-perfs." These were exhibited at the 1900 Paris Exposition, which has led to the common view that they were actually produced for the Exposition.

During the period 1900-06, there were many denominations surcharged with new values, many of which were unnecessary and rarely used commercially. A set of 1912 surcharges also exists, overprinted *05* or *10*. A wide-space variety occurs in this set, in constant positions in each half-sheet of 150 clichés: eight times for the *05* surcharge, two times for the *10* surcharge. Normal spacing is about 1.4mm between *05*, and 2.4mm between *10*. The wide-spacing variety is about 2mm between *05*, and 3mm between *10*.

The Group Type was gradually replaced by pictorial issues that began to appear as early as 1902 in some colonies.

[Contributed by Robert E. Picirilli. Robert G. Stone, "French Colonies, 1892-1910: The Allegorical Group Type (Commerce and Navigation)," *The*

Congress Book, 1962, pp. 67-100. Included are photographs and discussion of stamps and covers with technical details; Robert G. Stone and Edward Grabowski, "Collecting the French Colonies Group Type ("Navigation and Commerce")," *American Philatelist*, June 1984, pp. 618-632; Robert G. Stone, "French Colonies: The Allegorical Group Type— Some Further Notes," *France & Colonies Philatelist*, whole no. 118 (vol. 21, no. 1), pp. 2-5; Robert G. Stone, "Notes on the Usage of the Allegorical Group Type Stamps of French Colonies," *France & Colonies Philatelist*, whole no. 147 (vol. 28, no. 1), pp. 7-8.]

allekirjoitus [*Finn.*] signature.

Allemagne [*Fr.*] Germany.

Allemagne de l'Est [*Fr.*] East Germany (D.D.R.).

Allemagne de l'Ouest [*Fr.*] W. Germany (B.R.D.).

All-Up Service Common name of the Empire Air Mail Scheme, established in 1937. Its purpose was to transport all first-class mail sent from Great Britain to its Commonwealth members by airmail without extra charge. The service was discontinued at the outbreak of World War II.

Almanya [*Turk.*] Germany.

almindelig [*Dan.*] common.

alminnelig [*Nor.*] common.

alt [*Ger.*] old; [*Turk.*] bottom.

általános [*Hun.*] common.

alter (*v.*) Fraudulently changing something on a stamp to make it appear more valuable.

altera (*v.*) [*Rom.*] to alter.

alterar (*v.*) [*Span., Port.*] to alter.

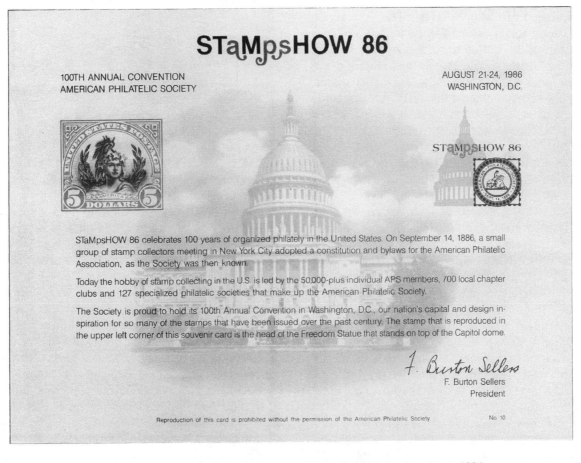

Souvenir card of the American Philatelic Society's 100th Anniversary in 1986

alterare (*v.*) [*Ital.*] to alter; (*f.*) [*Rom.*] alteration.

alteration A change made fraudulently to a stamp or cover to make it appear more valuable than it really is. For example, regumming a stamp without stating that it has been regummed is a fraudulent alteration. Another common type of alteration is the chemical treatment of a stamp to change colors or to remove them.

alterazione (*f.*) [*Ital.*] alteration.

alto (*m.*) [*Ital.*] top.

Alto Commissariato; A. Commissariato [*o/p*] Italian overprint on Yugoslav stamps. See *Lubiana*.

amarelo [*Port.*] yellow.

amarelo-âmbar [*Port.*] amber.

amarillo [*Span.*] yellow.

ambergeel [*Dut.*] amber.

American Philatelic Society The American Philatelic Society (A.P.S.) is the largest and one of the oldest philatelic organizations in the United States. The A.P.S. was founded on September 13, 1886, in New York City under the name American Philatelic Association. After several name changes, it permanently became the American Philatelic Society in 1908.

The American Philatelic Society moved to State College, Pennsylvania, in 1972. Its present building was dedicated in 1981.

The A.P.S. serves more than 50,000 individual members, 700 local chapter clubs, and 125 specialized philatelic societies. In addition to publishing a monthly journal, *The American Philatelist*, the association offers a wide assortment of philatelic handbooks and pamphlets. The A.P.S. operates a stamp expertizing service in conjunction with the American Stamp Dealers' Association. The Society's library contains thousands of books which are available to members, and the library staff provides competent research assistance. Exhibiting is encouraged at its annual conventions and at stamp shows given by its member clubs, and a judges' accreditation program has been established. Additional services and benefits include a speakers bureau, translation service, insurance program, an estate advisory service, and a stamp theft committee.

The American Philatelic Society is an outstanding organization which has served its members well for more than a century. For membership information, contact the American Philatelic Society, P.O. Box 8000, State College, PA 16801.

A.P.S. HomePage:

http://www.west.net/~stamps1/aps.html

Amerika Birleşik Devletleri [*Turk.*] United States of America (U.S.A.).

Amerikai Egyesült Államok [*Hun.*] United States of America.

Amerikan Yhdysvallat [*Finn.*] United States of America.

Amerikas Förenta Stater [*Swed.*] United States of America.

A.M.G./ F.T.T. *o/p* on Italian postage due stamp

A.M.G./ F.T.T. [*o/p*] Allied Military Government/ Free Territory (of) Trieste. Overprint on Italian stamps for use in Trieste from 1947 to 1954. At the time, the Free Territory of Trieste included the city of Trieste and nearby coastal areas to the west. As a result of the September 15, 1947, Peace Treaty, the province of Udine and parts of the provinces of Gorizia and Trieste were restored to Italian sovereignty; the city of Trieste (known as Zone A) passed under Allied administration; and the remainder of Venezia Giulia to the east passed to a Yugoslav Military Government (Trieste Zone B). The *A.M.G.-F.T.T.* overprint, in various styles, was applied to most Italian definitive and commemorative stamps of the period. Zone A was incorporated in Italy on November 15, 1954, and the *A.M.G.-F.T.T.* overprints were withdrawn.

[Contributed by Giorgio Migliavacca.]

A.M.G./ V.G. *o/p* on Italian stamp

A.M.G./ V.G. [*o/p*] Allied Military Government of Venezia Giulia. Overprint applied to Italian stamps used in the Allied-administered area of Venezia Giulia on the Italian-Yugoslav border which included Trieste, Gorizia, and Pola. This overprint was first used in September 1945 at the Renato Fortuna Press in Trieste. Stamps with this overprint ceased to be valid after September 30, 1947. They were replaced by *A.M.G.-F.T.T.* overprints at Trieste (October 1, 1947) by Italian definitive stamps at Gorizia, and by Yugoslavian stamps at Pola. Forgeries of the *A.M.G.-V.G.* overprints exist; the forgeries are usually longer than the genuine overprints.

[Contributed by Giorgio Migliavacca.]

amincissement (*m.*) [*Fr.*] thin spot; skinned spot.

amiti אֲמִתִּי [*Heb.*] genuine.

amtlich [*Ger.*] official.

an (*m.*) [*Rom., Fr.*] year.

anaparagogi αναπαραγωγή (*f.*) [*Grk.*] a copy; reproduction.

anaranjado [*Span.*] orange.

anbieten (*v.*) [*Ger.*] to offer.

anbud (*n.*) [*Swed.*] offer; bid.

anbudslapp (*r.*) [*Swed.*] bid sheet.

And.a Alta [*Span.*] *Andalucia Alta.* Pre-adhesive postmark in nineteenth-century Spain.

anepisimon ανεπίσημον [*Grk.*] unofficial.

Angebot (*n.*) [*Ger.*] an offer.

Angleterre [*Fr.*] England.

Anglia [*Pol., Rom.*] England.

añil [*Span.*] indigo.

anilin (*c.*) [*Dan.*] aniline.

Anilin (*m.*) [*Ger.*] aniline.

anilina (*f.*) [*Span., Ital.*] aniline.

aniline A colorless liquid poison used as the base of some water-soluble dyes and inks. These inks have a coal-tar base. When used on postage stamps, aniline ink is not poisonous, but it does dissolve when saturated with water. Stamps have sometimes been printed with aniline ink to prevent the reuse of those stamps once they have gone through the mail. Any attempt to erase or wash off the cancellation destroys the stamp's design.

Aniline ($C_6H_5NH_2$) is also known as *phenylamine.*

ank [*Hin.*] an issue, issuance.

anma tabakası [*Turk.*] souvenir sheet.

année (*f.*) [*Fr.*] year.

anno (*m.*) [*Lat., Ital.*] year.

annulation par découpage [*Fr.*] cut cancellation.

annuler (*v.*) [*Fr.*] to cancel.

annuleret efter ønske [*Dan.*] cancelled to order.

annullamento (*m.*) [*Ital.*] cancellation; obliteration.

annullare (*v.*) [*Ital.*] to cancel.

annullato di favore [*Ital.*] cancelled to order.

annullere (*v.*) [*Nor.*] to cancel.

annullering (*m.*) [*Nor.*] cancellation.

annullo (*m.*) [*Ital.*] postmark.

annullo a penna [*Ital.*] pen cancelled.

annullo a punzone [*Ital.*] punch cancellation.

annullo a taglio [*Ital.*] cut cancellation.

ano (*m.*) [*Port.*] year.

año (*m.*) [*Span.*] year.

anomaly Something that logically should not be the way it is.

A philatelic example is the Dutch stamp commemorating the creation of Braille and bringing attention to the plight of the blind. The Braille inscription is printed as black dots rather than being embossed as raised bumps the way Braille is normally produced. Since most sighted people do not know the Braille alphabet, they cannot read the inscription. Similarly, the blind cannot feel the printed letters, so they cannot read it either. Thus, the stamp displays an inscription that cannot be understood by virtually anyone.

The U.S. domestic stamp issued in 1988 is another such example. The uniqueness of domestic stamps lies in their failure to exhibit a specific denomination of value. In the United States they are printed when a postal rate increase is anticipated but the exact amount of increase is not yet known. The U.S. Postal Service prints a large capital letter (in this case, "E") in lieu of a denomination. When the rate increase is approved, the stamps are ready for use. The post office merely has to tell its customers what the value of the new stamp is (the "E" stamp cost 25 cents). But because the stamps do not display a specific value, the U.P.U. did not recognize them as being valid for international mailings until the mid-1990s, hence the name *domestic* stamps. The anomaly lies in the ironic choice of design of the "E" stamps: the planet Earth. This is virtually the only postage stamp which the U.S. ever printed that would *not* transport a letter to all parts of the globe at the time of its issuance, yet this is the one that carries a picture of our planet.

anomalies? Dutch Braille, U.S. Earth, and Dec. 32 meter

The meter impression in the illustration is another anomaly. Its date of December 32 is an impossibility, yet the letter which was metered in this manner actually passed through the mails.

Anomalies are not absolute. What may seem to be an anomaly to one collector may be perceived as totally normal and logical to someone else. They are strictly a matter of one's own opinion.

Ansichtskarte (*f.*) [*Ger.*] postcard.

antallasso ανταλλάσσω (*v.*) [*Grk.*] to trade.

anthonize (*verb*) Word coined in the 1980s referring to a government's attempt to force its people to do something they don't want to do. The term is derived from the Susan B. Anthony Dollar, which was introduced in 1979 as the first possible step in eliminating the one dollar note. Despite extensive promotion by the U.S. Treasury Department, the Anthony Dollar failed. It was much smaller than previous dollar coins and so closely resembled the quarter dollar in size and color that many people confused the two coins, passing off dollars as though they were quarters. The American people also thought the government was trying to anthonize them by eliminating the dollar bill, a very popular fixture in domestic American commerce.

This term has several philatelic connections. The American people felt "anthonized" by being pressured by the U.S. Postal Service to use 9-digit zip codes. Many citizens have enough trouble remembering the original 5-digit code; the additional four digits are regarded as an unnecessary nuisance.

Similarly, the issuance of non-denominated domestic stamps[*q.v.*] has been seen as a form of anthonization because they symbolize ever-increasing postal rates. The stamps are also very confusing to many Americans.

Susan B. Anthony

Anthony, Susan Brownell Women's rights advocate and crusader for women's suffrage. Born February 15, 1820, in Adams,

Massachusetts; died March 13, 1906, in Rochester, New York.

Susan B. Anthony believed passionately in the democratic values upon which the United States was founded, but she never had the right to exercise the most basic of them all— the right to vote. Anthony also used her experience as a teacher, journalist, and author in her tireless efforts to abolish slavery and in the temperance crusade.

She devoted her life fighting for the birthright of women and the privileges that are often taken for granted today: the right to vote, co-educational schools, the right to own property, and the opening of all professions on the basis of qualification and not gender.

Anthony helped establish the American Equal Rights Association in 1866 and the National Woman Suffrage Association in 1869. On November 28, 1872, she was arrested for voting illegally and was fined $100, a fine she never paid.

In 1906 at age 86, Susan B. Anthony died, with only four states having given women the right to vote. Finally in 1920, the centennial of her birth, the U.S. Congress passed the 19th Amendment to the Constitution which gave women in all states the right to vote.

In the 1970s Susan B. Anthony's name was used as a rallying symbol by various American gay and lesbian organizations in their quest for equal rights, because Anthony herself was a lesbian.

Anthony was elected to the Hall of Fame for Great Americans located at the Bronx Community College of City University of New York in 1950.

[Contributed by Pamela Makricosta. Florence Horn Bryan, *Susan B. Anthony: Champion of Women's Rights*; Phyllis J. Read & Bernard L. Witlieb, *The Book of Women's Firsts*; Matthew G. Grant, *Susan B. Anthony: Crusader for Women's Rights*.]

anticipo (*m.*) [*Ital.*] deposit.

anti-counterfeiting device Anything included in the design or method of production of a stamp which makes counterfeiting of that stamp more difficult or makes a forgery easier to detect. Silk threads embedded in the paper and watermarks are two commonly-seen examples.

anticuado [*Span.*] obsolete.

anulación (*f.*) [*Span.*] cancellation.

anulado con barras [*Span.*] barred.

anular (*v.*) [*Span.*] to cancel.

använd [*Swed.*] used.

ANZAC Commemoration (Australia)

ANZAC Commemoration Australian 2d stamp issued in 1935 to commemorate the twentieth anniversary of the ANZAC's landing at Gallipoli during World War I. The word is an acronym formed from the initials of *Australian-New Zealand Army Corps*. King George V named one of his horses Anzac in its honor. These troops were also active in World War II.

Anzahlung (*f.*) [*Ger.*] deposit.

anzahlungspflichtig [*Ger.*] deposit required.

A.O. [*Fr. o/p*] *Afrique Orientale* (East Africa) overprinted on 1918 Red Cross stamps of the Congo; Audit Office (on stamps of South Australia).

A.O.F. [*Fr. o/p*] *Afrique Occidentale Française* (French West Africa).

A.O.I. [*abbr.; o/p*] *Africa Orientale Italiana* (Italian East Africa). As an overprint, this abbreviation appears on some Italian stamps of the mid-1930s which converts them to postage due stamps for use in the Italian East Africa colonies. See *Somalia*.

août [*Fr.*] August.

aparcheomeno απαρχαιομένο [*Grk.*] obsolete.

apfelgrün [*Ger.*] apple green.

à pied [*Fr.*] literally, *on foot*. The portrayed person on a postage or revenue stamp is shown in a standing position. The illustration shows George Washington *à pied* on a stamp of Monaco.

apodido αποδίδω (*v.*) [*Grk.*] to attribute.

apodiksi απόδειξη (f.) [Grk.] receipt.

apodiksis prosforon απόδειξη προσφορών (f.) [Grk.] bid sheet.

appendice di propaganda bellica

appendice di propaganda bellica [Ital.] [literally *war propaganda appendix.*] Propaganda labels were incorporated into the design of Italian postage stamps from 1942-44. The stamp and the label are one contiguous item with no perforation in between. The left half of the label shows a standard postage stamp design, while the right half consists of a propaganda slogan and a related illustration. In one case, the postage stamp is on the bottom and the propaganda appendix is at the top.

aprile [Ital.] April.

apsogos άψογος [Grk.] perfect, flawless.

aquila (f.) [Ital.] eagle.

aquisição (f.) [Port.] acquisition.

år (n.) [Dan., Swed, Nor.] year.

ár [Hun.] price.

A.R. [Span.] *Aviso de Recepción* (Acknowledgement of Receipt).

árajánlat (v.) [Hun.] to bid (at an auction).

árajánlatot tesz [Hun.] (auction) bid.

Aralık [Turk.] December.

aralıklı delikli dantel [Turk.] interrupted perforation; syncopated perforation.

arancio [Ital.] orange.

arckép [Hun.] portrait.

ARF [Fr.] *Autriche Rayon Frontière* (Austrian Border Radius). Pre-adhesive postmark on mail originating from a post office near the Austrian border. It was usually seen on mail from Lombardy Venetia to the Kingdom of Sardinia and only on letters destined within five miles from the border.

árfolyam [Hun.] exchange rate.

argent (m.) [Fr.] silver; money.

Argentinien [Ger.] Argentina.

Arjantin [Turk.] Argentina.

árjegyzék [Hun.] price list.

ark (n.) [Dan., Nor., Swed.] pane; sheet (of stamps).

arka yüzü [Turk.] reverse.

arkusik okolicznościowy (m.); arkusik pamiątkowy (m.) [Pol.] souvenir sheet.

arkusz (m.) [Pol.] sheet (of stamps).

arrows: U.S. (documentary) & Great Britain

arrow Margin indicator resembling an arrow found on the selvage of some panes of stamps. Its purpose is to serve as a guide for cutting the pane into smaller, predetermined portions. A block of four or more stamps with the selvage and arrow marking intact is called an *arrow block.*

arruga (f.) [Span.] a crease, fold.

årstal (n.) [Dan.] date.

arte (m./f.) [Span.]; (f.) [Port.] art.

árverés [Hun.] auction, auction sale.

árverési katalógus [*Hun.*] auction catalogue.
árverési lap [*Hun.*] bid sheet.
arvo [*Finn.*] value.
arvokas [*Finn.*] valuable.
arvonalennus [*Finn.*] devaluation.

Juana de Asbaje

Asbaje, Juana de [a.k.a. *Sor Juana Inés de la Cruz* (*Sister Johanna Inés of the Cross*)]. Mexican poet, musician, scientist, and historian. Born 1648 or 1651 at San Miguel de Nepantla (near Mexico City); died of the plague in 1695 in the Convent of San Jerónimo.

Sister Johanna is regarded as the foremost Latin American poet of the seventeenth century and was called the "Tenth Muse" by her contemporaries. Her poetry reflects her deep religious faith.

One of the great intellects of her time, she conducted scientific experiments involving physics and astronomy and shared her observations with such European intellectuals as Sir Isaac Newton.

Although Sister Johanna lived in a convent, she managed to acquire a personal library of more than 4000 volumes. Two years prior to her death, her priest made her sell her collection and devote her life to normal religious endeavors.

Many of today's observers regard her as the world's first feminist because of her lifelong struggle against the establishment that sought to suppress women's intellect.

Although Sister Johanna's portrait appears on the popular Mexican 1000 peso note introduced in 1985, she is conspicuous in philately because of her absence. Despite being regarded as perhaps the most intellectual and accomplished woman ever born in Latin America, her portrait appears on only one rather inconsequential commemorative stamp of Mexico.

The philatelic plight of Sister Johanna raises the question of who is and who is not worthy of being featured on postage stamps. As a point of comparison, Elvis Presley appears on the stamps of several countries, including the most popular U.S. commemorative stamp in history.

[*Smithsonian World: Voices of Latin America* (script of television program), 1987, WETA (Washington, DC) & Smithsonian Institution; Angel Valbuena Briones, *Historia de la literatura española*, Vol. V: "Literatura hispanoamericana," 1969, Editorial Gustava Gili, S.A., Barcelona, Spain, pp. 126-139.]

asgarî teklif [*Turk.*] minimum bid.
askeri posta pulu [*Turk.*] military postage stamp.
assegno (*m.*) [*Ital.*] check, cheque; scrip.
assinatura (*f.*) [*Port.*] signature.
asta (*f.*) [*Ital.*] auction.
astro άστρο (*n.*) [*Grk.*] star.
AT [*Fr.*] *Autriche Transit* ("in Transit in Austria"). Abbreviation used as a pre-adhesive postmark.
ATF [*Fr.*] *Angleterre Transit Français* ("English mail via France"). Abbreviation used as a pre-adhesive postmark.
atrament (*m.*) [*Pol.*] ink.
atribución (*f.*) [*Span.*] attribution (the complete identification of a postage stamp, cover, or other philatelic item).
atribuição (*f.*) [*Port.*] attribution.
atribuir (*v.*) [*Span., Port.*] to attribute.
atrybucja (*f.*) [*Pol.*] attribution (the complete identification of a postage stamp, cover, or other philatelic item).
atrybuować (*v.*) [*Pol.*] to attribute.
åtta [*Swed.*] eight.
åtte [*Nor.*] eight.
attestere (brev) som portofrit (*v.*) [*Dan.*] to frank.
åtti [*Nor.*] eighty.
åttio [*Swed.*] eighty.
attribuer (*v.*) [*Fr.*] to attribute.
attribuera (*v.*) [*Swed.*] to attribute.
attribuire (*v.*) [*Ital.*] to attribute.

attribute (*v.*); **attribution** (*noun*) The determination and classification of a stamp, booklet, cover, or other philatelic item's issuing agency (country, private individual, or whatever), place of manufacture, denomination, date of issue, kind of paper, watermark, type, and variety. In some cases, other characteristics such as grade, error, or pedigree are also included in the attribution.

Anything that contributes to the complete and accurate identification of a philatelic item is part of its attribution. Until this identification is complete, the piece is referred to as *unattributed*.

attribuzione (*f.*) [*Ital.*] attribution.

au buste enfantin (Spain's Alfonso XIII)

au buste enfantin [*Fr.*] Bust of the king or queen as a child. The term especially refers to effigies of monarchs (e.g., Spain's King Alfonso XIII) who succeeded to the throne at a very young age and who remained on the throne long enough to require the updating of their effigies.

The stamp in this illustration, the Spanish colonial keytype of 1898, is also specifically referred to as *Curly Head* because of the young king's appearance. Alfonso was about twelve years old when this stamp was issued.

auf Briefumschlag; auf Umschlag [*Ger.*] on cover.

Aufdruck (*m.*) [*Ger.*] surcharge.

augustus [*Dut.*] August.

aukcja (*f.*) [*Pol.*] auction.

aukcja na oferty pocztowe [*Pol.*] mail bid sale.

auksjon (*m.*) [*Nor.*] auction; auction sale.

auksjonskatalog (*m.*) [*Nor.*] auction catalogue.

auktion (*r.*) [*Swed.*] auction.

Auktion per Postweg [*Ger.*] mail bid sale.

auktionsförsäljning (*r.*) [*Swed.*] auction sale.

auktionskatalog [*Swed., Dan.*] auction catalogue.

Auktionskatalog (*m.*) [*Ger.*] auction catalogue.

auktionsnummer (*n.*) [*Dan.*] (auction) lot.

auktionssalg (*n.*) [*Dan.*] auction sale.

Auktionsverkauf (*m.*) [*Ger.*] auction sale.

Ausgabe (*f.*) [*Ger.*] an issue, issuance.

ausgezeichnet [*Ger.*] excellent.

Aushilfsmarke (*f.*) [*Ger.*] provisional.

ausländisch [*Ger.*] foreign.

Auslandswährung (*f.*) [*Ger.*] foreign currency.

ausstellen (*v.*) [*Ger.*] to exhibit.

Ausstellung (*f.*) [*Ger.*] exhibition.

Australien [*Ger.*] Australia.

Ausztrália [*Hun.*] Australia.

Ausztria [*Hun.*] Austria.

autentico [*Ital.*] authentic, genuine.

auténtico [*Span.*] authentic, genuine.

autêntico [*Port.*] authentic, genuine.

authentisch [*Ger.*] authentic, genuine.

Automatenmarke (*f.*) [*Ger.*] Coil stamp dispensed by vending machines.

Autr [*Fr.*] *Autriche* ("Austria"). Abbreviation used as a pre-adhesive postmark.

Autriche [*Fr.*] Austria.

au verso [*Fr.*] on the back.

avbildning (*r.*) [*Swed.*] effigy.

avbrudt perforering (*m.*) [*Nor.*] interrupted perforation; syncopated perforation.

avbruten tandning (*r.*) [*Swed.*] interrupted perforation; syncopated perforation.

avec charnière [*Fr.*] hinged.

avgift (*r.*) [*Swed.*] fee.

avisportomærke (*n.*) [*Dan.*] newspaper stamp.

avril [*Fr.*] April.

axia αξία (*f.*) [*Grk.*] value.

ay'rech na'kuv עֵרֶךְ נָקוּב (*m.*) [*Heb.*] face value.

A.Z. [*o/p*] Ahmed Zogu (later King Zog I of Albania).

az bulunur [*Turk.*] scarce.

azul [*Span., Port.*] blue.

azul celeste [*Span.*] azure.

azul da Prússia [*Port.*] Prussian blue.

azul de Prusia [*Span.*] Prussian blue.

azul espliego [*Span.*] lavender.

azul real [*Span., Port.*] royal blue.

azul zafiro [*Span.*] sapphire blue.

azzurro oltremare [*Ital.*] ultramarine.

B b

B 1. *Brig* (Wallis Canton of Switzerland). Abbreviation used as a pre-adhesive postmark, usually found on mail from the Wallis region of Switzerland to destinations in the Kingdom of Sardinia (1814-16).

2. Overprint on stamps of Straits Settlements that indicates use at the British post office in Bangkok, Siam (now Thailand).

3. [with lily above] *Bordeaux*. French abbreviation used as a pre-adhesive postmark.

4. [within oval] Overprint or imprint on Belgium stamps indicating railway parcels.

B.A. [*abbr.*] British Administration. Used on 1950 emissions for Eritrea and Somaliland.

babérkoszorús [*Hun.*] laureate.

back-of-the-book Term often used by philatelists in reference to all postage stamps other than general issues. This category includes airmails, postage dues, revenues, newspaper stamps, occupation stamps, semipostals, locals, postal stationery, military stamps, and a host of others. The term is derived from catalogues which normally place the listing of such stamps after the general issues.

BAD. OE. C [*Ger.*] Abbreviation used as a pre-adhesive postmark on letters which benefitted from a reduced postal rate resulting from a postal treaty between Austria and Baden.

bakside [*Nor.*] reverse. *på baksiden*: on the back.

bal [*Hun.*] left (direction or position).

Balloon Postage Semi-official stamps issued by the United States in 1877 in conjunction with balloon flights performed by Samuel Archer King. Only two on-cover specimens are known to survive. These could be considered the world's first airmail stamps, although Italy is credited with having put out the first true airmail issues, some existing express stamps overprinted to accommodate an experimental service between Rome and Turin in 1917. See *airmail*.

Balloon Post of Paris The world's first official airmail service, which operated from September 23, 1870, to January 28, 1871. A total of 67 balloons left Paris at this period of the Siege of Paris during the Franco-Prussian War. Only 55 of the 67 balloons were intended to carry mail, but some pieces entrusted to the crew (called *aerostiers* or *aeronautes*) are known to have been carried on the other twelve flights. Other firsts associated with these flights include microfilming of messages to be returned to Paris by pigeon, privately-printed cards and stationery, and special editions of newspapers and journals intended to be flown out.

[Contributed by John E. Lievsay. Chaintrier, *Balloon Post of the Siege of Paris*, American Air Mail Society translation, 1976; Cohn, *The Flight of the "Ville d'Orleans"*; Brown, Cohn, & Walske, *New Studies of the Transport of Mails in Wartime France, 1870-71*.]

banda (*f.*) [*Span.*] strip (of stamps).

bande (*f.*) [*Fr.*] strip (of stamps).

bani (*m.pl.*) [*Rom.*] money.

Bargeld (*n.*) [*Ger.*] cash (ready money).

barna [*Hun.*] brown.

bärnstensfärgad [*Swed.*] amber (color).

barrado [*Span.*] barred.

barré [*Fr.*] barred.

barred (*adj.*) An overprint, usually of heavy black lines, which defaces some part of the stamp's design.

1. Some barred stamps are stock remainders which are defaced in this way and then are sold to dealers at discounted prices. They usually are worth less to collectors than either

mint or postally-used specimens. Notable exceptions include some stamps of North Borneo, the barred versions of which are listed separately in stamp catalogues.

barred stamps [#2]: post-Farouk and post-Hitler

2. In some cases, the purpose of barring is to block out the portrait of a deposed ruler so that the current stamps can be used until new ones are printed. Many stamps portraying Hitler received this treatment in 1945, as did Egyptian stamps in 1953 after the overthrow of King Farouk as well as Iranian stamps of 1979 after the ouster of the Shah.

Other methods of overprinting have also been used to achieve a similar objective. In 1922 when Ireland won its independence from Britain, the Irish government was permitted to use British stamps overprinted with Irish inscriptions to validate them for postage until the fledgling nation could print its own stamps. See *provisional* for an illustration.

The term *barred* is not used in reference to overprints memorializing recently-deceased monarchs or other people featured on stamps current at the time of their death. See *memorial overprint.*

3. Many precancelled stamps show various forms of barring, even though these are not usually referred to as barred stamps. U.S. precancels are noted for indicating the name of the city of origin between two black lines.

A group of special precancels known as *training stamps*[q.v.] were issued in Great Britain during the reign of King George VI. Two wide vertical black lines were overprinted on some definitives to invalidate them for postage or revenue. These stamps were made available to business colleges to give students hands-on experience.

bas (*m.*) [*Fr.*] bottom.
basilias βασιλιάς (*m.*) [*Grk.*] king.
basilissa βασίλισσα (*f.*) [*Grk.*] queen.
basso (*m.*) [*Ital.*] bottom.
bathmologo βαθμολογώ (*v.*) [*Grk.*] to grade.
bathmos βαθμός (*m.*) [*Grk.*] grade, condition.
Batı Almanya [*Turk.*] West Germany (B.R.D.).
bâtonné paper A seldom-used lined paper similar to that found in children's notebooks or lined writing pads. Some of the very crude watercolor stamps of Poonch (an Indian State) were produced with this paper.
B.a.V. [*Fr.*] *Bateau à Vapeur* (steamship). Abbreviation used as a pre-adhesive postmark.
Bayern [*Ger.*] Bavaria.
B.C. 1. [*abbr.*] Before Christ, as used in Western dating systems. In the Middle East, *B.C.E.* (Before Christian Era) and *C.E.* (Christian Era, the equivelant of A.D., *anno Domini*) are preferred.

2. [*abbr.*] British Columbia; British Colonies; British Commonwealth.
B.C.E. [*abbr.*] Before Christian Era. This and *C.E.* (Christian Era) are the preferred term in Jewish and Arab societies to designate B.C. and A.D. for Western dating systems.
B.C.M. [*abbr.*] British Consular Mail.
B.C.O.F. [*o/p*] British Commonwealth Occupation Force. Post-World War II overprint on Australian stamps intended for Australian troops stationed in Japan.
B.E.A. [*abbr.*] British East Africa.
B.eau Fr. de Bale [*Fr.*] *Bureau Française de Bale* ("French Post Office at Bazel [Switzerland]"). Abbreviation used as a pre-adhesive postmark.
bedrag (*n.*) [*Dut.*] amount.
B.E.F. [*abbr.*] British Expeditionary Force.
befejezetlen [*Hun.*] incomplete.
Befestigungsleiste (*f.*) [*Ger.*] (stamp) hinge.
belasting (*m.-c.*) [*Dut.*] tax.
belastingzegel (*m./c.*) [*Dut.*] fiscal stamp.
Belçika [*Turk.*] Belgium.
Belg [*Fr.*] *Belgique* ("Belgium"). Abbreviation used as a pre-adhesive postmark.
belge [*Turk.*] certificate.
Belgia [*Pol.*] Belgium.
Bélgica [*Span., Port.*] Belgium.

Belgien [*Ger.*] Belgium.

Belgio [*Ital.*] Belgium.

Belgique [*Fr.*] Belgium.

beløp (*n.*) [*Nor.*] amount.

belső [*Hun.*] intrinsic.

BENADIR [*o/p*] See *Somalia.*

benzine Highly volatile chemical used for the identification of watermarks. Because it can dissolve some inks, it must be used with care.

berlinerblå [*Swed., Dan.*] Prussian blue.

bernsteingelb [*Ger.*] amber.

beş [*Turk.*] five.

beschadigd [*Dut.*] damaged.

beschädigt [*Ger.*] damaged.

beschermend bod (*n.*) [*Dut.*] protective reserve bid.

Beschriftung (*f.*) [*Ger.*] inscription, lettering.

beskadiget [*Dan.*] damaged.

beställningssedel (*r.*) [*Swed.*] order form.

bestämning (*r.*) [*Swed.*] attribution.

bestelformulier (*n.*) [*Dut.*] order form.

Bestellformular (*n.*) [*Ger.*] order form.

bestemmende [*Nor.*] definitive.

bestillingsformular (*c.*) [*Dan.*] order form.

betét [*Hun.*] deposit.

Betrag (*m.*) [*Ger.*] amount.

betul [*Indo.*] authentic.

bevakningspris (*n.*) [*Swed.*] protective reserve bid.

beyaz [*Turk.*] white.

bez kleju [*Pol.*] ungummed.

bez podlepki [*Pol.*] unhinged; never hinged.

B.F. [*Fr.*] *Bureau Français* ("French Post Office"). Abbreviation used as a pre-adhesive postmark.

B.G. [*Ital. abbr.*] *bollo gazzette* (newspaper stamp).

B.I. [*abbr.*] British India.

biały [*Pol.*] white.

bianco [*Ital.*] white.

bicolor [*Span., Port.*] bicolored, bicoloured.

bid sheet Order form submitted by mail by someone wishing to place a bid at an auction or mail bid sale. Just as with live participation at an auction, the highest bidder is legally obligated to pay for those items successfully bid upon.

B.I.E. [*o/p*] *Bureau International d'Éducation* (International Bureau of Education). Overprinted on stamps of Switzerland.

bieden (*v.*) [*Dut.*] to bid (at an auction or mail bid sale).

biedformulier (*n.*); biedingsformulier (*n.*) [*Dut.*] bid sheet.

Bietempfehlung (*f.*) [*Ger.*] suggested bid.

bieten (*v.*) [*Ger.*] to bid (at an auction or mail bid sale).

bihira [*Tag.*] rare, scarce.

Bildnis (*n.*) [*Ger.*] effigy; portrait.

bilhete postal (*m.*) [*Port.*] postal card. The term for *postcard* in Portuguese is *cartão postal* (*m.*).

bilingual stamp (Canada)

bilingual pair (South Africa)

bilingual A stamp with inscriptions in two languages. English-French stamps of Canada are the examples most frequently cited. Stamps with inscriptions in three languages are called *trilingual*; stamps showing three of more languages can also be call *multilingual.*

In order to abide by U.S.P. regulations, stamps of most countries show a romanized version of that country's name if its official language uses some other alphabet (e.g., "Hellas" on Greek stamps and "Nippon" on Japanese stamps), or it may show the English version of its name to avoid confusion ("Finland" in addition to "Suomi" on Finnish stamps). These stamps are not considered bilingual. Also see *bilingual pair.*

bilingual pair A *se-tenant*[*q.v.*] pair of stamps in which the only difference in design is the language. The most commonly-found examples are the English-Afrikaans pairs of South African stamps. Afrikaans is a dialect of Dutch and is one of the two official languages of that country.

bilingue [*Ital.*] bilingual.

bilingüe [*Span.*] bilingual.

bilingv [*Rom.*] bilingual.

bilog [*Tag.*] round.

bilti m'zoheh בִּלְתִּי מְזוֹהֶה [*Heb.*] unattributed (not fully identified).

bilti-yadu'a בִּלְתִּי יָדוּעַ [*Heb.*] unknown.

bin [*Turk.*] thousand.

bipartido [*Port.*] bisected.

birbirine bitişik farklı pullar [*Turk.*] se-tenant.

birinci kalite kağıt [*Turk.*] wove paper.

Birlesik Kırallık [*Turk.*] United Kingdom (U.K.).

biseccionado [*Span.*] bisected.

bisect (*noun*); **bisected** (*adj.*) A stamp which has been cut in half and used on mail for half of its stated face value. Some countries have permitted this practice, especially during times of stamp shortages. A few, like Guatemala, have perforated stamps diagonally to facilitate separation. In the United States and elsewhere, the use of bisects has never been officially permitted, although some postmasters have tolerated the practice. Some letters bearing bisects probably passed through the mail undetected.

Stamps can be bisected diagonally, vertically, or horizontally. Some postage stamps have even been cut into three pieces (known as *trisects*) or four pieces (*quadrisects*).

Bisected stamps are virtually always collected on cover. It is nearly impossible to tell if a bisect removed from its cover actually passed through the mail in that manner or if it went through the mail intact and was bisected after its removal.

[Kenneth A. Wood, *This Is Philately*, Vol. I, p. 78.]

Bishop mark In 1861 Henry Bishop of Great Britain began cancelling stamps by indicating the day and month that the letter was received at the post office. This was among the world's first postmarks.

bisseto; bissecto [*Port.*] bisected.

B.I.T. [*Fr. o/p*] *Bureau International du Travail* (International Labor Office [of Geneva, Switzerland]). Overprinted on 1930 Belgian stamps and 1938 Swiss stamps.

bizonytalan származású [*Hun.*] unattributed.

bjuda (*v.*) [*Swed.*] to bid (at an auction).

blå [*Nor., Swed., Dan.*] blue.

bläck (*n.*) [*Swed.*] ink.

Black Jack (U.S.)

Black Jack Popular name for the 2c stamp issued in the United States from 1863 to 1875. It shows an over-sized portrait of Andrew Jackson[q.v.] and was printed in black ink, hence the nickname.

bläckmakulerad; bläckmakulerat [*Swed.*] pen cancelled.

blackout cancel Type of censored postmark used in east- and west-coast port cities of Canada during World War II. The location names within the date stamp of machine and handstamps were deleted In some cases, the rings were left blank; in other cases, the rings were filled in and printed solid black.

In theory, the blackout cancels were used to prevent the enemy from obtaining clues about shipping movements, convoy information, etc., from captured mail. But as Kenneth A. Wood points out, the Canadian government apparently failed to realize that most mail bears return addresses or corner cards, so the entire endeavor was a wasted effort.

See *censored mail*.

[Kenneth A. Wood, *This Is Philately*, Vol. I, pp. 143-44.]

black stamp Term for some proof issue stamps of Austria which are attached to news releases that describe new issues of Austrian stamps.

bład (*m.*) [*Pol.*] error.

blæk (*n.*) [*Dan.*] ink.
blågrønn [*Nor.*] cobalt (color).
blanc [*Fr.*] white.
blanco [*Span.*] white.
blankt papir (*n.*) [*Dan.*] glossy paper.
blasenartiges Papier (*n.*) [*Ger.*] Goldbeater's Skin[*q.v.*].
blau [*Ger.*] blue.
blauw [*Dut.*] blue.
błękit królewski [*Pol.*] royal blue.
błękit pruski [*Pol.*] Prussian blue.
blekk (*n.*) [*Nor.*] ink.
bleu [*Fr.*] blue.
Bleu [*Fr.*] literally, *blue*. Popular term for the common letter-rate stamps of France, 1850-76 (Scott #6, 15, 33, & 58). Because they were printed in huge quantities (and are relatively inexpensive compared to other values), they have been extensively studied for varieties and plating. Thus, they usually constitute the majority of stamps found in collections of French cancels. A lot described in a French sale as stamps *de coleur* means that no (or few) *bleus* are included.

[Contributed by John E. Lievsay. Suarnet, *Les Bleus de France*; Barat, *Le Nouveau "Bleus de France."*]
bleu azur [*Fr.*] azure blue.
bleu de Prusse [*Fr.*] Prussian blue.
bleu roi [*Fr.*] royal blue.

blind perf (U.S. coil stamps)

blind perf Type of perforation error in which the holes are not punched completely through the paper. There may be some partial penetration or there may be nothing more than a slight mark left by the perf pin. Under either circumstance, there is always some indication that an attempt was made to perforate the paper. Blind perfs may affect only one or two holes on a stamp, or they can affect an entire

row, giving the appearance that the stamp is at least partially imperforate.

This is in contrast to *missing perforations* which show no signs of any perforation having been attempted. Missing perfs are caused either by human error or a mechanical breakdown.

"blind" stamps: U.K. (due) and Spain (telegraph)

blind stamp A postage or revenue stamp with no mention of its country of origin, thus making the stamp difficult to attribute. Stamps of Great Britain have traditionally been "blind" as an honor bestowed by the U.P.U. in consideration of Britain's having been the first country to issue postage stamps.

Early stamps of many nations were "blind" or exhibited inscriptions in foreign alphabets that were indecipherable to Westerners. Since the 1970s, most nations have issued stamps showing romanized versions of their names, usually in English (for example, *Finland* as well as *Suomi* on Finnish stamps, and *Hellas* in addition to Ελλάς on the stamps of Greece).

Many "blind" stamps are postage dues, newspaper stamps, and other such specialized stamps and labels. Some nineteenth century Spanish and Spanish colonies stamps fall into this category. Many of them are inscribed with their purpose (telegraph, newspaper, or whatever) but do not indicate the name of the country.
bloc (*m.*) [*Fr.*] block (of stamps).
blocco (*m.*) [*Ital.*] block (of stamps); pane.
bloc commémoratif (*m.*) [*Fr.*] souvenir sheet.
bloc de quatre [*Fr.*] block of four.
block Unsevered group of three or more stamps with at least one stamp having both a vertical mate and a horizontal mate. A group of three or more attached stamps that are all in line (i.e.,

with nothing but vertical mates or horizontal mates) is called a strip.

If the block comes from the corner of the pane showing the plate number, it is called a plate number block and usually commands a higher price than a non-plate block or a group of individual or paired stamps of the same type.

blockade-run mail A special postal route during the U.S. Civil War (1861-1865) connecting Europe and the Confederate States. This route began on April 19, 1861, when President Abraham Lincoln declared a blockade of the Confederate States. There was never a time from 1861 to 1864 when the blockade completely closed the Confederate ports of Wilmington, Delaware, or of Charleston, South Carolina, and the ports of New Orleans, Louisiana, and Savannah, Georgia, remained open until early 1862. The only communication with Europe was carried on by the blockade runners of the government and private ship owners via Havana, Bermuda, and West Indies ports. The Confederacy adopted the regular rate (5 cents and 10 cents) plus the ship letter rate of 2 cents for single-weight letters for blockade-run letters addressed to any city in the Confederacy.

[Contributed by Richard Corwin. Lawrence L. Shenfield, *Confederate States of America: The Special Routes*, pp. 51-62; *Dietz Confederate State Catalog*, p. 199.]

bloco (*m.*) [*Port.*] block.

bloco comemorativo (*m.*) [*Port.*] souvenir sheet.

bloco de quatro [*Port.*] block of four.

blodröd [*Swed.*] blood (red).

blodrød [*Nor.*] blood (red).

blok (*c.*) [*Dan.*]; (*m.*) [*Pol.*]; (*n.*) [*Dut.*] block (of stamps).

blokk (*m.*) [*Nor.*] block (of stamps).

blok van vier (*n.*) [*Dut.*] block of four.

bloque (*m.*) [*Span.*] block (of stamps).

bloque de cuatro (*m.*) [*Span.*] block of four.

blu [*Ital.*] blue.

blu di Prussia [*Ital.*] Prussian blue.

blu savoia [*Ital.*] royal blue.

blutrot [*Ger.*] blood (red).

BM [*Fr.*] *Boîte Mobile* ("Traveling [Mail] Box"). Abbreviation used as a pre-adhesive postmark.

B.M.A. [*o/p*] British Military Administration. Overprint found on many stamps from around 1942 to 1952. In 1952 the "M." was dropped. This overprint is often followed by the name of a country (e.g., "B.M.A. SOMALIA" or "B.M.A. ERITREA").

B.M.A. ERITREA [*o/p*] British Military Administration Eritrea.

B.M.A. SOMALIA [*o/p*] British Military Administration Somalia. In May 1948 this replaced stamps overprinted "E.A.F." (East Africa Forces) issued for use in Somalia[*q.v.*]. In January 1950 the M. was dropped from "B.M.A."

B.N.A. [*abbr.*] British North America (Canada, Newfoundland, *et al*).

B.N.F. Castellorizo [*o/p*] *Base Navale Française Castellorizo* (French Naval Base, Castelrosso). Overprinted on stamps of French Levant in 1920 for the naval occupation of Castelrosso in the Aegean.

boardwalk margin (Ukraine)

boardwalk margin Oversized stamp with a normal image but an unusually wide margin. The example shown here is a government-in-exile stamp of Ukraine.

bobina (*f.*) [*Ital., Span.*] coil (of stamps).

B.O.C. [*Ger.*] *Bayerische-Österreichisch Correspondenz*. Abbreviation used as a pre-adhesive postmark. It was utilized in the 1840s on letters benefitting from a reduced postal rate as a result of the Austrian-Bavarian postal treaty. The postmark is also sometimes written *O.B.C.*

bod (*n.*) [*Dut.*] (auction) bid.

Bogen (*m.*) [*Ger.*] sheet (of stamps).

Bogenblatt (*n.*) [*Ger.*] pane (of stamps).

bollo di franchigia [*Ital.*] franchise stamp.

bom (*m.adj.*); **boa** (*f.adj.*) [*Port.*] good.
bon (*m.adj.*); **bonne** (*f.adj.*) [*Fr.*] good.
bon de commande [*Fr.*] order form.
bond paper Very high-quality paper used for some early stamp issues.

booklet pane (U.S.)

booklet One or more small panes of stamps bound together with a thin cardboard cover. On one end of each pane is a stub known as a *tab* which is used for stapling, gluing, or stitching the pages together. Booklets are produced by the post office and often sold in vending machines.

Although a few privately-produced advertising booklets were made in Great Britain as far back as 1891, the first government-issued booklets and the first to consist of bound panes came from Luxembourg in 1895. Luxembourg broke sheets down into individual panes and formed them into booklets. Many other nations soon followed suit, including the United States in 1900 and Great Britain in 1904. Some early booklets, especially from the U.S., show plate numbers on some of the panes.

Booklets usually contain from two to four panes, although some Canadian and U.S. duck stamps have been printed in booklet format. In that case, the "booklet" consists of one pane bearing one single revenue stamp.

Traditionally, collectors have preferred stamps with perforations on all four sides. Thus, many collectors dislike booklet stamps because the older stamps almost always had at least one straight edge. Booklet stamps are most often collected by booklet specialists who save the entire booklet or at least the entire pane.

An *exploded booklet* is one that has been taken apart and may or may not have been reassembled. Sometimes the booklet is exploded so that its panes can be displayed page by page, and sometimes the booklet is separated so that the panes can be sold individually. The stamps are normally not removed from the tab, because that lessens their value. Rare booklets are checked for explosion before they are purchased, in part to be sure that all the panes came from the same booklet. A booklet will generally show signs of having been taken apart and put back together, such as staple holes that are not in alignment. A booklet that has never been taken apart is called *unexploded*.

If the cardboard cover has a cellophane window so that at least one of the stamps contained therein can be seen, the item is called a *window booklet*[q.v.].

The most recent innovation in booklets was the introduction in the 1990s of self-adhesive stamp booklets. The United States pushed this idea very hard, especially on its Christmas stamps. Self-adhesives do not need perforations or rouletting to aid in separation. Yet the U.S. discovered that its 1989 25c "Flag" self-adhesives (sold by automatic teller machines) did not "look" like stamps because of their utilitarian straight edges. To make the Christmas booklet stamps more marketable, the U.S. started using an updated form of serpentine roulette[q.v.] to give the stamps a more "natural" appearance.

Another problem the U.S. encountered with its self-adhesive booklets was the mathematical problem of how to place twenty stamps on one long pane. A 4 x 5 arrangement would have required an almost square pane and would have been impractical for booklet use. The solution was to configure the stamps 3 x 7 but to make one label a non-postal tab. But some customers tried to use that label as postage, and their letters were returned. The solution to this problem was to place enough slices in the label so that any attempt to remove it from its backing paper would cause the label to come apart in several pieces.

Self-adhesive booklets pose an interesting question for philatelists: Are these items really booklets? Traditionally, the term *stamp booklet* has been defined as one or more small panes of stamps plus a cardboard cover that are stapled, glued, or stitched together. But self-adhesive booklets consist of a single small pane that is folded in half. Its ends may be glued together to prevent it from opening, or it may be sold in a straight flat piece that the user has to fold. A philatelic purist might argue that this item is *not* a booklet, yet if you go into any U.S. post office and ask to buy a booklet, this is what you will probably get.

booklet pane See *booklet*.

bootlegged mail Letters carried and delivered outside the regular government-sponsored postal service. This term is often used to describe letters sent prior to the advent of prepaid postage stamps.

bordeaux [*Fr.*] maroon.

Bordeaux issue When the Prussians mounted the Siege of Paris in September 1870, the rest of France was cut off from supplies of postage stamps which had been printed in Paris. An emergency issue of new stamps, by lithographic process, was produced at the mint at Bordeaux in 1870 and 1871. These are Scott #38-48 and the oft-forgotten #J2.

The issue is full of collectible shades, varieties, and interesting usages; it has been shown at gold medal level in international competition. For 110 years the subtleties of collecting the issue were hidden in journal articles and monographs only in French; the secrets were not shared with readers of English until 1981: Ruth & Gardner Brown, *The*

Bordeaux Issue of 1870-1871, published by the France & Colonies Philatelic Society.

[Contributed by John E. Lievsay.]

botten (*r.*) [*Swed.*] bottom.

boules de Moulins [*Fr.*] literally, *balls of Moulins*. In January 1871 during the Siege of Paris, an attempt to get letters into Paris was made by floating them down the Seine from Moulins to Paris in sealed zinc balls. A special tariff for this service was set at 1 franc (20c for postage and 80c to the promoters). However, no such letters were delivered in Paris until after the end of the siege.

[Contributed by John E. Lievsay. Yvert, *Catalogue Specialisé des Timbres de France*, Vol. 1, pp. 126-127.]

bovenkant (*m.-c.*) [*Dut.*] top.

B.R.A. [*o/p*] British Railway Administration. Overprinted on stamps of China in 1901 during the Boxer Rebellion. Included was a surcharge for railway express postal fees.

branco [*Port.*] white.

Brasilien [*Ger.*] Brazil.

braun [*Ger.*] brown.

brązowy [*Pol.*] brown.

Brésil [*Fr.*] Brazil.

brett (*m.*) [*Nor.*] a crease, a fold.

brev (*n.*) [*Swed., Dan.*] cover (in the philatelic sense). The term *på brev* means *on cover* in Swedish and Danish.

brevbudsauktion (*c.*) [*Dan.*] mail bid sale.

brevkort (*n.*) [*Dan., Nor., Swed.*] postal card. The term for *postcard* in Danish and Norwegian is *postkort* (*n.*); the word for *postcard* in Swedish is *vykort* (*n.*).

Briefgebühr (*f.*) [*Ger.*] postage.

briefkaart (*m./f./c.*) [*Dut.*] postcard.

briefomslag (*n.*) [*Dut.*] envelope.

Briefumschlag (*m.*) [*Ger.*] envelope; cover. The terms for "on cover" in German are *auf Briefumschlag* and *auf Umschlag*.

British Guiana One Cent Magenta Regarded by many as the world's most famous stamp. Only one specimen is known to exist.

The stamp was actually a provisional issued by the British Guiana postmaster in 1856 because a shipment of British stamps failed to arrive on time. The postmaster, E. T. E. Dalton, had stamps of 1c and 4c printed, the 1c version being the newspaper rate. The stamp's central design features a three-masted ship. Above the ship is the Latin inscription *Damus Petimus Que Vicissim* ("We give and expect in return"). The design is enclosed by an oblong rectangular frame with lines that do not meet at the corners. The country's name, the denomination, and the word "postage" are printed outside the frame. As an anti-forgery device, each stamp was initialed by a post office employee.

British Guiana One Cent Magenta (enlarged)

The only surviving specimen was discovered in 1873 when a young philatelist, L. Vernon Vaughan, found it among some family papers. The stamp was not attractive nor impressive and in fact had all four corners clipped. The boy sold it to a local collector for six shillings. Ten years later it was re-sold to a Scottish dealer who sold it to an English dealer who in turn sold it to Count Philippe von Ferrari (of automobile fame) for $750. In 1980 the 1c magenta became the first stamp to approach the million dollar mark when it was auctioned for $935,000 ($850,000 plus a 10% buyer's commission).

Despite being one of the dullest and most uninteresting stamps ever issued, it remains the most popular.

British Virgin Islands [abbreviated *B.V.I.*] The stamps of the British Virgin Islands belong to the extremely, and deservedly, popular group of West Indian stamps. One of the most famous collectors of all times said, "Among all the fascinating pages of the well-filled stamp album, few are so arresting to the collector and to the profane alike as those devoted to the stamps of the Islands of Virgins." This was the opinion of renowned stamp writer Fred J. Melville some eighty years ago.

2 modern stamps of British Virgin Islands

The first post office was opened in Tortola in 1787 at a time when stamps had not yet been invented. It was not until 1858 that a small quantity of adhesive stamps issued by Great Britain depicting Queen Victoria was supplied to the local post office. These stamps were postmarked with the letters "A 13" enclosed by bars; as such they are extremely rare.

In 1866, by popular demand, the post office of the British Virgin Islands issued two stamps, one denominated at 1 penny and the other at 6 pence. The following years stamps of 4d and 1 shilling were added. These stamps depicted St. Ursula. From 1890 to 1956, the British Virgin Islands enjoyed presidency status as a unit of the Leeward Islands colony. Stamps of the Leeward Islands were used concurrently with B.V.I. issues.

Since 1866 the British Virgin Islands has issued about 700 stamps. Since the 1970s most of the philatelic issues of this country have focused on thematic subjects such as sports, ships, stamps on stamps, coins on stamps, pirates, members of the royal family, authors, et al. This wide range of themes has contributed to the stamps' great popularity.

The links with the neighboring U.S. Virgin Islands and with the mainland U.S.A. have been celebrated on B.V.I. stamps, thus making this collection even more popular with the immense philatelic market in the United States. Specific issues have been devoted to celebrate the U.S.V.I. and B.V.I. Friendship Day and the Bicentennial of the American Revolution. Other stamps with an appeal for the American collector include the Quakers set issued in 1973; two values depict William Thornton, a native British Virgin Islander and architect of the Capitol Building in Washington, DC.

Some design elements of B.V.I. stamps are unique because they include either Queen Elizabeth's cameo (or, alternately, her cipher) and at the same time show a currency expressed in U.S. dollars, while the inscriptions clearly read British Virgin Islands. In 1959, the U.S. dollar, along with Eastern Caribbean currency, became the legal tender of the territory; the introduction of stamps with face value in U.S. dollars and cents was at first implemented by overprinting earlier definitive stamps. The dollar had enjoyed great popularity in the B.V.I. since 1917 when the United States purchased the Danish West Indies (St. Thomas, St. John, and St. Croix) and had become a de facto currency. In 1967, the local legislature passed a bill making the U.S. dollar the only legal tender.

Stamp issues of the British Virgin Islands have remained moderate both in the number each year and in face value, yet the designs are always very attractive and have a relevance to the people of the B.V.I. These stamps have shown a regular appreciation in value on the international philatelic market.

Also see *Missing Virgin*.

[Contributed by Giorgio Migliavacca. Vernon Pickering, *Early History of the British Virgin Islands, from Columbus to Emancipation*; Giorgio Migliavacca, "British Virgin Islands: Stamps and Postal History of the Reign of King George VI," *Second Annual B.V.I. Philatelic Exhibition*.]

brøkdel (*c.*) [*Dan.*]; (*m.*) [*Nor.*] (mathematical) fraction.

bronsefarget [*Nor.*] bronze (color).

Bruchteil (*f.*) [*Ger.*] fraction.

brugt [*Dan.*] used.

bruin [*Dut.*] brown.

brukt [*Nor.*] used.

brun [*Fr., Swed., Dan., Nor.*] brown.

bud (*n.*) [*Nor., Dan.*] bid (at an auction or mail bid sale).

budliste (*c.*) [*Dan.*] bid sheet.

bud uden øvre grænse accepteres ikke [*Dan.*] no unlimited bids accepted.

bueno [*Span.*] good.

bueno por... [*Span.*] good for....

buiten koers stelling [*Dut.*] demonetization.

buitenlands [*Dut.*] foreign.

buitenlandse valuta (*f.-c.*) [*Dut.*] foreign currency.

bulle [*Fr.*] manila (color).

bulletin de commande [*Fr.*] order form.

[#2] Bull's Eye [*olho-de-boi*] (Brazil)

Bull's Eye 1. [often written *bull's-eye* or *bullseye*; also known as *socked-on-the-nose*.] A perfectly-centered cancellation on a postage stamp which is made by the circular-dated (plus town name) portion of a machine canceller or of a rubber hand stamp. Bull's eye cancels can be collected by date, type, or city. Some specialists put together what are known as "calendar collections."

2. Common name for the first three general-issue stamps of Brazil (1843), so named because of their resemblance to the eye of a bull. They were issued in denominations of 30, 60, and 90 réis. The Portuguese name for "Bull's Eye" is *Olho-de-Boi*.

The third general issue of Brazil (1850) is known as Goat's Eye (*Olho-de-Cabra*). These stamps are sometimes known as the "poor man's Bull's Eyes" because they are less scarce and less expensive than the 1843 issues.

bun [*Rom.*] good.

bund (c.) [*Dan.*] bottom.

Bundesrepublik Deutschland [*Ger.*] Federal Republic of Germany (better known to English speakers as *West Germany*).

bunn (m.) [*Nor.*] bottom.

bureau; **bureau precancel** U.S. precancelled stamp produced by the Bureau of Engraving and Printing in large quantities for major post offices or as precancelled general issues. Precancels overprinted by the post offices themselves were referred to as *locals*. See *precancel*.

bureau de poste (m.) [*Fr.*] post office.

burelado [*Span.*] *burélage, burelé.*

with & without *burélage (burelé)* on U.S.S.R. stamps

burélage; **burelé** [*Fr.*] A network of fine lines, dots, or other devices. It can be overprinted to either side of a stamp or it can be used as a background design to make counterfeiting or reusing of that stamp more difficult. The Russian stamp in the illustration uses a subtle, inauspicious burélage, but some stamps show a burélage so intense that it almost completely obliterates the stamp's design. See *Winchester paper* for examples.

The words *burélage* and *burelé* are French words but are commonly used by English speakers, especially in Britain.

burelering (m.) [*Nor.*] *burélage, burelé.*

burilagem [*Port.*] *burélage, burelé.*

bursztynowy [*Pol.*] amber (color).

busta (f.) [*Ital.*] envelope; cover. The term for *on cover* in Italian is *su busta.*

busta primo giorno di emissione [*Ital.*] first day cover.

buste enfantin, au [*Fr.*] bust (of the king or

queen) as a child. See *au buste enfantin* for illustration.

Victoria "Butterfly" obliterator #15

Butterflies of Victoria The "butterfly" obliterators were used to cancel the first issues of Victoria (Australia). These brass obliterators were designed by Thomas Ham, who also engraved the first issues ("Half-Lengths").

Fifty obliterators, numbered from 1 to 50, were made and issued to the post offices according to routes ("Line of Road"). They all have a butterfly-shaped body with wings and a "V" underneath. The different post office numbers are found atop the body.

The butterfly obliterators were used for almost two years, commencing January 3, 1850, and were withdrawn around March of 1852. Some of them had special usages (e.g., emergency cancellations, advertised and unclaimed mail, and dead letter office cancellations) and almost half of them have never been recorded on covers.

[Contributed by Greg Herbert. J. R. W. Purves, "Victoria: The 'Butterfly' and 'Barred Oval' Cancellations, 1850-1855." Royal Philatelic Society of Victoria, 1965.]

buying blind Purchasing a stamp through an auction without having first personally seen it. Some auction houses (but not all) will allow blind purchases to be returned if found unsatisfactory. If the lot has been seen by the bidder prior to the bid's being placed, then the successful bidder is legally obligated to purchase the lot. Returns are not normally permitted.

büyük [*Turk.*] large.

Büyük Britanya [*Turk.*] Great Britain.

büyüteç [*Turk.*] magnifying glass.

BVCCARI [*o/p*] Overprint on stamps of Fiume[q.v.] to celebrate the February 1918 naval raid when Italian Commander Gabriele d'Annunzio sank several Austrian ships anchored at Buccari (Bakar).

B.V.I. [*abbr.*] British Virgin Islands[*q.v.*].

B.W.A. [*abbr.*] British West Africa.

B.W.I. [*abbr.*] British West Indies.

by (*v.*) [*Nor.*] to bid (at an auction or mail bid sale).

byde (*v.*) [*Dan.*] to bid.

bytte (*v.*) [*Nor.*] to trade.

C c

C 1. [*abbr.*] cent, céntimo, *et al;* chalky paper; common.

2. Abbreviation used as a pre-adhesive postmark. It refers to "control" handstamps used by postal authorities in various countries (Austria, Turkey, Italy, Iran, etc.) to show that a postal supervisor had checked to make sure the post rate (paid or to be paid) was accurate.

3. [*o/p*] *Campaña* (countryside). Overprinted on stamps of Uruguay in 1922.

Cabinet Noir (*m.*) [*Fr.*] literally, *black closet.* Reference to the censorship of mail in France in the late sixteenth century. See *censored mail.*

cachet 1. [*Fr.*] stamp (but not of the postal variety) or seal.

2. Decorative and ornate design added to an envelope for philatelic purposes. Cachets are most frequently found on first day covers[*q.v.*] and usually relate in some way to the theme of the affixed stamp.

Stamp clubs are a huge source of cachets. Many local and regional organizations issue cachets in conjunction with shows and other club-sponsored activities. The clubs have occasionally run into legal trouble when their cachets include Olympic rings, Disney characters, or other copyrighted designs.

Cachets are sometimes provided by the same postal agencies that issue stamps. Some collectors refer to these as "official" cachets, although the term is not universally accepted.

The cachet in the illustration was produced to help promote the U.S. Hanukkah[*q.v.*] stamp in 1996.

cachet featuring the 1996 U.S. Hanukkah stamp

caderneta (de selos) [*Port.*] booklet (of postage stamps).

cadre (*m.*) [*Fr.*] frame.

cal (*m.*) [*Pol.*] inch.

califica (*v.*) [*Rom.*] to grade.

CALIMNO; CALINO Overprints on Italian stamps used on the Dodecanese island of Calino. See *Aegean Islands*.

całość pocztowa (*f.*) [*Pol.*] cover (in the philatelic sense).

całostka pocztosa [*Pol.*] on cover.

całostka pocztowa (*f.*) [*Pol.*] postal card.

cambio (*m.*) [*Span.*] exchange rate; small change, pocket change [also called *menudo* (*m.*)].

cameo head of The Gambia

cameo head Small round or oval portrait included as the integral part of a stamp's design. It is so named because it resembles the style of cameo jewelry.

In order to give the cameo appearance, the head is usually embossed[*q.v.*] into the paper rather than printed with ink. The technique was used on some nineteenth century stamps, including those from The Gambia and Heligoland that portray Queen Victoria and some early Italian stamps featuring King Victor Emmanuel II.

The stamp in the illustration is sometimes called the *Gambia Cameo*.

Canadiana According to the *Canadian Philatelist*, the term "Canadiana" refers to a postage stamp or other postal item issued by a postage-issuing authority other than Canada itself which exhibits an element or device relating to Canada. The subject was thoroughly reviewed in an excellent five-part series by C. F. Black that appeared in the above-mentioned journal.

The illustration shows an early Canadian stamp featured on a modern Hungarian stamp.

Its purpose was to publicize CAPEX 78 held in Toronto.

[C. F. Black, "Canadiana," *Canadian Philatelist*, 1986: January-February, pp. 16-22; March-April, pp. 88-94; May-June, pp. 160-166; July-August, pp. 235-241; and September-October, pp. 316-323.]

"Canadiana" on Hungarian stamp

cancel (*v.*) The action of obliterating a postage stamp by a postal official so that the stamp cannot be used again.

cancelación (*f.*) [*Span.*] cancellation.

cancelación mediante corte [*Span.*] cut cancellation.

cancelación por taladro circular [*Span.*] punch cancellation

cancelado a la orden [*Span.*] cancelled to order.

cancelado a pluma [*Span.*] pen cancelled.

cancelar (*v.*) [*Span.*] to cancel.

cancellation; cancelation Obliteration placed on a postage stamp by a postal worker to invalidate the stamp for future use. It can also be the invalidation of a revenue stamp.

The first cancels were little more than pen marks, or they consisted of flowers, initials, or other simple designs applied with a rubber stamp.

Modern cancellations are usually in two sections. One part is the *postmark*, found on the left side of the cancel, which gives information. The other part is known as the *killer*, the portion of the cancellation which actually obliterates the stamp.

Cancellations of postage stamps are usually done with a hand-held rubber-stamp canceller or by means of a modern high-speed sorting machine. The postmarks generally include

cancelled-to-order stamps from Dhufar laminated as a bookmark

information about the city and post office where the cancellation took place, as well as the date. In the past, the time of day when the cancel was applied was also sometimes included, but this is rarely seen today. The killers have variously consisted of straight lines, wavy lines, flags, slogans, and other bits of information or decoration.

Even in today's world, some stamps are hand-cancelled with a pen. This usually occurs if the delivery person discovers that a letter has gone through the post office without being cancelled. In most countries, letter carriers are required to draw lines through the stamps in this situation. Stamps cancelled this way are usually not highly collectible but— by definition— they are regarded as cancelled stamps.

Examples of revenue stamps can be found hand cancelled, pen cancelled, punch cancelled, cut cancelled, and invalidated by way of a variety of ingenious means. Some are known to have been invalidated by having dates or other pieces of information hand-written on them.

cancelled to order [abbr.: c.t.o.] Stamps which are cancelled without ever having been attached to a cover or sent through the mail. Except for the cancellation, the stamps are mint fresh in every respect, including full original gum. Full panes are neatly postmarked and are sold by the issuing agencies to collectors and dealers at lower prices than what usable stamps would cost. In some instances, the special cancellation is actually added as the stamps are

being printed, thus making the cancellation part of the stamp's design. In sum, cancelled to order stamps are postage stamps with no legitimate postal value whatsoever that are essentially official "imitations" produced by governments for the lucrative philatelic market.

Catalogue prices are usually for postally-used stamps. But some countries have been producing the *c.t.o.*s on a regular basis, and catalogue prices often reflect this situation. In other words, genuine postally-used examples may command a higher premium than mint-fresh *c.t.o.*s.

The *c.t.o.*s from Dhufar in the illustration were sold to a company that put them into strips of four, laminated them, and then sold the finished item as a bookmark!

Canea, La See *La Canea.*

cantidad (*f.*) [*Span.*] amount; quantity.

çap [*Turk.*] diameter.

caparra (*f.*) [*Ital.*] deposit (of funds).

çaprazlı dantel [*Turk.*] lozenge roulette.

C.A.R. Overprint on the Imperial series of Italy. The acronym stands for *Città Aperta Roma* ("Rome Open City"). This overprint was deemed bogus from its first appearance on the market.

carimbagem (*f.*); **carimbo** (*m.*) [*Port.*] cancellation.

carimbar (*v.*) [*Port.*] to cancel.

carimbo de favor [*Port.*] cancelled to order.

carmesí [*Span.*] crimson.

carnet (*m.*) [*Fr.*] booklet (of stamps).

44

carré (*adj.*) [*Fr.*] square.

carta (*f.*) [*Ital.*] paper; [*Port.*] letter; cover (in the philatelic sense).

carta con fili di seta [*Ital.*] granite paper.

carta costolata (*f.*) [*Ital.*] ribbed paper.

carta di credito [*Ital.*] credit card.

carta gessata (*f.*) [*Ital.*] chalky paper.

carta liscia (*f.*) [*Ital.*] wove paper.

carta moneta (*f.*) [*Ital.*] paper money.

cartão de crédito [*Port.*] credit card.

cartão postal (*m.*) [*Port.*] postcard. The term for *postal card* in Portuguese is *bilhete postal* (*m.*).

carta patinata (*f.*) [*Ital.*] glossy paper.

carta unita (*f.*) [*Ital.*] wove paper.

carta vergata (*f.*) [*Ital.*] laid paper.

carte de credit [*Rom.*] credit card.

carte de crédit [*Fr.*] credit card.

carte postale (*f.*) [*Fr.*] postcard. The term for *postal card* in French is *entier postal* (*m.*).

cartero (*m.*) [*Span.*] mailman, postman.

carţi de credit acceptate [*Rom.*] credit cards accepted.

cartolina (*f.*) [*Ital.*] postcard.

cartolina postale (*f.*) [*Ital.*] postal card.

carto-philately: maps on stamps (Mexico, U.S.); stamp on map paper (Latvia, both sides)

carto-philately Study and collection of stamps incorporating maps in their designs. This field also includes such peripheral issues as the

Latvian stamps printed on the back of German military maps. (See *map paper*.) The term comes from the word *cartography*, the technical name for map-making.

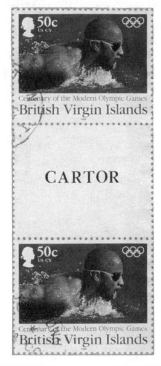

"CARTOR" on gutter label (B.V.I.)

Cartor Security printer that has produced stamps for many countries, including British colonies. Its name can be found imprinted on gutter labels such as the one pictured here from the British Virgin Islands.

cartouche (Angra)

cartouche 1. Rectangular area within a stamp design, usually at the bottom. It is provided by the designer to allow for the insertion of the name of the specific country for common-design type issues. An example are the "palm" stamps[q.v.] issued by France for six of its colonies (Dahomey, French Guinea, Ivory Coast, Mauritania, Senegal, and Upper Senegal & Niger) from 1906 to 1913/14. The designer left the cartouche blank so that the name of each colony could be added.

2. An oval or rectangular figure which shows the name of the ruler. In the 1960s, two types of Saudi Arabian stamps of a certain series were printed, the first showing the cartouche of King Saud. After he died, stamps were ultimately issued with the cartouche of his son, King Faisal.

casa de correos [*Span.*] post office.

casi [*Span.*] almost.

CASO Overprint on Italian stamps used on the Dodecanese island of Casos. See *Aegean Islands*.

castanho [*Port.*] brown.

Castellorizo [a.k.a. *Castelrosso.*] See *Aegean Islands*.

CASTELROSSO [*o/p*] On August 10, 1920, the Treaty of Sevres awarded Rhodes and Castellorizo to Italy. On July 11 of the following year, Italian stamps overprinted "CASTELROSSO" were issued. See *Aegean Islands* for additional information.

catálogo (*m.*) [*Span., Port.*] catalog, catalogue.

catalogo d'asta (*m.*) [*Ital.*] auction catalogue.

catálogo de subasta [*Span.*] auction catalogue.

catalogue d'encan; catalogue de vente aux enchères [*Fr.*] auction catalogue.

catalogus (*m./c.*); **cataloog** (*m./c.*) [*Dut.*] catalog, catalogue.

cataloguswaarde (*f./c.*) [*Dut.*] catalogue value.

Cat's Eye [known as *Olho-de-Gato* in Portuguese.] Series of Brazilian stamps issued from 1854 to 1861 in the values of 10, 30, 280, and 430 réis. Because of their bright colors, they are also called *Coloridos*.

cavallini (*m.pl.*) [*Ital.*] literally, *little horsemen*. Prepaid letter sheets of Sardinia, 1818-20. They are so-named because the paper used for them is impressed with the design of a horseman blowing a horn while at full gallop. In the strictest sense, the *cavallini* were

probably regarded as a tax rather than as postage, because the sum paid did not cover the delivery of the letter.

[Kenneth A. Wood, *This Is Philately*, Vol. I, p. 141; Prince Kandaouroff, *Collecting Postal History*.]

CB [*Fr.*] *Correspondence Baloise*. Pre-adhesive postmark which referred to mail from Basel, Switzerland.

C.C.C.P. [*Russ. abbr.*] Union of Soviet Socialist Republics. [These are actually Cyrillic letters that resemble Roman letters. They are the abbreviation of Союз Советских Социалистических Республик.]

C.Ch. [*Fr. abbr.*] *Cochin Chine* ([French] Cochin China).

CCV [*Ital.*] *Compagnia Corrieri Veneti* (Venetian Couriers Company). Abbreviation used as a pre-adhesive postmark.

C. di L.N. ARONA [*o/p*] See *C.L.N.*

c.d.s. [*abbr.*] circular date stamp.

cec (*n.*) [*Rom.*] check, cheque.

C.E.F. [*abbr.*] Cameroons Expeditionary Force; China Expeditionary Force.

çek [*Turk.*] check, cheque.

cem [*Port.*] hundred.

cena (*f.*) [*Pol.*] price.

cena katalogowa [*Pol.*] catalogue value.

cena licytowana (*f.*) [*Pol.*] a bid (at an auction or mail bid sale).

cena szacunkowa (*f.*) [*Pol.*] suggested bid.

cennik (*m.*) [*Pol.*] price list.

censored mail Censorship has a long and odious history going back to antiquity, and the word itself is of Roman origin. In modern times mail censorship has been exercised on several occasions to examine, suppress, or excise sensitive information for security and intelligence purposes. The practice of mail censorship dates back to the very inception of the postal service in ancient times and is in fact briefly mentioned by Greek and Roman writers. In one form or another, the practice continued through the centuries to re-emerge in northern Italy in the fourteenth and fifteenth centuries. Specific instructions were issued at Bologna, Italy, in 1376 regarding mail censorship. In 1590 France had its *Cabinet Noir,* and under Richelieu and Mazarin the practice flourished.

During the early 1700s mail censorship was also routinely carried out by the postal authorities in Milan, Italy, where the censor was supplied with a "press for letters... identical to the one the Post used" to re-seal perfectly the letters that had been examined. During the American and Napoleonic wars, Great Britain issued instructions to open and inspect any letter to or from the West Indies "if the Publick service required it."

The underlying principle in mail examination by government agents was secrecy, and the examiner was instructed to leave no evidence that the letter had been opened. Censor markings in the form of manuscript endorsements first appeared in Great Britain during the Jacobite Rebellion of 1745-46. During the Napoleonic era the English opened mail to and from their French prisoners of war and stamped it with an oval censor mark featuring the crown and the king's initials (G.R.) and inscribed with the words "Transport Office. Prisoners of War."

Censor marks had made their debut in France during the revolution and shortly thereafter in the New World where some letters emanating from Boston received an oval censor mark featuring a radiating eye and inscribed "Examined/ Marshal's Office Massachusetts (18)14." Early American censor marks include an oval stamper used during the Civil War and inscribed "Prisoners Letter/ Examined/ Elmira. N.Y."

During the South African campaign of 1899 to 1902, the British introduced an elaborate system of censorship, and various types of rubber stamps were used to indicate that mail had been censored. Interestingly enough, some of these censor markings were used on mail from Boer prisoners of war detained in Bermuda and St. Helena. Mail censorship was routinely enforced by all belligerent nations and even by neutral countries during World War I; rubber stamps and adhesive labels to re-seal letters were used to indicate that the letter had been opened. Censorship of mails reached an all-time high during World War II when just about every nation engaged in some form of

mail surveillance at one point or another. Among the strange philatelic items resulting from that war are the so-called *blackout cancels* of Canada, censor postmarks in which the location names within the circular date stamp were deleted.

In more recent times, mail censorship has been carried out by countries at war such as Egypt, Vietnam, Iran, Korea, Cuba, and Pakistan, to name a few. Censored mail is widely studied and collected by specialists throughout the world; the American Philatelic Society has a unit called the Civil Censorship Study Group, and in Europe there is a very active group in Germany called AGZ (Arbeitsgemeinschaft Zensurpost e. V.). Both clubs publish interesting bimonthly bulletins with many informative articles. From a postal history viewpoint, the theme of mail censorship includes both military and civil correspondence.

[Contributed by Giorgio Migliavacca.]

censor mark Rubber stamping, special postmark, adhesive label, or other marking used to indicate that a letter has been opened and inspected. See *censored mail*.

Censurado [*Span.*] Censored. A censor mark from Spanish-speaking countries. See *censored mail*.

Censura gubernativa (*f.*) [*Span.*] Government Censor. A censor mark from Spanish-speaking countries. See *censored mail*.

Censura militar (*f.*) [*Span.*] Censored by the Military. A censor mark from Spanish-speaking countries. See *censored mail*.

Censure Militaire (*f.*) [*Fr.*] Military Censor. A censor mark from French-speaking countries. See *censored mail*.

censurerad post (*r.*) [*Swed.*] censored mail.

censureret post [*Dan.*] censored mail.

cent 1. [*Fr.*] hundred.

2. Minor denomination valued at 1/100 of a dollar, rupee, or gulden. It has been used at various times by sixty-five nations, including Australia, Bahamas, Bermuda, Canada, Hong Kong, the Netherlands, New Zealand, and the United States.

centenaire (*m.*) [*Fr.*] centennial, centenary.

centenar (*n.*) [*Rom.*] centennial, centenary.

Censor cover (1945) mailed from Brazil (above); censored World War II prisoner of war mail (below)

centenario (*m.*) [*Ital., Span.*] centennial, centenary.

centenário (*m.*) [*Port.*] centennial, centenary.

centering: good, fair, and awful

centering A primary factor in determining a stamp's grade. Centering refers to the degree to which the four margins are (or are not) of equal width. Ideally, a stamp's design is located perfectly in the center of the paper with all four margins being precisely the same.

centesimo (*m.*) [*Ital.*] hundredth (fraction).

centésimo (*m.*) [*Span., Port.*] hundredth (fraction).

centième (*m.*) [*Fr.*] hundredth (fraction).

centimetro (*m.*) [*Ital.*] centimeter, centimetre.

centímetro (*m.*) [*Span.*] centimeter, centimetre.

cento [*Ital.*] hundred.

centrado [*Span., Port.*] centered.

centrage (*m.*) [*Fr.*] centering.

centragem (*f.*) [*Port.*] centering.

centralización (*f.*) [*Span.*] centering.

centrato [*Ital.*] centered.

centratura (*f.*) [*Ital.*] centering.

centré [*Fr.*] centered.

Cenzurat [*Rom.*] Censored. A censor mark found on mail opened and inspected in Romania. See *censored mail.*

cercadura (*f.*) [*Port.*] frame.

CERIGO/ OCCUPAZIONE MILITARE ITALIANA World War II overprint on stamps of Greece. It was privately applied and is of no legitimate philatelic interest.

cero [*Span.*] zero.

certificado (*m.*) [*Span., Port.*] certificate.

cesarz (*m.*) [*Pol.*] emperor.

çeşit [*Turk.*] variety.

C.G.H.S. [*Fr. abbr.*] *Commission de Gouvernment Haute Silésie.* (Government Commission of Upper Silesia).

C.G.R. [*o/p*] Cape Government Railways. Overprinted on stamps used for mail carried by train from Caledon, Cape Province, in 1911 and 1912.

chad The small bits of paper punched out of a sheet of stamps during the perforation process.

Chain Breaker (Slovenia)

Chain Breaker Allegorical figure which symbolizes breaking the chains of tyranny. This device is most commonly seen on some post-World War I stamps issued by Eastern European countries. The illustrated stamp is from Slovenia.

chalky paper Paper with a printing surface coated with kaolin which produces a thicker paper with a smooth, white, satiny finish. The printed image is much sharper than that of stamps printed on normal paper because the coating prevents the printer's ink from being absorbed into the paper's fibers during the stamp's manufacture.

Any attempt to remove the cancellation from the stamp so that it can be fraudulently re-used causes the stamp's design to smear or disintegrate. For this reason, a rather heavy chalky paper was widely used by the printing firm of De La Rue for British colonial issues.

The usage of a somewhat lighter type of chalky paper for some stamps of French colonies apparently came about for reasons other than just for security. A. Montader, a French stamp dealer, editor, and designer who had criticized the appearance of the colonial stamps, succeeded in influencing the printery to obtain a quantity of *papier couché* (as it is known in French) in 1914. This paper was used, by no discernible pattern, for various stamps of the colonies from 1914-24.

Soaking stamps produced on chalky paper should be avoided. The ink from which the design is printed can become dislodged from the surface of the paper, thus destroying the stamp's philatelic value. Similarly, the stamps can lose part of their design if they are rubbed, such as by the pages of an album.

Chalky paper is known as a type of *safety paper*[q.v.], i.e., any paper which is specially treated or is manufactured in such a way as to cause some sort of disintegration if any attempt is made to re-use the stamp.

[Contributed by Robert E. Picirilli. Robert G. Stone, "*Papier Couché*— The Chalky-paper Varieties of the French Colonies, 1915-24," *France & Colonies Philatelist*, whole no. 176 (vol. 35, no. 2), pp. 41-43. Gives additional detail, including a listing of all *papier couché* varieties; "Les Coloniaux françaises sur papier couché," *L'Écho de la Timbrologie*, no. 735 (15 août 1926). Lists all *papier couché* varieties.]

"Chalon Head" (Queensland, Australia)

Chalon, Alfred Edward Famous stamp designer. Born 1780 in Geneva, Switzerland; died in 1860.

Chalon studied in England and became Royal Academician in 1816. In 1837 he was appointed painter in water colors to Queen Victoria and did the famous painting of the monarch on her first visit to the House of Lords. The head served as a model for the series of colonial stamps widely known as "Chalon Heads."

[Contributed by Giorgio Migliavacca.]

chân dung [*Viet.*] effigy; portrait.
charactiristikon χαρακτηριστικόν (*n.*) [*Grk.*] attribution.
charneira (*f.*) [*Port.*] (stamp) hinge.
charneirado; com charneira [*Port.*] hinged.

charnela (*f.*) [*Span.*] (stamp) hinge.
charnière (*f.*) [*Fr.*] (stamp) hinge.
châtain [*Fr.*] chestnut (color).
chek чек (*m.*) [*Russ.*] check, cheque.
chelín (*m.*) [*Span.*] (British) shilling.
cheque (*m.*) [*Span., Port.*] check, cheque.
chèque (*m.*) [*Fr.*] check, cheque.
cheshbon חֶשְׁבּוֹן (*m.*) [*Heb.*] account.
child's play stamp See *Kinderpost*.
chilia χίλια (*n.pl.*) [*Grk.*] thousand.
China, Italian Post Offices See *Italian Post Offices in China*.
Chińska Republika Ludowa [*Pol.*] People's Republic of China (P.R.C.).
Chiny [*Pol.*] China.
chitanţă (*f.*) [*Rom.*] receipt.
chrimata χρήματα (*n.pl.*) [*Grk.*] money; cash.

Christmas seals of 1926 and 1952

Christmas seal Popular type of label sold during the Christmas season to raise money for tuberculosis and other lung diseases. The labels have traditionally been placed on the backs of Christmas cards to help "seal" the envelopes, hence the name.

The invention of Christmas seals is attributed to Einar Holböll, a Danish postal worker, who developed this idea in 1904. The concept was introduced to North America three years later by Emily Bissell, who was honored for her efforts on a U.S. commemorative postage stamp in 1980. Christmas seals have ultimately been printed and sold throughout the Christian world.

Christmas seals serve two purposes. First, they form a means of exchange. There is a great psychological difference between asking people to "buy" Christmas seals instead of asking them to "give" to a charity. Secondly, when these seals are affixed to Christmas cards, they become an effective way of promoting lung associations and of raising public consciousness about lung diseases.

Christmas seals usually show the Patriarchal Cross (a cross with one vertical line and two horizontal lines), symbolic of the fight against tuberculosis.

Christmas seals have no postal value and are not normally listed in standard stamp catalogues. They should not be confused with semi-postal stamps[q.v.], some of which allocate a portion of their purchase price to the war on lung disease.

Christmas stamps: Canada & U.S. (above); Cuba (below)

Christmas stamp Postage stamp with a Christmas motif issued during the Christmas mailing season. The first such stamps were issued by Canada in 1898. They were actually intended to commemorate the inauguration of Imperial Penny Postage on Christmas Day. Their "Christmas motif" was limited to the inscription *XMAS 1898* on stamps showing a map of the world with the British Empire indicated in red. The word "XMAS" is regarded as somewhat sacrilegious today, even though what appears to be a roman X is actually the Greek letter χ (chi), the first letter in the Greek word for "Christ" and an early symbol of Christianity (see *Christogram*).

By the mid-1990s, the United States Postal Service was actively promoting its self-adhesive Christmas stamps. This was a marketing gimmick to encourage people to send more Christmas cards, a tradition which is beginning to go out style, partly due to the advent of e-mail, but mostly because of the ever-increasing cost of purchasing and mailing greeting cards.

Christmas stamps have always been in the center of controversy in the United States where the government is constitutionally bound to a separation of Church and State. Many U.S. Christmas stamps show secular designs, but many others display religious themes, usually famous paintings honoring the birth of the Christ Child. Thus far, U.S. courts have upheld the constitutionality of these stamps.

In 1996, the United States issued its first stamps honoring Hanukkah[q.v.]. Initially, a few protests were raised regarding the appropriateness of issuing stamps with a religious theme, but the Hanukkah stamps ultimately proved to be very popular and quite successful.

The illustrations show the Canadian stamp of 1898 as well as more recent Christmas stamps of the U.S. and Cuba.

[C. F. Black, "A Quizzical Look at Canada," *Canadian Philatelist*, May-June 1983, pp. 154-5.]

Christogram Superimposition of the Greek letter χ (chi) over the letter P (rho), the first two letters in the Greek word for "Christ." The Christogram was a symbol used by early Christians as a way of identifying themselves to each other. It is featured on such stamps as the 1962 West German issue honoring the 150th anniversary of the Württemberg Bible Society.

Churchill, Sir Winston [né *Winston Leonard Spencer Churchill*.] British prime minister (1940-45 & 1951-55). Born November 30, 1874, in Blenheim Palace, Oxfordshire, England; died January 24, 1965, in London.

Winston Churchill was the son of Lord Randolph Churchill, third son of the seventh Duke of Marlborough, and Jennie Jerome Churchill, daughter of Leonard W. Jerome, a New York financier. She was part Iroquois Indian and the great-granddaughter of Reuben Murray, a lieutenant in George Washington's Continental Army.

Churchill was noted as being a poor student, and yet he was famous for his fantastic memory. As a young man he served in the British Army in India, South Africa, and the Sudan. Throughout his life he was a prolific writer. His many works include the four-volume *A History of the English-speaking Peoples* (1956-58).

the famous Churchill portrait on U.S. stamp

He was a multifaceted and talented man— a statesman, writer, painter, politician, journalist, and orator remembered as much for his failures as his successes. He was first elected to Parliament in 1900 as a Conservative, but he switched to the Liberal Party in 1904. In 1908 he became president of the Board of Trade in Herbert Henry Asquith's Liberal cabinet. As first lord of the admiralty (1911-15), one of Churchill's primary goals was the modernization of the navy. In 1924, he was appointed Chancellor of the Exchequer, and in 1925 presented his first budget which returned Britain to the gold standard.

Winston Churchill served as prime minister from 1940 to 1945. In response to Hitler's threat, the Grand Alliance was formed. In 1945 he met with Franklin D. Roosevelt and Joseph Stalin at the Yalta Conference.

Through his famous "Iron Curtain" speech in 1946, he called for a strong cooperation between Britain and the Unites States to stand as guardians of peace against Soviet expansionism. Churchill was also the leading advocate of a United States of Europe. He became prime minister again from 1951 to 1955. He received the Nobel Prize for Literature in 1953. In 1963 President John F. Kennedy declared him an honorary citizen of the United States.

Although Churchill is universally regarded as one of the great figures of World War II, his personal life was less than exemplary. He was a heavy drinker who could be quite belligerent when he consumed too much alcohol. On one occasion, Lady Astor chided him for being drunk. He replied, "Madam, tomorrow I shall be sober, but you will still be ugly."

Churchill died on January 24, 1965, in London and received a state funeral reserved only for members of the royal family.

In the history of British coinage, only two commoners have ever appeared on British coins: Oliver Cromwell and Winston Churchill, who was honored on a commemorative 5 shilling crown issued in the year of his death.

Churchill's portrait has been featured on a wide range of postage stamps issued by countries throughout the world. The U.S. stamp in the illustration is very popular because it shows the famous stern-looking photo of him taken during the darkest days of the war.

[Contributed by Pamela Makricosta. Duncan M. White (editor), *Caesar to Churchill: The Years of Fulfillment*; Kenneth G. Richards, *People of Destiny: Sir Winston Churchill*, p. 16; James A. Moncure (editor), *Research Guide to European Historical Biography, 1450 to Present*, p. 428; Frank W. Weis, *Lifelines: Famous Contemporaries from 600 B.C. to 1975*.]

C.I. [*abbr.*] Channel Islands.

ciemny [*Pol.*] dark.

cien; ciento [*Span.*] hundred.

çift [*Turk.*] pair.

C.I.H.S. [*Fr. abbr.*] *Commission Interalliée Haute-Silésie* (Inter-allied Commission of Upper Silesia). Overprinted or handstamped on German stamps used in Upper Silesia.

címlet [*Hun.*] denomination.

cimo (*m.*) [*Port.*] top.

Çin [*Turk.*] China.

Cina [*Ital.*] China.

cinabrio [*Span.*] vermilion.

cinci [*Rom.*] five.

cincizeci [*Rom.*] fifty.

cinco [*Span., Port.*] five.

Çin Cumhuriyeti [*Turk.*] Republic of China.

cinderellas: charity seals; trading stamp; exhibition label

postage stamp attached to non-postal label (cinderella)

cinderella A very broad field of philately which, in essence, includes any stamp-like postal item *except* government-issued adhesive postage stamps and the imprinted stamps on postal stationery. Cinderellas include revenue stamps, local stamps, fiscals, charity seals, gutter labels, hurricane stickers, promotional labels, bogus issues, etiquettes, tabs, exposition poster labels, propaganda and advertising labels, priority mail labels, and virtually anything else of this general nature. In other words, if it looks like a stamp but cannot be used as postage, it's a cinderella.

Despite not being valid for postage, cinderellas are often quite interesting and very collectible. They serve as a fascinating complement to the study of postage stamps.

Çin Halk Cumhuriyeti [*Turk.*] People's Republic of China (P.R.C.).

cincuenta [*Span.*] fifty.

cinq [*Fr.*] five.

cinquanta [*Ital.*] fifty.

cinquante [*Fr.*] fifty.

cinquefoil An ornament or design with five cusps, such as a rose with five petals. It is a device often found on English coins of the late Middle Ages and is occasionally seen on today's postage stamps.

cinqüenta [*Port.*] fifty.

cinque [*Ital.*] five.

cinquième (*m.*) [*Fr.*] fifth (the fraction).

cinzento [*Port.*] gray.

çizgili [*Turk.*] barred.

çizgili damga [*Turk.*] barred stamp.

clair [*Fr.*] light (*re:* color).

claro [*Span., Port.*] light (*re:* color).

clasificación (*f.*) [*Span.*] classification.

clasificar (*v.*) [*Span.*] to classify; to grade.

classement (*m.*) [*Fr.*] classification.

classer (*v.*) [*Fr.*] to classify; to grade.

classificare (*v.*) [*Ital.*] to classify.

classificazione (*f.*) [*Ital.*] classification.

cliché (*m.*) [*Fr.*] literally, (*photographic*) *exposure.* Its philatelic use refers to the method formerly used to produce stamps. In the early days of stamp production, a cliché was the portion of a printing plate that printed one single stamp. Clichés were laid together somewhat like the squares on a checkerboard. If, for example, a full sheet consisted of 400 stamps, then the printing plate required 400 clichés, usually arranged in four groups of 100 each.

Problems with clichés have created interesting errors. If a cliché became worn out or damaged, it could be replaced rather quickly. But occasionally, a replacement cliché was inserted upside-down. The faulty printed stamp and any stamp next to it together would create a *tête-bêche* pair. Some pairs made this way are quite valuable. There were also times when the replacement cliché was inserted sideways, creating a type of *tête-bêche* pair in which one stamp is rotated 90° relative to the other.

anti-fascist C.L.N. overprint

C.L.N. Inscription or overprint widely found on Italian stamps, especially those of the fascist *Repubblica Sociale Italiana* (R.S.I.) established by Benito Mussolini in 1943, or on *ad hoc* stamps issued by the various *Comitati di Liberazione Nazionale* (National Liberation Committees) which had been operating clandestinely on a large scale in Northern Italy until the end of World War II. Under the leadership of Ferruccio Parri, on November 1, 1943, a National Committee of Liberation (C.L.N.) was formed with recruits from the ranks of five anti-fascist parties. This gave momentum to the formation of similar C.L.N. committees and resistance movements throughout Northern Italy.

When the Allies liberated the area, their priority was to chase the retreating Germans. Not until late spring of 1945 was an Allied Military Government established in the area. However, a great degree of internal rule was mostly left in the hands of the various C.L.N.s. The largest C.L.N. (*Alta Italia*— "Upper Italy") had drafted an ordinance regulating the overprinting of stamps of the former R.S.I., but the measure never got off the ground due to greater issues and tasks needing urgent attention. In many cities, and even in small villages, C.L.N. stamps were issued by the various Committees, sometimes for political reasons but mostly as fund raisers at the instigation of local philatelists or stamp clubs. Those C.L.N. stamps with enough evidence to

lend to their legitimacy (i.e., actual postal use) have since been listed in Italian catalogues.

Other C.L.N. issues have raised a great deal of perplexities, although in recent years there has been a tendency to expand the list of legitimate C.L.N. stamps. Throughout the second half of the twentieth century, C.L.N. overprints have often been imitated by forgers as the result of high demand for the limited supply of original material which has lead to escalating prices.

Piacenza overprint

C.L.N. issues which have gained wide acceptance as legitimate stamps include Ariano Polesine in the Rovigo district; Arona in the Novara district; Barge (Cuneo); Maccagno (Varese); Parma; Savona; and Valle Bormida (Alessandria). Other C.L.N. issues, some controversial, include Aosta; Belluno; Cuvio (Varese); Garbagnate Milanese; Imperia; Massa Carrara; Nizza Monferrato; Piacenza; Ponte Chiasso (Como); Sesto Calende (Varese); Torino; Valle d'Ossola (Novara); Varesotto (Varese district); and an array of cinderellas or pseudo stamps.

Also see *MORTE ai Tedeschi invasori....*

[Contributed by Giorgio Migliavacca. Egido Errani and Maurizio Raybaudi Massilia, *Catalogo Specializzato dei Francobolli dei C.L.N.*]

CLN ITALIA POSTA PARTIGIANA Inscription of unissued C.L.N. stamps prepared at Parma, Italy.

C.L.N./ Ossola Libera/ 10.9.44 Overprint used by the Domodossola (Italy) National Liberation Committee. See *C.L.N.*

C.L.N./ POSTE ITALIANE/ ZONA AOSTA Inscription found on stamps issued at Aosta, Italy, in 1944. See *C.L.N.*

C.L.N./ SONDALO/ PRO/ TUBERCOLOTICI [*o/p*] See *C.L.N.*

C.L.N. Zona Aosta [o/p] See *C.L.N.*

CM [*Ital.*] *Corrier Maggior.* Pre-adhesive postmark used by the Venetian Postmaster General.

Co-Ci [o/p] *Commissariato Civile*, the Italian administrative commission for the area which included Slovenia during World War II. See *Lubiana.*

coil Long strip of stamps usually made to accommodate stamp vending machines or other types of machines that use postage stamps. Coil stamps virtually always show either vertical perforations or horizontal perforations but not both; i.e., two parallel sides are perforated but the other two have straight edges. A coil often consists of 500 stamps.

Some of the first coils were actually cut from imperforate panes supplied by the U.S. Post Office in the early 1900s. The strips were pasted together to form long coils and were perforated in special ways to accommodate the mechanical needs of the vending machines. See *Schermack perforation* for additional information and illustrations of the Schermack and Mail-O-Meter coil stamps.

For many years, the Dutch separated their coil stamps via *roltanding*, known to English speakers as interrupted[q.v.] or syncopated perforation, which kept the paper at separation points strong enough so that the stamps would not separate at the wrong time and jam the vending machine.

Whether a stamp comes from a coil or from a pane usually does not make a great deal of difference to the stamp's philatelic value, largely because most coil stamps are standard definitives printed in such huge quantities that it does not really matter where they come from. Of course, collectors who do not like straight edges will prefer pane stamps.

There are some instances, however, where coil stamps are much preferred. The best U.S. example is the group of stamps known as the Orangeburg Coil[q.v.], a coil of 500 Washington 3c definitives produced in 1911. Unlike other 3c coil stamps of its day, this one unique coil was perfed at 12 instead of the usual 8 1/2. The surviving specimens from that coil are con-sidered to be great rarities and sell for many thousands of dollars.

coin daté [*Fr.*] The dated corner block found on some sheets of French stamps. They are collected by French specialists much in the same manner as U.S. collectors save plate blocks. The *coin daté* is found on issues from 1924 to 1971.

[Contributed by John E. Lievsay. Marc Martin, "The Hulot Plates of France," France & Colonies *Philatelist*, No. 156, April 1974, pp. 25-35.]

coleção (*f.*) [*Port.*] collection.

colección (*f.*) [*Span.*] collection.

coleccionar (*v.*) [*Span., Port.*] to collect. [Note: the preferred spelling in Portuguese is *colecionar.*]

coleccionista (*m./f.*) [*Span.*] collector.

colecionador (*m.*) [*Port.*] collector.

colecionar (*v.*) [*Port.*] to collect.

colecţie (*f.*) [*Rom.*] collection.

colecţiona (*v.*) [*Rom.*] to collect.

colecţionar (*m.*) [*Rom.*] collector.

colis (*m.*) [*Fr.*] package.

colis postal [*Fr.*] parcel post.

collectionner (*v.*) [*Fr.*] to collect.

collectionneur (*m.*) [*Fr.*] collector.

college stamp 1. Local stamp[q.v.] used for a messenger service at Cambridge and Oxford Universities in Great Britain as far back as the mid-1600s. The service did not extend beyond the boundaries of those institutions.

The emission of the first adhesive postage stamps in Britain in 1840 generated renewed interest in this concept. From 1871 and 1884, Hertford, Keble, Merton, and Exeter Colleges issued their own "local" postal cards and envelopes.

2. Stamp-like labels or legitimate stamps with special precancellations used by business colleges for classroom purposes. See *training stamp.*

collezionare (*v.*) [*Ital.*] to collect.

collezione (*f.*) [*Ital.*] collection.

collezionista (*m./f.*) [*Ital.*] collector.

color changeling A stamp whose color has changed due to exposure to chemicals or light. The color alteration can be caused accidentally or intentionally.

colored line roulette (Thurn & Taxis)

colored (coloured) line roulette [also known by the French term *percé en lignes de couleur*.] A form of rouletting[q.v.] that is different from the other types in that the location of the piercing is indicated by rows of colored dashes printed over top of the short slits. Unlike perforations, which are normally very visible to the naked eye, some line rouletting is difficult to discern. The colored marks are printed simultaneously with the rest of the stamp's design to enable the user to find the separation points more quickly.

This method was rarely used. The most common examples are the stamps of Thurn und Taxis (Southern District). The different denominations were printed in different colors. Naturally, the colored dashes were printed in the same color as the rest of the stamp.

combination usage The terms *combination usage* and *mixed usage* refer to covers with stamps of more than one postal service. Covers franked with two or more different issues from the same country are sometimes called *mixed frankings*, but *multi-issue franking* would be a better choice.

The rarest type of mixed usage is true *mixed franking*, in which postage is prepaid with stamps of more than one authority. An example would be a cover with a Danish West Indies stamp payng local D.W.I. postage and a United States stamp paying packet postage to the U.S. from St. Thomas. This usage would have been valid before the G.P.U. or during the transition period immediately following, but afterwards there would be no reason for such franking.

A much commoner usage occurs when letters are forwarded. Before the G.P.U., if a letter was taken out of the mails and re-addressed, it had to start all over again and be refranked or have postage due collected, depending on local rules. Now, of course, a first-class letter can be forwarded, if unopened, without additional postage.

A third usage showing normal postage stamps of two countries can happen when these stamps are used to indicate that postage due is to be collected from the addressee. The usual practice of showing the additional amount to be paid was by manuscript rating or with a handstamp numeral. However, some places, including Greece and Puerto Rico, used stamps for this purpose fairly routinely.

[Contributed by H. L. Arnould.]

combinazione (*f.*) [*Ital.*] combination; *se-tenant*.

comb perforation Method of perforating sheets of stamps whereby three sides of the stamp are perforated at one time and the operation is repeated row by row or column by column until all sides of the stamps are perfed. This method is so named because each time the perforation process takes place, the arrangement of holes left in the paper resembles a comb.

The other types of perforations are harrow perforations, in which the entire sheet or pane is perforated at once, and line or guillotine perforations, which are punched one row at a time.

comemorativ (*adj.*) [*Rom.*] commemorative.
comemorativo (*m.; adj.*) [*Port.*] commemorative.
comerciar (*v.*) [*Span.*] to trade.
Comitato/ Liberazione/ Nazionale/ MACCAGNO [*o/p*] See *C.L.N.*
commémoratif (*adj.*) [*Fr.*] commemorative.
commemorative (*noun; adj.*) A stamp issued to honor a person or to mark a special event. Commemoratives are only available at the post office for a limited time. Some experts feel that the availability should be limited to eighteen months, but this is not a universally-accepted time span. Stamps that are available

for extended periods of time are called *definitives*.

Commemorative stamps are also featured on *souvenir sheets*[q.v.] and are almost always the types of stamps that are *cancelled to order*[q.v.]. Some commemoratives have created considerable controversy, such as the U.S. Nixon and AIDS stamps (see *protest cover*). The presence of Elvis Presley and Marilyn Monroe on U.S. commemoratives pleased many Americans (as well as people from all over the world) and angered many others. Regardless, the Elvis and Marilyn stamps were wildly popular with collectors and non-collectors alike and generated huge profits for the U.S. Postal Service.

Commemorative stamps sometimes honor people who made major contributions to society but whose names are virtually unknown to the general public. Many commemoratives (as well as definitives) from the United States fall into this category. The Soviet Union issued many stamps honoring people whose views would clearly have been anti-communist, such as Benjamin Franklin, Albert Einstein, and even Jesus Christ (a Da Vinci painting of Jesus and the Virgin Mary appeared on a 1971 Christmas stamp).

Many philatelists consider the first commemoratives to be the set of six denominations of 1888 and 1889 stamps of New South Wales which marked the hundredth anniversary of the first British settlement in Australia. These were the first adhesive stamps issued anywhere which mention the anniversary of a special event.

Commissione Provinciale Censura (*f.*) [*Ital.*] Provisional Censor Commission. A censor mark from Italian-speaking countries. See *censored mail*.

compound perforation A stamp whose horizontal and vertical perforations do not gauge the same. For example, some of the Russian issues of 1922 are listed in catalogues as "Perf 14 1/2 x 15." This means that the stamps are horizontally perfed at 14 1/2 and vertically perfed at 13. Compound perfing is done to avoid certain production problems.

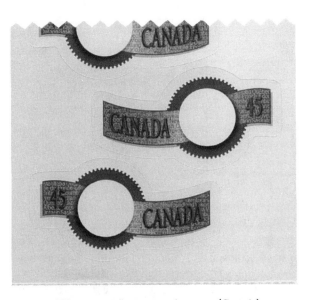

"Chiropractic" compound stamps (Canada): postal portions (above); decorative labels (below)

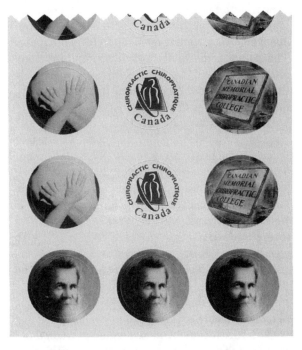

compound stamp Two-piece stamp which is assembled by the user. A decorative self-adhesive label is chosen from several possibilities and is attached to a postally-valid, self-adhesive stamp. That, in turn, is affixed to an envelope.

Canada used this idea in 1995 with its "booklet" of 45c stamps commemorating the hundredth anniversary of the chiropractic profession, a field founded by a Canadian. The concept is interesting, but the resulting stamps were among the strangest and ugliest ever issued by that nation.

comprador (*m.*) [*Span., Port.*] buyer.

comprar (*v.*) [*Span., Port.*] to buy.

comprare (*v.*) [*Ital.*] to buy.

compratore (*m.*) [*Ital.*] buyer.

comum [*Port.*] common.

común [*Span.*] common.

comune [*Ital.*] common.

Comunicaciones [*Span.*] Communications. Inscription found on early Spanish revenue stamps.

con charnela; con fijasello [*Span.*] hinged.

condition [also referred to as *grading*.] When describing a stamp's condition, factors such as centering, state of the gum, brightness (or fading) of color, heavy or unpleasant cancellation marks, quality of impression, and other similar characteristics are considered. Any specific faults, such as thin spots or tears, must be taken into account.

The following are the grades of stamps, ranging from worst to best:

—*poor:* A stamp in terrible condition, sometimes not even recognizable. Unless a stamp in poor condition is a great rarity, it is not generally regarded as collectible.

—*good:* A stamp that has tears, thins, or creases, is off-center, and lacks a pleasing appearance. From a collector's point of view, a stamp in good condition acts as a "filler" until a better specimen can be found (or afforded).

—*very good:* Considered the lowest acceptable grade for a collectible stamp. A stamp in very good condition is usually off-center and has one or two minor faults such as thin spots or creases that do not detract from the stamp's overall appearance. There are no large tears or face scrapes. Noticeable hinge marks can be expected. A used stamp of this grade might be heavily cancelled.

—*fine:* A stamp in this grade is slightly off-center but has no faults. The stamp is generally pleasing in appearance. It may have hinge marks and a somewhat heavy cancellation.

—*very fine:* There must be no faults of any kind, and the centering is nearly perfect. A very collectible specimen. It must have fresh color and no more than a light hinge mark with the remainder of the gum undisturbed. If perforate, the teeth should all be in good condition; if imperforate, the margins should be even and adequate.

—*extremely fine; superb:* This is the *crème de la crème*, a stamp with perfect centering, good color, neat perforations, and as close to perfect in every respect as a stamp can be. [Note: The term *superb* was created by dealers to make their *extremely fine* stamps seem better than the top grade would indicate and thus be more marketable. However, the term has become popular and is widely used.]

Confœderatio Helvetica [*Lat.*] Official Latin name of Switzerland. Stamps and coins are usually inscribed *Helvetia*. Switzerland has four official languages— German, French, Italian, and Romansh; to avoid confusion (as well as to circumvent local jealousies), the Latin designation is preferred.

conjoined busts: traditional & nontraditional placement

conjoined [also known as *accolated* or *jugate*.] Postage stamp design showing two or more heads or busts which face in the same direction and overlap.

This technique first appeared on Egyptian gold coins in the third century B.C. Ptolemy III and wife Berenice were portrayed in a conjoined fashion to indicate that they were co-rulers, yet with one having more status than the other. Because of the infrequency of having two people rule the same country simultaneously, conjoined portraiture on coins did not become a widely-needed technique during ancient and medieval times.

Although joint rule is no more common in the twentieth century than it was in previous times, the methods of deciding who appears on postage stamps and how they appear have changed immensely. Stamps are no longer the exclusive domain of kings and queens. When two or three commoners are portrayed on the same stamp in conjoined fashion, all of them are presumed to have equal status, so the positioning of the individuals relative to each other usually has no particular significance.

Yet even in the twentieth century the matter of positioning is very important when royalty is involved. If a reigning monarch is portrayed with someone else, then the ancient custom of placing the monarch's effigy in the forefront and of relegating the other person's portrait toward the back comes into play. If Queen Elizabeth II and Prince Philip are depicted together, Elizabeth will traditionally appear in the front.

A notable example of non-traditional positioning is the British Commonwealth omnibus issues of 1948-49 portraying King George VI and Queen Mother Elizabeth. In the strictest sense, George VI's status was greater than that of his wife, yet Elizabeth was shown in the forefront on these stamps honoring their silver wedding anniversary.

conjugado [*Port.*] accolated[q.v.], conjoined, jugate.

conmemorativo (*m.; adj.*) [*Span.*] commemorative.

con ó [*Viet.*] eagle.

conocidos (*m.pl.adj.*) [*Span.*] known. Usually used in the sense of a certain number of specimens known to exist, e.g., *cuatro conocidos* ("four known").

cont (*n.*) [*Rom.*] account.

conta (*f.*) [*Port.*] account.

contante (*m.*) [*Ital.*] cash (ready money).

contant (*adj.*) [*Dut.*] cash.

continuous silk thread paper A type of safety paper[q.v.] that exhibits one or more continuous colored silk threads which run the entire length of the stamp. Its purpose is to make forgeries more difficult. It is more commonly known as *Dickinson paper*[q.v.].

conto (*m.*) [*Ital.*] account.

contrafação (*f.*) [*Port.*] a counterfeit; a fake, forgery.

contraffazione (*f.*) [*Ital.*] a counterfeit.

contrassegno (*m.*) [*Ital.*] cash on delivery (C.O.D.).

contrefaçon (*f.*) [*Fr.*] a counterfeit; a fake, forgery.

CONTRO; Control Abbreviation used as a pre-adhesive postmark. See *C*.

Spanish stamp (both sides) with control number

control number Plate position numbers or serial numbers printed on the backs of stamps for purposes of internal control. Control numbers are most commonly found on some stamps of Spain issued from 1875 through the 1930s. The most unusual control numbers are found on the self-adhesive stamps of Tonga issued in the 1960s and 70s. Each number is printed on small separate self-adhesive "tab" affixed to the same piece of backing paper as the stamp.

conundrum Riddle or inexplicable situation that arises in philately.

COO; COS Overprints on Italian stamps used on the Dodecanese island of Kos. See *Aegean Islands*.

Copa Mundial de Fútbol [*Span.*] World Cup of Football (soccer).

coppia (*f.*) [*Ital.*] pair.

coppia invertita (*f.*) [*Ital.*] *tête-bêche* pair.

cor (*f.*) [*Port.*] color, colour.

cornice (*f.*) [*Ital.*] frame.

coroa (*f.*) [*Port.*] crown.

corona (*f.*) [*Span., Ital., Port.*] crown.

coronato di lauro [*Ital.*] laureate.

Coroncine (*f.pl.*) [*Ital.*] literally, *little crowns.* Nickname of the airmail semipostal official stamps issued by Italy for its colonies and Italy proper in 1934 which were overprinted with a small Savoy crown (from which the nickname was derived) and a one-line inscription reading "SERVIZIO DI STATO." They are among the most coveted stamps of the Italian colonial area, as only 750 of them were issued for each of the four colonies: Cyrenaica, Eritrea, Somalia, and Tripolitania.

correio (*m.*) [*Port.*] mail; post office.

correio aéreo (*m.*) [*Port.*] airmail.

correio de campanha [*Port.*] field post.

correo (*m.*) [*Span.*] mail.

correo aéreo (*m.*) [*Span.*] airmail.

correo de campaña [*Span.*] field post.

correspondencia censurada (*f.*) [*Span.*] censored mail.

corrispondenza censurata (*f.*) [*Ital.*] censored mail.

cortado [*Span.*] cut; rouletted.

cortado a serpentina [*Span.*] serpentine roulette.

cortado em dois [*Port.*] bisected.

cortado en cuadrado [*Span.*] cut square.

cortado en puntos [*Span.*] pin perforation, *percé en points.*

cortado en zigzag [*Span.*] serrated roulette, zigzag roulette, *percé en pointes, percé en scie.*

cortado quadrado [*Port.*] cut square.

corte em serpentina [*Port.*] serpentine roulette.

Todays' covers don't have to be dull!

corte em serra [*Port.*] serrated roulette.

corte percê [*Port.*] roulette, *perçage*.

cotele [*Fr.*] ribbed paper.

couleur (*f.*) [*Fr.*] color, colour.

coupé [*Fr.*] cut; bisected.

coupure d'entier postal [*Fr.*] cut square.

courant [*Fr.*] common.

couronne (*f.*) [*Fr.*] crown (royal headpiece; large silver coin).

courrier (*m.*) [*Fr.*] the mail.

courrier passé par la censure [*Fr.*] censored mail.

cover Any envelope, postcard, wrapper, box, tube, piece of postal stationery, or other similar item which is itself mail or is a container for mail and upon which postage is affixed or imprinted.

Covers can be as bland as a piece of junk mail or can be as complex and interesting as the envelope in the photo. The illustrated piece with its multiple stamps, souvenir sheets, etiquettes, etc., was mailed from Denmark to America by a collector with flair!

The term *on cover* refers to a stamp still attached to an envelope, postcard, or whatever. In some cases, the cover makes no difference to the stamp's value. On the other hand, a postcard that travelled to Europe on the Graf Zeppelin and still has its U.S. Zeppelin[*q.v.*] stamp intact is worth more than the cancelled stamp by itself.

A *first day cover*[*q.v.*] is a stamped envelope or other cover postmarked on the official date of its stamp's issuance or on the first day upon which that stamp is valid for postage.

cramoisi [*Fr.*] crimson.

credit cards accepted Statement that would be found on an order blank or catalogue indicating that MasterCard™, Visa™, American Express™, or whatever other credit cards are accepted in payment.

credit cards worden aangenomen [*Dut.*] credit cards accepted.

crédito (*m.*) [*Span., Port.*] credit.

cremefarben [*Ger.*] cream (color).

cremisi [*Ital.*] crimson.

CRNA GORA [ЦРНА ГОРА] [*Serb.-Cr.; o/p*] See *Montenegro*.

Croce Rossa [*Ital.*] Red Cross.

Croix Rouge [*Fr.*] Red Cross.

crosses: Maltese, Latin, Jerusalem, & *Croix de Guerre*

cross Ancient symbol found in many cultures. The tau (T-shaped) cross was a symbol of life to the ancient Egyptians; when combined with a circle, it represented eternity. To the ancient Greeks, the cross was a metaphor for the four indestructible elements of creation: air, earth, fire, and water.

The cross's greatest impact on philately has been as a symbol of Christianity and as such is often seen on stamps with religious themes. A Greek Cross printed in red is the symbol of the International Red Cross.

A cross with a more somber history is the swastika, the symbol of Nazi Germany. Throughout the centuries, the swastika has represented a wide spectrum of concepts ranging from the source of life to agriculture and has even been found in early Christian catacombs. Yet its philatelic involvement is clearly with World War II Germany.

There are more than twenty forms of crosses. The ones most likely to be seen on postage stamps are pictured in the illustrations.

The two French stamps show crosses associated with military decorations: the Maltese Cross and the *Croix de Guerre*. The two German stamps feature Protestant crosses: the Latin Cross and a stylized Jerusalem Cross (the emblem of the Evangelical Synod).

Also see *Christmas seal*.

cruciform shield Shield design arranged in the form of a cross. The cross forms a divider to show four separate devices. This is a useful configuration when, for example, the symbols of four political entities must be represented in the same shield.

Cruz Roja [*Span.*] Red Cross.

Cruz Vermelha [*Port.*] Red Cross.

Crveni krst Montenegro [*Serb.-Cr.*; *o/p*] Red Cross Montenegro. See *Montenegro*.

Cs. [*Hun. abbr.*] csomag (parcel). Overprinted on 1946 inflation stamps of Hungary to indicate validity.

CS [*Ital.*] *Corrispondenza Sarda*. Transit pre-adhesive postmark on letters from the Kingdom of Sardinia.

csekk [*Hun.*] check, cheque.

csillag [*Hun.*] star.

C.S.I.R./ VINCEREMO [*Ital.*] Overprint meaning *Italian Expeditionary Force in Russia/ We Will Win* which was printed on Rome-Berlin Axis stamps of Italy. This overprint is neither semi-official nor privately produced. It was simply a fabrication to lure inexperienced, naïve collectors.

C.S.1.R. [*Fr.*] *Correspondance Sarde 1 Rayon* ("Kingdom of Sardinia Mail First Radius"). Used on mail from the Kingdom of Sardinia to nearby nations. Similar pre-adhesive postmarks with the numbers 2nd through 7th Radius exist, depending on the distance of the final destination.

C.S.R.1. [*Fr.*] *Correspondance Sarde Rayon 1* [2 or *3*] ("Kingdom of Sardinia Mail Radius One [Two *or* Three]"). See *C.S.1.R.*

CT [*Ital.*] *Corrispondenza Ticinese*. Stamped on mail dating from 1837 to 1850 from the Ticino Canton (Kanton Tessin) of Switzerland to indicate it had not been prepaid.

c.t.o. [*abbr.*] cancelled to order[*q.v.*].

ctr. [*abbr.*] center, centre.

cu [*Rom.*] with.

cuadernillo (*m.*) [*Span.*] booklet (of stamps).

cuadrado (*m.; adj.*) [*Span.*] square.

cuadriculado [*Span.*] *quadrillé*.

cuarenta [*Span.*] forty.

cuarto (*m.*) [*Span.*] a fourth, quarter.

cuatro [*Span.*] four.

cu defect [*Rom.*] defective.

cuenta (*f.*) [*Span.*] account (financial or transactional); *a cuenta*: on account.

cuirassed (abbreviated *cuir.*) Protected by armor on the breast and shoulder.

culoare (*f.*) [*Rom.*] color, colour.

cumpăra (*v.*) [*Rom.*] to buy.

cumpărător (*m.*) [*Rom.*] buyer.

cupo [*Ital.*] deep (re: color).

Curly Head Spanish colonial keytype of 1898 featuring the curly-locked King Alfonso XIII, then about twelve years old. See *au buste enfantin* for illustration.

currency Any form of circulating coins or paper money, and in particular, those with legal tender status. It is a commercial term referring to any circulating money produced by a government or any official agency authorized to issue money.

Although many people (including numismatists) use the word as if it were synonymous with paper money, this is not the case. *Currency* can include circulating coins as well as many philatelic items which have been used as money (see *postage stamp currency*). The term *paper currency* as a reference to paper money is acceptable.

currency paper See *postage stamps on currency paper*.

curs de schimb (*n.*) [*Rom.*] exchange rate.

cută (*f.*) [*Rom.*] a crease, fold.

cut cancellation Slits or wedges that are cut into a stamp or piece of paper money to cancel or invalidate it. Although some postage stamps have been cut cancelled to prevent their reuse, this method has been more commonly applied to fiscal, telegraph, and other revenue stamps of nonpostal usage. The obvious problem in using this method to cancel postage stamps is that the mail itself incurs a certain amount of damage.

Slits were also applied to disinfected mail[q.v.] which sometimes affected the stamps. In this case, however, the process of slitting was not intended to be a form of cancellation.

cut square v. cut to shape

cut square The preferred method of removing an imprinted stamp from a piece of postal stationary. The area of paper that is clipped from the upper right-hand corner of the envelope is larger than the stamp itself, thereby allowing a border of blank paper around the stamp. Usually the cut-out is square or rectangular, while the imprinted stamp may be oval, round, octagonal, or virtually any other shape.

The less desireable possibility is *cut to shape*, in which the cut-out is the same shape and size as the stamp itself. Although there is sometimes a bit of blank border left around the imprinted stamp, most often the stamp is trimmed directly around its boundary. It must be noted, however, that early stamp albums were designed to encourage cutting to shape, which explains why many older imprinted stamps were cut this way.

cut to shape An undesirable method of removing an imprinted stamp from a piece of postal stationary by closely trimming it from its original cover. Usually there is no border of blank paper left around the stamp. The cut-out is the same shape and size as the stamp itself. Early stamp albums were designed to encourage cutting to shape, the reason why many older imprinted stamps were cut this way.

The preferred method is called *cut square*[q.v.]. The area of paper that is clipped from the upper right-hand corner of the envelope is larger than the stamp itself, thereby allowing a border of blank paper around the stamp. Usually the cut-out is square or rectangular, while the imprinted stamp may be oval, round, octagonal, or virtually any other shape.

C/V [*abbr.*] catalogue value.

CV DA TRIESTE [*Ital.*] *Col Vapore da Trieste* ("From Trieste by Steamship"). Pre-adhesive postmark.

CV DA VENEZIA [*Ital.*] *Col Vapore da Venezia* ("From Venice by Steamship"). Pre-adhesive postmark.

C.VL. [*Fr.*] *Correspondence Valaisanne.* Abbreviation used as a pre-adhesive postmark on mail from the Wallis region of Switzerland. This came as a result of the postal treaty of May 13, 1835, between the Wallis Canton and the Kingdom of Sardinia.

C.X.C. [*Serb.-Cr. abbr.*] Cyrillic overprint found on some stamps of Bosnia and Herzegovina which refers to Serbia, Croatia, and Slovenia. A similar overprint exists in the equivalent Roman letters *S.H.S.*

czarny [*Pol.*] black.

czek (*m.*) [*Pol.*] check, cheque.

czerwiec [*Pol.*] June.

czerwony [*Pol.*] red.

Czerwony Krzyż [*Pol.*] Red Cross.

czterdzieści [*Pol.*] forty.

cztery [*Pol.*] four.

czworoblok znaczków (*m.*) [*Pol.*] block of four.

D d

d. [*abbr.*] penny (or its plural form *pence*). Because the word *penny* is presumed to have been derived from *denarius*, an ancient Roman coin, the abbreviation of the traditional penny is "d." instead of "p." However, the "p." designation has been used since the switch-over to decimalization in 1970.

D.A.a£ [*Ital.*] *Debito Austriaco austriache Lire.* Accountancy mark in Austrian currency on mail in transit on Austrian territory, namely Lombardy-Venetia, to destinations in the Kingdom of Sardinia. The accountancy mark was introduced as a result of the postal treaty of 1853 between Austria and the Kingdom of Sardinia.

daftar harga [*Indo.*] price list.

daglig- (*adj.*) [*Dan.*] definitive.

dalawa [*Tag.*] two.

Damus Petimus Que Vicissim [*Lat.*] We give and expect in return. Inscription found on the British Guiana One Cent Magenta[*q.v.*], regarded as the world's rarest stamp.

dañado [*Span.*] damaged.

Danemark [*Fr.*] Denmark.

Dänemark [*Ger.*] Denmark.

danificado [*Port.*] damaged.

Danimarca [*Ital.*] Denmark.

Danmark [*Nor.*] Denmark.

danneggiato (*m.*) [*Ital.*] damaged.

dantel [*Turk.*] perforation.

dantellenmiş [*Turk.*] perforated.

dantelsiz [*Turk.*] imperforate.

data (*f.*) [*Port., Pol.*] date.

dato (*m.*) [*Nor.*] date.

datum (*n.*) [*Swed.*]; (*m.-c.*) [*Dut.*] date.

Datum (*n.*) [*Ger.*] date.

D.B.P. [*o/p*] Overprinted in the form of a script monogram on Russian "Arms" stamps of the Far Eastern Republic in 1919 and 1920.

D.D.R. [*Ger. abbr.*] *Deutsche Demokratische Republik* (German Democratic Republic). Known to English speakers as East Germany.

dead countries: Bavaria, Czarist Russia, East Germany

formerly dead country: Lithuania

dead country A nation which formerly issued postage stamps, coins, or banknotes but which no longer exists as a political entity.

The nineteenth century saw some stamp-issuing countries come and go (Hawaii, Confederate States of America, various German states, *et al*), but the twentieth century has witnessed an enormous number of such national "deaths." On the one hand, the Soviet Union, Czechoslovakia, Yugoslavia, and a number of other countries have become dead in the philatelic sense by splitting apart. On the other hand, East Germany and West Germany merged.

The illustrations show stamps of Bavaria, Czarist Russia, and East Germany, all of which could be considered philatelically dead. The stamp of Lithuania provides somewhat of a philatelic anomaly, because it represents a country that was dead but has risen from the ashes as a stamp-issuing entity. Lithuania, Latvia, Croatia, Estonia, Ukraine, and a host of other nations proved in the 1990s that death is not permanent in philately.

deasupra [*Rom.*] top.

décembre [*Fr.*] December.

déchiré [*Fr.*] torn.

déchirure (*f.*) [*Fr.*] a tear (as in a stamp or banknote).

dechomaste pistotikes kartes δεχόμαστε πιστωτικές κάρτες [*Grk.*] credit cards accepted.

decimo (*m.*) [*Ital.*] tenth (the fraction).

décimo (*m.*) [*Span., Port.*] tenth (the fraction).

decoration: the U.S. Purple Heart

decoration Medallic badge, ribbon, or sash ornament awarded for valor or as a prize. Unlike other types of awards, decorations are intended to be worn, not just displayed.

Military decorations are a very popular motif on stamps and postal stationery. The illustration shows the Purple Heart, a decoration awarded to American soldiers (or their families) who are killed or wounded in combat.

découpage (*m.*) [*Fr.*] Cut impressions of stamps, some in special colors, used in the pressbed by the printer to get uniform clarity of detail. It is also known as *mise-en-train* in French and is called *makeready* or *patching* in English.

[Contributed by John E. Lievsay.]

dedesubt [*Rom.*] bottom.

défaut (*m.*) [*Fr.*] defect.

defectivo; defeituoso [*Port.*] defective.

défectueux [*Fr.*] defective.

defectuoso [*Span.*] defective.

defeito (*m.*) [*Port.*] defect.

definitieve [*Dut.*] definitive.

définitif [*Fr.*] definitive.

definitive (*noun; adj.*) A regular-issue stamp that is printed and sold by the post office for a prolonged period of time. Depleted stocks may be renewed as often as necessary. Many collectors regard a definitive stamp as one that is available for at least eighteen months, although not all experts agree with that exact time requirement. Stamps issued for only a short time are called *commemoratives*.

definitivo [*Span., Port.*] definitive.

definitywny [*Pol.*] definitive.

defne yaprağı taçlı baş [*Turk.*] laureate.

defnostefis δαφνοστεφής [*Grk.*] laureate.

değer düşürme [*Turk.*] devaluation.

değerli [*Turk.*] valuable.

değiştirme [*Turk.*] alteration.

D.E.I. [*abbr.*] Dutch East Indies.

Dei Gratia [*Lat.*] By the Grace of God. Abbreviated *D.G.* or *Dei Gra.* Motto often seen in reference to the British monarch.

deka δέκα [*Grk.*] ten.

dekorasjon (*m.*) [*Nor.*] cachet.

Dél-Afrika [*Hun.*] South Africa.

De La Rue, Thomas Thomas De La Rue was already into the printing business before he moved from Guernsey to London in 1819. His firm gained its first contract to print fiscal stamps in 1853, but two years later De La Rue was contracted to print the first 4d stamp for Great Britain. Between 1855 and 1880, De La Rue printed all the British high denominations, and in 1880 the firm won the contract for the lower denominations. It was during the following three decades that the company enjoyed virtual monopoly.

Famous foreign stamps produced by De La Rue include Italy (1863), Confederate States of America (1862), Belgium (1865 and 1883), Egypt (1879), and Siam (1887).

[Contributed by Giorgio Migliavacca.]

deltion paraggelion δελτίον παραγγελιών (*n.*) [*Grk.*] order form.

demi (*adj.*) [*Fr.*] half.

démonétisation (*f.*) [*Fr.*] demonetization.

Demonetisierung (*f.*) [*Ger.*] demonetization.

demonetyzacja (*f.*) [*Pol.*] demonetization.

denaro (*m.*) [*Ital.*] money.

dengi деньги (*pl.*) [*Russ.*] money.

denominação (*f.*) [*Port.*] denomination.

dentado [*Span.*] (*m.*) perforation; (*adj.*) perforated.

dentado de peine [*Span.*] comb perforation.

dentado en línea [*Span.*] line perforation.

denteação (*f.*) [*Port.*] perforation.

denteação em linhas [*Port.*] line perforation.

denteação parcial (*f.*); **denteação irregular** (*f.*) [*Port.*] interrupted perforation; syncopated perforation.

denteado [*Port.*] perforation.

dentelé [*Fr.*] perforated.

dentellato [*Ital.*] perforated.

dentellato a roulette [*Ital.*] rouletted.

dentellatura (*f.*) [*Ital.*] perforation.

dentellatura a pettine [*Ital.*] comb perforation.

dentello (*m.*) [*Ital.*] perforation.

dentelure (*f.*) [*Fr.*] perforation.

dentelure en lignes [*Fr.*] line perforation.

dentelure en peigne [*Fr.*] comb perforation.

dentelure syncopée (*f.*) [*Fr.*] interrupted perforation; syncopated perforation.

deposito obbligatorio (*m.*) [*Ital.*] deposit required.

deposit required Statement on an auction bid sheet indicating that a deposit must be submitted with the bid in order for the bid to be considered. The amount of the deposit will be a specified percentage of the total bid. If the bid is successful, the deposit is applied to the price of the item. If the bid is unsuccessful, the deposit is returned. The purpose of a required deposit is to help insure that the highest bidder will honor his bid as he is legally obligated to do.

depositum (*n.*) [*Nor., Dan.*] deposit.

depositum nødvendig [*Nor.*] deposit required.

depositum nødvendigt [*Dan.*] deposit required.

dépôt (*m.*) [*Fr.*] deposit (of funds).

dépôt est requis, un [*Fr.*] deposit required.

depozit obligatoriu [*Rom.*] deposit required.

derde [*Dut.*] third.

derecha (*f.*) [*Span.*] right (direction or position).

dertig [*Dut.*] thirty.

desconhecido [*Port.*] unknown.

desconocido [*Span.*] unknown.

desember [*Nor.*] December.

desenho (*m.*) [*Port.*] design.

desenho ornamental (*m.*) [*Port.*] cachet.

de service [*Fr.*] official (in the philatelic sense).

design error See *error*.

Desinfiziert [*Ger.*] Disinfected. A term stamped on letters to show that they had been fumigated or in some other way disinfected against disease. See *disinfected mail*.

desmonetização (*f.*) [*Port.*] demonetization.

desmonetización (*f.*) [*Span.*] demonetization.

destinatário desconhecido [*Port.*] undeliverable; addressee unknown.

desuso (*m.*) [*Span.*] disuse; *en desuso*: obsolete.

desvalorização (*f.*) [*Port.*] devaluation.

deteriorat [*Rom.*] damaged.

deuda pública on Mexican fiscal

deuda pública (*f.*) [*Span.*] public debt. The term is often found as an overprint on various fiscal stamps.

Deutsche Besetzung Zara [*Ger.*; *o/p*] German Occupation of Zara. See *Zara [German occupation]*.

Deutsche Demokratische Republik [*Ger.*] German Democratic Republic. More commonly known to English speakers as *East Germany*.

Deutsche/ Militaer-/ Verwaltung/ Montenegro [*Ger.*] German Military Administration of Montenegro. German overprint (including denominations in Italian lire) produced in 1943 on Yugoslav stamps. See *Montenegro*.

Deutschland [*Ger.*] Germany.

deux [*Fr.*] two.

de valor [*Span.*] valuable.

devalüasyon [*Turk.*] devaluation.

devaluatie (*f.-c.*) [*Dut.*] devaluation.

devaluering (*c.*) [*Dan.*]; (*m.*) [*Nor.*] devaluation.

devalvaatio [*Finn.*] devaluation.

devalvatsiya девальвация (*f.*) [*Russ.*] devaluation.

devalvering (*r.*) [*Swed.*] devaluation.

devise (*f.*) [*Fr.*] motto.

Devise (*f.*) [*Ger.*] foreign exchange.

devise étrangère (*f.*) [*Fr.*] foreign currency.

deviză (*f.*) [*Rom.*] motto.

dewaluacja (*f.*) [*Pol.*] devaluation.

dewizy (*f.pl.*) [*Pol.*] foreign currency.

deyutsmark [*Tag.*] mark (German unit of currency).

dez [*Port.*] ten.

Dezember [*Ger.*] December.

dezembro [*Port.*] December.

D.G. [*Lat. abbr.*] By the Grace of God. Also abbreviated *Dei Gra.*

diadochikos arithmos διαδοχικός αριθμός (*m.*) [*Grk.*] serial number.

diafilassomeni prosfora διαφυλασσόμενη προσφορά [*Grk.*] protective reserve bid.

1897 Diamond Jubilee Label (Great Britain)

Diamond Jubilee Label Set of British charity labels produced in 1897 and 1898 by De La Rue. They were made at the urging of Queen Victoria's son, Edward, Prince of Wales (the future King Edward VII), who wanted a semipostal stamp issued in honor of his mother's fiftieth anniversary on the throne. The 1897 issues were valued at 1 shilling and at 2 shillings 6 pence, and the 1898 labels were issued at 2/6, 5/-, and 10/-.

Although he failed to convince postal authorities to give official sanction to the labels, he was able to persuade many merchants to sell them and to turn all proceeds over to the Prince of Wales's Hospital Fund on behalf of Queen Victoria. Many top stamp dealers, Stanley Gibbons among them, felt certain that the labels would eventually become semipostal stamps, yet such was not to be the case. Beautiful and philatelically important as they are, they were destined to become what Kenneth A. Wood calls the "almost" stamps.

[Kenneth A. Wood, *This Is Philately*, Vol. I, p. 214.]

dicembre [*Ital.*] December.

diciembre [*Span.*] December.

dieci [*Ital.*] ten.

Dienstmarke (*f.*) [*Ger.*] official stamp.

diepdruk (*n.*) [*Dut.*] intaglio.

Dieu [*Fr.*] God (in the Judaic-Christian sense).

diez [*Span.*] ten.

difetto (*m.*) [*Ital.*] defect.

difettoso [*Ital.*] defective.

digma δείγμα (*n.*) [*Grk.*] specimen.

di gran valore [*Ital.*] valuable.

dimoprasia δημοπρασία (*f.*) [*Grk.*] auction.

Dinamarca [*Span., Port.*] Denmark.

Dios [*Span.*] God (in the Judaic-Christian sense). The phrase *Por la gracia de Dios* ("By the Grace of God") is often used in reference to the Spanish monarch.

direito [*Port.*] right (direction or position).

disegno (*m.*) [*Ital.*] design, pattern.

diseño (*m.*) [*Span.*] design, pattern.

disinfected mail In the late Middle Ages, the world was devastated by pestilence. Disinfection of the mail became a valid link in the chain of sanitary precautions created by individual states hoping to protect their defenseless populations. Health precautions affecting couriers were first implemented in 1463 by the Republic of Siena, Italy; in 1490 the Duke of Mila issued regulations requiring a health passport for all couriers. In 1499, a man was arrested in Rome for attempting to "kill" the pope with a letter from an area infected with plague.

During the nineteenth century, historians noted that in 1493 the Supreme Health

Magistrate of Venice extended the sanitary precautions to couriers and to the letters they carried. But some modern scholars have argued that the measure only affected couriers and that the procedure of disinfecting the mail itself was introduced later in 1576. At this time the practice of disinfecting every paper that came from infected places became a regular feature of health precautions implemented by many countries throughout Europe.

Special equipment for the disinfection and fumigation of the letters was invented. Letters were normally opened and disinfected sheet by sheet; to save time, it was later decided to leave the letters closed and to make cuts or hole in them to allow the entrance of the disinfecting and purifying fumes.

In 1770, Russian postmasters were ordered to use waxed gloves when sorting letters coming from infected zones. Fumigation and similar disinfection of letters was also employed as early as 1600. To give an idea of the superstition surrounding contagion from mail, the Czar gave instructions for all letters addressed to him personally to be subjected to such treatment, and then to be recopied by various scribes several times to exclude all possibility of contagion.

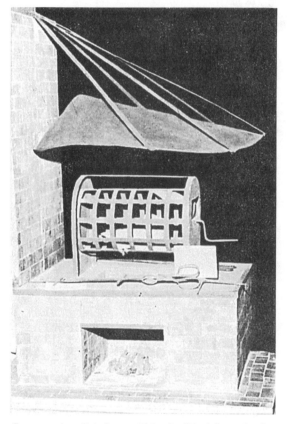

Stove used to disinfect mail in the Papel States in the 19th century [Photo courtesy Museo Postale Italiano, Rome.]

The most common procedure was fumigation of the letters by fumes (or more romantically called "perfumes" by contemporaries) obtained from juniper berries, scented resins, incense, myrrh, gum benzoin, and camphor. Another method consisted of spraying acids, chlorine, vinegar, or sulfur on the pages of the letters.

Handstamps used on mail to certify that it had been disinfected.

In the New World, the first quarantine measures were carried out in Santo Domingo in 1520. but the first evidence of disinfection of mail in the U.S.A. can only be traced back to 1822 when the Board of Health introduced a measure requiring disinfection of mail from cholera-infected places.

Disinfection of mail left signs which can still be easily seen. On some letters a brownish coloring and a few signs of burning appear. Wide white stripes reveal the use of special pincers with which the letters were held near the fire for fumigation. The most evident signs, however, remain the handstamps and sometimes the labels affixed by the various sanitary offices: *Sporca di dentro e netta di fuori* (Unclean inside but clean outside); *Profumata in Pontremoli* (Perfumed in Pontremoli); *Sigillum Sanitatis* (Seal of the Health [Authority]); *Desinfiziert* (Disinfected); *PURIFIÉ FRIOUL* (Purified at Frioul); *Purifié au Lazaret* (Purified at the Lazaretto); *GEREINIGET* (Purified); etc.

The procedure of disinfecting mail lessened after 1850, but as late as 1947 mail was still disinfected in North Africa. In 1952 the World Health Organization clearly stated that there is no need to subject mail to any sanitary measure. But at a time when people were terrorized by the plague, it is understandable that whoever received a letter at least had the consolation to learn from the stamp that his correspondence had been "perfumed." The study of disinfected mail is a very popular facet of postal history, and many important collections have been created on the subject. During the 1970s and 1980s, many books and studies have been published worldwide. The London-based Disinfected Mail Study Circle publishes a quarterly journal titled *Pratique*.

[Contributed by Giorgio Migliavacca. K.F. Meyer, *Disinfected Mail*; Giorgio Migliavacca, "The plague letter plot of 1499," *Pratique*, Vol. VI, #3; Giorgio Migliavacca, "Russian Health Practices of Disinfecting Mail Received from Infected Zones," *Postal History Journal*, February 1975.]

Disney, Walt Cartoon artist and producer of live-action and animated films. Born December 5, 1901, in Chicago, Illinois; died December 15, 1966, in Los Angeles, California, of undisclosed illness.

Walt Disney on U.S. stamp

Disney is best known for having created Mickey Mouse plus a whole stable of other wonderful cartoon characters, and he perfected the genre of the full-length animated cartoon in 1937 with his classic, *Snow White and the Seven Dwarfs*. He also built Disneyland in Anaheim, California, and founded one of the most successful motion picture studios in the world.

Disney scene on stamp of Mongolia

Long after his death, Disney's cartoon characters became the basis of an entire field of philately, even though purists may argue that most stamps featuring Disney scenes do not see postal use. Hundreds and hundreds of stamps showing Disney characters have been issued, but the vast majority are from Antigua, Dominica, Grenada, Togo, Maldives, Turks & Caicos Islands, Bhutan, Lesotho, Sierra Leone, and various other stamp factories that produce tons of stamps, mostly *c.t.o.s*, for philatelists and collectors of Disney memorabilia. All of these stamp designs are copyrighted by Disney and carefully licensed to stamp issuers, much the same way that Disney properties are licensed for tee-shirts, coffee mugs, and the toy industry.

The stamp in the illustration is one such example of a non-postal postage stamp. The scene, a classic from the 1940 movie *Fantasia*, shows Mickey Mouse as the Sorcerer's Apprentice. But the stamp was issued by Mongolia, a closed society where children probably have less exposure to Disney than almost any other place on earth. Despite their popularity, these stamps have little postal legitimacy and are only produced as a source of income for the small countries that issue them.

divisa (*f.*) [*Span.*] motto; foreign currency.

dix [*Fr.*] ten.

dixième (*m.*) [*Fr.*] tenth (the fraction).

DJ. [*o/p*] Djibouti. Overprinted on stamps of Obock in 1894.

djup [*Swed.*] deep (*re*: color).

dk. [*abbr.*] dark.

dobbelportrettert [*Nor.*] accolated, jugate, conjoined[*q.v.*].

doblez (*m.*) [*Span.*] a fold (as in a postage stamp or banknote).

dobra (*f.*) [*Port.*] a crease, fold.

docketing Extra writing on a cover stating when the letter was received, read, or filed. This can help establish the date of a cover if the date does not appear in any of the normal markings.

doctor blade A flexible steel blade used to remove excess ink from a printing plate, sleeve, or cylinder utilized to produce intaglio and photogravure stamps. Any bit of grit in the ink can be picked up by the blade, causing the cylinder to become scratched. The resulting constant plate flaw produces unwanted lines or other marks to appear on the stamps.

documentary stamp Revenue stamp affixed to or imprinted on a document to prove that a tax has been paid. This is in contrast to *proprietary stamps* which are tax stamps attached directly to a product.

Although many nations have issued tax stamps that fall into this category, the United States has probably issued the largest number of different types, and many have been overprinted for specific purposes (stock transfer, future use, etc.). Officially, the U.S. put out documentary stamps from 1862 until 1967. But the so-called "duck stamps," which are actually a form of documentary stamps, are still being released on an annual basis (see *migratory bird hunting stamp*).

U.S. documentary stamps

Mexican documentary stamp (*Documentos*)

documentos (*m.pl.*) [*Span.*] documents. Word found on Spanish-language documentary[*q.v.*] stamps.

Dodecanese Δωδεκάνησα [*Grk.*] literally, *Twelve Islands*. The term was used in ancient times for a group of islands in the Aegean Sea and was revived at the beginning of the 20th century. The islands in question are Casos, Karpathos, Kharki, Tilos, Symi, Nisiros, Atypalaia (Stampalia), Kos, Kalimnos, Leros, Lipsos, and Patmos. See *Aegean Islands* for philatelic information.

dodeka δώδεκα [*Grk.*] twelve.

doğruluk markası [*Turk.*] authentication mark.

Doğu Almanya [*Turk.*] East Germany (D.D.R.).

doi [*Rom.*] two.

dois (*m.adj.*) [*Port.*] two.

dokuz [*Turk.*] nine.

dół (*m.*) [*Pol.*] bottom.

dô-la [*Viet.*] dollar ($).

dolar דּוֹלָר (*m.*) [*Heb.*] dollar ($).

dólar (*m.*) [*Span., Port.*] dollar.

dollar Unit of currency created by the U.S. Coinage Act of April 2, 1792. The first coins of this denomination were struck two years later by the Philadelphia Mint.

The dollar is significant because it was the first unit of currency intended to be broken into decimal units, i.e., one dollar equaling one hundred cents. In today's world, most countries use a decimal system similar to this; in 1792, the practice was unheard of.

Postage stamps denominated in dollars have been issued at one time or another by Aitutaki, Anguilla, Antiqua, Australia, Bahamas, Barbados, Belize, Bermuda, British Virgin Islands, British West Indies, Brunei, Canada, Canal Zone (Panama), Cayman Islands, Confederate States of America, Cook Islands, Danish West Indies, Dominica, East Caribbean States, Eritrea, Ethiopia, Fiji, Grenada, Guyana, Hawaii, Hong Kong, Jamaica, Japan, Kiribati, Liberia, Malaysia, Marshall Islands, Montserrat, Namibia, Nauru Island, New Zealand, Newfoundland, Niue, Palau Islands, Panama-Palo Seco, Papua New Guinea, Philippines, Pitcairn Islands, Puerto Rico, St. Kitts, St. Lucia, St. Vincent, Sierra Leone, Singapore, Solomon Islands, Straits Settlements, Texas, Tuvalu, Thailand, Trinidad & Tobago, Turks & Caicos Islands, United Nations, United States, Western Samoa, and Zimbabwe.

[Walter Breen, *Complete Encyclopedia of U.S. and Colonial Coins*, pp. 423-84.]

dollario δολλάριο (*n.*) [*Grk.*] dollar.

domestic stamp A postage stamp that is not valid for international mailing because it does not show a specific denomination. This type of stamp is usually produced either to anticipate a postal rate increase or to cope with inflation or a monetary devaluation.

The United States is the country most guilty of issuing domestic stamps. The first came in 1978 and was denominated simply with the letter "A". Since then, every postal rate increase has seen the issuance of another "lettered" stamp ("B", "C", "D", etc.). Domestic stamps are always valued at the next rate of sending a one-ounce letter first-class to any part of the United States. Their purpose is to enable the U.S. Postal Service to have a large number of stamps in stock when a rate increase takes effect, but the stamps have to be printed months before the U.S.P.S. knows exactly how much the rate increase will be.

domestic stamps: cover of "G" stamp booklet (above); official stamp & "additive" stamp (below)

Domestic stamps are very unpopular with most Americans. Not only do the stamps cause confusion, but they are a graphic symbol of what Americans regard as an excessive number of postal rate increases.

The most confusing domestic stamp was an "additive" stamp issued in conjunction with the "F" stamp. The U.S.P.S. assumed that many people would still have a large number of 25c stamps on hand (the existing rate at the time) and would need to purchase stamps equal to the amount of the increase. The additive stamp's inscription reads, "This U.S. stamp, along with 25c of additional postage, is equivalent to the 'F' stamp rate." Since the one-ounce, first-class rate was increased from 25c to 29c, the additive stamp thus cost four cents and was (in theory) equal to a regular 4c stamp. Some collectors tried placing seven additive stamps plus a regular 1c stamp on letters to see if they would go through the mail. They did not. Virtually all the letters were returned for insufficient postage. When the collectors complained to their local postmasters, the postmasters usually agreed to accept letters franked with additive stamps. But by this time, the additives were declared invalid for postage and were no longer usable at all. Once again, the letters were returned for insufficient postage. If nothing else, the twice-returned letters surely rank among the most bizarre philatelic covers in U.S. postal history.

See *undenominated stamp*.

stamp with Dominical label (Belgium)

Dominical label [also known as *Sunday delivery label*.] Small label attached to the bottom of some Belgian stamps indicating that delivery was not to take place on a Sunday. The message was printed both in French (*Ne pas livrer le dimanche*) and Flemish (*Niet bestellen op zondag*). If the sender had no objection to

Sunday delivery, he or she could tear off the label before affixing it to an envelope. Stamps with these labels were first issued in 1896 and were available until 1914.

From 1925 to 1941, Bulgaria issued special stamps that were compulsory for delivery on Sundays or holidays. These are regarded as postal tax stamps because the revenue collected from them was used to support a sanatorium for employees of the postal, telegraph, and telephone services. One of the sanatorium's primary purposes was to treat tuberculosis.

donker [*Dut.*] dark; deep (*re:* color)

doorboord [*Dut.*] holed.

doorsteek (*m./c.*) [*Dut.*] roulette, *perçage*.

doorstoken [*Dut.*] rouletted, *percé*.

dopłata (*f.*) [*Pol.*] surtax.

doppio (*m.; adj.*) [*Ital.*] duplicate.

dört [*Turk.*] four.

dörtlü blok [*Turk.*] block of four.

dos [*Span.*] two.

doskonały [*Pol.*] perfect, flawless.

douăzeci [*Rom.*] twenty.

double (*m.; adj.*) [*Fr.*] duplicate.

double impression A stamp that has been partially or completely printed twice due to a mechanical failure. The doubling normally occurs on large areas of the stamp's design. Unlike double transfers[*q.v.*], double impressions can occur randomly.

double transfer Plate variety similar to a foreign transfer. When line-engraved intaglio stamps are being prepared, the design is rocked into the printing plate. Sometimes the transfer is faulty and the design has to be burnished out of the plate so that the plate can be reused. If the old design has not been completely expunged, whatever remains will show up on the stamp in addition to the new design that is rocked in. If the burnished plate is re-rocked with the design for a different stamp, bits of design elements from the old design (the one supposedly burnished out) will show up on the new design of the finished stamp. This is called *foreign transfer*, a condition that happens very infrequently. But if an identical stamp design is rocked in, the finished stamp will show signs of doubling in the areas where the old design remained. This is called a *double transfer* and is somewhat more common than foreign transfer.

If double transfer occurs, the same flaw will show up on every stamp produced with that plate because the problem has become a permanent part of the plate. This is different from a double impression[q.v.], a type of error which can occur randomly.

dove Christian symbol representing the Holy Ghost. In a more general sense, it also symbolizes spirituality or sublimation, i.e., the conversion of something inferior to something of a higher worth. It is also the universal symbol of peace.

The dove is found on various postage stamps and non-postal labels, often those issued at Christmas. Stamps of the Vatican frequently display this symbol.

[J. E. Cirlot, *A Dictionary of Symbols* (2nd Ed.), Philosophical Library, New York, p. 85.]

döviz [*Turk.*] foreign currency.

D.P.O. [*abbr.*] dead post office. A post office that is no longer in operation.

draadje (*n.*) [*Dut.*] silk thread.

drachm; drachma δϱάχμη [*Grk.*] Unit of currency used by modern Greece since 1831.

dreapta [*Rom.*] right (direction or position).

drei [*Ger.*] three.

dreißig [*Ger.*] thirty.

dreptunghiular [*Rom.*] rectangular.

drie [*Dut.*] three.

Drittel (*n.*) [*Ger.*] third (the fraction).

D.R.L.S. [*abbr.*] Despatch rider letter service.

droite (*f.*) [*Fr.*] right (direction or position).

dronning (*c.*) [*Dan., Nor.*] queen.

drop letter A letter delivered from the same post office at which it was mailed.

drottning (*f.*) [*Swed.*] queen.

drucken (*v.*) [*Ger.*] to print.

drukken (*v.*) [*Dut.*] to print.

drukować (*v.*) [*Pol.*] to print.

D.S.I.L. [*Ital.*] *Diritto Sardo Italiane Lire.* Accountancy mark in Italian lire on mail in transit by the Kingdom of Sardinia to an Austrian territory, e.g., from Spain to Milan via Genoa. The accountancy mark indicated the quota owed to the Sardinian Post Office. This accountancy mark was introduced as a result of the 1853 postal treaty between Austria and the Kingdom of Sardinia.

dua [*Indo.*] two.

duas (*f.adj.*) [*Port.*] two.

duck stamp See *migratory bird hunting stamp.*

due 1. [*Ital.*] two. 2. (*noun*) postage due[q.v.] label.

duizend [*Dut.*] thousand.

dunkel [*Ger.*] dark.

dunne plek (*f./c.*) [*Dut.*] thin spot, skinned spot.

Dünnstelle (*f.*) [*Ger.*] thin spot, skinned spot.

Duplex postmark Dual obliterator used in Great Britain from 1853 to 1906. The left-hand portion consisted of a circle containing the location where the stamp was cancelled as well as the date and time. The right-hand portion was also circular but consisted of horizontal rows of bars, sometimes with a post office number in the center. The left-hand section acted as the postmark and the right-hand part as the killer[q.v.].

duplicaat (*n.*) [*Dut.*] a duplicate.

duplicado (*m.; adj.*) [*Span., Port.*] duplicate.

duplicar (*v.*) [*Span., Port.*] to duplicate.

duplicare (*v.*) [*Ital.*] to duplicate.

duplicat (*n.; adj.*) [*Rom.*] duplicate.

duplikat (*n.*) [*Nor.*]; (*m.*) [*Pol.*] a duplicate.

Duplikat (*n.*) [*Ger.*] a duplicate.

duplisert (*adj.*) [*Nor.*] duplicate.

duplizieren (*v.*) [*Ger.*] to duplicate.

dupliziert (*adj.*) [*Ger.*] duplicate.

durch Federzug entwertet [*Ger.*] pen cancelled.

durchgestochen [*Ger.*] rouletted, *percé.*

durch Schnitt entwertet [*Ger.*] cut cancellation.

durch Schriftzug entwertet [*Ger.*] pen cancelled.

Durchstich (*m.*) [*Ger.*] roulette, *perçage.*

duży [*Pol.*] large.

dwa [*Pol.*] two.

dwadzieścia [*Pol.*] twenty.

dwujęzyczny [*Pol.*] bilingual.

dwukolorowy [*Pol.*] bicolored, bicoloured.

D.Y. [*Turk. abbr.*] *Demir Yol* (railroad).

dyb [*Dan.*] deep (*re:* color).

dyo δύο [*Grk.*] two.

dyp [*Nor.*] deep (*re:* color)

dziesięć [*Pol.*] ten.

E e

E [*Ger. o/p*] *Eisenbahn Behörden* ([to be used by] railway officials). Overprinted on 1908 stamps of Bavaria.

E.A.F. [*o/p*] East Africa Forces. Overprint used by Great Britain in 1943 on stamps issued for Italian Somaliland (see *Somalia.*). It replaced the overprint "M.E.F." (Middle East Forces), and was itself ultimately replaced with stamps overprinted "B.M.A. SOMALIA" (British Military Administration Somalia) in May 1948. In January 1950 the M. was dropped from "B.M.A."

eagles: U.S. & Mexico

eagle Symbol of high spiritual principle found on the postage stamps of many nations. It is the bird associated with courage, power, and war. Because the eagle lives in the full light of the sun, it is considered to be luminous in its essence and shares in the elements of air and fire. Its identification with the sun (which fertilizes female nature) makes it a symbol of masculinity.

In pre-Columbian America, eagles represented the struggle between the higher spirit and the lower world. The eagle with a serpent in its beak, as seen on Mexican stamps, follows this line of symbolism. That eagle, which represents the higher order, conquers the snake, a symbol of evil. According to ancient Aztec legend, the Aztecs were foretold to build their capital where they saw the eagle and the serpent. As per the legend, they found such an eagle and built their capital where Mexico City now stands.

[J. E. Cirlot, *A Dictionary of Symbols* (2nd Ed.), pp. 91-92.]

Earth stamp U.S. undenominated stamp issued in 1988 showing the planet Earth. Its postage value was 25 cents.

Featuring our planet on an undenominated stamp created somewhat of a philatelic anomaly. The stamp was printed in anticipation of a postal increase, but the exact amount of the increase was not yet known at the time of the printing. Because it was America's fifth such undenominated stamp, it was inscribed with the letter "E" in lieu of a value. For failure to state a specific denomination, the stamp was regarded by U.P.U. regulations as a "domestic" stamp which could only be used to carry mail within the United States. Although the U.P.U. regulations have since been changed, at the time of its issuance the Earth stamp might have pictured the entire planet, but it was not officially valid for taking mail beyond America's borders.

The Earth stamp created quite an unusual problem for the Internal Revenue Service (I.R.S.). The United States Postal Service agreed to apply a first-day cancellation dated March 28, 1988, on any mail bearing that stamp, even if the request was not made until early May. Income tax returns sent to the I.R.S. must be postmarked no later than April 15 of any given year, and the taxpayer incurs a fine if the return is sent late. A few tardy taxpayers tried to avoid the fine by affixing Earth stamps and by requesting first-day cancellation, thus giving their return the

74

appearance of having been mailed on March 28. Although the I.R.S. claimed that it would penalize taxpayers for doing that, no one really knows how many tardy taxpayers (if any) succeeded in pulling that stunt.

See *domestic stamp*.

écarlate [*Fr.*] scarlet.

échanger (*v.*) [*Fr.*] to trade.

echar al correo (*v.*) [*Span.*] to mail.

echt [*Ger., Dut.*] authentic, genuine.

Echtheitszeichen (*n.*) [*Ger.*] authentication mark.

Ecosse [*Fr.*] Scotland.

French stamp with *ecu*-denominated overprint

écu (*m.*) [*Fr.*] literally, *shield*.

1. Large silver coin struck intermittently in France from 1641 until the overthrow of the monarchy in 1793.

[Richard G. Doty, *The Macmillan Encyclopedic Dictionary of Numismatics*, pp. 116-17.]

2. Name chosen by the European Economic Community for its proposed common currency. The word *ecu* (usually written without the accent mark) is an acronym for "European Currency Unit."

The illustration shows a 1988 French stamp of 2.20 francs overprinted with the equivalent value of 0.31 ecu. [Note: In most non-English-speaking countries, commas are used to denote decimal places and periods are used to set off groups of thousands.]

Edward Name of eight British kings, two of whom played a role in philately.

1. Edward VII [a.k.a. the *Peacemaker*.] King of Great Britain and Ireland and Emperor of India (1901-10). Born November 9, 1841, at Buckingham Palace in London; died there on May 6, 1910.

Although Edward VII waited until he was fifty-nine years old to become king, he had actually taken over many ceremonial duties from his mother, Queen Victoria, after his father, Prince Albert, died in 1861. Yet he had been totally excluded from the meaningful elements of his future position.. When he finally became king, he was far more interested in pleasure than in affairs of state. His marriage to Princess Alexandra of Denmark was harmonious, yet his extra-marital affairs with numerous women, both at home and abroad, often caused scandal and gossip.

Because he was king for only a short time, the range of stamps with his portrait is somewhat limited. His face appeared on the stamps of Great Britain, New Zealand, Canada, Fiji, India, Straits Settlements, Victoria (southeastern Australia), Virgin Islands, and various other colonies and Commonwealth members. Among the most desirable stamps bearing his likeness is the magnificent £1 stamp (Scott 142).

Edward VIII

2. Edward VIII [né *Edward Albert Christian George Andrew Patrick David*; known as the *Duke of Windsor* after his abdication.] Uncrowned king of Great Britain and Northern Ireland, and Emperor of India (January 20-December 11, 1936; born June 23, 1894, at Richmond Park in Surrey, England; died May 28, 1972, in Paris.

Edward VIII had hoped to make the monarchy reflect the social attitudes of the time. Although he had little interest in politics, he was concerned about the plight of the masses. During World War I, he served in Italy, France, and Egypt but could not serve on the front lines due to his status as Prince of Wales.

Ten months after his accession to the throne, he made it known that he wished to marry an American, Wallis Simpson, twice divorced.

This marriage was so inconsistent with his position as Head of the Church of England that he was forced to choose. In announcing his abdication on December 11, 1936, he gave up the throne for, as in his own words, "the woman I love." From that time, he was known as "His Royal Highness, Prince Edward, Duke of Windsor."

Edward's unexpected abdication created turmoil with the designers of stamps, coins, banknotes, and all sorts of other official items. Some British stamps showing him as king were issued in 1936, but most other stamps that bear his portrait, such as those from Canada, were issued prior to that year while Goerge V was still alive and presented Edward as the Prince of Wales.

[Contributed by Ruth Ann Davis. *Encyclopedia Americana*, Vol. 9, pp. 745-46.]

E.E.F. [*abbr.*] Egyptian Expeditionary Force.

één [*Dut.*] one.

eerste-dagenveloppe (*f./c.*); **eerste-dagomslag** (*n.*) [*Dut.*] first day cover.

E.E.U.U. de Venezuela

E.E.U.U. [*Span. abbr.*] *Estados Unidos* (United States). Used, for example, on stamps of Venezuela (*E.E.U.U. de Venezuela*).

efigie (*f.*) [*Span.*] effigy.

efígie (*f.*) [*Port.*] effigy.

eftergummerad [*Swed.*] regummed.

efterligne (*v.*) [*Dan.*] to duplicate.

efterligning (*c.*) [*Dan.*] imitation.

egcharaksi εγχάραξη (*f.*) [*Grk.*] intaglio.

egenværdi [*Dan.*] intrinsic.

egenverdi [*Nor.*] intrinsic.

Egeo [*Ital.*] Aegean. The overprint "EGEO" is found on the Italian stamps of 25c and 50c which were authorized by the Commissioner for Civilian Affairs in September 1912 for use in the Aegean Islands, a territory under Italian rule during Italy's war with Turkey. Later overprints read "ISOLE ITALIANE DELL'EGEO" ("Italian Islands of the Aegean"). See *Aegean Islands* for additional information.

egy [*Hun.*] one.

Egyesült Királyság [*Hun.*] United Kingdom (U.K.).

egyirányba néző kettős portré [*Hun.*] conjoined[*q.v.*], accolated, jugate.

ehdotettu tarjous [*Finn.*] suggested bid.

ehiökortti [*Finn.*] postal card. [Note: the term for *postcard* in Finnish is *postikortti*.]

Einfassung (*f.*) [*Ger.*] frame.

eingefalzt [*Ger.*] hinged.

eingekapselte Briefmarke (*f.*); **eingekapselte Marke** (*f.*) [*Ger.*] encased postage stamp.

eingraviert [*Ger.*] engraved.

eins [*Ger.*] one.

Einschreibmarke (*f.*) [*Ger.*] registration stamp.

einstufen (*v.*) [*Ger.*] to grade.

einzigartig [*Ger.*] unique.

Éire [*Ire.*] Ireland.

Éireann [*Ire. o/p*] Irish overprint on stamps of Great Britian.

Éirí Amac Na Casca 1916 [*Ire.*] Irish Easter Rising 1916.

ejemplar (*m.*) [*Span.*] specimen.

ejemplar firmado (*m.*) [*Span.*] signed example.

ej skild [*Swed.*] unsevered.

ej utgiven [*Swed.*] not issued.

ekato εκατό [*Grk.*] hundred.

ekatommirio εκατομμύριο (*n.*) [*Grk.*] million.

ekatontaeterida εκατονταετηρίδα (*f.*) [*Grk.*] centennial, centenary.

ekdosi έκδοση (*f.*) [*Grk.*] an issue, issuance.

Ekim [*Turk.*] October.

eksemplar (*n.*) [*Nor.*] specimen.

ekspozycja (*f.*) [*Pol.*] exhibition.

ekte [*Nor.*] authentic, genuine.

elachisti prosfora ελάχιστη προσφορά (*f.*) [*Grk.*] minimum bid.

eladni (*v.*) [*Hun.*] to sell.

eladó [*Hun.*] seller.

elcserélni (*v.*) [*Hun.*] to trade.

elde etme [*Turk.*] acquisition.

elenco dei proprietari precendenti [*Ital.*] pedigree, provenance.

First Day Cover commemorating the coronation of Queen Elizabeth II

Elizabeth II (full name Elizabeth Alexandra Mary, of the house of Windsor.) Queen of Great Britain and Northern Ireland since 1952. Born in London in 1926 of (the future) King George VI and Queen Mother Elizabeth.

Unlike her namesake Elizabeth I, Queen Elizabeth II has never had to behead anyone to keep her throne. Her biggest threat is her own family. While Elizabeth II has always maintained the decorum of her position and is loved by the majority of her subjects, her children have scandalized their positions to the point of having weakened the very structure of the British monarchy. Only time will tell whether the throne will survive.

No matter what the future may bring, Elizabeth II has established an indelible place in philatelic history by having appeared on more different stamps than anyone else in history. In total, Queen Elizabeth's portrait has appeared on the postage stamps of the United Kingdom, Scotland, Wales & Monmouthshire, Alderney, Canada, New Zealand, Australia, the Bahamas, Bermuda, Seychelles, South Africa, Gilbraltar, Southern Rhodesia, Rhodesia & Nyasaland, Cook Islands, Guernsey, Jersey, Nigeria, Fiji, British West Africa, The Gambia, South Georgia, Falkland Islands, British Indian Ocean Territory, Kenya-Uganda-Tanzania, Leeward Islands, Hong Kong, British Caribbean Territories, British Honduras, Ceylon, Cyprus, Dominica, Mauritius, Jamaica, Malaya and British Borneo, Isle of Man, and Cayman Islands. Canada, Southern Rhodesia, and other nations used her portrait as early as 1935 when she was still Princess Elizabeth and her grandfather, King George V, was on the throne.

Elizabeth II has had the good grace to allow her stamps to age as she herself has aged (unlike her great-great-grandmother Victoria whose 18-year-old portrait still appeared on stamps even when Victoria was past eighty). Stamps show Elizabeth's progression from a young child to a mature dowager.

elli [*Turk.*] fifty.

elnök [*Hun.*] president.

előfizetés [*Hun.*] prepayment.

elokuu [*Finn.*] August.

elölap; előoldal [*Hun.*] front; obverse.

Elveția [*Rom.*] Switzerland.

e-mail Letters sent electronically via the World Wide Web. Advocates prefer e-mail to "snail mail" (i.e., post office mail) because mail sent electronically is instantaneous and relatively inexpensive and it can be sent to virtually any part of the world. Since e-mail does not involve the use of postage stamps or other related items, it may never have much of a role in philately except for its day-to-day usefulness to dealers and collectors.

embossing: stamps of Heligoland and West Germany

embossing The process of pressing a design into paper from the back in order to create a raised effect. Philatelically, this method is most commonly found in postal stationary but also is becoming increasingly popular as a way of adding style to postage stamps. An example is the German Red Cross stamp with a printed center surrounded by an embossed design. Most stamps featuring a cameo head[q.v.] have been produced in this way. One of the stamps in the illustration shows the embossed cameo of Queen Victoria on a stamp of Heligoland. Braille, which is occasionally added to postal items, must be embossed in order to be readable by the blind.

embrulho (*m.*) [*Port.*] package.

emettere (*v.*) [*Ital.*] to issue.

émettre (*v.*) [*Fr.*] to issue.

emisión (*f.*) [*Span.*] issue, issuance.

emisja (*f.*) [*Pol.*] issue, issuance.

emissão (*f.*) [*Port.*] issue, issuance.

emission An issue of a postage or revenue stamp or other philatelic item.

émission (*f.*) [*Fr.*] issue, issuance.

emissione (*f.*) [*Ital.*] issue, issuance.

emitir (*v.*) [*Span., Port.*] to issue.

emitować (*v.*) [*Pol.*] to issue.

emitteren [*Dut.*] to issue.

emlék- (*adj.*) [*Hun.*] commemorative.

emne [*Nor.*] topical; thematic.

emnespecificeret [*Dan.*] topical; thematic.

emperador (*m.*) [*Span.*] emperor.

empereur (*m.*) [*Fr.*] emperor.

Empire Air Mail Scheme A service whose purpose was to air ship all first-class mail between Britain and the various Commonwealth countries without extra charge. Commonly known as *All-Up Service*, it was initiated in Great Britain in 1937 but was discontinued at the outbreak of World War II.

emsalsiz [*Turk.*] unique.

en [*Nor., Swed.*] one.

ena ένα [*Grk.*] one.

encarnado [*Span.*] scarlet.

U.S. encased postage stamp

encased postage stamp One of two major categories of postage stamps which have circulated as money. Since the 1860s, sixteen countries have used stamps encapsulated in windowed tokens as a way to combat shortages of minor coins.

Encased postage stamps were born during the U.S. Civil War (1861-65). Economic panic forced hard money, even minor coins, out of circulation. To alleviate this shortage, the federal government authorized that stamps could be used in lieu of coins. Loose stamps were impractical for circulation because they easily became lost or torn. In 1862, John Gault, an inventor and entrepreneur from Boston, Massachusetts, devised an encasement that made the circulation of stamps more practical. The invention essentially consisted of placing a stamp between a brass disk and a mica window. The cost of the encasement was to be absorbed by local merchants who could place their advertising message on the back side of the token. His invention proved to be a marketing failure, however, because the government soon started issuing fractional currency notes and private merchants introduced a series of small unofficial coins known as Civil War tokens. The encased postage stamps were discontinued because they proved to be less economical and therefore less desirable than these other items.

Post-World War I Germany and Austria saw a revival of encased postage stamps. The economic chaos of that period resulted in the issuance of great quantities of emergency money known in German as *Notgeld*. Tens of thousands of different paper notes, metallic coins, and pieces of money fabricated from silk, coal, linen, leather, and a host of other substances were produced to deal with the uncontrollable inflation. Encased postage stamps were included in this avalanche of paper and non-paper currencies.

The second category of postage stamps which have circulated as money consists of stamps or paper notes resembling stamps which have been used "naked" without encapsulation or have been affixed to a piece of cardboard and have circulated in that fashion.

See *postage stamp money*.

[Albert Pick, *Briefmarkengeld*, 1970; Richard G. Doty, *The Macmillan Encyclopedic Dictionary of Numismatics*, pp. 122-123.]

enchère (*f.*) [*Fr.*] (auction) bid.

encomenda postal (*f.*) [*Port.*] parcel post.

encre (*f.*) [*Fr.*] ink.

en desuso [*Span.*] obsolete; in disuse.

endgültig (*adj*) [*Ger.*] definitive.

endommagé [*Fr.*] damaged.

end pair The last two stamps on a coil. The final stamp is pasted onto a strip of blank labels to allow the stamp to go far enough through the vending machine so that it can be dispensed. (See illustration.)

en el reverso [*Span.*] on the back.

enero [*Span.*] January.

en espera de aprobación [*Span.*] on approval.

engine turned Design mechanically engraved by a lathe process. See *guilloche*.

engomado de nuevo [*Span.*] regummed.

ensayo (*m.*) [*Span.*] essay.

ensipäivän kuori [*Finn.*] first day cover.

entalhe (*m.*) [*Port.*] intaglio.

entero postal (*m.*) [*Span.*] postal card. The term for *postcard* in Spanish is *tarjeta postal* (*f.*).

entier postal (*m.*) [*Fr.*] postal card. The term for *postcard* in French is *carte postale* (*f.*).

entrega especial stamp (Cuba)

entrega especial; entrega inmediata [*Span.*] special delivery. These terms also refer to some impressively-designed special delivery airmail stamps issued by many Spanish-speaking countries.

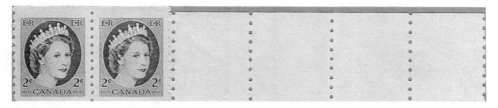

end pair (Canada)

entwerten (*v.*) [*Ger.*] to cancel.

Entwurf (*m.*) [*Ger.*] design.

envelope de primeiro dia [*Port.*] first day cover.

enveloppe (*f.*) [*Fr.*] envelope; cover (in the philatelic sense).

enveloppe du premier jour d'émission [*Fr.*] first day cover.

enviar por correo (*v.*) [*Span.*] to mail.

epäsäännöllinen [*Finn.*] irregular.

epätäydellinen [*Finn.*] incomplete.

epävirallinen [*Finn.*] unofficial.

epigrafi επιγραφή (*f.*) [*Grk.*] legend; inscription.

epitagi επιταγή (*f.*) [*Grk.*] check, cheque.

eplegrønn [*Nor.*] apple green.

épreuve (*f.*) [*Fr.*] essay.

eredeti [*Hun.*] original.

Erhaltungsgrad (*m.*) [*Ger.*] grade, condition.

erhvervelse (*c.*) [*Dan.*] acquisition.

erikoismerkki [*Finn.*] charity stamp.

Eritrea Eritrea, Italy's first African colony, was in ancient times part of the Ethiopian Empire and its natural gateway to the Red Sea. By the first century A.D., Massawa, the ancient Adulis of the Kingdom of Axum, was already known to the Western world. Throughout the following centuries, Ethiopia, a feudal empire dominated by the Christian Amhara, continued to press its claim to the coastal area. Moslem penetration of the area began in the sixteenth century.

During the first half of the nineteenth century, Turkish and Egyptian rule alternated at Massawa, but in 1865 it passed to Egypt until the Italian occupation. On November 15, 1869, two days before the inauguration of the Suez Canal, Italian explorer Giuseppe Sapeto and Rear-Admiral Acton negotiated an agreement for the lease of the Bay of Assab, a trading station at the northern end of the Straits of Bab-al-Mandab, and indigenous chieftains gave their approval.

In 1870 the Genoa-based Rubattino Steamship Company finalized the purchase of the area. During the years that followed, the borders of the Italian settlement were gradually extended. On Christmas Eve 1880, a ministerial ordinance established Italian sovereignty on Assab giving instructions for the operation of a postal agency. Initially, Italian stamps overprinted "ESTERO" were used and cancelled by a straight-line "BAIA DI ASSAB" postmark; later, current Italian definitive stamps were used.

Meanwhile, in 1882, the Italian government bought the Assab settlement from Rubattino. The Italian colony of Eritrea wan not officially established until January 1, 1890. The colony was named after the Erythræum Mare (the Red Sea) of Roman times.

"Colonia Eritrea" overprint

On January 1, 1893, eleven definitive stamps of Italy were issued with the overprint "Colonia Eritrea." The first pictorial stamps specifically designed for the colony were not issued until 1910 despite repeated attempts on the side of the governor to convince Rome to approve ten different bicolored stamps. For ten years he had been lobbying for a full-fledged pictorial series. But in the end, only four stamps utilizing monochrome designs (including those issued in 1914) were approved by Rome. The first design featured the Governor's Palace at Massawa flanked by two scarabei and surmounted by a diminutive shield charged with the Cross of Savoy. The other design featured a Senafe plowman with oxen.

Governor's Palace and Senafe plowman

In 1916 the introduction of new postal rates resulted in steady demand for 20c stamps. On the other hand, the surplus of 15c stamps of the 1910 pictorial duo was sizable, and a decision was made to utilize part of the surplus by overprinting the old denomination into 5c and 20c stamps. This was achieved by overprinting stocks at Asmara (5c on 15c) in red ink, and the bulk at Turin in black ink (20c on 15c). This emergency resulted in the 5c on 15c being the only stamp produced in the colony. The two basic designs were revived in 1928-29 when they were re-issued using the old plates but changing the perforation (11 instead of 13 3/4). Some of the non-adopted designs which were to form the 1910 series were later adapted for the ten pictorial stamps issued in 1930.

ERITREA overprint on Somali stamp

During World War I, the colony saw the Italian Red Cross stamps of 1916 overprinted for use in Eritrea, followed in 1922 by similar overprints on the "Victory" issue of Italy. The practice of overprinting Italian commemorative issues for the various colonies continued until 1931; an exception to this was the release in 1922 of the definitive series of Somalia overprinted "ERITREA." This most unusual overprinting metamorphosis which transformed the stamps of one colony into stamps for another colony originated from a colossal blunder by the Italian Security Printers who had misunderstood the instructions to reprint 80,000 stamps of the 1906 issue of Somalia with overprints introducing the Italian currency. In 1921 the printers produced some eight million stamps instead of 80,000. Since such a huge quantity could not be absorbed by Somalia alone, it was decided to use some of the 1921

reprints for Eritrea. In 1924 the same stamps were again overprinted, but this time the word "ERITREA" was in red for the 5c, 25c, and 1 Lira denominations, and in blue for the remaining four values. Apparently the black ink overprint did not stand out enough, and therefore different colors were adopted in 1924.

In 1933 a set of ten pictorial stamps showing locally-relevant designs were issued. A year later, selected denominations from the same series were overprinted "ONORANZE/ AL DUCA DEGLI/ ABRUZZI" in order to pay tribute to the late Luigi Amedeo of Savoy, a strong advocate of the colonialization of Somalia. On December 5, 1934, a clash between Italians and Ethiopians at the Walwal wells which Italian Somaliland authorities had occupied since 1930 supplied Mussolini with the pretext for invading Ethiopia. By May 1936 Ethiopia was under Italian control. An administrative reshuffling soon followed which created Italian East Africa (*Africa Orientale Italiana*) incorporating Eritrea, Ethiopia, and Somalia.

At the same time, a regular airmail service was established, and a series of airmail definitives of ten denominations was issued. Apart from two parcel post stamps, released in October 1936 and April 1937, these airmail stamps were the last Eritrean stamps to be issued in the colony. In 1938, specific stamps for Italian East Africa were issued and used concurrently with Eritrean stamps.

During the early months of 1941, British troops carried out their offensive, and by April 1 the capital of Eritrea, Asmara, was occupied by forces led by General Platt. Five days later Addis Ababa surrendered. On June 10, Assab, the last Red Sea port in Italian hands, was captured by an Indian battalion. Between 1942 and 1952, overprinted British stamps were used in Eritrea, the first of which with "M.E.F." (Middle East Forces) overprints (1942-48), and thereafter with "B.M.A. ERITREA" (British Military Administration Eritrea) and "B.A. ERITREA" (British Administration Eritrea) overprints.

unofficial stamp issued by Eritrean resistance (1978)

In 1952, Eritrean calls for independence were ignored and the country was federated with Ethiopia. Eritrean resistance continued but with little success until the Ethiopian emperor was ousted in 1974. Forces of the Eritrean People's Liberation Front marched into Asmara in 1991. Self-determination and admission to the United Nations as an independent country finally came in 1993. A set of four stamps publicizing a referendum for independence was issued by Eritrea on April 22, 1993. During the 1970s, a few sets of stamps inscribed "POSTE ERITREA LIBERA" had been issued by the insurgents, but those stamps never achieved official status in most catalogues.

[Contributed by Giorgio Migliavacca.]

EROI/ Monte San Martino/ Municipio di CUVIO [*o/p*] See *C.L.N.*

erottamaton [*Finn.*] unsevered.

design error [#1]: Christopher Columbus using a not-yet-invented telescope (St. Kitts-Nevis)

error Any major mistake on a stamp caused by human carelessness or mechanical breakdown.

1. Design errors are human errors. They happen when a designer misspells a word, uses a wrong portrait or device, adds something to a design that is inherently illogical, leaves out part of a design, or makes any other human-type mistake before the design is applied to the printing plate.

Stamps and overprints can both show misspellings. See *spelling error* for examples and illustrations. Errors of logic also can be found on stamps. The stamp pictured here from St. Kitts-Nevis shows a dramatic portrayal of Christopher Columbus searching for land through his telescope. Regretfully (for the stamp's designer), the telescope had not yet been invented! The U.S. stamp shows an interesting anomaly: the flag is waving in one direction while the smoke from the train is blowing in the opposite direction.

design errors [#1]: flag and smoke blowing in opposite directions (U.S.); Winchester paper (Venezuela)

Many collectors consider some uses of Winchester paper*[q.v.]* as a type of design error if the *burélage* is so intense that it totally obliterates the stamp's design.

Some supposed design errors are not really errors. Guernsey issued an eight-stamp series in 1972 and 1973 featuring mail boats*[q.v.]*. According to some catalogues, the 1973 issue showing the *Isle of Guernsey* is an error and that the boat is actually the *Isle of Sark*. In this case, the stamp is correct and the catalogues are at fault.

2. Production errors are often human errors, but they can also occur as the result of a mechanical malfunction. *Cliché[q.v.]* errors are human errors caused when a defective or worn cliché is replaced with a cliché of the wrong stamp or if the replacement *cliché* is inadvertently rotated 90° or 180°.

Among the most spectacular errors in philatelic history are the U.S. inverts[q.v.] of the early twentieth century. Inverts only happen on stamps of two or more colors. The paper has to be fed through the press a separate time to print each color in the design. If the sheet gets turned around as the paper is being fed into the press or if the printing plate has inadvertently been rotated, the image in that color is printed upside-down relative to everything else. The most famous of these is the so-called Jenny invert[q.v.], a 1918 24c airmail stamp showing a Curtiss Jenny biplane flying upside-down. Yet the strangest story may well involve the Pan-American Exposition inverts of 1901. Some specimens of the 1c Fast Lake Navigation and 2c Empire State Express stamps were inadvertently printed with their vignettes inverted. Somehow the Post Office heard the rumor that some of the 4c Electric Automobile issues of that same series had been inverted. For its own files, the Post Office authorized the intentional "reprinting" of a full sheet of 400 inverts of this stamp, some specimens of which eventually found their way into the general philatelic market. But as it turned out, the rumor had been false. Thus, the only existing examples of that inverted stamp are intentional errors.

[George Amick, *The Inverted Jenny: Mystery, Money, Mania*, p. 37.]

erro (*m.*) [*Port.*] error.

Ersttagsbrief (*m.*) [*Ger.*] first day cover.

értékes [*Hun.*] valuable.

Erwerbung (*f.*) [*Ger.*] acquisition.

esaminare qualitativamente (*v.*) [*Ital.*] to grade.

escarlata [*Span.*] scarlet.

escaso [*Span.*] scarce.

escasso [*Port.*] scarce, rare.

Escocia [*Span.*] Scotland.

Escócia [*Port.*] Scotland.

escudo (*m.*) [*Span., Port.*] shield.

Escuelas [*Span.*] Schools. Inscription found on early Venezuelan postal/revenue stamps.

escuro [*Port.*] dark; deep (*re*: color).

esemplare (*m.*) [*Ital.*] specimen.

espaço (*m.*); **espaçamento** (*m.*) [*Port.*] space; gutter (on a sheet of stamps).

Espagne [*Fr.*] Spain.

España [*Span.*] Spain.

Espanha [*Port.*] Spain.

espécime (*m.*) [*Port.*] specimen.

ESPLORAZIONE POLARE 1928/ RICERCHE DIRIGIBLE ITALIA A 1928 unofficial overprint on the 1.20 Lire air stamp of Italy purporting to celebrate Nobile's polar research flight in the Italia. The gummed side was overprinted *Esplorazione Polare/ NOBILE/ Dirigibile Italia - 1928*. Its private origin makes this overprint a mere curiosity of no philatelic relevance.

esporre (*v.*) [*Ital.*] to exhibit.

esposizione (*f.*) [*Ital.*] exhibition.

esquerdo [*Port.*] left (direction or position).

essai (*m.*) [*Fr.*] essay.

essay A new design for a postage stamp or other postal item that is rejected by postal authorities and never put into use or is accepted but with major modifications. The essay itself is usually a sample stamp made from a plate which shows the new design. An essay is not a forgery or cinderella because its existence is legitimate and official.

Estados Unidos de América (*abbr.*: E.U.A.) [*Span.*] United States of America (U.S.A.).

estampilla encapsulada (*f.*) [*Span.*] encased postage stamp.

estampilla de franquicia [*Span.*] franchise stamp.

estampilla de propaganda [*Span.*] propaganda stamp.

estampilla de telégrafos [*Span.*] telegraph stamp.

estampilla luminescente (*f.*) [*Span.*] tagged stamp.

estampilla postal (*f.*) [*Span.*] postage stamp.

estampilla provisional (*f.*) [*Span.*] a provisional.

ESTERO Overprint on Italian stamps. See *Eritrea*.

estragado [*Port.*] damaged.

estrangeiro [*Port.*] foreign.

estrela (*f.*) [*Port.*] star.

estrella (*f.*) [*Span.*] star.

Észak-Írország [*Hun.*] Northern Ireland.

état de conservation [*Fr.*] grade, condition.

États-Unis d'Amérique [*Fr.*] United States of America (U.S.A.).

Etelä-Afrikka [*Finn.*] South Africa.
ETF [*Fr.*] *Espagne Transit Française.* Abbreviation used as a pre-adhesive postmark on Spanish mail in transit from France.

etiquettes: U.S. and Israel

etiquette (*f.*) [*Fr.*] label; sticker. In philatelic terms, an *etiquette* is a gummed label or a label-shaped imprinted message on an envelope or aerogramme indicating that the letter or parcel is to go by airmail. These are known to have been used as far back as 1918 on the early airmail flights between Paris and St. Nazaire (France). In 1922 the Universal Postal Union recommended that they be used on all airmail letters. Countries issue etiquettes in their national colors and with the term for "airmail" written both in French (*par avion*) and in their own language. Some etiquettes have also been printed and distributed by international airlines.

As can be seen in the illustrated examples, some etiquettes carry a marketing message ("First, fast and reliable" on the U.S. version) or a special airmail symbol (e.g., the Israeli winged deer). Many different etiquettes exist, and they are eagerly collected by some specialists.

étoile (*f.*) [*Fr.*] star.
etos ἔτος [*Grk.*] year.
étranger [*Fr.*] foreign.
etterligning (*m.*) [*Nor.*] imitation.
etusivu [*Finn.*] obverse; front.
Europa On September 15, 1956, France, West Germany, Italy, Luxembourg, Belgium, and the Netherlands released their first omnibus[*q.v.*] issue of *Europa* stamps as an expression of European unity. The issuance of these stamps became an annual event, and dozens of other Western European countries began participating.

In addition to signifying unity, the stamps sometimes honor C.E.P.T., the Conference of European Postal and Telecommunications Administrations.

During the first years, all of the participating nations issued *Europa* stamps with identical designs. Now, the various *Europa* stamps produced in any given year conform to a common theme, but the actual designs differ so as to meet the needs of the individual countries. This change took place largely because of the difficulty in creating a motif each year that has important symbolic meaning and yet remains politically, religiously, and socially inoffensive to all of the countries involved. Furthermore, requiring a common design ran counter to the internal stamp-issuing policies of many of these nations.

1956 Europa issues: Italy and West Germany

In honor of the twenty-fifth anniversary of C.E.P.T., 35 member nations (or national subdivisions) agreed to use the same design on their 1984 *Europa* issues. Jacky Larriviére of Monaco submitted the accepted design, a stylized bridge motif.

[Edgar Lewy, "The 1984 *Europa* Bridge Design," *American Philatelist*, April, 1985, pp. 330-356. Photographs of all of the 1984 issues plus extensive technical details are included.]

Europa and the Bull Allegorical figure of Europa riding sidesaddle on a bull. Included in the depiction are a dolphin and angel. This design, honoring the direct elections to the European Parliament, is found on the 1984 British 16 pence and 20 1/2 pence stamps

Europa and the Bull (Great Britain)

which are *se-tenant* with the *Europa* issues of that year.

Also known as *Abduction of Europa*.

europino Monetary denomination chosen in the early 1950s by a group of Europeans interested in establishing a European federation. Although many unofficial silver coins were struck in Hamburg, Germany, in 1952, no valid postage stamps were ever issued in this denomination.

évaluer l'état de conservation (*v.*) [*Fr.*] to grade.

Ex Candoris Decus [*Lat.*] An ornament of dazzling whiteness (brightness).

exemplaar (*n.*) [*Dut.*] specimen.

exemplaire (*m.*) [*Fr.*] a specimen, copy.

exhibición (*f.*) [*Span.*] exhibition.

exhibir (*v.*) [*Span.*] to exhibit.

exibição (*f.*) [*Port.*] exhibition.

exile See *government-in-exile*.

expédier (*v.*) [*Fr.*] to mail; to send.

expertsignatur (*r.*) [*Swed.*] authentication mark.

exploded booklet A stamp booklet that has been taken apart. It may or may not have been reassembled. Sometimes the booklet is exploded so that its panes can be displayed page by page, and sometimes the booklet is separated so that the panes can be sold individually. The stamps are normally not removed from the tab, the piece of end paper used for stapling, stitching, or gluing the panes together.

Rare booklets are checked for explosion before they are purchased, in part to be sure that all the panes came from the same booklet. A booklet will generally show signs of having been taken apart and put back together, such as staple holes that are not in alignment. A booklet that has never been taken apart is called *unexploded*.

exposer (*v.*) [*Fr.*] to exhibit.

exposition (*f.*) [*Fr.*] exhibition.

exposición (*f.*) [*Span.*] exhibition.

1930 exposition label (A.P.S., Boston)

exposition label; exposition poster stamp Large ornate stickers issued to publicize national or international philatelic exhibitions. They are often called *poster stamps* because they resemble miniaturized posters. Most of them were printed (usually by engraving) in the 1920s and 1930s and are beautiful examples of philatelic art.

[Kenneth A. Wood, *This Is Philately*, Vol. I, pp. 253-4.]

expoziţie (*f.*) [*Rom.*] exhibition.

express stamp Payment of fee for special handling and expedient service.

extended tête-bêche Gutter pair[q.v.] in which the two stamps are upside-down relative to each other.

extranjero [*Span.*] foreign.

Eylül [*Turk.*] September.

eyrekh nakuv עֵרֶךְ נָקוּב (*m.*) [*Heb.*] face value.

ezer [*Hun.*] thousand.

F f

F. 1. [*abbr.*] forgery; fiscal; franc (French, Belgian and Swiss unit of currency).

2. [*o/p*] Overprinted on French stamps which were given free of charge to Spanish refugees in 1939; "1F" (one franc) surcharge on German stamps used in occupied France during World War I.

face comerţ (*v.*) [*Rom.*] to trade.

facsimile, both sides (Confederate States of America)

facsimile Copy of a stamp made for study or research purposes and not intended to defraud. The illustration shows one of the H. E. MacIntosh group of Confederate States of America facsimiles. A copy made with the purpose of defrauding is called a *forgery*.

facteur (*m.*) [*Fr.*] mailman, postman.

faire une mise; faire une offre (*v.*) [*Fr.*] to bid (at an auction or mail bid sale).

Faksimile (*n.*) [*Ger.*] reproduction; facsimile.

fällige Postgebühr (*f.*) [*Ger.*] postage due.

Fälschung (*f.*) [*Ger.*] a counterfeit; a fake, forgery.

falsificación (*f.*) [*Span.*] a counterfeit; a fake, forgery.

falso (*m.; adj.*) [*Span., Ital.*] fake, forgery.

falsyfikat (*m.*) [*Pol.*] a fake.

falszerstwo (*n.*) [*Pol.*] a counterfeit, fake, forgery.

Falte (*f.*) [*Ger.*] a fold or crease (in a piece of paper).

falten (*v.*) [*Ger.*] to crease.

fältpost (*r.*) [*Swed.*] field post.

fältpostfrimärke (*n.*) [*Swed.*] military postage stamp.

Falz (*m.*) [*Ger.*] (stamp) hinge.

"Famine" (Ukraine)

Famine Macabre allegory featured on 1923 semipostals of the Ukrainian Soviet Socialist Republic.

Farbe (*f.*) [*Ger.*] color, colour.

farge (*m.*) [*Nor.*] color, colour.

fare un'offerta (*v.*) [*Ital.*] to bid (at an auction).

färg (*r.*) [*Swed.*] color, colour.

farthing A small British coin valued at one fourth of a penny. Its name is derived from the *fourthling*, meaning "one fourth". The last of the modern farthings of Britain were dated 1956; they were demonetized in 1960.

Only a few British Commonwealth members such as Dominica issued stamps in the value of one farthing (or 1/4d), largely because the amount was too small for postal purposes. As a point of comparison, the smallest stamp ever issued by Great Britain was for a halfpenny (2 farthings). Hard as it is to believe, mailing a letter today is much cheaper than it was in the 1840s and 1850s when postage stamps first appeared on the scene. Adjusted for inflation, today's rates are about one-third of what they were in the mid-nineteenth century. So even in the 1840s, a farthing would not take a letter anywhere. By the time postal rates came down, inflation had increased the cost of everything to the point where a farthing would *still* not carry a letter anywhere. Hence, a denomination which played a major role in Britain's monetary history for 340 years played virtually no role whatsoever in its philatelic life.

farvestyrke (*c.*) [*Dan.*] shade (*re*: color).

fasces Bundle of rods, usually bound by a leather cord or strap, and topped with an ax blade. It was an ancient Roman symbol of strength and authority.

Among the stamps exhibiting the fasces are some World War II occupational air post stamps of Italy. In some cases, the fasces is part of the main design of the stamp; in other cases, it appears as an overprint.

Faserpapier (*n.*) [*Ger.*] granite paper.

fast [*Ger.*] almost.

fastsättare (*r.*) [*Swed.*] (stamp) hinge.

faţă (*f.*) [*Rom.*] front.

faux (*m.; adj.*) [*Fr.*] fake.

favörstämplat [*Swed.*] cancelled to order.

fazer uma oferta (*v.*) [*Port.*] to make an offer; to bid (at an auction or mail bid sale).

f.c. [*abbr.*] fiscal cancellation.

Fco [*Ital.*] Franco. Abbreviation used as a pre-adhesive postmark.

F.D.C. [*abbr.*] first day cover[*q.v.*].

febbraio [*Ital.*] February.

februar [*Dan., Nor.*] February.

Februar [*Ger.*] February.

februari [*Swed.*] February.

fecha (*f.*) [*Span.*] date.

Federation Internationale de Philatélie [F.I.P.] International Federation of Philately. International association of stamp organizations which sets rules and conditions governing international stamp exhibitions. Headquartered in Zürich, Switzerland, the Federation publishes a quarterly bulletin, *Flash*, which reports the activities of the various commissions as well as the schedule of future exhibitions. Formal meetings and congresses are held each year at one of the scheduled exhibitions.

fehér [*Hun.*] white.

Fehler (*m.*) [*Ger.*] defect; error.

feil (*m.*) [*Nor.*] error.

fejl (*c.*) [*Dan.*] error.

fekete [*Hun.*] black.

fekete piac [*Hun.*] black market.

fel (*n.*) [*Swed.*] error.

fél (*adj.*) [*Hun.*] half.

felaktig [*Swed.*] defective.

German military stamp w/ *o/p FELDPOST 2 kg*

Feldpost (*f.*) [*Ger.*] field post. Commonly-seen overprint or inscription on the World War I-era military stamps of Austria and the World War II "Hitler Head" military stamps of Germany. The stamp in the illustration was also overprinted with *2 kg*, indicating that it was good for free-franking soldiers' parcels of up to two kilograms.

[Kenneth A. Wood, *This Is Philately*, Vol. I, p. 263.]

fele valaminek [*Hun.*] half (the fraction).

felírás; felirat [*Hun.*] inscription; legend.

feltpost (*c.*) [*Dan.*]; (*m.*) [*Nor.*] field post.

felülbélyegzés [*Hun.*] overprint.

fem [*Nor., Swed., Dan.*] five.

femti [*Nor.*] fifty.

femtio [*Swed.*] fifty.

fénynyomás [*Hun.*] photogravure.

feuille (*f.*) [*Fr.*] sheet (of stamps).

feuille se soumission des offres [*Fr.*] bid sheet.

fevereiro [*Port.*] February.

février [*Fr.*] February.

FEZZAN Occupation Française French overprint added to some Italian and Libyan stamps in 1943. See *Libya*.

fieldpost Temporary military post office which operates in the field during wartime. See *Feldpost* and *military stamp*.

first day cover (China)

fijasello (*m.*) [*Span.*] (stamp) hinge.

filament de soie [*Fr.*] silk thread.

filateli (*c.*) [*Dan.*]; (*n.*) [*Nor.*]; (*r.*) [*Swed.*] filatately.

filatelia (*f.*) [*Ital., Span.*] philately.

filatélia (*f.*) [*Port.*] philately.

filatelie (*f./c.*) [*Dut.*] philately.

filatélie (*f.*) [*Fr.*] philately.

filatelico [*Ital.*] philatelic.

filatélico [*Span., Port.*] (*m.*) philatelist; (*adj.*) philatelic.

filatelist (*c.*) [*Dan.*]; (*m./f.*) [*Swed., Nor.*] philatelist.

filatelista (*m./f.*) [*Port., Ital., Pol., Span.*] philatelist.

filatelistisch [*Dut.*] philatelic.

filatelistisk [*Nor., Swed., Dan.*] philatelic.

filatelistyczny [*Pol.*] philatelic.

filatelistyka (*f.*) [*Pol.*] philately.

filigrana (*f.*) [*Span., Ital., Port.*] watermark.

filigrane (*m.*) [*Fr.*] watermark.

filo di seta [*Ital.*] silk thread.

final de estoque [*Port.*] remainder, stock remainder.

Finlandia [*Span., Ital., Pol., et al*] Finland.

Finlândia [*Port.*] Finland.

Finnország [*Hun.*] Finland.

fio de seda [*Port.*] silk thread.

fir de mătase (*n.*) [*Rom.*] silk thread.

fire [*Nor., Dan.*] four.

fireblok (*c.*) [*Dan.*] block of four.

fireblokk (*m.*) [*Nor.*] block of four.

firkantet (*adj*) [*Dan.*] square.

firma (*f.*) [*Span., Ital.*] signature.

first day cover [*abbr.*: F.D.C.] Stamped envelope or other cover which is postmarked on the official date of its stamp's issuance or on the first day upon which that stamp is valid for postage. Any such envelope is a first day cover, irrespective of whether it is purposely postmarked on the stamp's first day of validity to create a philatelic collectable, or whether the envelope contains normal mail and whose first-day cancellation is only a mere coincidence.

Occasionally, first day covers feature postage due stamps rather than postage stamps. See *postage due* for an illustration.

Many philateliciy-prepared F.D.C.s have colorful cachets[q.v.] which relate to the theme of the stamp. Sometimes post offices use special postmarks that indicate first-day status.

first-day-of-issue Idea borrowed from philately which has failed to gain popularity in numismatics. It consists of obtaining a banknote or other collectible certificate on its first day of issue, and then of having a post

first-day-of-issue postmarked U.S. $2 note

office worker affix a postage stamp to the note and apply a postmark. This is supposed to prove that the note was obtained on the first day it was released (a fallacy in itself, because banknotes are sometimes given out by banks before their official release date).

On April 13, 1976, many thousands of U.S. $2 bills suffered the fate of being postmarked. They were issued on that day as part of America's Bicentennial celebration. The U.S. government encouraged all this hoopla because it hoped that the $2 note would finally become accepted by the American people, thus easing the pressure on the Bureau of Engraving and Printing to produce $1 bills. The results, however, were not encouraging. First, the $2

bill failed to circulate, largely because it is regarded as bringing bad luck. Secondly, the postmarked notes failed to generate any numismatic interest. Many thousands are in the hands of collectors, but they seldom sell for much above their $2 face value.

first flight cover In the early days of airmail, first flight covers were prepared to commemorate the maiden flight of a new air route. Interesting cachets and stamps were often used. Many first flight covers were signed by the pilot. To prove that the cover had actually gone on board that specific flight, the post office at the plane's destination would cancel the envelope on the back as soon as the plane arrived.

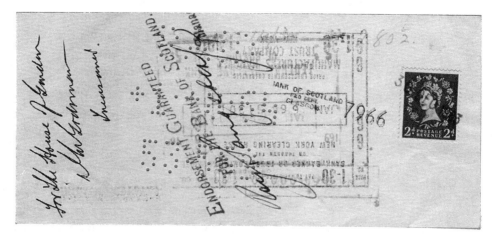

Great Britain fiscal stamp on check

First United Kingdom Aerial Post Postmark found on approximately 130,000 letters and postcards which were transported by air between London and Windsor, England, in September 1911. The service was known as "Coronation Airmail" because of its tie-in with the coronation of King George V and was the first airmail flown on a regular basis.

fiscal stamp [also known as a *revenue stamp*.] A tax stamp, often similar in design to a postage stamp. If it is affixed to a legal document to show that a tax or fee has been paid, it is called a *documentary stamp[q.v.]*. The stamp is then validated either by pen or by a non-postmark type of cancellation. If it is attached directly to a product for sale, it is called a *proprietary stamp[q.v.]*.

In the rare instances in which revenue stamps have been used provisionally as postage, they are referred to as *postal fiscals*. Proving that a fiscal has gone through the mail is usually difficult if the stamp has been removed from its original cover.

As the illustration on the previous page shows, regular postage stamps occasionally take the place of fiscal stamps. In this case, a British stamp (inscribed *POSTAGE + REVENUE* to indicate that it serves both purposes) was affixed and validated on the back of a check.

fita (*f.*) [*Port.*] strip (of stamps).

Fiume At the end of World War I, the Croatian port of Fiume (now called Rijeka) on the east side of the Northern Adriatic Sea became the subject of controvery between the new nation of Yugoslavia and Italy. Fiume dates back to Roman times when it was called *Tarsatica* or *Terra Fluminis Sancti Viti* (the river-land of St. Vitus); Fiume, in fact, means *river*.

At the end of the fifteenth century, Fiume was bought from the Emperor of Austria, Frederick III as a much-needed outlet on the sea. It later became Hungary's only major port when it was annexed to that country in 1776 by a decree of Empress Maria Theresa. In 1809 Fiume was incorporated in the Napoleonic province of Illyria, but in 1814 it was returned to Austria and eight years later re-assigned to Hungary. In 1848, despite the city's adverse

feelings to "croatisation," it became part of the Croatian Crownland. In 1870, the postal network was controlled by Hungary. Stamps of Austria were used at Fiume until 1871 when Hungarian stamps were introduced.

stamp showing Italian flag on Civic Tower of Fiume

In 1915, following the Treaty of London, Fiume was promised to Croatia while Italy was to annex Dalmatia. But when the "October Revolution" forced Russia to withdraw, Italy found herself bearing the burden. Thus, expectations of greater rewards were fueled by public opinion, and while Dalmatia had only marginal connections with Italy, Fiume had a strong ethnic presence of Italians. On October 28, 1918, the Italian flag was raised on the Civic Tower of Fiume (A4 type: Scott 30-32) heralding the strong wind of change. Two days later a plebiscite called for annexation to Italy, and inter-Allied armed forces (British, French, and American) had to intervene to prevent a clash.

From strictly a postal viewpoint, the *de facto* Italian annexation resulted in overprinting stocks of Hungarian stamps with the name *FIUME* in capital letters. This operation was carried out by letterpress for the post office stocks and was done by hand for privately-held part sheets or single stamps.

The provisional (overprinted) issue of Fiume (Scott 1-23) is familiar to specialists for its complexities. Many of these stamps are known with two distinct types of letterpress overprints, and as many as six distinct types of hand overprints. Scott 7 exists with hand overprints, but the rare letterpress type is known only with the overprint inverted (regular upright letterpress overprints of this stamp are forgeries). Forgeries abound, but Fiume overprints are not exceedingly difficult to assess once some genuine reference copies of each overprint are acquired.

Fiume stamp showing Gabriele d'Annunzio & overprint

Eventually Rome twisted the arm of the Allies, and on February 22, 1923, Fiume was annexed to Italy. The process was far from painless, as it involved the highly embarrassing intervention of Gabriele d'Annunzio (an Italian hero with a penchant for flamboyance) and his "Arditi" paramilitary force. As the Rapallo Treaty was signed (November 11, 1920), it became necessary to get rid of the belligerent poet and his Legionari. On Christmas Eve the Italian navy bombarded Fiume, and d'Annunzio and his men capitulated.

Between December 1918 and March 1924, Fiume issued no fewer than 280 stamps. With only one exception (Scott B4-B15), most of the series issued by Fiume from 1918 to 1923 have been forged. This proliferation of forgeries was fueled in the post-World War I years when demand for "war stamps" was at its peak.

o/p ZOFK - ZONA OCCUPATA FIUMANO KUPA

After the official annexation, Italian stamps were used at Fiume. In May 1941, Fiume-Kupa, on the outskirts of Fiume proper, was occupied and later annexed to the pre-existing Province of Fiume. A number of overprinted Yugoslav stamps were issued; some of the overprints include the initials *ZOFK - ZONA OCCUPATA FIUMANO KUPA* ("Fiume Kupa Occupied Zone") and *MAS*, the abbreviation for the Latin motto *Memento Avdere Semper* ("Remember always to be daring," which is also repeated in full on some stamps). These were typically struck as a continuous legend on the horizontal perforation line. Additionally, some overprints include the acronym *O.N.M.I.* (*Opera Nazionale Maternità Infanzia*, "National Organization for Maternity and Child Welfare") and the legend *BVCCARI* to celebrate the February 1918 naval raid when d'Annunzio sank several Austrian ships anchored at Buccari (Bakar).

After Mussolini's ousting (July 25, 1943), Italy signed an armistice with the Allies (September 8, 1943). However, Mussolini was able to establish a civilian government in Northern Italy called the Italian Social Republic. Fiume thus came under the new regime and stamps of this *Repubblica Sociale Italiana* were used in its province.

May 3, 1945 "RIJEKA" overprint

In May 1945, Yugoslav partisans liberated Fiume which reverted to its Croat name of Rijeka. Stocks of the Italian Social Republic stamps were overprinted with a Communist star over the sunrise, the bilingual inscription *FIUME RIJEKA*, and the liberation date May 3, 1945. Fiume then came under Yugoslav military rule and used the stamps of Istria. In 1947 the seaport was formally annexed to Yugoslavia.

[Contributed by Giorgio Migliavacca. Roy A. Dehn, "The Postal History of Fiume" (*Fiume Storia Postale*), as serialized in *Il Nuovo Corriere Filatelico*; "Fiume"

flag cancellations: Canada & the United States

section of *Catalogo Enciclopedico Italiano* (most of the information of which is taken from the 1956 Guglielmo Oliva catalogue, which in turn borrowed from the basic reference work on Fiume stamps compiled by Vincenzo Antoniazzo and Umberto Riccotti included in the *Catalogo Storico Descrittivo* published in 1923).]

fiyat [*Turk.*] price.

fiyat arttırmak (*v.*) [*Turk.*] to bid (at an auction or mail bid sale).

fiyat listesi [*Turk.*] price list.

fjärdedel (*r.*) [*Swed.*] a fourth, quarter.

fjerdedel (*c.*) [*Dan.*]; (*m.*) [*Nor.*] a fourth, quarter.

F.L. [*abbr.*] folded letter. Term especially used to describe mail sent prior to the advent of prepaid postage stamps.

fläck (*r.*) [*Swed.*] stain (on a stamp or banknote).

flag cancellation Cancellation with a killer[q.v.] which resembles the flag of that nation. Flag cancels were very popular in the first half of the twentieth century, especially in those countries whose flags bear a distinctive design, such as the United States and Canada. The "flags" sometimes contained slogans or announcements.

flag-of-truce mail -- 1. Any mail sent between countries or other geographic areas which are at war with each other. Unusual restrictions generally apply, such as limiting the mail to letters only or limiting the length of a mailed letter to one page.

2. A special postal route between the North and South via Fortress Monroe and Norfolk, Virginia, during a period from September 1861 to February 1862 at the time of the U.S. Civil War (1861-1865). Many covers show both Confederate (Southern) and Union (Northern) postage stamps as well as hand stamp markings. Some have coins attached to pay the 3 cents for Federal postage or 5 cents for Confederate postage.

[Contributed by Richard Corwin. Lawrence L. Shenfield, *Confederate States of America: The Special Routes*, pp. 12-15; *Dietz Confederate State Catalog*, p. 135.]

flammes (*f.pl.*) [*Fr.*] literally, *flames*. Slogan cancels, used for special occasions or for promotions in France and various colonies. Also called *flammes d'oblitération* or *flammes publicitaires*. Distinctions are sometimes made between permanent ones (used for months or years) and temporary ones (used for only a few days).

[Contributed by Robert E. Picirilli. Robert G. Stone, *"Flammes Publicitaries*: Slogan and Commemorative Cancels of the French Colonies, Union, and Overseas Departments," *France & Colonies Philatelist*, whole no. 111 (vol. 20, no. 4), pp. 25-27, 32.]

Fleck (*m.*) [*Ger.*] stain.

flekk (*m.*) [*Nor.*] stain; tarnish.

flerfärgad [*Swed.*] multicolored, multicoloured.

flerfarget [*Nor.*] multicolored, multicoloured.

fleur-de-lis on Boy Scout Emblem (Netherlands)

fleur-de-lis [*Fr.*] literally, *flower lily*. A type of heraldic flower which does not exist in nature although it looks somewhat like an iris. It has been a symbol of royalty since ancient times. During the Middle Ages the *lis* was emblematic of illumination and of religious faith. It was popular among Christian monarchs because its central flower rises straight up from a horizontal connector creating something that resembles a cross.

The *fleur-de-lis* is usually associated with France because it appeared on many French regnal coins and because the term itself is in French. However, when featured on postage stamps, it frequently symbolizes the Boy Scouts. The Dutch stamp in the illustration is one such example.

Flüchtlingshilfe Montenegro [*Ger.*] Overprint on 1944 provisional charity issues of German-controlled Montenegro for the aid of war refugees. See *Montenegro*.

fluoresceret frimærke (*n.*) [*Dan.*] tagged stamp.

fluoriscerande frimärke (*n.*) [*Swed.*] tagged stamp.

flygpost [*Swed.*] airmail.

flygpostfilateli (*n.*) [*Swed.*] aerophilately.

flygpostmärke (*n.*) [*Swed.*] air stamp, airmail stamp.

F.M. [*Fr. o/p*] *Franchise Militaire*. Overprint allowing French soldiers free-franking privileges.

foglaló [*Hun.*] deposit.

foglaló kötelező [*Hun.*] deposit required.

foglietto (*m.*) [*Ital.*] souvenir sheet.

foglio d'offerta [*Ital.*] bid sheet.

foglio quadrettato (*m.*) [*Ital.*] *quadrillé*.

fokozat [*Hun.*] grade, condition.

fold (*noun*) A crease in a piece of paper.

folha (*f.*) [*Port.*] sheet (of stamps).

folhinha filatélica (*f.*) [*Port.*] souvenir sheet.

Folkerepublikken Kina [*Nor., Dan.*] People's Republic of China (P.R.C.).

Folkrepubliken Kina [*Swed.*] People's Republic of China.

folosit [*Rom.*] used.

folt [*Hun.*] stain.

foncé [*Fr.*] dark.

fondo (*m.*) [*Span.*] bottom.

font [*Hun.*] pound (16 ounces avdp. or 12 oz. troy of weight; pound Sterling - £).

food coupon see *food stamp*.

food stamp [technically known as *food coupon*.] Certificate distributed on behalf of the U.S. Department of Agriculture to low-income people who meet certain qualifications. It is used for the purchase of food items, excluding such things as prepared (already cooked) foods, tobacco products, and alcoholic beverages.

According to law, these are not collectible items. Recipients are not legally permitted to sell them, and the food stamps may only be removed from their original booklets by a cashier at a supermarket or grocery store.

[Contributed by Faith H. Barnett. *State of Ohio Food Stamp Certification Handbook*; *Encyclopedia of Social Work* (1973), Vols. 1 & 2.]

forældet [*Dan.*] obsolete.

föråldrad [*Swed.*] obsolete.

förändra (*v.*) [*Swed.*] to alter.

forandre (*v.*) [*Nor.*] to alter.

forandring (*c.*) [*Dan.*]; (*m.*) [*Nor.*] alteration.

förändring (*r.*) [*Swed.*] alteration.

forato [*Ital.*] holed; rouletted.

foratura (*f.*) [*Ital.*] roulette.

foratura a serpentina [*Ital.*] serpentine roulette.

foratura à zigzag [*Ital.*] serrated roulette; zigzag roulette.

forbundet [*Nor.*] accolated, conjoined[q.v.].

foreign transfer Plate variety similar to a double transfer. When line-engraved intaglio stamps are being prepared, the design is rocked into the printing plate. Sometimes the transfer is faulty and the design has to be burnished out of the plate so that the plate can be reused. If the old design has not been completely expunged, whatever remains will show up on the stamp in addition to the new design that is rocked in. If an identical stamp design is rocked in, the finished stamp will show signs of doubling in the areas where the old design remained. This is called a *double transfer*. But if the burnished plate is re-rocked with the design for a different stamp, bits of design elements from the old design (the one supposedly burnished out) will show up on the new design of the finished stamp. This is called *foreign transfer*, a condition that happens very infrequently.

If foreign transfer occurs, the same flaw will show up on every stamp produced with that plate because the problem has become a permanent part of the plate. This is different from a double impression[q.v.], a type of error which can occur randomly.

foreldet [*Nor.*] obsolete.

Forenede Stater [*Dan.*] United States of America (U.S.A.).

Forente Stater [*Nor.*] United States of America.

foreslået bud (*n.*) [*Dan.*] suggested bid.

forfalskning (*c.*) [*Dan.*]; (*m.*) [*Nor.*] a counterfeit, fake, forgery.

förfalskning (*r.*) [*Swed.*] a counterfeit, fake, forgery.

forgalomból kivont [*Hun.*] demonetization; obsolete.

forgery A copy of a stamp made with the intent to defraud. The Buenos Aires stamp in the illustration is not marked as a fake and is a good enough copy to fool the uninitiated.

The two overprinted Fiume stamps represent a different type of forgery. In this case, the stamps are both real, but the *overprint* on the stamp at the right was forged. Both overprints were produced on a letterpress. The genuine specimen has serifs that are crisp and clear; the forged overprint has poorly-defined serifs, especially those at the top of the letter *M*. Because it is known to be a fake, the stamp has correctly been marked with the word "Forgery" so that it can never be sold as genuine.

A copy of a stamp that is made for research or study purposes with no intent to defraud is known as a *facsimile*[q.v.].

stamp forgery: Buenos Aires

overprint: genuine and forgery (Fiume)

forhåndsbetaling (*m.*) [*Nor.*] prepayment.

forkortelse (*c.*) [*Dan.*]; (*m.*) [*Nor.*] abbreviation.

förkortning (*r.*) [*Swed.*] abbreviation.

förmakulera [*Swed.*] precancel.

formulario de pedido (*m.*) [*Span.*] order form.

formulário de pedido (*m.*) [*Port.*] order form.

formularz ofertowy (*m.*) [*Pol.*] bid sheet.

formularz zamówienia (*m.*) [*Pol.*] order form.

foro (*m.*) [*Ital.*] hole.

foros φόρος (*m.*) [*Grk.*] tax.

försändelse (*r.*) [*Swed.*] cover (in the philatelic sense). The terms for *on cover* in Swedish are *på brev* and *på försändelse*.

forside (*c.*) [*Dan.*]; (*m.*) [*Nor.*] front; obverse.

förskottsbetalning (*r.*) [*Swed.*] prepayment.

forskudt takning (*c.*) [*Dan.*] interrupted perforation; syncopated perforation.

förstadagsbrev (*n.*) [*Swed.*] first day cover.

førstedagsbrev (c.) [Dan.]; (n.) [Nor.] first day cover.

förstoringsglas (n.) [Swed.] magnifying glass.

forstørrelsesglas (n.) [Nor., Dan.] magnifying glass.

Fortuna Variabilis / Omnia Cum Pondere Numero & Mensura [Lat.] Changing fortune / All things with weight, number and measurement.

Fortuna Volubilis Errat [Lat.] Fortune varies erratically.

forudbetaling (c.) [Dan.] prepayment.

förvärv (n.) [Swed.] acquisition.

fosforescende [Nor.] phosphorescent.

fosforescente [Ital., Span.] phosphorescent.

fosforescerande [Swed.] phosphorescent.

fosforescerend [Dut.] phosphorescent.

fosforiserende [Dan.] phosphorescent.

fosforyzujący [Pol.] phosphorescent.

fotoincisione (f.) [Ital.] photogravure.

fotograbado (m.) [Span.] photogravure.

fotogravyyri [Finn.] photogravure.

fout (f.-c.) [Dut.] defect; error.

foutief [Dut.] defective.

foxing Discoloration of a cover.

fraai [Dut.] fine (grade or condition).

fracción (f.) [Span.] fraction.

fractional currency Any of the U.S. notes issued from 1862-1876 bearing a denomination of less than one dollar. See *postage currency*.

fracţiune (f.) [Rom.] fraction.

fragko φράγκο (n.) [Grk.] franc (French unit of currency).

frakcja (f.) [Pol.] fraction.

frame The outer portion of a stamp's design which surrounds the portrait or vignette. It was usually printed in a different color from that of the vignette and is most commonly found on stamps issued prior to 1930.

França [Port.] France.

franchigia (f.) [Ital.] frank.

franchise militaire (f.) [Fr.] military postage stamp.

Francia [Ital., Span.] France.

Franciaország [Hun.] France.

Francja [Pol.] France.

franco (m.) [Port., Ital, Span.] franc (French unit of currency).

Franco, Francisco [né *Francisco Paulino Hermenegildo Teodulo Franco Bahamonde*; a.k.a. *El Caudillo* ("The Commander").] Spanish Chief of State (1947-75). Born December 4, 1892, in El Ferrol, Galicia (Spain); died of acute heart disease on November 20, 1975, in Madrid.

General Franco was leader of the Nationalist forces that overthrew the Spanish Democratic Republic in the Spanish Civil War (1936-39). He entered the army in 1907 at the age of fifteen. Because of his military capabilities, his rise through the military ranks was meteoric. In 1926, he became Europe's youngest Brigadier-General.

During World War II, Franco was sympathetic to the Axis but refused to officially enter the war, calling Spain's position "non-belligerent." But as the Allied armies started to advance, he drew back closer to a position of "neutrality." In 1947, after re-organizing the government and proclaiming Spain a monarchy, he made himself Chief of State, a position he kept until his death.

In July 1969 Franco chose Prince Juan Carlos de Borbón as his eventual successor. At Franco's death, Juan Carlos was sworn in as King Juan Carlos I on November 22, 1975.

During the years that he was in power, Franco appeared on many series of Spanish definitive stamps.

[Contributed by Ruth Ann Davis.]

francobollo (m.); **francobollo postale** (m.) [Ital.] postage stamp.

francobollo di beneficenza (m.) [Ital.] charity stamp.

francobollo di posta aerea [Ital.] airmail stamp.

francobollo di propaganda [Ital.] propaganda stamp.

francobollo di servizio [Ital.] official stamp.

francobollo fiscale (m.) [Ital.] fiscal stamp.

francobollo fluorescente (m.) [Ital.] tagged stamp.

francobollo per giornali [Ital.] newspaper stamp.

francobollo per pacchi [Ital.] parcel post stamp.

francobollo per posta militare [Ital.] military postage stamp.

francobollo per raccomandate [Ital.] registration stamp.

francobollo per telegrafo (*m.*) [*Ital.*] telegraph stamp.

frank [*Hun., Turk.*]; (*m.*) [*Pol.*] franc.

frank (*noun; verb*); **franking privilege** [Also known as *free-franking*.] The right or privilege of sending mail without paying postage.

Prior to the advent of prepaid postage stamps, free-franking was abused by anyone with the authority to do it, especially in Great Britain. In the eighteenth century, as much as one-half of all mail delivered in England was free-franked. An Act of Parliament was passed in 1764 to curb the abuse, but to little avail. It is even reported that Samuel Johnson wrote intimate letters to a Mrs. Thrale, but he addressed them to her husband because Mr. Thrale was allowed to send and receive letters free of charge!

Part of the reason the postage stamp was invented (and certainly a major reason why it first appeared in Great Britain) was to limit the abuse. The first stamps not only standardized rates but also helped reduce them. because a letter could now be sent to any part of Britain for a penny. The affordability and convenience of the stamps, along with tougher regulations as to who could have franking privileges, greatly reduced the amount of free mail and contributed to the postage stamp's success.

In today's world, franking privileges are usually given to top governmental officials, such as members of Congress and the President, for mail sent to their constituents. Under Universal Postal Union regulations, free-franking must be given to prisoners-of-war, military or civilians. And in many countries, soldiers on active duty are granted this right. Military mail is sometimes franked with the notation *O.A.S.* (On Active Service).

In everyday use, the verb *frank* is often used in the same sense as *affixed*: "the envelope was franked with a colorful stamp." This is not strictly correct because no free-franking privilege is invoked. Nevertheless, the word is commonly used in this way.

[Kenneth A. Wood, *This Is Philately*, Vol. I, p. 282-4.]

Frankatur (*f.*); **Frankaturunterschrift** (*f.*) [*Ger.*] frank.

frankering (*r.*) [*Swed.*] frank.

frankieren (*v.*) [*Ger.*] to frank.

Benjamin Franklin on Russian stamp

Franklin, Benjamin American author, printer, inventor, diplomat, and scientist, and one of the leaders of the American Revolution. Born January 17, 1706, in Boston, Massachusetts; died April 17, 1790, at his home in Philadelphia, Pennsylvania.

Although his talents encompassed many areas of human endeavor, Franklin is best remembered for his wisdom and diplomacy in effecting an alliance between France and the American colonies and later in bringing about a peace treaty forcing Great Britain to recognize American independence. An elder statesman of the American Revolution, he was the oldest man to sign the Declaration of Independence and the United States Constitution.

Born into a family of seventeen children, Franklin attended school just long enough to learn to read and write. Yet despite his limited education, he became the publisher of the *Pennsylvania Gazette* and the highly respected *Poor Richard's Almanac*.

In 1727 he formed the Junto, or Leather Apron Club, a social and philosophical club for young craftsmen. Four years later, the Junto Club's library became the basis for the Library Company of Philadelphia, regarded as the first circulating library in America.

Franklin obtained a lucrative printing contract to print Pennsylvania's paper money after he published a pamphlet in 1729 called *A Modest Inquiry into the Nature and Necessity of*

Paper Currency that called for the issuance of more paper money.

His long illustrious career in public office began at the age of thirty when he was chosen as Clerk of the Pennsylvania Legislature. He accepted a second office in 1737 when he became Philadelphia's Deputy Postmaster in order to improve the city's distribution of mail.

His life was not without controversy. His first son was born out of wedlock. The two disliked each other so much that the son took the side of the British during the American Revolution. Franklin's behavior in France when he was trying to obtain support for the American cause was far from exemplary, as he had quite a reputation for being a heavy drinker and womanizer. Even his experiments with lightning and electricity proved controversial, because many preachers in America and Europe believed that being hit by lightning was God's punishment for sinners, and that Franklin had no business interfering with the will of God.

Nevertheless, Benjamin Franklin will always be remembered as one of America's greatest patriots. Thomas Jefferson summed it up by calling him "the greatest man and ornament of the age and country in which he lived."

Benjamin Franklin has appeared on a multitude of U.S. postage and revenue stamps, and his portrait has been featured on the stamps of many countries, including the Soviet Union. Franklin and George Washington share the distinction of having been on America's first stamps, those issued in 1847. The five cent stamps bear the likeness of Franklin, and the ten cent stamps feature Washington.

[Contributed by Ruth Ann Davis. David C. Whitney (editor), *Founders of Freedom in America*.]

Frankreich [*Ger.*] France.

Frankrig [*Dan.*] France.

Frankrijk [*Dut.*] France.

Frankrike [*Nor., Swed.*] France.

franquear (*v.*) [*Span., Port.*] to frank.

franqueo (*m.*) [*Span.*] postage.

franqueo deficiente (*m.*); **franqueo insuficiente** (*m.*) [*Span.*] postage due.

franquicia postal (*f.*) [*Span.*] to frank.

franquicia postal militar (*f.*) [*Span.*] military postage stamp.

frånsida (*r.*) [*Swed.*] reverse.

Franţa [*Rom.*] France.

frazionato diagonalmente [*Ital.*] bisected.

frazione (*f.*) [*Ital.*] fraction.

freak A random variety or a minor error such as a misperf[*q.v.*] or ink smear.

free-franking The right or privilege of sending mail without paying postage. See *frank*.

Freiheit (*f.*) [*Ger.*] liberty.

fremd [*Ger.*] foreign.

Fremdwährung (*f.*) [*Ger.*] foreign currency.

frente (*m.*) [*Span.*] front.

fri-frankering (*c.*) [*Dan.*] franchise stamp.

frimærke (*n.*) [*Dan.*] (postage) stamp.

frimærkehæfte (*n.*) [*Dan.*] booklet (of stamps).

frimærkehængsel (*c.*) [*Dan.*] (stamp) hinge.

frimærkepenge [*Dan.*] encased postage stamp (such as the type used during the U.S. Civil War of 1961-65).

frimärke (*n.*) [*Swed.*] (postage) stamp.

frimärksmynt (*n.*) [*Swed.*] encased postage stamp.

frimerke (*n.*) [*Nor.*] (postage) stamp.

frimerke for offisielt bruk [*Nor.*] official stamp.

frimerkerull (*m.*) [*Nor.*] coil (of stamps).

fuchsinrot [*Ger.*] magenta.

fugitive ink Unstable ink that is prone to fade, smear, or dissolve, especially when exposed to water, carbon tetrachloride, or benzine. Ink of this type is sometimes utilized to prevent the stamp from being postally reused.

fumigated mail See *disinfected mail*.

fundo (*m.*) [*Port.*] bottom.

fünf [*Ger.*] five.

Fünftel (*n.*) [*Ger.*] fifth.

fünfzig [*Ger.*] fifty.

fungi on stamps See *mycophilately*.

funt szterling (*m.*) [*Pol.*] pound Sterling (£).

fuoricorso [*Ital.*] (*m.*) demonetization; (*adj.*) obsolete.

furo (*m.*) [*Port.*] hole.

F.V. [*abbr.*] face value.

fyra [*Swed.*] four.

fyrblock (*n.*) [*Swed.*] block of four.

fyrkantigt utklippt [*Swed.*] cut square.

G g

G [o/p] 1. Griqualand West. Overprinted on stamps of the Cape of Good Hope.

"G" official overprint (Canada)

2. Government/*Gouvernement*. Overprint on official stamps of Canada. It replaced the previous "official" overprint *O.H.M.S.* ("On His/Her Majesty's Service") as the result of complaints from French Canadians.

Ga [*Span. abbr.*] Pre-adhesive postmark from Galicia, Spain.

galben [*Rom.*] yellow.

Gales [*Span.*] Wales.

Galles [*Ital.*] Wales.

gammal [*Swed.*] old.

gammel [*Dan.*] old.

gat (*n.*) [*Dut.*] hole.

gauche (*f.*) [*Fr.*] left (direction or position).

gaură (*f.*) [*Rom.*] hole.

găurit [*Rom.*] holed.

gays and lesbians on stamps See *lambda-philately*.

gazete pulu [*Turk.*] newspaper stamp.

G.B. [*abbr.*] Great Britain.

G. C. paper See *grande consommation*.

GD-OT [*Ger./Cz. abbr.*] *Geschäfts Drucksache—Obchodni Tiskopiš* (commercial printed papers). Overprinted on newspaper stamps of Bohemia and Moravia in 1940 for use by commercial firms.

Gebot (*n.*) [*Ger.*] bid; bid sheet.

gebraucht [*Ger.*] used.

gebruikt [*Dut.*] used.

Gebühr (*f.*) [*Ger.*] fee.

Gebührenmarke (*f.*) [*Ger.*] fiscal stamp.

gebyr (*n.*) [*Nor., Dan.*] fee.

Gedenk- [*Ger.*] commemorative.

geel [*Dut.*] yellow.

geen ongelimiteerde biedingen geaccepteerd [*Dut.*] no unlimited bids accepted.

gecensureerde post (*f./c.*) [*Dut.*] censored mail.

Gefälligkeitsabstempelung (*f.*) [*Ger.*] cancelled to order.

gefalzt [*Ger.*] hinged.

gegraveerd [*Dut.*] engraved.

gehalveerd [*Dut.*] bisected.

geheim merk (*n.*) [*Dut.*] hidden mark, secret mark.

Geheimzeichen (*n.*) [*Ger.*] hidden mark, secret mark.

gelauwerd [*Dut.*] laureate.

gelb [*Ger.*] yellow.

gelbbraun [*Ger.*] buff.

Geld (*n.*) [*Ger.*] money.

Geldanweisung (*f.*) [*Ger.*] money order.

Geldeinheit (*f.*) [*Ger.*] monetary unit.

gelocht [*Ger.*] holed.

general issue Any postage stamp released for general use, such as a definitive stamp or commemorative stamp. This category does not include semipostals, airmails, postage dues, newspaper stamps, etc. Stamps of this nature are sometimes called "front-of-the-book" material because they are always listed first in catalogues ahead of the other afore-mentioned stamps.

General Postal Union See *Universal Postal Union*.

gennaio [*Ital.*] January.

gennemhulsannulering (*c.*) [*Dan.*] punch cancellation.

gennemstikning (*c.*) [*Dan.*] roulette, *perçage.*

gennemstukket [*Dan.*] rouletted, *percé.*

Geöffnet [*Ger.*] A censor mark from German-speaking countries. See *censored mail.*

George Name of six British kings, two of whom are extremely important in philately.

George V

1. George V (born June 3, 1865, in London; died January 20, 1936, at Sandringham House, Norfold) was the first British monarch to realize the need to become accessible to his subjects, starting a trend which has shown mixed results in the late twentieth century.

Although he was born into the house of Saxe-Coburg-Gotha, he renounced his German titles at the beginning of World War I and changed the royal name to the house of Windsor. As a sailor who had entered the Royal Navy in 1877 and had risen to the rank of vice admiral in 1903, George V took an active interest in the "War to end all wars" and achieved great popularity with his subjects. His military involvement is reflected in a group of stamps known as *Admirals*[*q.v.*]. These stamps were actually three separate unrelated series showing him in three different naval uniforms. One series was an eleven-denomination set from Canada (1911-25), another was a two-stamp set from New Zealand (1926), and the third was a thirteen-denomination set from Southern Rhodesia (1924-30), which also happened to be that nation's very first postage stamps.

George V not only inherited the title of king of Great Britain and Ireland but also that of emperor of India. He lost his reign of Ireland in the rebellion of 1922 but retained Northern Ireland as part of his domain. Some of the British definitives bearing his likeness were overprinted with a message in the Irish language for use in Ireland until that fledgling nation could print its own. This was done with the blessing of the British government. (See *provisional.*)

2. George VI was not groomed to be king. As second in line to the throne, everyone always assumed that his older brother Edward would be king. But, then, "everyone" did not assume that Edward would renounce his throne after only nine months to marry an American divorcée. Prepared or not, George VI became king of Great Britain and Northern Ireland and emperor of India in 1936.

George VI was born in Sandringham, Norfolk, on December 14, 1895. He married Lady Elizabeth Bowes-Lyon who would later be known to her many loving subjects as Queen Mother Elizabeth. Just as his father had done, George VI faced a major war and dealt with it admirably. He was a symbol of strength during World War II and helped his people overcome the Nazi aggression. George VI died on February 6, 1952, and was succeeded by his daughter, Elizabeth II.

George VI

The stamps of George VI are not particularly distinguished, but several of them are quite interesting. Among the most beautiful are the 1937 Coronation Issues of Australia which show both King George and Queen Mother Elizabeth in their coronation robes. Several British commemorative issues, especially those of 1951 which feature *St. George Slaying the Dragon*[*q.v.*] and the royal arms, are also magnificent. Among the most unusual of his stamps are the British definitives which were overprinted with heavy vertical black lines to invalidate them for postage so they could be used by students. (See *college training stamp*.)

geperforeerd [*Dut.*] perforated.

gerçek [*Turk.*] authentic.

GEREINIGET [*Ger.*] Purified. A term stamped on letters to show that they had been fumigated or in some other way disinfected against disease. See *disinfected mail*.

gerepareerd [*Dut.*] repaired.

Germania 1. [*Ital., Rom.*] Germany.

2. Allegorical figure symbolizing the German Empire which appeared on German definitives in 1920 and 1921. *Germania* was created by Paul Waldraff who used a painting of Wagnerian opera star Anna von Stratz-Führing.

gerouletteerd [*Dut.*] rouletted, *percé*.

geruit albumblad (*n.*) [*Dut.*] *quadrillé*.

gescheurd [*Dut.*] torn.

gestreept papier (*n.*) [*Dut.*] laid paper.

gestreiftes Papier (*n.*) [*Ger.*] laid paper.

gesyncopeerde perforatie (*f./c.*) [*Dut.*] syncopated perforation; interrupted perforation.

getal (*n.*) [*Dut.*] number.

getand [*Dut.*] perforated.

gewöhnlich [*Ger.*] common.

gewoon [*Dut.*] common; definitive.

gewoon papier (*n.*) [*Dut.*] wove paper.

gezähnt [*Ger.*] perforated.

ghost tagging Improper alignment of the phosphor tagging and the inked impression on a stamp. See *tagged stamp*.

giallo [*Ital.*] yellow.

Giappone [*Ital.*] Japan.

giro (*m.*) [*Span.*] money order.

Gitter (*n.*); **Gittermuster** (*n.*) [*Ger.*] *quadrillé*.

giugno [*Ital.*] June.

gizli işaret [*Turk.*] secret mark.

Glanzpapier (*n.*) [*Ger.*] glossy paper.

glassert papir (*n.*) [*Nor.*] glossy paper.

glättat papper (*n.*) [*Swed.*] glossy paper.

głęboki [*Pol.*] deep (*re*: color).

glossy paper Smooth and shiny paper that reflects luster.

G.N. [*Span. abbr.*] *Gobierno Oficial* ("Official Government"). Some official Venezuelan stamps of 1930-42 were perforated with these initials.

gnision γνήσιον [*Grk.*] genuine, authentic.

G.N.R. overprint on Italian stamp

G.N.R. [*Ital.*; *o/p*] Overprint found on 1929-42 definitive, airmail, special delivery, and war propaganda stamps of Italy. *G.N.R.* stands for *Guardia Nazionale Repubblicana* (National Republican Guard)— the military arm of the Fascist party decreed by Mussolini on December 8, 1943.

Goat's Eye (Brazil)

Goat's Eye Common name for the third general issue of Brazilian stamps (1850), so named because they resemble the eye of a goat. They are sometimes known as the "poor man's Bull's Eyes[*q.v.*]" because they are less scarce and less expensive than the 1843 issues. The Portuguese name for "Goat's Eye" is *Olho-de-Cabra*.

god [*Dan., Swed.*] good.

goed [*Dut.*] good.

goffratura (*f.*) [*Ital.*] embossing.

gök mavisi [*Turk.*] azure (blue).

Goldbeater's Skin A tough paper made somewhat transparent by rubbing it with resin. The design is printed in reverse on the gum side of the paper so that the design is actually viewed through the paper, rather than being printed on it. If the stamp is removed from the envelope, the design will suffer considerable disintegration.

This type of security paper[*q.v.*] was only used for the 1866 Prussian stamps of 10 and 30

Silbergroschen, and apparently was quickly deemed unsatisfactory for stamp production. The paper must have surely fulfilled its purpose, however, as very few of these stamps survive today in undamaged condition. In other words, philatelists could not remove these stamps from their covers any better than dishonest "recyclers" could.

The term *Goldbeater's Skin* is idiomatic to English and does not exist as such in any other language, including the original German. German-language catalogues refer to this paper as *blasenartiges Papier*.

gom (*n.*) [*Dut.*] gum.

goma (*f.*) [*Port., Span.*] gum.

goma original (*f.*) [*Port., Span.*] original gum.

gomma (*f.*) [*Ital.*] gum.

gomma originale (*f.*) [*Ital.*] original gum.

gomme (*f.*) [*Fr.*] gum.

gomme d'origine [*Fr.*] original gum.

goot (*f./c.*) [*Dut.*] gutter.

góra (*f.*) [*Pol.*] top.

Görögország [*Hun.*] Greece.

gotówka (*f.*) [*Pol.*] cash (ready money).

Gouda P. Gouda Post. Pre-adhesive postmark used from 1757 to 1793.

goú wáng [*Chin.-py.*] king.

Governatorato del Montenegro [*Ital.*] Governorship of Montenegro. Italian overprint produced during World War II on Yugoslav stamps. See *Montenegro*.

government-in-exile issue (Albania)

government-in-exile Rulers and ruling parties that are driven into exile sometimes issue postage stamps as a way of demonstrating their credibility and legitimacy. These stamps usually have no postal validity and are thus regarded by philatelists as a form of cinderellas[*q.v.*].

The illustrated stamp was issued by Albania's government-in-exile during World War II. Although a bogus stamp, it is a semipostal with its surtax intended for victims of the war. There are many variations of the Albanian spelling of that country's name (*Shqiperise, Shqipëria, Shqipëtare*, et al), but the spelling *Shqipnija* is limited to exile stamps and stamps issued under German administration.

government life insurance [New Zealand] See *life insurance stamp.*

G.P. de M. [*Span. abbr.*] *Gobierno Provisional de México* (Provisional Government of Mexico). Overprinted on 1916-18 stamps of Mexico.

GPE. [*abbr.*] Guadeloupe.

G.P.O. [*abbr.*] General Post Office.

G.P.U. [*abbr.*] General Postal Union. See *Universal Postal Union.*

Gr. Grenze (pre-adhesive postmark).

grå [*Nor., Swed., Dan.*] gray.

grabado [*Span.*] engraved.

grabado en acero (*m.*) [*Span.*] steel engraving.

Grã-Bretanha [*Port.*] Great Britain.

gräddfärgad [*Swed.*] cream (color).

grading See *condition.*

grado de conservación; graduación (*f.*) [*Span.*] grade, condition.

graduar (*v.*) [*Span.*] to grade.

Graf Zeppelin See *Zeppelin.*

grammatosimo γραμματόσημο (*n.*) [*Grk.*] postage stamp.

Grana Pre-adhesive postmark used in Granada, Spain.

Gran Bretaña [*Span.*] Great Britain.

Gran Bretagna [*Ital.*] Great Britain.

grand [*Fr.*] big, large.

grande [*Ital., Span., Port.*] big, large.

Grande Bretagne [*Fr.*] Great Britain.

grande consommation [*Fr.*; abbreviated *G. C. paper.*] Paper used to print French stamps during World War I. It was poor quality paper, off-white and often gray. A literal translation of the term, *large expenditure of material*, comes from the military, suggesting paper shortages and a reduction in quality.

[Contributed by John E. Lievsay.]

Austrian stamp on granite paper

granite paper Special paper that contains extremely short colored silk threads which function as an anti-counterfeiting device. Austria and Switzerland issued postage stamps made from this paper around the beginning of the twentieth century; some recent Swiss issues also exist.

Silurian paper is the specific name of a blue-grey colored granite paper containing blue threads.

Granite paper should not bae confused with silked paper[q.v.] which contains silk threads that are longer in length and generally fewer in number.

granitpapper (n.) [Swed.] granite paper.

gratis frimerke (n.) [Nor.] franchise stamp.

gratis label In January 1871 during the Franco-Prussian War, French General Bourbaki was beaten by the Prussians. He retreated into neutral Switzerland where his troops were promptly interned. The Swiss kindly provided the troops with a label for correspondence, inscribed in two lines, "Militaires Françaises Internes en Suisse" and then one line in bold type, "Gratis," letter pressed on violet paper. Overlooked by the French catalogues, this label is listed only in Zumstein; it is the first-ever stamp for carrying mail issued by one country to citizens of another.

[Contributed by John E. Lievsay. Victor Chanaryn, *The Posts of France in the Franco-German War of 1870-1871*, pp. 50-59.]

grau [Ger.] gray; (m.) [Port.] grade, condition.

graubraun [Ger.] drab (color).

gravada [Port.] engraved.

gravé [Fr.] engraved.

graverad [Swed.] engraved.

graveret [Dan.] engraved.

gravert [Nor.] engraved.

graviert [Ger.] engraved.

Grav.na Italian pre-adhesive postmark from Gravedona (1835-40 Lombardy).

gravură în oţel (f.) [Rom.] steel engraving.

gravure en creux [Fr.] intaglio.

gravure sur acier [Fr.] steel engraving.

Great Seal of the United States on special delivery stamp

Great Seal of the United States Official seal of the United States as adopted in 1782.

Unlike the seal of any other nation, the Great Seal of the United States has two sides. The obverse depicts an American eagle, symbolizing national sovereignty. On its breast is the national shield with its traditional 13 bars. In its right talon, the eagle grasps an olive branch of 13 leaves and 13 olives representing peace. The left talon clutches 13 arrows signifying the fight for liberty and independence. The eagle's beak holds a scroll with the Latin inscription *E Pluribus Unum*, the official U.S. motto meaning *From Many, One.* Above the eagle is a cluster of 13 stars surrounded by a cloud of glory. In each case, the number 13 refers to the 13 original colonies which banded together to form one government.

The reverse is dominated by an Egyptian-style pyramid, symbolic of permanence and strength. Yet this pyramid is unfinished, representing the young country and its promise to build and grow. The "Eye of Providence", based on an ancient Egyptian symbol of understanding and truth, sits atop the pyramid. At the bottom of the pyramid is engraved the date 1776, the year in which the Declaration of Independence was signed. This is regarded as the founding date of the U.S.A. Surrounding the pyramid are two additional Latin inscriptions: *Annuit cœptis* ("God has smiled on our undertakings") and *Novus ordo seclorum* ("New Order of the Ages").

Although the Great Seal was commissioned shortly after the signing of the Declaration of Independence on July 4, 1776, the final design was not adopted by the U.S. Congress until June 20, 1782.

Both sides of the Great Seal are depicted on the reverse of the U.S. one dollar notes which have been issued since the mid-1930s. The Seal is not a device commonly seen on U.S. stamps, but its front side (the eagle side) does appear on such issues as some recent official stamps, the 1934 air post/special delivery stamps, and a 1982 postal envelope commemorating the two hundredth anniversary of the Seal's adoption.

[*Funk & Wagnalls New Encyclopedia* (1984), Vol. 12, p. 157.]

Grecia [*Span., Ital., Rom.*] Greece.

Grécia [*Port.*] Greece.

Grecja [*Pol.*] Greece.

greşeală (*f.*) [*Rom.*] error.

G.R.I. [*Lat. abbr.*] *Georgius Rex Imperator* (George, King & Emperor). British occupation overprint on stamps of German New Guinea, Samoa, and the Marshall Islands in 1914.

Griechenland [*Ger.*] Greece.

Griekenland [*Dut.*] Greece.

grigio [*Ital.*] gray.

grijs [*Dut.*] gray.

gris [*Span., Fr.*] gray.

groef (*f./c.*) [*Dut.*] gutter.

groen [*Dut.*] green.

grøn [*Dan.*] green.

groot [*Dut.*] large.

Groot-Brittannië [*Dut.*] Great Britain.

groot zilverstuk (*n.*) [*Dut.*] crown (large silver coin).

groß [*Ger.*] large, big; great.

Großbritannien [*Ger.*] Great Britain.

grön [*Swed.*] green.

grønn [*Nor.*] green.

gros [*Fr.*] big, large.

Group Type See *Allegorical Group Type*.

grudzień [*Pol.*] December.

grün [*Ger.*] green.

G.R.V; Geo. V; G.V [*abbr.*] King George V of Great Britain.

G.R.VI; Geo. VI; G.VI [*abbr.*] King George VI of Great Britain.

guarantee mark on back of Fiume stamp

guarantee mark Handstamp or other marking applied to a stamp, usually by the issuing agency, to indicate that the stamp is genuine and is valid for postal use.

The illustration shows a guarantee mark that was handstamped on the back of some stamps of Fiume[*q.v.*]. It depicts the emblem of the Arditi, a snake biting its own tail.

guilloche on Hungarian stamp (above)
and on Israeli *tête-bêche* gutter pair (below)

guilloche (*m.*) [*Fr.*] Circular or symmetrical machine-generated pattern found on many banknotes, bonds, and various other types of certificates. It is occasionally seen on postage stamps and other philatelically-related items. Although these designs can be extremely attractive, especially when done in multiple colors, they are used on paper money and other official documents primarily because *guilloche* designs are hard to counterfeit. The patterns tend to be intricate with very fine and delicate lines.

The technique was created by Asa Spencer, an American inventor who built a geometrical lathe capable of engraving such a design onto a steel engraving plate. The patterns soon became popular and are now used worldwide.

The Hungarian stamp in the illustration shows a *guilloche* design taken from a Hungarian banknote. An entirely different use of this technique is seen on the Israeli *tête-bêche* gutter pair, where a circular *guilloche* pattern was printed on the gutter label.

guillotine perforation Type of perforation method in which one horizontal or vertical row is punched at a time. See *line perforation.*

gul [*Dan., Swed., Nor.*] yellow.

gum Adhesive affixed to the back of a postage stamp or other label. Traditionally, the gummed side of a stamp had to be moistened such as by licking to make the gum sticky. The new self-adhesive stamps use a different type of gum which does not have to be moistened by the user.

On older stamps, particularly those of the nineteenth century, the quality of the gum is a factor in determining the value of the stamp. Applying a hinge[q.v.] to a stamp damages the gum. Some stamps are fraudulently altered by regumming them to increase their value, but experts can usually determine if the gum is not original.

In the production of stamps, gum is usually applied before the stamps are printed. Occasionally, faulty sheet-feeding into the press causes stamps to be printed on the gummed side by mistake.

gum additives Coffee, corn starch, peach juice, apricot tea, and other coloring agents added in the process of regumming to imitate the original gum. These additives can be detected by exposing the gummed side of the stamp to ultraviolet light. See *regummed.*

gum alteration See *regummed.*

guma idealna (*f.*) [*Pol.*] never hinged.

guma oryginalna (*f.*) [*Pol.*] original gum.

gum manipulation Any intentional change made to the gum of a stamp, including total regumming, with the intent of defrauding a buyer into believing that the gum is original. See *regummed.*

gummering (*r.*) [*Swed.*] gum.

gummi (*c.*) [*Dan.*] gum.

Gummierung (*f.*) [*Ger.*] gum.

Güney Afrika [*Turk.*] South Africa.

gut [*Ger.*] good.

gutter Margin of paper, frequently blank, which separates the panes of stamps on a full sheet. If the sheet consists of 400 stamps, it is separated into 4 panes of 100 stamps each by cutting the vertical and horizontal gutter strips. The marginal paper on all four sides of the pane is known as *selvage,* but only the two strips that previously adjoined other panes are referred to as the *gutter.* Also see *gutter pair* and *tête-bêche.*

gutter pair with blank label (U.K.)

gutter pair Two stamps which are still attached to opposite sides of a piece of gutter paper. The non-postage label in between the two stamps may be blank, or it may show a design or give information. See *guilloche, Cartor,* and *tête-bêche* for additional examples.

gutter snipe A type of misperf[q.v.] which leaves a row of narrow, fully-perfed labels adjacent to a row of stamps.

A sheet being separated into four panes is supposed to be cut down the middle of the gutter, leaving a very narrow piece of selvage adjoining the stamps on both sides of the gutter. That selvage will be perforated on the stamp side and will have a straight edge on the other. But if the slicing is made too far to the left, right, top, or bottom, the gutter piece remains

gutter snipe: stamp with fully-perfed label

intact, as it is in the illustrated example. The sheet is sliced through the stamps on the other side of the gutter instead of through the gutter itself. In the stamp pictured here, the cut should have been made where the margin line is located.

gutter tête-bêche pair See *tête-bêche.*

G.W. [*o/p*] Griqualand West. Overprinted on stamps of the Cape of Good Hope.

gwiazda (*f.*) [*Pol.*] star.

gyűjtemény [*Hun.*] collection.

gyűjteni (*v.*) [*Hun.*] to collect.

gyűjtő [*Hun.*] collector.

gyűrődés [*Hun.*] a crease, a fold (as in a postage stamp or banknote).

H h

habilitado [*Span.*] literally, *qualified* or *validated*. An overprint indicating that a previous issue of stamp has been re-authorized for postal use. A surcharge is usually included which gives the stamp's new value. Hence, the complete overprint will read *Habilitado para 2c* (as in the case of the illustrated Cuban stamp), *Habilitado de 7 centavos* (on stamps of Costa Rica), *Habilitado Correos 25 Céntimos* (on Venezuelan telegraph stamps authorized for postal use), or some other similar inscription.

habilitado overprint (Cuba)

Stamps showing this overprint are called *provisionals*[*q.v.*]. They are usually (but not always) used as temporary substitutes during a stamp shortage caused by political change, postal rate increases, war, or whatever. The illustration shows a Batista-era Cuban stamp overprinted by the Castro regime in 1960 to be used until Castro could print his own.

Habilitado por la Nación [*Span.*] Validated for the Nation. Overprinted on provisional stamps of Spain in the late 1860s and early 1870s. Also seen overprinted in its abbreviated form, *H.P.N.*

hængslet [*Dan.*] hinged.

häfte (*n.*) [*Swed.*] booklet (of stamps).

Hagert. Md Pre-adhesive postmark from Hagerstown, Maryland (U.S.A.).

hajtás [*Hun.*] a crease, fold (as in a postage stamp or banknote).

hakiki [*Turk.*] genuine.

hakkô [*Jpn.*] an issue, issuance.

hål (*n.*) [*Swed.*] hole.

halagang nakatakda [*Tag.*] face value.

halb (*adj.*) [*Ger.*] half.

halbiert [*Ger.*] bisected.

Halbtaler (*m.*) [*Ger.*] crown (numismatic term for a large silver coin).

Hälfte (*f.*) [*Ger.*] half (the fraction).

halkaisija [*Finn.*] diameter.

hallitsija [*Finn.*] sovereign.

halogram See *halographic stamp.*

halographic stamp Adhesive postage stamp or imprinted stamp which is made by projecting a split laser beam onto specially-treated thin foil with a photosensitive surface. This type of pattern gives the illusion of a 3-D image, similar to that of the security device on a credit card. Stamps of this type have been issued by true stamp-issuing countries (such as the United States) and have seen actual postal use.

halv (*adj.*) [*Nor., Swed.*] half.

halvdel (*c.*) [*Dan.*] half (the fraction).

halvert [*Nor.*] bisected.

halvfems [*Dan.*] ninety.

halvfjerds [*Dan.*] seventy.

halvpart (*m.*) [*Nor.*] half (the fraction).

halvtreds [*Dan.*] fifty.

Hamilton, Alexander [called the *Prime Minister*, so completely did he dominate the government.] American statesman. Born (out of wedlock) on January 11(?), 1755, in Charlestown on the island of Nevis, British West Indies; died from being mortally wounded in a duel with Aaron Burr on July 12, 1804.

At an early age, Hamilton distinguished himself in a number of military missions and soon became aide-de-camp to General George

Washington. Later as a politician, Hamilton was a tireless, hard-boiled realist who believed that money was the key driving force and that government would not last unless the wealthy class could make money by it. This put him in constant conflict with Thomas Jefferson, who wanted the United States to remain a country of farmers and craftsmen instead of bankers and industrial workers.

In the presidential election of 1800, Jefferson and Aaron Burr, both political enemies of Hamilton, were tied in votes. The House of Representatives was called upon to break the deadlock. Hamilton urged his supporters to vote for Jefferson, his old enemy, instead of Burr, a man he considered to have dangerous ambitions.

Hamilton: St. Christopher-Nevis-Anquilla and the U.S.

In 1804 Hamilton again used his influence to prevent Burr's election, this time for the New York governorship. Burr, in turn, demanded retribution by challenging Hamilton to a duel. Hamilton was opposed to dueling because his son had been fatally shot in a duel in 1801. But as a public figure, Hamilton could not avoid the issue. The duel was fought on July 11, 1804, in Weehawken, New Jersey, the same place where Hamilton's son had died three years earlier. Hamilton did not take aim but shot harmlessly in the air. Burr shot Hamilton, mortally wounding him. Hamilton died the following day in New York City.

Hamilton's face is well known to Americans because it appears on the $10 bill. Yet his philatelic presence is minimal. Despite being a noted American patriot, his likeness has appeared on very few stamps, mostly postage and revenue stamps of the nineteenth century. Hamilton's situation raises the question of who is and who is not worthy of appearing on stamps. It seems inconceivable that people like Hamilton have had so little impact on philately, while Elvis Presley, Marilyn Monroe, and James Dean have become philatelic icons.

On a more positive note, Nevis, the place of his birth, honored Hamilton's 200th birthday by issuing a commemorative stamp in 1957.

[Contributed by Ruth Ann Davis. Roger Butterfield, *The American Past*.]

hamisítvány [*Hun.*] a counterfeit, forgery.

hamkha'ah הַמְחָאָה (*f.*) [*Heb.*] check, cheque.

hammastamaton [*Finn.*] imperforate.

hammaste [*Finn.*] perforation.

hammastettu [*Finn.*] perforated.

håndlagt papir (*n.*) [*Dan.*] laid paper.

handla med (*v.*) [*Swed.*] to trade.

handlować (*v.*) [*Pol.*] to trade.

handpenning erfordras [*Swed.*] deposit required.

hankinta [*Finn.*] acquisition.

han'pakah הַנְפָקָה [*Heb.*] an issue, issuance.

Hanukkah stamps: Israel (above) and U.S. (below)

Hanukkah stamp The first-ever joint issue between the United States Postal Service and the Israeli Postal Authorities featured two commemorative stamps honoring the Jewish holiday of Hanukkah— the Festival of Lights.

The American 32c stamp was designed by graphic artist Hannah Smotrich of Washington, D.C. The stamp depicts a menorah with nine multicolored candles symbolizing the eight days of lighting candles during Hanukkah and the one extra candle, or *shamesh*, which is used to light the other candles. Hanukkah is a time when the Jewish people celebrate religious freedom. They recall their victory over the religious oppression of the Syrian-Greeks in the year 165 B.C.E.

The Book of Maccabee in the Torah states the meaning of Hanukkah in verses 52 through 59 of Chapter 4: "Since the days of Judas Maccabeus, Hanukkah has been celebrated by lighting candles for eight days as a reminder of the cruse of oil which burned for eight days instead of one."

In Canton, Ohio, the Jewish Community Federation rushed to develop a design for the first day cover envelope. The designer of the envelope was Sister Paulette Kirschensteiner, a Humility of Mary Catholic nun. She is a fiber artist from Canton who designed art work for various synagogues and churches. The design depicts flames, a symbol in the joyous celebration of religious freedom, as well as the Hebrew statement, "A great miracle happened over there," referring to the cruse of oil miracle in Israel.

How was the Hanukkah stamp concept developed? Post Office clerk Ronald Scheiman of Holbrook, Long Island, New York, learned that the Postal Service was going to print a series of stamps representing various ethnic groups. He felt a stamp for Hanukkah should be included in this series. After many letters and requests, including one to the White House, the U.S. Postal Service finally decided to print 103 million 32c stamps featuring a menorah. It was expected that if demand for the stamp increased, the stamp would be reprinted annually.

Some opposition was generated by various secular groups. The Southern California District of the Workmen's Circle passed a resolution opposing the stamp. The director of that district, Eric Gordon, felt that the stamp blurred the separation between Church and State embodied in the First Amendment establishment clause. However, other organizations, such as the Anti-Defamation League (A.D.L.) and the American Civil Liberties Union (A.C.L.U.) did not cast any objections. The Jewish establishment was generally pleased about the stamp.

See *cachet* for an illustration of the Hanukkah envelope.

[Contributed by Bilha Ron.]

HAPAG [*Ger. abbr.*] *Hamburg-Amerikanische Paketfahrt-Aktien-Gesellschaft.* Reference to Hamburg American Line which issued 10c local stamps in 1875 for use on mail carried by their ships between the West Indian islands and various ports in Central and South America. They were withdrawn in 1879, but reprints have been issued periodically.

harç pulu [*Turk.*] fiscal stamp.

harga [*Indo.*] price; value.

harmad [*Hun.*] third (the fraction).

harminc [*Hun.*] thirty.

három [*Hun.*] three.

harrow perforation Type of perforation in which the entire sheet or pane is perforated at one time. This method is used mostly to perforate small souvenir sheets.

hârtie (*f.*) [*Rom.*] paper.

harvinainen [*Finn.*] rare.

harvinaisuus [*Finn.*] rarity.

hasta pública (*f.*) [*Port.*] auction.

használt [*Hun.*] used.

hat [*Hun.*] six.

hata [*Turk.*] error.

hatıra (*adj.*) [*Turk.*] commemorative.

hatıra tabakası [*Turk.*] souvenir sheet.

hátoldalon [*Hun.*] on the back.

hatsa'at m'khir minimum הַצָעַת מְחִיר מִינִימוּם (*f.*) [*Heb.*] minimum bid.

hatvan [*Hun.*] sixty.

haut (*m.*) [*Fr.*] top.

Haziran [*Turk.*] June.

H.B. [*Ger. abbr.*] Herzogtum Braunschweig (Germany). Pre-adhesive postmark.

H.Borg [*Swed. abbr.*] Pre-adhesive postmark from Helsingborg (Sweden).

H.B. Sanitats Stempel [*Ger. abbr.*] Health Authorities mark. Pre-adhesive postmark.

"heads of wheat" overprints (Hungary)

heads of wheat Name given to two different pictorial overprints seen on some 1919 and 1920 stamps of Hungary. The date 1919 is included in the overprint design.

health stamp (New Zealand)

health stamp Charity stamps that are sold at more than their postal value to raise money to promote good health and fight disease. Many countries have issued stamps for this general purpose, but New Zealand's Health semipostals are the best known. The New Zealand stamps have been released annually since 1929. They frequently portray children, often the younger members of the British royal family.

"Hear, O Israel..."

"Hear, O Israel..." שְׁמַע יִשְׂרָאֵל The first line of the essential Jewish creed (*Deut. 6:4*). These words (written in the Hebrew alphabet) appear in the form of a flame on a 1962 Israeli commemorative stamp. It was issued for Heroes and Martyrs Day, in memory of the six million Jewish victims of Nazi persecution.

Heft (*n.*) [*Ger.*] booklet (of stamps).

hefte (*n.*) [*Nor.*] booklet (of stamps).

heimisch [*Ger.*] domestic.

heinäkuu [*Finn.*] July.

helft (*f.-c.*) [*Dut.*] half (the fraction).

Heliogravüre (*f.*) [*Ger.*] intaglio.

hell [*Ger.*] light (*re*: color).

Hellas Ελλάς [*Grk.*] Greece.

helmikuu [*Finn.*] February.

Helvetia (Switzerland)

Helvetia [*Lat.*] 1. Switzerland. Because Switzerland has four official languages, stamps and coins of that nation are inscribed with its Latin name. The official name of the country is *Confœderatio Helvetica*.

2. Female allegorical figure representing the nation of Switzerland. She is seen on many older Swiss stamps as well as Switzerland's current coins.

Helv. Rep. [*Lat. abbr.*] Pre-adhesive postmark from the Swiss Republic.

hemelsblauw [*Dut.*] azure (blue).

hemligt märke (*n.*); **hemlig markering** (*r.*) [*Swed.*] secret mark.

hemmeligt mærke (*n.*) [*Dan.*] secret mark.

henføre til (*v.*) [*Dan.*] to attribute.

hengsel (*n.*) [*Nor.*] (stamp) hinge.

hengslet [*Nor.*] hinged.

herausgeben (*v.*) [*Ger.*] to issue (stamps, coins, etc.).

herdenkings- (*adj.*) [*Dut.*] commemorative.

herdenkingsblad (*n.*) [*Dut.*] souvenir sheet.

hergomd [*Dut.*] regummed.

hersker (*m.*) [*Nor.*] sovereign (i.e., a king or queen). The English word *sovereign* is used to refer to the gold coin of that designation.

hét [*Hun.*] seven.

hetven [*Hun.*] seventy.

HG Dutch border postmark.

hiányos; hibás [*Hun.*] defective.

hiba [*Hun.*] defect; error.

Hibernia [*Lat.*] Ireland.

hiç şarniyerlenmemiş [*Turk.*] never hinged.

Father Hidalgo (Mexico)

Hidalgo y Costilla, Fr. Miguel (known as *El Zorro,* "The Fox," by his classmates). Leader of the Mexican liberation movement. Born 1753 on the Hacienda San Diego Corralejo in the Bajio district near Guanajuato, Mexico; died by execution on May 8, 1811.

Father Hidalgo is remembered as the foremost liberator who fought to enable Mexico to gain its independence from Spain. He was ordained a priest in 1778. As a liberal, revolutionary thinker who was unconventional in performing his priestly duties, he had a hand in convincing the Catholic Church to relax somewhat its stern dogma which had created difficulties for him with the Church's hierarchy.

In championing the cause of the Mestizos and the Indians, Hidalgo joined a secret society dedicated to freeing Mexico from Spanish oppression. He wanted to reform the government, remove the Spanish-born agents from control, and free the working classes from the tyranny of slavery.

He rallied an army of Mestizos and Indians, but they were sadly lacking in discipline and their weapons consisted mostly of machetes.

The rebels, with Hidalgo as their leader, routed the mining town of Celaya and then followed that with a bloody attack on Guanajuato. After successful attacks on several other cities, his forces seemed invincible until they themselves were routed by a small band of Spanish soldiers near Guadalajara on January 11, 1811. Hidalgo fled north but was ultimately captured when he became trapped in a narrow ravine on March 21. After his capture, the Catholic Church and its Inquisition condemned him for heresy and sacrilege.

Father Hidalgo was executed by a firing squad on May 8, 1811, in the courtyard of a Jesuit College. In deference to his former priesthood, he was granted two requests: to be shot in the chest instead of in the back, and to face the firing squad unbound and without a blindfold. Before his execution, he embarrassed his captors by giving them candy.

Mexico honors Hidalgo by celebrating its Independence Day on September 16, the date in 1810 when he proclaimed his revolt. His portrait appears on a very wide range of postal items as well as on coins, paper money, and other public documents.

See *Josefa.*

[Contributed by Ruth Ann Davis. Clarke Newlon, *The Men Who Made Mexico.*]

hidden mark [also known as *secret mark.*] Any letter, number, or symbol incorporated into a stamp's design which is not intended to be readily seen. If the mark's inclusion is officially sanctioned, it is there to convey some special information. For example, most Canadian stamps produced since 1935 have the year of issuance hidden somewhere in figures so small they can usually only be seen through magnification.

One of the earliest uses of the hidden mark came in 1858 when each of the seven stamps issued by Naples included a secret mark within the design. Each hidden mark consisted of a different letter found in the engraver's name: G. MASINI.

Some hidden marks parallel the numismatic concept of a mintmark. Such was the case in 1873 when the United States first had its stamps printed by one company and then had the same series printed by a competing firm. The second company altered the design ever so slightly so that the stamps it produced would be distinguishable from those of its competitor.

Hitler's face— intentional or coincidental?

A far more dramatic use of the hidden mark surfaced in 1987 when collectors became aware that Kenneth Kipperman, a Jewish activist who was working as a free-lance engraver for the U.S. Bureau of Engraving and Printing, had hidden the Star of David in his design of Bernard Revel, a noted American Jewish scholar, for a one-dollar definitive. The discovery was first announced by *Linn's Stamp News* and was picked up by every major news service in the United States, thus giving philately some interesting and positive publicity. When asked if it would remove the star from future issues of that definitive, the B.E.P. stated that it would not change the design for fear of being accused of anti-Semitism. Although this was surely one consideration, the B.E.P.'s decision was probably based more on the realization that by not changing the design, many people, mostly non-collectors, would buy this high-priced

stamp as a novelty and not use it, thus giving the U.S. Postal Service an unexpected profit.

Mary Lyons— hidden leaf?

The Mary Lyon 2 cent definitive presents a different problem. There appears to be a tiny leaf hidden near the bottom of the stamp's design, yet the B.E.P. denies that the leaf was placed there intentionally. Officially, the leaf's inclusion was mere coincidence. Philatelists may never know for certain whether the leaf is some sort of secret mark or whether it happened totally by chance.

Lincoln's eyes and hat brim— a cocker spaniel's head?

Similarly, the 1964 German stamp showing the Castle Gate at Ellwangen seemingly shows the face of Hitler hidden in tree branches at the top. Officials claim that the resemblance to

hidden mark: The hidden Star of David is difficult to detect even in the greatly magnified photo shown above. The arrow points to the location of the star in Revel's beard. The photo at the left shows the same stamp at normal size.

Hitler is purely coincidental. But could it have been put there intentionally by a Nazi sympathizer? Again, philatelists may never know for sure.

On the U.S. National Archives stamp, Abraham Lincoln has a strange, dark, somber expression on his face, in stark contrast to Washington's bland white silhouette. Could Lincoln's pensive look be the result of the cocker spaniel drawn into the eyes and hat rim? When the stamp is seen right-side up, the dog is not obvious. But when the stamp is positioned on its side (as in the illustration), the dog's head is quite distinct. Is it there by chance or by intent?

Sir Rowland Hill (Great Britain)

Hill, Sir Rowland Creator of the adhesive postage stamp. Born December 3, 1795, in Kidderminster, England; died August 27, 1879, of natural causes.

In Hill's day, postal rates in Great Britain were so high that only the wealthy could afford to use the postal system. Yet so many of the wealthy enjoyed free-franking privileges that very few actually paid. In 1837 Hill published a treatise titled *Post Office Reform: Its Importance and Practicality*, his ideas on how to make the post office more efficient. He suggested that the mail be prepaid, that the charges be based on weight instead of the number of sheets, and that the rates be low enough to allow the non-wealthy to mail letters. Specifically, he proposed that one penny per half-ounce should be the flat rate for mailing a letter from any part of Great Britain to any

other part. He also urged the elimination of most of the free-franking privileges.

He also proposed that the mail should be placed in one and two penny-denominated envelopes (known as Mulready envelopes) that were addressed and sealed in the post office. If illiterate servants showed up with letters from their employers, small pieces of paper with the amount of postage printed on the front and an adhesive surface on the back could be affixed to the letter in lieu of using the Mulready envelope. Both the envelopes and the stamps were scheduled for release on January 1, 1840, but production problems delayed their introduction until May 6.

The ultra-fancy design on the Mulready envelopes proved to be too excessive even for Victorian tastes, and the envelopes were quickly abandoned. But the adhesive postage stamps became very popular with the public. The first stamps were imperforate and had to be separated with scissors. Perforation was not added until 1854, an idea proposed by Henry Archer and only minimally supported by Hill.

For his achievements, Rowland Hill was knighted by Queen Victoria. Upon his death in 1879, he was buried in Westminster Abbey.

[Kenneth A. Wood, *This Is Philately*, Vol. II, pp. 341-43.]

hilo de seda [*Span.*] silk thread.

himmelblå [*Nor., Dan.*] azure (blue).

himmelblau [*Ger.*] azure (blue).

himmelsblå [*Swed.*] azure (blue).

hindi ipinalabas [*Tag.*] not issued.

hinge Small rectangular piece of opaque glassine paper with a mild gum on one side. The gum is usually (but not always) peelable so as not to damage to the stamp. Hinges are used to attach postage stamps to the page of a stamp album. They may be purchased either flat or pre-folded.

When using stamp hinges, care must be taken not to moisten the hinge to an excessive degree. If too much moisture is applied, the excess moisture can allow the gum on the stamp to become sticky, thereby causing the stamp to attach itself directly to the album page and damaging the stamp. Only enough moisture should be applied so that the hinge will gently attach to both the stamp and the album.

Even when the hinge is applied with very great care, there will be some visible evidence of hinging when the hinge is ultimately removed. If two stamps are absolutely identical except that one has been hinged and the other has not, the never-hinged specimen will usually command a higher price than the other. Although hinges have been popular for a long time and a great many choice specimens show signs of hinging, there has been a trend in recent years for advanced collectors and investors to search out the choicest never-hinged specimens. Unfortunately, this trend has encouraged regumming and other manipulations of the gum.

hinnasto [*Finn.*] price list.

hinta [*Finn.*] price.

hintaluettelo [*Finn.*] price list.

history, postal See *postal history.*

Hiszpania [*Pol.*] Spain.

hitel [*Hun.*] credit.

hiteles [*Hun.*] authentic.

hitelkártya [*Hun.*] credit card.

hitelkártya-elfogadás [*Hun.*] credit cards accepted.

hivatalos [*Hun.*] official.

H.J.Z. [*o/p*] Hedjaz. Overprinted on 1919 stamps of Palestine for use by the Hedjaz Railway.

H.M.S. Her (His) Majesty's Ship. Among its various applications (philatelic and otherwise), this abbreviation was used as a pre-adhesive postmark.

höger [*Swed.*] right (direction or position).

hoja (*f.*) [*Span.*] sheet; pane.

hoja de licitación (*f.*); **hoja de oferta** (*f.*) [*Span.*] bid sheet.

hoja recuerdo (*f.*) [*Span.*] souvenir sheet.

højre [*Dan.*] right.

Holanda [*Span., Port., et al*] Holland, Netherlands.

honderd [*Dut.*] hundred.

honderdjarig [*Dut.*] centennial, centenary.

honderdste [*Dut.*] hundredth.

honorario (*m.*) [*Span.*] fee.

honorarium (*n.*) [*Dut.*] fee.

hors d'usage [*Fr.*] obsolete.

hotsa'ah mitokef הוֹצָאָה מְחוֹקֶף (*f.*) [*Heb.*] demonetization.

hoù bì de [*Chin.-py.*] monetary.

høyre [*Nor.*] right (direction or position).

høyrød [*Nor.*] carmine.

H.P. 1. Hamburg (Germany) Post, used as a pre-adhesive postmark. 2. Dutch Post.

H.P.N. [*Span. abbr.*] *Habilitado por la Nación* (Validated for the Nation). Overprinted on provisional stamps of Spain in the late 1860s and early 1870s.

H.R. [*Lat. abbr.*] Pre-adhesive postmark from the Swiss Republic.

H.R.S. [*abbr.*] Hudson River Steamer (pre-adhesive postmark from the U.S.).

Hrvatska [*Cr.*] Croatia.

H.S. [*abbr.*] hand stamp.

huáng dì [*Chin.-py.*] emperor.

huáng hòu [*Chin.-py.*] queen.

huecograbado (*m.*) [*Span.*] intaglio.

huhtikuu [*Finn.*] April.

huippu [*Finn.*] top.

huit [*Fr.*] eight.

hükümdar [*Turk.*] sovereign.

hul (*n.*) [*Dan.*] hole.

hull (*n.*) [*Nor.*] hole.

hullmakulering (*m.*) [*Nor.*] punch cancellation.

hull perforering (*m.*) [*Nor.*] pin perforation, *percé en points.*

hullstempel (*n.*) [*Nor.*] cut cancellation.

hulpzegel (*m./c.*) [*Dut.*] provisional.

hundert [*Ger.*] hundred.

Hundertjahrfeier (*f.*) [*Ger.*] centennial, centenary.

Hundertstel (*n.*) [*Ger.*] hundredth (the fraction).

hundra [*Swed.*] hundred.

hundraårsjubileum (*n.*) [*Swed.*] centennial, centenary.

hundradel (*n.*) [*Swed.*] hundredth.

hundre [*Nor.*] hundred.

hundredårsdag (*c.*) [*Dan.*] centennial, centenary.

hundrede [*Dan.*] hundred.

hundrededel (*c.*) [*Dan.*]; (*m.*) [*Nor.*] hundredth.

Hussey's Post New York delivery service which issued many local[q.v.] stamps during its operation from 1854 to 1880.

húsz [*Hun.*] twenty.

huutokauppa [*Finn.*] auction, auction sale.

huutokauppakohde [*Finn.*] (auction) lot.

huutokauppaluettelo [*Finn.*] auction catalogue.

hüvelyk [*Hun.*] inch.

hvid [*Dan.*] white.

hvit [*Nor.*] white.

hyphen-hole perforation Narrow rectangular perforation holes found on such issues as America's 1898 "Battleship" revenue series and on various types of special labels. The holes are difficult to recognize as perforations and are often mistaken for rouletting. Some catalogues mistakenly call them roulettes.

hyvä [*Finn.*] good.

hyväksyttäväksi [*Finn.*] on approval.

hyväntekeväisyysmerkki [*Finn.*] charity stamp.

hyphen-hole perfs (U.S. post office seals)

I i

I/ Symbol of the Peruvian monetary unit known as the *inti*. It was introduced in 1985 and equals 1,000 soles.

Ia [*abbr.*] Iowa (pre-adhesive postmark from the U.S.).

I.B. [*Indo. abbr.*] Republik Indonesia.

I. Balear [*Span. abbr.*] Islas Baleares. Pre-adhesive postmark from the Balearic Islands, a Spanish province located in the Mediterranean Sea east of Spain.

ickepostal sidostämpel [*Swed.*] cachet.

idatosimo υδατόσημο (*n.*) [*Grk.*] watermark.

I de Cuba [*Span. abbr.*] Isla de Cuba. Cuban pre-adhesive postmark.

idegen [*Hun.*] foreign.

identifikasjonsmerke (*n.*) [*Nor.*] attribution (the complete identification of a postage stamp, revenue stamp, cover, or other philatelic item).

idioma (*m.*) [*Span.*] language.

I.E.F. 'D' *o/p* on Turkish stamp

I.E.F. 'D' [*o/p*] Overprinted on Turkish revenue stamps in 1919 during the British occupation of Mosul (Iraq). They were for use by Indian troops of the Mesopotamia Force.

Ierland [*Dut.*] Ireland.

I. Filips [*Span. abbr.*] Islas Filipinas. Pre-adhesive postmark used in the Philippines.

igemonas ηγεμόνας [*Grk.*] sovereign.

iğne delikli dantel [*Turk.*] pin perforation, *percé en points.*

iki [*Turk.*] two.

iki renkli [*Turk.*] bicolored, bicoloured.

ikke identificeret [*Dan.*] unattributed.

ikke katalogført [*Nor.*] unpublished (not listed in any book or catalogue).

ikke udgivet [*Dan.*] not issued.

ikke utgitt [*Nor.*] not issued.

ikosi είκοσι [*Grk.*] twenty.

Il; Ill [*abbr.*] Illinois (pre-adhesive postmarks from the U.S.).

ilkgün zarfı [*Turk.*] first day cover.

illeték [*Hun.*] fee.

illinguellato [*Ital.*] unhinged.

ilmakirje [*Finn.*] aerogramme.

ilman liimaa [*Finn.*] ungummed.

ilman liimaketta [*Finn.*] unhinged.

I M India Mail. Abbreviation used as a pre-adhesive postmark.

I. Man [*abbr.*] Isle of Man. Pre-adhesive postmark.

imerominia ημερομηνία (*f.*) [*Grk.*] date.

imitacja (*f.*) [*Pol.*] imitation.

imitazione (*f.*) [*Ital.*] imitation.

Imp 1. [*Ital. abbr.*] *Impostazione* (posting site). 2. [*Fr. abbr.*] *Imprimés* (printed matters).

imperatore (*m.*) [*Ital.*] emperor.

imperf between The result that occurs when a sheet of stamps is perforated in one direction but not in the other. In some cases, only one single row of perforations is missing, creating a column of pairs of stamps with no perforations in between. Thus, a horizontal pair may be missing vertical perforations or a vertical pair may lack horizontal perforations. It is also possible for any number of rows of perforations to be missing from the pane, creating all sorts of misperfed configurations.

pair of imperf U.S. stamps

imperforate Stamps lacking perforation or rouletting[q.v.]; i.e., stamps produced without rows of small holes or without rows of tiny cuts in the paper to aid in separating the stamps.

All of the first postage stamps issued anywhere in the 1840s and early 1850s were imperforate and had to be separated with scissors. Henry Archer of England originated the idea of perforating stamps. Some British stamps in 1854 were the first to use this method.

Although the idea of perforation (or rouletting) eventually caught on everywhere, for many years some stamps were still issued imperforate. In the twentieth century, most imperf stamps were not intended to be that way and are regarded as freaks. In the case of blind perfs[q.v.], the perfing pins fail to penetrate the paper, giving the impression that the stamps are fully or partially imperforate. On coils stamps showing interrupted[q.v.] or syncopated perforation, some of the perforation is intentionally omitted to give the paper more strength so that the coils will not tear at the wrong time and jam the vending machine dispensing the stamps.

imperforate newspaper stamp (Bosnia & Herzegovina)

Whether or not a stamp is perforated can make a difference in its intended usage. The perforated version of the illustrated Bosnian stamp was used for regular postage. But when the same design was issued imperforate, it was intended as a newspaper stamp.

imperf sides (top & bottom) on U.S. coil stamps

imperf sides Coil stamps with parallel straight edges, either top and bottom or on the sides.

imposta sull'entrata (Italy)

imposta sull'entrata [*Ital.*] income tax. Inscription seen on some Italian revenue stamps.

imposto (*m.*) [*Port.*] tax.

impresión calcográfica (*f.*); **impresión intaglio** (*f.*) [*Span.*] intaglio.

impresión en relieve [*Span.*] embossing.

Impresos [*Span.*] Printed matter. Inscription found on early Philippine newspaper stamps.

impresso de oferta [*Port.*] bid sheet.

imprimir (*v.*) [*Span., Port.*] to print.

imprint Any inscription, denomination, portrait, frame, vignette, or other portion of a stamp's design which is printed at the time of the stamp's original production. This is in contrast to an *overprint* (stating a surcharge, provisional information, or whatever) which is added at a later time.

The one gray area is the addition of country names and values to a *key type*[q.v.], a generic design used by large colonial countries to supply stamps for their colonies. The basic design leaves only a space (a *cartouche*) for the colony name and another space (the *tablet*) for the denomination. The stamps go through the press a second time so that the appropriate colony name and value can be added.

bi-denominational imprinted stamp (Heligoland)

imprinted stamp Postage printed directly onto an air letter, postal card, or other piece of postal stationery. If imprinted stamps are trimmed from their covers, a certain amount of space should be left surrounding the stamp (see *cut square*). The method of trimming the stamp close is called *cut to shape* and is much less desired by collectors.

The Heligoland piece in the illustration is unusual because it was denominated in the currencies of two different countries: 1 1/2 British pence and 10 German pfennig.

impuesto (*m.*) [*Span.*] tax.

imputation (*f.*) [*Fr.*] attribution (the complete identification of a postage stamp, revenue stamp, cover, or other philatelic item).

imputer (*v.*) [*Fr.*] to attribute.

In [*abbr.*] Indiana. Used as pre-adhesive postmark.

ince çizgili kâğıt [*Turk.*] laid paper.

inchiostro (*m.*) [*Ital.*] ink.

închis [*Rom.*] dark.

incisione su acciaio [*Ital.*] steel engraving.

inconnu [*Fr.*] unknown.

indelen (*v.*) [*Dut.*] to classify.

indicator markings Any combination of letters, numbers, or words printed immediately to the left of a meter impression or a postage stamp which indicates that the user is entitled to a special low rate of postage. These rates are usually given to businesses that do bulk mailings or use special postal codes.

Canada initiated this practice on January 1, 1982, when it raised its first-class rate from 17 cents to 30 cents. Its postal service began offering a variety of rates to its business mailers. The mailers are required to obtain a special permit and then must print the appropriate indicator markings on the letters: "1A" indicates bulk mailings with specified mail preparation requirements (Optical Character Reader information, for example); "1B" is for mail that is sent in bulk quantities and is presorted; "BULK" is for third-class mailings in quantity.

Many other countries have similar indicator markings and require the users to fulfill certain obligations in order to be entitled to the lower postal rates. A commonly-found American indicator marking is "ZIP + 4", referring to the use of the 9-digit Zip Code. As can bae seen in the illustrations, some U.S. indicator markings are printed directly on the postage stamps themselves, eliminating the need to have them printed on the envelopes.

[James E. Kraemer, "Indicator Markings on Canadian Metered Mail," *Canadian Philatelist*, May-June 1985, pp. 190-4.]

indicium (pl.: *indicia.*) 1. Imprinted postage stamp on postal stationery. 2. Meter stamp impression.

Ind. Neer. [*Dut. abbr.*] Dutch Indies. Pre-adhesive postmark.

îndoitură (*f.*) [*Rom.*] a fold, crease.

indragning (*r.*) [*Swed.*] demonetization.

indskåret [*Dan.*] intaglio.

in duplo maken (*v.*) [*Dut.*] to duplicate.

inflation issues: Germany and Hungary

inflation issue Stamp issued during a period of hyper-inflation. The stamp's value, usually overprinted, can be an astronomically high number. Post-World War I stamps of Germany and post-World War II stamps of Hungary fall into this category.

Inghilterra [*Ital.*] England.

İngiliz lirası [*Turk.*] pound Sterling (£).

İngiltere [*Turk.*] England.

Inglaterra [*Span., Port.*] England.

inkt (*m.-c.*) [*Dut.*] ink.

inländisch [*Ger.*] domestic.

Inld pge [*abbr.*] inland postage. Abbreviation used as a pre-adhesive postmark.

inndraging (*m.*) [*Nor.*] demonetization.

inneboende [*Swed.*] intrinsic.

innpakning (*m.*) [*Nor.*] cover (in the philatelic sense). The term for *on cover* in Norwegian is *på original konvolutt*.

innskrift (*m.*) [*Nor.*] legend.

inofficiell [*Swed.*] unofficial.

Inschrift (*f.*) [*Ger.*] legend.

inscrição (*f.*) [*Port.*] inscription; legend.

inscripción (*f.*) [*Span.*] inscription; legend.

Inselpost [*Ger.; o/p*] Island post. See *Aegean Islands*.

inskrift (*r.*) [*Swed.*] legend.

inskriptio [*Finn.*] inscription.

inskrypcja (*f.*) [*Pol.*] inscription.

Instrucción on Venezuelan postal/revenue stamp

Instrucción [*Span.*] Instruction. Inscription found on early Venezuelan postal/revenue stamps.

insuficiencia de porte [*Port.*] postage due.

intaglio (*m.*) [*Ital.*] literally, *cut in*.

A method of printing postage stamps, paper money, or other printed material in which a mirror image of the design is etched onto a plate, the plate is inked, and the excess ink on the plate's surface is removed, leaving only the ink in the etchings. When paper is pressed against the plate, the ink within the etchings transfers to the paper, thus producing a normal image of the design.

When the etching is done manually with engraver's tools, the method known as *line engraving* is generally chosen. The portraiture or lettering is broken down into many small lines of varying lengths, thicknesses, and curvatures.

Photographs can be reproduced using a mechanical method known as *photogravure*. A screen is placed over the photo which breaks the picture into small black dots. The larger and denser the dots, the darker that particular area of the photo will be. Magazine and newspaper pictures are usually done with this method.

integral (*noun*) Precancelled stamp with the precancelling information printed instead of handstamped. See *precancel*

internazionale [*Ital.*] international.

interpanneau (*m.*) [*Fr.*] gutter.

interrupted perforation (Netherlands):
2 sides & all 4 sides

interrupted perforation [also known as *syncopated perforation*.] Type of perforation with some of the punched holes purposely omitted.

The Dutch stamps in the illustration are regarded as classic examples. The perforations were punched in groups of four with an imperforate "bridge" in between. On some stamps, the interrupted perfs occur on all four sides; on other stamps, two sides are syncopated while the remaining sides have normal perforation. The Dutch created this concept to prevent unwanted separation of stamps in vending machines. One of the Dutch terms for interrupted perforation is *roltanding*, which translates as "coil perforation."

Interrupted perforation has also been used on some privately perforated coil stamps of the United States. Several different arrangements of syncopated perfing can be found. See *Schermack perforation* for illustrations.

interspazio (*m.*) [*Ital.*] gutter.

inti Monetary unit of Peru. Introduced in 1985 as a way of fighting inflation, the inti equals 1,000 soles. Its symbol is I/.

intonso [*Ital.*] unsevered.

intrínseco [*Span., Port.*] intrinsic.

intrinsèque [*Fr.*] intrinsic.

intrinsisch [*Ger.*] intrinsic.

învechit [*Rom.*] obsolete.

inventaire restant [*Fr.*] remainder, stock remainder.

1901 Fast Lake Navigation invert (enlarged)

invert (*noun*) A stamp with part of its design printed upside-down.

When stamps are printed in two or more colors, each color has to be applied to the sheet by a separate run through the press. If the sheet is inadvertently turned around during one of the runs, that color will be printed upside-down relative to everything else on the stamp. In theory, it is also possible to create an invert by feeding the paper correctly but by turning the printing plate the wrong way.

1979 "C.I.A." invert (enlarged)

The early U.S. inverts (and there were many) are all bicolored. The frame of one color was normally printed first, and then the paper was fed in again to print the center vignette of another color. Some very popular rarities resulted from the mis-feeding of paper. The most famous of all is the Jenny invert[q.v.], a 1918 24c airmail stamp showing a Curtiss Jenny biplane flying upside-down. Another famous invert of that era is the 1901 1c Fast Lake Navigation stamp. A vertical pair is shown in the illustration.

Not all inverts are errors. The 1901 1c stamp and its 2c inverted counterpart were true errors, meaning that they were unintentionally printed and released. But the Post Office had received an erroneous report that some inverts of the 4c stamp of that same series had been issued. The P.O. then ordered 400 copies (i.e., one full sheet) of the invert to be reprinted for its files. Most of those artificially-created "errors" eventually ended up in private hands and are now available to collectors, albeit at a high price.

Inverts are not limited to pre-World War I stamps. The United States issued a multicolored $1 definitive in 1979 which seems to have fallen victim to a variety of errors. Some of the stamps were sold with colors missing while some others were released with one color inverted. A great deal of controversy surrounded the discovery of these stamps, because they had been purchased by the Central Intelligence Agency for internal use. The inverts were recognized by an employee who reimbursed the C.I.A. for the stamps and claimed them for himself.

Another controversy arose on the discovery of the inverted version of the 1995 U.S. 32c Richard Nixon stamp. According to claims made by the United States Postal Service, these stamps were actually printer's waste that were supposed to be destroyed. Instead, 160 inverted and misperfed Nixon stamps were stolen by an employee of the Suffern, New York, plant of the Banknote Corporation of America where the stamps were partially printed. The employee sold the stamps to two dealers for a total of $87,000 in cash plus $13,000 in additional rare stamps. The employee was arrested in 1996 on charges or theft of government property and the interstate transport of stolen property, and the U.S. Postal Service demanded the return of all 160 stamps. This was the first time that fully-perforated and gummed stamps had been identified as printer's waste by the U.S. Postal Service, and one of the rare times when any issuing agency has threatened confiscation of stamps once they were out in the mainstream.

inexpensive inverts: Italian due & U.S. 4c Hammarskjold

Contrary to what some collectors believe, not all inverts are expensive. The illustrated Italian postage due stamp with an inverted overprint of its value sells for only a few

dollars. The 1962 U.S. 4c stamp honoring U.N. Secretary General Dag Hammarskjold can be bought for less than 25 cents. The U.S. Postal Service had issued a few inverts of this stamp in error and then purposely printed many thousands of them to prevent the error from becoming a rarity.

The term *invert* generally refers to printing errors, but it is also possible for the watermark to be inverted if the paper has been fed incorrectly into the press. Minor errors of this type are usually of less interest to collectors than the major printing errors typified by the Jenny invert.

[George Amick, *The Inverted Jenny: Mystery, Money, Mania,* pp. 36-37; Maurice D. Wozniak, "U.S. wants its inverts back," *Stamp Collector,* December 30, 1996, pp. 1 & 23.]

invertido [*Port., Span.*] inverted.

invertito [*Ital.*] inverted.

investment club Any group of individuals who pool their financial resources to invest in rare stamps, coins, or other collectibles.

According to the laws of most Western countries, a "legal entity" is created whenever two or more people form a business relationship. Thus, any group wishing to form such a club should start by consulting a legal professional to learn what that group's rights and obligations are.

When an investment club is formed, certain decisions should be agreed upon in writing: who collects the money, who spends it, who decides which items will be purchased, where the purchases will be stored, how the profits (or losses) will be divided, etc. Provision must also be made for the loss of interest or death of a member.

[David L. Ganz, Jerrietta R. Hollinger, and Steven I. Welinsky, "Forming an Investment Club", *The Numismatist,* July 1990, pp. 1075-1076, et al.]

invio a scelta [*Ital.*] on approval.

io [*abbr.*] Iowa (pre-adhesive postmark from the U.S.).

ipotimisi υποτίμηση (*f.*) [*Grk.*] devaluation.

I.R. 1. [*abbr.*] Inland Revenue (Great Britain).

2. [*Ital. abbr.*] *Imperiale Reale* (Imperial Royal). Pre-adhesive postmark.

Irland [*Nor., Swed.*] Ireland.

Irlanda [*Span., Port., Ital.*] Ireland.

İrlanda [*Turk.*] Ireland.

Irlanda del Nord [*Ital.*] Northern Ireland.

Irlanda del Norte [*Span.*] Northern Ireland.

Irlande [*Fr.*] Ireland.

Irlande du Nord [*Fr.*] Northern Ireland.

Irlandia [*Pol.*] Ireland.

Irlandia Pólnocna [*Pol.*] Northern Ireland.

Irlanti [*Finn.*] Ireland.

Írország [*Hun.*] Ireland.

irregolare [*Ital.*] irregular.

irregular Something unusual or unintentional on a stamp which is generally regarded as an error.

isa [*Tag.*] one.

isandaan [*Tag.*] hundred.

işaret [*Turk.*] motto.

iscrizione (*f.*) [*Ital.*] inscription.

isipoumeni prosfora εισηγούμενη προσφορά (*f.*) [*Grk.*] suggested bid.

İskoçya [*Turk.*] Scotland.

Ísland [*Ice.*] Iceland.

ısmarlama formu [*Turk.*] order form.

ismeretlen [*Hun.*] unknown.

Iso-Britannia [*Finn.*] Great Britain.

ISOLA ITALIANA DI/ PAXO/ ANNO XIX World War II overprint on stamps of Greece. It was privately applied and is of no legitimate philatelic interest.

ISOLE ITALIANE DELL'EGEO [*Ital.; o/p*] Italian Islands of the Aegean. This overprint first appeared on three issues of Italian airmail stamps released on October 20, 1930. See *Aegean Islands*.

İspanya [*Turk.*] Spain.

İsrail [*Turk.*] Israel.

issue (*v.*) To produce and release a new stamp.

issue; issuance (*noun*) The production and release of a postage stamp which bears a new design or some other notable change.

İsveç [*Turk.*] Sweden.

İsviçre [*Turk.*] Switzerland.

I.T. Abbreviation used as pre-adhesive postmarks, both in the United States and Europe: Idaho Territory; Indiana Territory; Iowa Territory; [*Fr.*] *Italie Transit*.

Italia [*Ital., Span., Nor., et al*] Italy.

ITALIA/ ISOLA DI/ SANTA MAURA Overprint on stamps of Greece. It was privately produced during World War II. The overprint rendered the stamps totally useless.

Italian East Africa During its first hundred years of existence, the postage stamp has recorded an impressive amount of contemporary history, including the short but complete lifetime of an empire. Italy's colonial empire began with the 1882 acquisition of Assab (Eritrea), followed by the 1889 establishment of Italian Protectorates in southern Somalia[q.v.]. In 1890 the Italian colony of Eritrea[q.v.] was officially established, and in 1905 the same was done for Benadir and other areas of southern Somalia. Meanwhile, an Italian settlement at Tien-Tsin (China) had been established. Following a 1902 treaty with the Chinese government, the Tien-Tsin settlement was given to Italy "in perpetuity" and as such it became a *de facto* colony.

In 1911 Italy began to occupy Libya[q.v.], and the following year the Aegean Islands[q.v.] had also become Italian. The colony of Somalia was further expanded in 1926 when Britain agreed to cede Jubaland to Italy. Mussolini's dream of founding an Italian empire in East Africa was realized in 1936 following the occupation of Ethiopia. On May 5, 1936, Italian troops under Marshal Badoglio entered Addis Ababa, and four days later Italy issued a decree annexing Ethiopia.

On May 22 three stamps depicting King Victor Emmanuel III and inscribed "ETIOPIA" were issued. They were followed by four additional denominations on December 5. These stamps, however, had a short life span. Of the pre-existing 38 post offices in the Ethiopian Empire, only two (Harar and Dire Dawa) were functioning at the time of the Italian occupation. On June 1, an administrative reshuffle created Italian East Africa (*Africa Orientale Italiana*) amalgamating Ethiopia with Eritrea and Somalia. The newly-formed Viceroyalty of Italian East Africa included six governorships: Amhara, Eritrea, Harar, Galla & Sidama, Shoa, and Somalia. Between October and November 1936, recognition of the Italian conquest was given by Germany (October 25), Austria, Hungary, Japan, and Switzerland. The Duke of Aosta, a playboy of the Italian nobility known in international circles, was appointed Viceroy of Italian East Africa.

Mussolini on Italian East African airmail stamp

On February 7, 1938, definitive and airmail stamps for Italian East Africa were issued, but in view of huge stocks of Somalia and Eritrea's stamps, they were used concurrently to them. The pictorial series included 20 definitive stamps, 11 airmail values, and two air speed/special delivery stamps. Among the great variety of subjects depicted on this series, most collectors will recognize the head of Mussolini carved (à la Mount Rushmore?) on Mount Amba Aradam on the 50c, Lire 1.50, and Lire 10 denominations of the airmail set. It is significant that this monumental disfiguration of the natural landscape was perpetrated in the vicinity of Aduwa where the Italians had suffered a bitter defeat in 1896.

In April 1938 Great Britain also officially recognized the Italian conquest; France followed suit. On June 10, 1940, Mussolini issued declarations of war to Britain and France. At this time Italy had a force of 300,000 men under arms in her East African Empire. In January 1941 British troops in the Sudan began their offensive against Eritrea, and by April, Asmara, the capital of Eritrea, was taken by British forces led by General Platt. On May 18, 1941, the Duke of Aosta surrendered to General Platt at Amba Alagi.

Meanwhile, Rome had prepared new stamps depicting the conjoined profiles of Mussolini and Hitler to celebrate the Axis. Due to the Italian debacle, these stamps were never issued. Nevertheless, one of the most spectacular

blunders in philatelic history occurred on the planned 1 Lira airmail value. The designer (who had to contend with inscriptions in Italian, Arabic, and Amharic) placed the value tablet between the legend at the left and the profiles of Hitler and Mussolini at the right. Even

"Two peoples, one war" (misplaced tablet on the top)

today people often make fun of this stamp, regarding it as a philatelic practical joke. The legend "Two peoples, one war" and the value tablet reading "1 Lira" is read in natural sequence since the eye reads from left to right, followed by the spectacle of the two dictators in full military regalia. The pun was immediately spotted by the authorities and a new design placing the value tablet at the bottom left was approved but was never issued. Between 1942 and 1952 British stamps overprinted "M.E.F." (Middle East Forces) were used in Italian East Africa.

[Contributed by Giorgio Migliavacca.]

Italian Post Offices in China The stamps and postal history material of the Italian presence in China during the early part of the twentieth century is one of the most difficult areas to study in the world of philately. Only limited research has been carried out, and collectors know how difficult it is to purchase even the cheaper stamps of the Italian Post Offices in China.

The presence of Italian troops in China was motivated by the eagerness of the Italian government to flex its muscles as an international superpower. The Italian Navy had already visited the area. In 1899 Italy engaged in negotiations with China for the purpose of acquiring or leasing the harbor of San-Mun to turn it into a naval base. The Chinese government felt that the presence of Italian forces was of little or no relevance to them and rejected the proposal, thus infuriating Rome who went as far as giving an ultimatum.

But historical developments were favorable to the Europeans, who, in the process, had acquired settlements. In 1900 the "Boxers," a group of Chinese whose aim was to drive exploiting foreigners from the country, marched on Peking and assailed the foreign legations. The rebels burned down the Italian, Austrian, French, and Dutch legations. On August 14, a relieving force entered Peking and the Boxer Rebellion was quelled. However, the Chinese understood the necessity of reform, and in 1911 China became a republic.

When the international troops evacuated Peking, the Italians relocated to Tien-Tsin ("The Heavenly Ford") where on the pretext of buying accommodations, they actually ended up creating a true "settlement," although this was nothing new because Great Britain and France had already practiced the same strategy.

The Italian settlement ultimately reached a population of 17,000, consisting mostly of Chinese who preferred living there during the revolution which resulted in the overthrow of the ruling dynasty followed by a period of instability and civil wars.

The opening of post offices for civilians was sanctioned by Royal Decree No. 637 dated March 11, 1920, with retroactive effect. In reality, the Italian post offices in China opened on September 20, 1917, and survived until the end of 1922. Two first-class *ricevitorie* (post offices) were authorized by the Italian Foreign Affairs Ministry, one at Peking within the headquarters of the Italian Legation, and the other at Tien-Tsin within the settlement area. A first-class *ricevitoria* was a full-fledged post office with staff and date-stamps; it was entrusted with registered, insured, and express

mail, and offered a full range of services. The principals of these *ricevitorie* were the Italian consuls at Peking and Tien-Tsin respectively. The postal service was solely for the benefit of Italian personnel and the crews of Italian ships in the area.

"Pechino" & "Tientsin" *o/p* on Italian postage & express stamps

To better serve the two civilian post offices, the issuance of overprinted stamps was authorized. For this purpose, Italian definitive stamps were overprinted with the words "PECHINO" or "TIENTSIN" at Turin, Italy. These stamps were issued on December 1, 1917. It must be noted that earlier, the post offices were supplied with cds postmarks and registration stampers. However, in the interim, the Italian post offices in China locally overprinted a small supply of Italian stamps. Two-line registration stampers utilized on registration labels were adopted for this purpose. All inscriptions such as "R.R. POSTE ITALIANE/.....CINA" were omitted and the line reading "PECHINO" or "TIENTSIN" was used for these early overprints. They can be easily distinguished for their larger size: 19mm x 3mm. The following stamps of Italy's definitive series are known with the above-mentioned overprints: 5, 10, 15, 20, 20 on 10, 25, 30, and 50 cents— all are rare.

Subsequently, between September and November, another locally hand-overprinted issue took place. This time metal stampers (copper punches) manufactured in Peking and inscribed on two lines: "Pechino" or "Tientsin" on the top line and with the denomination in cents or dollars on the second line. These semi-official stamps caused some stir in the philatelic community, and the copper punches were officially destroyed at the Italian legation in Peking. The rarity of these stamps was enhanced by the loss of a large dispatch of mail due to the sinking on September 24, 1917, of a Chinese postal vessel that carried it.

Eventually the regular stamps (Italy's 1901-1916 series) overprinted by the Officina Carte Valori (Government Printing Works) at Turin with the wording "Pechino" and "Tientsin" in upper- and lower-case lettering were issued on December 1.

"Pechino" & "Tientsin" *o/p* on Italian postage dues

At the end of World War I, as Italy annexed the peninsula's territories of Trentino and Venezia Giulia which had previously been under Austrian rule, the Austrian citizens of these areas now became Italian citizens. Many had been serving in the Austrian army and a large quota was taken as prisoners-of-war by Russian troops and transferred to concentration camps in Siberia. The Italian legations in Peking and Tien-Tsin were instrumental in the transfer and repatriation of these POWs to a now-united Italy.

[Contributed by Giorgio Migliavacca. Giorgio Migliavacca, "A Concise Introduction to the Stamps and Postal History of the Italian Post Offices in China," *The Philatelic Shopper*, Vol. I, No. 1, June 1992.]

Italie [*Fr.*] Italy.

Italië [*Dut.*] Italy.

İtalya [*Turk.*] Italy.

Itä-Saksa [*Finn.*] East Germany (D.D.R.).

itur dafna עֲטוּר דַּפְנָה (*m.*) [*Heb.*] laureate.

iturevet [*Dan.*] torn.

Iugoslavia [*Rom.*] Yugoslavia, Jugoslavia.

Iugoslávia [*Port.*] Yugoslavia, Jugoslavia.

izquierda (*f.*) [*Span.*] left (direction or position).

Izrael [*Hun., Pol.*] Israel.

J j

jäännöserä [*Finn.*] remainder, stock remainder.

jaar (*n.*) [*Dut.*] year.

Jackm. L [*abbr.*] Jacmel. Pre-adhesive postmark.

Jackn. T. Jacksonville, Tennessee (U.S.A.). Abbreviation used as a pre-adhesive postmark.

Andrew Jackson

Jackson, Andrew [nicknamed *Old Hickory* by his troops because of his toughness.] U.S. Army general; later president of the United States (1829-37). Born March 15, 1767, in Waxhaws County, South Carolina; died of tuberculosis on June 8, 1845, at the Hermitage (his plantation home).

As seventh president of the United States, Jackson was the first to be called the "People's President." As founder of the Democratic Party, he was the first poor boy with little education to be elected to this high office.

His spectacular service in the War of 1812 was the turning point in his life. His victories over the Creek Indians at the Battle of Horseshoe Bend, Alabama, won him great acclaim. He was commissioned Major-General of the regular Army. His next assignment was to defend New Orleans where he decisively routed the British troops. In 1817, he captured Pensacola in Florida and stemmed the attacks of the Seminole Indians. For this, he was made first Governor of Florida.

Tiring of politics, Jackson wished to retire to private life, but his friends felt he was the only man who could break the power of the East in the national government. He was inaugurated president March 4, 1829.

In his second term of office, Jackson dissolved the Bank of the United States which he detested. He ordered government funds removed from it and deposited into state banks. Wild speculation occurred as they began to issue large quantities of paper money. Financial panic struck in 1837. The ensuing economic depression caused him (as well as many other Americans) to lose most of his money. His health grew progressively worse and he died at his Hermitage Home on June 8, 1845.

Philatelically, Jackson is best known for his portraiture on the Black Jack[*q.v.*] U.S. 2c stamps issued in 1862. Relative to the other stamp designs of its day, the portrait on these stamps is immense. Jackson's face is so big that it seems to jump right off the paper.

A more subdued version of Jackson's likeness appears on a wide array of nineteenth-century definitives. By the twentieth century, his popularity seems to have waned to the point where he was featured on only a handful of stamps, mostly on series honoring all the presidents.

[Contributed by Ruth Ann Davis. Charles van Doren (editor), *Webster's American Biographies*; *Compton's Encyclopedia and Fact Index*, Vol. 13.]

Jahr (*n.*) [*Ger.*] year.

Jaliva [*Span. abbr.*] Pre-adhesive postmark from San Felipe de Jaliva.

jäljennös [*Finn.*] reproduction.

jäljitelmä [*Finn.*] imitation.

janeiro [*Port.*] January.

januar [*Nor., Dan.*] January.

Januar [*Ger.*] January.

januari [*Dut., Swed.*] January.

Japão [*Port.*] Japan.

Japón [*Span.*] Japan.

Japonia [*Pol.*] Japan.

jarang [*Indo.*] rare, scarce.

jasny [*Pol.*] light (*re*: color).

jaune [*Fr.*] yellow.

jaune-citron [*Fr.*] lemon yellow; citron.

jeden [*Pol.*] one.

jedna czwarta (*f.*) [*Pol.*] fourth (the fraction).

jedna dziesiąta (*f.*) [*Pol.*] tenth.

jedna piąta (*f.*) [*Pol.*] fifth.

jedna setna (*f.*) [*Pol.*] hundredth.

jedna trzecia (*f.*) [*Pol.*] third.

jednostka monetarna (*f.*) [*Pol.*] monetary unit.

jedwabna nitka (*f.*) [*Pol.*] silk thread.

Jefferson, Thomas Third president of the United States (1801-1809) and the writer of the Declaration of Independence. Born April 13, 1743, at Shadwell, Albemarle County, Virginia; died July 4, 1826, at Monticello (his Virginia home).

The range of Jefferson's multiple interests and talents was incredible. Above all else a statesman and politician, he was also an outstanding writer, lawyer, architect, farmer, musician, classicist, linguist, naturalist, botanist, surveyor, geographer, ethnologist, and philosopher.

The Declaration of Independence, which he drafted for the Second Continental Congress in June 1776, reflects his political philosophies, especially where he declares that the tyrannical acts of the British government gave the American colonists the right to "dissolve the political bands" which tied them to England.

After the Revolutionary War was won, he held many positions in the fledgling American government. He was secretary of state (1790-94) in President Washington's first admin-istration, vice president (1797-1801) under John Adams, and finally president for two terms (1801-1805 and 1805-1809).

On the whole, America's founding fathers were not the best of friends. Jefferson in particular seems to have had a great many enemies, including John Adams, the man under whom Jefferson had served as vice president. When Adams was on his deathbed, he is reported to have said that his greatest regret was that he had not out-lived his old nemesis, Thomas Jefferson. Adams could not know that Jefferson had died several hours earlier. In a strange quirk of fate, John Adams and Thomas Jefferson, America's second and third presidents, both died on July 4, 1826, fifty years to the day after the signing of the Declaration of Independence. To add to the irony, James Monroe, America's fifth president, died exactly five years to the day later (July 4, 1831).

Jefferson appears on many definitive and special presidential issues of U.S. stamps, as well as on an array of miscellaneous postal items. Nevertheless, his philatelic presence is not nearly as great as that of Washington, Franklin, and several other key American patriots.

[Contributed by Ruth Ann Davis. David C. Whitney (editor), *Founders of Freedom in America.*]

jelkép [*Hun.*] symbol.

jelmondat [*Hun.*] motto.

Jenny invert A 1918 U.S. 24c airmail stamp with its center inverted. It is one of the most popular of all U.S. postage stamps.

The 6c, 16c, and 24c issues of 1918 were America's first airmail stamps and among the first airmails issued anywhere. The 24c version was intended for an experimental airmail service between Washington, DC, and New York City with an intermediate stop in Philadelphia. The first such flights were scheduled to take place on April 15 of that year but had to be postponed for a month. It was during that delay that the "Jennys" were printed.

The stamp is named for its central device, a Curtiss Jenny two-seater biplane that was anticipated for delivering mail. The small plane was neither beautiful nor stable, but it was the same plane used to train virtually all U.S. and Canadian combat pilots during World War I. The plane was inherently dangerous; in one single week in 1918, five people were killed in these planes, including the famous dancer Vernon Castle who was a flying instructor with Canada's Royal Flying Corps. They were also plentiful and seemed practical for the purpose of delivering the mail.

The 24c Jennys were rushed into production so they could be ready for the May 15 inaugural flights. In fact, the time between the initial announcement of the stamps and their first day of sale was less than a week. The stamps were given a patriotic look— red frame, white paper, and blue plane. The actual word "Airmail" was omitted, but the presence of the plane in flight made it clear that these were stamps intended for air delivery.

The Jenny invert (enlarged)

It was customary to print stamps in large sheets of 400 stamps, i.e., four panes of 100 each. In the case of the Jennys, however, small sheets of 100 were printed instead. It has been documented that at least nine of the sheets were printed with the Jenny upside-down, presumably because when the sheets with the red frames were fed into the press a second time to print the blue vignettes, they were fed in backwards. Eight of the sheets were caught and destroyed; one sheet somehow escaped the attention of inspectors.

On the morning of May 14, a 26-year-old stockbroker's clerk named William T. Robey went to the New York Avenue branch of the post office in Washington, DC, to buy some of the stamps for his collection. The Jennys he was shown were poorly centered, so he left and returned later in the day to examine another batch. To his surprise, he discovered a sheet with the Jenny inverted. After he paid for the sheet and left the post office, the postal clerk informed his superiors of the error. Sales of all Jenny stamps were discontinued until the remaining stocks could be checked, but no additional inverts were found.

Robey assumed that there were at least three more panes of inverts somewhere; he had no way of knowing that his stamps were not a pane but an actual sheet and that no other inverts of this type existed. A week after purchasing stamps at the post office, he sold them to Eugene Klein, a Philadelphia dealer, for $15,000. Robey probably would have held out for a higher price had he known that the other three panes did not exist.

Klein soon sold the sheet to Col. E. H. R. Green, son of the infamous Hetty Green (the "Witch of Wall Street") and a major collector and dealer of rare stamps and coins. Robey had attempted to contact Green originally, but Green was out of town at the time. Green purchased the sheet for $20,000 and then separated it into various blocks, pairs, individual specimens, etc., for resale. Today, we can account for eighty-five of those inverts. The others may be in the hands of private collectors who wish to remain anonymous. One authority described Col. Green's office as resembling a barn, and that Green was so disorganized that some of the stamps may simply have been discarded by mistake. It has also been reported that one specimen was inadvertently sucked into a vacuum cleaner and mangled. The specimen still exists, of course, but in decidedly less than mint fresh condition.

The American Philatelic Society often shows an exhibit of three inverted Jennys, two of which are genuine and the remaining specimen a forgery. Attendees of major stamp shows are asked to pick the fake. Of those people correctly identifying the forgery, one name is pulled and a prize is awarded.

The Jenny invert is one of the most fascinating stamps in U.S. history. It is also one of the most desired of all U.S. stamps and is destined to remain so.

[George Amick, *The Inverted Jenny: Mystery, Money, Mania.* This book is a very comprehensive review of the circumstances surrounding the issue, discovery, and sales of these intriguing stamps.]

Jer [*Fr. abbr.*] *Janvier* (January). Pre-adhesive postmark.

J.N.F. provisional stamp (Israel)

Jewish National Fund The Jewish National Fund (J.N.F.) was founded by the World Zionist Organization (W.Z.O.) in 1901 to raise capital for the purchase and preservation of land in what is now the State of Israel. The W.Z.O. has traditionally imposed a one shekel tax or membership fee. Before World War II, the shekel was valued at 2 shillings in the United Kingdom or 100 mils in Palestine Currency Board money. Because of the general poverty of Jews living in Eretz (Land of) Israel during the pre-independence period, the W.Z.O. facilitated partial payment of dues by issuing receipts for fractions of a shekel. These coupons have the name of the organization in Hebrew (*Keren Kayamet L'Yisroel*; literally, Fund for the Preservation of the People Israel) and are denominated in M.E.I. (mils Eretz Israel). As the British prepared to evacuate their Palestine Mandate in May 1948, they gave up their postal responsibilities. These were filled in by the Jewish Government (Yishuv). Because they did not have a supply of postage stamps, the Jews overprinted J.N.F. receipt coupons with דאר (*do'ar*, "postage") and used these in their stead. Shortly after independence on May 15, the Israelis replaced these makeshift postage stamps with the *Do'ar Ivri* (דֹּאַר עִבְרִי, Hebrew Post) series.

[Contributed by Simcha Kuritzky.]

język (*m.*) [*Pol.*] language.

jià gé [*Chin.-py.*] price.

jià mù biǎo [*Chin.-py.*] price list.

jobb [*Hun.*] right (direction or position).

Joegoslavië [*Dut.*] Yugoslavia, Jugoslavia.

John XXIII [né *Angelo Giuseppi Roncalli*; nicknamed *John-outside-the-walls* by the citizens of Rome.] Pope of the Roman Catholic Church (1958-63). Born November 25, 1881, in Sotto il Monte, near Bergamo, Italy; died in the Vatican on June 30, 1963.

Pope John XXIII was above all a pastor. He wanted Catholics to look on other Christians as members of the same family, the children of a common father. In the non-Catholic world, John XXIII is best remembered for having helped rescue many Jews, especially children, from Nazi-controlled Hungary during World War II.

Because John XXIII was only pope for five and a half years, he did not leave as much of a philatelic legacy as most other popes of the twentieth century. Yet the stamps issued during his reign cover a curious spectrum of subjects, ranging from draining marshes to commemorating the hundredth anniversary of the Vatican's newspaper to honoring a radio tower.

[Contributed by Ruth Ann Davis. Eric John (editor), *The Popes: A Concise Biographical History.*]

John Paul I [né *Albino Luciani*.] 263rd Pope of the Roman Catholic Church. Born 1912 in Forno di Canale, Italy; died at the Vatican in Rome on September 28, 1978.

Pope John Paul I, the first pope to choose a double name, died just 34 days after becoming pontiff. By dying so unexpectedly in 1978, he left a rather odd philatelic legacy. It is customary for the Vatican to issue *sede vacante*[q.v.] ("vacant see") stamps to note the death of a pope. Because of the time it takes to prepare the designs, these stamps, which show the year of the interregnum, are issued after the fact and are a form of commemoration. But John Paul's death provided two interregnal periods within the same calendar year. Hence, two 1978 *sede vacante* stamps were issued, but the second also shows the month (*Sett.*, September). This is one of the few times a month-year date has ever appeared on a postage stamp.

John Paul II [né *Karol Wojtyla*.] Pope of the Roman Catholic Church (1978-   ). Born May 18, 1920, in Wadowice, Poland.

Pope John Paul II is the first non-Italian pope since 1523. His election to the papacy had great political significance because he came from Poland, a country still under communist control at the time of his ascension.

John Paul II distinguished himself as being the most widely-traveled pope in history. Many of his journeys are commemorated on stamps, both of the Vatican and of the countries he has visited. Even Communist Poland honored his 1983 visit by issuing two commemorative stamps and a souvenir sheet.

joint issues: Australia and the United States

joint issue Stamps of similar design and purpose issued concurrently by two or more issuing agencies. The stamps usually promote a political concept (e.g., the Europa[q.v.] issues), a religious event (the U.S. and Israeli Hanukkah[q.v.] stamps), or a national anniversary.

The illustrated stamps were issued in 1988 to honor Australia's 200th Anniversary. The pair came from Australia and the United States. A curious difference is found in the word chosen to designate the event. The Australian stamp uses *Bicentenary*, while the U.S. stamp

shows *Bicentennial*, the term preferred by Americans. The 1959 St. Lawrence Seaway joint issue between the U.S. and Canada pushes this difference one more degree, because the Canadian version is bilingual. (See the *Quick Identifier* section for illustrations.) Thus, joint issues are usually similar but do not have to be identical.

The Europa issues are regarded among the most significant joint issues of all time, partly because more than two dozen countries have participated at least once, but mostly because this joint issuance has become an annual affair since its inception in 1956. From 1956 to 1973, the Europa stamps of all participating countries shared a common design; now they use a common theme.

jos [*Rom.*] bottom.

Josefina, *La Corregidora*

Josefina [née *Josefa Ortiz de Domínguez*; known by the popular title *La Corregidora*.] Key figure in Mexico's struggle for independence from Spain. Born 1770 in Vallodolid (now Morelia, capital of the State of Michoacán), Mexico; died 1829.

Josefina was a Creole of pure Spanish blood. She was born of well-to-do parents who gave her the standard education expected of young women of her class: music (piano), sewing, dancing, riding, etc. At the age of thirteen she married Don Miguel Domínguez, the *Corregidor* (Chief Administrator), a position of great political importance in the province of Querétaro.

During the Mexican rebellion against both the Spanish rule and the Spanish Inquisition,

Josefa and Don Miguel held many secret meetings in their home. Señora Domínguez planned lavish events at her home to conceal the plotting sessions that were being conducted in an adjoining room. She and her husband were actively engaged in the conspiracy headed by Father Miguel Hidalgo[q.v.] along with Captains Allende and Aldama.

On September 12, 1810, word reached Querétaro that traitors had revealed the plot to the authorities who immediately ordered the arrest of Miguel Hidalgo and his followers. At the risk of her life and that of her husband, *La Corregidora* (as she was affectionately called) sent word to Hidalgo that the plot had been discovered and that his arrest and probable execution were imminent.

When word reached Hidalgo, he made the immediate decision to start the rebellion. At first his forces were unstoppable and a cruel and bloody onslaught ensued in which the revolutionists emerged victorious. However, on March 21, 1811, Hidalgo's and his troops were ambushed in a narrow ravine heading to Guadalupe. Two months later Hidaglo was executed by a firing squad.

Without the determination and courage of *La Corregidora*, the fight for independence might have been delayed for many years. She is honored among her countrymen as the heroine of the rebellion and the precursor of Mexican independence.

Her likeness has appeared on many Mexican postage stamps, coins, banknotes, and other official items. Josefa is portrayed artistically as a strong woman of plain features, not unlike Susan B. Anthony's effigy on the U.S. dollar coins. Josefa's strong and chiseled face is itself a symbol of Mexico's struggle for independence.

[Contributed by Ruth Ann Davis. Clarke Newlon, *The Men Who Made Mexico*.]

joulukuu [*Finn.*] December.

jóváhagyással [*Hun.*] on approval.

J.S.D.; J.St.D. [*Fr. abbr.*] *Île Saint-Domingue* (Island of Santo Domingo). Abbreviation used as a pre-adhesive postmark.

Juana de Asbaje See *Asbaje, Juana de.*

jugate Also known as *accolated* or *conjoined.* Postage stamp design which shows two or more heads or busts that face in the same direction and overlap. See *conjoined* for additional information and illustrations.

Jugoszlávia [*Hun.*] Yugoslavia, Jugoslavia.

julho [*Port.*] July.

juli [*Dut., Swed., Nor., Dan.*] July.

Juli [*Ger.*] July.

julio [*Span.*] July.

julkaisematon [*Finn.*] unpublished.

jump strip (Canada)

jump pair Two adjacent coil stamps that are not in alignment relative to each other, i.e., the image on one is slightly higher or lower than that of its neighbor. A group of three or more stamps showing this characteristic is called a *jump strip.*

This variation occurs when coil stamps are produced on printing cylinders with two (or more) separate curved plates. If the plates are not properly aligned, a periodic shift in the position of the image is visible. The shift is called a *jump* because the design suddenly "jumps" up or down. As can be seen in the illustration, the second stamp in the strip is just slightly lower than the third stamp.

If the plates are not completely together, a colored line over top of the perforation row appears. The pair of stamps which share that line are called a *line pair* or a *line-gap pair.* Line pairs and jump pairs are most often found on coil stamps of Canada.

junho [*Port.*] June.

juni [*Dut., Swed., Nor., Dan.*] June.

Juni [*Ger.*] June.

junio [*Span.*] June.

juntos [*Port.*] together; unsevered.

K k

K Abbreviation used as pre-adhesive postmarks, both in the United States and in Europe: Kentucky; Kissingen; [with crown] Krakau.

kadrilli [*Turk.*] *quadrillé.*

kağıdın incelmiş yeri [*Turk.*] thin spot, skinned spot.

kahverengi [*Turk.*] brown.

Kaiser (*m.*) [*Ger.*] emperor.

kaiverrettu [*Finn.*] engraved.

kakaunti [*Tag.*] rare, scarce.

kaksi [*Finn.*] two.

kaksikielinen [*Finn.*] bilingual.

kaksikymmentä [*Finn.*] twenty.

kaksivärinen [*Finn.*] bicolored, bicoloured.

kaksois- (*adj.*) [*Finn.*] duplicate.

kaksoiskappale [*Finn.*] a duplicate.

kalemle iptal edilmiş [*Turk.*] pen cancelled.

kalkholdig paper (*n.*) [*Nor.*] chalky paper.

kambiyo kuru [*Turk.*] exchange rate.

kampahammastus [*Finn.*] comb perforation.

kamperforatie (*f./c.*); **kamtanding** (*f./c.*) [*Dut.*] comb perforation.

kam-perforering (*m.*) [*Nor.*] comb perforation.

kamtakning (*c.*) [*Dan.*] comb perforation.

kamtandning (*r.*) [*Swed.*] comb perforation.

Kanada [*Ger., Finn., Swed., Hun., Turk., et al*] Canada.

kangaroos (Australia)

kangaroo Generic name of 52 species of marsupial animals constituting the family *Macropodidæ* which are native to Australia and surrounding islands.

People throughout the world associate the kangaroo with Australia. The philatelic connection is very strong, because the Commonwealth of Australia's first stamps, a definitive series from 1913 comprised of fifteen denominations ranging from 1/2d to £2, feature a kangaroo superimposed over the map of Australia. Australians refer to these stamps as 'roos, the shortened version of the name they give to these popular animals.

An updated version (minus the map) appeared in 1942, along with stamps showing other native species of Australian animals (emu, koala, kookaburra, etc.).

kansainvälinen [*Finn.*] international.

kansallinen [*Finn.*] national.

kansallisuus [*Finn.*] nationaity.

kansio [*Finn.*] album.

kaparo [*Turk.*] deposit (of funds).

karmijnrood [*Dut.*] carmine.

karminröd [*Swed.*] carmine.

karminrot [*Ger.*] carmine.

karmosinröd [*Swed.*] crimson.

karmosinrød [*Nor.*] crimson.

karmozijnrood [*Dut.*] crimson.

karta kredytowa (*f.*) [*Pol.*] credit card.

karta pocztowa (*f.*) [*Pol.*] postal card. The terms for *postcard* in Polish are *pocztówka* (*f.*) and *widokówka* (*f.*).

kartal [*Turk.*] eagle.

kart postal [*Turk.*] postcard. The term for *postal card* in Turkish is *posta kartı.*

Kasım [*Turk.*] November.

käsiraha [*Finn.*] (monetary) deposit.

kasowanie (*n.*) [*Pol.*] cancellation.

kasowanie przez dziurkowanie (*n.*) [*Pol.*] punch cancellation.

kasowanie przez nacięcie (*n.*) [*Pol.*] cut cancellation.

kastanienbraun [*Ger.*] chestnut (color).

katalog [*Turk.*]; (*n.*) [*Dan., Swed.*]; (*m.*) [*Pol., Nor.*] catalogue, catalog.

Katalog (*m.*) [*Ger.*] catalogue.

katalog aukcyjny (*m.*) [*Pol.*] auction catalogue.

katalogos κατάλογος (*m.*) [*Grk.*] catalogue.

katalogos plistiriasmou κατάλογος πλειστηριασμού (*m.*) [*Grk.*] auction catalogue.

katalógus [*Hun.*] catalogue.

katalógus érték [*Hun.*] catalogue value.

katalogvärde (*n.*) [*Swed.*] catalogue value.

katalogværdi (*c.*) [*Dan.*] catalogue value.

katalogverdi (*m.*) [*Nor.*] catalogue value.

Katalogwert (*m.*) [*Ger.*] catalogue value.

katastasi κατάσταση (*f.*) [*Grk.*] grade, condition (of a stamp).

käteinen raha [*Finn.*] cash (ready money).

kati desenli [*Turk.*] definitive.

kaufen (*v*) [*Ger.*] to buy.

Käufer (*m.*) [*Ger.*] buyer.

käytetty [*Finn.*] used.

käytöstä poistettu [*Finn.*] obsolete.

keerdruk [*Dut.*] *tête-bêche*.

kehäkirjoitus [*Finn.*] legend.

Kehrdruck (*m.*) [*Ger.*] *tête-bêche*.

keisari [*Finn.*] emperor.

keiser (*m.*) [*Nor.*] emperor.

keizer (*m.-c.*) [*Dut.*] emperor.

kejsare (*m.*) [*Swed.*] emperor.

kejser (*c.*) [*Dan.*] emperor.

kék [*Hun.*] blue.

Kelet-Németország [*Hun.*] East Germany (D.D.R.).

keltainen [*Finn.*] yellow.

kendetegn (*n.*) [*Dan.*] attribution.

Kennedy, John Fitzgerald President of the United States (1961-63). Born May 29, 1917, in Brookline, Massachusetts; shot to death on November 22, 1963, in Dallas, Texas.

Born into a political family of Irish descent and Roman Catholic faith, J.F.K. was quiet and shy. It was expected that he would become a writer or teacher. However, when his brother Joe was killed in 1944 while serving in World War II, John turned to politics. John had also fought in that war, distinguishing himself as the captain of the U.S. Navy torpedo boat PT-109. He rescued several of his crewmen when the boat was rammed by a Japanese destroyer off the Solomon Islands.

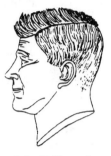

John F. Kennedy

Elected to the United States Senate in 1952, he was appointed to the powerful Foreign Relations Committee. He supported a program of aid to underdeveloped countries and worked for legislation to end corruption in the labor unions. In 1958 he won re-election to the Senate.

Upon being inaugurated president on January 20, 1961, J.F.K. initiated a program known as the "New Frontier" and established the Peace Corps.

The highlight of his brief presidency was his handling of the Cuban Missile Crisis in 1962 in which he succeeded in lessening Cold War tensions with the Soviet Union and avoided a possible atomic war.

Kennedy was assassinated by Lee Harvey Oswald in 1963. He will always be remembered for his famous words to the American people during his inaugural address in 1961: "Ask not what your country can do for you—Ask what you can do for your country."

Shortly after his death, the U.S. put out a memorial issue intended for legitimate postal use, as did Mexico, Ecuador, and a number of other nations. Unfortunately, many small countries such as Dominica, San Marino, Ajman, and Equitorial Guinea exploited Kennedy's death for their own profit by issuing mountains of "collectors'" stamps, few of which ever saw any real postal use.

[Contributed by Ruth Ann Davis.]

kennzeichnen (v.) [*Ger.*] to attribute.

Kennzeichnung (f.) [*Ger.*] attribution.

kenttäposti [*Finn.*] field post.

képmás [*Hun.*] effigy.

keräilijä [*Finn.*] collector.

kerätä (v.) [*Finn.*] to collect.

kereskedni (v.) [*Hun.*] to trade.

kersrood [*Dut.*] cerise.

kesäkuu [*Finn.*] June.

kesatuan moneter [*Indo.*] monetary unit.

kesef כֶּסֶף (m.) [*Heb.*] money; silver.

készpénz [*Hun.*] cash (ready money).

ketem כֶּתֶם (m.) [*Heb.*] stain; tarnish.

keter כֶּתֶר (m.) [*Heb.*] crown (royal headpiece; large silver coin).

kétnyelvű [*Hun.*] bilingual.

kétszeres; kettős (adj.) [*Hun.*] duplicate.

K.E. VII [*abbr.*] King Edward VII[q.v.] of Great Britain.

K.E. VIII [*abbr.*] King Edward VIII[q.v.] of Great Britain.

key types: German (Mariana Islands) & Portuguese (Guinea; due)

key type; keytype A standard design used by a colonial nation for the stamps of its colonies. Great Britain introduced the concept in the 1890s, and its earliest issues for the Commonwealth were regarded as dull and flat. France, Portugal, Germany, and Spain then issued similar stamps for their possessions with varying degrees of critical acclaim.

Key types are useful in keeping down the cost of producing stamps for many small colonies. The basic stamp design is created but with the name of the country and the stamp's value omitted. This original printing plate is called the *key plate*. It is also sometimes referred to as the *head plate* because it often

featured the head of the monarch. The stamps then go through the press a second time to have the country name and denomination added by what is known as the *duty plate*. In some cases, the duty plate does a good job of adding the additional information, and the finished stamp has an attractive appearance. In other cases, the addition resembles a crude overprint.

The first illustrated stamp shows a decent-looking German key type issued for the Mariana Islands. It features Kaiser Wilhelm's yacht, the *Hohenzollern*. The second illustration shows a much cruder example, the Portuguese postage due key type issued for Portuguese Guinea.

K.G.C.A. [*abbr.*] Karen Government Commission, Zone A (Carinthia).

KGL/POST/FRM [*Dan. abbr.*] *Konglilgt Postfrimaerke* (Royal Postage Stamp). Inscription on early Danish stamps.

K.G. V [*abbr.*] King George V[q.v.] of Great Britain.

K.G. VI [*abbr.*] King George VI[q.v.] of Great Britain.

kheshbon חֶשְׁבּוֹן (m.) [*Heb.*] account (financial or transactional).

kiadás; kibocsátás [*Hun.*] an issue, issuance.

kiadatlan [*Hun.*] unpublished.

kiadni; kibocsátani (v.) [*Hun.*] to issue.

kiállítani (v.) [*Hun.*] to exhibit.

kiállítás [*Hun.*] exhibition.

kibdilon κίβδηλον (n.) [*Grk.*] a fake, forgery.

kibocsátásra nem került [*Hun.*] not issued.

kicsi [*Hun.*] small.

kieli [*Finn.*] language.

Kiina [*Finn.*] China.

Kiinan kansantasavalta [*Finn.*] People's Republic of China (P.R.C.).

Kiinan tasavalta [*Finn.*] Republic of China (Taiwan).

kilenc [*Hun.*] nine.

kilencven [*Hun.*] ninety.

killer 1. Any obliteration lacking a date and post office information which is applied to postage stamps to prevent their reuse. The term particularly applies to the right-hand (barred) portion of the Duplex[q.v.] postmark used in Great Britain from 1853 to 1906, although it can also apply to any rubber-stamp markings used to cancel stamps as long as the markings do not include the date and city where the stamps were cancelled.

2. The portion of a modern cancellation that actually obliterates the stamp. It can take the form of wavy lines, flags, slogans, or other designs, but it does not include the date and post office indicator. The portion of the cancellation that tells where and when it was applied is called the postmark[q.v.].

Kina [*Nor., Dan., Swed.*] China.

Kína [*Hun.*] China.

Kínai Köztársaság [*Hun.*] Republic of China.

Kínai Népköztársaság [*Hun.*] People's Republic of China (P.R.C.).

Kinderpost (Austria), actual size

Kinderpost; Kinderstempel [*Ger.*] Child's "post office toy" stamp. These were miniature simulated stamps produced by various European countries to be included in play kits. The toy stamp in the illustration, shown at actual size, is a child's version of the 1890 Austrian definitive series.

Kipperman, Kenneth A Jewish activist who worked as a free-lance engraver for the U.S. Bureau of Engraving and Printing in the 1980s. In 1987 he secretly hid a tiny Star of David within the bearded area in his design of Bernard Revel, a noted American Jewish scholar, for a one-dollar definitive.

See *hidden mark* for additional information and an enlarged illustration.

kıraliçe [*Turk.*] queen.

király [*Hun.*] king.

királynő [*Hun.*] queen.

kiraz rengi [*Turk.*] cerise.

kirjaamislipuke [*Finn.*] registration stamp.

kirjekuori [*Finn.*] envelope.

kirjoitus [*Finn.*] inscription.

kırmızı [*Turk.*] red.

kirschrot [*Ger.*] cerise.

kirsebærfarget [*Nor.*] cerise.

kirsebærrød [*Dan.*] cerise.

kızıl [*Turk.*] carmine.

Kızıl Haç [*Turk.*] Red Cross.

kjøpe (*v.*) [*Nor.*] to buy.

kjøper (*m.*) [*Nor.*] buyer.

K.K.; K.u.K. [*Ger. abbr.*] *Kaiserliche und Königliche* (Imperial and Royal). Abbreviation on stamps of Austria and Austrian possessions.

Klagenf. Klagenfurt. Abbreviation used as a pre-adhesive postmark.

klasseren (*v.*) [*Dut.*] to classify; to grade.

klassificera (*v.*) [*Swed.*] to classify.

klassificere (*v.*) [*Dan.*] to classify.

klassifisere (*v.*) [*Nor.*] to classify; to grade.

klassificering (*r.*) [*Swed.*] classification.

klassifikasjon (*m.*) [*Nor.*] classification; grade, condition.

klassifizieren (*v.*) [*Ger.*] to classify.

klasyfikować (*v.*) [*Pol.*] to classify; to grade.

klein [*Ger.*] small.

kleur (*f.-c.*) [*Dut.*] color, colour.

Knick (*m.*) [*Ger.*] a fold, crease.

kobaltblau [*Ger.*] cobalt (blue).

købe (*v.*) [*Dan.*] to buy.

køber (*c.*) [*Dan.*] buyer.

kokhav כּוֹכָב (*m.*) [*Heb.*] star.

kokoelma [*Finn.*] collection.

kolekcja (*f.*) [*Pol.*] collection.

kolekcjoner (*m.*) [*Pol.*] collector.

kolekcjonować (*v.*) [*Pol.*] to collect.

kollektsioner коллекционер (*m.*) [*Russ.*] collector.

kollektsionirovat коллекционировать (*v.*) [*Russ.*] to collect.

kollektsiya коллекция (*f.*) [*Russ.*] collection.

kolmasosa [*Finn.*] third (the fraction).

kolme [*Finn.*] three.

kolmekymmentä [*Finn.*] thirty.

kolor (*m.*) [*Pol.*] color, colour.

Kolumbia [*Pol., Finn.*] Colombia.

Kolumbien [*Ger.*] Colombia.

kombinationspar [*Swed.*] *se-tenant*.

komplet [*Dan.*] complete.

kompletny [*Pol.*] complete.

konge (*c.*) [*Dan.*]; (*m.*) [*Nor.*] king.

kongeblå [*Nor., Dan.*] royal blue.

König (*m.*) [*Ger.*] king.

Königin (*f.*) [*Ger.*] queen.
königsblau [*Ger.*] royal blue.
koning (*m.-c.*) [*Dut.*] king.
koningin (*f.-c.*) [*Dut.*] queen.
koninklijk blauw [*Dut.*] royal blue.
konserveringsgrad (*c.*) [*Dan.*] grade, condition.
konst (*r.*) [*Swed.*] art.
kontant [*Dan., Nor.*] cash (ready money).
kontanter (*r.pl.*) [*Swed.*] cash (ready money).
konto (*n.*) [*Pol., Swed.*]; (*c.*) [*Dan.*]; (*m.*) [*Nor.*] account (financial or transactional).
Konto (*n.*) [*Ger.*] account.
konulu [*Turk.*] topical; thematic.
Konv. [*Ger. abbr.*] convoy. Abbreviation used as a pre-adhesive postmark.
konvolut (*c.*) [*Dan.*] envelope.
köpa (*v.*) [*Swed.*] to buy.
köpare (*m./f.*) [*Swed.*] buyer.
kopen (*v.*) [*Dut.*] to buy.
koper [*Dut.*] (*m.-c.*) buyer; (*n.*) copper (the metal).
koperta (*f.*) [*Pol.*] envelope; cover (in the philatelic sense).
koperta pierwszego dnia obiegu [*Pol.*] first day cover.
kopi (*c.*) [*Dan.*]; (*m.*) [*Nor.*] copy; reproduction.
kopia (*r.*) [*Swed.*]; (*f.*) [*Pol.*] copy; reproduction.
kopie (*f.-c.*) [*Dut.*] copy; reproduction.
Kopie (*f.*) [*Ger.*] copy; reproduction.
kopiera (*v.*) [*Swed.*] to copy.
kopiere (*v.*) [*Nor.*] to copy.
kopieren (*v.*) [*Ger.*] to copy.
kopiëren (*v.*) [*Dut.*] to copy.
kopio [*Finn.*] a copy.
kopioida (*v.*) [*Finn.*] to copy.
kopiować (*v.*) [*Pol.*] to copy; to duplicate.
köprülü çift [*Turk.*] gutter.
koristeellinen kirjekuori [*Finn.*] cachet.
korjattu [*Finn.*] repaired.
korona [*Hun.*]; (*f.*) [*Pol.*] crown (royal headpiece; large silver coin).
körsbärsröd [*Swed.*] cerise.
Kos One of the islands in the Dodecanese group. Italian stamps issued for this area were overprinted *COO* or *COS*. See *Aegean Islands*.
koteloitu postimerkki [*Finn.*] encased postage stamp.
kotka [*Finn.*] eagle.

köztársaság [*Hun.*] republic.
kral [*Turk.*] king.
krantenzegel (*m./c.*) [*Dut.*] newspaper stamp.
krediet (*n.*) [*Dut.*] credit.
kredietkaarten aanvaard [*Dut.*] credit cards accepted.
kredi kartı [*Turk.*] credit card.
kredi kartı kabul edilir [*Turk.*] credit cards accepted.
Kreditkarte (*f.*) [*Ger.*] credit card.
Kreditkarten akzeptiert [*Ger.*] credit cards accepted.
kreditkort (*n.*) [*Dan., Swed.*] credit card.
kreditkort gäller [*Swed.*] credit cards accepted.
kredittkort (*n.*) [*Nor.*] credit card.
kredittkort akseptert [*Nor.*] credit cards accepted.
Kreidepapier (*n.*) [*Ger.*] chalky paper.
Kreikka [*Finn.*] Greece.
Kriegsgefangenenpost [*Ger.*] prisoner of war mail[q.v.].
krijtpapier (*n.*) [*Dut.*] chalky paper.
kritat papper (*n.*) [*Swed.*] chalky paper.
król (*m.*) [*Pol.*] king.
królowa (*f.*) [*Pol.*] queen.
krona (*r.*) [*Swed.*] crown (royal headpiece; large silver coin).
krone (*c.*) [*Dan.*]; (*m.*) [*Nor.*] crown (royal headpiece; large silver coin). In Danish and Norwegian, a large silver coin is often referred to by the English word *crown* if it is foreign and *krone* if it was struck in Denmark or Norway.
Krone (*f.*) [*Ger.*] crown (royal headpiece; large silver coin).
kroon (*m.-c.*) [*Dut.*] crown (royal headpiece).
kruunu [*Finn.*] crown (royal headpiece; large silver coin).
krwistoczerwony [*Pol.*] blood (red).
kseno nomisma ξένο νόμισμα (*n.*) [*Grk.*] foreign currency.
kuitti [*Finn.*] receipt.
K.u.K.; K.K. [*Ger. abbr.*] *Kaiserliche und Königliche* (Imperial and Royal). Abbreviation on stamps of Austria and Austrian possessions.
kun faste bud akseptert [*Nor.*] no unlimited bids accepted.
kung (*m.*) [*Swed.*] king.

kungsblå [*Swed.*] royal blue.
kuningas [*Finn.*] king.
kuningatar [*Finn.*] queen.
kunst (*f.-c.*) [*Dut.*]; (*c.*) [*Dan.*]; (*m.*) [*Nor.*] art.
Kunst (*f.*) [*Ger.*] art.
kuntoluokka [*Finn.*] grade, condition.
kuorella [*Finn.*] on cover.
kuori [*Finn.*] cover (in the philatelic sense).
kupować (*v.*) [*Pol.*] to buy.
kurs (*m.*) [*Nor.*] exchange rate.
kurs wymiany (*m.*) [*Pol.*] exchange rate.
kuşe kâğıt [*Turk.*] glossy paper.
kusursuz [*Turk.*] perfect, flawless.
kuusi [*Finn.*] six.
kuusikymmentä [*Finn.*] sixty.
kuwarta [*Tag.*] money.
Kuzey İrlanda [*Turk.*] Northern Ireland.
kvadratisk (*adj.*) [*Nor., Dan.*] square.

kvadratiskt (*adj.*) [*Swed.*] square.
kvadrille (*c.*) [*Dan.*] *quadrillé.*
kvalitet (*c.*) [*Dan.*]; (*m.*) [*Nor.*] grade, condition.
kvalitetsbedømme (*v.*) [*Dan.*] to grade.
kvittering (*c.*) [*Dan.*]; (*m.*) [*Nor.*] receipt.
kvitto (*n.*) [*Swed.*] receipt.
kwadratowy (*adj.*) [*Pol.*] square.
kwalificeren (*v.*) [*Dut.*] to grade.
kwaliteitsaanduiding (*f.-c.*) [*Dut.*] grade, condition.
kwiecień [*Pol.*] April.
kwota (*f.*) [*Pol.*] amount.
Ky [*abbr.*] Current postal designation for the state of Kentucky (U.S.A.). It has also been used as a pre-adhesive postmark.
kymmenen [*Finn.*] ten.
kymmenesosa [*Finn.*] tenth (the fraction).
kyôbai [*Jpn.*] auction; auction sale.

L l

l. [*abbr.*] left (direction or position).

L 1. [*o/p*] Lansa (name of an air transport company). Overprinted on airmail stamps of Colombia in 1948. The stamps were used to prepay additional air fees.

2. Abbreviation used as a pre-adhesive postmark: Lendinara (Venetian province); Lerida (Spain); [with crown] Limoges (France); Louisiana (U.S.); [with crown] Lublin; Lyon (France).

La [*abbr.*] Current postal designation for the state of Louisiana (U.S.A.). It has also been used as a pre-adhesive postmark.

laagste bod (*n.*) [*Dut.*] minimum bid.

labas; limbag [*Tag.*] an issue, issuance.

LA CANEA overprint on Italian stamp

LA CANEA Overprint found on Italian stamps used in Crete during the early twentieth century. Canea, the capital of Crete, was under Italian protection following the 1897 military intervention of the European superpowers. The military operation was aimed at preventing a conflict between Turkey and Greece. From 1899 to 1908, Crete, one of the larger islands in the Mediterranean, was under the joint protection of Britain, France, Russia, and Italy. To reinforce the *status quo*, the four occupying powers issued stamps for their respective areas. Austria also had post offices in Crete, and between 1903 and 1914 issued distinctive stamps.

On July 10, 1900, just nineteen days before King Umberto I was assassinated, a 25c stamp depicting the Italian monarch and overprinted in red *1 PIASTRA 1* was issued for use at La Canea. A year later, another 25c stamp, this time depicting Umberto's son King Victor Emmanuel III and overprinted *LA CANEA/ 1 PIASTRA 1* was issued, followed on November 15, 1906, by a set of eleven definitive stamps of Italy with a similar overprint. A special delivery stamp with the same overprint was issued on November 5, and an additional six definitive stamps with LA CANEA overprint were issued between 1907 and 1912. The Italian post office was closed on December 31, 1914. On January 1, 1915, following the 1913 Treaty of London, Crete was handed over to Greece.

[Contributed by Giorgio Migliavacca.]

lachnos λαχνός (*m.*) [*Grk.*] lot (at an auction or mail bid sale).

lachsrosa [*Ger.*] salmon (color).

lagad [*Swed.*] repaired.

lagerkransad [*Swed.*] laureate.

lager tilåvers (*n.*) [*Nor.*] remainder, stock remainder.

Laibach Name given to Ljubljana by the Germans during World War II. See *Lubiana*.

laid paper One of the two major types of paper used for making postage stamps.

All paper exhibits a fibrous weave that results from the way in which it is manufactured. Wove paper, the single most common type used for stamps, has somewhat the appearance of woven cloth when held up to the light. Laid paper will show narrow parallel lines. It is less desirable than wove paper for stamps because it is generally more expensive and does not absorb printer's ink as well.

There are a few cases in which a limited number of specimens exist on laid paper of a stamp normally printed on wove paper. One of the most significant is the 1868 Canadian 2-cent stamp (green). A used specimen on wove paper sells for less than $65 (Canadian), but a similar example on laid paper is valued in excess of $60,000.

lambda-philately: Anthony, Grieg,
E. Roosevelt, & von Steuben

lambda-philately The study and collecting of stamps showing known or suspected homosexuals. The field also includes gay and lesbian collectors, dealers, engravers, and anyone else directly involved with the production, study, or sale of postage stamps.

This area of philately got its name from the Greek letter lambda (λ) which has come to represent the gay movement. Both the movement and the proliferation of stamps featuring homosexuals happened at about the same time. Although stamps portraying gays and lesbians were issued as far back as the nineteenth century, most have been printed since 1969, the year of the police raid on the Greenwich Village gay bar known as Stonewall which triggered much of today's gay political activity.

The list of people known or strongly suspected of being homosexual who have appeared on stamps includes Julius Caesar, Rock Hudson, Oscar Wilde, Horatio Alger, William Shakespeare, King James I of England, Leonardo da Vinci, Alexander the Great, Cicero, Desiderius Erasmus, Richard Wagner, Cecil Rhodes, Hans Christian Anderson, Herman Melville, Emily Dickinson, George Washington Carver, Maurice Ravel, Willa Cather, Cardinal Newman, Lord Byron, and many more. The two American stamps in the illustration show Susan B. Anthony and Baron von Steuben; the Soviet stamp portrays Norwegian composer Edvard Grieg.

It is sometimes difficult to imagine that certain countries with official anti-gay attitudes would issue stamps portraying people who are definitely known to be gay. For example, the Soviet Union issued several commemorative stamps featuring the great Russian composer Peter Ilich Tchaikovsky. Not only is it clearly documented that Tchaikovsky was gay, but he even committed suicide in part because he was unable to cope with his sexuality. Yet the Soviet Union, which regularly persecuted homosexuals, honored Tchaikovsky on their stamps. Similarly, Ireland, a country so fiercely Catholic that for years it refused to allow openly gay people to enter the country, has issued stamps honoring Oscar Wilde, a man who went to prison because of his homosexuality.

Entire philatelic exhibits have been built around this theme. Interest in this field is likely to increase in the future as more homosexuals come out of the closet and as more and more appear on postage stamps.

[Contributed by James Oliver.]

lanço (*m.*) [*Port.*] (auction) bid.

langued Heraldic term indicating an exposed tongue.

Länsi-Saksa [*Finn.*] West Germany (B.R.D.).

laos [*Tag.*] obsolete.

läpimitta [*Finn.*] diameter.

larawan [*Tag.*] portrait.

laskea liikkeeseen (*v.*) [*Finn.*] to issue.

laskos [*Finn.*] a fold.

LASSITHI/ (CRETA) Bilingual overprint (Italian/Greek) on the stamps of Rhodes.

Supposedly conceived in 1943, this overprint may have been privately produced long after the Italians had left Crete.

Late Oincta Profundit [*Lat.*] That which is joined together, stretches far and wide.

lathos λάθος (*n.*) [*Grk.*] error.

laur. [*abbr.*] laureate.

lauréat [*Fr.*] laureate.

laureate head

laureate Head crowned with a laurel wreath. The laurel is an ancient symbol of honor and victory and also serves to identify the hero with the motives and goals of his accomplishments. This motif has been used on a variety of stamps which honor ancient heroes or on stamps from countries whose monarchs wish to make themselves appear heroic, such as Napoléon III on some early French stamps.

[J. E. Cirlot, *A Dictionary of Symbols* (2nd Ed.), 1983, Philosophical Library, New York, p. 181.]

laureato [*Ital.*] laureate.

Laurier, Sir Wilfrid Canadian Prime Minister (1896-1911). Born November 20, 1841, in Saint-Lin (now Laurentides), Québec; died February 17, 1919, in Ottawa, Ontario.

Sir Wilfrid Laurier was the first French-Canadian Prime Minister of the Dominion of Canada. An advanced liberal with anticlerical and republican views, he dedicated his life to Canadian unity. Through his statesmanship and perseverance, he was able to bridge the gap between conservative churchmen and liberal politicians.

In 1874 he was elected to the Canadian House of Commons, and then in 1877 became minister of inland revenue. When he became Prime Minister in 1896, his primary objectives

were to bring all Canadians together on issues of church and state and to improve relations with the United States and Great Britain (while keeping Canada independent of Britain).

Laurier's land and emigration policies were among the primary achievements of his administration. His government settled boundary disputes between British Columbia and Alaska, created the precursor of the Canadian National Railways, and expanded trade. He governed during a period of great prosperity for which he provided the slogan, "The Twentieth Century belongs to Canada."

To his faithful followers, he was a hero. His great personal charisma, character, dignity, and dedication won him the admiration of Canadians and non-Canadians alike.

Sir Wilfrid Laurier

The illustration shows a caricatured likeness of Laurier as it appears on a 1972 commemorative stamp of Canada.

[Contributed by Ruth Ann Davis.]

lavendel [*Ger.*] lavender.

läviste [*Finn.*] roulette, *perçage*.

lävistetty [*Finn.*] rouletted, *percé*.

laxrosa [*Swed.*] salmon (color).

lazurowy [*Pol.*] azure.

L.C. [*abbr.*] Lower Canada. Abbreviation used as a pre-adhesive postmark.

leather postcard In the early 1900s, the W. S. Heal Company of New York produced a series of comic postcards made from leather. The concept did not seem to have survived the

leather postcard (United States)

Leitmotiv (*n.*) [*Ger.*] A brief musical theme associated with a specific character in Wagnerian operas. The term is sometimes used philatelically in reference to some particular device or design that recurs frequently on the postage or revenue stamps of a given country. Coats of arms and various national symbols (Mexican and American eagles, Canadian maple leaves, Australian kangaroos, etc.) fall into this category.

leke [*Turk.*] tarnish; stain.

lema (*f.*) [*Span., Port.*] motto.

lengua (*f.*) [*Span.*] language.

Vladimir Ilich Lenin

World War I era, but at least these postcards provide today's philatelists with a very different type of item to collect.

leértékelés [*Hun.*] devaluation.

left side of stamp When used as part of a description of a stamp, the terms *left* and *right* refer to positioning from the viewer's perspective, not the stamp's perspective.

legalacsonyabb ár [*Hun.*] minimum bid.

legaliseringsmerke (*n.*) [*Nor.*] authentication mark.

legenda [*Finn.*]; (*f.*) [*Port., Pol.*] legend.

Legende (*f.*) [*Ger.*] legend.

leggenda (*f.*) [*Ital.*] legend.

Leid [*abbr.*] Leiden (The Netherlands). Pre-adhesive postmark.

leikkaamalla mitätöity [*Finn.*] cut cancellation.

leilão (*f.*) [*Port.*] auction.

leilão por correspondência [*Port.*] mail bid sale.

Lenin, Vladimir Ilich né *Vladimir Ilich Ulyanov.* Russian statesman who created the Bolshevik Party and the Soviet state. Born April 22, 1870 (as per current calendar; April 10, 1870, on the calendar in use at that time) in Simbirsk (now Ulyanovsk), Russia; died January 21, 1924, in Gorkiy (near Moscow) of a paralytic stroke.

After the overthrow and execution of Czar Nicholas II in 1917, the Bolsheviks, led by Lenin, ultimately took control of Russia and renamed it the Union of Soviet Socialist Republics. His basic goal was to build a workers' state from what had been a peasant society. Lenin's political theory was a modified version of Marxism, especially in that he opposed both the feudal system of the Russian czars and the capitalist system of the West. In his eyes, both systems took power and land away from the workers. Unfortunately, the new socialist system to which he gave birth did not furnish sound economic answers. The twentieth century saw the Soviet Union become an increasingly large and militarily powerful nation, but one with an ever-worsening economy until its ultimate dissolution in 1991. It is even more unfortunate that the current nation of Russia inherited that weak economy with its multiple problems.

Because Lenin was regarded as a communist icon, his likeness appears on dozens of stamps of the Soviet Union, as well as many stamps of East Bloc countries and countries with varying degrees of communist sympathy. The fall of European communism will probably prove to be the end of Lenin as a philatelic figure; few future stamps are likely to be issued with his portrait.

[*Funk & Wagnalls New Encyclopedia* (1984), Vol. 16, pp. 54-56.]

lennätinmerkki [*Finn.*] telegraph stamp.

lente de aumento [*Span.*] magnifying glass.

lente d'ingrandimento (*f.*) [*Ital.*] magnifying glass.

lentoposti [*Finn.*] airmail.

lentopostimerkki [*Finn.*] air post stamp, airmail stamp.

lentopostimerkkien keräily [*Finn.*] aerophilately.

LEROS; LERO Overprints on Italian stamps used on the Dodecanese island of Leros. See *Aegean Islands*.

letét [*Hun.*] deposit.

lewa strona (*f.*) [*Pol.*] left (direction or position).

Lexnt. [*abbr.*] Lexington (Kentucky, U.S.A.). Abbreviation used as a pre-adhesive postmark.

Leyd [*abbr.*] Leiden (The Netherlands). Pre-adhesive postmark.

leyenda (*f.*) [*Span.*] legend.

L.F. [*Fr. abbr.*] *Lettere Française* (French Mail). Abbreviation used as a pre-adhesive postmark.

L.G. [*Fr. abbr.*] *Lettere Genevoise* (Geneva Mail). Pre-adhesive postmark.

libbra (*f.*) [*Ital.*] pound (unit of weight).

libertad (*f.*) [*Span.*] liberty.

liberté (*f.*) [*Fr.*] liberty.

Liberté, egalité, fraternité [*Fr.*] Liberty, equality, fraternity. Rallying cry of the French revolutionists in 1789. This motto has appeared on many French stamps, coins, and notes.

libra esterlina (*f.*) [*Span., Port.*] pound Sterling (£).

libranza (*f.*) [*Span.*] money order.

libretto di francobolli (*m.*) [*Ital.*] booklet of stamps.

librillo (*m.*) [*Span.*] booklet (of stamps).

Libyan stamp portraying Hitler and Mussolini

Libya Before the Italian colonization of the northern coast of Africa between Egypt and Tunisia, the name of Tripolitania was broadly used in the West to the whole of the territory belonging nowadays to Libya, and comprising Tripolitania proper, Cyrenaica and the Fezzan. Turkish power in Africa came to an end in 1881 with the French occupation of Tunisia except for the provinces of Tripoli and Benghazi where the Ottoman flag continued to fly. Turkish rule had been re-established in the coastal regions of Libya in 1835, following a long period under the Caramanli pashas when Tripoli became the most notorious hideout of the Barbary pirates.

Under Ottoman rule, the situation improved and Italy began to carry out regular trade with Cyrenaica and Tripolitania. Between 1869 and 1880, an Italian Consular Post Office at Tripoli, initially using current stamps of Italy and from 1874 on "ESTERO" overprints of the same, was the only link between the Jewish merchants and their contacts abroad. The activation of the Italian Post Office became necessary by the increasing number of Italian merchant ships calling at Tripoli, including those of the Rubattino and Florio lines. In 1901 a second Italian Consular Post Office was opened at Benghazi, Cyrenaica. Italian definitive stamps were used for the mail from this post office except for the 25c definitive stamp which was overprinted "BENGASI/ 1 PIASTRA." Between 1909 and 1911 the Consular Post Office at Tripoli used Italian definitive stamps overprinted "TRIPOLI DI BARBERIA." Ten stamps were issued for this post office with denominations in the widely-used Italian lira.

Meanwhile, in 1910 an Italian nationalist movement held its first congress in Florence advocating the occupation of Tripoli. With the pretext of safeguarding the life and property of Italian expatriates in Libya, on September 27, 1911, Rome sent an ultimatum to Constantinople, and two days later Italy declared war on Turkey after having been refused the transfer of sovereignty on Tripolitania.

On November 5 Italy decreed the annexation of Cyrenaica and Tripolitania. The following year the Italian navy occupied Rhodes and the Aegean Islands to impede the flow of supplies to the Turkish army in Libya. As a result, on October 18, 1912, Italy and Turkey signed a peace treaty at Ouchy, Switzerland, leaving Italy in possession of the Aegean Islands and the Turkish vilayets of Tripoli and Benghazi. In December 1912 seven definitive stamps of Italy overprinted "LIBIA" were issued in the new colony. Five additional denominations with the same overprint were issued in 1915. The newly acquired colony was a single entity under the ancient Greek name of Libya. The area included only the coastal zones, but in due course the Italian penetration of Libya continued, and by 1913 the new colony was divided into two separate administrative areas: Cyrenaica and Tripolitania. This was not immediately reflected by new stamps, but beginning on October 24, 1923, Cyrenaica and Tripolitania issued their own pictorial and commemorative stamps while definitive stamps inscribed or overprinted "LIBIA" were used in both countries.

On July 1, 1921, the first non-overprinted stamps inscribed with the legend "LIBIA" were issued; they consisted of two special delivery (*Espresso*) stamps, and a definitive series of 12 stamps commonly known as *Pittorica* ("Pictorial" series.). Overprinted stamps issued earlier continued to be used even after September 30 when they had been deemed obsolete. The 1c, 2c, and 5c denominations of the pictorial series featured a design by renowned painter Duilio Cambellotti who was later to design other stamps for Italy proper (notably, the 20c of the 1926 St. Francis series). The central subject of these low denominations is a Roman legionary holding a fasces and a spade. The 10c, 15c, and 25c were designed by Vittorio Grassi and depicted the mythical goddess of Abundance emerging from the Libyan desert while the Italian star shines in the background. The 30c, 50c, and 55c were designed by Paolo Paschetto and featured the bow of a Roman war-galley leaving the harbor of Tripoli which is shown in the background.

four Libyan stamps from the "Pictorial" series

The higher denominations in lire show a design by Giovanni Constantini featuring the allegorical figure of a winged Victory emerging from the altar of industry and labor and raising her crown over her head; the background shows a Libyan landscape. These stamps were reissued later with different perforations and later yet on unwatermarked paper.

A new series featuring the Libyan Sibyl by Michelangelo as seen in the Sistine Chapel was issued in 1924 (perf. 14); in 1926 this series was reprinted (perf. 11) and new denominations (1.75 Lire and 2.55 Lire) were added in 1931 (perf. 14).

1942 Libyan postage due,
unissued because of Axis defeat

In 1928 the first airmail stamp of Libya was issued followed by the inauguration of a regular air link with the colony. In 1934 Cyrenaica and Tripolitania were re-united into the single colony of Libya. British and French troops drove the Italians out of Libya during the 1942-43 offensive. The final blow to the Axis forces came in November 1942; the following month General Leclerc advanced with his Free France force from Chad into the South Fezzan. He then continued to move north until he joined up with the Eighth Army on January 24, 1943, in the vicinity of Garian.

On May 13, 1943, Marshal Messe ordered the surrender of the Axis forces which had by that time been pushed into Tunisia; altogether 250,000 prisoners were taken. Three days later Fezzan and Ghadames, which had been placed under French colonial administration since April 1943, utilized small stocks of Italian and Libyan stamps by overprinting them "FEZZAN Occupation Française" on three lines. In June and July the Sebha post office utilized the remainders of Italian and Libyan stamps by overprinting them by hand with rudimentary devices. These stamps of the French occupation of Fezzan were not available to civilians and were used by postal clerks for mail from the Free France force.

From June 1943 and continuing until 1950, British stamps overprinted "M.E.F." (Middle East Forces), initially used in Somalia and Eritrea under British occupation, were introduced in the northern areas of Libya. They were used in Tripolitania until July 1948 and in Cyrenaica until January 15, 1950. In 1944, after using the overprinted stamps issued during the emergency period, Fezzan adopted Algerian stamps between 1944 and 1946. Distinctive Fezzan-Ghadames stamps were issued in October 1946. As far as the northern areas of Libya were concerned, British stamps overprinted "B.M.A. TRIPOLITANIA" (British Military Administration Tripolitania) were introduced in July 1948. They were denominated in Military Administration Lire (M.A.L.). Two years later, when a civil administration took over, the letter M in the overprint was dropped. In 1950 Cyrenaica gained independence under the rule of the Emir Idris, the spiritual leader of the Senussi Order who had encouraged his followers to help the British. On December 24, 1951, Idris became the sole ruler of the newly-formed United Kingdom of Libya which included Cyrenaica, Tripolitania, Fezzan, and Ghadames.

[Contributed by Giorgio Migliavacca.]

licita (*v.*) [*Rom.*] to bid (at an auction or mail bid sale).

licitación (*f.*) [*Span.*] (auction) bid.

licitación mínima (*f.*) [*Span.*] minimum bid.

licitación sugerida (*f.*) [*Span.*] suggested bid.

licitar (*v.*) [*Span.*] to bid.

licitare (*f.*) [*Rom.*] (auction) bid.

licitaţie (*f.*) [*Rom.*] auction, auction sale.

licitaţie prin poştă (*f.*) [*Rom.*] mail bid sale.

licytować (*v.*) [*Pol.*] to bid.

liefdadigheidszegel (*m./c.*) [*Dut.*] charity stamp.

life insurance stamps (New Zealand)

life insurance stamp Official stamp of New Zealand issued for use by the Life Insurance Department of the New Zealand government. These stamps, introduced in 1891, all show lighthouses as their primary design, including many genuine lighthouses that can still be found on New Zealand's coast. Because of this distinctive feature and the quality of the work, these government life insurance stamps are highly regarded by collectors. As one of the illustrated examples on the previous page indicates, some of these stamps are available with surcharges.

lignée (*f.*) [*Fr.*] pedigree, provenance (list of previous and present owners).

liikkeeseen laskematon [*Finn.*] not issued.

liimake [*Finn.*] (stamp) hinge.

liimakkeellinen [*Finn.*] hinged.

liimaton [*Finn.*] ungummed.

lijnperforatie (*f./c.*); **lijntanding** (*f./c.*) [*Dut.*] line perforation.

lila [*Ger.*] lilac (color).

lim (*n.*) [*Nor.*] gum.

Abraham Lincoln

Lincoln, Abraham (nicknamed *Honest Abe* and *The Great Emancipator*). Sixteenth president of the United States. Born February 12, 1809, in Hardin County, Kentucky; shot by John Wilkes Booth on April 14, 1865, in Washington, D.C., and died the following morning.

Abraham Lincoln was president during the U.S. Civil War (1861-65), one of the most turbulent periods in American history. The war itself was fought primarily over the issue of slavery. In 1861 eleven of the southern states bonded together in an attempt to secede from the U.S.A. and to form a separate nation known as the Confederate States of America. It was the intent of the C.S.A. to permit the ownership of black slaves.

Lincoln's primary objective was to keep the Union intact. His second goal was to eliminate slavery throughout the country. In this latter regard, he issued the *Emancipation Proclamation* on January 1, 1863, which officially abolished slavery, although the proclamation had no practical effect until 1865 when the Confederacy was defeated.

Lincoln is regarded as one of the greatest U.S. presidents because he had worthy goals and was capable of achieving them. He proved himself a compassionate leader by being merciful to the defeated Confederacy and by doing everything possible to bring those states back into the mainstream of American society quickly and painlessly. Although many members of his own party strongly objected to these tactics, history has shown that he made the right decision.

Lincoln was shot to death while watching a play in the Ford Theater in Washington, D.C. He had just begun his second 4-year term as president. His assassin was John Wilkes Booth, a Southern sympathizer.

Abraham Lincoln appears on many definitive and commemorative U.S. postage stamps, as well as a variety of other postal items. Nicaragua, Niger, Guatemala, and several other countries have also issued stamps honoring Lincoln.

Lindbergh, Charles Augustus American aviator, engineer, and Pulitzer Prize winner who was the first person to make a non-stop solo flight across the Atlantic. Born February 4, 1902, in Detroit, Michigan; died August 26, 1974, on Maui, Hawaii.

Lindbergh's historic solo flight from New York to Paris in 1927 had a profound effect on philately because it spawned a wide range of commemorative airmail stamps, special overprints, and Lindy-flight covers. Flying,

Lindbergh cover (1928)

which was still in its infancy in the late 1920s, was considered a romantic and exciting endeavor, and Lindbergh's adventure sparked the imagination of the world. It is not surprising that so many philatelic tributes were paid to him.

Lindbergh: Cuba overprint & Panama airmail stamp

The two stamps in the illustration are a Panamanian stamp inscribed *HOMENAJE*

A LINDBERGH ("Homage to Lindbergh") and a Cuban stamp overprinted *LINDBERGH / FEBRERO 1928* ("Lindbergh/ February 1928"). The illustrated cover is quite unusual, because the handstamped cachet says *LINDBERGH AGAIN FLIES THE AIR MAIL*, suggesting that Lindbergh himself piloted the plane that carried that cover, and yet the envelope is franked with a U.S. 10c *LINDBERGH AIR MAIL* stamp that features Lindbergh's plane, *The Spirit of St. Louis.*

line-gap pair [also known simply as *line pair.*] A colored line printed between a pair of coil stamps indicating where one printing plate has ended and the next has started. The line appears over the row of perforations more or less by accident caused by the slight gap where the two plates meet. Line-gap pairs are found on coil stamps of Canada, the United States, and some other countries, and are prized by collectors.

line perforation Method of perforating panes or sheets of stamps by punching one vertical or horizontal row at a time. Stamps perfed in this manner are distinguishable by the overlapping of perforation holes at the corners of the stamps. This method is also known as *guillotine perforation*.

Other methods of perforation include *comb perforation* and *harrow perforation*.

line roulette [also known by the French term *percé en lignes*.] The most common and basic form of rouletting[q.v.]. The roulette slits have the appearance of a row of short dashes. If colored dashes are printed over top of the slits to make the rouletting more visible, then the method is called *colored line roulette*.

linietakning (c.) [*Dan.*] line perforation.

linjepapir (n.) [*Nor.*] laid paper.

linjeperforering (m.) [*Nor.*] line perforation.

linjetandad [*Swed.*] rouletted, *percé*.

linjetandad i sicksackmönster [*Swed.*] zigzag roulette.

linjetandning [*Swed.*] roulette, *perçage*.

lingua (f.) [*Ital.*] language.

linguella (f.) [*Ital.*] (stamp) hinge.

linguellato [*Ital.*] hinged.

Linienzähnung (f.) [*Ger.*] line perforation.

linjetandning (r.) [*Swed.*] line perforation.

links [*Ger., Dut.*] left (direction or position).

British Lion on stamps of Great Britain and New Zealand

lion Symbol of regal dignity, virility, and victory. Because of the lion's status as "king" among animals, it gained wide acceptance as a symbol of the ruling king or lord. In medieval heraldry, the lion was shown in many different poses and positions, especially in Great Britain where this symbol has always been popular.

Some of the most magnificent British and British Commonwealth stamps feature lions. The great beast shown on the British Empire Exhibition stamps of 1924 and 1925 and on three of the six New Zealand "Victory" issues of 1920 portray what is known as the British Lion.

LIPSO Overprint on Italian stamps used on the Dodecanese island of Lipsos. See *Aegean Islands*.

lira sterling לִירָה שְׁטֶרְלִינְג (f.) [*Heb.*] pound Sterling (£).

lisämaksu [*Finn.*] surtax.

lisäpainama [*Finn.*] overprint; surcharge.

lista de precios [*Span.*] price list.

lista de preços (f.) [*Port.*] price list.

liste de prix [*Fr.*] price list.

liste over tidligere eiere [*Nor.*] pedigree, provenance (list of previous and present owners).

listino prezzi [*Ital.*] price list.

listopad [*Pol.*] November.

listownik lotniczy (m.) [*Pol.*] aerogramme, air letter.

liten [*Nor., Swed.*] small.

lithography Printing technique developed in 1798 by Aloys Senefelder (1771-1834), a German map inspector. This method was the forerunner of modern offset printing.

Lithography is based on the principle that water and grease repel each other. An image (actually a reversed, "mirrored" image) was drawn on a piece of flat, polished limestone with a greasy crayon. The entire piece of limestone would then be wetted. The water would not stick to the image but would be absorbed into the porous surface of the bare limestone keeping it moist. A greasy ink would then be applied to the entire area but would only adhere to the greasy image. If a sheet of paper were pressed against this, the image (i.e., a "normal" image) would transfer to the paper.

The frequent use of the word "greasy" should not be misconstrued as meaning that the finished work was crude or sloppy. To the contrary, some very beautiful works of art exhibiting exquisite shading have been produced through this process. Yet the use of lithography as a means of printing stamps has usually proved unsatisfactory. The technique lacks the sharpness normally seen on stamps, and a flat appearance often results because of the relatively thin film of ink which gets transferred to the paper. If the work is not done by an expert, the paper can wrinkle during the printing process, resulting in a flawed reproduction.

Livingstone, David Scottish physician and missionary who is considered one of the most important modern explorers of Africa. Born March 19, 1813, in Blantyre, Scotland; died April 30(?), 1873, in Zambia.

After completing his medical studies in Glasgow in 1840, he was sent as a medical missionary by the London Missionary Society to South Africa. He and his family traveled into regions of Africa never before explored by white Europeans. He was the first European to locate the Zambezi River, Lake Ngami, Victoria Falls, Lake Nyasa, the Lualaba River, and many other key geographic spots.

His greatest contribution to society was his condemnation of the last remnants of black slavery, still practiced by the Arabs and Portuguese. Because of his work, his portrait was placed on the 1973 Great Britain 3p stamp.

[Pat Carrigan, "Clydesdale Bank Plans New Note Trio," *World Coins,* April 1973, p. 532; *Funk & Wagnalls New Encyclopedia* (1984), Vol. 16, pp. 168-69.]

livră (*f.*) [*Rom.*] pound (unit of weight; pound Sterling - £).

livre (*f.*) [*Fr.*] 1. pound, i.e., weight of 16 ounces (avdp.) or 12 ounces troy. Derived from the Latin word *libra*.

2. pound Sterling (£).

Ljubljana Administrative capital of Slovenia. See *Lubiana* (the name given to this city by the Italians during World World II).

ljust smutsbrun [*Swed.*] bister.

L.M. [*Ital. abbr.*] Pre-adhesive postmark: 1. Lago Maggiore (Northern Italy) lake mail. 2. *Lettera da Mare* (Sea Mail).

L.Mc.L. [*abbr.*] *Lady McLeod* steamship.

L. Murcia León Murcia (Spain). Abbreviation used as a pre-adhesive postmark.

L.N. Neuchatel Mail. Pre-adhesive postmark os Switzerland.

LNO [*Span. abbr.*] Logroño (Spain). Pre-adhesive postmark.

L N Rioja; **Lno Rioxa** [*Span. abbr.*] Logroño Rioja (Spain). Pre-adhesive postmarks.

locals [#1]: governmental (Bogotá) & private (Hussey's Post & I.P.S.A.)

local (*noun*); **local stamp** 1. Postage stamp valid only within a limited area or accepted only by a specified postal system. "Normal" postage must be added if the mail is to be delivered outside the local area.

Locals can be government-issued or can be printed and distributed by private companies. The first stamp pictured here shows a government-issued stamp from Bogotá, Colombia. It was made in 1889 and was only valid for use in that city. The second illustrated stamp is a private emission from Hussey's Post, a New York delivery service which issued stamps of this type during its operation from 1854 to 1880. The third example is much more recent. It is from the Independent Postal System of America, a private carrier that has issued many colorful and interesting local stamps.

Some collectors refer to U.S. domestic stamps[*q.v.*] as locals because they originally were not valid for international mailings. Technically this is correct. Nevertheless, it seems strange to call a stamp a "local" if it can be used to carry mail anywhere within one of the largest countries on earth and to a population of a quarter-billion people. Yet by strictest definition, the U.S. domestic stamps are indeed "locals."

2. A *local* is a U.S. precancelled stamp (with city and state overprinted) produced by post offices. Precancels printed in large quantities by the Bureau of Engraving and Printing are called *bureaus*. See *precancel*.

Loch (*n.*) [*Ger.*] hole.

Lochentwertung (*f.*) [*Ger.*] punch cancellation.

lock seal (U.S.)

lock seal Paper seal which was inserted in specially-made padlocks placed on doors of bonded liquor warehouses, freight cars, or whatever. Opening the lock destroyed the seal, proving that tampering had taken place. The seals bore serial numbers and were issued by the U.S. Internal Revenue.

L.O.F. [*o/p*] London-Orient Flight. Overprinted on Philippine airmail stamps in 1928.

lokakuu [*Finn.*] October.

lo mitkablot hatsa'ot bilti mugbalot לֹא מְתְקַבְּלוֹת הַצָּעוֹת בִּלְתִּי מוּגְבָּלוֹת [*Heb.*] no unlimited bids accepted.

lorbeerbekränzt [*Ger.*] laureate.

Los (*n.*) [*Ger.*] (auction) lot.

lösen [*Swed.*] postage due.

lösenmärke (*n.*) [*Swed.*] postage due stamp.

lot One or more items sold as a single unit at an auction or mail bid sale.

lote (*m.*) [*Span., Port.*] (auction) lot.

lotto (*m.*) [*Ital.*] (auction) lot.

Louise. Ky. Louisville, Kentucky (U.S.A.). Abbreviation used as a pre-adhesive postmark.

loupe (*f.*) [*Fr.*] magnifying glass.

Love stamp: Is the "O" a birth control pill?

Love stamp "Love" has been a recurring theme on U.S. commemoratives since 1973. These stamps have been issued often but not on an annual basis. When the U.S. Postal Service does issue them, they are generally released around the first of February to coincide with the sending of Valentine's Day cards. Some people found the 1973 issue (shown in the illustration) to be amusing, because they claimed that the letter "O" in the word "LOVE" resembles a birth control pill.

lozenge roulette Horizontal or vertical rows of X-shaped cuts between stamps on a sheet which allow the stamps to be easily separated. The entire row looks like a string of diamonds; hence, this method is also known as *diamond roulette*. As with all rouletting, no paper is removed during the manufacturing process as is the case with perforations.

In some British texts, the French words *percé en croix* or *percé en losanges* are frequently seen in lieu of the English terms.

L.R. 1 [*abbr.*] Letters Radius 1. Abbreviation used as a pre-adhesive postmark.

lt. [*abbr.*] light.

LT [*Ital. abbr.*] *Lettera Toscana* (Tuscany Mail). Pre-adhesive postmark.

L.T. [*abbr.*] Letter Transit.

Lubiana [**Italian and German occupations**] Ljubljana, the administrative capital of Slovenia, was occupied by Italian forces in April 1941 when Yugoslav definitive stamps depicting King Peter were overprinted *Co-Ci* (*Commissariato Civile*, the Italian administrative commission for the area). Two types of this overprint exist, one by letter press and one by hand. These were followed by new overprints reading *R. Commissariato/ Civile/ Territori Sloveni/ occupati/ LUBIANA* on Yugoslav stamps of King Peter. Italian occupation authorities also overprinted Yugoslavia's four-value 1940 Red Cross airmail set for ordinary use, once with the *R. Commissariato* and then with the *Alto Commissariato* wording.

Yugoslav stamp with *Co-Ci* overprint for Lubiana

Three postage due sets were issued overprinting Yugoslav postage dues of 1931: on April 26, 1941, with the *Co-Ci* overprint; on May 5, 1941, with the *R. Commissariato* overprint; and finally on June 30 with the *A. Commissariato* overprint. On September 9, 1943, following a secret armistice signed by Rome and the Allies, German troops took over Lubiana (as it was named by the Italians). Later that month a German task force freed Mussolini who was soon able to establish his fascist republic (*R.S.I.*) in northern Italy. As a result, some semblance of Italian control was considered and, among other things, the Italian lira continued to be the currency used on stamps of Lubiana.

In 1944 the province was renamed Laibach and definitive stamps of Italy were overprinted with the German eagle and a bilingual inscription, *PROVINZ LAIBACH— POKRAJINA LJUBLJANSKA.* A definitive series consisting of sixteen stamps with the same legend and depicting local scenes was issued in early 1945. Following the Italian collapse and for security reasons, in October 1943 Germany incorporated Laibach into its *Deutsche Dienstpost Adria* postal arrangement, and German stamps were introduced. Lubiana and four former Italian provinces of Venetia-Giulia (Gorizia, Trieste,

Pola, and Fiume) made up the *O.Z.A.K.* (*Operation Zone Adriatische Küstenland*, "Operation Zone of the Adriatic Coast"). During the spring and summer of 1944, many post offices ran out of stamps and revenue (fiscal) stamps were tolerated. In some instances, a postmark reading "Postage Paid" was adopted.

On April 3, 1945, the German front was pulverized; shortly thereafter Tito was able to gain control of Slovenia. The 1945 pictorial definitives mentioned above were overprinted with a star, the word *Slovenija* diagonally, the date *9.5.1945*, and *Jugoslavia* placed in a way as to cover the name of the province at both the top and bottom of the stamps. These stamps remained valid until June 30, 1945.

[Contributed by Giorgio Migliavacca.]

luchtpost (*f./c.*) [*Dut.*] airmail.

luchtpostblad (*n.*) [*Dut.*] aerogramme.

luchtpostfilatelie (*f./c.*) [*Dut.*] aerophilately.

luchtpostzegel (*m./c.*) [*Dut.*] air stamp, airmail stamp, air post stamp.

Lucite Dupont tradename for polymethyl methacrilate[*q.v.*].

Luemb [*abbr.*] Luxembourg. Pre-adhesive postmark.

luettelo [*Finn.*] catalog, catalogue.

luetteloarvo [*Finn.*] catalogue value.

luftpost (*c.*) [*Dan.*]; (*m.*) [*Nor.*] airmail.

Luftpost (*f.*) [*Ger.*] airmail.

luftpostfilateli (*c.*) [*Dan.*] aerophilately.

luftpostfrimærke (*n.*) [*Dan.*] air stamp, airmail stamp, air post stamp.

luftpostfrimerke (*n.*) [*Nor.*] air stamp, airmail stamp, air post stamp.

Luftpostleichtbrief (*m.*) [*Ger.*] aerogramme, air letter.

Luftpostmarke (*f.*) [*Ger.*] air stamp, airmail stamp, air post stamp.

Luftpostphilatelie (*f.*) [*Ger.*] aerophilately.

Lug. [*Ital. abbr.*] *Luglio* (July). Abbreviation used as a pre-adhesive postmark.

luglio [*Ital.*] July.

luminescerende postzegel (*m./c.*) [*Dut.*] tagged stamp.

lunastus maksu [*Finn.*] postage due.

luokitella (*v.*) [*Finn.*] to classify; to grade.

luokitus [*Finn.*] classification.

luotto [*Finn.*] credit.

luottokortit hyväksytään [*Finn.*] credit cards accepted.

luottokortti [*Finn.*] credit card.

lupa (*f.*) [*Span., Port., Pol.*] magnifying glass.

lupă (*f.*) [*Rom.*] magnifying glass.

luty [*Pol.*] February.

L.V. [*abbr.*] Vaud Mail (Switzerland). Preadhesive postmark.

lys [*Nor.*] light (*re:* color).

lyserød [*Dan., Nor.*] pink.

L.Z. [*abbr.*] Zürich Mail (Switzerland). Preadhesive postmark.

M m

M Abbreviation used as a pre-adhesive postmark: [with or without crown] Madrid (Spain); Maine (U.S.A.); Mecklenburg (Germany); Menin; Milano (Italy).

Ma [*abbr.*] Maryland (pre-adhesive postmark from the U.S.).

M.A. [*Span. abbr.*] *Ministerio de Agricultura* (Minister of Agriculture). Overprinted on official stamps of Argentina.

määrittää (*v.*) [*Finn.*] to attribute.

määrittelemätön [*Finn.*] unattributed.

määritys [*Finn.*] attribution.

maart [*Dut.*] March.

Sir John Alexander Macdonald

Macdonald, Sir John Alexander First Prime Minister of Canada (1867-73 and 1878-91). Born January 11, 1815, in Glasgow, Scotland; died June 6, 1891, in Ottawa, Ontario.

Sir John Macdonald emigrated from Scotland to Kingston (in what is now Ontario) in 1820. He became Prime Minister of the Province of Canada in 1857. Largely through his efforts and the efforts of Sir George Étienne Cartier and George Brown, the British Parliament passed the British North America Act in 1867, creating the Dominion of Canada. Macdonald became its first Prime Minister.

Under his direction, the Dominion quickly expanded to include the provinces of Manitoba, British Columbia, and Prince Edward Island. But Macdonald was forced to resign during the Pacific Scandal of 1873 in which the government was accused of taking bribes regarding railway contracts. He returned as Prime Minister five years later and retained that position until his death in 1891.

He always remained loyal to the British Commonwealth and directed his efforts to maintaining independence from the United States. He remained loyal to his motto, "A British subject I was born; a British subject I will die."

The illustration shows a caricatured likeness of Macdonald as it appears on a 1972 commemorative stamp of Canada.

[Contributed by Ruth Ann Davis.]

macenta [*Turk.*] magenta.

macchia (*f.*) [*Ital.*] stain (as on a postage stamp).

Machin definitive (Great Britain)

Machin Series Definitive stamps of Great Britain featuring the crowned head of Queen Elizabeth II. They were introduced on July 1, 1968. The design comes from a plaster cast made of the queen's profile by Arnold Machin.

The earliest Machin issues were among the last British stamps denominated in £/s/d values. They were also the first to use the decimal system in 1971. Since their inception, these stamps have been issued in approximately one hundred denominations (including non-denominated versions and denominations of regional issues). No other definitive series anywhere has come close to this number. The Machin definitives have also been issued in various colors and sizes; in pane, coil, and booklet formats; with and without advertising in the selvage; with and without tagging; and with numerous varieties, especially of the £1 stamps. In short, these stamps are not only beautiful, but they also encompass a huge and awesome area of British philately.

madraygah מַדְרֵגָה (*f.*) [*Heb.*] grade; condition.

Mag [*Ital. abbr.*] *Maggio* (month of May). Abbreviation used as a pre-adhesive postmark.

magán szükségpénz [*Hun.*] scrip.

maggio [*Ital.*] May.

Magyar [*Hun.*] Hungary.

Magyar (Kir) Posta [*Hun.*] Hungarian (Royal) Post.

Magyar Tanácköztársaság [*Hun.*] Hungarian Soviet Republic. Overprinted on 1919 stamps during the Bolshvik regime.

mai [*Fr., Nor.*] May.

Mai [*Ger.*] May.

mail (*v.*) To send a letter or parcel by way of the post office.

mail bid sale Type of auction sale where all bids are placed by mail; there is no live bidding done on the auction floor. The company conducting the sale usually places a minimum bid on the more expensive items. Unlike at a regular auction, purchases found to be unsatisfactory may usually be returned for a full refund, unless some provision has been made for prospective bidders to examine the items prior to the sale.

Mail Boat Series of eight stamps issued by Guernsey in 1972 and 1973 which show various ships that were used to transport mail during the past two centuries.

There is some controversy surrounding the stamp in the illustration. The inscription *Isle of*

Guernsey 1930 is correct, although at least one authority claims that the ship in question is actually the *Isle of Sark*.

[*Scott Postage Stamp Catalogue* (1987), Vol. 1, p. 200; C. F. Black, "Canadiana," *Canadian Philatelist*, March-April 1986, p. 92.]

Mail Boat: *Isle of Guernsey 1930* (Guernsey)

maio [*Port.*] May.

maj [*Pol., Swed., Dan.*] May.

Makel (*m.*) [*Ger.*] stain; blemish; fault.

makellos [*Ger.*] unblemished, faultless.

makeready Cut impressions of stamps, some in special colors, used in the pressbed by the printer to get uniform clarity of detail. It is also known as *découpage* or *mise-en-train* in French and is also called *patching* in English.

[Contributed by John E. Lievsay.]

maksu [*Finn.*] fee.

maksumääräys [*Finn.*] money order.

makulera (*v.*) [*Swed.*] to cancel.

makulering (*r.*) [*Swed.*] cancellation; obliteration.

makulering med hålslag [*Swed.*] punch cancellation.

M.A.L. [*abbr.*] Military Authority Lire. Overprint which accompanies a surcharge on stamps of Great Britain prepared for Tripolitania in 1948.

mala aérea (*f.*) [*Port.*] airmail.

mala postal (*f.*) [*Port.*] the mail.

mallikappale [*Finn.*] specimen.

mały [*Pol.*] small.

Man; Man.a; Mant.a; Man.va [*Ital. abbr.*] Mantova (Italy). Abbreviations used as pre-adhesive postmarks.

mancha (*f.*) [*Span., Port.*] stain (as on a postage stamp).

mandat (*m.*) [*Fr.*] money order.

mandat poştal (*n.*) [*Rom.*] postal money order.

block of Latvian stamps printed on the back of a German military map

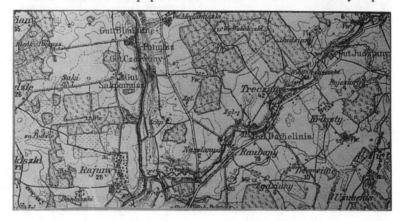

mangel (*m.*) [*Nor.*] defect.
mangelfull [*Nor.*] defective.
mangelhaft [*Ger.*] defective.
mångfald (*r.*) [*Swed.*] variety.
mangfoldighet (*m.*) [*Nor.*] variety.
manipulation of gum Any intentional change made to the gum of a stamp, including total regumming, with the intent of defrauding a buyer into believing that the gum is original. See *regummed*.
map paper Immediately following World War I, there was a severe shortage of paper throughout Eastern Europe. Latvia seems to have faced the greatest shortage. In order to maintain an adequate supply of postage stamps, stamps were printed on whatever paper was at hand, including the back of discarded money paper, wallpaper, and leftover maps. The illus-tration shows a block of ten Latvian stamps printed on the clean side of a German military map.

Also see *postage stamps on currency paper*.
marca da bollo [*Ital.*] fiscal stamp.
marca de agua (*f.*) [*Span.*] watermark (when used in reference to a banknote). The more general term (and the one used in philately) is *filigrana*.
marca de autenticação (*f.*) [*Port.*] authentication mark.
marca de autenticación (*f.*) [*Span.*] authentication mark.
marca secreta (*f.*) [*Span., Port.*] secret mark.
marché noir (*m.*) [*Fr.*] black market.
marco (*m.*) [*Span., Ital., Port., et al*] mark (German unit of currency); [*Span.*] frame (on a postage stamp).

marco [*Port.*] March.
marcophily The study and collecting of postmarks. See *postal history*.
mare [*Rom.*] large.
Marea Britanie [*Rom.*] Great Britain.
marg (*m.*) [*Nor.*] gutter.
marginalpapir (*n.*) [*Dan.*] gutter.

margin summation marking (Germany)

margin summation marking Calculation found in the top margin of German stamps issued during the first half of the twentieth century which indicates the total value of all the stamps in that column added to the total values of all columns to the left of it. For example, if a pane of 6 pfennig stamps is printed 10 x 10, then the first summation marking will read *,60* (= 60 pfennig or .60 of a mark; in most European countries, commas are used to designate decimals and periods are used to set off thousands). The second marking will read *1,20* (one mark 20 pfennig), the third will read *1,80*, the fourth *2,40*, etc. The tenth and final summation marking will say *6,00*. These summations were written in the selvage to eliminate the need for postal employees to figure out the price of a purchase if a customer only bought part of a pane of stamps.
margines zewnętrzny (*m.*) [*Pol.*] gutter.
maritime postmark Special cancel used for letters posted in an official post office maintained on board a ship. This is not the same as a *paquebot*[q.v.] or other marking used in most major seaports on loose letters collected on board ships to be deposited in a port post office for onward transmission.
marka (*f.*) [*Pol.*] mark (German currency).

márka [*Hun.*] mark (German currency).
markacyjny znak drukarski (*m.*) [*Pol.*] *burélage, burelé.*
Marke (*f.*) [*Ger.*] (postage) stamp; token.
markedsverdi [*Nor.*] intrinsic value.
Markenblock (*m.*) [*Ger.*] block.
markierte Briefmarke (*f.*) [*Ger.*] tagged stamp.
markka [*Finn.*] mark (German unit of currency).
marko μάρκο (*n.*) [*Grk.*] mark (German unit of currency).
marque d'affranchissement [*Fr.*] frank.
marque d'authenticité [*Fr.*] authentication mark.
marque secrète (*f.*) [*Fr.*] secret mark.
marraskuu [*Finn.*] November.
marrom [*Port. (Brazil)*] brown.
marrón [*Span.*] maroon; brown.
marrone [*Ital.*] brown.
mars [*Fr., Swed., Nor.*] March.
Mart [*Turk.*] March.
März [*Ger.*] March.
marzec [*Pol.*] March.
marzo [*Ital., Span.*] March.
Mas.; Mass [*abbr.*] Massachussetts (pre-adhesive postmarks from the U.S.).
MAS [*abbr.; o/p*] *Memento Avdere Semper,* "Remember always to be daring." Latin inscription which appears either in full or in abbreviated form on stamps of Fiume[q.v.].
Maschinenfrankatur (*f.*) [*Ger.*] frank.
Masini, Giuseppe Engraver who placed the seven letters (G. MASINI) of his name— one at a time— within the design of the seven stamps issued by Naples in 1858. This is one of the earliest known uses of the hidden mark[q.v.].
másolat [*Hun.*] a copy, reproduction; a duplicate.
Massa C. [*Ital. abbr.*] Massa Carrara (Tuscany). Pre-adhesive postmark.
matasellos (*m.*) [*Span.*] cancellation; postmark.
Matam. [*Span. abbr.*] Matamoros (Mexico). Abbreviation used as a pre-adhesive postmark.
mattgul [*Swed.*] buff (color).
Mavge [*Fr. abbr.*] Maubeuge (France). Pre-adhesive postmark.
maximaphily The study and collecting of maximum cards[q.v.].

maximum card (British Virgin Islands)

maximum card A picture postcard bearing a stamp and a postmark that are relevant to the subject depicted on the card. The stamp is affixed on the view-side of the postcard and is usually cancelled by a postmark that has some strong connection with the topic or theme depicted on the stamp. The "host" card must be a postcard published by a commercial publisher and not a photograph or an enlarged reproduction of the stamp itself. The picture on the card must be closely related to the subject depicted on the stamp.

Most of the early maximum cards dating back to the 1930s did not enjoy the privilege or possibility of having the stamp cancelled by a "matching" postmark. But since the early 1960s, special postmarks have been widely used by many postal administrations, and collectors of maximum cards have become more demanding. Maximum cards are quite useful to thematic collectors who wish to highlight certain details of the stamp design; a sensible and moderate use of maximum cards may enhance the visual aspect of thematic displays.

The study and collecting of maximum cards is called *maximaphily.* Anyone interested in this field may wish to contact the Maximum Card Study Unit of the American Topical Association, P.O. Box 11447, Norfolk, VA 23517, U.S.A., or the Associazione Italiana Maximafilia, Via 4 Novembre 17, 13019 Varallo Sesia VC, Italy. Maximaphily units of national stamp organizations also exist in Germany, Belgium, France, and Spain.

[Contributed by Giorgio Migliavacca.]

Mayıs [*Turk.*] May.

May.ne [*Fr. abbr.*] Mayenne (France). Pre-adhesive postmark.

mayo [*Span.*] May.

M.B. [*abbr.*] Mobile Box.

Mbledhja/ Kushtetuëse/ 12-IV-1939/ XVII [*Alb.*; *o/p*] Albanian overprint on Albanian stamps to serve as a reminder of the decision taken by a "puppet" Constituent Assembly which had met in April of 1939 to offer the Albanian crown to Italy's King Victor Emmanuel III. The roman numerals at the end of the overprint refer to the year of the fascist era. See *Albania.*

m/c [*abbr.*] multicolored, multicoloured.

Md. [*abbr.*] Current postal designation for the state of Maryland (U.S.A.). It has also been used as a pre-adhesive postmark.

Me [*abbr.*] Current postal designation for the state of Maine (U.S.A.). It has also been used as a pre-adhesive postmark.

medallion portrait Stamp portrait that resembles a medallic engraving. The earliest examples are some of the first issues of Belgium which are regularly referred to as *Medallions* due to their medallion-like portrayal of King Leopold I. However, the

St. Vincent stamp in the illustration is one of the best examples because of the three-dimensional quality of the design, including the truncation at the neck. George V's portrait is presented within an oval inner frame which resembles the ornate rim on a medallic piece.

medallion portrait (St. Vincent)

med fastsättare [*Swed.*] hinged.
med hål [*Swed.*] holed.
medianil (*m.*) [*Span.*] gutter.
medio (*adj.*) [*Span.*] half.
medium of exchange Anything which is accepted as a standard of value by all parties participating in a transaction. The valued item may have been chosen voluntarily by the participants or may have been forced upon them by legal decree (e.g., U.S. notes are "legal tender for all debts, public and private").

Although money is the most common medium of exchange in today's world, exchange has sometimes been transacted with such diverse items as coffee, live animals, shells, beads, tobacco, chocolate, and nails. Postage stamps have sometimes circulated in lieu of small change during periods of coin shortages, such as during the U.S. Civil War of 1861-65 (see *encased postage stamp*) and the Spanish Civil War of 1936-39 (see *postage stamp currency*).

M.E.F. [*o/p*] Middle East Forces. British overprint which appeared from 1942 to 1952 on stamps such as those used in Italian East Africa.
megenthitikos fakos μεγενθυτικός φακός (*m.*) [*Grk.*] magnifying glass.
megrendelőlap [*Hun.*] order form.
megrongált [*Hun.*] damaged.
mehrfarbig [*Ger.*] multicolored, multicoloured.
mei [*Dut.*] May.
meio (*adj.*) [*Port.*] half.

Golda Meir (Israel)

Meir, Golda [née *Goldie Mabovitz* (or *Mabovich*).] Israeli prime minister (1969-74). Born May 3, 1898, in Kiev, Russia (now Ukraine); died December 8, 1978, in Jerusalem.

Golda Meir started her career as a schoolteacher in Milwaukee, Wisconsin. An avowed Zionist, she and her husband moved to Palestine in 1921. She became active in Zionist affairs and in the labor movement. Throughout the 1930s and 1940s, she served in various Zionist organizations in Palestine, Europe, and the United States.

Her perilous secret meeting with King Abdullah of Jordan just before the Arab invasion in 1948 was a dramatic attempt for last minute conciliation. Appointed Minister of Labor in 1949, Golda initiated large-scale housing and road-building programs, and vigorously supported the policy of unrestricted immigration despite the great economic difficulties faced by the young Jewish State. As Foreign Minister (1956-65), she was often Israel's spokesperson at the United Nations. Among her main achievements in foreign relations was the extension of Israeli aid to the emerging African nations, and the establishment of friendly relations accomplished through personal visits to Liberia, Ghana, Nigeria, and the Ivory Coast.

After the death of Levi Eshkol in 1969, Golda Meir became the fourth Prime Minister of Israel. Originally thought to have been a stop-gap appointment, she went on to lead her party to victory in the next general elections.

She held this critical position, continuing to carry on indirect negotiations with Egypt, through the outbreak of the Yom Kippur War in 1973. Despite her eminence, she was and continues to be called simply "Golda."

[Contributed by Mel Wacks on behalf of the Magnes Museum.]

Méjico; México [*Span.*] Mexico.

Meksika [*Turk.*] Mexico.

Meksyk [*Pol.*] Mexico.

mektupla müzayede [*Turk.*] mail bid sale.

melago μεγάλο [*Grk.*] large.

melkein [*Finn.*] almost.

melko harvinainen [*Finn.*] scarce.

Memento Avdere Semper [*Lat.*] Remember always to be daring. Legend which appears either in full or in abbreviated form (*MAS*) on stamps of Fiume[*q.v.*].

memorial cover 1. Cover with a special cachet commemorating the death of a monarch, president, prime minister, or other special person. The cachet might be very beautiful and elaborate, or it might be a simple one-line statement indicating the person's demise. This item is also known as a *mourning cover*.

The death of Queen Victoria in 1901 probably generated more memorial covers, mourning souvenir cards, and other related articles than any other event in the twentieth century. The philatelic tribute was fitting, since Victoria had been the first person ever to be portrayed on a postage stamp.

2. An envelope with a black border which is used to mail a death notice.

[C. R. McGuire, "Canada Mourns Her Monarch," *Canadian Philatelist*, May-June 1984, pp. 215-221, and July-August 1984, pp. 278-294.]

menorah Candelabrum symbolizing the universe, used in Jewish worship. The menorah appears on one of the ancient coins of Antigonus Mattathias. In modern times, it has been featured on some of the stamps and coins of Israel, as well as the 1996 U.S. Hanukkah[*q.v.*] stamp.

mercancía residual (*f.*) [*Span.*] remainder, stock remainder.

early U.S. message card

mes (*m.*) [*Span.*] month.

Mesa [*Ital. abbr.*] Messina (Sicily). Pre-adhesive postmark.

mese (*m.*) [*Ital.*] month.

message card [also known as a *paid reply postal card.*] A two-part postal card which, in essence, consists of two individual postal cards attached together. The original sender uses the front part for the address and for the message, but the connected part is left blank. The receiver detaches the original, write his own response onto the second piece, and mails it.

When the message card is sent to another country, the Universal Postal Union requires its member nations to honor the mailing of the reply portion, even though the card's imprinted stamp is from a different country.

See illustration on previous page.

Messico [*Ital.*] Mexico.

met [*Dut.*] with.

metà (*f.*) [*Ital.*] half (the fraction).

metade (*f.*) [*Port.*] half (the fraction).

metered postage 1. Postage imprinted directly onto an envelope by means of a meter machine. These machines are often used by corporations to help keep track of postage costs and to deter unauthorized use of the company's postage by employees. Their use for international mail was authorized by the Universal Postal Union effective January 1, 1922.

2. Meter stamp (sometimes known as a *meter strip*) which is generated by a meter machine in a post office. In today's world, these machines are connected to scales which weigh the mail and then electronically tell the meter machine exactly how much postage is required. The machine prints a strip with the correct postage. This innovation is hated by many philatelists (because it bypasses the need for standard postage stamps), but it is fast and efficient and post office clerks are less likely to make mistakes.

met lauwerkrans [*Dut.*] laureate.

met plakker [*Dut.*] hinged.

mettere in mostra (*v.*) [*Ital.*] to exhibit.

Mex [*Span. abbr.*] Mexico. Abbreviation used as a pre-adhesive postmark.

mezat [*Turk.*] auction.

mezat kataloğu [*Turk.*] auction catalogue.

mezzo (*adj.*) [*Ital.*] half.

Mi [*abbr.*] Mississippi (pre-adhesive postmark from the U.S.).

mic [*Rom.*] small.

Mic; Mich [*abbr.*] Michigan (pre-adhesive postmarks from the U.S.).

Mic. T. [*abbr.*] Michigan Territory. Abbreviation used as a pre-adhesive postmark.

mie [*Rom.*] thousand.

międzynarodowy [*Pol.*] international.

mi ekdothenta μή εκδοθέντα [*Grk.*] not issued.

migrating phosphor Type of phosphor found on some 1972 Canadian stamps which tends to bleed onto other stamps, album pages, or whatever paper the phosphor touches. See *tagging*.

migratory bird hunting stamp (Canada)

migratory bird hunting stamp Revenue stamp issued by the United States and Canada which must be purchased on an annual basis and affixed to a hunting permit to allow a person to hunt ducks, geese, and other water fowl. These stamps are popularly known as *duck stamps* and are highly prized by collectors. The first were issued by the U.S. in 1934. Canada introduced its version in 1985. In both countries, proceeds from the sale of the stamps go to the conservation of wetland regions.

mikhuts l'makhazor מְחוּץ לְמַחֲזוֹר [*Heb.*] obsolete.

mikro μικρό [*Grk.*] small.

mil [*Span., Port.*] thousand.

Mil [*Ital. abbr.*] Milano (Lombardy). Pre-adhesive postmark.

milhão [*Port.*] million.

milímetro (*m.*) [*Span., Port.*] millimeter, millimetre.

milione [*Ital.*] million.

militært frimerke (*n.*) [*Nor.*] military postage stamp.

militaire postzegel (*m./c.*) [*Dut.*] military postage stamp.

militärfrimärke (*n.*) [*Swed.*] military postage stamp.

militärpost (*r.*) [*Swed.*] field post.

Militärpostmarke (*f.*) [*Ger.*] military postage stamp.

miljoen [*Dut.*] million.

miljoona [*Finn.*] million.

mille [*Fr., Ital.*] thousand.

millésime [*Fr.*] A single-digit number representing the year of printing. It is found between the panes at the second row of French stamps printed in the format of six panes of 25 stamps per sheet. It was used from 1890 to 1926. Philatelic pieces showing the *millésime* are collected by French specialists as a cross-gutter piece: stamp, gutter with number, stamp. Also see *coin daté*.

Although the word *millésime* can be translated into most European languages, it has no equivalent in English and is traditionally written in its French form by English speakers.

[Contributed by John E. Lievsay.]

millimetri [*Finn.*] millimeter, millimetre.

millimetro (*m.*) [*Ital.*] millimeter, millimetre.

millió [*Hun.*] million.

miniatyrark (*n.*) [*Swed.*] souvenir sheet.

minimibud (*n.*) [*Swed.*] minimum bid.

minimum bid The lowest acceptable bid as determined by the seller in an auction or mail bid sale.

minimum müzayede değeri [*Turk.*] protective reserve bid.

minimumsbud (*n.*) [*Dan.*] minimum bid.

minne- [*Nor.*] commemorative.

minnes- [*Swed.*] commemorative.

minnesblock (*n.*) [*Swed.*] souvenir sheet.

minstebud (*n.*) [*Nor.*] minimum bid.

minstepris (*m.*) [*Nor.*] minimum price; protective reserve bid.

minta [*Hun.*] design; specimen.

Mir; Mira [*Ital. abbr.*] Mirandola (Italy). Abbreviations used as pre-adhesive postmarks.

Mis.; Miss. [*abbr.*] Mississippi (pre-adhesive postmarks from the U.S.).

mise (*f.*) [*Fr.*] (auction) bid.

mise ajoutée; mise de protection [*Fr.*] protective reserve bid.

mise-en-train [*Fr.*] Cut impressions of stamps, some in special colors, used in the pressbed by the printer to get uniform clarity of detail. It is also known as *découpage* in French and is called *makeready* or *patching* in English.

[Contributed by John E. Lievsay.]

mise suggérée (*f.*) [*Fr.*] suggested bid.

miso μισό (*n.; adj.*) [*Grk.*] half.

misperfs: Guatemala and the United States

misperf Shortened form of *misperforation*. Any misalignment of the perforation on a stamp. This is regarded as a freak rather than an error because it is usually a random happening and does not create a major variety. A *boardwalk margin*[q.v.] is the effect seen on an oversized stamp with a normal-size image but an unusually wide margin caused by incorrect perfing.

Missing Virgin Nickname given to one of the greatest rarities of West Indian philately. In 1890, twenty-three years after its issuance, the British Virgin Islands 1 shilling error (with the letterpress-printed figure of the Virgin omitted, Scott 8c) was discovered in London in the old Booksellers Row. The stunning error, of which only a handful exist, soon received its nickname.

In describing the rare stamp, Harmers stated that five copies of the "Missing Virgin" are known to exist, one of which resides in the collection of Her Majesty Queen Elizabeth II. All five specimens have trimmed edges on one or two sides.

Virgins: Missing and normal (B.V.I.)

However, other sources, including Vernon Pickering's *Early History of the British Virgin Islands* and British specialist William Frazer indicate that seven copies of this stamp are known to exist. Some experts insist that the discrepancy stems from re-counting the same item twice.

As to the real status of this rarity, there are many conflicting opinions. The Stanley Gibbons catalogue listed it in 1897 as an "error" but omitted it in its 1900 edition. In 1911 it was described as a printer's trial, and by 1923 it had re-gained its status as an "error." Sir John Wilson in his opus on the Royal Philatelic Collection placed the stamp in the "unissued" category.

Fred J. Melville, one of the early scholars of British Virgin Islands philately and a famous stamp writer, describes the rarity as a "proof"; L.N. and M. Williams tend to agree with Melville, while Yardley— an ardent collector of the turn of the century— said that this variety was not issued and refers to it as a printer's waste. Robson Lowe, the eminent author of the Encyclopædia of Empire Postage Stamps, has revealed that he had "always thought that at least some of the Missing Virgins were proofs as [he] found a copy in a collection of proofs which had no issued stamps." Norman Williams believes that the Missing Virgin was a perforation trial.

In any event, the "freak" probably occurred when two stamp sheets got stuck together during the printing process, thus causing the underlying sheet not to receive the impression of the Virgin. In actuality, the central figure of the Virgin was typographed in black as a second and last operation after the stamp sheet had been printed with the background consisting of sun's rays enclosed by a crimson border.

[Contributed by Giorgio Migliavacca. L. N. Williams, "The mystery of the Missing Virgin," in *Stamps*, London, August 1987, vol. 4, no. 4, pp. 37-39; Giorgio Migliavacca, "West Indian Stamps continue to attract new collectors," in *Stamps* (U.S.A.). vol. 249, #9, November 26, 1994; Giorgio Migliavacca, "The magic of West Indian stamps: Rarity and Beauty," *Liat Islander* (London/Antigua), #35, May 1995, pp. 27-30; Vernon Pickering, *Early History of the British Virgin Islands. Missing Virgin* photo courtesy Harmers of London.]

Missionary stamp Common name of 1851 stamps of Hawaii. They are so-named because they are almost always found on correspondence from American missionaries in Hawaii to their friends back in the United States. The stamps were issued in denominations of 2c, 5c, and 13c.

The 2c stamps of this series were printed as newspaper stamps to be used on newspapers and other printed material sent to the U.S. mainland. Very few were used and even fewer were saved. Only fifteen specimens are known to survive, making this one of the world's great philatelic rarities.

mit [*Ger.*] with.

mitad (*f.*) [*Span.*] half (the fraction).

mitätöinti [*Finn.*] cancellation.

Mittigkeit (*f.*) [*Ger.*] centering.

mivkhar מִבְחָר (*m.*) [*Heb.*] variety.

mixed franking; mixed usage A cover exhibiting postage that has been prepaid with stamps of more than one issuing authority. See *combination usage.*

m'khir מְחִיר (*m.*) [*Heb.*] price.

m'khiron מְחִירוֹן (*m.*) [*Heb.*] price list.

ML [*Span. abbr.*] Málaga (Spain). Pre-adhesive postmark.

M.L. [*abbr.*] maple leaf.

MM [*Ital. abbr.*] Milano (Lombardy). The letters are shown in the form of a monogram and used as a pre-adhesive postmark.

Mo [*abbr.*] Current postal designation for the state of Missouri (U.S.A.). It has also been used as a pre-adhesive postmark.

Mod; Moda [*Ital. abbr.*] Modena (Italy). Pre-adhesive postmarks.

modası geçmiş [*Turk.*] obsolete.

modificare (*f.*) [*Rom.*] modification; alteration.

modification (*f.*) [*Fr.*] modification; alteration.

modulo di offerta [*Ital.*] bid sheet.

modulo d'ordine [*Ital.*] order form.

mois (*m.*) [*Fr.*] month.

moitié (*f.*) [*Fr.*] half (the fraction).

Moldavian Bull

Moldavian Bull Popular name of the Romanian 27, 54, 81, and 108 parale stamps, issued by the principality of Moldavia on July 15, 1858. The design shows Romania's coat of arms (an ox head and a post horn) in a circle inscribed ПОРТО СКРИСОРИ (Letter Postage). Although collectors have nicknamed these stamps the Moldavian *Bulls*, in actuality the animal depicted is an aurock, an extinct ox which once lived in Eastern Europe.

The stamps were printed in mini-sheets of thirty-two stamps (four horizontal rows of eight stamps). Yet the press was so small that it could only print two rows at a time, requiring that the paper be turned around for the second printing. Thus, the finished sheets had eight vertical *tête-bêche* pairs in the middle. Only one such configured pair is known to have been postally used.

This stamp is one of the world's great rarities. A total of 6,016 27p specimens were printed before a rate change late in 1858 caused them to be discontinued. Some 2,325 were destroyed. Of the 3,691 specimens sold for postage, fewer than one hundred are known to survive today.

Molly Pitcher overprint

Molly Pitcher overprint Often called the "poor man's commemorative." Standard U.S. 2c definitives were overprinted with the words *MOLLY PITCHER* in 1928 to honor the 150th anniversary of the Battle of Monmouth, New Jersey, fought during America's Revolutionary War, and especially to honor Molly Pitcher, the heroine of the battle. The resulting stamps appeared cheap and tacky. The consensus of opinion was that the stamps were an inappropriate way to honor anyone. Mercifully, this concept has long since been discarded.

Mon [*abbr.*] Monmouth. Abbreviation used as a pre-adhesive postmark.

monada chrimaton μονάδα χρημάτων [*Grk.*] denomination.

monadikos μαναδικός [*Grk.*] unique.

Monat (*m.*) [*Ger.*] month.

money order stamp See *postal money order stamp*.

money of account Unit of currenty or denomination of money which exists only for accounting purposes. There are usually no postage stamps issued in those amounts.

An example is the *mill*, a sum equal to one-tenth of a U.S. cent or one-thousandth of a dollar. This unit of money is seen frequently in financial and legal documents but has never been used as the denomination of a U.S. stamp, even though stamps denominated at 1/2 cent, 1 1/4 cents, 2 1/2 cents, etc., have been issued.

An example that is even more well known is the British *guinea*, a sum equal to 21 shillings (whereas the old pound sterling consisted of 20 shillings). Although coins were issued in that denomination at one time, the modern use of that unit was strictly as money of account. Until the adoption of the new pound in 1970, prices of luxury items were quoted in guineas rather than pounds to give the seller a five percent bonus.

monograms: Netherlands & British Virgin Islands

monogram Symbol of a king or queen, usually a crowned version of the monarch's initials.

The first illustrated stamp is somewhat unusual because it shows the monogram of a university. The crowned *AG* represents the University of Groningen in The Netherlands. The stamp honors that institution's 350th anniversary.

The second stamp is more traditional. The crowned E[II]R is the monogram of Queen Elizabeth II (*Elizabeth II Regina*). This symbol is often seen on stamps issued by British colonies, in this case British Virgin Islands.

montant (*m.*) [*Fr.*] amount.

Montenegro [Italian and German occupations] Italian troops occupied Montenegro in April 1941. Overprints on fourteen Yugoslav definitive stamps with the Italian and Serbo-Croatian versions of the province's name were issued on June 13, 1941. The Serbo-Croatian inscription includes the date of the invasion— April 17, 1941— and the year of the fascist era— XIX.

Montenegro overprint on Yugoslav stamp

The same haste, inexperience, and wartime shortages in local printing establishments that produced overprint errors and varieties in Lubiana and later in Zara[*q.v.*] also resulted in constant varieties here. Only the low denominations were on sale at the post office; the bulk of the entire issue was held back and later sold to stamp dealers at a high premium with the excuse that the proceeds were to benefit the country.

ЦРНА ГОРА ("Monte Negro")
o/p on Italian stamp

To add insult to injury, in June nine definitives, one airmail, and five postage dues were overprinted in Cyrillic with the inscription ЦРНА ГОРА (*CRNA GORA*, "Monte Negro"). The bilingual wording of the first overprint featuring the fascist year, followed by overprints on stamps depicting the Italian monarch, hurt national sensitivies of Montenegrins, and a new approach had to be implemented. Queen Helena (*née* Petrović), the consort of King Victor Emmanuel III, was also a Montenegrin, and a special administrative arrangement had to be adopted.

both sides of one of the 10 stamps celebrating
the Montenegrin national poem

On October 3, 1941, Mussolini issued a special decree making Montenegro an Italian Governorship. The special status on Montenegro under Italian occupation is also reflected by its stamps, which include a set issued on May 25, 1943, commemorating Prince Bishop Petrovič Njegoš, author of the Montenegrin national poem. Each of the ten stamps bore a few lines of the poem inscribed on the back. Undoubtedly Queen Helena had a lot of influence in all of this, and having a famous Sicilian stamp collector at the top of the newly-established Governorship made things easier. Earlier issues include the four 1940 Legionnaire stamps of Yugoslavia overprinted in January 1942 with the inscription *Governatorato/ dell Montenegro/ Valore in Lire*. This set exists with the scarcer black overprint as well as with the overprint in red; 100 and 200 sets respectively were overprinted. The same situation relates to the Yugoslav Red Cross airmail stamps of 1940, overprinted on January 9, 1942, with the inscription *Governatorato/ dell Montenegro* for one series in black and another series in red, 400 and 200 sets respectively.

King Peter definitives were used again in 1942 to produce a 9-stamp set overprinted

Governatorato/ dell Montenegro/ Valore LIRE in black. The 1 din(ar) is known with a slightly different overprint where the word *LIRE* is noticeably smaller. This rare variety is believed to have originated from a printers' test sheet that was inadvertently left in the stockpile supplied to the post office. Additionally, eleven denominations of the same definitive series received the same overprint in red. The first signs of rebellion came as early as July 13, 1941, when Montenegrin partisans shot up an Italian convoy near Kolasin and besieged garrisons at Danilovgrad and Bioca. A more massive attack came in May 1942.

Deutsche Militaer- Verwaltung Montenegro overprint

In September 1943, following the announcement that Italy had signed an armistice with the Allies, the Germans took over the territory. In December, the on-duty German Field Postmaster overprinted five of Italy's ten-value regular occupation issues (Scott 2N37-41) and five of the six airmail issues (Scott 2NC18-22) with *Nationaler/ Verwaltungsausschuß/ 10.XI.1943* three-line overprint. Prior to that time (November 22), nine Yugoslav 1939-40 King Peter stamps (five 3 dinar and four 4 dinar values) were overprinted with new values in Italian lire and with the inscription *Deutsche/ Militaer-/ Verwaltung/ Montenegro*. These overprints were executed by Obod, the Montenegrin state printers in Cetinje. In addition, the Field Postmaster authorized four separate semi-postal and two airmail semi-postal sets in 1944 bearing a *Crveni krst/ Montenegro* overprint with a red cross and new value, and also a *Flüchtlingshilfe/ Montenegro* overprint as provisional charity issues in aid of war refugees. Montenegro was liberated in November 1944 by partisan troops under Marshal Tito.

[Contributed by Giorgio Migliavacca.]

møntenhed (c.) [*Dan.*] monetary unit; denomination.

Montev.; Mont:vo [*Span. abbr.*] Montevideo (Uruguay). Pre-adhesive postmarks.

month Very few stamps show the month as well as the year of issue. One of the few exceptions is the date on the Vatican's September 1978 *sede vacante*[*q.v.*] coins. The month was needed because two popes died within the same calendar year. The stamps dated simply 1978 (in roman numerals) were in honor of Pope Paul VI; the second issue dated September 1978 (*Sett. 1978*) were specifically in memory of John Paul I.

M.O.P. [*abbr.*] Military Post Office.

MQE. [*abbr.*] Martinique.

morado [*Span.*] purple.

moreno [*Span.*] brown.

mörk [*Swed.*] dark.

mørk [*Nor., Dan.*] dark.

mørkebrun [*Dan.*] bister.

"MORTE" inscription

MORTE/ ai Tedeschi invasori/ e Fascisti traditori! *DEATH to the invading Germans and Fascist traitors!* Inscription/overprint on Alto Varessotto C.L.N. issues of Italy. See *C.L.N.*

mostra (f.) [*Ital.*] exhibition.

Mo. T. [*abbr.*] Missouri Territory. Pre-adhesive postmark.

mot etterkrav [*Nor.*] cash on delivery (C.O.D.).

motif (m.) [*Fr.*] design.

motsa מוֹצָא (m.) [*Heb.*] pedigree, provenance (list of previous and present owners).

mourning cover Cover with a special cachet commemorating the death of a famous person. See *memorial cover.*

mourning stamps: Hindenburg, George II, Queen Astrid

mourning stamp Postage stamp showing an inscribed or overprinted black border or other symbolic device to memorialize a person who has recently died. This procedure is often done for people who appear on stamps at the time of their death. The illustration shows three of the most famous example: Von Hindenburg (Germany, 1934), King George II (Greece, 1947), and Queen Astrid (Belgium, 1935).

M.R.C. overprint (Argentina)

M.R.C. [*Span. abbr.*] *Ministerio de Relaciones Culturales* (Ministry of Cultural Relations). Overprint on 1913-1939 official stamps of Argentina.

Mss. [*abbr.*] Massachussetts (pre-adhesive postmark from the U.S.).

Mt [*abbr., various languages*] Mount. Among its philatelic applications, it has been used as a pre-adhesive postmark.

M.T. Abbreviation used as a pre-adhesive postmark (U.S.): Michigan Territory; Minnesota; Mississippi Territory; Missouri Territory.

muestra (*f.*) [*Span.*] specimen.

muisto- (*adj.*) [*Finn.*] commemorative.

muistoarkki [*Finn.*] souvenir sheet.

muotoilu [*Finn.*] design.

musical notation: Jaime Laredo [*la-re-do*] (Bolivia)

musical notation: *O Canada*

musical notation 1. Two series of 1960 Bolivian stamps (six regular and six airmails) honoring Bolivian violinist Jaime Laredo are unique, because Laredo's name is written in musical notation instead of in words. If a diatonic scale (do-re-mi-fa-sol-la-ti-do) is sung in the key of C, then the name Laredo ("la-re-do") is written on a musical staff as the notes A-D-C. This is exactly how they appear on the stamps.

2. Stamp device consisting of a portion of a musical work, a technique used occasionally to honor great composers or famous musical works. The illustrated *se-tenant* pair highlights three Canadian composers on one stamp and features the first four notes of Canada's national anthem, *O Canada*, on the other.

In 1956, East Germany issued two commemorative stamps to honor composer Robert Schumann. Included in the stamps' background was a piece of his music. But a work of Franz Shubert was used by mistake. A corrected version was released a month later.

musta [*Finn.*] black.

muste [*Finn.*] ink.

Muster (*n.*) [*Ger.*] specimen.

mutsmad מְצֻמָּד [*Heb.*] accolated, conjoined[*q.v.*].

müzayede ile satış [*Turk.*] auction sale.

M.V.i.R. overprint (Romania)

M.V.i.R. [*Ger. abbr.*] *Militar Verwaltung in Rumanien* (Military Administration in Romania).

mycophilately A thematic branch of philately devoted to collecting and studying stamps featuring mushrooms, fungi, mycologists, and related areas.

The term was first used in the 1970s by Giorgio Migliavacca and later adapted when he published a short-lived magazine titled *Mycophilatelia*. Mushrooms have been featured on a number of recent stamps, postmarks, and postal stationery. In 1948, Japan issued a 5 yen stamp featuring distillery towers and stylized yeast cells (*Saccharomyces*); more familiar fungi appeared on stamps issued ten years later by Romania. Since then, just about every country has issued stamps featuring mushrooms. Russia, Romania, and several other countries have also issued postal stationery depicting mushrooms. Italy, France, Czechoslovakia, Spain, and various other postal authorities from time to time have adopted postmarks celebrating mycological events such as forays, fairs, congresses, etc.

In 1991 Stanley Gibbons published a thematic catalogue titled *Collect Fungi on Stamps* which lists all known stamps depicting mushrooms. The standard listing is then followed by a fungal species section which allows collectors to identify from either the English name or the systematic (mycological)

maximum card showing an example of mycophilately

name those stamps which have illustrated a specific type of fungus. Lichens and mycorrhizas are treated in separate sections of the catalogue.

Catalogues devoted entirely to stamps, postmarks, and postal stationery featuring mushrooms or fungi-related topics have been published in Italy (the Modolo and Gatti catalogues), France, Germany (Arnold catalogue), Spain, and Czechoslovakia. Thematic/topical associations such as the American Topical Association and their French, German, and Italian counterparts include units of mycophilatelists.

myyjä [*Finn.*] seller.

myyntiarkki [*Finn.*] pane (of stamps).

N n

N Abbreviation used as a pre-adhesive postmark: [with crown] Nantes (France); Newport (England); Norfolk (England).

nabywca (*m.*) [*Pol.*] buyer.

Nachdruck (*m.*) [*Ger.*] reprint; reproduction.

Nachgebühr (*f.*) [*Ger.*] postage due.

nachgummiert [*Ger.*] regummed.

Nachnahme (*f.*) [*Ger.*] cash on delivery (C.O.D.).

nacinanie (*n.*) [*Pol.*] roulette, *perçage*.

nacinanie krzyżowe (*n.*) [*Pol.*] lozenge roulette.

nacinanie serpentynowe (*n.*) [*Pol.*] serpentine roulette.

nacinanie zygzakowate (*n.*) [*Pol.*] zigzag roulette; serrated roulette.

nacinany [*Pol.*] rouletted, *percé*.

nacionalidad (*f.*) [*Span.*] nationality.

naderwanie (*n.*) [*Pol.*] a tear (as in a stamp or cover).

naderwany [*Pol.*] torn.

nadir [*Turk.*] rare, scarce.

nadruk (*m.*) [*Pol.*] overprint.

nagy [*Hun.*] large.

Nagy-Britannia [*Hun.*] Great Britain.

nagyító [*Hun.*] magnifying glass.

nahezu [*Ger.*] almost.

najniższa cena (*f.*) [*Pol.*] minimum bid.

nakit [*Turk.*] cash (ready money).

na lewo [*Pol.*] left (direction or position).

nåltandning (*r.*) [*Swed.*] pin perforation, *percé en points*.

namaak (*m.-c.*) [*Dut.*] imitation.

namaaksel (*n.*) [*Dut.*] a fake.

não [*Port.*] no; not.

não classificado [*Port.*] not classified; unattributed.

não denteado [*Port.*] imperforate.

não emitido [*Port.*] not issued.

não publicado [*Port.*] unpublished (not listed in any book or catalogue).

não se aceitam propostas sem limites [*Port.*] no unlimited bids accepted.

Nap; Napli [*Ital. abbr.*] Naples (Italy). Pre-adhesive postmarks.

napis (*m.*) [*Pol.*] inscription.

Napoléon Name of two French rulers and one pretender.

1. Napoléon I [né *Napoleone*, translated in French to *Napoléon Bonaparte*; nicknamed *Le Petit Caporal*, the "Little Corporal."] Military leader and self-proclaimed emperor of France. Born August 15, 1769, in Ajaccio on the island of Corsica; died May 5, 1821, at Longwood on St. Helena.

Napoléon Bonaparte's presence in philately is essentially limited to his appearance on a few twentieth-century commemorative stamps.

2. Napoléon II [né *Napoléon Francis Joseph Charles* (1811-1832); nicknamed *l'Aiglon* ("Little Eagle")]. Son of Napoléon Bonaparte and his second wife Marie Louise, daughter of Francis I of Austria. Napoléon II was a pretender to the throne who never took power, and he played virtually no role in philately.

3. Napoléon III [né *Louis Napoléon Bonaparte*.] French emperor. Born April 20, 1808, in Paris; died in exile on January 9, 1873, at Chislehurst, England.

Napoléon III was the son of King Louis and Queen Hortense of Holland, and was thus a nephew of Napoléon Bonaparte. Because the Bonaparte family was banished from France, the young Louis Napoléon was educated in Switzerland and Bavaria.

He was sentenced to life in prison for two unsuccessful attempts to overthrow the French government of King Louis Philippe but escaped in 1846. When Louis Philippe was ousted in 1848, Louis Napoléon ran for the presidency of the new French republic and won an astonishing victory. When the new French constitution forbade him to run for a second 4-year term, he assumed dictatorial powers and extended his term to ten years. By 1852 he had gained enough personal support to re-establish the French Empire and to name himself Emperor Napoléon III (Napoléon Bonaparte's son had been accorded the title *Napoléon II*; see #2 above).

Napoléon III's rule is generally regarded as having been a failure, both for his domestic policies and especially because he led France to a devastating loss in the Franco-Prussian War of 1870. His regime was overthrown on September 4, 1870, and he died in exile in England in 1873.

Although Louis Napoléon's likeness appears on many of the French stamps issued from 1852 until 1871, his real philatelic legacy did not really materialize until long after his death. When he failed to defeat the Prussians in 1870, they imposed a huge war indemnification on France which nearly bankrupted the country. The French did not forget this. A half century later, France convinced its allies to impose enormous payments on Germany and Austria after World War I. This helped create the hyperinflation of the early 1920s which resulted in the issuance of stamps with outrageously huge values (e.g., 50 *billion* marks).

[Contributed by Ruth Ann Davis. *Compton's Encyclopedia and Fact Index*, Vol. 17, pp. 8-13 et al.]

na prawo [*Pol.*] right (direction or position).

narodowość (*f.*) [*Pol.*] nationality.

narodowy [*Pol.*] national.

Nash. [*abbr.*] Nashville (Tennessee, U.S.A.). Pre-adhesive postmark.

Nationaler Verwaltungsausschuß [*Ger.*] National Administration Committee. German overprint produced in 1943 on Italian stamps. See *Montenegro*.

Nationalität (*f.*) [*Ger.*] nationality.

nationaliteit (*f.-c.*) [*Dut.*] nationality.

nationalitet (*r.*) [*Swed.*] nationality.

naula [*Finn.*] pound (16 ounces). [Pound Sterling (£) is *punta*.]

näyte [*Finn.*] specimen.

näyttely [*Finn.*] exhibition.

nazionale [*Ital.*] national.

nazionalità (*f.*) [*Ital.*] nationality.

N.B. [*abbr.*] New Brunswick (Canada). Among its various postal applications, it is an abbreviation used as a pre-adhesive postmark.

N.C. [*abbr.*] Current postal designation for the state of North Carolina (U.S.A.). It was also used as a pre-adhesive postmark.

N-C.E. [*Fr. abbr.*] *Nouvelle-Caledonie* (New Caledonia).

N. Dorog [*Hun. abbr.*] Nagy Dorog (Hungary). Pre-adhesive postmark.

neatribuit; nedeterminat [*Rom.*] unattributed.

necunoscut [*Rom.*] unknown.

Nederland [*Dut.*] The Netherlands. The official Dutch name *Koninkrijk der Nederlanden.*

Nederländerna [*Swed.*] Netherlands, Holland.

ne-emis [*Rom.*] not issued.

negen [*Dut.*] nine.

negentig [*Dut.*] ninety.

negro [*Span.*] black.

negru [*Rom.*] black.

négy [*Hun.*] four.

negyed [*Hun.*] fourth, quarter.

négyszögletes [*Hun.*] rectangular; square.

negyven [*Hun.*] forty.

N.E.I. [*abbr.*] Netherlands East Indies.

nelikulmainen [*Finn.*] square.

neljä [*Finn.*] four.

neljäkymmentä [*Finn.*] forty.

neljäsosa [*Finn.*] fourth; quarter.

Németország [*Hun.*] Germany.

nem hivatalos [*Hun.*] unofficial.

nemzeti [*Hun.*] national.

nemzetközi [*Hun.*] international.

Nennwert (*m.*) [*Ger.*] denomination; face value.

neoficial [*Rom.*] unofficial.

nepublicat [*Rom.*] unpublished.

neregulat [*Rom.*] irregular.

nero [*Ital.*] black.

nesher נֶשֶׁר (*m.*) [*Heb.*] eagle.

net price A price that cannot be further discounted.

netwerk (*n.*) [*Dut.*] *burélage, burelé.*

neu [*Ger.*] new.

Neudorf [*Ger. abbr.*] Wiener Neudorf (Austria). Pre-adhesive postmark.

neuf [*Fr.*] nine; new.

neuf sans charnière [*Fr.*] never hinged.

neun [*Ger.*] nine.

Neuseeland [*Ger.*] New Zealand.

Neuvostoliitto [*Finn.*] Soviet Union.

newspaper stamps: Bosnia-Herzegovina & U.S.

newspaper stamp Special postage stamp used for sending newspapers and other printed materials through the mail. In some cases, part of the cost of the stamp has been applied to a news tax, thus making the stamps both postal and revenue in nature.

The first newspaper stamp was put out by Austria in 1851. The first U.S. newspaper stamp (1965) was an incredible 51mm x 95mm in size, making it one of the largest stamp of any kind ever issued. In 1875 the size was reduced to that of the stamp in the illustration. These smaller stamps featuring female allegorical figures were used until newspaper stamps were discontinued in the United States in 1898.

The stamp of Bosnia & Herzegovina in the illustration served a double purpose. When issued perforated, it was a standard postage stamp; when issued imperforate, it was intended for newspapers. Under either circumstance, it is a difficult stamp for collectors to identify because it has no written inscription to indicate its issuing agency, just as the earliest newspaper stamps from Austria bore no identifying inscription.

[Kenneth A. Wood, *This Is Philately*, Vol. III, pp. 736-37.]

N.F. [*o/p*] Nyasa-Rhodesian Force. Overprinted on stamps of Nyasaland Protectorate for the temporary occupation of German East Aftrica (1916).

NFF [*abbr.*] Natal Field Force.

ngày tháng [*Viet.*] date.

NGR [*abbr.*] Natal Government Railways. Punch-perfed on stamps of Natal.

Niag. [*abbr.*] Niagara (U.S./Canada). Pre-adhesive postmark.

postage currency of Nicholas II (Russia)

Nicholas II [né *Nicholas Alexandrovich Romanov*] Last czar (or *tsar*) of Russia, and the only czar who played any significant role in philately. Born May 18, 1868, in St. Petersburg, Russia, to Czar Alexander III and Marie Fyodorovna; died by execution on July 16, 1918.

Nicholas II became czar in 1894 upon the death of his father. His wife was Princess Alix of Hesse-Darmstadt who took the name of Alexandra Fyodorovna. The couple had one son and four daughters.

Though ill-prepared politically and militarily, Nicholas II ruled from 1894 to 1917. After his military defeat by Japan, he took little notice of the many warnings he received of future trouble such as the student riots of St. Petersburg in 1899, and the rebellions all over the country that began in 1905 due to the harsh conditions under which the peasants and city dwellers lived. As a result of the unrest, Nicholas issued a manifest on October 30, 1905, in which he promised to establish an elected legislative body— the State Duma— and guaranteed civil liberties to his subjects.

During the reign of Nicholas II, Russia became a major industrial power; science, music, and literature flourished; and the Trans-Siberian railroad was completed. In 1914 Russia entered World War I, largely to help defend its Slavic neighbor Serbia. Military losses, the threat of famine, and the disorganization of the economy led to the riots of 1917. The communist uprising was lead by Lenin and Trotsky and began on October 25, 1917. Nicholas and his family were held under house arrest, and were executed on July 16, 1918, thus ending the rule of the czars.

Alexander III, Nicholas's father, had left a very minor philatelic legacy by only issuing stamps showing the royal crest. The greatest challenge to philatelists is to tell the difference between early Russian and early Finnish issues.

Nicholas, however, issued a series of definitive stamps honoring many of Russia's heroes. Some of the stamps in that series also feature some of that nation's great architectural treasures, such as the Kremlin, the Winter Palace, and the Romanov Castle.

A severe coin shortage in the 1910s forced Nicholas to issue small pieces of currency that resembled postage stamps and, in fact, were printed with stamp dies. These *postage currency*[q.v.] notes were identical to the stamps of its day on the face but were printed on thin cardboard, were left ungummed, and exhibited an inscription on the back stating that the pieces were to be used as a substitute for small silver coins. The presence of the royal insignia gave them legitimacy. Some people mistakenly glued the notes to envelopes and used them as postage stamps.

[Contributed by Ruth Ann Davis. Frank W. Weis, *Lifelines: Famous Contemporaries from 600 B.C. to 1975*, p. 373; Duncan M. White (editor), *Caesar to Churchill: The Years of Fulfillment*; Chester L. Krause and Clifford Mishler, *Standard Catalog of World Coins* (1985), p. 1804.]

nicht amtlich [*Ger.*] unofficial.

nicht ausgegeben [*Ger.*] not issued.

nicht zugeschrieben [*Ger.*] unattributed.

niebieski [*Pol.*] blue.

niedoręczalny [*Pol.*] undeliverable.

Niedrigstgebot (*f.*) [*Ger.*] minimum bid.

nie gefalzt [*Ger.*] never hinged.

niegumowany [*Pol.*] ungummed.

niekompletny [*Pol.*] incomplete.

Niemcy [*Pol.*] Germany.

Niemcy Wschodnie [*Pol.*] East Germany (D.D.R.).

Niemcy Zachodnie [*Pol.*] West Germany (B.R.D.).

nieoddzielony [*Pol.*] unsevered.

nieoficjalny; nieurzędowy [*Pol.*] unofficial.

nieokreślony [*Pol.*] unattributed.

nieperforowany [*Pol.*] imperforate.

nie przyjmuje się zleceń bez limitu [*Pol.*] no unlimited bids accepted.

niepublikowany [*Pol.*] unpublished (not listed in any book or catalogue).

nieregularny; nietypowy [*Pol.*] irregular.

niet afgescheurd [*Dut.*] unsevered.

niet compleet [*Dut.*] incomplete.

niet gepubliceerd [*Dut.*] unpublished (not listed in any book or catalogue).

niet toegeschreven [*Dut.*] unattributed.

niet uitgegeven [*Dut.*] not issued.

nieuw [*Dut.*] new.

Nieuw-Zeeland [*Dut.*] New Zealand.

nieużywany [*Pol.*] unused.

nie wprowadzony do obiegu [*Pol.*] not issued.

nieząbkowany [*Pol.*] imperforate.

nieznany [*Pol.*] unknown.

nimellisarvo [*Finn.*] denomination; face value.

nimikirjoitus [*Finn.*] signature.

nio [*Swed.*] nine.

Nippon [*Jpn.*] Romanized word for Japan. As per current U.P.U. regulations, *Nippon* is now printed on Japanese stamps.

Nisan [*Turk.*] April.

NISIROS; NISIRO Overprints on Italian stamps used on the Dodecanese island of Nisiros. See *Aegean Islands*.

nitti [*Nor.*] ninety.

nittio [*Swed.*] ninety.

N.J. [*abbr.*] Current postal designation for the state of New Jersey (U.S.A.). It has also been used as a pre-adhesive postmark.

N'Jork [*abbr.*] New York. Misspelled abbreviation used as a pre-adhesive postmark.

NL [*Dut. abbr.*] *Nederland* (Netherlands). 1. Dutch pre-adhesive postmark. 2. Overprinted with a surcharge on 1953 stamps of Denmark converting them to semipostals. Money raised from the surcharge was used to help Dutch flood victims.

no atribuido [*Span.*] unattributed.

noce [*Ital.*] chestnut (color).

no emitido [*Span.*] not issued.

no entregable [*Span.*] undeliverable.

no envelope [*Port.*] on cover. [Note: the Portuguese word *no* means "on the" in English; the English word "no" is translated into Portuguese as *não*.]

noir [*Fr.*] black.

noll [*Swed.*] zero.

nolla [*Finn.*] zero.

nominal номинал (*m.*) [*Russ.*] denomination.

nominal (*m.*) [*Pol.*] denomination.

nominale waarde (*f.-c.*) [*Dut.*] face value.

nominellt värde (*n.*) [*Swed.*] face value.

nomismatiki monada νομισματική μονάδα (*f.*) [*Grk.*] monetary unit.

non attribué [*Fr.*] unattributed.

non attribuito [*Ital.*] unattributed.

non catalogato [*Ital.*] unpublished (not listed in any book or catalogue).

non dentelé [*Fr.*] imperforate.

non dentellato [*Ital.*] imperforate.

non emesso [*Ital.*] not issued.

non-émis [*Fr.*] not issued.

non gommato [*Ital.*] ungummed.

non linguellato [*Ital.*] not hinged; never hinged.

non livrable [*Fr.*] undeliverable.

non publié [*Fr.*] unpublished (not listed in any book or catalogue).

non staccato [*Ital.*] unsevered.

noodzegel (*m./c.*) [*Dut.*] a provisional.

Noord-Ierland [*Dut.*] Northern Ireland.

Noorwegen [*Dut.*] Norway.

no publicado [*Span.*] unpublished (not listed in any book or catalogue).

Nordirland [*Ger., Swed., Dan.*] Northern Ireland.

Nord-Irland [*Nor.*] Northern Ireland.

Noreg [*Nor.*] Norway.

Norge [*Swed., Nor., Dan.*] Norway.

Norja [*Finn.*] Norway.

N. Orl. [*abbr.*] New Orleans (Louisiana, U.S.A.). Pre-adhesive postmark.

Noruega [*Span., Port.*] Norway.

Norvège [*Fr.*] Norway.

Norvegia [*Ital.*] Norway.

Norwegen [*Ger.*] Norway.

Norwegia [*Pol.*] Norway.

no se aceptan licitaciones sin límite; no se aceptan pujas sin límite [*Span.*] no unlimited bids accepted.

no separado [*Span.*] unsevered.

not issued 1. Postage stamp or other item which is produced by a government or other issuing agency but is never released to the public, such as the gasoline rationing coupons that the U.S. produced by the millions in the early 1970s but never distributed.

2. Anticipated items which the issuing agency fails to produce for whatever reason. In 1987 South Africa announced the imminent release of a commemorative stamp showing the name of God in Hebrew and Arabic. Because this was a strong violation of Jewish tradition, protests by Jews prompted the government to cancel the issuance.

nou [*Rom.*] new.

nouă [*Rom.*] nine.

nouăzeci [*Rom.*] ninety.

Noua Zeelandă [*Rom.*] New Zealand.

no unlimited bids accepted Bidders at an auction or mail bid sale are not permitted to offer to pay a percentage above the actual highest bid from the floor rather than to submit a specific bid themselves.

In the 1940s and '50s, unlimited bidding was popular with many multi-millionaire collectors, especially King Farouk of Egypt, who expected to purchase anything they bid on. The auctioneer would be told in advance that Farouk (or whomever) wanted a certain item on auction for his collection and that he would pay a specified percentage above the highest actual bid.

Unlimited bidding has two drawbacks. First, it creates great animosity among the bidders on the floor when they realize they cannot purchase the item no matter how high they bid. Secondly, what happens if *two* people place an unlimited bid on the same item? Obviously one of the unlimited bids has to be rejected, but whose? Farouk's bid was virtually always accepted because of his tremendous clout. He was such a "high roller" that no auction house dared offend him by rejecting his bid.

nouveau [*Fr.*] new.

Nouvelle-Zélande [*Fr.*] New Zealand.

novanta [*Ital.*] ninety.

Nova Zelândia [*Port.*] New Zealand.

nove [*Port., Ital.*] nine.

novembre [*Fr., Ital.*] November.

novembro [*Port.*] November.

noventa [*Span., Port.*] ninety.

noviembre [*Span.*] November.

novo [*Port.*] new.

Nowa Zelandia [*Pol.*] New Zealand.

nowodruk (*m.*) [*Pol.*] reprint.

N.P. [*abbr.*] Newport (Rhode Island, U.S.A.). Pre-adhesive postmark.

N.P.B. [*abbr.*] News Paper Branch. A London cancel seen on some early British stamps.

N.R. [*abbr.*] no record, no records.

N.S.W. [*abbr.*] New South Wales.

nuance (*f.*) [*Fr.*] shade (*re*: color).

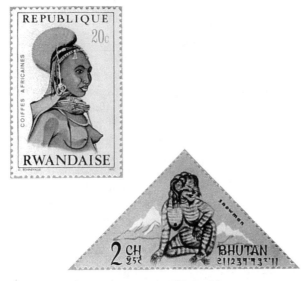

nudity on stamps: *Beauty* (Rwanda) .....
and the Beast (Bhutan)

nudity on stamps Nudity is a very popular feature of many postage stamps. More than forty nations have issued stamps showing some form of nudity, including many small countries that print stamps only to satisfy the demands of collectors.

Among the earliest stamps to exhibit nudity were the 1896 Greek stamps issued to commemorate the resumption of the Olympic Games[*q.v.*]. The portrayal of nude men on the stamps was logical, because male athletes did not wear clothing when they participated in the various Olympic events in ancient times. Women were neither permitted to participate nor were they even allowed to watch!

actual photo of topless woman (Eritrea)

In the days of the ancient Greeks and Romans, nudity appeared on works of art as a celebration of the human form. Similarly, nudity is often seen in the paintings and sculptures of the late Middle Ages and even into the twentieth century. Many of these works of art, classical to modern, appear on postage stamps. In most cases, the stamps are attractive and in good taste, and they have not generated a great deal of controversy.

Nudity is a common element on stamps issued by certain countries of Africa, Polynesia, and other parts of the world where the sight of a naked body is not as shocking as it is in the Western World, especially in English-speaking countries. The illustrated stamp of Rwanda showing a topless native woman might shock Americans, but it would not shock people from Rwanda. Yet even the citizens of Bhutan might be taken aback by the rather brutal portrayal of an Abominable Snowman on some of their stamps.

The 1934 Eritrean stamp pictured here is unusual because it shows an actual photo of a topless young woman. This is one of the earliest examples of true nudity on stamps.

It is generally accepted, both in philately and numismatics, that the most outrageously graphic character ever to appear on a stamp, coin, or banknote is Tangaroa, the Polynesian god of creation and fertility. Cook Islands featured him in blatant frontal nudity on some popular postage stamps. But he received far more "exposure" by appearing on several different types of $1 coins struck from 1972 to 1996 and on the $3 note introduced in 1993. The back of the notes showed Ina, a naked sea maiden. The illustrated photo is taken from one of the $3 notes which, hard as it is to believe, actually circulated. Many people were offended by Tangaroa's appearance (especially since Queen Elizabeth's head appears on the other side of the $1 coins), but the stamps, coins, and banknotes were highly marketable and generated a considerable profit for Cook Islands' treasury. The design was abandoned in 1996, not because of public outcry but because the currency of Cook Islands became virtually worthless. The tiny nation now uses the money of New Zealand. Cook Islands still produces stamps and a few banknotes, but the designs are more subdued and much more "proper."

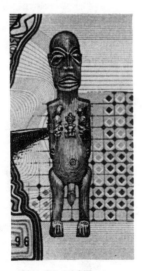

Cook Islands' Tangaroa

The two accompanying pages of illustrations of nude stamps reveal the wide range of styles and purposes. On the page titled *Female Nudity on Stamps*, all of the stamps except for the one from Spain are specialty stamps, mostly cancelled-to-order, intended for the lucrative philatelic market. Paraguay has issued many dozens of stamps featuring famous paintings, not all of which include nudity. Probably not too many of the stamps have actually seen postal use, but at least they were available for that purpose.

On the other hand, the stamps of Ajman, Manama (a dependency of Ajman), and Fujeira tell a very different tale. These shiekdoms, along with the other members of the United Arab Emirates (Dubai, Abu Dhabi, Sharjah, Umm al-Qiwain, and Ras al Khaima), had been guilty of creating a flood of agent-inspired collectors' stamps prior to the formation of the U.A.E. in 1971. Many of those stamps are unlisted in current catalogues because they have no real postal legitimacy. It is a true philatelic anomaly that so many stamps showing naked women would be issued by Moslem countries whose own female citizens are often required to wear veils and to be fully clothed while in public.

The illustrated Spanish stamp has seen much postal use. It features *La Maja Desnuda* ("The Naked *Maja*"), perhaps the most famous work of the Spanish painter Francisco de Goya. The *Maja* is regarded as a great Spanish treasure and currently resides in the Prado Museum in Madrid. Spanish stamps, not unlike Spaniards themselves, are somewhat conservative. *La Maja Desnuda* appears on Spanish stamps not because of its nudity but because of its magnificence.

The stamps on the page titled *Male Nudity on Stamps* cover a wide range of purposes. Frontal male nudity is seldom seen on stamps unless it is a reproduction of ancient art or unless the male figure is some sort of mythological god. The Costa Rican stamp would seemingly fall into the latter category, yet what it shows is little more than a piece of ancient Indian art.

The U.S. exhibition poster stamp in the illustration was certainly not intended for postal use, but it is probably the most "naked"

FEMALE NUDITY ON STAMPS

Ajman

Spain

Manama

Paraguay

Romania

Paraguay

Hungary

Fujeira

Romania

MALE NUDITY ON STAMPS

Hungary

Costa Rica

Hungary

U.S. (non-postal label)

Paraguay (male & female figures)

Canada

Poland

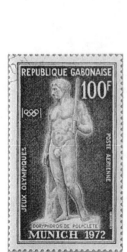

Gabon

Equatorial Guinea

Gabon

U.S. philatelic item a collector is apt to find. The United States and the Soviet Union, two of the most prolific producers of postage stamps, never issued any stamps that would legitimately fit into the category of nudity. Perhaps the U.S. never got over the fiasco created in 1916 when the U.S. mint began issuing quarter-dollar coins showing Miss Liberty with one breast exposed. The public outcry was so great that the mint redesigned the coins in 1917 and placed Liberty in a full suit of armor. The United States has not issued a coin, stamp, or note since that time showing even the slightest hint of nudity.

Canadian stamps have traditionally been quite conservative. The airmail stamp in the illustration shows the Greek mythological character Daedalus naked but properly draped.

The Polish stamp shows a scene from an ancient Greek vase. Its purpose is to honor the tenth session (1970) of the International Olympic Academy. The Gabon stamps feature more Greek art and were issued to commemorate the 1972 Olympic Games held in Munich. The stamps from Paraguay and Equatorial Guinea were prepared for collectors and saw little if any actual postal use.

The Hungarian stamp is perhaps the most interesting of the group. It was put out to honor the 1958 World's Fair held in Brussels, Belgium. The stamp shows the most famous tourist attraction in Brussels— the statue of a small boy urinating into a fountain. The reason why anyone would design something like this has been lost to history. All that is known for certain is that the boy has been relieving himself into that fountain for several hundred years. If such a thing were created today, the artist would probably be accused of dealing in child pornography. Yet the statue and the fountain hold a unique place in the realm of European art, and this bizarre stamp with the statue's likeness may well be the only postage stamp anywhere to show urination in progress.

[Contributed by James Oliver.]

Nueva Zelanda; Nueva Zelandia [*Span.*] New Zealand.

nueve [*Span.*] nine.

nuevo [*Span.*] new.

nul [*Dan., Dut.*] zero.

null [*Nor.*] zero.

Null (*f.*) [*Ger.*] zero.

număr (*n.*) [*Rom.*] number.

număr de serie (*n.*) [*Rom.*] serial number.

numer (*m.*) [*Pol.*] number.

numerar (*n.*) [*Rom.*] cash (ready money).

numero (*m.*) [*Ital.*]; [*Finn.*] number.

número (*m.*) [*Span., Port.*] number.

numéro (*m.*) [*Fr.*] number.

número de serie [*Span.*] serial number.

número de série [*Port.*] serial number.

numéro de série [*Fr.*] serial number.

numero di serie (*m.*) [*Ital.*] serial number.

numer serii (*m.*) [*Pol.*] serial number.

numismatics The examination and study of coins, banknotes, medals, tokens, and primitive forms of money. Numismatics has played an important role in philately because of the large number of postage stamps issued by dozens of countries which have featured coins, paper money, medals, and military decorations. There have also been times when postage stamps were used as emergency money (see *scrip* and *postage stamp currency*), when they were pictured on money (*postage currency*), or when they were attached to money (*first-day-of-issue note*). Occasionally, coin designs (*St. George Slaying the Dragon*) or coin designers (*Saint-Gaudens, Augustus*) have been featured on stamps.

nuovo [*Ital.*] new.

nußbraun [*Ger.*] bister (color).

ny [*Nor., Dan., Swed.*] new.

N.Y. [*abbr.*] Current postal designation for the state of New York (U.S.A.) and a common abbreviation for New York City. It has also been used as a pre-adhesive postmark.

nyans (*r.*) [*Swed.*] shade (*re:* color).

Nya Zeeland [*Swed.*] New Zealand.

nyelv [*Hun.*] language.

nyolc [*Hun.*] eight.

nyomtatni (*v.*) [*Hun.*] to print.

Nyugat-Németország [*Hun.*] West Germany (B.R.D.).

nyugta [*Hun.*] receipt.

nyutgåva (*r.*) [*Swed.*] reprint.

O o

O [*abbr.*] Ohio (U.S.A.). Pre-adhesive postmark.

O.A.S. [*abbr.*] On Active Service. Indication of free-franking privilege by military personnel on active duty.

O.A.T. [*abbr.*] Onward Air Transmission.

O.B. [*abbr.*] Official Business. Indicates official use (as the term is understood in philately).

O.B.C. [*Ger. abbr.*] *Österreichisch-Bayerische Correspondenz.* Abbreviation used as a pre-adhesive postmark. It was utilized in the 1840s on letters benefitting from a reduced postal rate as a result of the Austrian-Bavarian postal treaty. The postmark is also sometimes written *B.O.C.*

obcy [*Pol.*] foreign.

oben [*Ger.*] top.

obeställbar [*Swed.*] undeliverable.

obestämt [*Swed.*] unattributed.

obiegowy [*Pol.*] definitive.

obliteração por favor [*Port.*] cancelled to order.

obliterado à pena [*Port.*] pen cancelled.

obliteration 1. The part of the cancellation known as the *killer* that invalidates the stamp so that it cannot be reused for postage. The term is most commonly used when the cancellation is particularly heavy, thereby blackening out a sizable portion of the stamp's design.

2. An overprint, usually of heavy black lines, which defaces some part of the stamp's design. In most cases, the purpose is to block out the portrait of a deposed ruler so that the current stamps can be used until new ones are printed. Many stamps portraying Hitler received this treatment in 1945, as did Egyptian stamps in 1953 after the overthrow of King Farouk. Stamps with this overprint are also known as *barred* stamps. In 1925, the portrait of Ahmab

Shah was heavily obliterated on Iranian stamps to wipe out his effigy.

3. The blackening out of a non-current denomination accompanied by the overprinting of the new denomination (known as a *surcharge*).

oblitération (*f.*) [*Fr.*] cancellation (of a stamp); postmark; obliteration.

oblitération au poinçon [*Fr.*] punch cancellation.

oblitération par coupure [*Fr.*] cut cancellation.

obliterazione (*f.*) [*Ital.*] obliteration.

oblitéré à plume; oblitéré à stylo [*Fr.*] pen cancelled.

oblitéré de complaisance [*Fr.*] cancelled to order.

oblitérer (*v.*) [*Fr.*] to cancel.

Ocak [*Turk.*] January.

OCCUPAZIONE ITALIANA A 1942 overprint on stamps of Egypt to celebrate the Italian occupation of the Oasis of Siwa. It was privately applied and is of no legitimate philatelic interest.

ochenta [*Span.*] eighty.

ocho [*Span.*] eight.

octobre [*Fr.*] October.

octubre [*Span.*] October.

odcién (*m.*) [*Pol.*] shade (*re*: color).

ödemeli [*Turk.*] cash on delivery (C.O.D.).

odmiana (*f.*) [*Pol.*] variety.

odontomètre (*m.*) [*Fr.*] Name given to the first perforation gauge by its creator, Dr. J. A. Legrand, in the mid-1860s. See *perforation.*

odwrócony [*Pol.*] inverted.

oferi (*v.*) [*Rom.*] to offer.

oferować (*v.*) [*Pol.*] to offer.

oferta (*f.*) [*Span., Pol., Port.*] an offer, bid.

ofertă (*f.*) [*Rom.*] offer.

oferta cenowa (*f.*) [*Pol.*] (auction) bid.

ofertă de rezervă (pentru protecție) (*f.*) [*Rom.*] protective reserve bid.

oferta de salida (*f.*) [*Span.*] minimum bid.

oferta mínima (*f.*) [*Port.*] minimum bid.

oferta recomendada (*f.*) [*Span.*] suggested bid.

ofertă sugerată (*f.*) [*Rom.*] suggested bid.

oferta sugerida (*f.*) [*Port.*] suggested bid.

oferte nelimitate de licitație neacceptate [*Rom.*] no unlimited bids accepted.

offerera (*v.*) [*Swed.*] to offer.

offerta (*f.*) [*Ital.*] an offer.

offerta (ad un'asta) (*f.*) [*Ital.*] (auction) bid.

offerta minima (*f.*) [*Ital.*] minimum bid.

offerta minima di riserva [*Ital.*] protective reserve bid.

offerta suggerita (*f.*) [*Ital.*] suggested bid.

offerte illimitate sono proibite [*Ital.*] no unlimited bids accepted.

official stamps: Mexico (*o/p*); U.S. (adhesive & imprinted)

official stamp Stamp issued by a government for use by its own employees or agents when sending official government correspondence. The stamp may be in the form of an adhesive label or may be directly imprinted on an envelope (i.e., postal stationary). Some "officials" (as they are known) are sold in post offices while others are not.

The U.S. stamp at the left in the illustration clearly specifies that any unauthorized use will result in a penalty of $300. The official stamps of most countries do not include a legal warning, yet using them for private use usually leads to a punishment.

The illustration at the right is an imprinted stamp from a U.S. official stamped envelope dating back to the 1870s.

The Mexican stamp is a regular 1932 airmail stamp overprinted with the Spanish word *OFICIAL* to make it an official stamp.

officieel [*Dut.*] official.

officiële zegel (*m./c.*) [*Dut.*] official stamp.

officiell [*Swed.*] official.

offisiell [*Nor.*] official.

offre (*f.*) [*Fr.*] an offer; (auction) bid.

offre minimum (*f.*) [*Fr.*] minimum bid.

oficina de correos [*Span.*] post office.

oficjalny [*Pol.*] official.

o.g. [*abbr.*] original gum.

Ogn. [*abbr.*] Oregon (U.S.A.). Pre-adhesive postmark.

ogummerad [*Swed.*] ungummed.

O.H.B.M.S. [*o/p*] On His Britannic Majesty's Service. Overprinted in 1915 on German East African revenue stamps.

O.H.E.M.S. [*o/p*] On His Exalted Majesty's Service. Overprinted on Egypt's official stamps in 1922 and 1923.

O.H.H.S. [*o/p*] On His Highness's Service. Overprinted on Egypt's official stamps from 1907 to 1922.

O.H.M.S. *o/p* (Canada)

O.H.M.S. [*abbr.; o/p*] On Her [His] Majesty's Service. Indicator of official use. It can be found as an overprint on a stamp or rubber-stamped onto a cover. "O.H.M.S." was ultimately abandoned in favor of the single letter "G" (Government or *Gouvernement*) because of complaints from French Canadians who said that "O.H.M.S." had no meaning in French.

ohne Gummierung [*Ger.*] ungummed.

ohut kohta [*Finn.*] thin spot, skinned spot.

oikea [*Finn.*] right (direction or position).

okolicznościowy (*adj.*) [*Pol.*] commemorative.

oktober [*Dut., Nor., Dan., Swed.*] October.

Oktober [*Ger.*] October.

O.L. [*Fr. o/p*] *origine locale* (local origine). Overprinted as a control mark on stamps of Monaco.

Olanda [*Ital., Rom.*] Holland, Netherlands.

Olaszország [*Hun.*] Italy.

Olho-de-Boi [*Port.*] Bull's Eye[*q.v.*]. Popular name for the first three general-issue stamps of Brazil (1843), so named because of their resemblance to the eye of a bull. They were issued in denominations of 30, 60, and 90 réis.

Olho-de-Cabra [*Port.*] Goat's Eye. Common name for the third general issue of Brazilian stamps (1850). They are sometimes known as the "poor man's Bull's Eyes[*q.v.*]" because they are less scarce and less expensive than the 1843 issues.

Olho-de-Gato [*Port.*] Cat's Eye. Series of Brazilian stamps issued from 1854 to 1861 in the values of 10, 30, 280, and 430 réis. Because of their bright colors, they are also known as *Coloridos*.

olijfgroen [*Dut.*] olive green.

olimiterade bud accepteras ej [*Swed.*] no unlimited bids accepted.

oliv; olivgrün [*Ger.*] olive.

Oltre Giuba The area west of the River Juba, known as Jubaland (Oltre Giuba) and now forming the westernmost part of the Somali Republic (or what remains of it), had been explored by Germans and Italians in the nineteenth century and subsequently became a British possession. The acquisition of Jubaland was a veritable comedy of diplomatic errors where Italy missed very favorable opportunities through incompetent negotiators. In the end, Oltre Giuba was ceded to Italy on June 28, 1925, as a token of gratitude for her role in World War I in compliance with the secret Treaties of London (April 26, 1915) and St. Jean de Maurienne (April 20, 1917). Article XIII of the Treaty of London made provisions for an equitable compensation to Italy in the event of the British and French colonial dominions being augmented at the expense of

Germany. The newly-acquired territory had a short-lived autonomous administration headed by a High Commissioner, and on July 1, 1926, was annexed to Somalia.

OLTRE GIUBA *o/p* on Italian stamp

Stamps with a one-line "OLTRE GIUBA" overprint were issued on June 29, 1925. But what may baffle collectors is that Oltre Giuba had to issue a whole range of stamps including definitives, special delivery, parcel post, postage due, and even stamps for postal money orders. This was in compliance of instructions for an autonomous administration during the transition to annexation to Somalia.

Oltre Giuba stamp showing map

The only rare stamp of Oltre Giuba is the perforation variety of the 60c "Giubileo" stamp (perf. 13 1/2). A set of seven stamps was issued on April 21, 1926, to commemorate the annexation of Oltre Giuba to Somalia; this is an inexpensive but rather useful set since it depicts a map of the area. Given the short life of Oltre Giuba, it is quite understandable that used stamps are much scarcer than mint ones, and those on commercial or private mail are much coveted by collectors.

[Contributed by Giorgio Migliavacca. Giorgio Migliavacca, *The Stamps of Somalia and their Story*.]

Olympic stamps: Greece & Gabon (above); U.S. (below)

Freestyle Wrestling

Wrestling has 10 weight divisions. It is the only sport with a maximum weight limit: wrestlers must be less than 286 pounds. The United States has earned more medals than any other nation.

Olympics The modern Olympic Games are a revival of the ancient Olympian Games which took place in Ancient Greece as far back as 776 B.C. The modern games were first held in Athens, Greece, in 1896. They have been conducted every four years since that time except for 1916, 1940, and 1944 when they had to be postponed because of the World Wars.

The Winter Olympics were initiated in 1920 for sports requiring ice or snow. From 1920 until 1992, Winter and Summer Games were held in the same years. But starting in 1994, the Winter Olympics started being scheduled in the even-numbered years in between those of the Summer Games.

Since their revival, most modern games have been commemorated on stamps. Greece issued stamps in 1896 which showed naked men from ancient times participating in sport. This is an accurate rendition, because all of the athletes in the ancient games were men and they did perform in the nude. Women were not per-

mitted to participate nor were they even allowed to watch!

Over the next century, Olympic stamps had become a big business. Proceeds from the sale of these stamps were intended to help make the games self-sustaining. Because of this, the use of the Olympic name, the logo showing the five rings, and everything else directly relating to the Olympics is legally protected and is licensed out to stamp-issuing agencies which pay hefty fees. Except for Disney stamps, no group of stamp designs is more carefully protected.

1936 Olympic cancellation (Berlin, Germany)

The illustrations show one hundred years of Olympic stamps. The small stamp is an 1896 version from Greece, the stamp to its right was put out in 1972 by Gabon, and the third stamp was issued in 1996 by the United States. It was part of a souvenir sheet which represented many different Summer Olympic sports. Both sides of the U.S. stamp are shown here, because a brief description of the sport is printed on the back of the stamp.

Special cancellations have also been used to commemorate the Olympics. The postcard shown here was mailed in 1936 and exhibits an Olympic cancel used to publicize the games which were held in Berlin that year.

Both the 1896 and 1996 stamps shown here were issued by the host nation. As the Gabon stamp shows, this has not always been the case. Since roughly 200 countries have taken part in the various modern games, it is only appropriate that so many of them would honor this popular event by issuing postage stamps.

omnibus issues: portion of Queen Elizabeth II Coronation Set

omnibus issues A group of stamps, usually sharing a common design, which are issued by a group of issuing agencies to commemorate a special event. The concept goes as far back as the nineteenth century when Portugal released Vasco da Gama omnibus issues in 1898 for itself and its colonies. The first truly successful omnibus issues were the 1935 King George V Silver Jubilee stamps issued by various British colonies. Collectors immediately took a fancy to them, and they quickly rose in value.

In 1956, six members of the European Community (France, West Germany, Italy, Luxembourg, Belgium, and The Netherlands) began the tradition of issuing annual *Europa*[*q.v.*] stamps symbolizing European unity, a custom which continues today. Since that time, dozens of other nations have been included. At first, all participants issued stamps with similar designs; today, the stamps share a common theme but the designs vary.

The illustrated stamps are part of the 1953 Queen Elizabeth II Coronation Set. Sixty-two nations (of whatever size) issued stamps identical to these. Sixteen other nations issued one or more stamps of different designs, but those stamps are also included in the omnibus set. In all, the set consists of 106 stamps.

omslag (*n.*) [*Dan., Dut.*] cover (in the philatelic sense).

O Murcia [*abbr.*] Orihuela Murcia (Spain). Pre-adhesive postmark.

omvendt [*Dan.*] inverted.

on [*Turk.*] ten.

onbekend [*Dut.*] unknown.

onbestelbaar [*Dut.*] undeliverable.

önceden iptal edilmiş [*Turk.*] precancel.

onderkant (*m.-c.*) [*Dut.*] bottom.

onderwerp [*Dut.*] topical; thematic.

1 N 1 shilling (pre-adhesive postmark).

1 N 6 1 shilling 6 pence (pre-adhesive postmark).

ongegomd [*Dut.*] ungummed.

ongeperforeerd; ongetand [*Dut.*] imperforate.

ongepubliceerd [*Dut.*] unpublished (not listed in any book or catalogue).

O.N.M.I. [*o/p*] *Opera Nazionale Maternità Infanzia*, "National Organization for Maternity and Child Welfare." Overprint on stamps of Fiume[q.v.].

ön ödeme [*Turk.*] prepayment.

onofficieel [*Dut.*] unofficial.

onomastiki aksia ονομαστική αξία (*f.*) [*Grk.*] face value.

ONORANZE/ AL DUCA DEGLI/ ABRUZZI

[*o/p*] Three-line overprint appearing on some Somali definitives reprinted in May 1934 of the pictorial set of 1932. The inscription was added to solemnize (although with a 14-month delay) the state funeral of Luigi Amedeo of Savoy— a devoted explorer of the Arctic and Equatorial Africa. The Duke was instrumental in convincing industrialists to invest huge sums in the agricultural development of Somalia. It was his express wish to be buried there. See articles on *Somalia* and *Eritrea*.

onorario (*m.*) [*Ital.*] fee.

on the back On the reverse side of a stamp, i.e., the side of the stamp where the gum is normally found.

ontwaardigd met pen [*Dut.*] pen cancelled.

ontwerp (*n.*) [*Dut.*] design.

onuitgegeven [*Dut.*] not issued.

onvolledig [*Dut.*] incomplete.

Oost-Duitsland [*Dut.*] East Germany (D.D.R.).

Oostenrijk [*Dut.*] Austria.

o/p; opt.; optd. [*abbr.*] overprint, overprinted.

op brief [*Dut.*] on cover. The term *zegel op brief* is usually found in catalogues.

op de achterkant; op de achterzijde [*Dut.*] on the back.

opdruk (*m.-c.*) [*Dut.*] overprint.

op envelop [*Dut.*] on envelope; on cover.

operforerad [*Swed.*] imperforate.

opłata (*f.*) [*Pol.*] fee.

opłata pocztowa (*f.*) [*Pol.*] postage.

opnieuw gegomd [*Dut.*] regummed.

op omslag [*Dut.*] on envelope; on cover.

opp ned [*Nor.*] inverted.

opptrykk (*m.*) [*Nor.*] reprint.

opschrift (*n.*) [*Dut.*] motto.

opt [*Rom.*] eight.

optzeci [*Rom.*] eighty.

opublicerad [*Swed.*] unpublished (not listed in any book or catalogue).

op zicht [*Dut.*] on approval.

mint pair from the Orangeburg Coil (photo enlarged)

Orangeburg Coil A unique coil of 500 U.S. stamps released in 1911. The design is the standard Type I variety of the George Washington 3c definitive printed in deep violet. Unlike similar coils of this stamp which were perfed 8 1/2 vertically, this one single coil was was perforated 12.

Only one such coin was produced. It was sold to the Bell Pharmaceutical Company of Orangeburg, New York, which used the stamps from that coil to mail samples of patent medicines to physicians. One of the recipients, Dr. Jason Samuel Parker, was an avid stamp collector. He not only recognized this stamp as a new variety, but he wrote a letter of inquiry to the president of the company who in turn sent Dr. Parker a mint pair (see illustration).

The Orangeburg Coil, as it has become known, is the scarcest of all U.S. coil stamps and is among the most desired U.S. stamps of any kind.

[Kenneth A. Wood, *This Is Philately*, Vol. II, pp. 522-23.]

order form Printed form as supplied by a stamp dealer to assist the customer in making a purchase.

orderstämplat [*Swed.*] cancelled to order.

ordinario [*Ital.*] ordinary; definitive (in the philatelic sense).

originale [*Ital.*] original.

original gum [*abbr.:* O.G.] The gum which was applied to a stamp when it was manufactured. This description indicates that the stamp has not been regummed nor manipulated to hide hinge marks or other gum disturbances or imperfections.

The term does not imply, however, that the stamp has never been hinged nor that the gum is in perfect condition. Original gum can show imperfections, including hinge marks.

originalgummering (*n.*) [*Swed.*] original gum.

originalgummi (*c.*) [*Dan.*] original gum.

Originalgummi (*m./n.*) [*Ger.*] original gum.

originalt lim (*n.*) [*Nor.*] original gum.

origineel [*Dut.*] original.

originele gom (*n.*) [*Dut.*] original gum.

örn (*r.*) [*Swed.*] eagle.

ørn (*c.*) [*Dan.*]; (*m.*) [*Nor.*] eagle.

Oroszország [*Hun.*] Russia.

Ortiz de Domínguez, Josefa [a.k.a., *La Corregidora.*] see *Josefina.*

orts- [*Swed.*] topical; thematic.

Ortspostmarke (Gemona)

Ortspostmarke After the Battle of Caporetto (World War I, October 1917), the Austrians were able to re-capture territories occupied by Italy. These territories included the Friuli region, the Cadore area, and certain areas between Treviso and Venice. In these areas the only postal service that was functioning was that of the occupying army, but this was reserved only to the military. A postal service for civilians was re-activated on April 25, 1918, at Agordo, Ampezzo, Auronzo, Casarsa, Cividale, Codroipo, Gemona, Latisana, Longarone, Maniago, Moggio, Palmanova, Pieve di Cadore, Portogruaro, San Daniele, San Giorgio di Nogara, San Pietro al Natisone, San Vito, Spilimbergo, Tarcento, Tolmezzo, and Udine.

The service was very poor and disorganized. To improve on the situation, Udine, the only major post office among those named above, decided to create the Ortspostmarken— or local stamps— and organize a network of "authorized delivery" employing civilians for the purpose.

This would have created some revenue to get the service going. It was decided to boost revenue by creating special stamps inscribed/overprinted with the name of each of the post offices in the occupied areas. Huge quantities of revenue stamps were found and utilized for the purpose by overprinting them with the different names of eighteen post offices. The revenue stamps depict the Savoy coat of arms and are imperforate. The overprint includes the coat of arms of Austria and Hungary which were deemed large enough to cover the Savoy coat of arms.

Four denominations were adopted: 1c (postcards); 2c (letters); 3c (registered letter fee); and 4c (printed matters exceeding 50 grams). In actuality, a set of four stamps for eighteen of the post offices was prepared for issue. On June 15, 1918, the new service was inaugurated, but it lasted only a few hours because Vienna immediately vetoed the stamps and suspended the service.

[Contributed by Giorgio Migliavacca.]

oryginalny [*Pol.*] original.

oryol орел (*m.*) [*Srb., Bul.*]; орёл (*m.*) [*Russ.*] eagle.

orzechowobrązowy [*Pol.*] bister (color).

orzeł (*m.*) [*Pol.*] eagle.

O.S. [#1] *o/p* (Australia)

O.S. 1. [*o/p*] On Service. Indication of official use on Australian stamps.

2. [*Nor. abbr.*] *Offentlig sak.* Official use.

oscuro [*Span.*] dark.

osef אֹסֶף (*m.*) [*Heb.*] collection.

osiem [*Pol.*] eight.

osiemdziesiąt [*Pol.*] eighty.

ostaa (*v.*) [*Finn.*] to buy.

ostaja [*Finn.*] buyer.

ostemplować (*v.*) [*Pol.*] to cancel.

ostemplowanie (*n.*) [*Pol.*] cancellation.

ostemplowany dla kolekcjonerów [*Pol.*] cancelled to order.

Österreich [*Ger.*] Austria.

Østerrike [*Nor.*] Austria.

Österrike [*Swed.*] Austria.

Østrig [*Dan.*] Austria.

Östtyskland [*Swed.*] East Germany (D.D.R.).

Østtyskland [*Dan.*] East Germany.

Øst-Tyskland [*Nor.*] East Germany.

osztály [*Hun.*] grade, condition.

osztályozás [*Hun.*] classification.

öt [*Hun.*] five.

ottanta [*Ital.*] eighty.

otte [*Dan.*] eight.

otto [*Ital.*] eight.

ottobre [*Ital.*] October.

ötven [*Hun.*] fifty.

otwór (*m.*) [*Pol.*] hole.

oud [*Dut.*] old; ancient.

outremer [*Fr.*] ultramarine.

outubro [*Port.*] October.

Ouvert par l'Autorité Militaire [*Fr.*] Opened by military authority. See *censored mail*.

overnight delivery stamp (U.S.)

overnight delivery stamp Type of express stamp introduced in the United States in 1983. Express Mail overnight delivery service was created to enable the U.S. Postal Service to compete more effectively against United Parcel Service, Federal Express, and other commercial delivery companies.

The stamps do not show an inscription stating their purpose and, in fact, are good for any postal use requiring such a large amount of postage. The first issues in 1983 were sold in one-pane booklets of three stamps, although a customer could buy one or two single stamps.

The denominations of current stamps are determined by how much it costs to send a two-pound envelope by overnight express to any point in the United States. The first stamps in 1983 were valued at $9.35. Two years later the rate was $10.75. But by 1988, the stamps dropped to $8.75, one of the few times that a postal rate has actually gone down. The decrease was necessitated because the commercial services had reduced their rates, forcing the U.S.P.S. to stay competitive.

Although the 1983 $9.35 stamps were readily available at any U.S. post office in 1983 and 1984, not a great many were saved, largely due to the stamp's high price. Within only a few years, the collector value of this stamp exceeded $20. The $8.75 stamps also rose in collector value rather quickly, in part because the stamps were only on sale for a short time.

overprint [abbreviated *o/p, opt., optd.*] Any inscription, value, portrait, device, or other portion of a stamp's design which is printed at some point in time after the stamp's original printing. Overprints are usually in black ink, although some are found in various colors.

1 overprint with 3 purposes (Serbia);
3 overprints with 3 purposes (Cape Verde)

The most common overprint is the *surcharge*[q.v.], an overprinted number indicating a modification of the stamp's stated value. In a few cases the surcharge confirms the previous value, but usually the surcharge shows a change.

An overprint can also indicate that the stamp is a *provisional*[q.v.], i.e., a previously-issued stamp or non-postal label which is temporarily being authorized for postal use until new stamps can be printed. A well-known example is the Irish inscription overprinted on British stamps in 1922 permitting those stamps to be used in the new republic until actual Irish stamps could be issued. In another case, the fledgling State of Israel overprinted Jewish National Fund[q.v.] receipts in 1948 so they could be used postally as provisionals.

1 *o/p* on two stamps (Italian *o/p* on Greek stamp)

Barred stamps are overprinted with black lines to obliterate something. Egypt overprinted bars on King Farouk's face after his overthrow in 1953 and then used the stamps until different ones could be provided. Stamps showing the Shah of Iran and Adolph Hitler ultimately got the same treatment.

precancel (U.S.); commemorative *o/p* (Colombia)

Stamps showing people who have recently died are sometimes overprinted with wreaths or a black border as a form of memorial. One such example is the series overprinted in this way to honor King George II of Greece who died in 1947. Some regular stamps have been overprinted with necessary information to convert them to *semipostals*[q.v.]. U.S. *precancels*[q.v.] were overprinted with the name

of the city and state. Some 1988 French stamps were overprinted with the value *0,31 écu*, the European Currency Unit equivalent of the imprinted value of 2.20 francs (see *écu*). Stamps issued by the British for use in India were often overprinted in the local language with the name of the Indian state where the stamps could be used.

block of dues with bilingual *o/p* (Slovenia)

Overprints can be bilingual. The block of four Slovenian stamps were turned into postage dues by being overprinted as they are shown here. The word *porto* is written both in the Romanized version of the Serbo-Croatian language and in Cyrillic.

During wartime, many stamps have been overprinted to validate them for use in occupied territories. Some Italian occupation overprints of World War II show one single overprint spread out over a pair of Greek stamps (see illustration).

The Colombian stamp in the illustration, issued on July 19, 1945, is actually a makeshift commemorative which shows the faces of Joseph Stalin, Franklin D. Roosevelt, and Winston Churchill. The U.S. *Molly Pitcher*[q.v.] overprint of 1928 is sometimes called the "poor man's commemorative," because merely overprinting a current definitive instead of issuing a new commemorative stamp seemed like a cheap and inappropriate way to honor someone.

The overprint on one of the illustrated stamps not only gives a surcharge that confirms the previous value, but it changes the country name from Yugoslavia to Serbia and turns a regular stamp into an airmail.

The most unusual example of overprinting shown here is the Cape Verde stamp with three separate and distinct overprints. The first was a surcharge changing the value from 200 réis to 130 réis; the second is the word *REPUBLICA* overprinted diagonally; and the third is a new surcharge that reduces the old surcharge of 130 réis down to *$04* (= four céntimos).

These are the most common uses of overprints, but this list is hardly complete. There are probably a hundred reasons why overprints are placed on stamps. A collector could devote an entire lifetime to the study of overprints without learning everything there is to know.

Also see *posthorn*, *O.H.M.S.*, *A.M.G.*, *O.S.*, and *Ortspostmarke*.

overschot (*n.*) [*Dut.*] remainder, stock remainder.

øverst [*Nor.*] top.

övertryck (*n.*) [*Swed.*] overprint.

overtryk (*n.*) [*Dan.*] overprint.

overtrykk (*n.*) [*Nor.*] overprint.

ovpt. [*abbr.*] overprint.

O.Z.A.K. [*Ger. abbr.*] *Operation Zone Adriatische Küstenland*. Operation Zone of the Adriatic Coast, a consolidation of Lubiana (the Italian name for Ljubljana) and the four former Italian provinces of Venetia-Giulia (Gorizia, Trieste, Pola, and Fiume) created by Germany during World War II. See *Lubiana*.

oznaczenie pocztowe (*n.*) [*Pol.*] postmark.

P p

P 1. Abbreviation used as a pre-adhesive post-mark in many parts of the world: paid, postage paid; [with or without crown] Paris (France); Pennsylvania (U.S.A.); Philadelphia (Pennsylvania, U.S.A.); Poland; Prague (Bohemia; now Czech Republic).

2. [*o/p*] Consular overprint on Colombian semi-official airmails sold in Panama; *Perak* [with star and crescent], overprinted on stamps of Straits Settlements.

Pa [*abbr.*] Pre-adhesive postmark: Padova (Italy); Pennsylvania (U.S.A.).

paar (*n.*) [*Dut.*] pair.

Paar (*n.*) [*Ger.*] pair.

paars [*Dut.*] purple.

på brev [*Swed., Dan.*] on cover.

pacchi postali [*Ital.*] parcel post. The term for *parcel post stamp* in Italian is *francobollo per pacchi*.

See *parcel post stamp* for an illustration of a two-part San Marino stamp of this type.

pacco (*m.*) [*Ital.*] package.

pacote (*m.*) [*Port.*] package.

P. a D. [*abbr.*] paid to destination. Abbreviation used as a pre-adhesive postmark.

på försändelse [*Swed.*] on cover.

pagamento alla consegna [*Ital.*] cash on delivery (C.O.D.).

pagamento antecipado (*m.*) [*Port.*] prepayment.

pagamento anticipato (*m.*) [*Ital.*] prepayment.

pagbaba ng halaga [*Tag.*] devaluation.

pago adelantado (*m.*) [*Span.*] prepayment.

pago contra reembolso [*Span.*] cash on delivery (C.O.D.).

paid reply postal card See *message card* and *postal card*.

paiement anticipé (*m.*) [*Fr.*] prepayment.

paiement contre remboursement [*Fr.*] cash on delivery (C.O.D.).

paiements par carte de crédit acceptés [*Fr.*] credit cards accepted.

pāi mài [*Chin.-py.*] auction.

painaa (*v.*) [*Finn.*] to print.

painel (*m.*) [*Port.*] pane (of stamps).

pair Two attached stamps. If they are side-by-side, they are a *horizontal pair*. If they are matched top and bottom, they are called a *vertical pair*. If they are printed upside-down relative to each other, they are referred to as *tête-bêche*[*q.v.*]. If their designs differ, they are *se-tenant*[*q.v.*]. If their only difference is the language, they are a *bilingual pair*[*q.v.*]. If the entire piece consists of two postage stamps plus a non-postal label (blank or printed) in between, the item is called a *gutter pair*[*q.v.*]. Pairs also exist with combinations of these characteristics, e.g., a *tête-bêche gutter pair* or *se-tenant tête-bêche pair*.

Three or more attached stamps in a row are called a *strip*. Three or more stamps together with at least one having both a vertical mate and a horizontal mate are called a *block*[*q.v.*].

Being paired does not normally increase stamps' value unless the pairing indicates something unusual or unless the stamps represent a great rarity. A *tête-bêche* pair caused by a *cliché*[*q.v.*] error is worth more than two equivalent separated stamps. In this case, if the stamps are separated, there is no way to prove that they came from an error printing. Some great rarities are worth more in pairs. The mint pair from the Orangeburg Coil[*q.v.*] given to Dr. Jason Samuel Parker, the man who first identified those stamps, is worth more than two individual specimens from that same group.

paire (*f.*) [*Fr.*] pair.

País de Gales [*Port.*] Wales.

Países Bajos [*Span.*] Netherlands, Holland.

paket (*n.*) [*Swed.*] package.

Paket (*n.*) [*Ger.*] package.

Paketmarke (*f.*) [*Ger.*] parcel post stamp.

Paketpost (*f.*) [*Ger.*] parcel post.

paketpostmärke (*n.*) [*Swed.*] parcel post stamp.

pakke (*m.*) [*Nor., Dan.*] package.

pakkepost (*c.*) [*Dan.*]; (*m.*) [*Nor.*] parcel post.

pakkepost mærke [*Dan.*] parcel post stamp.

pakkepostmerke (*n.*) [*Nor.*] parcel post stamp.

pakketpost (*m./c.*) [*Dut.*] parcel post.

pakketpost-zegel (*m./c.*) [*Dut.*] parcel post stamp.

Pal. [*Ital. abbr.*] Palerma (Italy). Pre-adhesive postmark.

palios παλιός [*Grk.*] old.

palkkio [*Finn.*] fee.

palm stamps [also known by the French name *palmiers.*] A common design set issued for colonies in French West Africa (replacing the Allegorical Group Type[*q.v.*]) from 1906 until replaced by the Pictorial issues[*q.v.*] of 1913 or 1914. The name is taken from the palm tree design on the middle values. The lower values feature Captain Louis Faidherbe, and the upper values show Dr. N. Eugène Ballay. The postage dues (*timbres-taxe*) associated with the set portray two natives. All designs had blank cartouches for the colonies' names to be imprinted in red or black, depending on denomination. Many of the middle and upper values are printed on colored paper.

Stamps of these designs were issued for six colonies: Dahomey, French Guinea, Ivory Coast, Mauritania, Senegal, and Upper Senegal & Niger. The low values (portraying Faidherbe) were issued for all six colonies at 1, 2, 4, 5, and 10 centimes, plus 15c for Senegal and Upper Senegal & Niger, and an extra 2c for Senegal. The middle values (palms) include 20, 25, 30, 35, 45, 50, and 75 centimes, with 40c added for Mauritania, Senegal, and Upper Senegal & Niger (the structure in the other three colonies did not call for this rate). The upper values (Ballay) in all six colonies included 1, 2, and 5 francs. The postage dues were for 5, 10, 15, 20, 30, 50, and 60 centimes as well as 1 franc (except that Upper Senegal & Niger did not have the 30 centimes). In all, these total 96 values for the postage issues and 47 for the dues.

The low values were primarily for rates on printed matter and internal mail; the middle values for letters outside the colony and registered mail. The higher values matched no common rates and were only rarely needed for unusually heavy items. Consequently, the low values (on postcards) and middle values are generally more common on cover than the others, although none is especially plentiful, given the short period of time they were in use. Among those that are especially scarce is the 30c Mauritania, with much of the printing said to have been lost at sea in a shipwreck.

The collector can find, with some difficulty, a number of varieties, including proof sheets without gum, imperforates, and with the country name missing or doubled— although various ones of these exist only for certain values and certain countries. For Ivory Coast, five stamps (4c postage; 30, 50, and 60 centimes plus 1 franc dues) exist perforated 11. Their issuance is a curiosity and is considered suspect. The French dealer who "discovered" them claimed they were perforation trials, officially made. Others have suggested that these were trimmed and perforated proofs, but the paper is unlike that of other proofs.

Postal stationery of the Faidherbe type was issued: cards at 5 and 10c and envelopes at 10c. Just one item of the palms type was issued, the 25c envelope for French Guinea.

[Contributed by Robert E. Picirilli. Robert G. Stone, "The Palms Stamps (*Palmiers*) of French West Africa," *France & Colonies Philatelist*, whole no. 147 (vol. 28, no. 1), pp. 5-6; André Michon, "Côte d'Ivoire 1892-1944, un Demi-Siècle de Variétés," *Le Monde des Philatélistes*, #401 (Octobre 1986), pp. 76-78; "For the Record," *France & Colonies Philatelist*, whole no. 171 (vol. 34, no. 1), pp. 13-14.]

pålydende (*n.*) [*Nor.*] denomination.

pålydende verdi [*Nor.*] face value.

pamiątkowy (*adj.*) [*Pol.*] commemorative.

pananalapi ng ibang bansa [*Tag.*] foreign currency.

paneel (*n.*) [*Dut.*] pane (of stamps).

panneau (*m.*) [*Fr.*] pane (of stamps).

på original konvolutt [*Nor.*] on cover.

papa [*Turk., Tag.*]; (*m.*) [*Ital., Span., Port.*] pope (of the Roman Catholic Church).

papă (*m.*) [*Rom.*] pope.

papas πάπας (*m.*) [*Grk.*] pope.

pape (*m.*) [*Fr.*] pope.

papel (*m.*) [*Span., Port.*] paper.

papel avergoado (*m.*) [*Port.*] laid paper.

papel avitelado (*m.*) [*Span.*] wove paper.

papel enrugado (*m.*) [*Port.*] laid paper.

papel esmalte (*m.*) [*Port.*] glossy paper.

papel estucado (*m.*) [*Span.*] chalky paper.

papel granito (*m.*) [*Span.*] granite paper.

papel lustrado (*m.*) [*Port.*] glossy paper.

papel porcelana (*m.*) [*Port.*] chalky paper.

papel tecido (*m.*) [*Port.*] wove paper.

papel verjurado (*m.*) [*Span.*] laid paper.

paper-yabber longa big fella hawk [*pidgin Eng.*] airmail.

papier (*m.*) [*Fr., Pol.*] paper.

Papier (*n.*) [*Ger.*] paper.

papier błyszczący (*m.*) [*Pol.*] glossy paper.

papier brillant (*m.*) [*Fr.*] glossy paper.

papier couché (*m.*) [*Fr.*] chalky paper.

papier glacé (*m.*) [*Fr.*] glossy paper.

papier gładki (*m.*) [*Pol.*] wove paper.

papier granitowy (*m.*) [*Pol.*] granite paper.

papier kredowany (*m.*) [*Pol.*] chalky paper.

papier mélangé de fils de soie [*Fr.*] granite paper.

papier ordinaire (*m.*) [*Fr.*] ordinary paper; wove paper.

papier prążkowany (*m.*) [*Pol.*] laid paper.

papier vergé (*m.*) [*Fr.*] laid paper.

papier żeberkowany (*m.*) [*Pol.*] laid paper.

papież (*m.*) [*Pol.*] pope.

papillons [*Fr.*] literally, *butterflies. Papillon* was the name given to the thin slips of paper bearing messages that were carried by balloon out of the besieged city of Metz during the Franco-Prussian War (1870-71). The blockade lasted from August 19 to October 27, 1870. Two balloon services operated from September 5 to October 3.

The little slips of paper that constituted the airmail are called *papillons*. Uncertainty exists over whether they were named after Dr. E. Papillon who inspired the service, or if the name resulted from their small and light appearance (like butterflies).

The 5 cm x 10 cm *papillons* were bundled into packages and launched in the balloons. They are all stampless and devoid of Metz postmarks. A few of them bear either framed or unframed P.P. (postage paid) markings, a free-frank privilege accorded to military mail. Some recovered *papillons* were postmarked and mailed from where they landed, being forwarded in a special envelope (*enveloppe de réexpédition*).

[Contributed by Greg Herbert. Ernst Cohn and Cyril Harmer, "Metz Papillons: George T. Robinson's Airmail of 1870," American Philatelic Congress, Vol. 39, September 28-30, 1973.]

papir (*n.*) [*Nor., Dan.*] paper.

papír [*Hun.*] paper.

papir med silketråde [*Dan.*] granite paper.

på prøve [*Nor., Dan.*] on approval.

Papst (*m.*) [*Ger.*] pope.

Paq. [*Fr. abbr.*] *paquebot*[q.v.] (steamer; mail boat). Pre- and post-adhesive postmark.

Paq. fr. [*Fr. abbr.*] *paquebot*[q.v.] *français.* Pre- and post-adhesive postmark.

paquebot [*Fr.*] literally, *steamer* or *boat packet.* Philatelically, it refers to a mail boat.

A marking on loose letters collected on board ships in most major seaports to be deposited in a port post office for onward transmission. The use of such markings has been provided under U.P.U. rules since about 1894. The form of such markings varies, including such things as *navire, packetboat, paquete, ship-letter, loose letter, steamboat letter, packet letter,* etc. These markings are not typically used for letters posted in an official post office maintained on ship, which use special cancels (often called *maritime* postmarks).

[Contributed by Robert E. Picirilli. Robert G. Stone, "On the *Paquebot* Marks of French Colonial Ports," *France & Colonies Philatelist,* whole no. 159 (vol. 31, no. 1), pp. 1-4.]

paquete (*m.*) [*Span.*] package.

Paq. Reg. [*Fr. abbr.*] regular paquebot. Pre-adhesive postmark.

par (*m.*) [*Span., Port.*]; (*n.*) [*Nor., Swed., Dan.*] pair.

Par Abbreviation used as a pre-adhesive post-mark: Paris (France); Parma (Italy).

para (*f.*) [*Pol.*] pair.

para birimi [*Turk.*] monetary unit.

paranın değerini düşürmek [*Turk.*] demonetization.

páratlan [*Hun.*] unique.

Par Ballon Monté [*Fr.*] By piloted balloon. Postal marking on mail sent out of Paris by balloon while that city was under siege during the Franco-Prussian War. Covers marked in this way are highly prized by collectors because these were the first letters to be transported by way of the world's first official airmail service, the Balloon Post of Paris[*q.v.*]. The service operated from September 23, 1870, to January 28, 1871.

parcel post Service offered by post offices for sending boxes and parcels.

parcel post stamp (San Marino)

parcel post stamp Special stamp issued by many countries for sending boxes, packets, and parcels within the postal system. Among the most interesting of these are the *pacchi postali* stamps from Italy and San Marino. The left half of the stamp was attached to the portion of the documentation that remained with the package, and the right half was attached to the receipt which was kept by the sender.

pardo [*Span.*] brown; drab.

parlak kâğıt [*Turk.*] glossy paper.

parfait [*Fr.*] perfect, flawless.

parit פָּרִיט (*m.*) [*Heb.*] (auction) lot.

parte inferior (*f.*) [*Span.*] bottom.

parte superior (*f.*) [*Span.*] top.

parti (*n.*) [*Nor.*] (auction) lot.

parvis sammenstilt [*Nor.*] accolated, conjoined[*q.v.*], jugate.

pasek (znaczkowy) (*m.*) [*Pol.*] strip (of stamps).

Passed by Censor A common censor mark from English-speaking countries. See *censored mail.*

pas séparé [*Fr.*] unsevered.

patacconi [*Ital.*] literally, *large pieces of rubbish.* Nickname of a short-lived jumbo-sized set of stamps issued by Somalia in 1934. The 12-stamp set publicized the Second Exhibition of Colonial Art at Naples.

patching Cut impressions of stamps, some in special colors, used in the pressbed by the printer to get uniform clarity of detail. It is also known as *découpage* or *mise-en-train* in French and is also called *makeready* in English.

[Contributed by John E. Lievsay.]

pătrat [*Rom.*] square.

pătrime (*f.*) [*Rom.*] a fourth, quarter.

PATRIOTI VALLE BORMIDA Overprint and inscription on Italian stamps. See *C.L.N.*

patru [*Rom.*] four.

patruzeci [*Rom.*] forty.

påtryk (*n.*) [*Dan.*] overprint.

påtrykt frimærkeafklip (*n.*) [*Dan.*] cut square.

Paul VI [né *Giovanni Battista Montini.*] Pope of the Roman Catholic Church (1963-78). Born September 26, 1897, in Concessio, Italy; died August 6, 1978, at Castel Gandolfo.

Pope Paul VI was the son of a well-to-do, middle-class newspaper editor, banker, and member of Parliament. After training at Milan and Georgian University in Rome, Montini was ordained to the priesthood in May 1920. His work from 1923 until 1932 was in the Secretariat of State working closely with Eugenio Pacelli, the future Pius XII. In 1937, Montini was promoted to the position of *sostituto* (Under-Secretary of State). Pope Pius confirmed him in this position as one of Pius's first acts as pope. This was the beginning of a close relationship between the two which lasted until 1954.

In 1954, Montini was appointed Archbishop of Milan which signified a break with Pius XII after twenty-five years of cooperation. The reason for the break is unknown. In Milan, he undertook visits to all of his 912 parishes, established some 100 new churches, and a Diocesan Office for Social and Pastoral action. His vital pastoral experience as Archbishop of Milan eventually resulted in his election to the Papacy.

Prior to the enclave of cardinals following the death of Pope John XXIII, Montini made his own position quite clear that the initiatives of Pope John XXIII must be followed up. On the morning of July 21, 1963, Montini was presented to Rome and to the world as Paul VI. His realistic, objective approach followed the deeply human sympathetic approach of Pope John XXIII. Pope Paul declared that the Roman Curia needed to be adapted to the modern age. To look critically at an institution with which one is so closely related requires much courage, honesty, and independence of thought— virtues which he possessed in great abundance.

Pope Paul VI appears on many Vatican stamps, as well as stamps from throughout the Christian world. Vatican stamps of the Pope Paul VI era are noted for their international themes.

[Contributed by Ruth Ann Davis. Eric John (editor), *The Popes: A Concise Biographical History*.]

paus (*m.-c.*) [*Dut.*] pope.

Pava [*Ital. abbr.*] Pavia (Italy). Pre-adhesive postmark.

pave (*c.*) [*Dan.*]; (*m.*) [*Nor.*] pope.

påve (*m.*) [*Swed.*] pope.

Pax et Justitia See *Peace & Justice*.

Pays Bas [*Fr.*] Holland, Netherlands.

październik [*Pol.*] October.

P.C.C.P. [*Russ. abbr.*] Russian Soviet Socialist Republic. [These are actually Cyrillic letters that resemble Roman letters.]

P.D. [*Fr. abbr.*] *Payé à Destination* (Paid to Destination).

Peace & Justice (St. Vincent)

Peace & Justice [*Pax et Justitia* (*Lat.*).] A masterpiece of engraving which was originally created in 1880 by William Ridgway for a 5 shilling stamp issued by St. Vincent. The *Peace & Justice* design has been described by many experts as one of the best in the entire history of stamps.

Pearl Black Crown Coin with the denomination of one crown issued in 1990 by the Isle of Man to commemorate the 150th anniversary of the emission of the British *Penny Black* stamp, the world's first adhesive, prepaid postage stamp. The coins were struck by the Pobjoy Mint which developed a special black satin finish that it applied to the background areas of the coin to give the stamp design the appearance of black ink on paper as the original stamp had looked when it was issued in 1840. Never before had this Pearl Black coloration been used on a coin.

The Isle of Man authorized the mint to strike an unlimited number of uncirculated copper-nickel coins, plus 50,000 proof specimen pieces in copper-nickel, and 30,000 sterling silver proof crowns. All of these pieces exhibit the Pearl Black backgrounds. Additionally, a limited number of presentation pieces in gold and platinum were offered, but these are completely metallic in color and do not include the Pearl Black coloration.

["Isle of Man: Pearl Black Crown Bridges Numismatics and Philately," *The Numismatist*, October 1990, pp. 1554-6.]

pecete (*f.*) [*Rom.*] seal.

PECHINO Overprint on Italian stamps. See *Italian Post Offices in China*.

pedido (*m.*) [*Span.*] order form.

pedigree [also known as *provenance*.] A complete list of all former and present owners of a philatelic item, including books or journals. When a stamp is extremely rare but not unique, a pedigree or partial pedigree reference is often used to pinpoint which specific specimen is under discussion (e.g., "from the Col. Green collection" or "Farouk specimen").

Most collectors only care about the pedigrees of stamps which are exceedingly scarce or expensive, unless a more common item was previously owned by a famous person.

pedone (*m.*) [*Ital.*] foot-messenger[*q.v.*].

peel (*v.*) To pull a stamp off an envelope, preferably without damaging the stamp. This is not the preferred way to remove stamps from covers. Special chemical solutions are available which do a much better job.

Pegasus

Pegasus According to Greek mythology, Pegasus was a winged horse which sprang from the blood of Medusa, the Gorgon, when Perseus cut off her head with magic weapons given to him by the gods. Bellerophon rode Pegasus when he fought against the Chimaera. The winged horse symbolizes the power of natural forces to convert evil into good.

Pegasus is a popular device seen on airmail stamps, such as those from Italy.

pen cancellation (Italy)

pen cancelled Obliteration and invalidation of a postage or revenue stamp by hand with a pen rather than with a rubber stamp or with some other more standard canceler. The Italian stamp in the illustration was actually cancelled with a pencil.

Pendiente de Censura [*Span.*] Pending censorship on arrival. A censor mark from Spanish-speaking countries. Also sometimes written as *A Censurar en Destino*. See *censored mail* for additional information.

pengeanvisning (*m.*) [*Nor.*] money order.

pence period The years 1851-1859 when Canadian stamps bore denominations in pence (from the English sterling system) rather than in cents (from the decimal system adopted in 1858 and upon which the coinage system was based).

peninta πενήντα [*Grk.*] fifty.

Penn [*abbr.*] Pennsylvania. (pre-adhesive postmark from the U.S.).

penneannulering (*c.*) [*Dan.*] pen cancelled.

block of Penny Blacks (enlarged)

Penny Black The world's first prepaid, adhesive postage stamp, introduced on May 6, 1840, by Great Britain. The Penny Black and the Twopence Blue (released two days later) feature the portrait of Queen Victoria. The design came from a medal engraved by William Wyon in 1837.

The concept of the modern postage stamp is credited to Sir Rowland Hill who introduced a number of postal reforms. Part of the stamp's purpose was to reduce the widespread abuse of free-franking privileges in Britain. The stamps helped to standardize postal rates and even to reduce those rates, making the postal system accessible to everyone.

Both stamps were printed in sheets of 240. This might seem a bit strange by today's standards, but it must be remembered that in the nineteenth century, a pound Sterling equaled 240 pence. Hence, a full sheet of Penny Blacks sold for exactly £1 and a sheet of Twopence Blues for £2.

To prevent forgery, the stamps were printed with plate position designations in the stamps' bottom corners. The letter in the bottom left corner indicated the row, and the letter in the bottom right showed the column. Hence, the stamp in the upper left-hand corner of the sheet was marked *AA*, the stamp to its right *AB*, then *AC*, etc. The first stamp in the second row was given the letters *BA*, the one to its right *BB*, and so forth. The stamp in the bottom right-hand corner was *TL*.

The original stamps were imperforate. Stamps were not officially perforated until 1853. And again, British stamps were the first to use this process.

Penny Post Private postal service established in London in 1680 by William Dockwra. His organization had more than 400 receiving stations. His system used a flat rate of prepaid postage and his carriers made frequent deliveries. He used a triangular *Penny Post Paid* postmark and was among the first to use a handstamp to indicate the time of day that the letter was handled.

Unfortunately, his endeavor proved to be too successful, because in 1682 the Duke of York (then England's postmaster general and later King James II) decreed that Dockwra was infringing on the State's postal monopoly. The Duke then seized the business, leaving Dockwra out in the cold.

A form of the Penny Post was revived in Edinburgh and Dublin in 1773 and later in other cities. It was also the concept upon which Sir Rowland Hill reformed the postal system in Great Britain in 1840, which included the emission of the Penny Black*[q.v.]* and Twopence Blue, the world's first postage stamps.

Pensa. F. [*abbr.*] Pensacola, Florida (U.S.A.). Pre-adhesive postmark.

pente πέντε [*Grk.*] five.

pénzegység [*Hun.*] monetary unit.

pénzrendszer [*Hun.*] monetary system.

pequeno [*Port.*] small, little.

pequeño [*Span.*] small, little.

perçage (*m.*) [*Fr.*] roulette.

percé [*Fr.*] rouletted.

percé en points [*Fr.*] pin perforation.

percé en scie [*Fr.*] serrated roulette; zigzag roulette.

percé en serpentin [*Fr.*] serpentine roulette.

perfecto [*Span.*] perfect, flawless.

perfeito [*Port.*] perfect, flawless.

U.S. & U.K. perfins (both sides)

perfin [short for *perf*orated *in*itials.] Popular name, especially in America, of postage or revenue stamps perforated with a company's initials or logo to prevent the theft of those stamps by employees.

This procedure was approved as early as 1869 in Great Britain. A machine invented by Joseph Sloper was capable of perforating the stamps without destroying them for postal use. The concept was approved in the United States in 1908, and at least 6,000 perfin patterns are known to have been used since that date. All told, at least two hundred countries approved their use, encompassing some 40,000 types worldwide.

strip of perfin U.S. documentary stamps (both sides)

Some philatelists have built impressive collections of perfins; other collectors merely regard perfins as damaged stamps. Generally speaking, perfins sell for considerably less than identical stamps without internal perforations.

Perfins became so popular to corporate managers because they served their purpose well. The perfins were especially useful to large companies which were prone to suffer this type of thievery. As an example, the illustrated U.S. stamp with the initials "PRR" came from the Pennsylvania Railroad, a very large corporation in its day.

British collectors prefer to call this item a *spif*, an acronym for *Stamps Punched with the Initials of Firms*." Still others prefer to call these items *punch-perforated stamps*.

Occasionally, stamps have been punched-perforated for reasons other than to prevent theft. Some official stamps of Canada were punched-perfed with the initials *OHMS* ("On His [Her] Majesty's Service"). Similarly, some Australian stamps have been punched *OS* ("On Service"). And some stamps have been punched with a single small hole to indicate telegraph use.

perforación (*f.*) [*Span.*] perforation.

perforación sincopada (*f.*) [*Span.*] syncopated perforation; interrupted perforation.

perforacja (*f.*) [*Pol.*] perforation.

perforacja grzebieniowa (*f.*) [*Pol.*] comb perforation.

perforacja igłowa (*f.*) [*Pol.*] pin perforation.

perforacja liniowa (*f.*) [*Pol.*] line perforation.

perforacja nieciągła (*f.*); **perforacja rolkowa** (*f.*) [*Pol.*] interrupted perforation; syncopated perforation.

perforado [*Span.*] perforated.

perforasyon [*Turk.*] perforation.

perforatie (*f./c.*) [*Dut.*] perforation.

perforatie-afstempeling (*f./c.*) [*Dut.*] punch cancellation.

perforazione a losanghe [*Ital.*] lozenge roulette.

perforazione a punti [*Ital.*] pin perforation, *percé en points*.

perforazione interrotta (*f.*) [*Ital.*] interrupted perforation; syncopated perforation.

perforation Rows of tiny holes punched into the paper between the columns and rows of stamps on a sheet to allow easy separation of the stamps. If actual bits of paper (called *chad*) are removed and discarded, the process is called perforation. If cuts are made into the paper but no chad is removed, the process is called rouletting[q.v.].

Early stamps were *imperforate* and had to be cut apart with scissors or torn against a metal straight edge. During the first fourteen years of postage stamp production (1840-1854), no stamps anywhere were issued with perforation or rouletting, presumably because no one had thought of the idea. The first person to do so was Henry Archer of England who built the first perforating machine. Although Rowland Hill[q.v.], the "inventor" of the prepaid adhesive postage stamp, is reported to have been somewhat unenthusiastic about the concept, the first perforated stamps appeared in Great Britain in 1854. The idea caught on and has been used worldwide ever since.

There are several types of perforation. The method of perforating the entire sheet or pane at one time is called *harrow perforation*. This technique is seldom used today except for small souvenir sheets.

Another style is *comb perforation*. Three sides of the stamp are perforated at one time and the operation is repeated row by row or column by column until all sides of the stamps are perfed. This method is so named because each time the perforation process takes place, the arrangement of holes left in the paper resembles a comb.

Line or *guillotine perforation* is a method by which the holes are punched one row or column at a time. This process is very slow and cumbersome and leaves noticeable doubled holes at the corners of the stamps.

The same type of corner doubling results from *L-type perforation*, a more modern version of the line perforation. The configuration of holes from one cut resembles the letter "L."

Because stamps are currently printed at such a fast rate, new technology had to be developed to avoid slowing down the process. One such technological improvement uses a perforating disk which punches the sheets as they come off the press. This is a very efficient method because the printing and perforating are done in one process instead of two.

Rough perforation[q.v.] is the name given to the ragged appearance of the edges of detached stamps caused by inadequate means of perforation or rouletting. Many stamps exhibiting this condition have been separated by means of *pin perforation*, rows of pinholes punched into the sheets. Although called perforations, these holes are actually roulettes[q.v.], as no paper is removed when the punctures are made.

Interrupted[q.v.] (or *syncopated*) *perforation* is a special method of perfing coil stamps used in vending machines. Some of the holes are intentionally omitted to strengthen the paper between the stamps so that the coil does not tear and jam the machine. Although the Dutch used this method with the greatest success, the idea actually goes back to the early 1900s when a number of private vending machine companies in the United States bought imperforate panes of stamps from the U.S. Post Office, cut the stamps into strips, pasted the strips together into coils, and perfed the stamps in such a way that they would go through the machines. See *Schermack perforation* for additional information and illustrations.

Round holes are the norm, of course, but a few stamps, especially revenues or other non-postage labels, have been perfed with square, diamond, or rectangular holes. The rectangular perfing on the U.S. 1898 "Battleship" revenue series is difficult to recognize as perforation. It is called *hyphen-hole perforation* and is often mistaken for rouletting.

Not all perforation holes are spaced the same. Perforation gauges measure the number of perforations per two centimeters. This system was developed by Dr. J. A. Legrand in the mid-1860s and has been used ever since. His system used a scale ranging from perf 7 to perf 16 with half-steps allowed.

For various production reasons, the horizontal and vertical perfing on some stamps is not the same. When they differ, this is called *compound perforation* and both gauges are listed in catalogues. For example, some of the French Bordeaux issues of the 1870s are listed as "Perf 14 x 13 1/2." In other words, the stamps are horizontally perfed at 14 and vertically perfed at 13 1/2.

Blind perforations occur when perfing pins fail to penetrate the paper properly. In some cases, only a few holes are affected; in other cases, an entire row is missing. In order for this to be called blind perforation, there have to be some pin marks visible, even if the pins did not actually penetrate the paper. But if a row is missing and there are no signs of pin marks, then that portion of the pane is regarded as imperforate.

[Kenneth A. Wood, *This Is Philately*, Vol. II, pp. 550-54; R. J. Sutton, *The Stamp Collector's Encyclopaedia*, p. 229.]

Philately: booklet pane of U.S. stamps honoring stamp collecting

perforation gauge Gauge used to quickly and easily determine the number of perforations on all sides of a stamp. The gauge tells the number of perforations per 2 centimeters. See *perforation.*

perfore edilmiş [*Turk.*] perforated.

perforerad [*Swed.*] perforated.

perforering [*Nor., Swed.*] perforation.

perforert [*Nor.*] perforated.

perforowany [*Pol.*] perforated.

perfuração (*f.*) [*Port.*] perforation.

perfurado [*Port.*] perforated.

peringatan (*adj., noun*) [*Indo.*] commemorative.

peso (*m.*) 1. [*Span., Ital., Port.*] weight.

2. Current or former unit of currency of Argentina, Cambodia, Chile, Colombia, Costa Rica, Cuba, Dominican Republic, Culion Island, Curaçao, El Salvador, Guatemala, Guinea-Bissau, Honduras, Mexico, Paraguay, Peru, Philippines, Puerto Rico, and Uruguay.

The silver Spanish-American *peso de a ocho* ("piece of eight") which circulated in the eighteenth century helped inspire the creation of the U.S. dollar in 1792.

petit [*Fr.*] small.

pfennig 1. The German version of the French denier, English penny, or Spanish dinero. It was a small silver coin used from the tenth to the late thirteenth centuries.

2. Minor denomination introduced in 1948 in West Germany (B.D.R.) and now used in unified Germany. One hundred pfennig equal one Deutsche Mark.

Pfund Sterling (*n.*) [*Ger.*] pound Sterling (£).

P.G.S. [*abbr.*] Perak Government Service.

phenylamine Technical name for aniline, a colorless liquid poison used as the base of some water soluble dyes and inks. When used on postage stamps, aniline ink is not poisonous, but it does dissolve when saturated with water. Stamps have sometimes been printed with aniline ink to prevent the re-use of those stamps once they have gone through the mail. Any attempt to erase or wash off the cancellation destroys the stamp's design.

Phenylamine is denoted chemically as $C_6H_5NH_2$.

Phi; P.H.I. [*abbr.*] Philadelphia (Pennsylvania, U.S.A.). Pre-adhesive postmark.

philatélie (*f.*) [*Fr.*] philately.

Philatelie (*f.*) [*Ger.*] philately.

philatélique [*Fr.*] philatelic.

philatéliste (*m.*) [*Fr.*] philatelist.

philatelistisch [*Ger.*] philatelic.

philately The examination and study of postage stamps, revenues, postal stationery, postage due stamps, covers, and other postal-related items, as well as relevant literature. In the strictest sense, the word has no commercial connotation. An investor who does not study stamps is not a true philatelist, but someone who researches stamps, covers, and the like but without actually collecting them can claim the title.

However, the distinction between a "philatelist" and a "stamp collector" is not universal. In many languages, the exact translation of the word "philatelist" is itself the common term for "stamp collector."

philately: Stamp Day (U.S.S.R.) &
F. D. Roosevelt with his stamp collection (Nicaragua)

philometrist Philatelist who specializes in philometry, the study of postal permit imprints and metered mail markings.

philometry Area of philately specializing in the study and collecting of meter impressions and postal permit imprints. A participant is known as a *philometrist*.

phosphor A substance which emits light when exposed to radiation such as ultraviolet rays. Its philatelic application lies in *tagging*, a technique by which fluorescent material is applied to a stamp when it is manufactured so that the stamp will emit a certain type of light when exposed to ultraviolet rays. The light given off can be machine read, thereby expediting the handling of mail. See *tagged stamp*.

phosphorescent Exhibiting phosphorescence, i.e., the ability to emit light when subjected to radiation.

phosphoreszierend [*Ger.*] phosphorescent.

Phrygian cap Cloth head-piece originating in the ancient country of Phrygia, now part of Turkey. The cap was worn by freed slaves in Roman times to indicate their liberation.

Ms. Liberty wearing a Phrygian cap

During the French Revolution, the cap was adopted not only as a symbol of immolation (killing as a sacrifice) but also as a symbol of freedom. Americans continued this tradition by issuing a number of coins, revenue stamps, and various other official items portraying the personification of Liberty wearing a Phrygian cap and laurel wreath.

[J. E. Cirlot, *A Dictionary of Symbols* (2nd Ed.), 1983, Philosophical Library, New York, p. 254; *Funk & Wagnalls New Encyclopedia* (1984), Vol. 20, p. 407.]

P.I. [*abbr.*] perforated initials (i.e., *perfins*[*q.v.*]); poorly inked.

pictorial issue Generally, any stamp with a pictorial design. The name is often applied to a broad variety of stamps of French colonies. In its most narrow sense, it applies to sets originally issued for six colonies in French West Africa (replacing the "palm" stamps[*q.v.*]) from 1913/1914 through the late 1930s, depending on the colony. For all six colonies the stamps' designs are similar, consisting of an ornamental frame that includes tablets for values, colony names, etc., and an enclosed "pictorial" scene, typically in a different color. The scenes pictured are as follows:

    Dahomey: man climbing oil palm;
    French Guinea: ford at Kitim;
    Ivory Coast: Ebrié Lagoon;
    Mauritania: travelers crossing desert;
    Senegal: Sengalese preparing food;
    Upper Senegal & Niger: camel and rider.

The stamps of this design belonging to Upper Senegal & Niger also exist overprinted for Niger Territory, Upper Volta, and French Sudan, reflecting subsequent territorial divisions.

Because of the length of time covered by these issues, there are many stamps, including reissues in various colors, overprinted values, etc. The collector can obtain a number of varieties, including misregistered centers, chalky paper (see *papier couché*), booklets, gutter pairs (layout: four panes per sheet, separated by gutters), imprint blocks, overprints missing, etc. Most of the issued stamps are fairly easy to obtain on covers: regular postage, registered letters, airmail, etc.

[Contributed by Robert E. Picirilli.]

pięć [*Pol.*] five.

pięćdziesiąt [*Pol.*] fifty.

pied (*m.*) [*Fr.*] foot. The term *à pied*[q.v.] refers to the portrayed person on a stamp or coin shown in a standing position.

piega (*f.*) [*Ital.*] a crease, fold.

pieni [*Finn.*] small.

pikilia ποικιλία (*f.*) [*Grk.*] variety.

pinaka-larawan [*Tag.*] effigy.

pinakamababang tawad [*Tag.*] minimum bid.

pinces (*f.pl.*) [*Fr.*] tongs.

pincett (*r*) [*Swed.*] tongs.

pin perforation Rows of pinholes which allow for the separation of stamps. Although called perforations, these holes are actually roulettes[q.v.], as no paper is intentionally removed when the punctures are made.

This method proved to be one of the least efficient means of separating stamps, because the stamps will seldom tear along the pinhole lines. Even when they do tear straight, they leave a very rough edge.

pin perforation (Central China)

Pin perforation is often called *rough perforation* and is also known by the French term *percé en points*. *Sewing machine perforation* refers specifically to those pin perforations actually made by the bobbing needle of a sewing machine, such as some of the early twentieth century stamps of Colombia.

pinzas (*f.pl.*) [*Span.*] tongs.

Pinzette (*f.*) [*Ger.*] tongs.

piros [*Hun.*] red.

Pizz.e [*Ital. abbr.*] Pizzighettone (Lombardy). Pre-adhesive postmark.

plakker (*m./c.*) [*Dut.*] (stamp) hinge.

plate number block A block of stamps, usually four, which comes from the corner of the pane showing the plate number. The selvage with the plate number must still be attached to the

plate number block (U.S.)

stamps. Plate number blocks usually command higher prices than non-plate blocks or groups of individual or paired stamps of the same type.

play stamp See *Kinderpost.*

plet (*c.*) [*Dan.*] stain.

pli (*m.*) [*Fr.*] a crease, fold; cover (in the philatelic sense).

plistiriasmos πλειστηριασμός (*m.*) [*Grk.*] auction sale.

pliu (*n.*) [*Rom.*] a fold, crease.

P.L.L. [*Ger. abbr.*] *Polizei* (police). Punch-perfed on German stamps used as Prussian police official stamps.

pneumatic post stamp (Italy)

pneumatic post Local mail service established in London, Berlin, Marseilles, Paris, Vienna, Philadelphia, Chicago, and elsewhere. Its first practical use was in London (1863); its last in New York City (1953). Mail was sucked through vacuum tubes from a sending point to a receiving station where it was treated as special delivery mail. This system was often utilized to speed mail from a post office to a railway station. And in some cases, its purpose was to expedite the transport of important mail by circumventing the postal system, not unlike some of the reasons that faxes and e-mail are used today.

The Italian pneumatic postal system was very ambitious with operations in Rome, Naples, Turin, Genoa, and Milan. Italy introduced stamps in 1913 inscribed *Posta Pneumatica.* Italian stamps of this nature were issued until 1966.

P.O. [*abbr.*] post office. Used as an overprint in South Australia prior to the introduction of *O.S.* ("On Service") in 1874 as an official mail designation. It has many uses in today's world, including the commonly-seen abbreviation *P.O. Box* for "Post Office Box."

poached egg label Dummy test stamps produced in Great Britain to test vending machines. These "stamps" were produced in coils. They are so named because the center shows a dark oval instead of the monarch's likeness. See *test stamp.*

pochodzenie (*n.*) [*Pol.*] pedigree, provenance (list of previous and present owners).

poco común [*Span.*] somewhat common.

poczta (*f.*) [*Pol.*] post office.

poczta lotnicza (*f.*) [*Pol.*] airmail.

poczta paczkowa (*f.*) [*Pol.*] parcel post.

poczta polowa (*f.*) [*Pol.*] field post.

pocztówka (*f.*) [*Pol.*] postcard.

podatek (*m.*) [*Pol.*] tax.

poddelka подделка (*f.*) [*Russ.*] a counterfeit, fake.

podlepka (*f.*) [*Pol.*] (stamp) hinge.

podpis (*m.*) [*Pol.*] signature.

podrabiać (*v.*) [*Pol.*] to alter.

podrobienie (*n.*); **podróbka** (*f.*) [*Pol.*] alteration.

pohja [*Finn.*] bottom.

pohjahinta [*Finn.*] minimum bid.

pohjapainanta [*Finn.*] *burélage, burelé.*

pohjatarjous [*Finn.*] protective reserve bid.

Pohjois-Irlanti [*Finn.*] Northern Ireland.

poikkeavuus [*Finn.*] anomaly.

pokratkowany [*Pol.*] *quadrillé.*

pokwitowanie (*n.*) [*Pol.*] receipt.

Pol. [*Pol. abbr.*] *Polska* (Poland). Pre-adhesive postmark.

pół (*adj.*) [*Pol.*] half.

pola [*Indo.*] pattern.

polegada (*f.*) [*Port.*] inch.

policromo [*Ital., Span., Port.*] multicolored, multicoloured.

polisi mesou tachidromiou πώληση μέσω ταχυδρομείου [*Grk.*] mail bid sale.

politimos πολύτιμος [*Grk.*] valuable.

pollice (*m.*) [*Ital.*] inch.

polowa (*f.*); **połówka** (*f.*) [*Pol.*] half (the fraction).

połówkowy (znaczek) [*Pol.*] bisected.

polvekeläviste [*Finn.*] zigzag roulette.

pomarańczowy [*Pol.*] orange (color).

pond sterling (*n.*) [*Dut.*] pound Sterling (£).

porteado [*Port.*] postage due.

porte de correos [*Span.*] postage.

porte franco (*m.*) [*Port.*] franchise stamp.

porto (*n.*) [*Swed.*]; (*m.*) [*Nor.*]; (*c.*) [*Dan.*]; (*m./c.*) [*Dut.*] postage.; (*n.*) [*Pol.*] postage due.

Porto (*n.*) [*Ger.*] postage.

Portofreiheitsmarke (*f.*) [*Ger.*] franchise stamp.

portofrihetsmärke (*n.*) [*Swed.*] franchise stamp.

Portogallo [*Ital.*] Portugal.

Portomarke (*f.*) [*Ger.*] postage due stamp.

portomerke (*n.*) [*Nor.*] postage due stamp.

portr. [*abbr.*] portrait.

portræt (*n.*) [*Dan.*] portrait.

porträtt (*n.*) [*Swed.*] portrait.

portret (*n.*) [*Dut., Rom.*]; (*m.*) [*Pol.*] portrait; effigy.

portret podwójny ("gemmowy") [*Pol.*] conjoined[*q.v.*], accolated, jugate.

portrett (*n.*) [*Nor.*] portrait; effigy.

portvrijdomzegel (*m./c.*) franchise stamp.

Post (*f.*) [*Ger.*] the mail.

posta aerea (*f.*) [*Ital.*] airmail.

posta da campo [*Ital.*] field post.

postage currency Name given to the first general emission of U.S. fractional currency notes issued from August 21, 1862, to May 27, 1863. These small-size notes were printed in denominations of 5, 10, 25, and 50 cents. They were called *postage currency* because they actually picture 5 and 10 cent U.S. postage stamps.

During the early years of the U.S. Civil War (1861-65), in response to the political uncertainty of the time, the banking industry suspended the redemption of paper money for coin. The net effect of this action was to place a premium on coins vis-à-vis paper money, which resulted in a widespread hoarding of coins by the public.

All forms of coinage were involved in the hoarding, not just coins of silver and gold. This created a serious situation for merchants, who were unable to make change to carry on the normal course of their business.

Merchants and the general public did whatever they could to deal with the problem. They even tried barter. The most significant idea from the standpoint of the development of fractional currency, was the public's resort to postage stamps as change. These had the

obvious advantage of existing in small enough denominations. They also had the equally obvious disadvantage of gummed backs, which became sticky and soiled after only a short period of circulation.

U.S. postage currency

The solution, generally credited to General Francis E. Spinner, Treasurer of the United States during the Lincoln administration, was the issuance of a form of fractional notes similar in appearance to the "circulating" postage stamps they were designed to replace.

In all there were five different issues, or major design types, printed from 1862 until 1876, when production of these notes ceased. The designs were changed with some frequency in response to an alarming rate of counterfeiting— in itself an interesting comparative commentary on times then and now. Modern counterfeiters seldom bother with any denominations lower than a twenty dollar bill, whereas their Civil War counterparts busied themselves with denominations as low as three and five cents.

The first of these notes were designed in such a manner so as to convince the public that they were legitimate substitutions for postage stamps, but far more suitable for circulation. Also, some of the notes resembled postage stamps in that they had perforated edges.

These first fractional notes were actually issued illegally under the Act of Congress of July 17, 1862. That Act only permitted the acceptance of postage stamps as currency but did not authorize the printing of notes, even if those notes pictured the images of postage stamps.

The second general issue (October 10, 1863 to February 23, 1867; denominations of 5, 10, 25, and 50 cents), third (December 5, 1864 to August 16, 1869; 3, 5, 10, 25, and 50 cents), fourth (July 14, 1869 to February 16, 1875; 10, 15, 25, and 50 cents), and fifth (February 26, 1874 to February 15, 1876; 10, 25, and 50 cents) were officially titled *Fractional Currency* rather than *Postage Currency*. The change in name was part of the Congressional Act of March 3, 1863, which not only authorized the emission of the second and subsequent issues of these notes, but also legalized the Postage Currency (first issue) notes.

The retirement of Fractional Currency started in 1876, with the Act of Congress of April 17, 1876, calling for the emission of fractional silver coins to redeem fractional currency.

[Contributed by John and Nancy Wilson. Taken from their article "United States Postage and Fractional Currency," *The Centinel*, Vol. 28, No. 3, Fall 1980, pp. 15-28.]

postage due Stamp-like label affixed to an envelope to indicate insufficient postage on delivered mail. Postage dues are technically defined as labels because they are not a form of prepaid postage for carrying the mail, yet they are often referred to as postage due *stamps* by collectors and non-collectors alike.

The first dues were issued by France in 1859. Most major countries started this practice within the following two decades, although Great Britain did not issue its first postage due stamps until 1914. In 1912 the U.S.

issued parcel post dues. The following year they became valid for use as regular postage due stamps. Shortly thereafter, they were discontinued.

postage dues: Canada, U.K. U.S. (parcel post), Austria, & Slovenia

The purpose of postage due labels is to alert postal carriers to collect the deficient amount from the addressee. Not all countries have handled this matter the same. In the United States, the amount of postage due equals the amount of the deficiency, but in Great Britain, the postage due amount is doubled.

The rise and fall of postage dues in the United States is typical of what has happened worldwide— the U.S. issued its first in 1879 and its last in 1986. In essence, they outlived their usefulness. Using hand-stamps or metered postage-due slugs is faster and easier than fishing out the correct amount of due stamps. Although some countries still issue these, they have become largely a relic of the past.

Several dues from different nations are shown in the illustration. The designs tend to be rather bland and with emphasis on the large value number. Also illustrated is a very unlikely item: a first day cover of postage dues from Ghana. These five labels were the first dues to be inscribed with the country's name (as previous dues were overprinted). The postmark is November 29, 1958, even though the official release date was not until December 1.

Postage due labels are sometimes called *unpaid letter stamps*.

[Fred Boughner, "Postage due stamps outlive usefulness," *Linn's Stamp News*, August 25, 1986, p. 53; John M. Hotchner, "Modern postage due stamps very collectible," *Linn's Stamp News*, January 19, 1987, p. 6.]

postage/revenue stamp Type of stamp issued mostly by Great Britain and British Commonwealth countries which can be used either as a postage stamp or as a revenue tax stamp. Both words are inscribed on the face of the stamp. British stamps of 1881 are inscribed *Postage and Inland Revenue*. Also see *fiscal stamp*.

postage/inland revenue (U.K.); postage/revenue (N.Z.)

postage stamp currency; postage currency General term for any postal item which has circulated as money, usually during wartime when coins have been hoarded. Forty-three countries have used some form of postal currency, either issued with the official sanction of the government or done unofficially by private citizens as a way of overcoming coin shortages. The following are three of the best-known examples:

1. During the U.S. Civil War (1861-65), there was a great shortage of small circulating coins. In addition to the issuance of small tokens by merchants and others, postage stamps were used to alleviate the shortage. Some were

first day cover of postage dues (Ghana)

Latvian postage stamps printed on discarded banknote paper

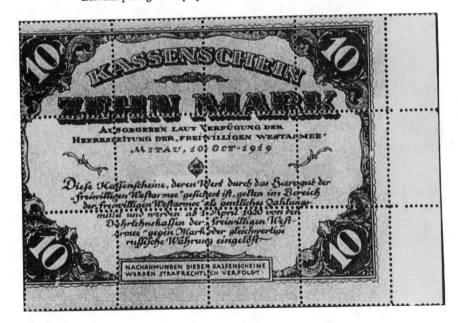

encased in mica containers (see *encased post-age stamp*); others were affixed to advertising cards and circulated as if they were paper money (see *scrip*). If the advertising card had ten cents' worth of uncancelled postage stamps, then it was legitimately worth ten cents in trade.

2. Czar Nicholas II faced a severe coin shortage during World War I. He authorized the production of small banknotes made from

postage stamp dies to alleviate the shortage. The face of the notes are identical to the stamps, but the backs are not gummed and the notes are printed on thin cardboard instead of normal postage stamp paper. Also, the backs of the notes carry an inscription stating that the items are notes worth a certain amount of kopecks in trade. Similar mini-notes were issued for Ukraine.

Russian postage currency notes

These notes are erroneously listed in many world stamp catalogues as postage stamps. Although they are not stamps, they were sometimes glued onto envelopes and used as postage.

Spanish Civil War-era postage currency

3. Postage stamps were affixed to round disks of thin cardboard and circulated as coins during the Spanish Civil War (1936-39). The royal crown printed on the disk indicates that these items were authorized by the government and were not simply concocted by private citizens.

postage stamps on currency paper World War I left a severe shortage of paper throughout Europe. In some countries, paper could not be wasted under any circumstances.

Latvia was one of the places hit the hardest; its limited supply of paper had to be distributed judiciously. Preference had to be given to paper currency in order to keep the economy intact, and practically none was left for the production of postage stamps. Thus, stamps were printed on any paper that the printers could find. During the post-war period, some stamps were printed on the back of old German military maps and some on leftover wallpaper.

The item in the illustration is a block of twelve Latvian Red Cross semi-postal stamps printed on discarded money paper. The stamps on the front are perfectly normal and are perforated in the usual way. The back of the block, however, shows a full banknote. The banknote side is gummed just as the back side of any group of stamps would be.

posta kartı [*Turk.*] postal card. The term for *postcard* in Turkish is *kart postal*.

postal card A piece of postal stationery somewhat resembling a commercial postcard. Postal cards usually have a postage stamp imprinted on the front and include room for an address. The back of the card is blank so that a message can be added (although some postal cards have been issued that do not follow this format).

The first postal card was produced by the Austrian Postal Administration and was introduced to the public on October 1, 1869. Its creator was a Dr. Emmanuel Herrmann who suggested it in a letter published in January of that year in the *Neue Freie Presse*, a Viennese newspaper. Many other countries quickly followed suit, including Germany, Luxembourg, Switzerland, Great Britain, and Finland (1870); Belgium, The Netherlands, and Denmark (1871); Sweden, Norway, and Russia (1872); and France, Spain, Japan, and the United States (1873).

The use of postal cards evolved to the point where some nations, especially the United States, began issuing postal cards bearing imprinted commemorative stamps. Perhaps a more significant innovation was the use of these cards by private firms for advertising

postal card with advertising message

purposes. Since they became used in mass-mailings, they could be considered among the world's first junk mail. Interestingly, the illustrated piece was part of an international promotion to sell stamp catalogues.

The paid reply postal card (also known as a *message card*) was an offshoot of the standard postal card. It consists of a folded two-part item, in essence two postal cards attached to each other. The original sender uses one part for the address and for the message. The receiver detaches the original, writes his own response onto the second piece, and mails it. A curious thing happens when these are sent internationally— both halves of the card bear postage from the same country but are mailed in two different countries. The Universal Postal Union requires its members to accept and deliver the reply portion of these cards even though their indicia (the imprinted postage stamps) are from another country.

[Kenneth A. Wood, *This Is Philately*, Vol. II, p. 598-9.]

postal fiscal Revenue used provisionally as postage. Postal fiscals are normally collected on cover, because it is difficult if not impossible to prove that a revenue stamp has actually seen postal use if it has been removed from its cover.

postal history The earliest postal history collections were formed at the beginning of the twentieth century when specialists began to show a moderate interest in postmarks, cancellations, postal rates, and handwritten postal symbols and/or rates. The study of postmarks developed as an offshoot of the stamps, and by the 1930s interest began to spread backward in time to the period before the invention of adhesive stamps. This fascinating aspect of philately gained momentum in the 1960s and has since been one of the most active sectors of the hobby.

Postal history collections contain material carried by, and related to, official, local, and/or private mails. Such collections usually emphasize routes, rates, markings, usages, and other postal aspects, services, functions, and activities related to the history of the development of postal services. A postal history collection consists of covers, used postal stationery, used postage stamps with clear and legible postmarks, and other postal documents illustrating a given aspect of postal history. If and when they bear some relevance to the research, then it is permissible to include maps, proclamations, and memorabilia in a postal history collection. However, it is very important for the beginner to understand that postal history collections do not illustrate *general* history through postal documents; the purpose of a postal history collection is to illustrate aspects of the history of the *postal service* through postal documents. History itself— especially social history— has certainly impacted upon the postal service. This can be a very fascinating aspect of the narration, but it is not its main aim. For example, a cover from Allied troops with a D-Day postmark can be featured in a postal history collection devoted to the postal service during World War II because it would add interest and perspective. But such a cover should not become the focal point of the entire collection. In this respect a 1944 cover from the U.S.A. and addressed to a country or territory occupied by Germany or Japan, with a postal marking indicating that it was returned to the sender as undeliverable owing to war events, has greater interest than a D-Day cover.

Examples of postal history collections include pre-adhesive (pre-philatelic) postal services; the development of local, regional, national, or international postal services; military mail; prisoner of war mail; disinfected mail; censored mail; mail sent through forwarding agents; postage due mail; disaster mail; railway mail; maritime mail; inland waterway mail (river or lake mail); traveling post offices mail; official mail; free frank mail; etc. Collections may be planned chronologically, geographically, or by mode of transport/service. Collections devoted only to postmarks belong to a category called *marcophily* which is considered by purists as a sub-branch of postal history.

The scope of a postal history collection is usually much broader than that of a marcophily collection. When starting a postal history collection, it is important to keep in mind that some limitations may be necessary in order to achieve not only completion but also a captivating display of postal documents that will hold the attention of the viewer. A neophyte may be tempted to start a collection focusing on the postal history of the United States, Europe, or China, but this is obviously exceedingly difficult to achieve. Beyond geographical limitations, the new collector will also learn that limiting a postal history collection to a certain historical period may help. The following are a few suggestions of well-defined collections: The Postal History of Washington, DC, 1776-1876; The Postal History of Iowa; The Postal History of Rome from the Renaissance to 1871; River Mail in the U.S.A.; Disinfected Mail of Austria; Military Mail of the Vietnam War; Special Delivery Mail of the U.S.A.; etc. In the process of putting together such a collection, the collector learns that achieving a well-coordinated and comprehensive postal history display is time-consuming— but the rewards are great.

The stimulus for research results in intellectual enrichment, while the ability to place a given cover in the right context and to show its importance (and sometimes rarity) may also produce financial benefits in the long run. To claim that postal history is an academic discipline would overstate the case; any postal historian knows that his field comes to life only in the context of a wider understanding of history and geography, and also a deep knowledge of the economy and traditions of the country and time he is researching. Treated thus, postal history is both pleasant and constructive.

The A.P.S. (American Philatelic Society, P.O. Box 8000. State College, PA 16803 U.S.A.) has several affiliates and units specializing in postal history. Other worldwide organizations include the Associazione Italiana di Storia

Postale (A.I.S.P.), Via Clerici 10, 20121 Milan, Italy; the Postal History Society, P.O. Box 3, St. Neots, Cambs, PE19 2HQ, U.K.; the Society of Postal Historians, Cavendish House, 153-157 London Road, Derby, DE1 2SY, U.K.; and the Postal History Society of Canada, 216 Mailey Drive, Carleton Place, Ontario K7C 3X9, Canada. Postal history societies exist in many countries including France, Switzerland, Austria, Germany, Australia, etc.

[Contributed by Giorgio Migliavacca.]

postal money order stamp (Italy)

postal money order stamp [also known simply as *money order stamp*.] First adopted by Holland in 1884, postal money order stamps were issued to facilitate the payment of duties (fees) on money orders. They were also issued by El Salvador (1895), Spain (1915), Spanish Morocco (1918), and Newfoundland (1918).

Similar stamps were simultaneously issued by Italy, San Marino, Tripolitania, Cyrenaica, Eritrea, and Somalia on July 1, 1924. All were denominated in Italian currency except for Somalia. In 1925 a set of money order stamps was issued for Oltre Giuba (Trans-Juba; Jubaland), followed in 1926 by a second set for Somalia, this time denominated in lire. San Marino utilized the money order stamps of Italy and overprinted them to suit the need, this being the only case of Italian stamps being overprinted for use in San Marino. The Italian inscription on them— *Segnatasse Vaglia* (Postage Due for Postal Money Orders)— is a bit deceptive because they were actually used to pay duty on orders following a change in the money order form. For security reasons, selling these stamps to the public was rigorously forbidden by Italian postal authorities, and their use was strictly internal.

In 1926 a new form that did not require such an elaborate procedure was devised, and on July 1, 1926, money order stamps were discontinued. Shortly after that date, the stamps were made available to collectors. Although not included in the listings of Scott, these stamps are widely collected in Europe where catalogues duly list them.

postal note stamp Set of 18 stamps issued by the United States in 1945. They were affixed to postal money orders to make up odd amounts. The series was discontinued in 1951.

U.S. postal savings stamp & official mail stamp

postal savings stamp From 1911 until 1966, the U.S. Post Office Department issued savings stamps which were credited to a postal savings account. These became especially popular during World War II because they were used to raise money for the war effort. The savings stamp in the illustration falls into that category and, in fact, bears the date 1941. The main figure in the design is known as a Minuteman, the nickname given to citizen soldiers during the American Revolution.

Similar stamps, part of the United States War Savings program, were issued by the U.S. Treasury Department from 1917 to 1943. They were redeemable for U.S. Treasury War Certificates or War Bonds.

From 1954 to 1970, the government sold United States Savings Stamps which could be exchanged for U.S. Savings Bonds. Most of the purchasers were school children.

On a related note, in 1911 the Post Office began issuing official postal savings mail stamps which were used to prepay postage on official correspondence of the U.S. Post Office's Postal Savings Division. These stamps were discontinued on September 23, 1914.

postal stationery Any piece of paper with an imprinted postage stamp that is issued by a legitimate stamp-issuing agency. Postal stationery includes envelopes, postal cards, message cards (paid reply postal cards), aérogrammes (air letters), return receipt cards, and any other post office-issued items with imprinted postage.

In the strictest sense, the term *postal stationery* can also apply to post office-issued stationery which lacks indicia, but most collectors limit themselves to items which do have imprinted postage.

Postamt (*n.*) [*Ger.*] post office.

postane [*Turk.*] post office.

postanvisning (*c.*) [*Dan.*] postal money order.

POSTA PARTIGIANA ALTO VARESOTTO Inscription on C.L.N.[q.v.] stamps of Italy.

posta tarihi [*Turk.*] postmark.

postauksjon (*m.*) [*Nor.*] mail bid sale.

postautalvány [*Hun.*] postal money order.

Postbote (*m.*) [*Ger.*] mailman, postman.

postcard A commercially-produced souvenir, usually made of thin cardboard, which shows a picture on one side and provides spaces for a message and for an address and stamp on the other.

Postcards became popular in the nineteenth century and have remained so ever since. Early examples show beautiful artwork as well as exquisite scenes, as the 1903 Swiss postcard in the illustration can attest. During that era, some very interesting postcards were also made of wood or leather[q.q.v.].

Around 1900, individualized postcards could be made with one's own picture on it. As can be seen from the illustration, the people being photographed for postcards took them as seriously as if they were posing for a family portrait. The people receiving these postcards regarded them as a personal gift, not just a cheap souvenir. Unlike today's postcards which are often read and discarded, individualized postcards were usually kept for many years, serving as a remembrance of that person. As a point of fact, the postcard in the illustration is the only surviving photo of this lady (the author's great-grandmother).

Some postcards are highly treasured because of where they have been. See *Zeppelin* for an example of a postage stamp whose collector's value has been enhanced because it is still on cover, and the cover in question is a very well-traveled postcard.

individualized postcard, circa 1900

A *maximum card*[q.v.] is a postcard bearing a stamp and a postmark that are relevant to the subject depicted on the card. The stamp is affixed on the view-side of the postcard and is usually cancelled by a postmark that has some strong connection with the topic or theme depicted on the stamp. The "host" card must be a postcard from a commercial publisher and not a photograph or an enlarged reproduction

Swiss picture postcard (1903)

of the stamp itself. The picture on the card should be related to the subject depicted on the stamp.

The term "postcard" should not be confused with "postal card," an item of postal stationery produced and sold by the post office. A postal card has the stamp already printed on it; a postcard does not.

post code; postal code System of standardizing addresses to simplify the patterns and methods of mail distribution and to enable the mail to be sorted by mechanical or electronic equipment. The post code in some countries is completely numerical, such as the ZIP Code[q.v.] used since 1963 by the United States. Other nations, among them Canada and Great Britain, use a combination of letters and numerals. The first post code was introduced by the Federal Republic of Germany in 1961. Since that time, most major countries have adopted some form of this system.

Many nations have issued stamps featuring their post codes, not to "honor" the codes but to encourage people to use them.

post code: Netherlands and Canada

poste aérienne (*f.*) [*Fr.*] airmail.
poste de campagne; poste militaire [*Fr.*] field post.
Poste/ Italiane/ Imperia/ Liberata/ 24-2-45 [*o/p*] See *C.L.N.*

Posten (*m.*) [*Ger.*] (auction) lot.

poste restante (*f.*) [*Fr.*] general delivery. Seen in abbreviated form (*Pte. Rte.*) as a preadhesive postmark.

poster label Large ornate sticker issued to publicize national or international philatelic exhibitions. See *exposition label* for additional information and illustration.

postförskott (*n.*) [*Swed.*] cash on delivery (C.O.D.)

postfrimærke (*n.*) [*Dan.*] postage stamp.

postfris [*Dut.*] unhinged; never hinged.

postfrisk [*Nor., Swed.*] unhinged; never hinged.

Postgebühr (*f.*) [*Ger.*] postage.

posthorn overprint (Germany)

posthorn; post horn Symbol of the mail, made popular by an 1872 design on Norwegian stamps. The exact reason why the posthorn has come to symbolize the mail has been lost to history. One theory goes like this: In the late days of the Renaissance, production of paper and the transport of mail were reserved privileges of the ruling class. As towns grew into cities, butchers had to go into the countryside to get fresh meat— and they announced their presence by blowing a horn. "Carry a message back into town? Certainly, m'lord. I'll bring the answer back next week, so just listen for my horn." The butcher's horn thus became equated with message service which ultimately evolved into the mail.

The stamp in the illustration is a 1947 German stamp overprinted with continuous posthorns to authorize it for use in the British and American zones.

[Contributed by John E. Lievsay.]

posthus (*n.*) [*Dan.*] post office.

postihuutokauppa [*Finn.*] mail bid sale.

postikortti [*Finn.*] postcard. [Note: the term for *postal card* in Finnish is *ehiökortti.*]

postileima [*Finn.*] postmark.

postimaksu [*Finn.*] postage.

postimaksuvapausmerkki [*Finn.*] franchise stamp.

postimerkki [*Finn.*] postage stamp.

postino (*m.*) [*Ital.*] mailman, postman.

postituore [*Finn.*] unhinged; mint fresh.

Postkarte (*f.*) [*Ger.*] postal card.

postkontor (*n.*) [*Swed., Nor.*] post office.

postkort (*n.*) [*Nor., Dan.*] postcard. The term for *postal card* in Danish and Norwegian is *brevkort* (*n.*).

postmark The portion of a cancellation which tells where and when the cancellation was applied. Usually the postmark consists of a circle into which is indicated such information as the post office, zip or postal code, date, and time.

In 1861 Henry Bishop of Great Britain began cancelling stamps by indicating the day and month that the letter was received at the post office. This was among the world's first postmarks and is called a *Bishop mark* by collectors.

Unlike the killer[*q.v.*], which is the part of the cancellation that actually obliterates the stamp, the contemporary postmark is not intended to cover the stamp but is placed on part of the envelope's blank space at the left of the stamp. However, many examples can be found in which the postmark has been used as an obliterator.

postmerk (*n.*) [*Dut.*] postmark.

post office seal (U.S.)

post office seal Adhesive label used to reseal a letter or parcel which has become damaged in transit, was opened by mistake by post office employees, or was never sealed in the first place. The U.S. Post Office Department also used them to secure registered mail against tampering.

post office sheet Mini-sheet of 150 stamps, cut from a full sheet of 300. The post office sheet is divided into five panes of twenty-five stamps each (five by five).

poststämpel (*r.*) [*Swed.*] postmark.

poststempel (*n.*) [*Dan., Nor.*]; (*m./c.*) [*Dut.*] postmark.

posttarief (*n.*) [*Dut.*] postage.

postväxel (*r.*) [*Swed.*] postal money order.

postwissel (*m./c.*) [*Dut.*] postal money order.

postzegel (*m./c.*) [*Dut.*] postage stamp.

postzegelboekje (*n.*) [*Dut.*] booklet (of stamps).

postzegelrol (*f./c.*) [*Dut.*] coil (of stamps).

postzegelverzamelaar (*m./c.*) [*Dut.*] stamp collector.

potwierdzenie odbioru (*n.*) [*Pol.*] receipt.

pouce (*m.*) [*Fr.*] inch.

pound; pound sterling [£] Unit of currency of Great Britain. The term originated in eighth-century Anglo-Saxon Britain as a monetary unit known as the *sterling* which was worth 1/240 of a pound of silver. Two hundred forty sterlings were referred to as a *pound of sterling* and then simply a *pound sterling*.

The pound was redeemable in silver until 1717 when Britain temporarily went on the gold standard and redeemed the pound in gold. Britain abandoned the gold standard in 1797, re-established it in 1816, abandoned it again during World War I, restored it in 1925, and finally did away with it forever in 1931.

The symbol for the pound sterling [£] resembles the letter "L" because it comes from the Latin word *libra* meaning "pound."

pour approbation [*Fr.*] on approval.

pourpre [*Fr.*] purple.

P.O.W. post See *prisoner of war mail*.

powtórnie gumowany [*Pol.*] regummed.

pozostałość magazynowa (*f.*) [*Pol.*] remainder, stock remainder.

P.P. [*abbr.*] Penny Post[q.v.]; postage paid. Among its various philatelic applications, this abbreviation has been used as a pre-adhesive postmark.

P.R. [*Ital. abbr.*] *Posta da Roma* (Mail from Rome). Pre-adhesive postmark.

præannulleret [*Dan.*] precancel.

præpareret papir (*n.*) [*Dan.*] chalky paper.

Prägedruck (*m.*) [*Ger.*] embossing.

Prägevorlage (*f.*) [*Ger.*] pattern.

Prägung (*f.*); **Prägungen** (*f.pl.*) [*Ger.*] coinage.

prangko [*Tag.*] franc (French unit of currency).

prasasti [*Indo.*] inscription.

Präsident (*m.*) [*Ger.*] president.

prawa strona (*f.*) [*Pol.*] right (direction or position).

prawdziwy [*Pol.*] genuine.

prawie [*Pol.*] almost.

pre-adhesive cover See *stampless cover*.

preannullering (*n.*) [*Nor.*] precancel.

four United States precancels

precancel Postage stamp with inscribed or overprinted information indicating that a letter with that stamp affixed does not have to go through the cancellation process at the post office. Precancels have been used on certain mail to save time and money. A *precancel* can also be defined as an adhesive or imprinted stamp that is cancelled prior to mailing. In addition to postage stamps, some revenue stamps have been precancelled.

The first known precancelled stamps were the original issues of U.S. stamps that were precancelled by the postmaster in Wheeling, Virginia (now West Virginia), who used a seven-line grid in red ink to precancel a block or four stamps at a time. The second country to issue precancels was France in 1868. Since that time, dozens of nations have used this concept.

Starting in 1903, U.S. post offices began overprinting the city and state where the stamp could be used. This practice was discontinued in 1978. Individual post offices usually overprinted their own precancels. These are known as *locals*. The Bureau of Engraving and Printing in Washington, DC, overprinted some of the stamps in bulk for major post offices which needed large quantities of these stamps. Those are referred to as *bureaus*.

The 1974 U.S. Christmas self-adhesives were also precancels, and they had the word *PRECANCELED* imprinted on them. The United States has also issued a variety of *bulk rate, presorted first class*, and *authorized nonprofit organization* stamps which are bureau precancels intended in one way or another to save money for the mailers.

In 1931 Canada started issuing precancels marked with numbers that correspond to a specific city. Other nations have used a variety of means to designate their stamps for precancelling purposes.

precancelado (*m.; adj.*) [*Span.*] precancel.

précieux [*Fr.*] valuable.

precio (*m.*) [*Span.*] price.

precio de reserva [*Span.*] protective reserve bid.

preço (*m.*) [*Port.*] price.

preço mínimo de adjudicação [*Port.*] protective reserve bid.

Preis (*m.*) [*Ger.*] price.

Preisliste (*f.*) [*Ger.*] price list.

preobliterazione (*f.*) [*Ital.*] a precancel.

pre-philatelic cover See *stampless cover*.

prescurtare (*f.*) [*Rom.*] abbreviation.

presque [*Fr.*] almost.

preto [*Port.*] black.

preußischblau [*Ger.*] Prussian blue.

prezzo (*m.*) [*Ital.*] price.

preţ (*n.*) [*Rom.*] price; (auction) bid.

prijs (*m.-c.*) [*Dut.*] price.

prijslijst (*m.-c.*) [*Dut.*] price list.

primer día de emisión [*Span.*] first day of issue.

P.R. in R. [*Ital. abbr.*] *Posta Toscana in Roma* (Tuscany Post in Rome). Abbreviation used as a pre-adhesive postmark.

printers' waste Poorly printed or otherwise defective stamps that should be destroyed by the printers. This material is in contrast to errors and varieties that legitimately escape inspection and are sold at post offices.

priority mail Concept developed by the U.S. Postal Service to compete against overnight deliveries provided by Federal Express and United Parcel Service. In theory, priority mail requires two days for delivery and is cheaper than overnight delivery provided by the two commercial carriers. Although it is true that priority mail is less expensive than overnight delivery by FedEx or U.P.S., it is equally true that the two-day delivery is not always accomplished. Priority mail's average delivery time is two to three days and some items get to their destinations in one. But priority mail often requires five to six days, prompting many citizens to accuse the U.S. Postal Service of false advertising.

Stamps are issued on a regular basis for the exact amount of postage that is needed to send a priority mail envelope (the type supplied by the post office) anywhere in the United States. These envelopes are not weighed; all of them go at the rate required for mailing a two pound parcel by priority mail. Priority mail stamps are not limited to that purpose and, in fact, are not even called "priority mail stamps" by the U.S. Postal Service. The stamps are issued in those denominations for the convenience of customers and can be used to send any letter or package requiring that much postage.

The U.S. Postal Service also provides global priority mail to selected foreign countries. Global priority mail envelopes *are* weighed, and the cost of postage varies depending on the destination.

pris (*n.*) [*Swed.*]; (*c.*) [*Dan.*]; (*m.*) [*Nor.*] price.

prislista (*r.*) [*Swed.*] price list.

prisliste (*c.*) [*Dan.*]; (*m.*) [*Nor.*] price list.

prisoner of war mail Letters or parcels addressed to or sent by internees of prisoner of war (P.O.W.) camps during wartime periods.

As per the International Convention relating to prisoners of war, P.O.W. mail was supposed to be exempt from all postage fees. However,

prisoner of war mail with censor markings

many countries have modified this policy because of abuses by many of the prisoners. For example, during World War II some P.O.W.s sent their dirty laundry home to be washed and returned, all postage free. This abuse prompted such countries as Canada to decree that P.O.W. letters could be sent without postage stamps being affixed, but packages must be sent with the regular prepaid postage which any non-interned person would be required to pay.

Prisoner of war mail is always subject to censorship. After the mail is examined by the censors, a designation to this effect is usually rubber-stamped on the cover.

[National Postal Museum, "Mail Arrangements for Prisoners of War and Internees Held in Canada During World War II," *Canadian Philatelist*, Part 1: November-December 1982, pp. 345-356; Part 2: January-February 1983, pp. 16-21.]

private die proprietary stamp See *proprietary stamp.*

Privatgeldschein (*m.*); **Privatschein** (*m.*) [*Ger.*] scrip.

privatpenge (*pl.*) [*Dan.*] scrip.

prix (*m.*) [*Fr.*] price.

próba (*f.*) [*Pol.*] essay.
Probe (*f.*) [*Ger.*] pattern.
Probedruck (*m.*) [*Ger.*] essay.
procedencia (*f.*) [*Span.*] pedigree; provenance.
proef (*f./c.*); **proefdruk** (*m./c.*) [*Dut.*] proof; essay.
Profumata in Pontremoli [*Ital.*] Perfumed in Pontremoli. Inscription stamped on letters to show they had been fumigated to prevent the spread of disease. Starting around the fifteenth century, the word "perfumed" (or its equivalent in many languages) was a euphemism for "fumigated." See *disinfected mail.*

Pro Juventute: 1947 Swiss set; Brazilian semipostal

Pro Juventude [*Lat.*] For Youth. Series of charity semipostals issued annually (except 1914) by Switzerland since 1913. The annual emission now consists of four stamps with a related theme. Proceeds go towards child welfare and other charitable causes involving the young. Other countries such as Brazil have

issued stamps with this inscription and for this purpose.
propaganda frimerke (*n.*) [*Nor.*] propaganda stamp.
propagandamærke (*n.*) [*Dan.*] propaganda stamp.
Propagandamarke (*f.*) [*Ger.*] propaganda stamp.
propagandamärke (*n.*) [*Swed.*] propaganda stamp.

propaganda stamps: Iraq and Cuba

propaganda stamp Any stamp which deliberately exhibits written or pictorial information or allegations intended to further the issuing agency's cause or to damage an opposing cause. The cause itself may be political, religious, economic, or military, or it may involve the aspirations of an individual. Since the 1980s, Iran has issued a sizable number of propaganda stamps, some of which attack the United States, and Iraq has put out many stamps promoting Saddam Hussein.
propagandazegel (*m./c.*) [*Dut.*] propaganda stamp.

U.S. proprietary stamps: "Battleship" & I.R.S.

proprietary stamp Revenue stamp attached directly to certain items to show that a tax was paid. In the United States, playing cards, perfumes, and a variety of other items were taxed in this manner. The stamps helped seal the item's container. The first time the box was opened, the stamp was "invalidated" by being torn in half.

Taxes on such items were initiated in 1862 during the U.S. Civil War, and the tax money was used to support the war effort. From 1862 until 1883, private manufacturers were permitted to print their own tax stamps (known as *private die proprietary stamps*) which included the company's name and trademark. The tax law was repealed in 1883, thus ending the need for firms to produce these stamps.

Some items were still taxed in this way, however, and the United States continued to issue its own proprietary stamps from 1871 to 1919, the most popular of which are the magnificent 1898 "Battleship" stamps. That design also appears on other types of U.S. revenues. The final issues of 1919 are designated as "U.S. Internal Revenue."

propuesta (*f.*) [*Span.*] an offer, proposal.

prosfora προσφορά (*f.*) [*Grk.*] (auction) bid.

prosfores anef oriou den apodechonte προσφορές άνευ ορίου δέν αποδέχονται [*Grk.*] no unlimited bids accepted.

protective reserve bid An auction bid made by the auctioneer on behalf of the seller of the lot in order to bring the price up to a level acceptable to the seller. This is usually done only if the bids from the floor are very low and the auctioneer does not believe that the bids will rise significantly. If no one offers a bid higher than the reserve bid, then the lot goes unsold.

protest cover Any envelope or other piece of mail upon which a message has been written in protest of a stamp design, postal rate increase, or other matter which the writer wishes to bring to the attention of the post office. In an immediate sense, these protest covers are usually only seen by postal workers who have no decision-making authority. Yet their presence is usually brought to the attention of news services or other organizations which make the protest known to the public.

Protest covers could theoretically circulate in any democratic country. Yet the majority

seem to come from the United States, largely because of the controversial nature of so many American stamps issued in the 1990s. The illustrated cover protests the issuance of the U.S. commemorative honoring Richard Nixon. The stamp was intentionally affixed upside-down on the envelope and the words "NO NIXON STAMP" were typed underneath. A large number of anti-Nixon protest covers were mailed throughout the U.S. in late 1995 and early 1996, partly because many Americans still opposed Nixon's failure to bring a faster end to the Vietnam War, but mostly because of his resignation as President to avoid being impeached over his involvement in the Watergate scandal.

Nixon protest cover (partial)

While political liberals sent out anti-Nixon covers, conservatives were protesting the issuance of the U.S. AIDS stamp. Using a variety of methods, Jerry Falwell and other right-wingers loudly protested the emission of this stamp, making the erroneous claim that

AIDS is a gay disease and stating their belief that AIDS is God's punishment of homosexuals.

Liberals and conservatives alike protested the release of stamps honoring Elvis Presley, Marilyn Monroe, and James Dean, three Hollywood icons whose personal lives and accomplishments hardly made them seem worthy of being honored on postage stamps. Many Americans who found themselves unintentionally using these stamps created protest covers by writing disparaging comments on the envelopes.

The creation of protest covers proves one thing: controversy does not hurt the sale of stamps. The Elvis stamp is the best-selling commemorative in history. Thousands of AIDS stamps have been encapsulated with pins attached so they can be worn on a lapel in place of an actual AIDS ribbon. The three other stamps mentioned above have also sold very well, especially the Marilyn Monroe issue. In sum, millions of these controversial stamps were purchased but never used for postage, generating huge profits for the U.S. Postal Service.

[Contributed by James Oliver.]

prøveeksemplar (*n.*) [*Dan.*] specimen.

prøvefrimærke (*n.*) [*Dan.*] essay.

prøvemønt (*c.*) [*Dan.*] pattern.

provenance A complete list of all former and present owners of a philatelic item (including books or journals). See *pedigree*.

proveniens (*r.*) [*Swed.*] pedigree, provenance.

PROVINZ LAIBACH— POKRAJINA LJUBLJANSKA [*o/p*] See *Lubiana*.

provisional (*noun*) A readily available stamp which is overprinted to change its denomination or issuing agency. The stamp may then be used as a temporary replacement until stamps of the correct type can be provided. Several different examples of overprinted provisionals are illustrated:

1. The first exhibits a surcharge, i.e., an overprint showing a denomination different from that originally assigned to the stamp. In this case, a postal envelope with an imprinted stamp valued at 6 cents has been revalued to 5 cents.

provisionals: [#1] revalued U.S. imprinted stamp; [#2] Irish overprint

2. The second example is an English stamp circa 1922 which was overprinted to make it acceptable for use in the Irish Free State until the fledgling nation could print its own. The inscription translates as *Provisional Government of Ireland.*

provisional: [#3] pair of U.S. domestic booklet stamps

3. A very different category of provisional stamps emerged in the 1970s. In 1978 the United States issued the first of a series of domestic stamps[q.v.], i.e., stamps lacking a specified denomination in anticipation of a postage rate increase. The stockpiled stamps, bearing a letter of the alphabet in lieu of a denomination, would then cost whatever the new rate would be for sending a one-ounce, first class letter. Israel followed suit in 1984 by issuing a domestic stamp in conjunction with its devaluation of the Israeli shekel. Both the U.S. and Israeli stamps were intended to be temporary issues, partly because their lack of a stated denomination made the stamps confusing to the users and partly because U.P.U. regulations originally prohibited the use of non-denominated stamps for international mailings, although this rule was changed in the 1990s.

provisionnel; provisoire [*Fr.*] provisional.

provisorisk utgave (*m.*) [*Nor.*] provisional.

provisorium (*n.*) [*Swed.*] provisional.

provmynt (*n.*) [*Swed.*] pattern.

proweniencja (*f.*) [*Pol.*] pedigree, provenance (list of previous and present owners).

prowizoryczny (*adj.*) [*Pol.*] provisional.

prøyssisk blå [*Nor.*] Prussian blue.

przedpłata (*f.*) [*Pol.*] prepayment.

przedruk (dopłaty) (*f.*) [*Pol.*] surcharge.

przepołowiony (*adj.*) [*Pol.*] half.

przestarzały [*Pol.*] obsolete.

przesyłka cenzurowana (*f.*) [*Pol.*] censored mail.

prześwitka (*f.*) [*Pol.*] thin spot, skinned spot.

przyjmujemy karty kredytowe [*Pol.*] credit cards accepted.

przypisywać (*v.*) [*Pol.*] to attribute.

P.S.B. [*abbr.*] by steamboat. Pre-adhesive postmark.

pseudo tête-bêche A pair of stamps with one stamp rotated 90 degrees relative to the other. An example is the French Colonies 10 centimes Eagle. There are no known examples of this technique having been used intentionally. The rotation is an error caused by mis-alignment of the plates.

In a normal tête-bêche[*q.v.*] pair, each stamp is upside-down (i.e., rotated 180 degrees) relative to the other. This arrangement is usually done on purpose and is not an error.

P.S.I./ MANTOVA + (surtax) [*o/p*] *P.S.I. = Piena Sovranità Italiana* ("Full Italian Sovereignty"). See *C.L.N.*

Pte. Rte. [*Fr. abbr.*] *poste restante* (general delivery). Pre-adhesive postmark.

Pt. pd. [*abbr.*] postage paid. Among its various philatelic applications, this abbreviation has been used as a pre-adhesive postmark.

PTS [*Span. abbr.*] 1. pesetas (Spanish unit of currency). 2. pre-adhesive postmark used to designate Potosí (Bolivia).

publikálatlan [*Hun.*] unpublished (unlisted in any book or catalogue).

pubs; publicité [*Fr.*] Words of advertising found on the selvage of some French stamps printed in booklet form. The advertisement may be repeated above and below each stamp in the pane, or it may be different stamp by stamp.

[Contributed by John E. Lievsay.]

puheenjohtaja [*Finn.*] president.

puja (*f.*) [*Span.*] (auction) bid.

pul defteri; pul karnesi [*Turk.*] booklet (of stamps).

pulgada (*f.*) [*Span.*] inch.

pul koleksiyonculuğu [*Turk.*] philately; stamp collecting.

pullara ait [*Turk.*] philatelic.

pul meraklısı [*Turk.*] philatelist; stamp collector.

punainen [*Finn.*] red.

Punainen Risti [*Finn.*] Red Cross.

punch cancelled U.S. internal revenue stamp

punch cancellation Invalidation of a banknote, bond, or philatelic item by punching one or more holes through it. This method was most often used in the nineteenth century to prevent notes and other certificates from being re-circulated once they had been redeemed. Its twentieth century application was limited mostly to post-World War I emergency currency.

This is not a practical method of cancelling postage stamps for the obvious reason that the act of punching holes through the stamp also punches holes through the contents of the envelope. Nevertheless, some revenue stamps have been punch cancelled to invalidate them.

punch-perforated stamp Postage or revenue stamp perforated with the initials or logo of a company. See *perfin.* The common British term for this type of individualized stamp is *spif.*

pund sterling [*Dan., Swed.*] pound Sterling (£).

punta [*Finn.*] pound Sterling (£).

punto delgado (*m.*) [*Span.*] skinned spot; thin spot.

puoli (*adj.*) [*Finn.*] half.

puolikas [*Finn.*] half (the fraction).

PURIFIÉ AU LAZARET [*Fr.*] Purified at the Lazaretto. **PURIFIÉ FRIOUL** [*Fr.*] Purified at Frioul. Inscriptions stamped on letters to show that they had been fumigated or in some other way disinfected against disease. See *disinfected mail*.

purper [*Dut.*] purple.

purpur [*Ger.*] purple.

púrpura [*Port., Span.*] purple.

purpurrot [*Ger.*] crimson.

Q q

Q [*abbr.*] Québec (Canada). Pre-adhesive postmark.

Q.E. II [*abbr.*] Queen Elizabeth II.

QEVERIJA/ DEMOKRAT./ W SHQIPERISE 22-X-1944 [*Alb.*] Albanian overprint on Italian stamps intended to celebrate the liberation of Albania from the Germans. October 22, 1944 (i.e., 22-X-1944) was the date upon which General Hoxha proclaimed Albania a democratic republic. See *Albania.*

qint; quind *et al* [*Alb.*] Minor unit of currency in Albania.

quadrado (*adj.*) [*Port.*] square.

quadratisch (*adj.*) [*Ger.*] square.

quadrato (*adj.*) [*Ital.*] square.

quadriculado [*Port.*] *quadrillé.*

quadrisect One portion of a stamp cut into quarters, each of which is affixed to an envelope and used for one-fourth of the stamp's original face value. This custom is no longer authorized anywhere, but it was used occasionally in the nineteenth century. Bisects (half of a stamp) and trisects (a third of a stamp) were somewhat more common.

qualidade (*f.*) [*Port.*] grade; quality.

quadrillé (*adj.*) [*Fr.*] Stamp album pages covered with fine horizontal and vertical lines similar to the configuration on graph paper. The lines enable the collector to mount stamps with more straightness and balance than if the stamps were mounted on blank sheets. The use of *quadrillé* pages also greatly enhances the neatness and proper arrangement of competitive stamp exhibits.

quadrillé paper Paper watermarked with cross lines in the form of rectangles. A paper similar to this was used for French 15c issues in 1892. The "watermark" was actually applied with oil or a transparent varnish.

quadriptych Block or strip of four individual stamps that together form one single design. A strip of three individual stamps forming one design is called a *triptych.*

quadriptych (U.S.)

qualità (*f.*) [*Ital.*] grade; quality.

quaranta [*Ital.*] forty.

quarante [*Fr.*] forty.

quarenta [*Port.*] forty.

quart (*m.*) [*Fr.*] fourth (fraction), quarter.

quartina (*f.*) [*Ital.*] block of four.

quarto (*m.*) [*Ital., Port.*] fourth (fraction), quarter.

quatre [*Fr.*] four.

quatre-vingt-dix [*Fr.*] ninety.

quatre-vingts [*Fr.*] eighty.

quatro [*Port.*] four.

quattro [*Ital.*] four.

quetzal Unit of currency of Guatemala introduced in 1925 and nominally equivalent to the United States dollar.

The resplendent quetzal (*Pharomacrus mocinno*) is the national bird of Guatemala and is a member of the trogon family. Its range is limited to Central America, and it is renowned for its long green tail feathers.

As the illustration shows, the quetzal is found on many beautiful stamps of Guatemala.

[Contributed by Halbert Carmichael.]

Quittung (*f.*) [*Ger.*] receipt.

q.v. [*Lat. abbr.*] *quod vide* (which see). Cross-reference designation in a dictionary or encyclopedia. The abbreviation *q.q.v.* is a multiple cross-reference.

Q.V. [*abbr.*] Queen Victoria.

quetzal (Guatemala)

R r

r. [*abbr.*] right (direction or position).

R [*abbr.*] 1. [*Span.*] *registro* (registered). 2. [*Fr.*] Réunion, a French colony. 3. [*o/p*] revenue. When overprinted, it converts a Northern Rhodesian postage stamp to a fiscal.

raadje (*n.*) [*Dut.*] roulette, *perçage*.

Rac. [*Ital. abbr.*] *raccomandata* (registered). Pre-adhesive postmark.

række (*c.*) [*Dan.*] strip (of stamps).

rahan poistaminen käytöstä [*Finn.*] demonetization.

railroad cancel A postal cancellation applied by a railway post office (R.P.O.), a working post office aboard a moving train.

railway stamp (Belgium)

railway stamp 1. Special railway parcel post stamp issued by Belgium on a regular basis since 1879. Many hundreds of varieties exist and most are quite beautiful. The stamps generally show allegorical figures or pictures of actual locomotives. The French and Flemish bilingual inscription on the illustrated stamp of 1902 reads *Chemins de Fer/ Spoorwegen* (Railroad). Since World War II, the stamps' designs have also included the letter "B" within an oval.

2. A type of British express stamp intended for use on letters carried by various railway companies. These stamps were used in addition to regular postage stamps.

rainha (*f.*) [*Port.*] queen.

raising the cross Symbolic act of taking possession of a territory. Frequently seen in vignettes showing Christopher Columbus dedicating newly-discovered lands to Spain. A philatelic example is the 2c issue from the U.S. Columbian Exposition Series of 1893.

raising the cross (U.S.)

rajoittamattomia tarjouksia ei hyväksytä [*Finn.*] no unlimited bids accepted.

ramka (*f.*) [*Pol.*] frame.

ramme (*c.*) [*Dan.*]; (*m.*) [*Nor.*] frame.

randat papper (*n.*) [*Swed.*] laid paper.

Randschrift (*f.*) [*Ger.*] inscription; motto; legend.

Ranska [*Finn.*] France.

rar [*Ger., Rom.*] rare, scarce.

rareté (*f.*) [*Fr.*] rarity.

rareza (*f.*) [*Span.*] rarity.

rarità (*f.*) [*Ital.*] rarity.

raro [*Span., Ital.*] rare, scarce.

rasgado [*Span., Port.*] torn.

rasgadura (*f.*); **rasgón** (*m.*) [*Span.*] a tear (as in a postage stamp or cover).

rautenförmiger Durchstich (*m.*) [*Ger.*] lozenge roulette.

ravfarget [*Nor.*] amber (color).

ravgul [*Dan.*] amber (color).

rayon limitrophe (*m.*) [*Fr.*] border radius. Seen in abbreviated form (*R.L.*) as a pre-adhesive postmark.

R. Commissariato [*o/p*] Italian overprint on Yugoslav stamps. See *Lubiana*.

R. de C. [*Span. abbr.*] *Recargo de Construcción* (Construction Surcharge). Overprinted on Nicaraguan stamps indicating a compulsive tax for the rebuilding of the Managua General Post Office.

re (*m.*) [*Ital.*] king.

recapito impossibile [*Ital.*] undeliverable.

rechteckig [*Ger.*] rectangular.

rechthoekig [*Dut.*] rectangular.

rechts [*Ger., Dut.*] right (direction or position).

recibo (*m.*) [*Span., Port.*] receipt.

recipisă (*f.*) [*Rom.*] receipt.

Recom. [*Fr. abbr.*] *recommandé* (registered). Pre-adhesive postmark.

recommandert stempel (*n.*) [*Nor.*] registration stamp.

reçu (*m.*) [*Fr.*] receipt.

Redt. [*abbr.*] returned. Among its various philatelic applications, this abbreviation has been used as a pre-adhesive postmark.

reembolso postal [*Port.*] cash on delivery (C.O.D.)

re-emisión (*f.*) [*Span.*] re-issuance.

re-emissão (*f.*) [*Port.*] re-issuance.

re-engomado [*Span.*] regummed.

Reg. [*abbr.*] 1. registered. 2. [*Ital.*] pre-adhesive postmark used to designate Reggio (Northern Italy).

Regatul Unit [*Rom.*] United Kingdom (U.K.).

rege (*m.*) [*Rom.*] king.

regent (*c.*) [*Dan.*] sovereign.

régi [*Hun.*] old.

Regie P. [*Ital. abbr.*] Royal Post (Italy). Pre-adhesive postmark.

regina (*f.*) [*Ital., Lat.*] queen.

regină (*f.*) [*Rom.*] queen.

Regio Uffizio Corrier Maggiore [*Ital.*] Royal Office of the General Postmaster. Seen in abbreviated form (*ROMC*) as a pre-adhesive postmark.

Regio Ufficio della Posta [*Ital.*] Royal Post Office. Seen in abbreviated form (*R.U.D.P.*) as a pre-adhesive postmark from Lombardy.

registratiezegel (*m./c.*) [*Dut.*] registration stamp.

registration label Adhesive label which designates the registration number and other pertinent information needed to send an item by registered mail. Registration stamps usually display a large letter "R."

registration label (Cyprus)

Although its purpose is not that of a postage stamp, between 1892 and 1913 Iran occasionally used registration labels as 1 chahi stamps. Registration labels of New Guinea were used for postage in 1914 after that country was overrun by the Germans.

registration marks Lines printed in the margins of sheets of multicolored stamps which must pass through the printing process more than once. They are normally seen as intersecting lines, sometimes within a circle. Their purpose is to act as a guide to help the printer position the sheet properly during the various passes through the printing press.

registration stamp (Panama)

registration stamp Stamp issued for the specific purpose of paying a fee on registered mail. Only a few countries have printed this type of stamp. In the late nineteenth and early twentieth centuries, Colombia and Panama issued stamps resembling registration labels[*q.v.*]. A space was provided for writing the registration number. Both of these countries also overprinted regular or airmail stamps with the letter "R" (*Registro* in Spanish) to authorize them as registration stamps.

The United States issued a 10c registration stamp in 1911. It was discontinued two years later.

registreringsmærke (*n.*) [*Dan.*] registration stamp.

REGNO D'ITALIA/ MBRETNIJA SHQIPTARE [*Ital./Alb.*; *o/p*] Bilingual inscription overprinted onto Italian *Imperiale* stamps of 1929. Some 50,000 sets were printed in 1940 and sent to Albania aboard an Italian vessel that was sunk en route by enemy action; only about 200 sets are said to have survived. See *Albania*.

Regno Unito [*Ital.*] United Kingdom (U.K.).

Reg.o [*Ital. abbr.*] Reggio (Northern Italy). Pre-adhesive postmark.

regomado [*Port.*] regummed.

regommé [*Fr.*] regummed.

regula [#2]: horizontal and diagonal (Netherlands)

regula 1. [*Lat.*] rule.

2. [*Eng.*] The line separating the numerator from the denominator in a fraction. Also known as *fraction line*. The illustrations show two Dutch stamps, one with a horizontal regula in the fraction and the other with a diagonal regula. On some stamps, the regula is seen as a wavy line.

[Alan Herbert, "Coin Clinic," *Numismatic News*, December 19, 1989, p. 46.]

regummed This term is used in the philatelic jargon in reference to a stamp that presents gum (or traces of gum) that is not original. Regumming unused stamps fraudulently enhances the value of a stamp without gum or one whose gum is affected by hinge or hinge remnants or other blemishes. This is done because "mint, never hinged" stamps usually command higher prices than their hinged counterparts. Stamps affected by stains or foxing can be "cleaned" and then regummed. Because regumming can turn a $1 stamp into a $50 stamp, there is a great temptation on the part of some people to do so.

Many of the regummed stamps seen on the market today were "cosmetically" enhanced in the 1960s and 1970s when the stamp market for "mint, never hinged" stamps was at its peak. During the 1980s, the supply of hinged stamps started thinning out, and the factors affecting supply and demand narrowed the price gap between hinged and never hinged stamps. Collectors also became increasingly aware of the existence of regummed stamps and usually required a certificate for the more expensive acquisitions. This precaution still remains the best way to reduce the risk of buying a stamp that has been regummed or whose gum has been manipulated in some form.

As in any aspect of human endeavor, there are skilled regummers and careless ones. In most instances, the average collector may be able to detect if a stamp has been regummed. For a correct diagnosis, one must look at the color and type of gum applied on other stamps of the same set or of the same year of issue. Gum variations do exist, but they are infrequent enough to justify some suspicion. Secondly, most stamp sheets are gummed before being perforated; but when a perforated stamp is regummed, the new gum will inevitably fall off the teeth and within the perforation holes. By gently rubbing the tip of a finger on the perforation tips of a regummed stamp, the tips will feel rather sharp. A good magnifier will also reveal the excess gum. This is a common problem with most regummed stamps, and there is very little the average regummer can do to hide this important clue. However, regummers have refined their skills, and a 15x magnifier may be needed to search for gum remnants within the perforation holes and on the tiny paper fibers of the teeth.

Examination of the gummed side under an ultraviolet light may also be helpful in diagnosing a regummed stamp. This will be easier if the gummed side of the suspected never-hinged stamp can be compared with that of a hinged copy of the same stamp with original gum.

Stamp experts are also aware that additives such as coffee, corn starch, peach juice, apricot tea, and other coloring agents are added to the gum used by the regummer to imitate the original gum. These additives can be detected by an "exercised" eye when the gummed side is exposed to ultraviolet light. In some cases the original gum is manipulated or redistributed to hide a blemish or traces of a hinge.

No matter how skillfully executed, manipulation and redistribution of gum will reveal itself under 15x magnification and/or ultraviolet light. When buying expensive mint stamps, collectors should exercise due caution and demand a recent certificate from a reputable expert or expert committee clearly stating that the stamp is "mint never hinged and has original gum." The absence of this terminology may be the source of regretful controversy. Additionally, collectors are advised to read carefully all the "fine print" regarding "terms and conditions of sale" in auction catalogues and dealers' price lists. If there is any doubt, a new certificate should be demanded as a condition of purchase; any hesitation on the side of the selling party will be quite revealing. Where possible regumming is concerned, one ounce of prevention is worth ten pounds of cure.

[Contributed by Giorgio Migliavacca.]

regummerad [*Swed.*] regummed.

regummieret [*Dan.*] regummed.

regummiert [*Nor.*] regummed.

rei (*m.*) [*Port.*] king.

Reihe (*f.*) [*Ger.*] series.

Reihenbezeichnung (*f.*) [*Ger.*] serial number.

reikä [*Finn.*] hole.

reikämitätöinti [*Finn.*] punch cancellation.

reimpresión (*f.*) [*Span.*] reprint.

reimpressão (*f.*) [*Port.*] reprint.

réimpression (*f.*) [*Fr.*] reprint.

reina (*f.*) [*Span.*] queen.

reine (*f.*) [*Fr.*] queen.

Reino Unido [*Span., Port.*] United Kingdom.

rekening (*f.-c.*) [*Dut.*] account (financial or transactional).

rekommenderingsmärke (*n.*) [*Swed.*] registration stamp.

remainder [also known as *stock remainder.*] Obsolete stamps dumped onto the philatelic market by their issuing agency, often at prices below face value. Some are overprinted with bars or marked in some other way to show that they are no longer current. Others are given a quasi-postmark, presumably to deceive collectors. Remainders are not highly regarded by philatelists.

remsa (*r.*) [*Swed.*] strip (of stamps).

remse (*m.*) [*Nor.*] strip (of stamps).

renta interior: 2-part revenue stamps (Mexico)

renta interior (*f.*) [*Span.*] internal revenue. Mexico issued a series of two-part internal revenue stamps in the 1920s and '30s, some with interesting overprints.

renversé [*Fr.*] inverted.

repeytynyt [*Finn.*] torn.

réplica (*f.*) [*Port.*] a duplicate; replica; reproduction.

reprint 1. Stamp printed from an original plate after the official issues have been discontinued. Reprints are made for official files, as souvenirs, or to satisfy collector demands. These stamps may be printed in colors unlike those of the originals, offered imperforate, or may show some other characteristic to differentiate them from the original stamps.

2. Term sometimes used in reference to fresh printings of current stamps to renew depleted stocks. This definition is commonly used but is not preferred by philatelists.

Reproduktion (*f.*) [*Ger.*] copy; reproduction.

reproduzieren (*v.*) [*Ger.*] to copy; to reproduce.

Repubblica Democratica Tedesca [*Ital.*] East Germany (D.D.R.).

Repubblica Federale Tedesca [*Ital.*] West Germany (B.R.D.).

Repubblica Popolare Cinese [*Ital.*] People's Republic of China (P.R.C.).

república (*f.*) [*Span., Port.*] republic.

República de ... [*Span., Port.*] Republic of .... [Note: If the name of the country that follows always uses its gender designation, then the word *de* may be changed to incorporate some form of the word *the*. For example, "Republic of Brazil" is written in Portuguese as *República do Brasil*.]

República de China [*Span.*] Republic of China (Taiwan).

República Democrática de Alemania [*Span.*] East Germany (D.D.R.).

República Federal de Alemania [*Span.*] West Germany (B.R.D.).

Republica Populară Chineza [*Rom.*] People's Republic of China (P.R.C.).

Republik China [*Ger.*] Republic of China. The name *Taiwan* is more commonly used in German.

Republiken Kina [*Swed.*] Republic of China (Taiwan).

Republikken Kina [*Nor., Dan.*] Republic of China (Taiwan).

république (*f.*) [*Fr.*] republic.

République de Chine [*Fr.*] Republic of China (Taiwan).

République Populaire de Chine [*Fr.*] People's Republic of China (P.R.C.).

requer-se um depósito [*Port.*] deposit required.

resello (*m.*) [*Span.*] surcharge.

reserve bid see *protective reserve bid*.

Reserveschutzgebot (*n.*) [*Ger.*] protective reserve bid.

resmi [*Turk.*] official.

resmî pul [*Turk.*] official stamp.

restant de stock [*Fr.*] remainder, stock remainder.

Restbestand (*m.*) [*Ger.*] remainder, stock remainder.

restlager (*n.*) [*Swed., Dan.*] remainder, stock remainder.

resztka (*f.*) [*Pol.*] remainder, stock remainder.

retouche (*f.*) [*Fr.*] alteration.

retoucher (*v.*) [*Fr.*] to alter.

retrato (*m.*) [*Span., Port.*] portrait.

rettangolare [*Ital.*] rectangular.

reva (*r.*) [*Swed.*] a tear (as in a piece of paper).

revalidado [*Span.*] re-validated.

revenue stamp Adhesive label similar in size and design to a postage stamp. It is affixed to a legal document to show that a tax or fee has been paid. See *fiscal stamp*.

revet [*Nor.*] torn.

rey (*m.*) [*Span.*] king.

"R.F." on French stamps: overprinted & imprinted

R.F. [*Fr. abbr.*] *République Française* (French Republic).

R.F.D. [*abbr.*] Rural Free Delivery (as used in the United States).

R.H. [*Fr. abbr.*] *République d'Haïti* (Republic of Haiti).

R.H./Official [*o/p*] Royal Household/ Official. Britain's King Edward VII restored the monarch's free-franking privilege which his mother, Queen Victoria, had relinquished. For a few months in 1902, this overprint was applied to 1/2d and 1d stamps for use by the staff at the royal residence.

Rhodes Greek island off the coast of Turkey. Ten postal administrations have operated there, giving the island a rich philatelic history. From 1845 to 1948, Austria, Great Britain, Egypt, France, Germany, Greece, India, Italy, Russia, and Turkey have variously maintained postal facilities there.

During that period, the greatest philatelic presence came from Italy, which had seized Rhodes along with the other Dodecanese islands from Turkey in 1912. Italy kept control of the islands until 1963. A set of nine definitive stamps inscribed "RODI" was issued on May 19, 1929. The same designation was used later for airmail, express, postage due, and parcel post stamps. See *Aegean Islands* for additional information about Rhodes and related topics.

R.I. [*abbr.*] Current postal designation for the state of Rhode Island (U.S.A.). It has also been used as a pre-adhesive postmark.

ricevitoria (*f.*) [*Ital.*] post office. See *Somalia* and *Italian Post Offices in China.*

ricevuta (*f.*) [*Ital.*] receipt.

rift (*c.*) [*Dan.*]; (*m.*) [*Nor.*] a tear (as in a postage stamp or cover).

right side of stamp When used as part of a description of a stamp, the terms *left* and *right* refer to positioning from the viewer's perspective, not the stamp's perspective.

rigommato [*Ital.*] regummed.

Rijeka [*Cr.*] Name given by the Croatians to the port of Fiume[*q.v.*].

riparato [*Ital.*] repaired.

riproduzione (*f.*) [*Ital.*] reproduction.

riquadro (*m.*) [*Ital.*] frame.

R.I.S. [*Indo. abbr.*] *Republik Indonesia Serikat.*

Riß (*m.*) [*Ger.*] a tear (in a piece of paper).

ristampa (*f.*) [*Ital.*] reprint.

ristiläviste [*Finn.*] lozenge roulette.

ritaglio (*m.*) [*Ital.*] cut square.

ritka [*Hun.*] rare, scarce.

ritkaság [*Hun.*] rarity.

rito ρητό (*n.*) [*Grk.*] motto.

ritratto (*m.*) [*Ital.*] portrait.

R.L. [*abbr.*] Pre-adhesive postmark: [*Fr.*] *Rayon Limitrophe* (border radius); [*Ital.*] *Repubblica Ligure* (Genoese Republic, Italy).

R.M.S. [*abbr.*] Railway Mail Service.

rød [*Nor., Dan.*] red.

Röda Korset [*Swed.*] Red Cross.

rødbrun [*Dan.*] maroon.

Røde Kors [*Nor., Dan.*] Red Cross.

Rode Kruis [*Dut.*] Red Cross.

Rodi [*Ital.*; *o/p*] Rhodes (Italian colony). The term appears on a set of nine definitive Italian stamps issued for the Aegean Islands on May 19, 1929. The same designation was used later for airmail, express, postage due, and parcel post stamps. See *Aegean Islands.*

roi (*m.*) [*Fr.*] king.

rojo [*Span.*] red.

rok (*m.*) [*Pol.*] year.

roleta (*f.*) [*Span.*] roulette, *perçage.*

Rolle (*f.*) [*Ger.*] coil (of stamps).

rollo (*m.*) [*Span.*] coil (of stamps).

rolo (*m.*) [*Port.*] coil (of stamps).

roltanding (*f./c.*) [*Dut.*] interrupted perforation; syncopated perforation. This term was coined to describe Dutch coil stamps which were perforated with some of the holes intentionally missing so the stamps could be more easily dispensed by vending machines.

Rom. [*Ital. abbr.*] Romagna (Italy). Pre-adhesive postmark.

roman numerals [sometimes written as *Roman numerals* with the first word capitalized.] Numbering system used by ancient Romans. The "numbers" are composites of letters of the alphabet, usually (but not always) capitalized. Roman numerals and their arabic counterparts are as follows: I (1), II (2), III (3), IV (4), V (5), VI (6), VII (7), VIII (8), IX (9), X (10), XI (11), XII (12), XIII (13), XIV (14), XV (15), XVI (16), XVII (17), XVIII (18), XIX (19), XX (20), XXI (21), XXII (22), ..., XXX (30), XXXI (31), ..., XL (40), XLI (41), ..., L (50), LI (51), ..., LX (60), ..., LXX (70), ..., LXXX (80), ..., XC (90), ..., C (100), CI (101), CII (102), ..., CC (200), CCI (201), ..., CCC (300), ..., CD (400), ..., D (500), ..., DC (600), ..., DCC (700), ..., DCCC (800), ..., CM (900), ..., M (1000), MI (1001), ..., MM (2000), ..., MMM (3000), ..., $\bar{V}$ (5000), ..., $\bar{X}$ (10,000), ..., $\bar{C}$ (100,000), ..., $\bar{M}$ (1,000,000), etc. There is no roman numeral equivalent for zero.

In the modern world, a few countries have used roman instead of arabic numerals for dates or denominations to give a certain flair to their stamps. The first *sede vacante*[*q.v.*] Vatican stamps of 1978 (the ones honoring the death of Pope Paul VI) show the year in roman numerals (MCMLXXVIII), but the second set of stamps (for Pope John Paul I) gives the month and the year in standard Italian form (*Sett. 1978*).

One of America's first stamps shows the denomination in the form of a roman numeral. The 1847 5c stamp gives the numerical value of 5, but the 10c stamp lists its value as *X.*

The most common philatelic use of roman numerals is their attachment to the names of monarchs and popes. Thousands of different stamps have been issued during the reigns of King Edward VII, King George V, King George VI, Queen Elizabeth II, Pope John XXIII, Pope Paul VI, Pope John Paul I, Pope John Paul II, Czar Nicholas II, Kaiser Wilhelm II, King Victor Emmanuel II, and a great many others. Even though their names (and numbers) do not usually appear on the stamps themselves, references to these popes and monarchs are found frequently in catalogues and in all types of philatelic literature. The names with their roman numeral designations do often appear on cachets, mourning covers, and other philatelic materials.

ROMC [*Ital. abbr.*] *Regio Uffizio Corrier Maggiore* (Royal Office of the General Postmaster). Pre-adhesive postmark.

rood [*Dut.*] red.

Eleanor Roosevelt (U.S.)

Roosevelt, Eleanor [née *Anna Eleanor Roosevelt.*] Wife of U.S. President Franklin D. Roosevelt. Born October 11, 1884, in New York City; died November 7, 1962, also in New York City.

Although Eleanor Roosevelt gained national recognition by being the wife of F.D.R., she became prominent in her own right as a social activist, author of many books and newspaper columns, and popular lecturer. She also became U.S. representative to the United Nations.

She was one of the most influential political liberals of her day, being regarded as much more liberal than her husband. She constantly strived to promote racial equality. At one point she resigned from the Daughters of the American Revolution when Marion Anderson, a black operatic singer, was denied use of D.A.R. facilities. Largely through Eleanor's efforts, the recital was ultimately performed in front of the Lincoln Memorial to an audience numbering in the hundreds of thousands.

Eleanor Roosevelt's life was not without controversy. Letters written by her to her female secretary suggest that the two may have had a lesbian relationship. (See *lambdaphilately.*)

Because of her tireless efforts to help humanity, many nations throughout the world have issued stamps in her honor.

Franklin D. Roosevelt, the philatelist (Monaco & Rwanda)

Roosevelt, Franklin Delano President of the United States (1933-45). Born January 30, 1882, in Hyde Park, New York; died suddenly on April 12, 1945, in Warm Springs, Georgia.

F.D.R., as he was affectionately called, was elected to four terms as president of the United States. His nomination in 1932 turned solely on the Great Depression issue. On March 4, 1933, he was inaugurated president of a nation on the verge of panic. His inaugural address inspired new confidence with his famous statement that "the only thing we have to fear is fear itself." He followed by declaring a national bank holiday to stop disastrous runs, and on the same day began a program of sweeping legislation known as the "New Deal." A reorganization of government functions and powers occurred which created many agencies known as the "alphabet agencies" such as the F.D.I.C. (Federal Deposit Insurance Corporation) and the S.S.A. (Social Security Administration).

By 1937 the New Deal was encouraging recovery and a cutback in government spending. But within two years foreign policy was engaging more attention than domestic problems. Roosevelt had maintained a policy of neutrality, but Japanese aggression in China, as well as the rise of Adolf Hitler in Germany and Benito Mussolini in Italy, brought about a deterioration of U.S. relations.

In 1940 Roosevelt won an unprecedented third term. But in 1941 the international situation worsened. Hitler had overrun most of Europe, and the Japanese were approaching a level of absolute strength in the Atlantic. Opposition to Roosevelt increased as he persisted in giving aid to the Allies but without committing U.S. troops.

Finally on December 7, 1941, Japanese aircraft attacked the U.S. Naval Base at Pearl Harbor in Hawaii. The next day, the president obtained a declaration of war from Congress. The course of the war was marked by a series of meetings with heads of state such as Winston Churchill and Joseph Stalin to plan the strategy of the war.

By this time, Roosevelt's health had become a serious problem. In 1921 he was stricken with polio myelitis. He had very little use of his legs and remained crippled throughout his life. He traveled to Warm Springs, Georgia, to rest for an upcoming meeting in San Francisco. Two weeks before the scheduled meeting, he suddenly died.

F.D.R. was both loved and hated, admired and feared. A consummate politician and a bold, courageous president, he left his mark on the nation and on the world.

Roosevelt was not only one of the most highly respected political leaders of the twentieth century, he was also the best-known philatelist. His love and knowledge of stamps was so great that some nations issued commemorative stamps showing him examining his stamp collection. The illustrated examples are from Monaco and Rwanda.

Because of the role he played in leading the Allies to victory in World War II, F.D.R. is featured on the stamps of dozens of countries, real and imaginary (see *government in exile* for a photo of an Albanian exile stamp showing F.D.R.). On many stamps, he is matched with Churchill, Stalin, and other WWII notables.

Nearly forty years after his death, F.D.R. became embroiled in a philatelic controversy. In 1982 a U.S. commemorative stamp was issued portraying F.D.R. with his ever-present cigarette and cigarette holder. Tobacco opponents protested, arguing that this portrayal sent the wrong message to young people. When plans were being made ten years later to issue another commemorative, the U.S. Postal Service intended again to show Roosevelt holding a cigarette. This time, however, the outcry was loud enough to force the U.S.P.S. to scrap that design and use something less controversial.

Franklin Roosevelt's wife Eleanor is also a philatelic icon and has appeared on a large number of worldwide stamps (see *Roosevelt, Eleanor*).

Franklin and Eleanor Roosevelt were two of the most influential people of the twentieth century, and they left an indelible mark on the field of philately. As long as postage stamps are collected and studied, the Roosevelts will never be forgotten.

[Contributed by Ruth Ann Davis. Charles van Doren (editor), *Webster's American Biographies*; Ted Morgan, *FDR: A Biography*.]

rosa [*Ital., Span., Swed., et al*] pink.

rosado [*Span.*] pink.

rose; roze [*Dut.*] pink.

Rosja [*Pol.*] Russia.

rosso [*Ital.*] red.

rosso ciliegia [*Ital.*] cerise.

rosso sangue [*Ital.*] blood red.

roşu [*Rom.*] red.

rot [*Ger.*] red.

rotbraun [*Ger.*] maroon.

Rotes Kreuz [*Ger.*] Red Cross.

rotgelb [*Ger.*] henna.
rotocalco (*m.*) [*Ital.*] intaglio.
rotolo (*m.*) [*Ital.*] coil (of stamps).
rouge [*Fr.*] red.
rouge sang [*Fr.*] blood (red).

rough perforation (China)

rough perforation Ragged appearance of the edges of detached stamps caused by inadequate means of perforation or rouletting. The right-hand side of the illustrated pair of Chinese stamps shows particularly bad separation. See *pin perforation*.

rouleau (*m.*) [*Fr.*] coil (of stamps).

serrated roulette (German military air labels)

roulette; rouletting Rows of variously shaped slits cut into the paper between the columns and rows of stamps on a sheet to facilitate the separation of those stamps. In rouletting, the sheet is pierced but no actual paper is removed, as is the case with perforations[*q.v.*]. British speakers frequently refer to rouletting by its French name, *percé* ("pierced").

Roulettes are not the same as perforations, even though philatelists often carelessly interchange the two words. In the strictest philatelic sense, perforations are tiny circles or rectangles of paper that are punched out of the sheet and discarded. Roulettes are piercings that do not leave any bits of leftover paper for disposal.

The most common and basic form of rouletting is the *line roulette* (*percé en lignes*). These slits have the appearance of a row of short dashes.

Pin roulettes (*percé en points*) are usually referred to in catalogues as *pin perforations* or even as *sewing machine perforations*, yet the method truly is a form of rouletting because no paper is intentionally removed. It is simply a row of pinpricks. In the case of sewing machine roulettes, the holes are actually made with the bobbing needle of a sewing machine. Pin rouletting may well be the least efficient separation method of all, because the stamps seldom want to tear along the rows of holes. The separation leaves such a ragged edge that many collectors and catalogues call this technique *rough perforation*.

Early Finnish stamps are excellent examples of *serpentine roulette* (*percé en serpentine*) with continuous deep S-shaped cuts. A more subtle version of this technique has surfaced in the 1990s when self-adhesive stamps were introduced in the United States and elsewhere. These new stamps are cut with a type of serpentine roulette that simulates traditional perforations to give the stamps a more "normal" appearance.

Lozenge roulette (*percé en losanges*) is a row of X-shaped cuts that in a sense form a double roulette. Because the rouletting resembles a string of diamonds, it is also known as *diamond roulette*. This was not a practical way of separating stamps and was rarely used.

If the slits are parallel rather than being in a continuous line, the rouletting is called *oblique* (*percé en lignes obliques*). The short piercings are slanted, which gives the technique its name. This was another impractical method that saw little use.

Arc roulette (*percé en arc*) and *serrated roulette* (*percé en scie*) are similar in concept, yet their appearance is quite different. While the arc roulette incisions are curved, similar to serpentine rouletting but not nearly as extreme, the serrated roulette demonstrates triangular cuts resembling the teeth of a saw. Serrated roulette (or serrate roulette) is also known as *zigzag roulette* (*percé en zigzag*) due to the abrupt turns and angles that the name would imply.

Colored line roulette (*percé en lignes de couleur*) is different from the other types in that the location of the piercing is indicated by rows of colored dashes printed over top of the short slits. Unlike perforations, which are normally very visible to the naked eye, some line rouletting is difficult to discern. The colored marks are printed simultaneously with the rest of the stamp's design (and, of course, in the same color) to enable the user to find the separation points more quickly.

roulette en losanges [*Fr.*] lozenge roulette.

roulette en zigzag [*Fr.*] zigzag roulette, *percé en scie.*

round adhesive stamp (Qatar)

round Relatively common shape for imprinted stamps, but a seldom-used shape for adhesives.

Most round adhesive stamps are issued by small agent-driven nations who issue these stamps as gimmicks to entice the lucrative philatelic market. They seldom— if ever— see actual postal use. Such was the case with the illustrated stamp from Qatar which was printed in wild colors on aluminum foil.

rovescio (*m.*) [*Ital.*] reverse; on the back.

rövidítés [*Hun.*] abbreviation.

Royaume Uni [*Fr.*] United Kingdom (U.K.).

roze; rose [*Dut.*] pink.

różowy [*Pol.*] pink.

R.S.I. [*Ital. abbr.*] *Repubblica Sociale Italiana* (Italian Social Republic) a political entity created by Mussolini in 1943.

R.S.M. [*Ital. abbr.*] *Repubblica di San Marino* (Republic of San Marino).

rückseitig [*Ger.*] on the back.

rudeformet gennemstik (*n.*) [*Dan.*] lozenge roulette.

R.U.D.P. [*Ital. abbr.*] *Regio Ufficio della Posta* (Royal Post Office— Lombardy). Pre-adhesive postmark.

ruitvormige tanding (*f./c.*) [*Dut.*] lozenge roulette.

rulle (*c.*) [*Dan.*]; (*r.*) [*Swed.*] coil (of stamps).

Ruotsi [*Finn.*] Sweden.

rupt [*Rom.*] torn.

ruptură (*f.*) [*Rom.*] a tear (in a piece of paper).

Rusia [*Span.*] Russia.

ruskea [*Finn.*] brown.

Rusland [*Dan., Dut.*] Russia.

Russland [*Nor.*] Russia.

Rußland [*Ger.*] Russia.

ruudutettu [*Finn.*] *quadrillé.*

Ryssland [*Swed.*] Russia.

rzadki [*Pol.*] rare, scarce.

rzadkość (*f.*) [*Pol.*] rarity.

S s

s. [*abbr.*] shilling.

S [*abbr.*] 1. specimen; surcharge; Selangor. 2. Pre-adhesive postmark: shilling; ship; Seville (Spain).

saanti [*Finn.*] acquisition.

sadasosa [*Finn.*] hundredth.

sælger (*c.*) [*Dan.*] seller.

sælgers minimumpris [*Dan.*] protective reserve bid.

safirblå [*Nor., Dan., Swed.*] sapphire blue.

safety paper Any postage or revenue stamp paper which is specially treated or is manufactured in such a way as to make counterfeiting more difficult or to cause some sort of disintegration if any attempt is made to re-use the stamp.

Among the various types of safety papers are,

—*chalky paper* with its heavy coating that prevents the printer's ink from being absorbed into the paper's fibers during the printing process. Any attempt to remove the cancellation causes the stamp's design to smear.

—*Goldbeater's Skin*, a tough paper made somewhat transparent by rubbing it with resin. The design is printed in reverse on the gum side of the paper. In theory, if the stamp is removed from the envelope, the design will suffer major disintegration. This idea was not particularly successful, as it was only used on the 1866 10- and 30-Silbergroschen stamps of Prussia.

—*bâtonné paper*, a rarely-utilized lined paper similar to that found in cheap notebooks. Some of the ultra-crude watercolor stamps of Poonch (an Indian State) were manufactured on this paper. There is some argument, however, that this paper was used more because of its availability than because of its safety feature.

—*granite paper* with numerous short colored silk threads embedded in the pulp during the paper's manufacture. It is most commonly found on Austrian and Swiss stamps made around the beginning of the twentieth century.

—*silked paper*, similar to the granite paper described above but with fewer and longer pieces of brightly colored silk embedded in the paper. The high rag content paper with its blue and red threads upon which U.S. paper money is printed falls into this catagory.

—*continuous silk thread paper* with its one or more long silk threads running the entire length of the stamp. This technique is much more commonly found in paper money, where the thread is usually referred to as a *security line*.

—*Winchester paper* with its overwhelming network of dark semi-circles. In essence, the paper is printed twice, first with the thick curved lines and then with the stamp's intended design. The security device is so intense that the stamp's design is partially obliterated. Some of the 1932-1938 Venezuelan stamps were produced on this paper.

Special papers are not the only security devices used to prevent forgeries or re-use. Punch and cut cancellations[*q.v.*] fall into this catagory, as do aniline[*q.v.*] and other unstable inks.

Sage; Type Sage Series of French stamps of 1876-1900 (Scott #64-108), with additional listings for Colonies-general issues, and surcharged for various Offices and specific colonies. The stamps feature allegorical designs of Peace and Commerce. They were created by Jules-Auguste Sage who won a French government competition held in 1875 for a new stamp design.

The set has two rarities: the 1c on Prussian blue paper, and the 25c types I & II *se-tenant*. The scarcity of these stamps may explain why they have never been shown in international competition.

[Contributed by John E. Lievsay. Joany, Storch, Brun, & Françon, *Timbres-Poste au Type Sage*; Schreiber, "Type Sage," *Linn's Stamp News*, November 19, 1990; John E. Lievsay, "What's In a Name?" *Opinions II*.]

sägezahnartiger Durchstich [*Ger.*] serrated roulette, zigzag roulette, *percé en pointes; percé en scie*.

saggio (*m.*) [*Ital.*] essay.

sahra postası [*Turk.*] field post.

S.A.I.D.E. [*Fr. o/p*] *Service Aérien Internationale d'Egypte* (International Air Service of Egypt). Overprinted in 1948 on stamps of Egypt to validate them for airmail use.

Augustus Saint-Gaudens

Saint-Gaudens, Augustus Sculptor and coin designer. Born 1848 in Dublin, Ireland; died 1907 in the United States.

Saint-Gaudens was one of the most noted sculptors of his day. His output included the statue of American admiral David Glasgow Farragut in Madison Square, New York City; the portrait figure of Abraham Lincoln in Chicago; the *Adams Memorial* in Rock Creek Cemetery, Washington, DC; and the famous equestrian statue of General William Tecumseh Sherman in New York's Central Park. He also created the design of the U.S. double eagles ($20 gold pieces) minted from 1907 to 1933. This magnificent portrayal of Liberty is regarded as America's most beautiful coin. The design was revived in the mid-1980s and has been used on U.S. gold bullion coins since 1986.

Saint-Gaudens is portrayed on the 1940 3c issue of the Famous Americans series of U.S. stamps. His double eagle design is featured on the U.S. 1991 29c commemorative honoring the 100th anniversary of the American Numismatic Association (see *numismatics* for an illustration of the first day cover).

St. George Slaying the Dragon (Great Britain)

St. George Slaying the Dragon Reverse design seen on British gold sovereigns and some large silver coins since 1817. It has also been featured on the 1951 10 shilling commemorative stamp of Great Britain. This magnificent design was the creation of Benedetto Pistrucci, who was criticized for not making the dragon formidable enough and for allowing the saint to appear naked. St. George, patron saint of England, is shown on horseback and is wearing only a cloak and a helmet, probably the last piece of armor he is likely to have wanted when fighting a dragon.

Whatever the St. George motif lacks in logic, it makes up for in beauty. It is truly an attractive and enduring design and still appears on some British gold coins today.

[Graham P. Dyer, "Five Centuries of the British Gold Sovereign," *The Numismatist*, March 1989, p. 396.]

St. Kitts St. Kitts, the oldest British colony in the West Indies, issued its first postage stamps in April 1870 when 1 penny and 6 pence stamps, representing the most widely-used postal rates, were offered. Stamps were not really a novelty in St. Kitts in 1870, however, because Nevis had preceded its sister island with its own stamps in 1861.

In the period between 1858 and 1860, the agency of the British Post Office in St. Kitts used stamps of Great Britain depicting Queen Victoria. Such stamps are quite rare and recognizable by the postmark used to cancel them: an "A 12" numeral postmark enclosed by bars. In 1860, control of the postal service passed to the local authorities.

stamp of St. Kitts

St. Kitts stopped using stamps of its own in October 1890 when uniform stamps for the Leeward Islands were introduced. In 1903 the island claimed a loss in revenue and was allowed to use the first stamps for the combined colony of St. Kitts and Nevis. These were used concurrently with the general issues of the Leeward Islands.

St. Kitts-Nevis and Anguilla formed one of the Presidencies of the Leeward Islands, and in 1952 stamps bearing the names of the three islands were introduced. St. Kitts-Nevis-Anguilla came into existence as a separate colony in 1956; in February 1967 it became an Associated State of the British Commonwealth.

Early in 1980 the government of St. Kitts and Nevis decided to have separate stamps issued; this continued after their independence in 1983. The popularity of St. Kitts' stamps is confirmed by the constant demand for them by the international philatelic market; these stamps regularly appreciate in value.

History, folklore, tradition, arts, and the cultural heritage of the island are regularly featured on these fascinating stamps. Nature is a dominant theme, ranging from the set depicting green monkeys (1978) to the 18-stamp definitive set devoted to indigenous birds (1981) to a more recent set of stamps featuring underwater life.

[Contributed by Giorgio Migliavacca.]

şaizeci [*Rom.*] sixty.

Saksa [*Finn.*] Germany.

salakauppa [*Finn.*] black market.

saldo (*m.*) [*Port.*] remainder, stock remainder.

sälja (*v.*) [*Swed.*] to sell.

säljare (*m./f.*) [*Swed.*] seller.

sällsynt [*Swed.*] rare, scarce.

samenhangend [*Dut.*] se-tenant.

samla (*v.*) [*Swed.*] to collect.

samlare (*m./f.*) [*Swed.*] collector.

samle (*v.*) [*Nor., Dan.*] to collect.

samler (*m.*) [*Nor.*]; (*c.*) [*Dan.*] collector.

samling (*c.*) [*Dan.*]; (*r.*) [*Swed.*]; (*m.*) [*Nor.*] collection.

sammantryckt [*Swed.*] se-tenant.

sammeln (*v.*) [*Ger.*] to collect.

sammensat [*Dan.*] accolated, conjoined[q.v.], jugate.

sammentryk (*n.*) [*Dan.*] se-tenant.

Sammler (*m.*) [*Ger.*] collector.

Sammlung (*f.*) [*Ger.*] collection.

sampu [*Tag.*] ten.

sanat [*Turk.*] art.

sanomalehtipostimerkki [*Finn.*] newspaper stamp.

sans charnière [*Fr.*] unhinged.

sans gomme [*Fr.*] ungummed.

santimetre [*Turk.*] centimeter, centimetre.

saphirblau [*Ger.*] sapphire blue.

şapte [*Rom.*] seven.

şaptezeci [*Rom.*] seventy.

Sar.; Sard. [*Ital. abbr.*] Kingdom of Sardinia. Pre-adhesive postmarks.

S. Ar. [*Span. abbr.*] Sevilla Aracena (Spain). Pre-adhesive postmark.

S.A.R. [*abbr.*] South African Railways.

sárga [*Hun.*] yellow.

sarı [*Turk.*] yellow.

sarja [*Finn.*] an issue, issuance; series.

sarjanumero [*Finn.*] serial number.

şarniyer [*Turk.*] (stamp) hinge.

şarniyerli [*Turk.*] hinged.

şarnıyersiz [*Turk.*] unhinged.

sas [*Hun.*] eagle.

şase [*Rom.*] six.

Saseno During World War I, Albania had been overrun by seven different armies. Following a period of anarchy and unrest, and with the help of Italy, the country stabilized itself. At the Versailles Peace Conference, Italy invoked Article XIII of the Secret Treaty of London (April 26, 1915) which made provisions for an "equitable compensation" to Italy in the event of the British colonial dominions being augmented at the expense of Germany and her allies. Additionally, Articles V, VI, and VII envisaged the possibility of substantial acquisitions of Albanian territory of Italy. Later, a similar treaty between France and Italy was signed at St. Jean de Maurienne (April 20, 1917).

Italian stamp with SASENO overprint

Italy's demand for a mandate over Valona and Central Albania was rejected, and eventually Italy was allowed to retain the tiny island of Saseno, dominating the harbor of Valona. In due course Saseno assumed greater strategic importance when Italy decided to use it as a naval base. In April 1923 a set of eight stamps consisting of 1901-1922 definitives of Italy overprinted SASENO was issued for use on mail from the island. The only noteworthy variety in this set is a double overprint on the 1 Lira denomination.

[Contributed by Giorgio Migliavacca.]

sata [*Finn.*] hundred.

satavuotinen [*Finn.*] centennial, centenary.

satu [*Indo.*] one.

satuan mata wang [*Indo.*] denomination.

Sav [*abbr.*] Savannah (Georgia, U.S.A.). Pre-adhesive postmark.

savings stamp See *postal savings stamp*.

savtakning [*Dan.*] serrated roulette, *percé en pointes*, *percé en scie*.

S. Ay. [*Span. abbr.*] Sevilla Ayamonte (Spain). Pre-adhesive postmark.

S.B.; S. Boat [*abbr.*] steamboat. Pre-adhesive postmarks.

S.c. [*abbr.*] Small crown (*re:* watermarks).

S.C. Current postal designation for the state of South Carolina (U.S.A.). It has also been used as a pre-adhesive postmark.

scambiare (*v.*) [*Ital.*] to trade.

schaars [*Dut.*] scarce.

scharlachrot [*Ger.*] scarlet.

scharlakansröd [*Swed.*] scarlet.

scharlaken [*Dut.*] scarlet.

Scheck (*m.*) [*Ger.*] check, cheque.

schedio σχέδιο (*n.*) [*Grk.*] pattern; design.

Schermack perforation (left); Mail-O-Meter perf (right)

Schermack perforation Type of interrupted perforation developed by the Schermack Mailing Machine Company.

In the early 1900s, Schermack (as well as several other private companies) convinced the U.S. Post Office Department to provide imperforate sheets of current 1c and 2c stamps which could be cut and pasted into coils and with special perforations to permit the coils to be fed through stamp vending machines. Stamps with normal perforations had proven to be unsatisfactory, because the stamps tended to separate at the wrong time and constantly jammed the machines.

The Schermack system placed two deep rectangular cuts on each side. The holes did not aid separation but were intended primarily to engage sprockets to enable the dispensing machines to function. Unlike most of today's stamp machines, the Schermack machines used double coils (two stamps across and however many stamps deep) and dispensed stamps in pairs.

The Schermack Company later became known variously as the Mailometer Co., Mail-om-eter Co., and the Mail-O-Meter Co. Under these names, the company produced coil stamps from 1906 to 1927. A version known as the *Mail-O-Meter perforation* is shown in the illustration on the right. Five round holes were punched in each side of the stamp. Many varieties of perforations exist, because Schermack and its competitors were sometimes contacted by customers with special requests. A few of the varieties are quite scarce and are seldom seen on cover.

It must be emphasized that the Schermack-*cum*-Mailometer Co. and its competitors did not actually print stamps; that job was left to the U.S. Post Office Department. Schermack's role was to supply vending machines and to cut and perforate genuine imperforate sheets of U.S. stamps in such a way that the stamps could be utilized by the machines.
[Kenneth A. Wood, *This Is Philately*, Vol. II, pp. 554-5; Richard McP. Cabeen, *Standard Handbook of Stamp Collecting*, pp. 97-99.]

scheur (*m.-c.*) [*Dut.*] a tear (in a stamp or cover).

schismeno σχισμένο [*Grk.*] torn.

schisimo σχίσιμο (*n.*) [*Grk.*] a tear.

Schnittentwertung (*f.*) [*Ger.*] cut cancellation.

Schottland [*Ger.*] Scotland.

schwarz [*Ger.*] black.

Schweden [*Ger.*] Sweden.

Schweiz [*Dan., Ger.*] Switzerland.

scrip [Acronym for *Substitute Currency Received In Payment*.] The term was coined in the 1930s to describe tokens or paper notes issued by companies, private individuals, or governmental agencies as a temporary replacement for legitimate money. These items are not counterfeits and are not intended to deceive or defraud anyone. Rather, they are most often issued in times of economic stress to alleviate a shortage of circulating money. Users normally understand the scrip's purpose.

Although the term goes back to the 1930s, the concept has been around for more than a hundred years. The U.S. Civil War of 1861-65 spawned several types of scrip, some of which included postage stamps. One type was the short-lived *encased postage stamp*[q.v.], an advertising piece made by enclosing an unused stamp between a brass disk and a mica window. The cost of making the piece was absorbed by the merchant who placed his advertising message on the back of the disk.

The illustrated item shows another type of advertising scrip, also from the U.S. Civil War. This merchant simply affixed 10 cents' worth of unused stamps to a piece of paper with his advertising message printed on it. Because the stamps were valid and uncancelled, the scrip circulated freely as if it were a 10 cent coin.

In 1932 Canada began issuing stamps inscribed *POSTAL SCRIP* which were used for remitting small amounts and could be redeemed

advertising scrip (U.S. Civil War)

at any Canadian post office. These are now redeemable only when attached to money orders. The United States released a similar set of 18 stamps in 1945 called *postal note stamps*. They were affixed to postal money orders to make up odd amounts. The series was discontinued in 1951.

Also see *postage currency* and *postage stamp currency*.

[Contributed by Simcha Kuritzky. Photo courtesy John and Nancy Wilson.]

[#1] "scroll" issue (Canada)

scroll 1. Fancy curved device found within the frame of some stamps. The 1928-29 definitive series of Canadian stamps exhibiting this characteristic are normally referred to as the *scroll* issues.

[Michael Madesker, "The *Scroll* Booklets of Canada," *Canadian Philatelist*, January-February 1986, pp. 37-46.]

2. Unusual British postmark showing a curved name panel in place of the circular date stamp. The best known is called the *Stamford Mercury*.

scuro [*Ital.*] dark; deep (*re*: color).

S.D. [*o/p*] Stamp Duty. Fiscal overprints on 1891 stamps of Hong Kong, although some were postally used.

S.D.C. [*Span. abbr.*] Santo Domingo de la Calzada (Spain). Pre-adhesive postmark.

S.D.D. (Σ.Δ.Δ.) [*Grk.*; *o/p*] Romanized as *Stratiotiki Dioikisis Dodecanissou* (Military Administration of the Dodecanese Islands). Overprint found on Greek stamps first issued April 1, 1947, when Greece was given control of Rhodes. See *Aegean Islands*.

S. de N.; S.D.N. [*Fr. abbr.*] *Société des Nations* (League of Nations).

se aceptan tarjetas de crédito [*Span.*] credit cards accepted.

[#2] Easter Seal

seal 1. Device with a cut or raised emblem used to certify a signature or to authenticate a document, or an engraved medallion which can be pressed into wax to officially seal envelopes or authenticate documents.

2. An adhesive label with no postal validity given in fund-raising campaigns and intended to be attached to the reverse side of greeting cards. They are intended to give publicity to the charities being promoted. The most widely-known types are the Christmas Seal[*q.v.*], used to benefit the fight against tuberculosis and other lung diseases, and the Easter Seal, used to help crippled children.

sechs [*Ger.*] six.

sechzig [*Ger.*] sixty.

secret mark Any letter, number, or symbol incorporated into a stamp's design which is not intended to be readily seen. See *hidden mark*.

1978 Vatican *sede vacante* issues: 1st & 2nd interregna

sede vacante [*Ital.*] literally, *vacant see*. The period between the death of an ecclesiastical ruler and the appointment of his successor. Philatelically and numismatically, the term refers to stamps or coins which are issued during this period. The tradition began in the

Middle Ages in various cities in Europe which were controlled by religious leaders who also enjoyed temporal power.

In today's world, the term is used almost exclusively in reference to the death of the pope. Vatican City regularly issues special coins and stamps during interregnal periods, such as in 1963 at the death of Pope John XXIII.

The issuance of *sede vacante* stamps and coins in 1978 was complicated by the death of John Paul I within about a month of his ascension to the papacy. In keeping with tradition, the Vatican did issue several different stamps and a 500 lire coin at the death of Paul VI, and then produced a distinct set of stamps and a different 500 lire coin two months later upon the death of John Paul I. Interestingly, the "living" stamps portraying John Paul I were not forthcoming until December 1978 after the latter interregnum issues were printed and distributed. In other words, stamps representing his death preceded those representing his life.

The second set of interregnum stamps in 1978 contains a very unusual inscription for a postage stamp— the month and year of issue. In order to differentiate between the two *sede vacante* series, the latter gives the month (*Sett.*, the abbreviation for September in Italian) and the year 1978 in arabic numerals. The year on the first series was written in roman numerals (MCMLXXVIII).

[Richard G. Doty, *The Macmillan Encyclopedic Dictionary of Numismatics*, pp. 294-5; Ewald Junge, *World Coin Encyclopedia*, p. 228; *Scott Postage Stamp Catalogue* (1990), Vol. 4, p. 917.]

Sega. [*Span. abbr.*] Segovia (Spain). Pre-adhesive postmark.

segnatasse (*m.*) [*Ital.*] postage due.

segno segreto (*m.*) [*Ital.*] secret mark.

sei [*Ital.*] six.

Seidenfaden (*m.*) [*Ger.*] silk thread.

seis [*Span., Port.*] six.

seitsemän [*Finn.*] seven.

seitsemänkymmentä [*Finn.*] seventy.

seks [*Nor., Dan.*] six.

seksti [*Nor.*] sixty.

self-adhesives: Christmas precancel (U.S.); banana (Tonga)

self-adhesive stamp Any adhesive stamp that does not have to be moistened before it is affixed to a cover.

A self-sticking stamp would seem to be a logical idea, yet it took stamp-issuing authorities a very long time to develop it. This is an idea whose time came, went, and finally returned.

Tonga, an island nation in the South Pacific, issued a large number of unusual stamps in the 1960s and '70s. Among them were a strange variety of self-sticking stamps, including some shaped like a banana. Many of these stamps even had separate self-adhesive "tabs" with control numbers. Some of the Tonga self-adhesive stamps were ultimately used on covers which became part of the revival of Niuafo'ou Island's tin can mail[q.v.].

The United States experimented with a self-adhesive, precancelled Christmas stamp in 1974, but the stamps proved very unpopular. For one thing, many people did not know what they were and tried to lick them. For another thing, the gum was so intense that it soaked through the paper, turning many of the stamps yellow. The experiment was temporarily abandoned.

During that same Christmas and again in 1975 and 1978, Norfolk Island issued sets of self-adhesive commemoratives. The stamps themselves are in the shape of the island, and the reverse side of the backing paper shows a design with a message (see illustration). These stamps were popular as souvenirs but obviously did not see extensive postal use.

The next U.S. attempt came in the late 1980s. The U.S. Postal Service issued a packet of self-adhesives which could be purchased at automatic teller machines. The general public liked the stamps but resented having to pay a surcharge that was tacked on when the stamps were bought at A.T.M.s.

self-adhesive: Norfolk Island commemorative (both sides)

By the mid-1990s, self-sticking stamps had become an established product in the United States and elsewhere. For marketing purposes, the U.S.P.S. gave the new stamps a type of serpentine roulette, not because rouletting was needed for separating the stamps but merely to simulate perforations so that the stamps would have more of a "stamp-like" appearance. (See *serpentine roulette* for illustrations and additional information.)

The United States ran into a problem with its 20-stamp booklets. The booklet pane is configured 3 x 7, so one of the labels has to be something other than a postage stamp. Many consumers inadvertently tried to use those "odd" labels as postage, only to have their letters returned. To correct this, the non-postal labels are now cut with slits that cause them to self-destruct if they are removed from the booklet pane.

The general public loves self-adhesives for their convenience; collectors tend to hate them because of the difficulties in storing them in traditional albums. But new albums are being designed to accommodate these stamps, and collectors are learning to accept the inevitable fact that these self-adhesive stamps are here to stay.

[Wayne L. Youngblood, "What new options do self-sticks offer?" *Stamp Collector*, April 21, 1997, p. 5.]

selge (*v.*) [*Nor.*] to sell.

selger (*m.*) [*Nor.*] seller.

sello (*m.*) [*Span.*] 1. postage stamp. 2. seal (in the philatelic sense).

sello aéreo (*m.*) [*Span.*] airmail stamp.

sello de beneficencia [*Span.*] charity stamp.

sello de certificado [*Span.*] registration stamp.

sello de correo (*m.*) [*Span.*] postage stamp.

sello de franqueo insuficiente [*Span.*] postage due stamp.

sello de franquicia [*Span.*] franchise stamp.

sello de propaganda [*Span.*] propaganda stamp.

sello de telégrafos [*Span.*] telegraph stamp.

sello encapsulado (*m.*) [*Span.*]; **selo encapsulado** (*m.*) [*Port.*] encased postage stamp (such as the type used as an emergency substitute for small coins during the U.S. Civil War of 1861-65).

sello fiscal (*m.*) [*Span.*] fiscal stamp.

sello fosforescente (*m.*); **sello luminescente** (*m.*) [*Span.*] tagged stamp.

sello pegado al sobre [*Span.*] (postage stamp) on cover.

sello para encomienda postal; **sello para paquete postal** [*Span.*] parcel post stamp.

sello postal (*m.*) [*Span.*] postage stamp.

sello provisional (*m.*) [*Span.*] a provisional.

sello servicio oficial [*Span.*] official stamp.

selo (*m.*) [*Port.*] stamp; seal (in the philatelic sense).

selo bisseto (*m.*) [*Port.*] bisected stamp.

selo de beneficência; selo de caridade [*Port.*] charity stamp.

selo de correio (*m.*) [*Port.*] postage stamp.

selo de correio aéreo [*Port.*] airmail stamp.

selo de guerra [*Port.*] war stamp (i.e., military postage stamp).

selo de porteado [*Port.*] postage due stamp.

selo de serviço oficial (*m.*) [*Port.*] official stamp.

selo de telégrafo (*m.*) [*Port.*] telegraph stamp.

selo fiscal (*m.*) [*Port.*] fiscal stamp.

selo militar (*m.*); **selo de franquia militar** (*m.*) [*Port.*] military postage stamp.

selo para encomenda postal [*Port.*] parcel post stamp.

selo para jornais [*Port.*] newspaper stamp.

selo postal (*m.*) [*Port.*] postage stamp.

selten [*Ger.*] rare, scarce.

Seltenheit (*f.*) [*Ger.*] rarity.

sem charneira [*Port.*] unhinged; never hinged.

sem denteação [*Port.*] imperforate.

sem goma [*Port.*] ungummed.

semipostals: Germany (o/p); Swiss *Pro Juventute*

semipostal [also known as a *charity stamp*.] Postage stamp that also acts as a receipt for the prepayment of an additional (nonpostal) fee, usually to benefit a charity. Anyone purchasing a stamp of this type at the post office is not only obtaining postage to mail a letter but is also making a contribution to some specific charity or to some other worthy cause such as aiding disabled war veterans.

Semipostals can usually be identified quickly because most of them show two values, such as 5c + 3c. In this case, five cents is the postage value and three cents is the amount earmarked for charity.

The first semipostal was issued in 1890 by the British Post Office and was actually a postal card commemorating the fiftieth anniversary of the Penny Black. The card sold for 6 pence, i.e., a penny for postage and 5 pence for a postal workers' fund. New South Wales is credited with having issued the first true semipostal stamps. Two were released in 1897 to honor Queen Victoria's Diamond Jubilee. The stamps became immediately unpopular with collectors because their denominations were for 1d and 2 1/2d, but their surcharges were for 1 shilling and 2 shillings 6 pence, respectively. In other words, the surcharges were twelve times the postage value. The surtax went to aid sufferers of tuberculosis (or "consumptives," as they were known in those days), a cause which became very popular worldwide for charity stamps.

In time, most countries began to realize that semipostal stamps would only generate profits for charity if the surcharges were less than the postage values. Belgium and a few other countries have resisted this trend, but the majority of semipostals charge more for postage than for charity.

Semipostals are usually commemorative stamps with the charity information inscribed, but they can also be general issues with special overprints. The illustrated stamp is a post-World War I German definitive overprinted *für Kriegsbeschädigte* ("for war disabled"). Charity stamps benefiting the International Red Cross sometimes show an actual red cross either imprinted or as an overprint.

Some of the better-known semipostals are the New Zealand "Health"[q.v.] stamps, first issued in 1929, and the annual Swiss Pro Juventute[q.v.] sets, initiated in 1913 (see illustration). French Red Cross stamps, which go back to 1914, are also very popular.

The concept of charity stamps is quite foreign to American collectors, because the

United States, despite being one of the world's most prolific issuers of postage stamps, has never issued any semipostals. Canada and Great Britain have released very few.

Also see *surcharge*.

semnătură (*f.*) [*Rom.*] signature.

sensurert post (*m.*) [*Nor.*] censored mail.

senttimetri [*Finn.*] centimeter, centimetre.

senza gomma [*Ital.*] ungummed.

S.E.O.F. [*Ital. abbr.*] *Servizio Estero Oltre Frontiera* (Foreign Service Beyond Border). Pre-adhesive postmark.

separasjon (*m.*) [*Nor.*] separation.

separation The method by which stamps can be easily detached one from another. Most modern stamps are manufactured with rows of tiny holes punched out of the paper. This method of separation is called *perforation*[q.v.]. If rows or zig-zags of cuts are made into the sheet without actually removing any paper, then the separation is called a *roulette*[q.v.]. When individual stamps must be cut from the sheet or pane with scissors because the manufacturing process has not allowed for ready separation, then the stamps are known as *imperforate*.

seppelöity (laakeriseppele) [*Finn.*] laureate.

sept [*Fr.*] seven.

septiembre; setiembre [*Span.*] September.

sepuluh [*Indo.*] ten.

seratus [*Indo.*] hundred.

se requiere un depósito [*Span.*] deposit required.

serie (*f.*) [*Ital., Span.*] series.

Serie (*f.*) [*Ger.*] series.

série (*f.*) [*Fr., Port.*] series.

serienummer (*n.*) [*Nor., Swed.*] serial number.

seri numarası [*Turk.*] serial number.

Serpentinendurchstich (*m.*) [*Ger.*] serpentine roulette.

serpentine roulette [also commonly known (especially to British collectors) by the French name, *percé en serpentine*.]

1. An infrequently-used roulette[q.v.] with deep continuous S-shaped cuts. The most notable examples are the 1860 stamps of Finland which exhibit four varieties of depths and shapes of the serpentine configurations.

Most surviving specimens have some teeth[q.v.] missing; untorn specimens are usually worth at least several times as much as those which are damaged.

serpentine roulette: *then* (Finland) & *now* (U.S.)

2. An updated version of this technique surfaced in the 1990s when self-adhesive stamps became popular in the United States and elsewhere. These new stamps are seperated with a more subtle type of serpentine roulette that simulates traditional perforations to give the stamps a "normal" appearance. This style of serpentine rouletting is used strictly to enhance the marketability of the stamps and not for the purpose of making the separation of them easier.

serrated roulette [also known by the French term *percé en scie*.] Form of rouletting[q.v.] which consists of triangular cuts resembling the teeth of a saw.

sérült [*Hun.*] damaged.

servicio de paquetes postales [*Span.*] parcel post.

Servizio Estero Oltre Frontiera [*Ital.*] Foreign Service Beyond Border. Seen in abbreviated form (*S.E.O.F.*) as a pre-adhesive postmark.

servizio veloce (*m.*) [*Ital.*] speedy service. Seen in abbreviated form (*SV*) as a pre-adhesive postmark.

sesenta [*Span.*] sixty.

sessanta [*Ital.*] sixty.

setembro [*Port.*] September.

se-tenant [*Fr.*] Two or more adjacent stamps which differ in design, language, color, size, denomination, or any combination of the above; in other words, two or more attached stamps which are not identical.

se-tenant booklet pane (U.S.)

Many countries now offer booklets in which all the stamps on the pane are different, even though the stamps usually share the same topical area such as flowers or famous singers.

se-tenant pair (Canada)

Se-tenant gutter pairs are two adjacent stamps separated by a selvage label. The gutter piece may be blank or may exhibit wording or a design.

This term should not be confused with *tête-bêche* which refers to two adjoining stamps, each of which is upside-down relative to the other. There exist examples of pairs of stamps which are simultaneously *se-tenant* and *tête-bêche*.

Also see *bilingual pair.*

set off Partial design of a freshly-printed stamp that transfers to the gum of the sheet above it caused when the sheets are stacked before the ink is dry. A similar effect can happen if a sheet is missed as they are going through the press. The impression from the printing plate is left on the underlying bed and is then transferred to the back of the next sheet as it is being printed.

Sev. [*Span. abbr.*] Seville (Spain). Pre-adhesive postmark.

sewing machine perforation A type of pin perforation[q.v.] in which the rows of pinpricks used for separating the stamps are produced by the bobbing needle of an actual sewing machine apparatus.

Tibet stamps of the early 1930s are reported to have been rouletted this way, although some catalogues merely describe these stamps as having pin perforations. Other such rouletted stamps, e.g., the Colombian Cartagena and Barranquilla issues of 1902 and 1903 and several early issues of Colombian registration stamps, are listed in the various catalogues as having sewing machine perforations.

Although this technique is regularly called sewing machine *perforation*, the term is really a misnomer. In the strictest philatelic sense, the method is a form of *rouletting*[q.v.], as there are no small bits of paper punched out that must be discarded.

The term *sewing machine perforation* is also sometimes incorrectly used as a general synonym for *pin perforation*, which refers to any rouletting of stamps via rows of pinholes, irrespective of the method used to apply those punctures to the paper.

[Samuel Grossman, *Stamp Collecting Handbook*, p. 57; *Scott Postage Stamp Catalogue* (1987), Vol. 2, p. 630 & p. 660, and Vol. 4, p. 785.]

sex [*Swed.*] six.

SF [*Ital. abbr.*] *strada ferrata* (railroad). Pre-adhesive postmark.

S.F. [*Swed. abbr.*] *Soldater Frimärke* (Soldiers' stamp). Overprinted on stamps issued to the Swedish armed forces.

sfragida σφραγίδα (f.) [*Grk.*] seal (as defined in philately).

S.G. [*abbr.*] Stanley Gibbons. These initials followed by a number indicate a stamp's catalogue number in the Stanley Gibbons catalogue.

shade Generic philatelic term for the tint, hue, or intensity of color of the ink with which a stamp has been printed. The various shade designations as they are listed in catalogues (*magenta, orange, grey-green, light blue,* etc.) refer to original unfaded colors of ink. In other words, the shade indicates the exact color which the stamp had the day it was printed.

Designating the proper shade can become a problem if the manufacturer's work is not of considerable quality. Several definitive series of Spanish stamps provide a prime example. The color may be pale and washed out or may be so vivid that it seems to bleed onto the paper. Yet nearly every catalogue in the world gives these stamps identical designations, failing to indicate any difference in color intensity.

Obviously, any philatelist who is partially or totally color-blind will experience great difficulty in distinguishing among the various shades of ink. A lesser-known problem is the effect of aging on the human eye. As people grow older, the fluid in their eyes begins to turn yellow, thus creating a filter through which people must see colors. The effect of this yellowing is most pronounced in the way older people perceive the color blue. The same shade of blue will look more greenish to a 70-year-old than to a 20-year-old. Collectors do not realize this change of color vision is happening to them, because the yellowing develops slowly over a long period of time. Older philatelists who are about to buy or sell an expensive stamp, the value of which could vary greatly depending upon a slight difference in shade, should have that stamp examined by a younger expert.

shelo pursam שֶׁלֹּא פּוּרְסָם [*Heb.*] unpublished (not listed in any book or catalogue).

shelo ya'tsa l'hanpakah שֶׁלֹּא יָצָא לְהַנְפָּקָה [*Heb.*] not issued.

sheqalim plural of *shekel* (or *sheqel*).

shill Phony bidder at an auction who bids against the real bidders in order to prop up the price. He does this on behalf of either the seller or the auction house.

shilling [abbreviated *s.*] Minor denomination used at one time or another by Australia, British Honduras (Belize), Biafra, British Virgin Islands, British West Africa, Cyprus, Dominica, East Africa, El Salvador, Fiji, Gambia, Ghana, Great Britain, Guernsey, Ireland, Isle of Man, Jamaica, Jersey, Kenya, Malawi, Mozambique, New Guinea, New Zealand, Nigeria, Rhodesia, Rhodesia & Nyasaland, St. Vincent, Somalia, South Africa, Southern Rhodesia, Trinidad, Uganda, and Zambia.

Originally known as a *testoon*, the silver shilling was introduced in England by Henry VII around 1504 to compete with the Italian *testone*. The name *shilling* was applied to the testoon in 1549 during the brief reign of Edward VI. The exact origin of the word shilling is uncertain, but the word was used as early as the ninth century as a unit of account.

During most of its history, the shilling was valued at twelve pence or 1/20 of a pound. After the decimal conversion of 1970, the equivalent value became five new pence.

shinplaster Common term for any of the U.S. notes issued from 1862-1876 bearing a denomination of less than one dollar. See *postage currency.*

Shqipëria; Shqipërise; Shqipëtare; Shqipnija *et al* [*Alb.*] Albania. On postage stamps, the name of the country is also found written in a variety of forms, including *R.P.E. Shqipërise* or abbreviated *P.R.SH.* [Note: the letters *R.P.E.* stand for "People's Republic of."]

The spelling *Shqipnija* is unique because it is only found on bogus stamps put out by the government in exile or stamps issued under German administration.

S.H.S. [*Serb.-Cr. abbr.*] *Serbia, Hrvata, Slovenia* (Serbia, Croatia, Slovenia). Overprinted on stamps of Bosnia and Herzegovina. Also seen written in the Cyrillic letters C.X.C.

sicksackformat genomstick [*Swed.*] zigzag roulette.

sieben [*Ger.*] seven.

siebzig [*Ger.*] seventy.

siedem [*Pol.*] seven.

Siegel (*n.*) [*Ger.*] seal (in the philatelic sense).

siete [*Span.*] seven.

Sigillum Sanitatis [*Lat.*] Seal of the Health (Authority). An inscription stamped on letters to show that they had been fumigated or in some other way disinfected against disease. See *disinfected mail.*

sign. [*abbr.*] signature, signatures.

sikkerhetsfibre [*Nor.*] silk thread.

sikk sakk roulett [*Nor.*] zigzag roulette; serrated roulette.

silked paper Small pieces of brightly colored silk thread are sometimes embedded in the paper upon which stamps and paper money are printed as a device for making counterfeiting more difficult. The technique can also be used as a decorative device. The illustrated example is the 1967 U.S. "Peace" Lions International 5c issue printed on gray paper with blue threads.

Paper containing very tiny pieces of silk thread is known as *granite paper*[q.v.].

silked paper (U.S.)

silketråd (*c.*) [*Dan.*] silk thread.

Silurian paper The specific name of a blue-grey colored granite paper containing blue threads.

siman mayim סִימָן מֵימִי (*m.*) [*Heb.*] watermark.

símbolo (*m.*) [*Span., Port.*] symbol.

sin atribución [*Span.*] unattributed (not fully identified).

sin charnela [*Span.*] unhinged; never hinged.

sin dentar [*Span.*] imperforate.

sin fijasello [*Span.*] unhinged; never hinged.

sin goma [*Span.*] ungummed.

sininen [*Finn.*] blue.

sinoberød [*Nor.*] vermilion.

sinistra (*f.*) [*Ital.*] left (direction or position).

sisma סִיסְמָה (*f.*) [*Heb.*] motto.

sjælden [*Dan.*] rare, scarce.

sjældenhed (*c.*) [*Dan.*] rarity.

sjekk (*m.*) [*Nor.*] check, cheque.

sjelden [*Nor.*] rare, scarce.

sjeldenhet (*m.*) [*Nor.*] rarity.

sju [*Nor., Swed.*] seven.

sjuttio [*Swed.*] seventy.

skadad [*Swed.*] damaged.

skade [*Nor.*] damaged.

skat (*c.*) [*Dan.*] tax; treasure.

skatt (*r.*) [*Swed.*]; (*m.*) [*Nor.*] tax; surcharge.

skatte-frimerke (*n.*) [*Nor.*] fiscal stamp.

skattemärke (*n.*) [*Swed.*] fiscal stamp.

skinned spot Damage caused by the careless removal of a stamp from its cover or of a hinge from the stamp which leaves part of the stamp paper thinner than normal. Since the damage occurs on the back side of the stamp, it is not always visible when the stamp is viewed from the front.

Also called *thin spot* or simply a *thin.*

skjult merke (*n.*) [*Nor.*] secret mark.

Skócia [*Hun.*] Scotland.

skopiowany (*adj.*) [*Pol.*] duplicate.

Skotland [*Dan.*] Scotland.

Skottland [*Nor., Swed.*] Scotland.

skrót (*m.*) [*Pol.*] abbreviation.

skyldig porto (*m.*) [*Nor.*] postage due.

slange gennemstik (*n.*) [*Dan.*] serpentine roulette.

slangenroulette (*n.*) [*Dut.*] serpentine roulette.

slangetagging [*Nor.*] serpentine roulette.

S L B [*Span. abbr.*] San Lucas de Barromeda (Spain). Pre-adhesive postmark.

slogan cancellation Cancellation with a killer[*q.v.*] that contains a message such as "Use ZIP Codes" or "Mail Early for Christmas."

slutgiltig [*Swed.*] definitive.

smaragdgroen [*Dut.*] emerald green.

smaragdgrün [*Ger.*] emerald green.

Samantha Smith (U.S.S.R.)

Smith, Samantha American teenager who traveled to the Soviet Union in 1983 in search of world peace. Born June 29, 1972, in Houlton, Maine; died August 25, 1985, in a plane crash near Augusta, Maine.

In November 1982 at the age of ten, Samantha Smith wrote a letter to Yuri Andropov, the newly-appointed leader of the Soviet Union. She told him of her fear that the United States and the U.S.S.R. would get into a nuclear war. To her surprise, not only did Andropov respond to the letter but he even invited her to visit the Soviet Union. In the summer of 1983, Samantha and her parents did visit Moscow, Leningrad (St. Petersburg), and a children's camp in the Crimea, all at the expense of the Soviet government.

Both in the United States and in the Soviet Union, Samantha's trip brought a great deal of attention to the issues of world peace. After returning home, she was interviewed frequently by the news media and (with the help of her father) even wrote a book about her experiences. She also hosted a television show on the Disney Channel.

Because of the exposure she received, Samantha was offered a role in "Lime Street," a television series starring Robert Wagner. The first four episodes were filmed in Virginia and passed uneventfully. The fifth episode was filmed in London. As she and her father were returning home on the evening of August 25, 1985, the plane taking them on a connecting flight from Boston to Augusta, Maine, crashed, killing everyone on board.

In tribute to Samantha Smith, the Soviet Union not only issued a stamp in her honor (pictured here) but also named a diamond, a planet, a flower, and a mountain after her. The State of Maine erected a full-scale bronze statue of her near the capitol building in Augusta. A plaque in front of the statue bears this inscription: "Samantha Reed Smith, June 29, 1972 — August 25, 1985, Maine's young ambassador of goodwill."

[Anne Galicich, *Samantha Smith: A Journey for Peace.*]

snail mail Disparaging term coined in the 1990s to refer to letters sent by way of government-sanctioned post offices. This expression is popular among advocates of e-mail and faxes, because mail sent electronically is instantaneous and relatively inexpensive, whereas post office services worldwide have gained the reputation for being slow, costly, and inefficient.

S.O. [*abbr.*] 1. Stamp Office. Fiscal overprints on 1891 stamps of Hong Kong, although some were postally used. 2. [punch-perfed with crown on stamps of Great Britain] Stationery Office.

S.O. 1920 [*Fr. o/p*] *Silésie Orientale 1920.* Overprinted on stamps of Czechoslovakia and Poland for the 1920 plebiscite in East Silesia.

soberano (*m.*) [*Span., Port.*] sovereign.

sobra (*f.*); **sobras de «stock»** (*f.pl.*) [*Port.*] remainder, stock remainder.

sobre (*m.*) [*Span.*] envelope.

sobrecarga (*f.*) [*Span.*] surcharge; surtax; [*Port.*] postmark.

sobrecarta (*f.*) [*Port.*] envelope; cover (in the philatelic sense).

sobre el reverso [*Span.*] on the back, on the reverse.

sobreestampa (*f.*); **sobreimpressão** (*f.*) [*Port.*] overprint.

sobreimpresión (*f.*) [*Span.*] overprint.

sobre postal (*m.*) [*Span.*] cover (in the philatelic sense).

sobre primer día de emisión [*Span.*] first day cover.

sobretasa (*f.*) [*Span.*] surcharge.

sobretaxa (*f.*) [*Port.*] surcharge; surtax.

socked-on-the-nose See *Bull's Eye.*

soeverein (*m.-c.*) [*Dut.*] sovereign.

soixante [*Fr.*] sixty.

soixante-dix [*Fr.*] seventy.

sokszorosítani (*v.*) [*Hun.*] to duplicate.

sol 1. [*Turk.*] left (direction or position). 2. (*m.*) [*Span.*] sun.

soldatenzegel (*m./c.*) [*Dut.*] military postage stamp.

soldaterfrimærke (*n.*) [*Dan.*] military postage stamp.

soldaterfrimærker (*n.*) [*Dan.*] field post.

SOLLUM/ 14 IX 40 A 1940 overprint on stamps of Libya. It was privately applied and is of no legitimate philatelic interest.

soma (*f.*) [*Port.*] amount.

Somali airmail stamp (1936)

Somalia Although Europeans knew the northern coast of Somaliland from ancient times, the southern coast, later known as Benadir, was familiar only to Arabs. Benadir was a widely-used term for the coastal areas of Somalia consisting of Mogadishu, Brava, Merka, and Warsheik. The name "Somalia" (*soo-maal* = go milk; *sa-maal* = cow milk) was first introduced to the Italian public by Pavia-born Luigi Robecchi-Bricchetti (1855-1926). Negotiations to acquire the area from the Sultan of Zanzibar commenced in 1885; these came to fruition in 1889 after the Sultanates of Obbia and Mijurtina had signed similar agreements giving Italy nominal control of the Somali coast from the Juba River to Cape Guardafui. Originally a part of Kenya, Jubaland (Oltre Giuba or Trans-Juba) was ceded by Great Britain in 1925, its major asset being Kismayu (Chisimaio), the safest anchorage on the Somali coast (see *Oltre Giuba*).

Somalian stamps with BENADIR inscription

In 1903 the first stamps of the Italian protectorates in Somaliland were issued bearing the inscription "BENADIR." Somalia was the first Italian territory to have stamps specifically designed for it from the very beginning. Originally issued in Indian currency, these stamps were later overprinted in Italian currency and subsequently in Somali currency. To add to the confusion, supplies of what would appear to be the 1906 "centesimi" overprints were sent to Eritrea after overprinting them with the name of that colony. In reality the Government Security Printers in Turin had misunderstood the instructions issued by the Ministry of the Colonies. Instead of 80,000 stamps, some 8 million were produced in 1921! These replicated the 1906 "Lire and centesimi" overprints. Neither the Ministry nor the Security Printers wished to take the blame, and in the end, it was realized that the only sensible solution was to utilize this surplus of stamps by overprinting them for the intended colony and also for Eritrea. In 1923 the surplus overprints were further utilized by applying an overprint cancelling the Italian currency. Therefore, stamps born with denominations in the indigenous currency and then overprinted with Italian currency now reverted to the original currency by means of an additional overprint.

It must be noted that throughout these vicissitudes, Italian stamps overprinted "SOMALIA" or "SOMALIA ITALIANA" had been introduced. Nevertheless, the Benadir lions and elephants series continued to proclaim its origin as the legend "BENADIR" remained unaltered and unobliterated. One feature of the stamp collection of Somalia Italiana, as was the case for most of the other large colonies, is the predominance of overprinted commemorative issues of Italy. The central authority thought this was an expedient, inexpensive, and profitable way to "milk" collectors. Most of these commemorative issues formed colonial omnibuses which were easy to market. Their scarcity in used condition is a clear indication that they saw insignificant genuine postal use for commercial mail. From 1925 to 1927, northern Somalia was the scene of military operations which came to a very dramatic finale on November 6, 1927, when Osman Mahmud surrendered his sword to Governor De Vecchi and renounced his rights as sultan.

After securing northern Somalia, the colony now had an area of 600,000 square kilometers and a population of some 750,000. The pictorial and commemorative stamps of Somalia reflect the propaganda concerns of the fascist regime in Rome. However, this did not prevent the issue of a number of aesthetically pleasant and geographically relevant stamps. Such is the case of the 18-value 1932 pictorial definitive designed by Piero Franco, an Italian artist residing in the colony.

Selected denominations of the pictorial set of 1932 were reprinted in May 1934 with the inscription "ONORANZE/ AL DUCA DEGLI/

ABRUZZI" added to them to solemnize, with a 14-month delay, the state funeral of Luigi Amedeo of Savoy— a devoted explorer of the Arctic and Equatorial Africa. The Duke was instrumental in convincing industrialists to invest huge sums in the agricultural development of Somalia. It was his express wish to be buried in Somalia.

The 1934 12-stamp set publicizing the Second Exhibition of Colonial Art at Naples inaugurated the short-lived jumbo-sized stamps nicknamed *patacconi* (large pieces of rubbish). Somalia's first airmails appeared in 1934 when the planned Rome-Mogadishu air link was to expedite postal communications with the Italian colonies of North Africa, Eritrea, and Somalia.

Italian Somalia stamp with inverted overprint (enlarged)

To conclude the shower of stamps issued for the philatelically-memorable flight, a stamp was issued on St. Martin's Day (November 11, 1934), the king's actual birthday, for the return flight from Mogadishu to Rome. The 25 centesimi Colonial Expo airmail stamp was overprinted with a three-line "11 NOV. 1934 — XIII/ SERVIZIO AEREO/ SPECIALE" surmounted at the left by the Savoy crown. The Roman XIII refers to the thirteenth year of the fascist era. In all, the king's visit to Italian Somaliland in conjunction with the first flight, resulted in the issue of fifty-two stamps.

The Second World War began with the Italian invasion of British Somaliland (1940), but the following year Lord Wavell carried out a retaliatory maneuver and was able to overrun Italian Somaliland. On April 13, 1942, the first stamps of Great Britain were issued in Somalia. These were the five dark colored low-value definitives overprinted "M.E.F." (Middle East Forces). At the beginning of 1943, these stamps were replaced by a longer series overprinted "E.A.F." (East Africa Forces) to be followed by a further series overprinted "B.M.A. SOMALIA" (British Military Administration Somalia) in May 1948. In January 1950 the M. was dropped from "B.M.A."

Great Britain administered Italian Somaliland until 1950 when it was handed back to Italy on a ten-year mandate from the United Nations. Preparations for independence were set in motion during the 1950s, both in British Somaliland and the former Somalia Italiana. Full independence was given to the British colony on June 26, 1960; on July 1 it joined with the former Italian area to create the independent Somali Republic.

[Contributed by Giorgio Migliavacca. Giorgio Migliavacca, *The Stamps of Somalia and their Story*.]

Sondermarkenblock (*m.*) [*Ger.*] souvenir sheet.

sönderriven [*Swed.*] torn.

sono accettate le carte di credito [*Ital.*] credit cards accepted.

sorozat [*Hun.*] series.

sorszám [*Hun.*] serial number.

sort [*Dan.*] black.

sortbørsmarked (*n.*) [*Dan.*] black market.

sötét [*Hun.*] dark.

sotilaspostimerkki [*Finn.*] military postage stamp.

soumission minimum (*f.*) [*Fr.*] minimum bid.

Sousa, John Philip American bandmaster and composer. Born November 6, 1854, in Washington, DC; died March 6, 1932, in Reading, Pennsylvania.

Sousa became director of the United States Marine Band in 1880 and held that position for twelve years. From 1892 until his death in 1932, he directed and managed his own musical organization, Sousa's Band, which was

regarded as the finest concert band in the world.

Sousa (U.S.) and sousaphone (Czechoslovakia)

The "March King," as he was known, wrote approximately 150 marches plus a wide array of operettas, ballads, and other works. His best-known march is *The Stars and Stripes Forever*, probably the most popular piece of patriotic music ever written.

Sousa's likeness appears on one of the 1940 Famous Americans issues. The sousaphone, named after him, is featured on a rather curious 1974 stamp of Czechoslovakia issued to honor the Prague and Bratislava Music Festivals.

sous condition [*Fr.*] on approval.

Southn. Letter Unpaid A special postal route from South to North from June 27 to July 11, 1861, through the Louisville, Kentucky, Post Office during the U.S. Civil War. The mail was handstamped *SOUTHn. LETTER UNPAID* in a bluish green ink and included either a due 3 (rubber stamping indicating 3 cents of postage due) for domestic mail or a due 24 for foreign mail. As of June 1, 1861, all mail between the seceded state and the Union had been suspended, and the Nashville, Tennessee, to Louisville route was one of the last to close. Very few examples of the marking exist and are highly prized by collectors.

[Contributed by Richard Corwin. Lawrence L. Shenfield, *Confederate States of America: The Special Routes*, pp. 5-11; *Dietz Confederate State Catalog*.]

souvenirark (*n.*) [*Nor., Dan.*] souvenir sheet.

souverain (*m.*) [*Fr.*] sovereign.

souvenir sheet: Blind Awareness (Brazil)

souvenir sheet A small sheet of postally-valid stamps which is issued as a commemoration. Souvenir sheets are usually very colorful and have relevant information or decorations printed in the margin surrounding the stamps. The sheet may hold only one single stamp or may have as many as twenty-five.

Luxembourg issued the first souvenir sheet in 1906 to mark the accession of Grand Duke William IV to the throne. That sheet held ten stamps. Since that time, virtually every stamp-issuing entity has released at least one souvenir sheet. Some recent ones have been quite unusual, such as the Gabon souvenir sheet printed on a thin slice of wood.

The Brazilian souvenir sheet pictured here is also unusual. It is one of several issued by that country to promote blind awareness. Part of the inscription on this sheet is embossed in braille and can actually be read by the blind.

Souverän (*m.*) [*Ger.*] sovereign.

Sovjetsamveldet [*Nor.*] Soviet Union (U.S.S.R.).

Sovjet-Unie [*Dut.*] Soviet Union.

Sovjetunionen [*Dan.*] Soviet Union.

sovrano (*m.*) [*Ital.*] sovereign.

sovrapprezzo (*m.*) [*Ital.*] surcharge.

sovrastampa (*f.*) [*Ital.*] overprint.

sovrastampato a righe tipografiche [*Ital.*] barred.

sovratassa (*f.*) [*Ital.*] surcharge; surtax.

Sowjetunion [*Ger.*] Soviet Union.

S.P. [*Fr. o/p*] *Service Public.* Overprinted on 1881-1899 Luxembourg stamps to indicate official usage.

Spagna [*Ital.*] Spain.

Spania [*Nor.*] Spain.

Spanien [*Ger., Dan.*] Spain.

spanio σπάνιο [*Grk.*] rare, scarce.

Spanje [*Dut.*] Spain.

Spanyolország [*Hun.*] Spain.

special printings The proper term denoting impressions from official plates to accommodate requests from "official" sources. For example, the term encompasses the impressions of French stamps (some as few as 600 copies) made for Sir Rowland Hill in 1862,

Post Minister Granet in 1887, and the Regents of the Bank of France from 1877 to 1879. These are not mass-produced printings like "Seebecks" but are instead truly special printings.

[Contributed by John E. Lievsay.]

specimen A sample stamp that a government puts out to introduce a new issue. It is usually overprinted as such and is supplied to the Universal Postal Union for distribution to member countries for purpose of identification. Some are remaindered[q.v.] and thus become available to collectors.

spellatura (f.) [Ital.] thin spot, skinned spot.

spelling error: missing "f" in *faune* (Canada)

spelling errors: *Les Inuits* (Canada); *OIHO* (U.S. precancel)

spelling error A type of design error that can be found either on stamps or on overprints.

Dealing with foreign languages can create spelling problems. One version of the 1927 Greek stamp honoring Sir Edward Codrington gives his name simply as "Sir Codrington," a strange form which is never used in Great Britain. Although not really a misspelling, it is a cultural error that falls into the same general category. The error probably occurred because the man's name is printed in the roman alphabet on a stamp otherwise printed in Greek. The mistake was later corrected.

Another language problem arose in Canada. On a series of stamps featuring Native Canadian art, the Indian group is listed as *Inuit* in English and *Les Inuits* in French. The tribe

complained that their name was correct in the English version but misspelled in French because it should not have been made plural.

A more obvious problem arose with the Canadian Migratory Wildlife series. The first letter in the French word for "wildlife" (*faune*) was omitted on some of the stamps showing the belted kingfisher. Corrected and misspelled versions exist.

Misspelled words can also be found on postal stationery, cachets, and other philatelic items. The illustration shows an example of a misspelling on an overprint. The precancel at the top is correct ("OHIO"), but the overprint at the bottom reads "OIHO."

Spem Reducis, Mentibus Anxiis [*Lat.*] Hope of return to anxious minds.

Sperati, Jean de [*né* Giovanni] Creator of "imitations" of many nineteenth century classic stamps. He was arrested in 1942 for shipping eighteen supposedly valuable stamps out of France in violation of customs law. His trial was a sensation as authoritative witnesses testified to the great value of the "genuine" stamps. In 1954 the British Philatelic Association bought him out. It then published *The Work of Jean de Sperati* (London, 1955, 2 vol.) exposing the imitations and telling how to detect them. Not all of his creations were imitations of valuable stamps; in fact, some of his creations are more valuable than genuine specimens.

[Contributed by John E. Lievsay. "Jean de Sperati: Master Forger" and Robertson, "The Sperati Forgeries," pp. 21-36, *The Philatelic Foundations Quarterly*, Vol. 8, No. 1, January-March 1990.]

spese postali (*f.pl.*) [*Ital.*] postage.

spif [acronym for *Stamps Punched with the Initials of Firms.*] Term preferred by British collectors for postage stamps punched-perfed with a corporation's initials to prevent theft. See *perfin.*

S.P.M. [*Fr. abbr.*] St. Pierre and Michelon. Overprinted on French stamps of 1885-1892.

Sporca di dentro e netta di fuori [*Ital.*] Unclean inside but clean outside. An inscription stamped on letters to show that they had been fumigated or in some other way disinfected against disease. See *disinfected mail.*

Sprache (*f.*) [*Ger.*] language.

språk (*n.*) [*Swed., Nor.*] language.

spre aprobare [*Rom.*] on approval.

sprog (*n.*) [*Dan.*] language.

sprzedający (*m.*) [*Pol.*] seller.

sprzedawać (*v.*) [*Pol.*] to sell.

sprzedaż aukcyjna [*Pol.*] auction sale.

spy Espionage is a profession rarely honored on stamps, yet there is a surprisingly large number of stamps which portray spies. The honorees are usually given such elegant titles as "resistance fighters" or even "revolutionary heroes," but their true function was to spy for their cause.

East Germany has probably produced more "spy" stamps than any other nation. A group of semi-postals issued in the late 1950s and early 1960s glorified various communist sympathizers who spied for the Soviet Union during World War II. Included were Elvira Eisenschneider, Arvid and Mildred Harnack, Kathe Kiederkirchner, Adam Kuckhoff, and others, many of whom were members of the so-called *Red Orchestra.* The surtax from these stamps contributed to the maintenance of memorials for victims of the Nazis.

[Stephen Esrati, "Spies on Stamps," *Canadian Philatelist*, January-February 1984, pp. 36-38.]

S.S. [*Span. abbr.*] San Sebastian (Spain). Pre-adhesive postmark.

staalgravure [*Dut.*] steel engraving.

Stahlstich (*m.*) [*Ger.*] steel engraving.

stålgravering (*c.*) [*Dan.*]; (*m.*) [*Nor.*] steel engraving.

stålgravyr (*r.*) [*Swed.*] steel engraving.

ställa ut (*v.*) [*Swed.*] to exhibit.

staloryt (*m.*) [*Pol.*] steel engraving.

Stamford Mercury The best known of the unusual British postmarks showing a curved name panel in place of the circular date stamp.

Stammbaum (*m.*) [*Ger.*] pedigree, provenance (list of former and present owners).

STAMPALIA Overprint on Italian stamps used on the Dodecanese island of Atypalaia (Stampalia). See *Aegean Islands.*

stampare (*v.*) [*Ital.*] to print.

stamp club An organization where collectors meet to discuss their collections and to share their general views on philately.

Although stamp collecting remains quite popular, stamp clubs have been on the decline since the early 1970s. Even the clubs that have survived often experience poor attendance, apathy, and financial difficulties. Most significantly, few young people are participating, turning such organizations into senior citizens' groups.

Some of these problems are the result of a declining membership. A stamp club increases its membership by promoting itself in whatever way it can, usually by starting with the local newspapers. The newspapers will almost always cover a club's events if the organization's officials merely make the request. Flyers placed on public bulletin boards, including on university campuses, and club newsletters sent to prospective members are also excellent promotional materials. The philatelic desks in post offices will almost always allow local clubs to leave flyers promoting club activities.

Boring meetings are another problem area for most philatelic associations. The single best way to alleviate boredom is to ask the club's own members to speak on whatever topic interests them the most. Although the more experienced members may be able to speak knowledgeably about technical topics, the beginners and newer members should also be encouraged to speak. Their enthusiasm may more than compensate for their lack of experience, and their active participation may well generate the interest that will keep them involved in the hobby and in the organization throughout their lifetimes.

Young people will not participate unless they are shown how fascinating and intriguing the hobby really is. Adult volunteers from the club can speak at schools and can set up small exhibits. The club can easily devise youth activities, including junior competitive exhibits. In all respects, the young people must be made to feel welcome. Without an infusion of young people, the hobby will not survive.

stampless cover 1. A piece of mail, usually a folded letter, which was sent by post prior to

stampless cover (1850)

the advent of prepaid, adhesive postage stamps. Since postage stamps were introduced at different times in different countries (1840 in Great Britain, 1843 in Brazil, 1847 in the United States, 1850 in Austria, etc.), the era of *pre-adhesive covers* (as they are also known) did not end on one single day.

Even after stamps were introduced in a given country, some letters continued to be sent without stamps. The cover in the illustration, which traveled from Milan to Galliavola, Piedmont (Kingdom of Sardinia), is one such example. The cover is dated August 5, 1850, two months and four days after Lombardy-Venetia issued its first stamps.

As the illustrated example shows, pre-stamp covers contained much of the same information found on today's mail. First, the cover shows the name and address of the person for whom the letter was intended. Second, modern mail displays a postmark; the illustrated example has three: *NOVARA* (Piedmont); *MILANO*; and *ARF*, the French abbreviation for *Autriche Rayon Frontière* ("Austrian Border Radius"), indicating that the letter was destined for a post within five miles of the Austrian-Piedmontese border. And third, as with modern mail, written on this cover is an indication that postage was paid and for how much. The large endorsement resembling the letter "N" tells us that upon the letter's arrival, the addressee had to pay a fee of four centisimi, even though postage from Milan to the Piedmontese border had been paid by the sender (as dictated by the postal convention between Sardinia and Austria, March 14, 1844). Aside from not having a stamp, the only other thing missing which would appear on today's mail is the return address, but placing one's own name and address on the cover was not customary in pre-adhesive days.

Stampless covers are also sometimes called *pre-philatelic covers*, but this is a poor choice of terminology because many philatelists, especially those involved with postal history[q.v.], have a deep interest in this field. From an historical perspective, we cannot understand and appreciate the need for postage stamps

unless we understand what the postal system was like without them.

2. In the most generic sense, a stampless cover is any piece of mail lacking an adhesive or imprinted stamp which has gone through any nation's postal system. The term does not include letters whose stamps accidentally fell off; the term is limited to letters and parcels that were intentionally mailed without postage.

Under some unusual circumstances, stampless covers have appeared in the twentieth century. One of the most common examples is prisoner-of-war mail[q.v.]. Participating member nations of the Universal Postal Union[q.v.] are required to allow prisoners-of-war to send mail free of charge, and those nations are also required to accept such mail without reimbursement. Similarly, soldiers active during wartime have had free-franking privileges. Their mail is sometimes marked *O.A.S.* (On Active Service).

stämpling (*r.*) [*Swed.*] obliteration.

stamp tongs See *tongs*.

stamtræ (*n.*) [*Dan.*] pedigree, provenance (list of former and present owners).

stânga [*Rom.*] left (direction or position).

Stanton, Edwin McMasters U.S. Attorney General and Secretary of War. Born December 19, 1814, in Steubenville, Ohio; died of pneumonia in Washington, D.C., on Dec. 24, 1869.

Edwin M. Stanton performed as U.S. Attorney General under President James Buchanon in the late 1850s. In 1862 he became Secretary of War in Abraham Lincoln's cabinet. Stanton distinguished himself through efficiency and hard work and contributed significantly to the ultimate military success of the Union (the North) in the U.S. Civil War (1861-65). He quickly became regarded as a Civil War hero.

Upon the assassination of Lincoln in 1865, Vice President Andrew Johnson ascended to the presidency. Johnson greatly disliked Stanton and removed him from his cabinet without the approval of Congress. The Congress reinstated Stanton, but Johnson dismissed him again, prompting the House of

Representatives to impeach Johnson. Although the Senate failed to ratify the impeachment by only one vote, thus saving Johnson's presidency, Johnson's political career was damaged beyond repair, and General Ulysses S. Grant was elected president in 1868.

At Grant's first opportunity, he appointed Stanton to the U.S. Supreme Court, a goal Stanton had cherished all his professional life. The coveted seat was still to elude Stanton, however, because he died just a few days before he was to be sworn in as Associate Justice.

Stanton was one of the first people ever featured on a U.S. postage stamp. His portrait appears on the vermilion, orange vermilion, and scarlet vermilion 7 cent definitives issued from 1871-1880 and a series of stamped envelopes of the same period.

[R. Scott Carlton, *The Numismatist*, "A Numismatic Journey Through Steubenville," July 1991, pp. 1054-60; *Funk & Wagnalls New Encyclopedia* (1984), Vol. 24, p. 317.]

Stany Zjednoczone Ameryki Pólnocnej [*Pol.*] United States of America (U.S.A.).

stary [*Pol.*] old.

Statele Unite al Americii [*Rom.*] United States of America (U.S.A.).

Stati Uniti d'America [*Ital.*] United States of America.

stea (*f.*) [*Rom.*] star.

stamp printed on steel foil (Bhutan)

steel Material upon which few stamps have been printed. Among the rare exceptions is the stamp in the illustration from Bhutan which was manufactured on steel foil. It is part of a series issued in 1969 to honor the history of steel making.

stella (*f.*) [*Ital.*] star.

stemma στέμμα (*n.*) [*Grk.*] crown (royal headpiece).

stempelmærke (*n.*) [*Dan.*] fiscal stamp.

stempling (*c.*) [*Dan.*] cancellation.

stentryk (*n.*) [*Dan.*] lithography.

ster (*m.-c.*) [*Dut.*] star.

sterlina (*f.*) [*Ital.*] pound Sterling (£).

Stern (*m.*) [*Ger.*] star.

Steuer (*f.*) [*Ger.*] tax.

S. Tiago [*Span. abbr.*] Santiago (Chile). Pre-adhesive postmark.

Stichzähnung (*f.*) [*Ger.*] pin perforation; *percé en points*.

stille ut (*v.*) [*Nor.*] to exhibit.

stjärna (*r.*) [*Swed.*] star.

stjerne (*m.*) [*Nor.*]; (*c.*) [*Dan.*] star.

sto [*Pol.*] hundred.

stock book Special type of stamp album used as a temporary storage for stamps until they are properly identified or classified. The pages of a stock book have long horizontal pockets made of either manila paper or transparent acetate into which the stamps are placed until they are ready to find homes in a regular stamp album. Stock books may be spiral bound or may consist of pages which fit into a 3-ring binder.

stock remainder See *remainder*.

stok bakiyesi [*Turk.*] remainder, stock remainder.

stor [*Nor., Swed.*] large.

Storbritannia [*Nor.*] Great Britain; United Kingdom (U.K.).

Storbritannien [*Dan., Swed.*] Great Britain; United Kingdom.

stortandad [*Swed.*] lozenge roulette.

strafport (*m./c.*) [*Dut.*] postage due.

strafportzegel (*m./c.*) [*Dut.*] postage due stamp.

straight edge An imperforate side of a stamp that is otherwise perforated. This is usually not an error. A straight edge occurs if the outer edge of a sheet is not perforated. Stamps printed along the margin will have one straight edge; corner stamps will have two (forming a right angle). Booklet stamps are particularly likely to have straight edges. Coil stamps often have two straight edges, but they are on opposite sides. Coil stamps with parallel straight edges are said to have *imperf sides*.

revenue stamp with straight edge on bottom

Because collectors dislike stamps with straight edges, most current stamps are printed with selvage on all four sides which allows every stamp on the pane to be fully perfed. Even self-adhesive stamps, which do not require perforation for separation, are sometimes cut with a modified form of serpentine roulette[q.v.] to give the stamps the appearance of being perforated.

străin [*Rom.*] foreign.

straniero [*Ital.*] foreign.

strappato [*Ital.*] torn.

strappo (*m.*) [*Ital.*] a tear (in a piece of paper).

Streifen (*m.*) [*Ger.*] strip (of stamps).

strip 1. Group of three or more stamps in a row, attached either vertically or horizontally.

2. Common name for an adhesive meter stamp.

striscia (*f.*) [*Ital.*] strip (of stamps).

strook (*f./c.*) [*Dut.*] strip (of stamps).

STT-VUJA; STT-VUJNA; S.T.TRSTA [*abbr.*] Inscribed or overprinted on Yugoslavian stamps from 1948 to 1954 for use in Trieste.

stuletni (*m.*) [*Pol.*] centennial, centenary.

stupid-philately The collection and study of philatelic and philatelically-related items whose very existence is so absurd that they logically should never have been issued. State of Illinois revenue stamps that must be purchased by dope pushers and pasted onto illegal drugs sold to junkies surely fall into this category. Revenue from this source is referred to as *pot tax*.

subasta (*f.*) [*Span.*] auction.

S.U. [*abbr.*] Sungei Ujong (a Malayan state).

subasta por correo [*Span.*] mail bid sale.

Şubat [*Turk.*] February.

Subducendis Rationibus [*Lat.*] Calculations must be made.

su busta [*Ital.*] on cover.

succino [*Span.*] amber (color).

Sudáfrica; Suráfrica [*Span.*] South Africa. Also written as *África del Sur* (although the accent over the capital "A" is usually omitted).

Sud Africa [*Ital.*] South Africa.

Südafrika [*Ger.*] South Africa.

Suecia [*Span.*] Sweden.

Suécia [*Port.*] Sweden.

Suède [*Fr.*] Sweden.

Suedia [*Rom.*] Sweden.

Suíça [*Port.*] Switzerland.

Suisse [*Fr.*] Switzerland.

Suiza [*Span.*] Switzerland.

sujeito a aprovação [*Port.*] on approval.

sukatfarget [*Nor.*] citron; lemon (color).

sukupuu [*Finn.*] pedigree, provenance (list of former and present owners).

suma (*f.*) [*Span., Pol.*] amount.

summa [*Finn.*] amount.

Suomi [*Finn.*] Finland.

suorakulmainen [*Finn.*] rectangular.

suosioleimattu [*Finn.*] cancelled to order.

supratipar (*n.*) [*Rom.*] overprint.

surcharge [*Eng.; Fr.*] 1. An overprint[q.v.] that changes (or confirms) the imprinted face value of a stamp. Most surcharges are found on adhesive stamps, but some have also been applied to the imprinted stamps on postal stationery. The surcharge on the illustrated Cuban stamp changes the value from 2 to 3 centavos. The stamp with the airplane overprint is part of a set. The multiple overprint changes the country from Yugoslavia to Serbia, and the airplane indicates airmail use. Two of the five stamps have their values confirmed by way of the overprint (including the illustrated example), while the other three show different surcharges.

When used in French, the word sometimes refers to any overprint, surcharge or otherwise, even though this usage is not strictly correct.

surcharges: [#1] Cuba & Serbia; [#2] D.D.R. semipostal

2. The second value shown on a semipostal stamp, i.e., the amount earmarked for a specific charity. If the compound value is stated as *20c + 10c*, then the 20 cents is for postage and the 10 cents is surcharged for charity. In this case, the surcharge is usually an imprinted number, but there are examples of regular postage stamps overprinted to make them semipostal. The next stamp in the illustration is an East German commemorative overprinted with a surtax for the erection of national memorials at the World War II concentration camps of Buchenwald, Ravensbruck, and Sachsenhausen.

sur enveloppe [*Fr.*] on envelope; on cover.

surimpression (*f.*) [*Fr.*] overprint.

surtaxe (*f.*) [*Fr.*] surtax; postage due.

S. UT [*Span. abbr.*] Sevilla Utrera (Spain). Pre-adhesive postmark.

sută [*Rom.*] hundred.

sutime (*f.*) [*Rom.*] hundredth.

suurennuslasi [*Finn.*] magnifying glass.

suuri [*Finn.*] large.

suveran (*m.*) [*Rom.*] sovereign.

suverän (*m./f.*) [*Swed.*] sovereign.

suweren (*m.*) [*Pol.*] sovereign.

S V [*Ital. abbr.*] *servizio veloce* (speedy service). Pre-adhesive postmark from Tuscany.

Svájc [*Hun.*] Switzerland.

svalutazione (*f.*) [*Ital.*] devaluation.

svart [*Nor., Swed.*] black.

svarta börsen (*r.*) [*Swed.*] black market.

svartebørs (*m.*) [*Nor.*] black market.

Svédország [*Hun.*] Sweden.

Sveits [*Nor.*] Switzerland.

Sveitsi [*Finn.*] Switzerland.

Sverige [*Swed., Nor., Dan.*] Sweden.

Svezia [*Ital.*] Sweden.

Svizzera [*Ital.*] Switzerland.

S.W.A. [*abbr.*] South West Africa.

Sweden Three Skilling Yellow Classic Swedish stamp that sold for 2,875,000 Swiss francs ($2.27 million U.S.) on November 8, 1996. The buyer chose to remain unknown.

Much about the stamp itself is also known. It was originally purchased by Swedish dealer H. Lichtenstein from George Wilhelm Bæckman, then a 14-year-old schoolboy, for seven Swedish crowns (about $2 U.S.). Bæckman had discovered it on a letter sent to his grandmother.

The exact origin of the stamp is not known for certain, but most experts theorize that it was a cliché error, caused when a 3 skilling banco cliché was inadvertently used to replace a damaged 8 skilling cliché. But the color is not exactly right for an 8 skilling stamp, resulting in the claim by Gilbert Svensson, former director of the Swedish Postal Museum, that the stamp is a fake. Some have suggested that the stamp was chemically altered to appear yellow. The top row of perforations has been reperfed, adding to the controversy.

But other experts have examined the stamp and declared it genuine, based on the ink, paper, and cancellation. Only one thing is certain: If it is a fake, it is the most expensive philatelic fake in the world!

[John Lindholm, "Three Skillings— And nearly three million Swiss francs," *The Posthorn*, November 1996, pp. 147-9.]

Sydafrika [*Dan., Swed.*] South Africa.

Syd-Afrika [*Nor.*] South Africa.

synkopierte Lochung (*f.*) [*Ger.*] syncopated perforation.

système monétaire (*m.*) [*Fr.*] monetary system.

system monetarny (*m.*) [*Pol.*] monetary system.
sytti [*Nor.*] seventy.
syv [*Dan.*] seven.
syyskuu [*Finn.*] September.
szakadás [*Hun.*] a tear (in a piece of paper).
szakadt [*Hun.*] torn.
szám [*Hun.*] number.
számla [*Hun.*] account (financial or transactional).

száz [*Hun.*] hundred.
szerzemény [*Hun.*] acquisition.
sześć [*Pol.*] six.
szín [*Hun.*] color, colour.
Szkocja [*Pol.*] Scotland.
Szovjetúnió [*Hun.*] Soviet Union (U.S.S.R.).
sztuka (*f.*) [*Pol.*] art.
Szwajcaria [*Pol.*] Switzerland.
Szwecja [*Pol.*] Sweden.

T t

T 1. Mark used universally to indicate *postage due*. It is seen overprinted, hand-stamped, hand-printed, and in various other forms. See *T-in-Triangle*.

2. [*o/p* in circle] Huacho provisional (Peru).

3. Abbreviation used as a pre-adhesive postmark: [*Fr.*] *taxe* (tax; postage due); Tennessee (U.S.A.); Torifa (Spain); transit.

T [-in-Triangle] A mark used by France and its colonies to indicate postage due. It was introduced in the early 1800s in France, although not used extensively until after G.P.U.-U.P.U., and in the colonies in the last quarter of the nineteenth century. Many stamps from the 1880s to the 1940s also have been struck with the "T"-in-Triangle, although the reasons are not always understood. In many instances, these may have been used in lieu of postage due stamps as a result of shortages, but one also suspects philatelic manipulation.

[Contributed by Robert E. Picirilli. Robert G. Stone, "On the Use of the "T"-in-Triangle Mark on Postage Stamps," *France & Colonies Philatelist*, whole no. 180 (vol. 36, no. 2), pp. 33-45.]

T.A. [*Ital. abbr.*] *Transito Austriaco* (Austrian Transit). Pre-adhesive postmark.

tab Any piece of selvage still attached to a stamp.

1. As the word is most commonly used, a tab is a selvage label which has some special information or for whatever reason is intended to remain attached to the adjoining stamp.

Among the best known are the tabbed stamps of Israel. The tabs are usually attached to the bottom row of stamps, although some are attached at the sides. The tabs usually feature something that is related to the design on the stamp. For example, the stamp in the illustration shows a butterfly, and the connected tab shows the caterpillar from which the butterfly will eventually evolve.

Israeli stamp with tab [#1]

Many current tabs contain a message encouraging people to use postal codes. The illustrated tab has a different type of message: "Your mailman deserves your help. Keep harmful objects out of your letters."

U.S. stamp with message tab [#1]

2. The end section of a booklet[*q.v.*] pane used for fastening the pane into the booklet. These

pieces are stapled, glued, or stitched to hold the booklet together. Philatelists prefer to collect booklet panes with the tabs still attached.

tablet 1. A block of space on some stamps where the value is printed. The tablet can be square, rectangular, hexagonal, oval, round, or a stylized shape. Tablets are often found on *key types*, i.e., a generic design used by colonial countries to supply stamps for their colonies. The basic design leaves only a space called a *cartouche* for the colony name and a tablet for the denomination. The stamps go through the press a second time so that the colony name and value can be added.

2. Common name of Eugéne Louis Mouchon's French key type known as *Peace and Commerce*. It is called a *tablet* because of the presence of a large and very conspicuous tablet (as defined above) in the design.

tache (*f.*) [*Fr.*] a stain (on a postage stamp or cover).

tagged stamp A stamp treated with luminescent material that gives off specific colors when exposed to ultraviolet light. The wave length of these colors activates electronic equipment which expedites the processing of mail. The tagging may come in the form of bars, frames, or other devices, or the phosphorescent substance may be mixed into the ink or paper before the stamp is manufactured. In some cases, a phosphorescent coating is placed on the entire surface of the paper. *Untagged* stamps are those which have not been treated with phosphor in any manner.

The first tagged stamps were produced experimentally in 1959 by Great Britain. Since then, many countries have adopted this method.

The tagging on some British stamps is easy to spot because it takes the form of two vertical black bars on the reverse side. In a few cases, otherwise identical stamps have been produced with and without tagging. Some tagged stamps from the United States are distinguishable from their untagged versions by the noticeably yellowed appearance of the paper caused by the application of the phosphor material. The color of the paper of the untagged stamp is very white.

Tagging sometimes produces errors. Many Canadian stamps circa 1972 were treated with a phosphor (known as *migrating phosphor*) that tends to bleed onto other stamps, album pages, or whatever paper the phosphor touches. Another error, ghost tagging, is the result of the phosphorescent tagging and the inked impression not being properly aligned.

tahra [*Finn.*] stain; tarnish.

tähti [*Finn.*] star.

taide [*Finn.*] art.

taitos [*Finn.*] a crease or fold (as in a piece of paper).

taittaa (*v.*) [*Finn.*] to crease.

Tajwan [*Pol.*] Taiwan; Republic of China.

takasivulla [*Finn.*] on the back.

takket [*Dan.*] perforated.

takning (*c.*) [*Dan.*] perforation.

takse pulu [*Turk.*] postage due stamp.

tammikuu [*Finn.*] January.

tam tanımlanmamış [*Turk.*] unattributed (not fully identified).

tanding (*f./c.*) [*Dut.*] perforation.

tandning (*r.*) [*Swed.*] perforation.

tanımlama [*Turk.*] attribution (the complete identification of a philatelic item, including books).

Tanska [*Finn.*] Denmark.

Ţara Galilor [*Rom.*] Wales.

tarak dantel [*Turk.*] comb perforation.

target cancellation Cancellation consisting of two or more concentric circles which resemble a target.

tarih [*Turk.*] date.

tarjeta de crédito [*Span.*] credit card.

tarjeta postal (*f.*) [*Span.*] postcard. The term for *postal card* in Spanish is *entero postal* (*m.*).

tarjota (*v.*) [*Finn.*] to offer; to bid (at an auction).

tarjous [*Finn.*] an offer; a bid (at an auction or mail bid sale).

tarjouslista [*Finn.*] bid sheet.

tasavalta [*Finn.*] republic.

tassa (*f.*) [*Ital.*] tax.

tatlo [*Tag.*] three.

tauschen (*v.*) [*Ger.*] to trade.

tausend [*Ger.*] thousand.

taustakuviointi [*Finn.*] *burélage, burelé.*

ta'ut טָעוּת *(f.)* [*Heb.*] error.
taxa *(f.)* [*Port.*] fee; tax.
taxe *(f.)* [*Fr.*] tax.
täydellinen [*Finn.*] complete.
Te [*abbr.*] Tennessee (U.S.A.). Pre-adhesive postmark.
tebeşir kağıdı [*Turk.*] chalky paper.
tedavülden kaldırmak [*Turk.*] demonetization.
tedavüle çıkarılmamış [*Turk.*] not issued.
tegnforklaring *(m.)* [*Nor.*] legend.
teklif [*Turk.*] (auction) bid.
telegraafzegel *(m./c.)* [*Dut.*] telegraph stamp.
Telegrafenmarke *(f.)* [*Ger.*] telegraph stamp.
telegrafmærke *(n.)* [*Dan.*] telegraph stamp.
telegrafmärke *(n.)* [*Swed.*] telegraph stamp.
telegraph stamp Stamp-like label used to prepay telegraph fees. Although they are a form of revenue stamps, they are often found in postage stamp collections.

Some countries have taken regular postage stamps and overprinted them or punched one single small hole through them to designate them as telegraph stamps. Many telegraph stamps, especially from the United States, were privately issued (see illustration).

privately-issued telegraph stamps (U.S.)

tematico [*Ital.*] topical, thematic.
temático [*Span., Port.*] topical, thematic.
tematyczny [*Pol.*] topical, thematic.
Temmuz [*Turk.*] July.
tentoonstelling *(f.-c.)* [*Dut.*] exhibition.
T.E.O. [*Fr. o/p*] *Territoires Ennemis Occupés* (Occupied Enemy Territories). Overprinted on French stamps for Syria in 1919.

This souvenir cover is highly suitable to a thematic collection on "Chess." The stamp depicts the historic chess tournament with living pieces held every year at Marostica (Northern Italy).

teräskaiverrus [*Finn.*] steel engraving.
terbitan [*Indo.*] an issue, issuance.
tercio (*m.*) [*Span.*] third (the fraction).
tercer (*m.adj.*); **tercera** (*f.adj.*) [*Span.*] third.
terne [*Fr.*] drab (color).
terzo (*m.*) [*Ital.*] third (the fraction).
tessera τέσσερα [*Grk.*] four.

testing labels (U.K. & U.S.)

testing label; testing stamp Labels resembling coil stamps produced by stamp-issuing agencies for the purpose of testing vending machines. Great Britain issued the first of these in the mid-1930s. Their design was an oval green blob inside a frame. Because of their appearance, they were called *poached egg stamps*. Some came into the hands of philatelists, and a few even went through the mail. Later issues were inscribed "For testing purposes only." A similar inscription is found on U.S. coil testing stamps.

tête-à-tête [*Fr.*] literally, *head to head*. Two separate portraits which face each other on a stamp. See *vis-à-vis* for additional information and an illustration.

tête-bêche pair (German)

tête-bêche [*Fr.*] literally, *head-spade*.

Two adjacent stamps that are printed upside-down relative to each other. They may be similar in design, or their designs can be different (known as *se-tenant*). A *tête-bêche gutter pair* consists of two *tête-bêche* stamps separated by a selvage label. The gutter piece may be blank (as in the illustration) or may contain some form of printing (see *guilloche*).

tête-bêche gutter pair (El Salvador)

Many stamps are intentionally printed in a *tête-bêche* format, but a few are created by accident as the result of the faulty placement of a *cliché*[*q.v.*] on the printing plate. There are also examples known of pairs showing one stamp rotated 90° relative to the other.

T.H. [*abbr.*] Territory of Hawaii. Perfed initials on Hawaiian stamps for official use.

thematic collecting Thematic collecting is the development of a theme or subject entirely through stamps, postmarks, covers, and all types of related appropriate philatelic material. Thematic collecting is an offshoot of topical collecting where the main purpose is to arrange stamps by the topic or subject they depict (animals, birds, flowers, trains, etc.). Thematic philately requires imagination and good knowledge of both the theme and philatelic items related to it. The end result is not a book where the illustrations are supplied by stamps and philatelic items but an original treatment of the subject matter with an innovative and creative approach.

It is of vital importance to have a clear and logical plan of the collection in order to have a precise guideline in the development and treatment of a given theme. Most collectors, however, prefer to accumulate all types of philatelic material related to a chosen theme and only later realize that they have acquired material that has little use or relevance. Philatelic materials used in a thematic collection include stamps, stamp booklets, postal stationary, franking meters, and their modifications (overprint, surcharges, perfins, etc., only if they are related to the theme), cancellations, registration labels, supplementary postal markings or labels (e.g., censorship, disinfection, crash mail), reply coupons, and pre-stamp covers.

Ideally, the most suitable philatelic materials include stamps which have a direct link to the theme, covers that have gone through the mails (as opposed to mass-produced first day covers and souvenir covers). Imperforate stamps, varieties, errors, deluxe proofs, proofs, and essays are important only if they add a new element to the development of a theme. It is true that this type of material can often increase the value of the collection. But if it does not provide new and relevant thematic information, it is only redundant and ostentatious. Nowadays collectors are bombarded by what appears to be a never-ending series of topical/thematic stamps issued by postal administrations around the world. In reality the thematic collector need not fall prey to these commercial gimmicks. For example, showing all the stamps (perforate and imperforate), proofs, and essays depicting doves is fine for a topical collection, but in a thematic collection one stamp depicting a dove will suffice, especially if it shows something special like the rare Basel Dove. The theme should be well developed, perhaps depicting the dove's habitat, nesting habits, eggs, doves' varieties and sub-types, etc.

The use of maximum cards in a thematic collection should be limited to a few significant items, mainly to enhance the understanding of the thematic information. Captions and descriptions should be concise. Thematic collectors would be wise to give priority to the lesser expensive material in order to build the "backbone" of their theme. Later they can visit dealers and stamp shows to acquire the more expensive material including those items that give a special touch to their collections. At stamp shows the budding thematist also has the chance to view thematic collections on display and to learn more about this facet of the stamp hobby. Instead of a rare FDC or a block of four, the thematic collector should spend his money on a cover that has actually gone through the mails and which shows stamps and postmarks that have special significance to the development of the theme.

Guidelines may seem boring and restrictive, but in reality they help the collector to focus on the theme of his choice while keeping the outlay of cash within reason. Double-checking the information included in a thematic collection is extremely important; accepting what one source says on a given subject may lead to including inaccurate information. The standard reference for all collectors is a stamp catalogue; we tend to believe that whatever is printed in a catalogue is gospel truth. Seasoned collectors know that a good deal of misinformation and various inaccuracies are perpetrated by all catalogues. Thorough research will not only reveal inaccuracies and inconsistencies but may also lead to a new path to follow in developing an original and eye-catching thematic collection.

For additional information on thematic collecting, contact the following organizations: American Topical Association (A.T.A.), P.O. Box 630, Johnstown, PA 15907, U.S.A.; British Thematic Association (B.T.A.), 107 Charterhouse Street, London, EC1M 6PT, U.K.; and Centro Italiano Filatelia Tematica, Via Tavanti 8, 50134 Florence, Italy. Very active thematic organizations exist in many countries, including France, Spain, Germany, Switzerland, Belgium, Holland, India, etc. For more information on these organizations, contact the International Federation of Philately (F.I.P.), Zollickerstrasse 128, CH-8008 Zürich, Switzerland.

[Contributed by Giorgio Migliavacca.]

thematisch [*Ger.*] topical.

thin (*noun*); **thin spot** [also called *skinned spot.*] Damage caused by the careless removal of a stamp from its cover or of a hinge from the stamp which leaves part of the stamp paper thinner than normal. Since the damage occurs on the back side of the stamp, it is not always visible when the stamp is viewed from the front. Thin spots reduce a stamp's value.

13^/ Zona/ Partigiana/ PIACENZA [*o/p*] See *C.L.N.*

3-D image on stamp (Yemen)

three-dimensional stamp Plasticized stamp which gives the perception of depth when viewed at different angles. Stamps of this type are usually made for collectors by small agent-driven countries and rarely see postal use.

This should not be confused with halographic stamps which are made by projecting a split laser beam onto specially-treated thin foil with a photosensitive surface. This type of pattern gives the illusion of a 3-D image, similar to that of the security device on a credit card. Stamps of this type have been issued by true stamp-issuing countries (such as the United States) and have seen actual postal use.

ti [*Nor., Dan.*] ten.

tidningsmärke (*n.*) [*Swed.*] newspaper stamp.

tief [*Ger.*] deep (*re:* color).

tien [*Dut.*] ten.

tiende [*Dut.*] tenth.

tiendedel (*c.*) [*Dan.*]; (*m.*) [*Nor.*] tenth (the fraction).

TIEN-TSIN Overprint on Italian stamps. See *Italian Post Offices in China.*

tiers (*m.*) [*Fr.*] third (the fraction).

tijdelijke zegel (*m./c.*) [*Dut.*] a provisional.

tilapäisseteli [*Finn.*] scrip.

tilauslomake [*Finn.*] order form.

tilbud (*n.*) [*Nor., Dan.*] an offer.

tilbudsskjema (*n.*) [*Nor.*] bid sheet.

tilby (*v.*) [*Nor.*] to offer.

tilbyde (*v.*) [*Dan.*] to offer.

til gennemsyn [*Dan.*] on approval.

Tilgungsentwertung (*f.*) [*Ger.*] obliteration.

tili [*Finn.*] account (financial or transactional).

tilintetgørelse [*Dan.*] obliteration.

tillagt egenskap (*m.*) [*Nor.*] attribution (the complete identification of a philatelic item).

tillegg (*n.*) surcharge.

tillegge (*v.*) [*Nor.*] to attribute.

tilleggsskatt (*m.*) [*Nor.*] surtax.

till påseende [*Swed.*] on approval.

tilskrive (*v.*) [*Nor.*] to attribute.

timbre de bienfaisance [*Fr.*] charity stamp.

timbre de franchise [*Fr.*] franchise stamp.

timbre de propagande [*Fr.*] propaganda stamp.

timbre de service [*Fr.*] official stamp.

timbre embouté (*m.*) [*Fr.*] tagged stamp.

timbre fiscal (*m.*) [*Fr.*] fiscal stamp.

timbre officiel [*Fr.*] official stamp.

timbre-poste (*m.*) postage stamp.

timbre-poste enchassé [*Fr.*] encased postage stamp (such as the type used as an emergency substitute for small coins during the U.S. Civil War of 1861-65).

timbre-poste militaire [*Fr.*] military postage stamp.

timbre pour colis postal [*Fr.*] parcel post stamp.

timbre pour journaux [*Fr.*] newspaper stamp.

timbre pour la poste aérienne [*Fr.*] air stamp, airmail stamp.

timbre pour lettre recommandée [*Fr.*] registration stamp.

timbre préoblitéré (*m.*) [*Fr.*] a precancel.

timbre-taxe (*m.*) [*Fr.*] postage due stamp.

timbre-télégraphe [*Fr.*] telegraph stamp.

timbro di affrancatura insufficiente (*m.*) [*Ital.*] postage due stamp.

timbro di autenticazione (*m.*) [*Ital.*] authentication mark.

timbro di tassazione (*m.*) [*Ital.*] postage due stamp.

timbro postale (*m.*) [*Ital.*] postmark.

timi τιμή (*f.*) [*Grk.*] price.

timi katalogou τιμή καταλόγου [*Grk.*] catalogue value.

tin can mail Mail carried by swimmers to and from ships anchored off the island of Niuafo'ou (Tonga) from 1921 to 1932. After a swimmer was killed by a shark, the procedure was changed. From that point on, mail was placed in 50-pound biscuit tins and taken to the ships by canoe. This activity continued until 1946 when the island was evacuated due to a volcanic eruption.

Over the years many interesting and very collectible covers came from this strange mail service, largely due to the efforts Walter George Quensell who lived on the island from 1919 until the 1946 evacuation. Many of these covers were his creations, especially those of 1931 to 1934. Those envelopes, franked with the stamps of Tonga, are noted for being rubber-stamped with "TIN CAN MAIL" and for having *paquebot*[*q.v.*] markings.

Islanders were able to return to Niuafo'ou in 1958. A few years later, the Matson Lines resumed tin can mail service as a marketing gimmick for its Pacific Far East Line.

Tin Hat (Belgium)

Tin Hat Series of 1919 Belgian stamps showing King Albert I[*q.v.*] wearing a trench hat. These stamps were intended as a tribute to the king who had actively taken charge of the Belgian army during World War I and had conducted a successful delaying action against the invading Germans. He gained great respect from the Belgians by remaining with his troops throughout the war.

tinta [*Hun.*]; (*f.*) [*Span., Port.*] ink.

Tinte (*f.*) [*Ger.*] ink.

tio [*Swed.*] ten.

tipo de cambio (*m.*) [*Span.*] exchange rate.

tira (*f.*) [*Port.*] strip (of stamps).

tire track cancellation (Belgium)

tire track cancellation Roller cancellation with a design resembling the tread on a tire.

tíz [*Hun.*] ten.

tized [*Hun.*] tenth.

tjänstefrimärke (*n.*) [*Swed.*] official stamp.

tjenestefrimærke (*n.*) [*Dan.*] official stamp.

tjue [*Nor.*] twenty.

tjugo [*Swed.*] twenty.

to [*Nor., Dan.*] two.

TOBRUCH/ 21.6.1942-XX A 1942 overprint on Axis stamps of Libya. This overprint is completely bogus. It was little more than a poorly-conceived fabrication to mesmerize collectors.

toeschrijving (*f.-c.*) [*Dut.*] attribution.

tofarget [*Nor.*] bicolored, bicoloured.

tofarvet [*Dan.*] bicolored, bicoloured.

tökéletes [*Hun.*] perfect.

tongs Tweezer-like utensil used for the handling of stamps in a collection. Using tongs makes examining stamps easier and reduces the possibility of damaging the stamps while they are being handled.

tono (*m.*) [*Span.*] shade (*re:* color).

Tönung (*f.*) [*Ger.*] shade (*re:* color).

tooth Tiny projection of paper that remains when stamps are separated along their perforation lines. If the stamps have been torn apart, the teeth will be at least slightly irregular. If the stamps have been cut apart with scissors or a knife, the teeth will be very straight and neat.

The quality of the teeth is important on all stamps. It is especially important on the 1860 stamps of Finland which were separated by serpentine roulette[q.v.]. Most surviving specimens have some teeth missing; untorn specimens are usually worth at least several times as much as those which are damaged.

tópico [*Span., Port.*] topical; thematic.

topique [*Fr.*] topical, thematic.

tosproget [*Dan.*] bilingual.

toughra

toughra; tughra Monogram configured from the sultan's name and title in the Arabic language. It became the royal cipher of the sultans of Turkey. It was introduced on Ottoman coinage in the fifteenth century as a substitute for the ruler's effigy which, according to Islamic law, may not appear on coins.

The *toughra* eventually was used on the postage stamps of Turkey, Saudi Arabia, and Hejaz-Nejd. It is prominently displayed on an eight-sided Turkish stamp issued for the Army in Thessaly (see illustration).

T.P.O. [*abbr.*] Traveling post office.

training stamp [also known as *college training stamp*.] Stamp-like labels or specially-precancelled legitimate stamps used by business colleges to give students hands-on experience in dealing with postage stamps. Around 1900 in the United States, some colleges began printing fictitious stamps as well as simulated paper money for classroom use. French examples of training stamps are also known.

precancelled training stamp (Great Britain)

Great Britain took a different approach. Some of its legitimate George VI definitives of various values were overprinted with two vertical lines which acted as a form of precancel to effectively invalidate the stamps for postal use. These should not be confused with the British tagged stamps of 1959 (portraying, of course, Queen Elizabeth II instead of King George VI). The tagged stamps were printed with two phosphorescent vertical lines on the back.

transition Any group of stamps from a pane, coil, or booklet that shows a change from one form to another. For example, a coil that is partially misperfed, i.e., the perforations are in the wrong place, may suddenly become imperforate. A group of coil stamps showing that type of changeover is called a *transition strip*.

transit mark Postmark applied to a piece of mail while it is on route between its place of mailing and its destination. Transit marks are usually applied to the back of the letter or parcel.

Trans-Mississippi mail A special postal route across the Mississippi River connecting the eastern and western Confederate states during the U.S. Civil War (1861-1865). This route existed from April 1862 through April 1865. Three major express carriers are known to have transported this mail: the Cushing Express Mail, the 5th Texas Regiment, and the Government Express Mail. At first, Cushing charged a fee of 20 cents in addition to the regular postage but raised the fee all the way to $5 per letter in March 1864.

[Contributed by Richard Corwin. Lawrence L. Shenfield, *Confederate States of America: The Special Routes*, pp. 63-94; *Dietz Confederate State Catalog*, p. 202.]

trapezoidal stamp (Monaco)

trapezoidal Quadrilateral geometrical figure having only two sides parallel. Shape seldom used for postage stamps.

travelogue stamps: Versailles, Paris, & Ghent

travelogue A thematic collection of postage stamps featuring tourist attractions. It usually relates to one's own travel experiences. The

illustrated stamps might be collected by someone who has visited Paris, France, or Ghent, Belgium.

[R. Scott Carlton, "A Philatelic Travelogue," *Global Stamp News*, November 1990, pp. 28-31.]

tre [*Ital., Swed., Dan., Nor.*] three.

tredive [*Dan.*] thirty.

trei [*Rom.*] three.

treinta [*Span.*] thirty.

Trennung (*f.*) [*Ger.*] separation.

trenta [*Ital.*] thirty.

trente [*Fr.*] thirty.

trepado [*Span.*] perforated.

tres [*Span.*] three; [*Dan.*] sixty.

três [*Port.*] three.

tressure Hexagon-shaped figure but with concave sides. If a fleur-de-lis appears at each point, it is called a *fleured tressure*.

tretti [*Nor.*] thirty.

trettio [*Swed.*] thirty.

tria τρία [*Grk.*] three.

triangular airmail stamp (Netherlands)

triangular Seldom-used shape of postage stamps. Stamps of odd shapes or materials have usually been issued by small countries trying to capitalize on the lucrative philatelic market. Yet the majority of triangular stamps have come from "normal" stamp-issuing countries, and the stamps in question have usually seen legitimate postal use.

The illustrated stamp is a 1933 airmail stamp from The Netherlands. It was issued for use on special flights. Its triangular shape made it more identifiable for its intended purpose.

The United States resisted issuing triangular stamps until 1997, in part because triangular stamps tend to leave a lot of wasted selvage on the sheet. The U.S. solved this problem by creating a configuration in which four contiguous stamps occupy a square space of paper. Each square was perforated from corner to corner creating four triangular stamps in a modified *tête-bêche* format. The north and south pair was printed in red and the east-west pair in blue.

[Barry Krause, "Triangles help make collecting interesting," *Stamp Collector*, April 28, 1997, p. 5.]

Trieste Zone A See *A.M.G./ F.T.T.*

trilingual A stamp with inscriptions in three languages. The Hebrew-English-Arabic stamps of Israel are among the most common examples.

Stamps with inscriptions in two languages are called *bilingual*; stamps showing three of more languages can also be call *multilingual*.

triptych: *Spirit of '76* (U.S.)

triptych Strip of three individual stamps that together form one single design. The term comes from Medieval Europe where it was used to describe a three-paneled painting.

The illustration shows a triptych from the U.S. Bicentenntial. The three stamps show a representation of the popular *Spirit of '76*.

A block or strip of four individual stamps forming one design is called a *quadriptych*[q.v.].

trisect One portion of a stamp cut into thirds, each of which is affixed to an envelope and used for one-third of the stamp's original face value. This custom is no longer authorized anywhere, but it was somewhat common in the nineteenth century. Bisects (half of the stamp) were more common.

triskeles

triskeles Configuration of three legs extending outward from the center. It is emblematic of the Isle of Man and appears on its regional issue stamps of 1958-71.

trois [*Fr.*] three.

troquelado [*Span.*] rouletted.

troquelado en forma de rombos [*Span.*] lozenge roulette.

troquelado en puntos [*Span.*] pin perforation, *percé en points*.

trou (*m.*) [*Fr.*] hole.

trykksaksfrimerke (*n.*) [*Nor.*] newspaper stamp.

trzy [*Pol.*] three.

T. Tard [*Fr. abbr.*] *Trop Tard* (Too Late). Pre-adhesive postmark.

tughra See *toughra*.

tulajdonítás; tulajdonság [*Hun.*] attribution.

tumma [*Finn.*] dark.

tunn fläck (*r.*) [*Swed.*] thin spot, skinned spot.

tunnuskuva [*Finn.*] symbol.

tuntematon [*Finn.*] unknown.

turchese [*Ital.*] turquoise blue.

türkischblau [*Ger.*] turquoise blue.

turquesa [*Span.*] turquoise blue.

turuncu [*Turk.*] orange (color).

tusen [*Nor., Swed.*] thousand.

tusind [*Dan.*] thousand.

två [*Swed.*] two.

tvådelad [*Swed.*] bisected.

tvåfärgad [*Swed.*] bicolored, bicoloured.

twee [*Dut.*] two.

tweekleurig [*Dut.*] bicolored, bicoloured.

twintig [*Dut.*] twenty.

tynd plet [*Dan.*] thin spot, skinned spot.

tynn flekk [*Nor.*] thin spot, skinned spot.

tysiąc [*Pol.*] thousand.

Tyskland [*Nor., Dan., Swed.*] Germany.

tyve [*Dan.*] twenty.

U u

U. 1. [*abbr.*] used.

    2. [*Ital. abbr.*] Udine (Italy). Pre-adhesive postmark.

U.A.R. [*abbr.*] United Arab Republic.

Überdruck (*m.*) [*Ger.*] overprint.

überdruckt [*Ger.*] overprinted; barred.

ubrudt [*Dan.*] unsevered.

üç [*Turk.*] three.

U.C. [*abbr.*] Upper Canada. Pre-adhesive postmark.

uçak ile [*Turk.*] airmail.

uçak postası pulu [*Turk.*] airmail stamp.

uçak pulu toplama [*Turk.*] aerophilately.

U.C. Co. [*abbr.*] Upper Columbia Company. This Canadian firm issued local stamps in 1898 for prepayment of fees on letters carried by steamboat between the British Columbia towns of Golden and Windermere on the Columbia River.

udenlandsk [*Dan.*] foreign.

udgivelse (*c.*) [*Dan.*] an issue, issuance.

U.D.P. [*Ital. abbr.*] *Ufficio della Posta* (Post Office). Pre-adhesive postmark.

ufficiale [*Ital.*] official.

ufficio postale (*m.*) [*Ital.*] post office.

ufficio postale militare (*m.*) [*Ital.*] field post.

ufficioso [*Ital.*] unofficial.

ufullstendig identifisert [*Nor.*] unattributed.

ugummieret [*Dan.*] ungummed.

uhængslet [*Dan.*] unhinged.

uhengslet [*Nor.*] unhinged.

uitgeknipt vierkant (*n.*) [*Dut.*] cut square.

Új-Zéland [*Hun.*] New Zealand.

ukendt [*Dan.*] unknown.

ukjent [*Nor.*] unknown.

ulimet [*Nor.*] ungummed.

ulkomainen [*Finn.*] foreign.

Ultramar [*Span.*] Overseas. Inscription found on early stamps of Cuba.

um (*m.adj.*); **uma** (*f.adj.*) [*Port.*] one.

umändern (*v.*) [*Ger.*] to alter.

Umänderung (*f.*) [*Ger.*] alteration.

Umschlag (*m.*) cover (in the philatelic sense). The terms for *on cover* in German are *auf Umschlag* and *auf Briefumschlag*.

Umschrift (*f.*) [*Ger.*] legend.

un (*m.adj.*) [*Fr., Span.*] one.

una (*f.adj.*) [*Ital., Span.*] one.

unattributed A philatelic item which has not been fully identified. A complete identification of the piece, including such elements as the issuing agency, date of issue, watermark, grade, pedigree, etc., is known as its *attribution*.

Unbegrenzte Bietgebote werden nicht entgegengenommen [*Ger.*] no unlimited bids accepted.

unbekannt [*Ger.*] unknown.

unbenutzt [*Ger.*] unused.

undenominated stamps: Israel & U.S.

undenominated stamp Postage stamp which does not state any specific value. In the nineteenth century, this was done as a way of reducing the cost of printing stamps. In recent times, such stamps have been produced either to anticipate a postal rate increase or to cope with a monetary devaluation.

    In the 1850s, 1860s, and 1870s, the British colonies of Mauritius, Barbados, Trinidad, and the Ionian Islands found that they could save money on the printing of stamps by sometimes preparing only one set of plates and by using that one set with different colored inks. Each color represented a different denomination, even though that denomination was not actually printed anywhere on the stamp. In Barbados, for example, the green or yellow green stamps were worth one-half penny, the blue stamps of the same design cost one penny, the identical slate blue stamps were valued at twopence, and brownish red equaled fourpence. Barbados, Mauritius, and Trinidad saved additional money by printing stamps of the same design: Britannia sitting on sugar bags.

Inflation and devaluation have prompted some countries to issue undenominated stamps. The rampant inflation of the 1940s induced China and South China to issue a set of four undenominated stamps. Each of the four stamps was intended for a different purpose: regular mail, air mail, registered mail, and express mail. The cost of the stamps at the post office fluctuated daily as the value of the yuan (their unit of currency) fell.

Israel's inflation and ultimate devaluation of the Israeli shekel necessitated the issuance of an undenominated stamp in 1982. Its selling price at the post office varied.

In recent years the United States and Canada have issued undenominated stamps in anticipation of postal rate hikes. In each case, the postal services needed to have large numbers of stamps in readiness for the day when the rate hikes would be approved. However, there was no guarantee as to exactly how high the rate increase would be. When the rate hike was approved, the stamps were declared to be worth the equivalent of the cost of sending a one-ounce, first-class letter. The undenominated stamps were used until denominated stamps of the proper value could be printed in sufficient quantities.

Since the 1970s, the United States has issued a fairly wide assortment of undenominated stamps, thanks to its frequent rate hikes. The issues have included panes of regular stamps, coils, and official stamps, all printed in large quantities. These stamps are easily recognizable due to the large capital letter printed in lieu of a stated value ("A" equals 15 cents, "B" equals 18 cents, "C" equals 20 cents, *et al*).

One important feature of undenominated stamps is that historically they were valid only for domestic mail (and hence are often referred to as *domestic stamps*). According to former U.P.U. regulations, stamps intended for international use must display a specific value. The U.P.U. finally changed its rules in the mid-1990s, thus permitting "domestic" stamps to be used for international mailings.

The 1988 U.S. "Earth" stamp created an unusual problem for the Internal Revenue Service (I.R.S.). The United States Postal Service agreed to apply a first-day cancellation dated March 28, 1988, on any mail bearing that stamp, even if the request was not made until early May. Income tax returns sent to the I.R.S. must be postmarked no later than April 15 of any given year, and the taxpayer incurs a fine if the return is sent late. A few tardy taxpayers tried to avoid the fine by affixing Earth stamps and by requesting first-day cancellation, thus giving their return the appearance of having been mailed on March 28. Although the I.R.S. claimed that it would penalize taxpayers for doing that, no one really knows how many tardy taxpayers (if any) succeeded in pulling that trick.

See *domestic stamp*.

["Undenominated Stamps," *American Philatelist*, April 1985, pp. 341-2.]

underfrankeret [*Dan.*] postage due.

underfrankeringsstempel (*n.*) [*Dan.*] postage due stamp.

underskrift (*m.*) [*Nor.*]; (*c.*) [*Dan.*] signature.

undertryck; **undertryckt** [*Swed.*] *burélage, burelé*.

undertryk (*n.*) [*Dan.*] *burélage, burelé*.

une (*f.adj.*) [*Fr.*] one.

uneingefalzt; **ungefalzt** [*Ger.*] unhinged.

unexploded booklet A stamp booklet that has never been taken apart and reassembled. An *exploded* booklet is one that has been disassembled, either so it could be displayed

Stamps honoring the Universal Postal Union: Great Britain, Hungary, and Bahawalpur

pane by pane or so the panes could be sold individually.

Rare booklets are checked for explosion before they are purchased, in part to be sure that all the panes came from the same booklet. A booklet will generally show signs of having been taken apart and put back together, such as staple holes that are not in alignment.

Ung. [*Ger. abbr.*] Ungarn (Hungary). Pre-adhesive postmark.

Ungarn [*Ger.*] Hungary.

ungeripptes Papier (*n.*) [*Ger.*] wove paper.

ungetrennt [*Ger.*] unsevered.

ungezähnt [*Ger.*] imperforate.

União Soviética [*Port.*] Soviet Union (U.S.S.R.).

unico [*Ital.*] unique.

único [*Span., Port.*] unique.

unidade monetária [*Port.*] monetary unit.

unidad monetaria (*f.*) [*Span.*] monetary unit.

uniek [*Dut.*] unique.

uniikki [*Finn.*] unique.

unik [*Nor., Swed.*] unique.

unikatowy [*Pol.*] unique.

Unione delle Repubbliche Socialiste Sovietiche [*Ital.*] Soviet Union (U.S.S.R.).

Unión de Repúblicas Socialistas Soviéticas; Unión Soviética [*Span.*] Soviet Union (U.S.S.R.).

unique Only one specimen known to exist, either because only one single piece was originally produced or because multiple examples were produced but all were later destroyed except one.

If no specimens are known to survive, the stamp or other item is referred to in catalogues as *unknown*, even if it is certain that at least one was printed.

unité monétaire (*f.*) [*Fr.*] monetary unit.

Uniunea Sovietică [*Rom.*] Soviet Union (U.S.S.R.).

Universal Postal Union Organization which sets rules and standards to facilitate the handling and delivery of international mail.

On May 11, 1863, postal representatives from Austria, Belgium, Costa Rica, Denmark, France, Great Britain, the Hanseatic cities (Northern German region), Italy, The Netherlands, Portugal, Prussia, Sandwich Islands, Spain, Switzerland, and the United States met in Paris to discuss common problems involving the transport of international mail. This meeting ultimately led to the drafting of a treaty which was signed by participating nations at the Postal Congress of 1874. The purpose of the treaty was to simplify and standardize international postal rates, to prohibit the shipment of narcotics and other specified items, to guarantee participants that they would be reimbursed for transporting foreign mail through their postal systems, to assure the return of undeliverable mail, and to guarantee freedom of transit throughout the entire territory covered by union members.

The organization was formally established as the General Postal Union in 1875, a name that was changed in 1878 to Universal Postal Union. In 1947 it became a specialized agency of the United Nations and is responsible for the international postal activities of nearly every independent country on earth. The U.P.U. is now headquartered in Bern, Switzerland.

The Universal Postal Union has dealt with such issues as persuading nations at war to allow prisoner-of-war mail to pass without any postal charge (a major success for the U.P.U.), of convincing all participants to standardize the colors of their stamps (basically a failure), and for requiring all members to recognize and accept other nations' postage on paid reply postal cards[q.v.] (also a success). It was also through U.P.U. efforts that Finland now lists itself both as *Finland* (the English word) as well as *Suomi* (its name in Finnish), Greece is stated as *Hellas* (in the Roman alphabet) in addition to its original Greek name *Ελλάς*, and Japan uses the romanized name *Nippon*. Until the romanized names were used, stamps from those (and other) nations were excessively difficult to identify.

Many countries have issued magnificent commemorative stamps honoring the U.P.U., a few of which are shown here. The British stamp honors the organization's 75th anniversary, and the Hungarian stamp was put out for the U.P.U.'s centennial. Both the Hungarian stamp and the stamp from Bahawalpur show the distinctive U.P.U. Emblem.

unknown Not known to exist in any collection. In some cases there is a question as to whether the piece was ever actually produced. In other cases, it is certain that at least one was made but none can be accounted for.

uno (*m.adj.*) [*Ital., Span.*] one.

unpaid letter stamp See *postage due.*

unpublished A postage stamp, revenue stamp, or any other philatelic item which is unlisted in any book or catalogue.

unregelmäßig [*Ger.*] irregular.

unsevered Two or more stamps which are still attached one to another exactly as they were produced.

unten [*Ger.*] bottom; below, beneath.

unterbrochene Lochung (*f.*) [*Ger.*] interrupted perforation.

Unterdruck (*m.*) [*Ger.*] *burélage, burelé.*

Unterschrift (*f.*) [*Ger.*] signature.

unu [*Rom.*] one.

unveröffentlicht [*Ger.*] unpublished (not listed in any book or catalogue).

unvollständig [*Ger.*] incomplete.

unzustellbar [*Ger.*] undeliverable.

uofficiel [*Dan.*] unofficial.

uperforert [*Nor.*] imperforate.

upp-och-ner vänd [*Swed.*] inverted.

U.P.U. [*abbr.*] Universal Postal Union[q.v.].

upubliceret [*Dan.*] unpublished.

uralkodó [*Hun.*] sovereign.

uregelmæssig [*Dan.*] irregular.

urząd pocztowy (*m.*) [*Pol.*] post office.

urzędowy [*Pol.*] official.

usado [*Span., Port.*] used.

usagé [*Fr.*] used.

usato [*Ital.*] used.

25c US CY (British Virgin Islands)

US CY [*abbr.*] United States Currency. Abbreviation used to signify that a stamp is denominated in American money instead of the currency of the issuing country. It is commonly found on the stamps of the British Virgin Islands.

uszkodzenie (*n.*) [*Pol.*] defect; damage.

uszkodzony [*Pol.*] damaged; defective.

utakket [*Dan.*] imperforate.

utforming (*m.*) [*Nor.*] design.

utgåva (*r.*) [*Swed.*] an issue, issuance.

utklipp (*n.*) [*Nor.*] cut square.

utklippt stämpel (*r.*) [*Swed.*] cut cancellation.

utslettelse (*n.*) [*Nor.*] obliteration.

utstedelse (*m.*) [*Nor.*] an issue, issuance.

uudelleen liimoitettu [*Finn.*] regummed.

Uusi-Seelanti [*Finn.*] New Zealand.

używany [*Pol.*] used.

V v

V 1. [*abbr.*] Victory; valuable.

2. Abbreviation used as a pre-adhesive postmark: Valencia (Spain); Venezia (Venice, Italy); Vicenza (Italy).

Va. [*abbr.*] Current postal designation for the state of Virginia (U.S.A.). It has also been used as a pre-adhesive postmark.

väärennös [*Finn.*] a counterfeit; fake; forgery.

vaglia (*m.*) [*Ital.*] postal money order.

værdifuld [*Dan.*] valuable.

vævet papir (*n.*) [*Dan.*] wove paper.

vahingoittunut [*Finn.*] damaged.

vaihtokurssi [*Finn.*] exchange rate.

valaminek az alja [*Hun.*] bottom.

választék [*Hun.*] variety.

vale por ... [*Span.*] good for ....

vale postal (*m.*) [*Port.*] postal money order.

valeur (*f.*) [*Fr.*] value.

valeur de catalogue [*Fr.*] catalogue value.

VALEUR D'ECHANGE [*Fr., o/p*] literally, *value of exchange.* Overprint converting three stamps of Ivory Coast and two of French Guinea to monetary use, resulting from a 1920 copper shortage.

For the Ivory Coast, the stamps were separated and pasted onto perforated cardboard in sheets of twenty. The overprinted monetary values of 5, 10, and 25 centimes corresponded to the stamps' original face value (Scott #45, 47, 52). Two printings produced these totals: 5c, 60,000; 10c, 50,000; and 25c, 40,000. They were withdrawn from circulation in 1925.

For French Guinée, the words VALEUR D'ECHANGE but without the stated values were overprinted on the 5 and 10 centime values (Scott #66 and 68).

[Contributed by Robert E. Picirilli. "Ivory Coast Stamp Money," *The Stamp Collectors' Fortnightly*, June 21, 1947; "Dans la Côte d'Ivoire," *L'Écho de la Timbrologie*, 30 juin 1930 (no. 828); "The Ivory Coast 1919-20 Emergency Currency, Made from Stamps," *France & Colonies Philatelist*, whole no. 64 (vol. 11, no. 4), front page; "Ivory Coast," *Scott's Monthly Journal*, March 1925, p. 3; H. Janton, *L'Écho de la Timbrologie*, avril-mai 1974, (nos. 1443-1444).]

valeur nominale (*f.*) [*Fr.*] face value.

välgörenhetsfrimärke (*n.*) [*Swed.*] charity stamp.

valgspråk (*n.*) [*Nor.*] motto.

väliö [*Finn.*] gutter.

valioso [*Span., Port.*] valuable.

valkoinen [*Finn.*] white.

valoare (*f.*) [*Rom.*] value.

valoare de catalog (*f.*) [*Rom.*] catalogue value.

valoare nominală (*f.*) [*Rom.*] denomination; face value.

valódi [*Hun.*] genuine.

valor (*m.*) [*Span., Port.*] value; denomination.

valör (*r.*) [*Swed.*] denomination.

valor de cambio (*m.*) [*Span.*] exchange rate.

valor de catálogo (*m.*) [*Span., Port.*] catalogue value.

valore (*m.*) [*Ital.*] value; denomination.

valore di catalogo (*m.*) [*Ital.*] catalogue value.

valoros [*Rom.*] valuable.

változtatás [*Hun.*] alteration.

vanbringelig [*Dan.*] undeliverable.

vandmærke (*n.*) [*Dan.*] watermark.

vanha [*Finn.*] old.

vanlig [*Swed.*] common.

vannmerke (*n.*) [*Nor.*] watermark.

vänster [*Swed.*] left (direction or position).

vânzător (*m.*) [*Rom.*] seller.

varausmaksu [*Finn.*] deposit.

varausmaksu vaaditaan [*Finn.*] deposit required.

värde (*n.*) [*Swed.*] value.

Va Real [*Port. abbr.*] *Vila Real* (Royal Villa). Pre-adhesive postmark of Portugal.

väri [*Finn.*] color, colour.

variant (*m.-c.*) [*Dut.*] variety.

variantti [*Finn.*] variety.

variedad (*f.*) [*Span.*] variety.

varietà (*f.*) [*Ital.*] variety.

varietate (*f.*) [*Rom.*] variety.

variété (*f.*) [*Fr.*] variety.

variëteit (*m.-c.*) [*Dut.*] variety.

vásárló [*Hun.*] buyer.

vásárolni (*v.*) [*Hun.*] to buy.

vasen [*Finn.*] left (direction or position).

Västtyskland [*Swed.*] West Germany (B.R.D.).

vattenmärke (*n.*) [*Swed.*] watermark.

vävt papper (*n.*) [*Swed.*] wove paper.

vecchio [*Ital.*] old.

vechi [*Rom.*] old.

veck (*n.*) [*Swed.*] a fold.

veelkleurig [*Dut.*] multicolored, multicoloured.

veertig [*Dut.*] forty.

viejo [*Span.*] old.

veiling (*f.-c.*); **veilingverkoop** (*m./c.*) [*Dut.*] auction, auction sale.

veilingcatalogus (*m.-c.*) [*Dut.*] auction catalogue.

veinte [*Span.*] twenty.

veldpost (kantoor) (*n.*) [*Dut.*] field post.

velgørenhedsfrimærke (*n.*) [*Dan.*] charity stamp.

velho [*Port.*] old.

vélin (*m.*) [*Fr.*] wove paper.

Velinpapier (*n.*) [*Ger.*] wove paper.

Venäjä [*Finn.*] Russia.

venda em leilão [*Port.*] auction sale.

vender (*v.*) [*Span., Port.*] to sell.

vendedor (*m.*) [*Span., Port.*] seller.

vendere (*v.*) [*Ital.*] to sell.

vendeur (*m.*) [*Fr.*] seller.

vendita all'asta (*f.*) [*Ital.*] auction sale.

vendita all'asta per posta [*Ital.*] mail bid sale.

venditore (*m.*) [*Ital.*] seller.

vendre (*v.*) [*Fr.*] to sell.

venstre [*Nor., Dan.*] left (direction or position).

venta en subasta (*f.*) [*Span.*] auction sale.

vente à l'encan; vente aux enchères [*Fr.*] auction; auction sale.

vente à prix nets [*Fr.*] French mail sale using fixed prices.

vente aux enchéres par correspondance [*Fr.*] mail bid sale.

venti [*Ital.*] twenty.

veraltet [*Ger.*] obsolete.

verbonden [*Dut.*] accolated, conjoined[*q.v.*], jugate.

verborgen merk (*n.*) [*Dut.*] hidden mark.

Verbriefte Schuldverpflichtung (*f.*) [*Ger.*] scrip, private scrip.

verde [*Span., Ital., Port., Rom.*] green.

verde manzana [*Span.*] apple green.

verde mela [*Ital.*] apple green.

verde smeraldo [*Ital.*] emerald green.

verdi [*Nor.*] value.

verdifull [*Nor.*] valuable.

verdubbelen (*v.*) [*Dut.*] to duplicate.

Vereinigtes Königreich [*Ger.*] United Kingdom.

Vereinigte Staaten von Amerika [*Ger.*] United States of America.

vereint [*Ger.*] accolated, conjoined[*q.v.*], jugate.

Verenigde Staten van Amerika [*Dut.*] United States of America.

Verenigd Koninkrijk [*Dut.*] United Kingdom.

vergrootglas (*n.*) [*Dut.*] magnifying glass.

Vergrößerungsglas (*n.*) [*Ger.*] magnifying glass.

verhandelen (*v.*) [*Dut.*] to trade.

Verificato per Censura [*Ital.*] A common censor mark from Italian-speaking countries. See *censored mail*.

veritabil [*Rom.*] authentic, genuine.

véritable [*Fr.*] authentic, genuine.

verkaufen (*v.*) [*Ger.*] to sell.

Verkäufer (*m.*) [*Ger.*] seller.

verkopen (*v.*) [*Dut.*] to sell.

verkoper (*m.-c.*) [*Dut.*] seller.

verkrijging (*f./c.*) [*Dut.*] acquisition.

vermeil Gold-plated silver, or gold-silver alloy. In its philatelic context, it is a medal level at competition, ranking below gold and above silver.

vermelho [*Port.*] red.

vero [*Finn.*] tax.

veromerkki [*Finn.*] fiscal stamp.

verouderd [*Dut.*] obsolete.

Versteigerung (*f.*) [*Ger.*] auction.

vert [*Fr.*] green.

vert-émeraude [*Fr.*] emerald green.

vert-pomme [*Fr.*] apple green.

vervalsing (*f.-c.*) [*Dut.*] a counterfeit, fake, forgery.

Vervelle Popular name of a 1F French stamp, Scott #8c, first issue in pale vermilion color. When Hulot, the platemaker, died, his nephew disposed of an accumulation of proofs and essays. Included in the lot was a partial sheet (139 stamps) in this color on ungummed paper. A dealer of the time, Vervelle (from whom the stamp was named), acquired this material in 1892 and split the sheet into blocks and singles for sale to collectors. These stamps were never sold in post offices but traditionally are listed as part of the issue.

[Contributed by John E. Lievsay. Kramer, *French Philatelic Facts*, 1949, (first of a series of little booklets published 1949-51; reprinted as Billig *Handbook*, Vol. 29, p. 202.]

verzamelaar (*m.-c.*) [*Dut.*] collector.

verzameling (*f.-c.*) [*Dut.*] collection.

vésett [*Hun.*] engraved.

vesileima [*Finn.*] watermark.

Vest-Tyskland [*Nor.*] West Germany (B.R.D.).

vevemønstret papir (*n.*) [*Nor.*] wove paper.

viallinen [*Finn.*] defective.

Vic. [*Ital. abbr.*] Vicenza (Italy). Pre-adhesive postmark.

Vichy issues Stamps of France and colonies issued while France was under the German government during World War II. Vichy is the name of the town where the puppet government of France was established by armistice signed on June 22, 1940, under Marshal Philippe Pétain.

These stamps appear without the initials "RF" (*République Française*) previously found on stamps of France and her colonies. For many colonies, questions exist whether the stamps were regularly sold and used there.

[Contributed by Robert E. Picirilli. "Vichy Air Mails Were Postally Used in French West Africa Before 1951," *Western Stamp Collector*, June 22, 1954, pp. 3-4.]

Victoria Queen of the United Kingdom of Great Britian and Ireland from 1837 to 1901 and Empress of India, 1876-1901. Born May 24, 1819, in Kensington Palace, London; died January 22, 1901 in London.

Victoria became queen at the age of eighteen upon the death of her uncle, King William IV, who had no legitimate heirs. Her reign of 63 years made hers the longest of any monarch in British history and one of the longest anywhere in Europe. Many thousands of British subjects were born and died having only known her as their monarch.

Queen Victoria

Victoria was neither brilliant nor witty, but she was very conservative, stable, and patriotic, making her the personification of the English ideal of her time. Her personality and demeanor were a perfect match for what British citizens of the nineteenth century wanted, so it is no surprise that this period became known as the Victorian Era. The Victorian Age, as it was also known, was marked by prosperity and the rise of the middle class. In many respects, Victoria truly was the "Fairie Queene" as she was portrayed on the 1839 gold £5 coin known as *Una and the Lion*.

Queen Victoria has the distinction of being the first person ever to be portrayed on a government-issued, pre-paid, adhesive postage stamp. Her presence on the Penny Black[*q.v.*] of 1840 makes her one of the most significant people in philatelic history.

Victoria's popularity was enhanced by the success of the British military. During her long reign, many diverse parts of the world became

Victory cover (China)

part of the British Empire on which, as it was said, "the sun never sets." The vastness of this empire contributed greatly to Victoria's importance in philatelic history. Not only did she appear on the vast number of British stamps expected from someone who would reign for sixty-three years, but she also was portrayed on many stamps issued in local denominations found in the far-off corners of the Empire.

Victoria's descendants included forty grandchildren, some of whom ultimately married into nearly every royal family in Europe. In a sense this could be called Victoria's curse, because she carried the gene responsible for hemophilia. The best-known recipient to suffer this affliction transmitted by Victoria was Alexis, son of the Russian Czar Nicholas II[q.v.], who was killed along with his entire family in 1918 by the Bolsheviks.

During her very long reign, mint officials changed her effigy twice on coins so that she and her portrait would both "age" (although not at the same rate). The same was not done for stamps. The Penny Black shows Victoria as she appeared as a young woman of twenty-one. But when Victoria turned eighty, the same youthful portrait was still being used.

Victoria was loved and respected by her many subjects. Her death in 1901 inspired the creation of many mourning covers and memorial cachets.

Queen Victoria was a classic. She will live forever in philately.

Victory cover Envelope or other cover prepared as a philatelic souvenir or a personal remembrance of a military victory or armistice. The stamps are postmarked on the day of that event. In many respects, these items resemble first day covers, except that FDCs are planned far enough ahead so that cachets can be prepared. Victory covers are somewhat more spontaneous; the "cachet" is usually little more than a typed or hand-written message.

Victory stamps: post-WWI (N.Z.) & WWII (Philippines)

Victory stamp Definitive stamp with a special overprint or a commemorative stamp issued to encourage patriotism during wartime or issued immediately after the war as part of a victory celebration. Most stamps of this nature came during or after the two World Wars. There are many examples, mostly from English-speaking countries.

The illustration shows a post-World War I Victory stamp of New Zealand. It is part of a series of six stamps, each with a different design, which was issued in 1920. The other illustrated stamp is one of several World War II Philippine Islands stamps overprinted *VICTORY* in 1944 and 1945.

Vielfalt (*f.*) [*Ger.*] variety.

vier [*Ger., Dut.*] four.

Viererblock (*m.*) [*Ger.*] block of four.

Vierkantausschnitt (*m.*) [*Ger.*] cut square.

Viertel (*n.*) [*Ger.*] fourth, quarter.

vierzig [*Ger.*] forty.

vieux [*Fr.*] old.

vignette .... frame

vignette 1. The center portion of a stamp design which is of a different color from that of the surrounding frame. It is comprised of a portrait or other pictorial design, and it usually shades off gradually into the frame or unprinted paper. The vignette/frame combination is found on many stamps printed prior to 1930 and on a few issued since that time.

Because the vignette and frame are of different colors, the stamps are printed with two separate runs through the printing press. If the wrong end of the sheet is fed into the press during one of those runs, the vignette will appear upside-down. This mistake produces what collectors call an *invert*. Some very desirable stamps, especially from the United States, have been created this way. (See *invert* and *Inverted Jenny*.)

2. Any pictorial design on a stamp, banknote, or bond that shades off gradually onto the surrounding blank paper.

3. Term used in France to describe a non-postage label containing a pictorial design.

viisi [*Finn.*] five.

viisikymmentä [*Finn.*] fifty.

viivahammaste [*Finn.*] line perforation.

viivattu [*Finn.*] barred.

vijf [*Dut.*] five.

vika [*Finn.*] defect.

vingt [*Fr.*] twenty.

vinte [*Port.*] twenty.

violaceo [*Ital.*] purple.

virallinen [*Finn.*] official.

Virgin See *Missing Virgin*.

Virgin Islands See *British Virgin Islands*.

virhe [*Finn.*] error.

virheetön [*Finn.*] perfect.

virkapostimerkki [*Finn.*] official stamp.

vis-à-vis: Hitler & Mussolini (Italy)

vis-à-vis [*Fr.*] literally, *opposite*. Two separate portraits which face each other on a stamp. The French term *tête-à-tête* is also used.

This style is rarely seen on stamps, in part because it tends to be esthetically displeasing. The configuration appears confrontational. Conjoined[q.v.] portraits tend to make a better appearance.

A better reason why this technique is seen infrequently is because its usage has seldom been appropriate. Vis-à-vis portraits signify two co-rulers or two rulers of equal status, a political arrangement which has seldom been seen since the advent of the postage stamp. The Italian stamp in the illustration shows a rare exception: Hitler and Mussolini. No type of conjoined portraiture would have sufficed, because whoever would have been placed in the forefront would have been given superior status over the other on that stamp.

vit [*Swed.*] white.

vízjegy [*Hun.*] watermark.

vlek (*m.-c.*) [*Dut.*] stain.

Volksrepublik China [*Ger.*] People's Republic of China (P.R.C.).

volledig [*Dut.*] complete.

vollständig [*Ger.*] complete.

volmaakt [*Dut.*] perfect.

voorafstempeling (*f./c.*) [*Dut.*] a precancel.

voorgesteld bod (*n.*) [*Dut.*] suggested bid.

Vorausentwertung (*f.*) [*Ger.*] precancel.

Vorauszahlung (*f.*) [*Ger.*] prepayment.

vouw (*f.-c.*) [*Dut.*] a crease, fold.

V.R. [*Lat. abbr.*] *Victoria Regina* (Latin name of Queen Victoria).

vraket utkast [*Nor.*] essay.

V.R.I. [*Lat. abbr.*] *Victoria Regina Imperatrix* (Victoria, Queen & Empress).

vuosi [*Finn.*] year.

vuosiluku [*Finn.*] date.

vuurrood [*Dut.*] scarlet.

vykort (*n.*) [*Swed.*] postcard. The term for *postal card* in Swedish is *brevkort* (*n.*).

W w

w/ [abbr.] with.

W (with crown) [Pol. abbr.] Warszawa (Warsaw, Poland). Pre-adhesive postmark.

waarmerk (f./c.) [Dut.] authentication mark.

Wahlspruch (m.) [Ger.] motto, slogan.

Walia [Pol.] Wales.

wariant (m.) [Pol.] variety.

war propaganda appendix From 1942-1944 many Italian stamps were printed with a self-contained propaganda message. In most cases, the left half of the adhesive label shows a standard postage stamp design, while the right half contains a propaganda message surrounded by a related illustration. In one case, the postage stamp is on the bottom half and propaganda appendix is at the top. In every case, the postage half and the propaganda half are one contiguous entity with no perforations in between. Also in every case, the postage portion had previously been issued as a separate stamp without the accompanying appendix.

The Italian name for this item is *appendice di propaganda bellica*[q.v.].

war tax stamps [#2] (British Honduras)

war tax stamp 1. Spanish stamps of 1874-79 and 1897-98 which bear the inscription *IMPUESTO DE GUERRA* or *IMPTO DE GUERRA* (War Tax). They represented a fiscal tax on mail and were required to be used in addition to postage stamps. This inscription was also used as an overprint on Puerto Rican stamps during the Spanish-American War (1898).

2. Postage or revenue stamps of many British colonies which were overprinted *WAR*, *WAR TAX*, or *WAR STAMP* during World War I to raise money for the war effort. Sometimes the overprint included a specific sur-charge which was earmarked for defense use.

Washington, George [nicknamed *The Father of His Country*]. General of the American forces in the American Revolutionary War and first president of the United States. Born February 22, 1732, in Westmoreland County, Virginia (then a part of the British colonies in America); died December 14, 1799, at Mount Vernon, Virginia, reportedly from over-exposure to the elements.

Washington was not a brilliant student and he received little in the way of formal education, yet he was a hard worker and an avid reader. He became self-taught by reading extensively on such subjects as agriculture, military history, and geography. At the age of seventeen Washington was asked to join a team of surveyors. He showed great aptitude for this profession and spent the next several years surveying for the local Virginia landowners.

His knowledge of surveying helped him enter the Virginia militia where he quickly rose to the rank of lieutenant colonel. He was ultimately given command of that militia and was instrumental in keeping the Virginia frontier safe during the war between France and England in the mid-1750s. After the war, he was elected to the House of Burgesses where he served for more than ten years.

Because of his tough stand against unpopular British policies, Washington was elected as a Virginia delegate to the First Continental Congress in 1774 and to the Second Congress in 1775. When fighting broke out between the Massachusetts colonists and English troops in 1775, the Congress appointed Washington to command its newly-formed army, in part to promote unity between Virginia and the New England colonies.

G. Washington on early U.S. 10c stamp (enlarged)

From 1775 until the Americans finally achieved victory at the Battle of Yorktown in 1781, Washington led his troops through a long string of successes and failures. He is best remembered today for his famous crossing of the Delaware River with his poorly-clad soldiers on Christmas night, 1776. The next morning they pulled a successful surprise attack on the British at Trenton, a battle which became one of the turning points of the war.

Because of his proven leadership abilities and his wide-spread popularity and because he was an outspoken advocate for developing a strong central federal government, Washington became elected as the first U.S. president in 1788 and was re-elected in 1792. He declined a third term. He is the only U.S. president not to belong to any political party.

To a large degree, the nature of the presidency was designed around his own personal talents and beliefs. For example, he created the concept of the presidential cabinet,

something which had not been provided by the Constitution.

George Washington is probably the most significant person in U.S. philatelic history, in the sense that he has appeared on far more U.S. commemoratives, definitives, revenues, postage currency notes, imprinted envelopes, and every other conceivable type of philatelic item than anyone else. He and Benjamin Franklin[q.v.] were featured on America's first stamps in 1847, Franklin being on the 5c stamp and Washington on the 10c version.

A series of twelve stamps was issued in 1932 to commemorate the 200th anniversary of his birth. The stamps, each showing a different portrait of Washington, ranged in value from 1/2c to 10c.

The U.S. Bicentennial in 1976 produced an avalanche of stamps from the U.S. and elsewhere honoring Washington as well as many other heroes of the American Revolution. Most notable is a series of four souvenir sheets which capture some of the most significant moments of the Revolution. Washington, of course, is prominently featured on those sheets.

George's wife Martha is also portrayed on stamps, including the 1 1/2c stamp which is part of the Presidential Issue series of 1938.

Was K [*abbr.*] Washington, Kentucky (U.S.A.). Pre-adhesive postmark.

Wasserzeichen (*n.*) [*Ger.*] watermark.

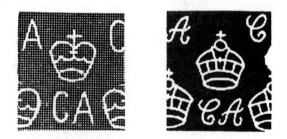

2 typical British Colonial watermarks
(Crown Agents for the Colonies)

watermark A design incorporated in stamp paper during its manufacture. Watermarked paper is usually preferred by postal authorities and security printers as an added safeguard against forgery. Watermarks consist of deliberate thinning or thickening in the paper substance. This is achieved by using special devices to put extra pressure on the paper during its manufacture. In machine-made paper, the device most often used for obtaining thinnings is a "dandy roll" (or hollow roller) with a watermark pattern consisting of metal "bits" attached to (or hand-sewn on) the surface of the roller. This is by far the most common procedure to produce watermarked paper.

Embroider working on a watermark drum
[Photo courtesy Istituto Poligrafico e Zecca]

The opposite process— cavities carved in the dandy roll— produces thickenings of the paper resulting in a "relief" watermark that is thicker than the surrounding paper. A combination watermark— thinnings and thickenings of the paper— is also known. The first adhesive postage stamp in the world, the British 1 penny black and its 2 pence twin, issued May 6, 1840, were printed on watermarked paper.

[Contributed by Giorgio Migliavacca.]

watermark tray Black plastic tray which is used in the detection and classification of watermarks on stamps. The color black is normally chosen so that the watermark will appear darker than the surrounding paper and thus can be more clearly seen. This is the opposite effect of what is usually visible when a stamp or any piece of paper is held up to the light. The watermark, being a thinned area, will normally appear lighter than the surrounding paper and is more difficult to detect.

watermerk (*n.*) [*Dut.*] watermark.

Weeping Princess A variety of 1935 Canadian 1 cent stamp showing the young Princess Elizabeth with a noticeable teardrop beneath her right eye. The tear presumably resulted from some sort of accidental plate damage. The faulty stamps came from Plate 1, position 21 on the sheet's upper right-hand pane.

Collectors apparently discovered the error before the Canadian Bank Note Company officials did, and as many specimens as possible were grabbed for collections. When the officials became aware of the variety, they ordered the plate to be retooled. The retouched specimens can be distinguished from the normal stamps because of minute irregularities in the dots and shading.

The stamps in question were part of the 1935 set issued to commemorate the Silver Anniversary of the reign of King George V.

[Hans Reiche, "Thoughts About a *Weeping Princess*," *Canadian Philatelist*, March-April 1985, pp. 106-7.]

Weihnachten [*Ger.*; *o/p*] Christmas. The overprint "WEIHNACHTEN 1944" is found on some 5c definitive stamps of the Italian colony of Rhodes. See *Aegean Islands*.

weiß [*Ger.*] white.

weldadigheidzegel (*m./c.*) [*Dut.*] charity stamp.

Werbemarke (*f.*) [*Ger.*] propaganda stamp.

Winchester paper: the sublime to the ridiculous (Venezuela)

West-Duitsland [*Dut.*] West Germany (B.R.D.).

w.f. [*abbr.*] wrong font (a typesetting error).

widokówka (*f.*) [*Pol.*] postcard. The terms for *postal card* in Polish are *karta pocztowa* (*f.*) and *całostka pocztowa* (*f.*).

Wielka Brytania [*Pol.*] Great Britain.

wielki [*Pol.*] large.

wielobarwny; wielokolorowy [*Pol.*] multicolored, multicoloured

wijzigen (*v.*) [*Dut.*] to alter.

wijziging (*f.-c.*) [*Dut.*] alteration.

Winchester paper Security paper printed with a heavy network of thick bluish semi-circles. The paper goes through the printing press twice, first to receive the maze of curved lines and then to go through the normal stamp production process. This paper proved unsatisfactory for postage stamp use, as the underprinted curves were so intense as to obliterate a large portion of the stamp's design.

Many Venezuelan stamps issued from 1932-1938 were printed on this paper with varying degrees of success (as can be seen from the illustrations).

window booklet Stamp booklet with a cover containing a cellophane window that enables the postal employee and the customer to see one or more of the enclosed stamps. This concept is popular in Great Britain.

Wis [*abbr.*] Wisconsin (U.S.A.). Pre-adhesive postmark.

wiśniowy [*Pol.*] cerise.

wit [*Dut.*] white.

Włochy [*Pol.*] Italy.

wmk. [*abbr.*] watermark.

w/o [*abbr.*] without.

Wohlfartsmarke (*f.*) [*Ger.*] charity stamp.

wolność (*f.*) [*Pol.*] liberty.

wood Substance seldom found in philatelic collections.

1. In the early 1900s, souvenir postcards were manufactured from thin sheets of wood. The illustrated example also has a small flower attached which is held in place with a nail. In most countries today, this card could not legally be sent through the mail because the nail protruding from it would be regarded as a hazard.

2. A few recent collector-targeted souvenir sheets have been printed on thin pieces of wood. Aside from being curiosities, these items have very little philatelic significance.

Work of Jean de Sperati, The Book published by the British Philatelic Association in 1955 to

window booklet (U.K.)

expose the imitations of philatelic rarities created by the famous forger Jean de Sperati. Information is also included on how to detect the forgeries.

Also see *Sperati, Jean de.*

wycentrowany; wyśrodkowany [*Pol.*] centered.

wycinek (*m.*) [*Pol.*] cut square.

wydanie (*n.*) [*Pol.*] an issue, issuance.

wydanie prowizoryczne (*n.*) [*Pol.*] provisional.

wydawać (*v.*) [*Pol.*] to issue.

wyobrażenie (*n.*) [*Pol.*] pattern.

wystawa (*f.*) [*Pol.*] exhibition.

wystawiać (*v.*) [*Pol.*] to exhibit.

wzór (*m.*) [*Pol.*] pattern; design.

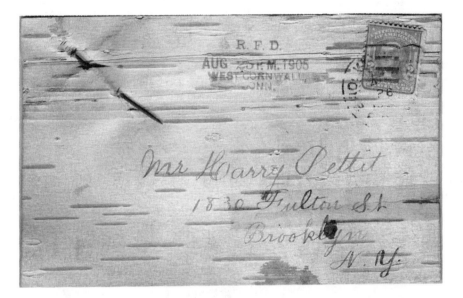

wooden postcard (1905) with a flower held by a nail

X x Y y

xelin (*m.*) [*Port.*] (British) shilling.
xiāo xiàng [*Chin.-py.*] effigy; portrait.
xī hǎn [*Chin.-py.*] rarity.
xīng [*Chin.-py.*] star.
xìn yòng kǎ [*Chin.-py.*] credit card.
xī shǎo [*Chin.-py.*] scarce.

Y 1. [*Span. o/p*] *Ynterior* (misspelling of *Interior*). Overprinted on Spanish (Havana) stamps in 1857 for use in Cuba and Puerto Rico.
2. [*abbr.*] Yorkshire (England). Pre-adhesive postmark.
yakhid b'mino יָחִיד בְּמִינוֹ [*Heb.*] unique.
Y.A.R. [*abbr.*] Yemen Arab Republic.
yayınlanmamış [*Turk.*] unpublished (not listed in any book or catalogue).
yazı [*Turk.*] inscription; legend.
Yeni Zelanda [*Turk.*] New Zealand.

yerro (*m.*) [*Span.*] error.
yhdeksän [*Finn.*] nine.
yhdeksänkymmentä [*Finn.*] ninety.
yhdistetty [*Finn.*] accolated, conjoined[*q.v.*], jugate.
Yhdistynyt kuningaskunta [*Finn.*] United Kingdom.
yıl [*Turk.*] year.
yīng bàng [*Chin.-py.*] pound Sterling (£).
yirmi [*Turk.*] twenty.
Yisra'el יִשְׂרָאֵל [*Heb.*] Israel.
yitur dafnah עָטוּר דַּפְנָה (*m.*) [*Heb.*] laureate.
y'khidah kaspit יְחִידָה כַּסְפִּית (*f.*) [*Heb.*] monetary unit.
yksi [*Finn.*] one.
yläosa [*Finn.*] top.
yleinen [*Finn.*] common.
Yunanistan [*Turk.*] Greece.
yüz [*Turk.*] hundred.
yüzüncü yıl dönümü [*Turk.*] centennial, centenary.

Z z

Z 1. Overprinted in monogram form on stamps of Russia intended for Armenia.

2. [*Dut. abbr.*] Zeeland (Holland). Pre-adhesive postmark.

Za [*Span. abbr.*] Zaragoza (Saragossa, Spain). Pre-adhesive postmark.

zaag-tanding (*n.*); **zaagvormige roulette** (*f./c.*) [*Dut.*] serrated roulette, *percé en pointes*, *percé en scie*.

ząbkowanie (*n.*) [*Pol.*] perforation.

ząbkowany [*Pol.*] perforated.

zaffiro [*Ital.*] sapphire (color).

zafiro [*Span.*] sapphire (color).

Zahl (*f.*) [*Ger.*] number.

Zahlungsanweisung (*f.*) [*Ger.*] money order.

Zähnung (*f.*) [*Ger.*] perforation.

zalmkleurig [*Dut.*] salmon (color).

zamk [*Turk.*] gum.

zamksız [*Turk.*] ungummed.

Z.A.R. [*Afrikaans abbr.*] *Zuid Afrikaansche Republiek* (South African Republic).

Deutsche Besetzung Zara o/p on Italian stamp

Zara [German occupation] Zara was part of the Austro-Hungarian Empire until early November 1918 when it was taken over by Italian forces. At the conclusion of World War I, the area became an Italian enclave on Yugoslav territory. After the official announcement of the signing of an armistice with the Allies on September 8, 1943, the Dalmatian area under Italian control was taken over by the Germans. Although formally still under the administration of Mussolini's R.S.I., Zara was actually under German rule.

Stamps from the *Imperiale* Series, war propaganda stamps, airmail stamps, special delivery stamps, and postage due stamps of Italy (1929-42) were locally overprinted by the E. de Schoenfeld Press with the words "Deutsche/ Besetzung/ Zara" (German Occupation of Zara). The local printer was unable to produce a uniform job due to lack of required fonts in large quantity. As a result, the overprinting plates presented a variety of fonts causing an extraordinary number of varieties and sub-types. A month later, on November 4, more Italian definitives, war propaganda, and special delivery stamps were overprinted by a continuous overprint "ZARA" within bands of lines.

It soon became apparent that too many stamps had been overprinted for a population of hardly 20,000. In reality, the high denominations never arrived at the post office but instead went straight to dealers' stockbooks and collectors' albums. Only 24 or the 58 stamps issued at Zara in 1943 are known to have been postally used, while most of the top denominations ended up on philatelic covers or plain *ctos*.

The general post office, which had already been damaged by an air raid on November 28, was completely destroyed by bombing on December 16, and all existing stock was destroyed. The evacuation of the urban area was concluded on December 31. On October 31, 1944, German forces withdrew from the area and Yugoslav partisans took over. In January 1945 it was annexed to

Yugoslavia, a unilateral move that received formal approval with the February 10, 1947, Treaty of Paris.

Although not listed by Scott, the stamps of the German occupation of Zara are listed by most major catalogues. Very dangerous forgeries of the overprints exist. The utmost care should be exercised in acquiring used examples, and expertization is highly recommended for all issues.

[Contributed by Giorgio Migliavacca. Emanuele M. Gabbini, *Storia Postale de Zara*, Edizioni Nico; E. Ludin, *The Zara Stamps and their Forgeries*; Lauson H. Stone, "Yugoslavia Postal History During World War II," *Postal History Journal*, #81-83.]

zarf [*Turk.*] cover (in the philatelic sense).

zarf üzerinde [*Turk.*] on cover.

za zgodą [*Pol.*] on approval.

zbieracz (*m.*) [*Pol.*] collector.

zbiór (*m.*) [*Pol.*] collection.

zehn [*Ger.*] ten.

Zeichnung (*f.*) [*Ger.*] design; model.

Zeitungsmarke (*f.*) [*Ger.*] newspaper stamp.

zeldzaam [*Dut.*] rare.

zensierte Post (*f.*) [*Ger.*] censored mail.

Zensur (*f.*) [*Ger.*] censor. See *censored mail*.

Zentimeter (*m.*) [*Ger.*] centimeter, centimetre.

zentriert [*Ger.*] centered.

Zeppelin An entire area of philately has been built around the huge German dirigibles known as the Zeppelins. Although mail sent via lighter-than-air vehicles had taken place as early as 1870 (see *Balloon Post of Paris*) and airplanes had been transporting mail since around 1908 (see *airmail*), the public was enthralled by the around-the-world flight made by the mighty Graf Zeppelin in 1929.

By 1930, many countries issued Zeppelin stamps either to commemorate its 1929 flight or to be used as postage for mail carried on it. The United States issued a series of three stamps in 1930 for mail transported on the first Europe/Pan-American Zeppelin flight scheduled for May of that year. The stamps

U.S. postcard transported on the *Graf Zeppelin*

were valued at 65c, $1.30, and $2.60. The illustration shows a Zeppelin cover which made the voyage, a postcard franked with a 65c stamp. The various rubber-stamped markings document the occasion.

The U.S. issued a 50c Zeppelin stamp in 1933 in conjunction with the ship's flight from Europe to Miami, then to Akron and Chicago, and then back to Europe. Envelopes and postcards with these stamps affixed form just a small part of the many interesting worldwide covers created in the 1920s and '30s for mail which traveled on the Graf Zeppelin. Before it was decommissioned in the late 1930s, the Zeppelin had traveled more than a million miles and had carried 235,300 pounds of mail. Decades later, Germany, Bermuda, Liechtenstein, and other nations issued commemorative stamps featuring the Zeppelin as well as other German and U.S. dirigibles.

German dirigibles were filled with volatile hydrogen rather than "safe" helium because the Germans simply did not have enough helium at their disposal. The ship built to succeed the Zeppelin was the grandiose Hindenburg, a huge and magnificent craft which suffered the misfortune of catching on fire and exploding on May 6, 1937, in Lakehurst, New Jersey.

The Graf Zeppelin II, a ship even larger than the original Graf Zeppelin, was built and is known to have carried some mail. A few Zeppelin II covers exist. But the fate of the Hindenburg and the rise of the Nazis essentially put an end to a fascinating period in philatelic history.

zerrissen [*Ger.*] torn.

zes [*Dut.*] six.

zestaw (*m.*) [*Pol.*] (auction) lot.

zeszycik znaczkowy (*m.*) [*Pol.*] booklet (of stamps).

zegel op brief [*Dut.*] on cover.

zhēn huò [*Chin.-py.*] authentic, genuine.

Zhōng Guó [*Chin.-py.*] China.

zieleń koloru jabłka [*Pol.*] apple green.

zielony [*Pol.*] green.

zig-zag gennemstik (*n.*) [*Dan.*] zigzag roulette.

zigzag roulette A type of rouletting[*q.v.*] in which the roulette cuts resemble the teeth of a saw.

This term is rarely used in English. Its other English name, *serrated roulette*, is more common, as are its French equivalents, *percé en scie, percé en pointes*, and *percé en zigzag*.

zinnoberrot [*Ger.*] vermilion.

Mr. ZIP (U.S., selvage)

ZIP code Acronym for *Zone Improvement Program*. Postal code introduced in the United States in 1963 to simplify the patterns and methods of mail distribution. The ZIP code is placed immediately after the city and state in an address. It originally consisted of a five-digit number but was expanded to nine digits in 1983 to include a hyphenated four-digit tag. The first number in the five-digit portion indicates a major geographic section of the U.S. or its territories. The next two digits narrow the area to a major post office or sectional center in a specific state. The final two digits identify a small post office or the delivery station of a major post office.

Prior to the introduction of the ZIP code (and to the creation of official state abbreviations), an area of Chicago covered by a particular post office might be listed as "Chicago 9, Illinois." With the ZIP code, it would be designated "Chicago, IL 60609." The new four-digit tag indicates a specific street address, office number, post office box, or whatever. That same address in Chicago might now be "Chicago, IL 60609-0524."

As part of its promotion to convince the American public to use ZIP codes, the U.S. Postal Service created a cartoon character named Mr. ZIP. He appeared on the selvage of many stamps in the 1960s and 1970s.

zitronengelb [*Ger.*] citron (color).

Zjednoczone Królestwo [*Pol.*] United Kingdom.

złoty [*Pol.*] Polish unit of currency.

znaczek (*m.*) [*Pol.*] (postage) stamp.

znaczek gazetowy (*m.*) [*Pol.*] newspaper stamp.

znaczek kapslowy [*Pol.*] encased postage stamp.

znaczek lotniczy (*m.*) [*Pol.*] airmail stamp.

znaczek luminescencyjny (*m.*); **znaczek "świecący"** (*m.*) [*Pol.*] tagged stamp.

znaczek na cele dobroczynne [*Pol.*] charity stamp.

znaczek opłaty pocztowej (*m.*) [*Pol.*] postage due stamp.

znaczek pocztowy (*m.*) [*Pol.*] postage stamp.

znaczek poczty lotniczej [*Pol.*] airmail stamp.

znaczek poczty paczkowej (*m.*) [*Pol.*] parcel post stamp.

znaczek poczty wojskowej (*m.*) [*Pol.*] military postage stamp.

znaczek propagandowy (*m.*) [*Pol.*] propaganda stamp.

znaczek skarbowy (*m.*) [*Pol.*] fiscal stamp.

znaczek telegraficzny (*m.*) [*Pol.*] telegraph stamp.

znaczek urzędowy (*m.*) [*Pol.*] official stamp.

znaczek zwalniający od opłaty pocztowej [*Pol.*] franchise stamp.

z nadrukiem kasującym [*Pol.*] barred.

znak autentyczności [*Pol.*] authentication mark.

znak sekretny (*m.*); **znak gwarancyjny** (*m.*) [*Pol.*] secret mark.

znak wodny (*m.*) [*Pol.*] watermark.

ZOFK [*o/p*] *ZONA OCCUPATA FIUMANO KUPA* ("Fiume Kupa Occupied Zone"). Italian overprint on stamps of Fiume[*q.v.*].

Zoll (*m.*) [*Ger.*] inch.

żółty [*Pol.*] yellow.

zonder plakker [*Dut.*] unhinged.

Zone Improvement Program See *ZIP code.*

Zuid-Afrika [*Dut.*] South Africa.

zümrüt yeşili [*Turk.*] emerald green.

zur Ansicht [*Ger.*] on approval.

zur Post geben (*v.*) [*Ger.*] to mail.

Zusammendruck (*m.*) [*Ger.*] *se-tenant.*

Zuschlagmarke (*f.*) [*Ger.*] surtax.

Zuschreibung (*f.*) [*Ger.*] attribution.

zwanzig [*Ger.*] twenty.

zwart [*Dut.*] black.

zwei [*Ger.*] two.

zweifarbig [*Ger.*] bicolored, bicoloured.

zweisprachig [*Ger.*] bilingual.

Związek Radziecki (Z.S.R.R.) [*Pol.*] Soviet Union.

Zwischensteg (*m.*) [*Ger.*] gutter.

Greek Alphabet

All words in Modern Greek

Α α

Αγγλία England.
άγνωστος unknown (no specimens are known to exist in any collection).
αγοράζω (v.) to buy.
αγοραστής buyer.
αδιαχώριστον unsevered.
αεροεπιστολή (f.) aerogramme.
αεροπορικόν (n.) airmail.
αεροπορικόν γραμματόσημον (n.) airmail stamp.
αεροφιλοτελισμός (m.) aerophilately.
ακυρώνω (v.) to cancel.
ακύρωση κοπής (f.) cut cancellation.
ακύρωση μετά εντολής cancelled to order.
ακύρωσις (n.) cancellation.
αλλοδαπός foreign.
ανάγλυφον (n.) embossing.
αναμνηστικό φύλλο (n.) souvenir sheet.
αναπαραγωγή (f.) copy; reproduction.
Ανατολική Γερμανία East Germany (D.D.R.).
ανατύπωση (f.) a reprint.
ανεπίσημον unofficial.
ανεστραμμένη εκτύπωση tête-bêche.
ανεστραμμένο inverted.
ανιλίνη aniline.
ανοικτόχρωμο light (re: color).
αξία (f.) value.
απαράδοτο undeliverable.
απαρχαιομένο obsolete.
απόδειξη (f.) receipt.
αποδίδω (v.) to attribute.
απόκτηση (f.) acquisition.
απόχρωση (f.) shade (re: color).

αριθμός (m.) number.
Αργεντινή Argentina.
αριστερός left (direction or position).
Απρίλιος April.
άσπρο white.
άστρο (n.) star.
ατελές incomplete.
Αύγουστος August.
Αυστραλία Australia.
Αυστρία Austria.
αυτοκράτορας (m.) emperor.
αχρησιμοποίητο unused.
άψογος perfect.

Β β

βαθμός (m.) grade, condition.
βαθύ deep (re: color).
βασιλιάς (m.) king.
βασίλισσα (f.) queen.
Βέλγιο Belgium.
βιβλιαράκι (n.) booklet (of stamps).
βιολέ violet (color).
βυσσινί crimson.

Γ γ

Γαλλία France.
Γερμανία Germany.
γιαλιστερό χαρτί (n.) glossy paper.
Γιουγκοσλαβία Yugoslavia, Jugoslavia.
γκρί gray.
γλώσσα (f.) language.
γνήσια γόμμα (f.) original gum.
γνήσιον genuine, authentic.
γόμμα (f.) gum.
γράμμα (n.) the mail; a letter.
γραμματόσημο (n.) postage stamp.
γραμματόσημο δημοσίου (n.) fiscal stamp.

γραμματόσημο εσωκλειόμενο (n.) encased postage stamp.

γραμματόσημο εφημερίδας newspaper stamp.

γραμματόσημο με προσαρτημένη ετικέττα tagged stamp.

γραμματόσημον για δέμα (n.) parcel post stamp.

Δ δ

Δανία Denmark.

δαφνοστεφής laureate.

δείγμα (n.) specimen.

δέκα ten.

δέκατον tenth (the fraction).

Δεκέμβριος December.

δελτίον παραγγελιών (n.) order form.

δέμα (n.) package.

δεξιός right (direction or position).

δεχόμαστε πιστωτικές κάρτες credit cards accepted.

δημοκρατία (f.) republic.

Δημοκρατία τής Κίνας Republic of China.

δημοπρασία (f.) auction; auction sale.

διακοπτομένη διάτρησις (f.) interrupted perforation.

διάτρησις διά βελόνης (f.) pin perforation; *percé en points.*

διάτρισις κτένας comb perforation.

διατρυπωμένο perforated.

διαφυλασσόμενη προσφορά reserve bid.

διαχωρισμός (m.) separation.

δίγλωσσος bilingual.

διεθνής international.

διπλασιάζω (v.) to duplicate.

διπλοτυπωμένο (adj.) duplicate.

διπλότυπον a duplicate.

διπλώνω (v.) to fold.

διχοτομισμένο bisected.

δίχρωμο bicolored, bicoloured.

δολλάριο (n.) dollar.

δοκίμιο essay.

δύο two.

Δυτική Γερμανία West Germany (B.R.D.).

Ε ε

εβδομήντα seventy.

εγχάραξη (f.) intaglio.

εθνικός national.

εθνικότητα (f.) nationality.

εικονογραφία (f.) portrait.

είκοσι twenty.

ειρήνη (f.) peace.

εισηγούμενη προσφορά (f.) suggested bid.

εκατό hundred.

εκατομμύριο (n.) million.

εκατονταετηρίδα (f.) centennial, centenary.

εκατοστό (n.) centimeter.

εκατοστόν hundredth.

εκδίδω (v.) to issue.

έκδοση (f.) an issue, issuance.

έκθεση (f.) exhibition.

εκθέτω (v.) to exhibit.

ελαιόχρουν olive (green).

ελαττωματικό defective.

ελάχιστη προσφορά (f.) minimum bid.

Ελβετία Switzerland.

ελευθερία (f.) liberty.

Ελλάς Greece.

ένα one.

ενάριθμα postage due.

ενάριθμον γραμματόσημον (n.) postage due stamp.

εννέα nine.

εξαλειφόμενον (n.) obliteration.

εξήντα sixty.

έξι six.

επαναγομμαρισμένο regummed.

επιγραφή (f.) legend; inscription.

επιδιορθωμένο repaired.

επί επιστολής on cover.

επικεντρομένο centered.

επιπρόσθετος φόρος (m.) surtax.

επισήμασμα (n.) surcharge.

επίσημον γραμματόσημον (n.) official stamp.

επίσημος official.

επισφράγισης (f.) overprint.

επιταγή (f.) check, cheque.

ερυθροκάστανο maroon.

Ερυθρός Σταυρός Red Cross.

έτος year.
ευθεία διάτρησις (f.) line perforation.

Ζ ζ

ζευγάρι (n.) pair (of stamps).

Η η

ηγεμόνας sovereign.
ημερομηνία (f.) date.
Ηνωμένον Βασίλειον United Kingdom (U.K.).
Ηνωμένες Πολιτείες τής Αμερικής United States of America (U.S.A.).

Ι ι

Ιανουάριος January.
Ισπανία Spain.
Ισραήλ Israel.
Ιούλιος July.
Ιούνιος June.

Κ κ

καθετες ραβδώσεις barred.
Καναδάς Canada.
καρμινόχρωμο carmine.
κατάλογος (m.) catalog, catalogue.
κατάλογος πλειστηριασμού (m.) auction catalogue.

κατάσταση (f.) grade, condition.
κάτω bottom.
κερασί cerise.
κεχριμπαρένιο amber (color).
κίβδηλον (n.) a fake, forgery.
Κίνα China.
κιτρινο yellow.
κοινός common.
κόκκινο red.
κοκκινόχρους magenta.
Κολομβία Colombia.
κομμάτι τών τεσσάρων block of four.
κορνίζα (f.) frame.
κορυφή (f.) top.
κυανόν azure (blue).

Λ λ

Λαϊκή Δημοκρατία τής Κίνας People's Republic of China (P.R.C.).
λάθος (n.) error.
λαχνός (m.) (auction) lot.
λέπτυνση (f.) thin spot, skinned spot.
λεύκωμα (n.) album.
λιθογραφία (f.) lithography.
λίρα (f.) lira; pound Sterling.
λογαριασμός (m.) account (financial or transactional).
λογοκριμένο ταχυδρομείο (f.) censored mail.
λουλάκι indigo.
λουρίδα (f.) strip (of stamps).

Μ μ

Μάϊος May.
μαναδικός unique.
μάρκο (n.) mark (German unit of currency).
Μάρτιος March.
μαύρο black.

Μεγάλη Βρεττανία Great Britain.
μεγάλο large.
μεγάλο κομμάτι block (of stamps).
μεγενθυτικός φακός (m.) magnifying glass.
μελάνι (n.) ink.
Μεξικό Mexico.
μέ ρουλέττα rouletted, *percé*.
μέ σαρνιέρα hinged.
μεταβάλλω (v.) to alter.
μεταξωτή κλωστή (f.) silk thread.
μεταχειρισμένο used.
μή αποδιδόμενο unattributed (not fully identified or classified).
μηδέν (n.) zero.
μή εκδοθέντα not issued.
μή εκδοθέν unpublished (not listed in any book or catalogue).
μήνας (m.) month.
μικρό small.
μίμηση (f.) imitation.
μισό (n.; adj.) half.
μονάδα χρημάτων denomination.
μπλέ blue.
μπλοκάκι (n.) pane (of stamps).
μυστικό σημάδι (n.) secret mark.

N ν

Νέα Ζηλανδία New Zealand.
Νοέμβριος November.
νομισματική μονάδα (f.) monetary unit.
Νορβηγία Norway.
Νότιος Αφρική South Africa.

Ξ ξ

ξένος foreign.
ξένο νόμισμα (n.) foreign currency.
ξεφλουδίζω (v.) to peel.

O o

ογδόντα eighty.
οδόντωση (f.) perforation.
οδοντομένο perforated.
οικιακός domestic.
Οκτώβριος October.
οκτώ eight.
Ολλανδία The Netherlands, Holland.
ομοίωμα (n.) effigy.
ονομαστική αξία (f.) face value.
όπισθεν on the back.
οπισθότυπος (m.) reverse.
ορθογώνιο rectangular.
οριστικόν (adj.) definitive.
Ουαλία Wales.

Π π

παλιός old.
πάπας (m.) pope (of the Roman Catholic Church).
πέμπτον fifth (the fraction).
πενήντα fifty.
πέντε five.
περιθώριο (n.) gutter.
Περού Perú.
πεσέτα (f.) peseta (Spanish unit of currency).
πέσο (n.) peso (unit of currency used by many countries in Latin America).
πίστωση (f.) credit.
πιστωτική κάρτα (f.) credit card.
πλαστό (n.) a forgery, fake, counterfeit.
πλειστηριασμός (m.) auction sale.
πλεκτόν (n.) wove paper.
πλήρες complete.
πληρωμή επί παραδόσεως cash on delivery (C.O.D.).
ποικιλία (f.) variety.
πολύτιμος valuable.

πολύχρωμο multicolored, multicoloured.
Πορτογαλία Portugal.
πορτοκαλί orange.
πορτραίτο (*n.*) portrait.
πορφυρούν purple.
ποσόν (*n.*) amount.
ποσοστό αβαρίας ασφαλισμένου γραμματοσήμου franchise stamp.
πουλώ (*v.*) to sell.
πράσινο green.
πράσινο-μπλέ turquoise; greenish-blue.
προακύρωσις (*n.*) precancel.
πρόεδρος president.
προπαγανδιστικόν γραμματόσημον (*n.*) propaganda stamp.
προπληρωμή (*f.*) prepayment.
πρόσοψη (*f.*) front.
προσφέρω (*v.*) to bid; to offer.
προσφορά (*f.*) an offer; a bid (at an auction or mail bid sale).
προσφορές άνευ ορίου δέν αποδέχονται no unlimited bids accepted.
προσωρινά χαρτονομίσματα (*n.pl.*) scrip.
προσωρινόν (*n.*) provisional.
Πρώσσικο κυανούν Prussian blue.
πρωτότυπος original.
πτυχή (*f.*) a fold, crease.
πυθμένας bottom.
πώληση μέσω ταχυδρομείου mail bid sale.
πωλητής seller.

Ρ ϱ

ρητό (*n.*) motto.
ρόδινο pink.
ρολό γραμματοσήμων coil (of stamps).
ρομβοειδής τροχίσκος lozenge roulette.
ρουλέττα (*f.*) roulette, *perçage*.
ρουλέττα ζιγκ-ζαγκ (*f.*) serrated roulette, zigzag roulette, *percé en pointes, percé en scie*.
ρουλέττα σερπεντίνα serpentine roulette, *percé en serpentin*.
Ρωσσία Russia.

Σ σ ς

Σαουδική Αραβία Saudi Arabia.
σαράντα forty.
σαρνιέρα (*f.*) hinge.
σειρά (*f.*) series.
Σεπτέμβριος September.
σετενάντ se-tenant.
σημείο ασφαλείας (*f.*) burélage, burelé.
σκοτεινός dark.
Σκωτία Scotland.
Σοβιετική Ένωση Soviet Union.
Σουηδία Sweden.
σπάνιο rare, scarce.
σπανιότητα (*f.*) rarity.
στέμμα (*n.*) crown (royal headpiece).
στρατιωτικά γραμματόσημα military postage stamp.
στρατιωτικό ταχυδρομείο (*n.*) field post.
συγκοπτομένη διάτρσις (*f.*) syncopated perforation.
συλλέγω (*v.*) to collect.
συλλέκτης collector.
συλλογή (*f.*) collection.
σύμβολο (*n.*) symbol.
συνδεδεμένο accolated, conjoined[*q.v.*], jugate.
σύντμηση (*f.*) abbreviation.
συστημένο γραμματόσημον (*n.*) registration stamp.
σφραγίδα (*f.*) postmark.
σφραγίς (*n.*) cachet.
σφραγισμένο διά οπών (*n.*) punch cancellation.
σφραγισμένο με πέννα pen cancelled.
σχέδιο (*n.*) pattern; design.
σχίσιμο (*n.*) a tear (in a piece of paper).
σχισμένο torn.

Τ τ

ταξινομία classification.
ταξινομώ (*v.*) to classify.
ταυτόσημα topical; thematic.

ταχυδρομείο (*n.*) post office.
ταχυδρομείον δεμάτων (*n.*) parcel post.
ταχυδρομική κάρτα (*f.*) postcard; postal card.
ταχυδρομικό τέλος (*n.*) postage.
ταχυδρόμος (*m.*) mailman, postman.
ταχυδρομώ (*v.*) to mail.
τέσσερα four.
τέταρτον (*n.*) fourth.
τετραγωνική κοπή (*f.*) cut square.
τετραγωνικό (*adj.*) square.
τέχνη (*f.*) art.
τηλεγραφικόν γραμματόσημον (*n.*) telegraph stamp.
τιμή (*f.*) price.
τιμή καταλόγου catalogue value.
τιμή συναλλάγματος exchange rate.
τιμοκατάλογος (*m.*) price list.
τσιμπίδα (*f.*) tongs.
τρία three.
τριάντα thirty.
τρίτον (*n.*) third (the fraction).
τροποποίηση (*f.*) alteration.
τρύπα hole.
τσακίζω (*v.*) to crease.
τσάκισμα (*n.*) a crease, a fold.
τυπογραφία (*f.*) typography.
τυπώνω (*v.*) to print.

Υ υ

υδατόσημο (*n.*) watermark.
υπογραφή (*f.*) signature.
υπό εγκρίσει on approval.
υπόλοιμα (*n.*) remainder, stock remainder.
υποτίμηση (*f.*) devaluation.

Φ φ

φαιό gray.
φάκελλος (*m.*) envelope; cover.
φάκελλος κρώτης ημέρας κυκλοφορίας first day cover.
Φεβρουάριος February.
φιλανθρωπικόν γραμματόσημον charity stamp.
φιλοτελικός (*adj.*) philatelic.
φιλοτελισμός (*m.*) philately.
φιλοτελιστής (*m.*) philatelist.
φόρος (*m.*) tax.
φράγκο (*n.*) franc (French unit of currency).
φύλλο (*n.*) sheet (of stamps).
φωσφορίζων phosphorescent.
φώσφορος (*m.*) phosphor.

Χ χ

χαλασμένο damaged.
χαρακτηριστικόν (*n.*) attribution.
χαρακωμένο χαρτί (*n.*) laid paper.
χαρτί (*n.*) paper.
χαρτί σκληρό (*n.*) granite paper.
χίλια (*n.pl.*) thousand.
χιλιοστό (*n.*) millimeter, millimetre.
χιλιοστόν thousandth.
Χόνγκ Κόνγκ Hong Kong.
χρήματα (*n.pl.*) money; cash.
χρόνος (*m.*) year.
χρώμα (*n.*) color, colour.
χωρίς γόμμα ungummed.
χωρίς οδόντωση imperforate.
χωρίς σαρνιέρα unhinged; never hinged.

Cyrillic Alphabet

Primarily words in Russian,
Serbian, and Bulgarian

А а

авиапочта (*f.*) [*Russ.*] airmail.
август [*Russ.*] August.
Австралия [*Russ.*] Australia.
Австрия [*Russ.*] Austria.
автентичен [*Bul.*] authentic, genuine.
Азєрбайджан [*Azer.*] Azerbaijan.
албум (*m.*) [*Serb.*] album.
альбом (*m.*) [*Russ.*] album.
Александр [*Russ.*] Alexander.
алый [*Russ.*] scarlet.
Англия [*Russ.*] England.
анилин (*m.*) [*Russ.*] aniline.
апрель [*Russ.*] April.
атрибуция (*f.*) [*Russ.*] attribution (complete
 identification of a philatelic item).
аукцион (*m.*) [*Russ.*] auction.
аукционная продажа (*f.*) [*Russ.*] auction sale.
Аустралија [*Serb.*] Australia.
Аустрија [*Serb.*] Austria.
аутентичан [*Serb.*] authentic, genuine.
аэрограмма (*f.*) [*Russ.*] aerogramme.
аэрофилателия (*f.*) [*Russ.*] aerophilately.

Б б

без клея [*Russ.*] ungummed.
без наклейки [*Russ.*] unhinged; never hinged.

беззубцовая [*Russ.*] imperforate.
белый [*Russ.*] white.
Бельгия [*Russ.*] Belgium.
бео [*Serb.*] white.
берлинская лазурь [*Russ.*] Prussian blue.
бирюзовый [*Russ.*] turquoise.
благотворительная марка (*f.*) [*Russ.*] charity
 stamp.
благотворительный налог (*m.*) [*Russ.*] surtax.
бланк (*m.*) [*Russ.*] order form.
бледно-лиловый [*Russ.*] lavender.
блок (*m.*) [*Russ.*] block.
Бог (*m.*) [*Bul., Serb., Russ.*] God (in the Judaic-
 Christian sense).
бонови (*m.pl.*) [*Serb.*] scrip.
боја (*f.*) [*Serb.*] color, colour.
большой [*Russ.*] large.
Босна и Херцеговина [*Serb.-Cr.*] Bosnia and
 Herzegovina.
Бразилия [*Russ.*] Brazil.
браун [*Serb.*] brown.
број (*m.*) [*Serb.*] number.
бронзовый [*Russ.*] bronze (color).
бумага (*f.*) [*Russ.*] paper.
бумага верже (*f.*) [*Russ.*] laid paper.
България [*Bul.*] Bulgaria.
Български [*Bul.*] Bulgarian.
бывший в употреблении [*Russ.*] used.

В в

ван оптицаја [*Serb.*] not issued.
вар (*m.*) [*Serb.*] stain (on a stamp or cover).
веленевая бумага (*f.*) [*Russ.*] wove paper.
Велика Британтја [*Serb.*] Great Britain;
 United Kingdom (U.K.).
велик; велики [*Serb.*] large.
Великобритания [*Russ.*] Great Britain; United
 Kingdom.
Велс [*Serb.*] Wales.
верх (*m.*) [*Russ.*] top.
видоизменять (*v.*) [*Russ.*] to alter.
водени жиг (*m.*) [*Serb.*] watermark.

водяной знак (*m.*) [*Russ.*] watermark.

Восточная Германия [*Russ.*] East Germany (D.D.R.).

вредност (*f.*) [*Serb.*] value.

вредност означена у каталогу [*Serb.*] catalogue value.

врх (*m.*) [*Serb.*] top.

выпуск (*m.*) [*Russ.*] an issue, issuance.

выпускать (*v.*) [*Russ.*] to issue.

вырезка (*f.*) [*Russ.*] cut square.

выставка (*f.*) [*Russ.*] exhibition.

выставлять (*v.*) [*Russ.*] to exhibit.

възпоменателен (*adj.*) [*Bul.*] commemorative.

Г г

газетная марка (*f.*) [*Russ.*] newspaper stamp.

гарантована понуда (*f.*) [*Serb.*] protective reserve bid.

гашеная (без прохождения почты) [*Russ.*] canceled to order.

гашение (*n.*) [*Russ.*] cancellation.

гашение компостером [*Russ.*] punch cancellation.

гашение надрезом (*n.*) [*Russ.*] cut cancellation.

гашеный вручную [*Russ.*] pen canceled.

гербовая марка (*f.*) [*Russ.*] fiscal stamp.

Германия [*Russ.*] Germany.

глянцевая бумага (*f.*) [*Russ.*] glossy paper.

глубокая печать (*f.*) [*Russ.*] intaglio.

год (*m.*) [*Russ.*] year.

година (*f.*) [*Serb.*] year.

Голландия [*Russ.*] Holland, Netherlands.

гравирование по стали (*m.*) [*Russ.*] steel engraving.

гравированный [*Russ.*] engraved.

гребенчатая перфорация (*f.*) [*Russ.*] comb perforation.

Греция [*Russ.*] Greece.

грешка (*f.*) [*Serb.*] error.

Грчка [*Serb.*] Greece.

гуммировка (*f.*) [*Russ.*] gum.

Д д

давни [*Serb.*] old; ancient.

Дания [*Russ.*] Denmark.

дата (*f.*) [*Russ.*] date.

датум (*m.*) [*Serb.*] date.

два [*Russ., Serb.*] two.

двадесет [*Serb.*] twenty.

двадцать [*Russ.*] twenty.

две [*Bul.*] two.

двојезичан [*Serb.*] bilingual.

двухцветный [*Russ.*] bicolored, bicoloured.

двуязычный [*Russ.*] bilingual.

девалвација (*f.*) [*Serb.*] devaluation.

девальвация (*f.*) [*Russ.*] devaluation.

девиз (*m.*) [*Russ.*] motto.

девиза (*f.*) [*Serb.*] foreign currency.

девяносто [*Russ.*] ninety.

девять [*Russ.*] nine.

действительный [*Russ.*] intrinsic.

декабрь [*Russ.*] December.

декоративный узор (*m.*) [*Russ.*] cachet.

демонетизация (*f.*) [*Russ.*] demonetization.

денежная единица (*f.*) [*Russ.*] monetary unit.

денежный перевод (*m.*) [*Russ.*] money order.

деньги (*pl.*) [*Russ.*] money.

десет [*Bul., Serb.*] ten.

десетина (*f.*) [*Serb.*] tenth (the fraction).

десно [*Serb.*] right (direction or position).

десятая часть (*f.*) [*Russ.*] tenth (the fraction).

десять [*Russ.*] ten.

дефект (*m.*) [*Serb., Russ.*] defect.

дефектный [*Russ.*] defective.

дефицитный [*Russ.*] rare, scarce.

дизајн (*m.*) [*Serb.*] design; pattern.

динар (*m.*) [*Serb.*] [*abbr.:* дин.] dinar, Yugoslavian unit of currency.

долар (*m.*) [*Serb.*] dollar ($).

доллар (*m.*) [*Russ.*] dollar ($).

доплата (*f.*) [*Russ.*] surcharge.

Држава С.Х.С. [*Serb.-Cr.*] Inscription found printed or as an overprint on some stamps of Bosnia and Herzegovina. *C.X.C.* are Cyrillic letters referring to Serbia [Срба], Croatia [Хрвата (*Hrvata*)], and Slovenia [Словенаца]. Romanized overprints also exist: *Država S.H.S.*

E e

едно [*Bul.*] one.
Екатерина [*Russ.*] Catherine.
Елизавета [*Russ.*] Elizabeth.
Енглеска [*Serb.*] England.

Ж ж

жёлтый [*Russ.*] yellow.
желтовато-зеленый [*Russ.*] apple green.
желтовато-коричневый [*Russ.*] manila (color).
жут [*Serb.*] yellow.

З з

зазубренная; зубчатая пробивка (*f.*) [*Russ.*] zigzag roulette, *percé en pointes*, *percé en scie*.
замазывание (*n.*) [*Russ.*] obliteration.
за одобрение [*Bul.*] on approval.
Западная Германия [*Russ.*] West Germany (B.R.D.).
Западни Немачка [*Serb.*] West Germany (B.R.D.).
запис (*m.*) [*Serb.*] inscription.
застарео [*Serb.*] obsolete.
зачёхленная марка (*f.*) [*Russ.*] encased postage stamp (such as the type used as an emergency substitute for small coins during the U.S. Civil War of 1861-65).
заявка на торгах (*f.*) [*Russ.*] bid sheet.
збирка (*f.*) [*Serb.*] collection.
званичан [*Serb.*] official.
звезда (*f.*) [*Russ., Serb.*] star.
зелен [*Serb.*] green.
зелёный [*Russ.*] green.

зубцовка (*f.*) [*Russ.*] perforation.
З.У.Н.Р. [*Russ. abbr.*] overprint on some stamps of Austria referring to Western Ukraine.

И и

идеальный [*Russ.*] perfect, flawless.
извилистая пробивка (*f.*) [*Russ.*] serpentine roulette.
изврстан [*Serb.*] excellent.
издавати; издатн (*v.*) [*Serb.*] to issue.
издање (*n.*); **изливање** (*n.*) [*Serb.*] an issue, issuance.
изложба (*f.*) [*Serb.*] exhibition.
изложити (*v.*) [*Serb.*] to exhibit.
Израел [*Serb.*] Israel.
Израиль [*Russ.*] Israel.
изумрудный [*Russ.*] emerald (color).
имитация (*f.*) [*Russ.*] imitation.
император (*m.*) [*Russ., Serb.*] emperor.
иностранная валюта (*f.*) [*Russ.*] foreign currency.
иностранный [*Russ.*] foreign.
интаглио (*m.*) [*Serb.*] intaglio.
интернациональный [*Russ.*] international.
Ирландия [*Russ.*] Ireland.
искусство (*n.*) [*Russ.*] art.
Испания [*Russ.*] Spain.
Источна Немачка [*Serb.*] East Germany (D.D.R.).
Италија [*Serb.*] Italy.
Италия [*Russ.*] Italy.
июль [*Russ.*] July.
июнь [*Russ.*] June.

J j

Јапан [*Serb.*] Japan.
један [*Serb.*] one.

jединствен [*Serb.*] unique.
jезик (*m.*) [*Serb.*] language.
Jугославиja [*Serb.*] Yugoslavia, Jugoslavia.
Jужна Африка [*Serb.*] South Africa.

К к

Канада [*Russ., Serb.*] Canada.
карминный [*Russ.*] carmine.
Карпатська-Украïна [*Russ.*] Carpatho-Ukraine. Overprinted on stamps of Czechoslovakia.
каталог (*m.*) [*Bul., Russ., Serb.*] catalog, catalogue.
каталог аукциона (*m.*) [*Russ.*] auction catalogue.
каталог лицитациje (*m.*) [*Serb.*] auction catalogue.
кауциja обавезна [*Serb.*] deposit required.
каштановый [*Russ.*] chestnut (color).
квадратный (*adj.*) [*Russ.*] square.
квартблок (*m.*) [*Russ.*] block of four.
квитанция (*f.*) [*Russ.*] receipt.
Кина [*Serb.*] China.
Китай [*Russ.*] China.
класификациja (*f.*) [*Serb.*] classification.
класифицирати (*v.*) [*Serb.*] to classify.
классификация (*f.*) [*Russ.*] classification.
классифицировать (*v.*) [*Russ.*] to classify.
клеймо (*n.*) [*Russ.*] authentication mark.
кляссер (*m.*) [*Russ.*] *quadrillé.*
книгопечатание [*Russ.*] typography.
книжка марок (*f.*) [*Russ.*] booklet (of stamps).
кобальтово-синий [*Russ.*] cobalt blue.
колекциja (*f.*) [*Serb.*] collection.
колекционар (*m.*) [*Serb.*] collector.
коллекционер (*m.*) [*Russ.*] collector.
коллекционировать (*v.*) [*Russ.*] to collect.
коллекция (*f.*) [*Russ.*] collection.
комеморативан (*adj.*) [*Serb.*] commemorative.
конверт (*m.*) [*Russ.*] envelope; cover.
конверт первого дня (*m.*) [*Russ.*] first day cover.

копейка (*f.*) [*Russ.*] [*pl.:* копейки] kopek.
копия (*f.*) [*Russ.*] a copy.
коричневый [*Russ.*] brown.
королева (*f.*) [*Russ.*] queen.
король (*m.*) [*Russ.*] king.
корона (*f.*) [*Bul., Russ.*] crown (royal head-piece).
краљ (*m.*) [*Serb.*] king.
Краљевство С.Х.С. [*Serb.-Cr.*] [abbreviated version of Краљевство Срба, Хрвата и Словенаца] Kingdom of Serbia, Croatia, and Slovenia.
краљица (*f.*) [*Serb.*] queen.
красновато-коричневый [*Russ.*] henna.
красный [*Russ.*] red.
Красный Крест (*m.*) [*Russ.*] Red Cross.
кредитна карта (*f.*) [*Serb.*] credit card.
кредитне карте важе [*Serb.*] credit cards accepted.
кредитная карточка (*f.*) [*Russ.*] credit card.
кредитные карточки принимаются [*Russ.*] credit cards accepted.
кровавый [*Russ.*] blood (color).
крузейро (*n.*) [*Russ.*] cruzeiro (Brazilian unit of currency).
крузеро (*m.*) [*Serb.*] cruzeiro.
круна (*f.*) [*Serb.*] crown (royal headpiece; large silver coin).
крупан [*Serb.*] large.
купац (*m.*) [*Serb.*] buyer.
купити; куповати (*v.*) [*Serb.*] to buy.

Л л

лазурный [*Russ.*] azure.
лауреат [*Serb.*] laureate.
лево [*Serb.*] left (direction or position).
левый [*Russ.*] left (direction or position).
лиловый [*Russ.*] purple.
лимонный; лимонно-желтый [*Russ.*] citron; lemon (color).
линейная перфорация (*f.*) [*Russ.*] line perforation.
лист (*m.*) [*Russ.*] sheet; pane (of stamps).

литография (*f.*) [*Russ.*] lithography.
лице (*n.*) [*Serb.*] front; obverse.
лицевая сторона (*f.*) [*Russ.*] front; obverse.
лицитација (*f.*) [*Serb.*] auction; auction sale.
лицитација путем поште [*Serb.*] mail bid sale.
лупа (*f.*) [*Bul., Russ., Serb.*] magnifying glass.
льготная марка (*f.*) [*Russ.*] franchise stamp.

многоцветный [*Russ.*] multicolored, multicoloured.
монета (*f.*) [*Bul., Russ.*] coin; [*Serb.*] currency.
Москва [*Russ.*] Moscow.
мото (*m.*) [*Serb.*] motto.
мраморная бумага (*f.*) [*Russ.*] granite paper.
мрачан [*Serb.*] dark.
мрља (*f.*) [*Serb.*] tarnish (on a coin or medal); stain (on a postage stamp or banknote).

М м

май [*Russ.*] May.
мален [*Serb.*] small.
маленький [*Russ.*] small.
малиновый [*Russ.*] crimson.
марка (*f.*) [*Bul., Serb., Russ.*] postage stamp; mark (German unit of currency).
марка авиапочты (*f.*) [*Russ.*] air stamp; airmail stamp.
марка доплаты (*f.*) [*Russ.*] postage due stamp.
марка, разрезанная пополам [*Russ.*] bisected (stamp).
марка полевой почты (*f.*) [*Russ.*] military postage stamp.
марка почтовой оплаты (*f.*) [*Russ.*] postage payment stamp.
марка правительственной почты (*f.*) [*Russ.*] official stamp.
марочный лист (*m.*) [*Russ.*] sheet (of stamps).
март [*Russ.*] March.
мастило (*n.*) [*Serb.*] ink.
међународни [*Serb.*] international.
Мексика [*Russ.*] Mexico.
Мексико [*Serb.*] Mexico.
меловая бумага (*f.*) [*Russ.*] chalky paper.
месяц (*m.*) [*Russ.*] month.
меченая марка (*f.*) [*Russ.*] tagged stamp.
милиметар (*m.*) [*Serb.*] millimeter, millimetre.
миллиметр (*m.*) [*Russ.*] millimeter, millimetre.
милион [*Serb.*] million.
миллион (*m.*) [*Russ.*] million.
минимальное предложение цены (*n.*) [*Russ.*] minimum bid.

Н н

надпечатка (*f.*) [*Russ.*] overprint.
надпись (*f.*) [*Russ.*] inscription; legend.
назнака (*f.*) [*Serb.*] attribution (the complete identification of a stamp, cover, or other philatelic item).
назначити порекло (*v.*) [*Serb.*] to attribute.
најнижа понуда (*f.*) [*Serb.*] minimum bid.
најнижи [*Serb.*] bottom.
наклейка (*f.*) [*Russ.*] stamp hinge; postal label.
наклейка заказной почты (*f.*) [*Russ.*] registration stamp.
наличје (*n.*) [*Serb.*] reverse.
налог (*m.*) [*Russ.*] tax.
наложенный [*Russ.*] accolated, conjoined[*q.v.*], jugate.
наложенный платёж [*Russ.*] cash on delivery (C.O.D.).
на полеђини [*Serb.*] on the back.
нарицательная стоимость [*Russ.*] face value.
Народна Република Българиа [*Bul.*] People's Republic of Bulgaria. [Usually abbreviated Н.Р.България on stamps.]
Народна Република Кина [*Serb.*] People's Republic of China (P.R.C.).
наруџбеница (*f.*) [*Serb.*] order form.
на увид [*Serb.*] on approval.
национальный [*Russ.*] national.
националност [*Serb.*] nationality.
национальная принадлежность (*f.*) [*Russ.*] nationality.
нацрт (*m.*) [*Serb.*] design.

незваничан; неслужбени [*Serb.*] unofficial.
неидентифицированный [*Russ.*] unattributed (i.e., not fully identified).
неисправан [*Serb.*] defective.
неисправност (*f.*) [*Serb.*] defect.
недоставляемый [*Russ.*] undeliverable.
неизвестный [*Russ.*] unknown (in any collection).
неизданный [*Russ.*] not issued.
неиздат [*Serb.*] not issued.
неиспользованный [*Russ.*] unused.
Немачка [*Serb.*] Germany.
немецкая марка (*f.*) [*Russ.*] mark (German unit of currency).
необјављен [*Serb.*] unpublished (not listed in any book or catalogue).
необычный [*Russ.*] irregular.
неопредељен [*Serb.*] unattributed (i.e., not fully identified).
неопубликованный [*Russ.*] unpublished (not listed in any book or catalogue).
непознат [*Serb.*] unknown.
непотпун [*Serb.*] incomplete.
нерасцепленный [*Russ.*] unsevered.
неофициальный [*Russ.*] unofficial.
неполный [*Russ.*] incomplete.
Нидерланды [*Russ.*] Netherlands, Holland.
Николай [*Russ.*] Nicholas.
низ (*m.*) [*Russ.*] bottom.
Новая Зеландия [*Russ.*] New Zealand.
нови [*Serb.*] new.
Нови Зеланд [*Serb.*] New Zealand.
новчана јединица (*f.*) [*Serb.*] denomination; monetary unit.
новчана уплатница (*f.*) [*Serb.*] money order.
новчани систем [*Serb.*] monetary system.
новый [*Russ.*] new.
номер (*m.*) [*Russ.*] number.
номинал (*m.*) [*Russ.*] denomination.
номинална вредност (*f.*) [*Serb.*] face value.
Норвегия [*Russ.*] Norway.
Норвешка [*Serb.*] Norway.
ноябрь [*Russ.*] November.
Н.Р.България [*Bul.*] People's Republic of Bulgaria. The *H.P.* is the abbreviation for Народна Република.
нула [*Serb.*] zero.
нуль (*m.*) [*Russ.*] zero.

О о

обичан [*Serb.*] common.
обменный курс (*m.*) [*Russ.*] exchange rate.
образец (*m.*) [*Russ.*] pattern.
обратная сторона (*f.*) [*Russ.*] reverse.
обыкновенный [*Russ.*] common.
овенчан [*Serb.*] laureate.
ограничене понуде [*Serb.*] no unlimited bids accepted.
один [*Russ.*] one.
одличан [*Serb.*] excellent (grade or condition).
одузимање вредности новчићу [*Serb.*] demonetization.
октябрь [*Russ.*] October.
оливковый [*Russ.*] olive (color).
определять (*v.*) [*Russ.*] to attribute.
оранжевый [*Russ.*] orange (color).
оригинал [*Russ.*] original.
оригиналан [*Serb.*] original; genuine.
остатки (*m.pl.*) [*Russ.*] remainder, stock remainder.
отечественный [*Russ.*] domestic.
отклеивать (*v.*) [*Russ.*] to peel.
открытка (*f.*) [*Russ.*] postcard; postal card.
отличный [*Russ.*] excellent (grade or condition).
отправлять почтой (*v.*) [*Russ.*] to mail.
отреставрированный [*Russ.*] repaired.
оттенок (*m.*) [*Russ.*] shade (*re*: color).
отцентрированное изображение (*n.*) [*Russ.*] centered.
официальный [*Russ.*] official.
ошибка (*f.*) [*Russ.*] error.
оштећен [*Serb.*] damaged.

П п

набавка (*f.*) [*Serb.*] acquisition.
пакет (*m.*) [*Russ.*] package.
пакетная почта (*f.*) [*Russ.*] parcel post.
памятный (*adj.*) [*Russ.*] commemorative.

папа (*m.*) [*Bul., Serb., Russ.*] pope (of the Roman Catholic Church).

папир (*m.*) [*Serb.*] paper.

папирна новчаница (*f.*) [*Serb.*] paper money.

пара (*f.*) 1. [*Serb.*] para (a minor unit of currency of Serbia, Montenegro, and Yugoslavia). 2. [*Russ.*] pair (of stamps).

пари (*f.pl.*) [*Bul.*] money.

паричен [*Bul.*] monetary.

партија (*f.*) [*Serb.*] (auction) lot.

партия (*f.*) [*Russ.*] (auction) lot.

педесет [*Serb.*] fifty.

первый слой клея [*Russ.*] original gum.

перевернутая марка [*Russ.*] inverted (stamp).

перегуммированный [*Russ.*] regummed.

перепечатка (*f.*) [*Russ.*] reprint.

Перу [*Russ., Serb.*] Peru.

перфорированный [*Russ.*] perforated.

пезо (*m.*) [*Serb.*] peso (Spanish-American unit of currency).

песета (*f.*) [*Russ., Serb.*] peseta (Spanish unit of currency).

песо (*n.*) [*Russ.*] peso (Spanish-American unit of currency).

пет [*Bul., Serb.*] five.

петдесет [*Bul.*] fifty.

петина (*f.*) [*Serb.*] fifth (the fraction).

Петр [*Russ.*] Peter.

печат (*m.*) [*Serb.*] seal.

печатать (*v.*) [*Russ.*] to print.

печать (*f.*) [*Russ.*] seal; cancellation.

пинцет (*m.*) [*Russ.*] tongs.

плав; плаветан [*Serb.*] blue.

повреждённый [*Russ.*] damaged.

погашать (*v.*) [*Russ.*] to cancel.

подделка (*f.*) [*Russ.*] a counterfeit; a fake, forgery.

подделывать (*v.*) [*Russ.*] to counterfeit.

подлинный [*Russ.*] authentic, genuine.

подпись (*f.*) [*Russ.*] signature.

покидан [*Serb.*] torn.

покупатель (*m.*) [*Russ.*] buyer.

покупать (*v.*) [*Russ.*] to buy.

полевая почта (*f.*) [*Russ.*] field post.

полный [*Russ.*] complete.

половина (*f.*) [*Russ.*] half (the fraction).

половинный (*adj.*) [*Russ.*] half.

половица (*f.*) [*Serb.*] half (the fraction).

половичан (*adj.*) [*Serb.*] half.

полоска (*f.*) [*Russ.*] strip (of stamps); gutter.

полосчатый [*Russ.*] barred.

полтина (*f.*) [*Russ.*] poltina.

полтинник (*m.*) [*Russ.*] poltinnik.

полушка (*f.*) [*pl.:* полушки] [*Russ.*] polushka.

поништавање рупицама или урезом [*Serb.*] cut cancellation.

понуда (*f.*) [*Serb.*] an offer; a bid (at an auction or mail bid sale).

понудити (*v.*) [*Serb.*] to offer; to bid.

порванный [*Russ.*] torn.

порез (*m.*) [*Serb.*] tax.

порекло (*n.*) [*Serb.*] pedigree, provenance (list of previous and present owners).

портрет (*m.*) [*Russ., Serb.*] portrait; effigy.

Португалија [*Serb.*] Portugal.

Португалия [*Russ.*] Portugal.

потайной знак (*m.*) [*Russ.*] secret mark.

потврда (*f.*) [*Serb.*] certificate.

потпис (*m.*) [*Serb.*] signature.

потпун [*Serb.*] complete.

поцепотина (*f.*) [*Serb.*] a tear (in a stamp).

почетна понуда (*f.*) [*Serb.*] suggested bid.

почта (*f.*) [*Russ.*] mail; postage; post office.

почта, прошедшая цензуру (*f.*) [*Russ.*] censored mail.

почтальон (*m.*) [*Russ.*] mailman, postman, letter carrier.

почти [*Russ.*] almost.

почтовая карточка (*f.*) [*Russ.*] postal card.

почтовая марка (*f.*) [*Russ.*] postage stamp.

почтовая плата (*f.*) [*Russ.*] postage.

почтовая пометка на марке доплаты [*Russ.*] precancel; postal mark on postage due stamp.

почтовая служба (*f.*) [*Russ.*] postal service.

почтовые марка (*f.*) [*Russ.*] parcel post stamp.

почтовый сбор (*m.*) [*Russ.*] postage due.

почтовый штемпель (*m.*) [*Russ.*] postmark.

прави [*Serb.*] genuine.

правоугаони [*Serb.*] rectangular.

правый [*Russ.*] right (direction or position).

предлагаемая цена (*f.*) [*Russ.*] suggested bid.

предлагать (*v.*) [*Russ.*] to offer.

предлагать цену (*v.*) [*Russ.*] to bid (at an auction or mail bid sale).

предложение (*n.*) [*Russ.*] an offer.

предложение цены (*n.*) [*Russ.*] (auction) bid.

предложения цен ограниченны [*Russ.*] no unlimited bids accepted.

предохранительная сеть (*f.*) [*Russ.*] burélage, burelé.

председник (*m.*) [*Serb.*] president.

президент (*m.*) [*Bul., Russ.*] president.

прейскурант (*m.*) [*Russ.*] price list.

прерывистая перфорация (*f.*) [*Russ.*] syncopated perforation; interrupted perforation.

признаница (*f.*) [*Serb.*] certificate; receipt.

пријава за учествовање на лицитацији [*Serb.*] bid sheet.

примерак (*m.*) [*Serb.*] specimen.

приобретение (*n.*) [*Russ.*] acquisition.

проба (*f.*) [*Russ.*] essay.

пробивка (*f.*) [*Russ.*] roulette, *perçage*.

пробитый [*Russ.*] rouletted, *percé*.

пробный образец (*m.*) [*Russ.*] specimen.

продавати (*v.*) [*Serb.*] to sell.

продавать (*v.*) [*Russ.*] to sell.

продавац (*m.*) [*Serb.*] seller.

продавец (*m.*) [*Russ.*] seller.

продати (*v.*) [*Serb.*] to sell; to trade.

происхождение (*n.*) [*Russ.*] pedigree, provenance (list of previous and present owners).

промена (*f.*) [*Serb.*] alteration.

пропагандистская марка (*f.*) [*Russ.*] propaganda stamp.

процена (*f.*) [*Serb.*] grade, condition.

прямоугольный [*Russ.*] rectangular.

пурпурно-красный [*Russ.*] magenta.

пятая часть (*f.*) [*Russ.*] fifth (the fraction).

пятно (*n.*) [*Russ.*] stain (on a stamp or cover).

пять [*Russ.*] five.

пятьдесят [*Russ.*] fifty.

Р р

разделение (*n.*) [*Russ.*] separation.

разновидность (*f.*) [*Russ.*] variety.

разноликост (*f.*) [*Serb.*] variety.

разрыв (*m.*) [*Russ.*] a tear (in a stamp).

разрывать (*v.*) [*Russ.*] to tear.

раритет (*m.*) [*Russ., Serb.*] rarity.

распродажа по почте (*f.*) [*Russ.*] mail bid sale.

рачун (*m.*) [*Serb.*] account (financial or transactional).

редак [*Serb.*] rare, scarce.

редкий [*Russ.*] rare.

резервная цена (*f.*) [*Russ.*] protective reserve bid.

репродукция (*f.*) [*Russ.*] reproduction.

република (*f.*) [*Serb.*] republic.

Република Кина [*Serb.*] Republic of China (Taiwan).

республика (*f.*) [*Russ.*] republic.

Республика Китай [*Russ.*] Republic of China (Taiwan).

рисунок (*m.*) [*Russ.*] design.

розолвый [*Russ.*] pink.

ромбовидная пробивка (*f.*) [*Russ.*] lozenge roulette.

Россия [*Russ.*] Russia.

рубль (*m.*) [*pl.:* рубли] [*Russ.*] rouble, ruble.

рулон (*m.*) [*Russ.*] coil (of stamps).

румен [*Serb.*] red.

рупица (*f.*) [*Serb.*] hole.

Русија [*Serb.*] Russia.

рядьк [*Bul.*] rare, scarce.

С с

савршен [*Serb.*] perfect, flawless.

Санкт-Петербург [*Russ.*] St. Petersburg (Russia).

сантим (*m.*) [*Bul./Fr.*] centime (a minor French denomination). The earliest Bulgarian stamps (1879) were valued at 5, 10, 25, and 50 centimes, plus 1 franc (100 centimes). Later stamps of that country (starting 1881) used the *stotinka* (стотинкь) as the minor denomination.

сантиметр (*m.*) [*Russ.*] centimeter, centimetre.

састављен [*Serb.*] accolated, conjoined[*q.v.*].

светлый [*Russ.*] light (*re:* color).

светящийся [*Russ.*] phosphorescent.

свилена нит (*f.*) [*Serb.*] silk thread.

свота (*f.*) [*Serb.*] amount.

сентиметар (*m.*) [*Serb.*] centimeter, centimetre.

сентябрь [*Russ.*] September.

серийный номер (*m.*) [*Russ.*] serial number.

серија (*f.*) [*Serb.*] series.

серијски број на новчаници [*Serb.*] serial number.

серия (*f.*) [*Russ.*] series.

сертификат (*m.*) [*Russ.*] certificate.

серый [*Russ.*] gray.

симбол (*m.*) [*Serb.*] symbol.

символ (*m.*) [*Russ.*] symbol.

синий [*Russ.*] blue.

сиреневый [*Russ.*] lilac (color).

ситан [*Serb.*] small.

Сједињене Америчке Државе [*Serb.*] United States of America (U.S.A.).

складка (*f.*) [*Russ.*] a fold, crease.

скраћеница (*f.*) [*Serb.*] abbreviation.

скупљати (*v.*) [*Serb.*] to collect.

скупоцен [*Serb.*] valuable.

службен; службени [*Serb.*] official.

с наклейкой [*Russ.*] hinged.

Советский Союз [*Russ.*] Soviet Union (U.S.S.R.).

Совјетски Савез [*Serb.*] Soviet Union.

Соединенные Штаты Америки [*Russ.*] United States of America (U.S.A.).

соединённый [*Russ.*] accolated, conjoined[*q.v.*], jugate.

сокращение (*n.*) [*Russ.*] abbreviation.

сорок [*Russ.*] forty.

сортировать (*v.*) [*Russ.*] to grade; to sort.

состояние (*n.*) [*Russ.*] grade; condition.

сотая часть (*f.*) [*Russ.*] hundredth (the fraction).

Союз Советских Социалистических Республик (С.С.С.Р.) [*Russ.*] Union of Soviet Socialist Republics (U.S.S.R.).

списак (*m.*) [*Serb.*] catalog, catalogue.

спојен [*Serb.*] accolated, conjoined[*q.v.*], jugate.

Србија [*Serb.*] Serbia.

С.С.С.Р. [*Russ. abbr.*] [Союз Советских Социалистических Республик] Union of Soviet Socialist Republics (U.S.S.R.).

ставка (*f.*) [*Serb.*] (auction) lot.

стандартный (*adj.*) [*Russ.*] definitive; standard.

ствари [*Serb.*] intrinsic.

степен (*m.*) [*Serb.*] grade, condition.

сто [*Bul., Russ., Serb.*] hundred.

стогодишњица (*f.*) [*Serb.*] centennial, centenary.

столетие (*n.*) [*Russ.*] centennial, centenary.

стоти [*Serb.*] hundredth (the fraction).

стотинкь [*Bul.*] [*pl.*: стотинки; *abbr.*: стот.] stotinka (a minor monetary denomination of Bulgaria).

стран; страни [*Serb.*] foreign.

страни новац (*m.*) [*Serb.*] foreign currency.

суверен (*m.*) [*Russ., Serb.*] sovereign.

сувенирный листок (*m.*) [*Russ.*] souvenir sheet.

сумма (*f.*) [*Russ.*] amount.

С.Х.С. [*Serb.-Cr. abbr.*] Cyrillic overprint found on some stamps of Bosnia and Herzegovina which refers to Serbia, Croatia, and Slovenia. A similar overprint exists in the equivalent Roman letters *S.H.S.* [The "H" stands for *Hrvata*, the Serbo-Croatian word referring to Croatia.]

сцепка (*f.*) [*Russ.*] se-tenant.

счёт (*m.*) [*Russ.*] account (financial or transactional).

Т т

Тайвань [*Russ.*] Taiwan (Republic of China).

Тајван [*Serb.*] Taiwan (Republic of China).

тантуз (*m.*) [*Serb.*] token.

телеграфная марка (*f.*) [*Russ.*] telegraph stamp.

таман [*Serb.*] dark.

тематический [*Russ.*] topical.

тёмно-бордовый [*Russ.*] maroon; dark claret.

тёмно-жёлтый [*Russ.*] buff; dark yellow.

тёмно-коричневый [*Russ.*] bister; dark brown.

тёмно-синий [*Russ.*] sapphire (color); dark blue.

тёмный [*Russ.*] dark; deep (re: color).

тет-беш (*m.*) [*Russ.*] tête-bêche.

төгрөг [*Mong.*] tukhrik (Mongolian unit of currency).

тиснение (*n.*) [*Russ.*] embossing.

точечная перфорация (*f.*) [*Russ.*] pin perforation, *percé en points.*

требуется задаток (*m.*) [*Russ.*] deposit required.

третья часть (*f.*) [*Russ.*] third (the fraction).

трећина (*f.*) [*Serb.*] third (the fraction).

три [*Bul., Russ., Serb.*] three.

тридесет [*Serb.*] thirty.

тридцать [*Russ.*] thirty.

туђи [*Serb.*] foreign.

тысяча (*f.*) [*Russ.*] thousand.

търг (*m.*) [*Bul.*] auction.

У у

увенчанный [*Russ.*] laureate.

угравиран [*Serb.*] engraved.

узорак (*m.*) [*Serb.*] specimen.

Уједињено Краљевство [*Serb.*] United Kingdom (U.K.).

Україна [*Ukr.*] Ukraine.

ультрамариновый [*Russ.*] ultramarine.

уметност (*f.*) [*Serb.*] art.

уникальный [*Russ.*] unique.

уоквирена, оклопљена марка [*Serb.*] encased postage stamp (such as the type used as an emergency substitute for small coins during the U.S. Civil War of 1861-65).

устаревший [*Russ.*] obsolete.

утончение (*n.*) [*Russ.*] thin spot, skinned spot.

Уэльс [*Russ.*] Wales.

Ф ф

фактура (*f.*) [*Serb.*] order form; account (financial or transactional).

фалсификат (*m.*) [*Serb.*] a counterfeit; a fake, forgery.

фальшивомонетчик (*m.*) [*Russ.*] counterfeiter.

фарба (*f.*) [*Serb.*] color, colour.

февраль [*Russ.*] February.

филателист (*m.*) [*Russ.*] philatelist.

филателистический [*Russ.*] philatelic.

филателия (*f.*) [*Russ.*] philately.

Финляндия [*Russ.*] Finland.

Финска [*Serb.*] Finland.

фиолетовый [*Russ.*] indigo.

фосфор (*m.*) [*Russ.*] phosphor.

фотогравюра (*f.*) [*Russ.*] photogravure.

франк (*m.*) [*Russ., Serb.*] franc (French, Swiss, etc., unit of currency).

франкъ [*Bul.*] franc (denomination of the earliest Bulgarian stamps, issued in 1879).

франкировать (*v.*) [*Russ.*] to frank.

франкировка (*f.*) [*Russ.*] frank.

Франция [*Russ.*] France.

Француска [*Serb.*] France.

фунт (*m.*) [*Russ.*] pound (16 ounces of weight; pound Sterling - £).

фунта (*f.*) [*Serb.*] pound (16 ounces of weight; pound Sterling - £).

фунт стерлингов [*Russ.*] pound Sterling (£).

Х х

хартија (*f.*) [*Serb.*] paper.

хиљада [*Serb.*] thousand.

Холандија [*Serb.*] Holland, Netherlands.

Ц ц

цар (*m.*) [*Serb.*] emperor; czar.

царь (*m.*) [*Russ.*] emperor; czar.

цвет (*m.*) [*Russ.*] color, colour.

цена (*f.*) [*Bul., Russ., Serb.*] price.

цена по каталогу (*f.*) [*Russ.*] catalogue value.
ценность (*f.*) [*Russ.*] value.
ценный [*Russ.*] valuable.
ценовник (*m.*) [*Serb.*] price list.
ценоразпис (*m.*) [*Bul.*] price list.
црвен [*Serb.*] red.
црн [*Serb.*] black.
црна берза (*f.*) [*Serb.*] black market.
Црна Гора [*Serb.-Cr.*] Montenegro.

Ч ч

частный сертификат (*m.*) [*Russ.*] scrip.
часть (*f.*) [*Russ.*] fraction.
червонец (*m.*) [*Russ.*] chervonetz.
чест [*Serb.*] common.
чек (*m.*) [*Bul., Serb., Russ.*] check, cheque.
чернила (*n.pl.*) [*Russ.*] ink.
чёрный [*Russ.*] black.
чёрный рынок (*m.*) [*Russ.*] black market.
четверть (*f.*) [*Russ.*] fourth (the fraction), quarter.
четвртаст (*adj.*) [*Serb.*] square.
четвртина (*f.*) [*Serb.*] fourth (the fraction), quarter.
четири [*Bul., Serb.*] four.
четрдесет [*Serb.*] forty.
четыре [*Russ.*] four.

Ш ш

Швейцария [*Russ.*] Switzerland.
Швеция [*Russ.*] Sweden.
шёлковая нить [*Russ.*] silk thread.
шест [*Serb.*] six.
шесть [*Russ.*] six.
Шкотска [*Serb.*] Scotland.
Шотландия [*Russ.*] Scotland.
штампање поврх текста [*Serb.*] overprint.

Ю ю

Югославия [*Russ.*] Yugoslavia, Jugoslavia.
Южная Африка [*Russ.*] South Africa.

Я я

язык (*m.*) [*Russ.*] language.
январь [*Russ.*] January.
янтарный [*Russ.*] amber (color).
ярко-синий [*Russ.*] royal blue; bright blue.

Hebrew Alphabet

Unlike European languages, Hebrew reads from right to left. In order to accommodate the natural flow of the Hebrew language, columns are snaked from right to left and pages turn in reverse order from that of English. But to satisfy the requirements of a book intended for English speakers, pages are numbered in accordance with English usage. Hence, this section begins on page 311 and ends on page 305.

The letters of the Hebrew alphabet are consonants while the vowels appear in the form of diacritical marks. In everyday usage, Hebrew words do not normally show vowel points. Inscriptions on postage stamps, coins, and banknotes are almost always written exclusively in consonants. For reference purposes, Hebrew words in this glossary are shown in their complete form, including vowels.

Although English verbs are given here in their infinitive form (as they are throughout this dictionary), Hebrew verbs are in the plene *form, i.e., third person male singular past tense which corresponds to the three-letter root of the word.*

Hebrew grammar often requires that letters be added to the beginnings of words, such as to infinitives which always start with the letter ל. If a particular word in Hebrew cannot be found under its first letter, it may be found under its second letter, although usually with some slight modification in spelling.

שְׁנַיִם two
שַׁעַר הַחֲלִיפִין exchange rate (m.)
שַׁעֲתוּק reproduction (m.)
שָׂפָה language (f.)
שֶׁקֶל shekel, sheqel (ancient Judaic coin; also a coin of modern Israel).
שֵׁרוּת דֹּאַר צְבָאִי field post
שִׁשָּׁה six
שִׁשִּׁים sixty

ת

תַּאֲרִיךְ date (m.)
תּוֹרָה Torah
תַּחְתִּית bottom (f.)
תְּכֵלֶת azure
תְּכֵלֶת סַפִּיר sapphire (color)
תֶּכֶן design (m.)
תִּכְנוּן שֶׁלֹּא יָצָא לְבִצּוּעַ essay
תַּעֲרוּכָה exhibition (f.)
תִּקּוּן כַּסְפִּי monetary reform
תַּשְׁלוּם fee (m.)
תַּשְׁלוּם בְּעֵת הַמְּסִירָה cash on delivery (C.O.D.)
תַּשְׁלוּם מֵרֹאשׁ prepayment (m.)
תִּשְׁעָה nine
תִּשְׁעִים ninety
תַּת-גִּלָּיוֹן pane (m.)

[ש continued from page 306]

שֶׁבֶר (mathematical) fraction (m.)
שְׁוֶדְיָה Sweden (f.)
שְׁוַיִץ Switzerland (f.)
שׁוּלַיִם gutter (m.)
שׁוּק שָׁחוֹר black market (m.)
שׁוּרַת בּוּלִים strip (of stamps) (f.)
שָׁחוֹר black
שְׁטָר certificate (m.)
שָׁכִיחַ common
שִׁכְפֵּל to duplicate (v.)
שֶׁלֹּא יָצָא לְהַנְפָּקָה not issued
שֶׁלֹּא פּוּרְסַם unpublished (a stamp or other philatelic item not listed in any book or catalogue).
שָׁלוֹם peace (m.)
שָׁלַח בַּדֹּאַר to mail (v.)
שַׁלִּיט sovereign (m.)
שְׁלִישׁ third (the fraction) (m.)
שָׁלֵם complete
שְׁלֹשָׁה three
שְׁלֹשִׁים thirty
שְׂמֹאל left (direction or position)
שְׁמוֹנָה eight
שְׁמוֹנִים eighty
שְׁמַע יִשְׂרָאֵל "Hear, O Israel..." (the first line of the essential Jewish creed, Deut. 6:4).
שָׁנָה year (f.)
שָׁנִי scarlet

ק

receipt (f.) קַבָּלָה
cobalt קוֹבַּלְט
Colombia (f.) קוֹלוּמְבִּיָה
buyer (m.) קוֹנֶה
catalog, catalogue (m.) קָטָלוֹג
auction catalogue (m.) קָטָלוֹג מְכִירָה פּוּמְבִּית
small קָטָן
emperor (m.) קֵיסָר
a crease or fold (m.) קֶמֶט ;(m.) קֶפֶל
Canada (f.) קַנַדָה
to buy (v.) קָנָה
booklet (m.) קוּנְטְרֵס
to fold (v.) קִפֵּל
abbreviation (m.) קִצּוּר
cruzeiro (Brazilian currency) (m.) קְרוּזֶירוֹ
torn קָרוּעַ
a tear (e.g., in a stamp) (m.) קֶרַע
to tear (v.) קָרַע
cachet (m.) קִשּׁוּט

ר

top (m.) רֹאשׁ
multicolored, multicoloured רַבְגּוֹנִי
square (adj.) רָבוּעַ
fourth (the fraction), quarter (m.) רֶבַע
Russia (f.) רוּסִיָה
acquisition (f.) רְכִישָׁה
republic (f.) רֵפּוּבְּלִיקָה
People's Republic of China (P.R.C.) (f.) רֵפּוּבְּלִיקָה הָעַמָּמִית שֶׁל סִין
Republic of China (Taiwan) (f.) רֵפּוּבְּלִיקָה שֶׁל סִין
official רִשְׁמִי

ש

remainder, stock remainder (f.) שְׁאֵרִית מְלַאי
seven שִׁבְעָה
seventy שִׁבְעִים

chestnut (color) עַרְמוֹנִי
maroon עַרְמוֹנִי-כֵּהֶה
tenth (the fraction) (f.) עֲשִׂירִית
ten עֲשָׂרָה
twenty עֶשְׂרִים
ancient עַתִּיק
a copy, reproduction (m.) עֹתֶק

פ

February פֶבְּרוּאָר
damaged פָּגוּם
Portugal (f.) פּוֹרְטוּגָל
devaluation (m.) פִּחוּת
Finland (f.) פִינְלַנְד
domestic פְּנִים
peso (Spanish-American currency) (m.) פֶּסוֹ
peseta (monetary unit of Spain) (f.) פֶּסֶטָה
deposit (of funds) (m.) פִּקָדוֹן
deposit required פִּקָדוֹן דָרוּשׁ
pruta, prutah (unit of Israeli money) פְּרוּטָה
(auction) lot (m.) פָּרִיט
franc (French unit of currency) (m.) פְרַנְק
steel engraving (m.) פִּתּוּחַ פְּלָדָה
embossing פִּתּוּחַ תַּבְלִיט

צ

color, colour (m.) צֶבַע
bronze (color) צֶבַע אָרָד
lemon (color) צֶבַע הַלִּימוֹן
cream (color) צֶבַע קְרֶם
front (m.) צַד הַקִּדְמִי
reverse (m.) צַד הַשֵּׁנִי
yellow צָהֹב
se-tenant צֶמֶד בּוּלִים שׁוֹנִים
tête-bêche צֶמֶד הֲפוּכִים
block (f.) צְמוּדָה
block of four (f.) צְמוּדַת אַרְבַּע
France (f.) צָרְפַת

[מ continued from page 308]

מָכַר to sell (v.)

מַלְבֵּנִי rectangular

מֶלֶךְ king (m.)

מַלְכָּה queen (f.)

מֶלְקָט tongs (m.)

מְמוּדְבָּק hinged

מַמְלָכָה הַמְאֻחֶדֶת United Kingdom (U.K.) (f.)

מְמֻרְכָּז centered

מִן הַמִּנְיָן definitive

מְנוֹרָה menorah

מְנֻקָּב perforated

מַס tax (m.)

מִסְגֶּרֶת frame (f.)

מַס יֵסֶף surtax (m.)

מִסְפָּר number (m.)

מִסְפָּר סִדּוּרִי serial number (m.)

מַעֲטָפָה envelope; cover (f.)

מַעֲטֶפֶת בּוּלִים מִיּוֹם-רִאשׁוֹן הַהַנְפָּקָה first day cover

מַעֲרֶכֶת הַכְּסָפִים monetary system (f.)

מְצֻיָּן excellent

מְצֻמָּד accolated, conjoined, jugate (two or more portraits overlapped and facing in the same direction on a stamp or coin).

מְקוֹרִי original

מֶקְסִיקוֹ Mexico (f.)

מִרְכּוּז centering (m.)

מַרְס March

מַרְק mark (German unit of currency) (m.)

מֻשְׁלָם perfect, flawless

מְשֻׁמָּשׁ used

מְתֻקָּן repaired

נ

נָאֶה fine (grade or condition)

נָדִיר rare, scarce

נוֹבֶמְבֶּר November

נוֹרְבֶּגְיָה Norway (f.)

נִיוּ זִילַנְד New Zealand (f.)

נְיָר paper (m.)

נְיָר אָחִיד wove paper (m.)

נְיָר גִּירִי chalky paper (m.)

נְיָר מַבְרִיק glossy paper (m.)

נְיָר מְצֻלָּע laid paper (m.)

נְיָר עִם סִיבֵי מֶשִׁי (לְהָגֵן מִזִיּוּף) granite paper

נִקּוּב perforation (m.)

נִקּוּב בְּצוּרַת מְעֻיָּן lozenge roulette

נִקּוּב דּוֹלֵג (m.) interrupted perforation; syncopated perforation

נִקּוּב מְסָרֵק comb perforation (m.)

נִקּוּב סִכָּה pin perforation (m.)

נִקּוּב קַו line perforation (m.)

נָשִׂיא president (m.)

נֶשֶׁר eagle (m.)

ס

סָגֹל violet

סִדְרָה series (f.)

סָחַר to trade (v.)

סִימָן מֵימִי watermark (m.)

סִימָן נִסְתָּר secret mark (m.)

סִיסְמָה motto (f.)

סְכוּם amount (m.)

סֵמֶל symbol (m.)

סֶנְטִימֶטֶר centimeter, centimetre (m.)

סֶפְּטֶמְבֶּר September

סְפָרַד Spain (f.)

ע

עִבְרִית Hebrew (language)

עָגֹל round

עָטוּר דַפְנָה laureate

עַל הַגַב on the back

עָמֹק deep (re: color)

עִנְבָּר amber (color)

עֲרָב הַסְּעוּדִית Saudi Arabia (f.)

עֵרֶךְ value (m.)

עֵרֶךְ בְּשׁוּק intrinsic value (m.)

עֵרֶךְ נָקוּב denomination; face value (m.)

עֵרֶךְ קָטָלוֹגִי catalogue value (m.)

no unlimited bids לֹא מִתְקַבְּלוֹת הַצָּעוֹת בִּלְתִּי מוּגְבָּלוֹת
accepted (at an auction or mail bid sale).

unofficial	לֹא-רִשְׁמִי
white	לָבָן
lilac	לִילָךְ
pound Sterling (£) (f.)	לִירָה שְׁטֶרְלִינְג
lithography (f.)	לִיתוֹגְרַפְיָה
ungummed	לְלֹא דֶבֶק
on approval	לְנִסָּיוֹן
defective	לָקוּי
a defect (m.)	לִקּוּי

מ

hundred	מֵאָה
May	מַאי
Golda Meir	מֵאִיר, גּוֹלְדָה
hundredth (the fraction) (f.)	מֵאִית
variety (m.)	מִבְחָר
Shield of David (m.)	מָגֵן דָּוִד

Red Shield of David (insignia of (m.) מָגֵן דָּוִד אָדֹם
the Israeli Chapter of International Red Cross).

magenta	מָגֶנְטָה
hinge	מַדְבֵּקָה
on cover	מֻדְבָּק לְמַעֲטָפָה
barred	מֻדְפָּס בְּפַסִּים
grade, condition (f.)	מַדְרֵגָה
inverted	מְהֻפָּךְ
seller (m.)	מוֹכֵר

pedigree (list of all previous and (m.) מוֹצָא
present owners of a collectible item).

obsolete	מָחוּץ לְמַחֲזוֹר
price (m.)	מְחִיר
price list (m.)	מְחִירוֹן
cancelled to order	מֻחְתָּם לְפִי הַזְמָנָה
coin; currency (m.)	מַטְבֵּעַ
foreign currency (m.)	מַטְבֵּעַ זָר
classification (m.)	מִיּוּן
mil (unit of Israeli currency)	מִיל
million	מִילְיוֹן
millimeter, millimetre (m.)	מִילִימֶטֶר
to classify (v.)	מִיֵּן
auction; auction sale (f.)	מְכִירָה פּוּמְבִּית

mail bid sale מְכִירָה פּוּמְבִּית דֶּרֶךְ הַצָּעוֹת לִשְׁלֹחוֹת בְּדוֹאַר

unique	יָחִיד בְּמִינוֹ
monetary unit (f.)	יְחִידָה כַּסְפִּית
to attribute (v.)	יִחֵס
right (direction or position)	יָמִין
January	יָנוּאָר
Japan (f.)	יָפָן
green	יָרֹק
old	יָשָׁן
Israel (f.)	יִשְׂרָאֵל

כ

dark	כֵּהֶה
star (m.)	כּוֹכָב

Western Wall (usually referred by כֹּתֶל הַמַּעֲרָבִי
gentiles as the *Wailing Wall*).

ultramarine	כָּחֹל עַז
blue	כָּחֹל
royal blue	כָּחֹל מַלְכוּתִי
Prussian blue	כָּחֹל פְּרוּסִי
almost	כִּמְעַט
money; silver (m.)	כֶּסֶף
duplicate (adj.)	כָּפוּל
a duplicate (m.)	כֵּפֶל
emerald (color)	כְּצֶבַע בָּרֶקֶת
credit card (m.)	כַּרְטִיס אַשְׁרַאי
credit cards accepted	כַּרְטִיסֵי אַשְׁרַאי מִתְקַבְּלִים
carmine	כַּרְמִין
inscription	כְּתוֹבִית
orange	כָּתֹם
stain (m.)	כֶּתֶם

crown (royal headpiece or large (m.) כֶּתֶר
silver coin)

ל

nationality (m.)	לְאֹם
national	לְאֻמִּי
unsevered	לֹא מְנֻתָּק
imperforate	לֹא מְנֻקָּב
unused	לֹא מְשֻׁמָּשׁ

[ה *continued from page 310*]

to bid (at an auction or at a mail (v.) הִצִּיעַ מְחִיר
bid sale).

Red Cross הַצְּלָב הָאָדֹם

an offer (f.) הַצָּעָה

suggested bid (f.) הַצָּעָה מֻצַּעַת

protective reserve bid (f.) הַצָּעָה שְׁמוּרָה מוּגֶנֶת

(auction) bid (f.) הַצָּעַת מְחִיר

minimum bid (f.) הַצָּעַת מְחִיר מִינִימוּם

Benjamin (Theodor) Zeev Herzl הֶרְצֵל, בִּנְיָמִן זְאֵב

ו

Wales (f.) וֵיְלְס

Chaim Weizmann וַיְצְמָן, חַיִּים

Venezuela (f.) וֶנֶצוּאֵלָה

pink וָרֹד

ז

pair (m.) זוּג

a fake, forgery (m.) זִיּוּף

olive (color) זַיִת

magnifying glass (f.) זְכוּכִית מַגְדֶּלֶת

foreign זָר

phosphorescent זַרְחוֹנִי

phosphor (m.) זַרְחָן

ח

package (f.) חֲבִילָה

centennial, centenary (f.) חֲגִיגַת שְׁנַת הַמֵּאָה

new חָדָשׁ

month (m.) חֹדֶשׁ

silk thread חוּט מֶשִׁי

brown חוּם

---

bister חוּם כֵּהֶה

hole (m.) חוֹר

seal (device with a cut or raised (m.) חוֹתָם
emblem used to certify a signature or
authenticate a document, or a medallion of this
type that can be pressed into wax to give
official validity to envelopes or documents).

postmark (f.) חוֹתֶמֶת דֹּאַר

cachet (f.) חוֹתֶמֶת נִלְוֵית

frank (f.) חוֹתֶמֶת פָּטוֹר

obliteration (f.) חוֹתֶמֶת פְּסִילָה

postage due חַיָּב דְּמֵי-דֹּאַר

skinned spot, thin spot (m.) חַלּוֹן

five חֲמִשָּׁה

fifty חֲמִשִּׁים

Hanukkah חֲנֻכָּה

bisected חָצוּי

half (adj.) חֲצִי

half (the fraction) (m.) חֵצִי

imitation (m.) חִקּוּי

engraved חָרוּת

irregular חָרִיג

account (financial or transactional) (m.) חֶשְׁבּוֹן

signature (f.) חֲתִימָה

ט

order form (m.) טֹפֶס הַזְמָנָה

bid sheet (m.) טֹפֶס הַצָּעָה

turquoise טוּרְקִיז

error (f.) טָעוּת

typography (f.) טִפּוֹגְרַפְיָה

י

Yugoslavia, Jugoslavia (f.) יוּגוֹסְלַבְיָה

Greece (f.) יָוָן

July יוּלִי

June יוּנִי

attribution (the complete identi- (m.) יִחוּס
fication of a stamp or other philatelic item).

precancel (noun) (m.) בִּטוּל מֵרֹאשׁ
to frank (v.) בִּיֵּל
international בֵּין-לְאֻמִּי
Belgium (f.) בֶּלְגִּיָה
unhinged בְּלִי מַדְבֵּקָה
unknown (not listed in any book or בִּלְתִּי יָדוּעַ
catalogue).
unattributed בִּלְתִּי מְזוֹהֶה
incomplete בִּלְתִּי מֻשְׁלָם
undeliverable בִּלְתִּי נִתָּן לִמְסִירָה
David Ben-Gurion בֶּן גוּרְיוֹן, דָּוִד
holed בַּעַל-חוֹר
valuable בַּעַל-עֵרֶךְ
Brazil (f.) בְּרָזִיל
Great Britain (f.) בְּרִיטַנְיָה הַגְּדוֹלָה
Soviet Union (U.S.S.R.) (f.) בְּרִית הַמּוֹעֲצוֹת

ג

large גָּדוֹל
shade (re: color) (m.) גּוּוָן
postcard גְּלוּיָה מְצֻיֶּרֶת
postal card (f.) גְּלוּיַת-דֹּאַר
sheet (of stamps) (m.) גִּלָּיוֹן
souvenir sheet (f.) גִּלְיוֹנִית זִכָּרוֹן
coil (m.) גְּלִיל בּוּלִים
Germany (f.) גֶּרְמַנְיָה
East Germany (D.D.R.) (f.) גֶּרְמַנְיָה הַמִּזְרָחִית
West Germany (B.R.D.) (f.) גֶּרְמַנְיָה הַמַּעֲרָבִית

ד

post office דֹּאַר
mail (m.) דֹּאַר ; דּוֹאַר
airmail (m.) דֹּאַר אֲוִיר
parcel post (m.) דֹּאַר חֲבִילוֹת
Hebrew Post דֹּאַר עִבְרִי
cerise דֻּבְדְּבָנִי
gum (m.) דֶּבֶק
regummed דֶּבֶק מְחֻדָּשׁ
original gum (m.) דֶּבֶק מְקוֹרִי

censored mail (m.) דְּבַר דֹּאַר מְצֻנְזָר
pattern (m.) דֶּגֶם
bicolored, bicoloured דּוּ-גּוֹנִי
specimen (f.) דֻּגְמָא
dollar ($) (m.) דּוֹלָר
bilingual דּוּ-לְשׁוֹנִי
mailman, postman (m.) דַּוָּר
ink (m./f.) דְּיוֹ
portrait (m.) דְּיוֹקָן
crimson דָּמִי
postage דְּמֵי דֹּאַר
Denmark (f.) דַּנְמַרְק
intaglio; photogravure (m.) דְּפוּס שֶׁקַע
quadrillé דַּף מְרֻשָּׁת שֶׁל אַלְבּוֹם
December דֶּצֶמְבֶּר
rouletted; percé דָּקוּר
roulette; perçage (m.) דִּקּוּר
serrated roulette; zigzag (m.) דִּקּוּר סְכָסָךְ
roulette; perçage en scie
serpentine roulette (m.) דִּקּוּר סֶרְפֶּנְטִין
to grade (v.) דֵּרֵג
South Africa (f.) דְּרוֹם אַפְרִיקָה
liberty (m.) דְּרוֹר

ה

to print (v.) הִדְפִּיס
a reprint (f.) הַדְפָּסָה נוֹסֶפֶת
overprint (m.) הֶדְפֵּס מֵעַל
surcharge הֶדְפֵּס עַל (שֶׁל עֵרֶךְ)
burélage, burelé (m.) הֶדְפֵּס רֶקַע
Holland, The Netherlands (f.) הוֹלַנְד
Hong Kong (f.) הוֹנְג-קוֹנְג
demonetization (f.) הוֹצָאָה מְתוּקֶּף
commemorative issue הוֹצָאַת זִכָּרוֹן
to cancel (v.) הֶחְתִּים
cancellation הַחְתָּמָה
check, cheque (f.) הַמְחָאָה
money order (f.) הַמְחָאַת כֶּסֶף
to issue (v.) הִנְפִּיק
an issue, issuance הַנְפָּקָה
to copy (v.) הֶעְתִּיק
separation (f.) הַפְרָדָה
to exhibit (v.) הִצִּיג
to offer (v.) הִצִּיעַ

Hebrew Alphabet

All words in Modern Hebrew

This section is formatted in accordance with accepted Hebrew usage. Pages and columns flow from right to left and all Hebrew entries are right-justified exactly as they are found in standard Israeli dictionaries.

See page 304 for additional information and explanations.

א

agora, agorah (Israeli unit of currency) אֲגוֹרָה
aerogramme (f.) אִגֶּרֶת אֲוִיר
magenta אָדֹם-אַרְגָּמָן
red אָדֹם
August אוֹגוּסְט
Austria (f.) אוֹסְטְרִיָה
Australia (f.) אוֹסְטְרַלְיָה
October אוֹקְטוֹבֶּר
one (f.adj.) אַחַת ;(m.adj.) אֶחָד
Italy (f.) אִיטַלְיָה
indigo אִינְדִיגוֹ
inch (unit of measure equal to 2.54 cm.) (m.) אִינְץ'
Albert Einstein אַיְנְשְׁטַיְן, אַלְבֶּרְט
(Republic of) Ireland (f.) אִירְלַנְד
Northern Ireland (f.) אִירְלַנְד הַצְּפוֹנִית
God (in the Judaic-Christian sense) (m.) אֵל
album (m.) אַלְבּוֹם
thousand (m.) אֶלֶף
art (f.) אָמָנוּת
authentic, genuine; real אֲמִתִּי
England (f.) אַנְגְּלִיָה
aniline (m.) אֲנִילִין
collection (m.) אֹסֶף
to collect (v.) אָסַף

---

collector (m.) אַסְפָן
pope (of the Roman Catholic Church) (m.) אַפִּיפְיוֹר
zero אֶפֶס
never hinged אַף פַּעַם לֹא מְמוּדְבָּק
gray אָפֹר
April אַפְּרִיל
four אַרְבָּעָה
forty אַרְבָּעִים
purple; heliotrope אַרְגָּמָן
lavender אַרְגָּמָן-כְּחַלְחַל
Argentina (f.) אַרְגֶּנְטִינָה
United States of America (U.S.A.) (f.) אַרְצוֹת הַבְּרִית
credit (m.) אַשְׁרַאי

בּ

light (re: color) בָּהִיר
philately (f.) בּוּלָאוּת
aerophilately (f.) בּוּלָאוּת-דֹּאַר אֲוִיר
topical בּוּלָאוּת שֶׁל נוֹשֵׂא מְסוּיָם
philatelic בּוּלָאִי
philatelist (m.) בּוּלָאִי
encased postage stamp (m.) בּוּל בְּצוּרַת נַרְתִּיק
(such as the type of token used as an emergency substitute for small coins during the U.S. Civil War of 1861-65).
postage stamp (m.) בּוּל דֹּאַר
air stamp; airmail stamp (m.) בּוּל דֹּאַר-אֲוִיר
parcel post stamp (m.) בּוּל דֹּאַר חֲבִילוֹת
military postage stamp (m.) בּוּל דֹּאַר צְבָאִי
postage due stamp (m.) בּוּל דְּמֵי דֹּאַר
fiscal stamp (m.) בּוּל הַכְנָסָה
provisional (noun) (m.) בּוּל זְמַנִּי
newspaper stamp (m.) בּוּל לְמִשְׁלוֹחַ עִתּוֹנִים
telegraph stamp (m.) בּוּל מִבְרָק
tagged stamp (m.) בּוּל מְסָמָן
franchise stamp (m.) בּוּל פְּטוֹר
charity stamp (m.) בּוּל צְדָקָה
registration stamp (m.) בּוּל רִשּׁוּם
official stamp (m.) בּוּל שֵׁרוּת
propaganda stamp (m.) בּוּל תַּעֲמוּלָה
cut cancellation (m.) בִּטּוּל בְּחִתּוּךְ
punch cancellation (m.) בִּטּוּל בְּנִקּוּב
pen cancelled בִּטּוּל בַּעֵט

Quick Identifier

The Quick Identifier enables the philatelist to determine quickly and easily the place of origin of hundreds of hard-to-identify stamps. This section also provides illustrations of many common philatelic terms.

The pages titled *Philatelic Terminology* are a pictorial guide to the technical vocabulary used in philately today. Many collectors are unfamiliar with much of the terminology of this field, especially French terms used by English speakers. By looking at the *Philatelic Terminology* pages, the collector can tell at a glance the difference between a *tête-bêche* pair, *se-tenant* pair, gutter pair, bilingual pair, etc.

The remainder of the Quick Identifier contains photos of hundreds of stamps which are difficult to place. The words in parentheses indicate the nature of a stamp (semi-postal, official, newspaper, parcel post, *et al*) if it was issued for any reason other than normal postal use.

The information in brackets gives clues to the determination of the stamp's origin. It may contain the name of the country in that nation's own language (*Suomi* for Finland, *Hellas* or *Ελλάς* for Greece, ישראל for Israel, etc.), or it may indicate some other inscription, symbol, denomination, overprint, or other special device or characteristic. Words in the Hebrew, Greek, and Cyrillic alphabets are only included when they are simple and recognizable by an English speaker.

Some of the bracketed information shows indicators that are unique to certain countries but not to specific regions. For example, the year *1949* on a Chinese stamp signifies that it came from some area now part of the P.R.C. Stamps inscribed 1949 originated in East China, Central China, South China, etc. Since these stamps often show nothing else that would help an English speaker, seeing 1949 printed on the stamp narrows the possibilities considerably.

Due to space limitations, lengthy inscriptions are shortened in the *Quick Identifier* by adding dashes after the first letter of the words. The overprint on the Hungarian Szeged issue has been shortened here from *MAGYAR NEMZETI KORMÁNY* to *M— N— K—* for lack of space.

In addition to the *Quick Identifier*, collectors can also use the main body of this dictionary to identify and place many thousands of stamps. For example, although there are many ways of spelling the name of Albania (*Shqipëria, Shqipëtare, R.P.E. Shqiperise*, etc.), the main body states that the spelling *Shqipnija* refers specifically either to a bogus stamp produced by the government in exile or to a stamp issued under German administration.

QUICK IDENTIFIER: **Philatelic Terminology**

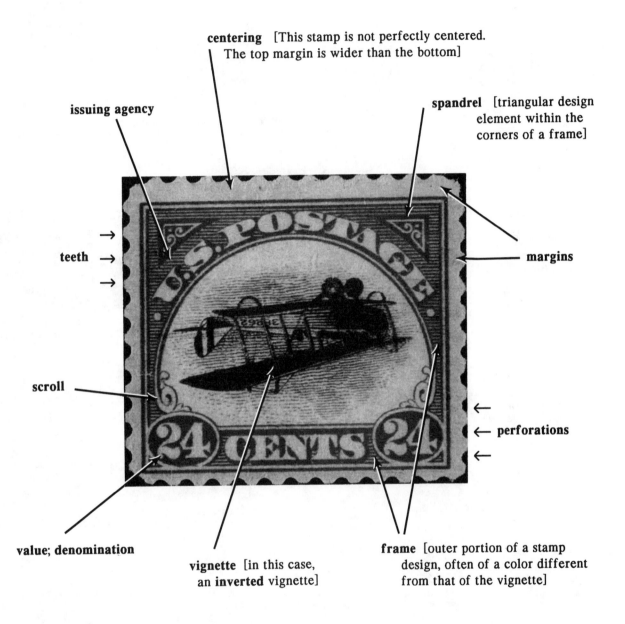

centering [This stamp is not perfectly centered. The top margin is wider than the bottom]

spandrel [triangular design element within the corners of a frame]

issuing agency

teeth →

margins

scroll

perforations ←

value; denomination

vignette [in this case, an **inverted** vignette]

frame [outer portion of a stamp design, often of a color different from that of the vignette]

popular name: **Jenny invert**[q.v.]

QUICK IDENTIFIER: Philatelic Terminology

semi-postal (France)

official stamp (U.S.)

official (overprint) (N. Zealand)

undenominated stamp
w/ tab (Israel)

surcharge (Liechtenstein)

overnight delivery (express) stamp (U.S.)

Red Cross stamp (Iceland)

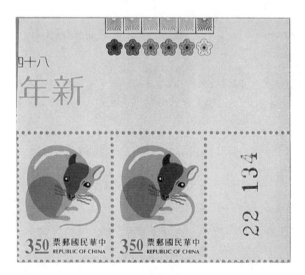

corner pair (Republic of China); **bilingual inscription;**
color registration marks [6 flowers & boxes in the **selvage** at the top];
plate number [in the selvage at the right]

airmail (air post) stamp (Italy)

airmail overprint (Serbia)

training school stamp
(Great Britain)

precancel (U.S.)

QUICK IDENTIFIER: Philatelic Terminology

non-postal label (U.S.)

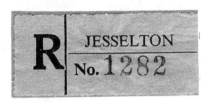

registration label (North Borneo)

occupation stamp
(Finnish occupation of Karelia)

triptych (Vatican) [strip of 3
individual stamps forming one single design]

quadriptych (U.S.) [block or strip of 4
individual stamps forming one single design]

first day cover (Spain; in Spanish: *PRIMER DIA DE EMISION*)
cachet [fancy design on the left-hand portion of the envelope which relates to the theme of the stamp]

QUICK IDENTIFIER: Philatelic Terminology

military stamp (Austria)

encased postage stamp (U.S. Civil War)

postage due (Angola)

(horizontal) bilingual pair (S. Africa)

tête-bêche pair (Israel)

perfin; spif (U.S.) [both sides]

(vertical) se-tenant pair (Brit. Vir. Is.)

joint issue (U.S. & Canada); the Canadian stamp is also **bilingual**

stamp w/ imperf **propaganda label** (Italy)

railway stamp (Belgium; "B" *o/p*)

gutter pair (Cuba); separated by **perforation**

documentary (revenue) stamps (U.S.); separated by **roulette**

QUICK IDENTIFIER: Western Europe

GREAT BRITAIN
[head of Queen Victoria]

GREAT BRITAIN
[head of King George V]

GREAT BRITAIN
[head of King Edward VIII]

G.B. (training school stamp)
[George VI w/ 2 vertical black bars]

G.B. (postage/revenue)
[head of Queen Elizabeth II]

G.B. (postage due)

G.B. (postage due)
[TO PAY]

G.B. (inland revenue)
[o/p GOVT PARCELS]

IRELAND (provisional)
[Irish o/p on G.B. stamp]

IRELAND
[ÉIRE]

IRELAND
[Éire]

FRANCE (precancel)
[o/p AFFRANCHts/ POSTES]

FRANCE
[RF]

FRANCE
[REPVBLIQVE FRANÇAISE]

FRANCE (postage due)
[CHIFFRE - TAXE]

FRANCE
[RF]

QUICK IDENTIFIER: Western Europe

BELGIUM (mourning)
[BELGIQUE/ BELGIË]

BELGIUM
[head of King Leopold I]

BELGIUM (occupation by)
[o/p Malmédy]

BELGIUM (railway)
["B" *within oval circle*]

ITALY
[FRANCO BOLLO]

ITALY (pneumatic post)
[POSTA PNEUMATICA]

ITALY (propaganda)
[w/ imperf propaganda label]

ITALY (parcel post)
[o/p Valevole per le stampe]

VENEZIA GIULIA (occup. of)
[o/p A.M.G/ V.G.]

SAN MARINO (postage due)
[SEGNATASSE]

NETHERLANDS (surcharge)
[NEDERLAND + o/p]

NETHERLANDS (postage due)
[TE BETALEN]

PORTUGAL
[CORREIO/ REIS]

PORTUGAL (franchise)
[PORTE FRANCO]

PORTUGAL (franchise)
[PORTE FRANCO]

PORTUGAL (postage due)
[PORTEADO]

QUICK IDENTIFIER: Western Europe

MONACO (precancel)
[MONACO/ AFFRANCHts/ POSTES]

SWITZERLAND
[HELVETIA]

SWITZERLAND (postage due)
[*mountains & cross*]

LIECHTENSTEIN

ICELAND
[ÍSLAND]

ICELAND (surcharge)
[ÍSLAND; *o/p* 1 GILDI/ '02-'03]

ICELAND
[ÍSLAND]

LUXEMBOURG (occupation of)
[*o/p* LUXEMBURG *on German stamp*]

NORWAY
[NORGE]

NORWAY (official)
[OFF. SAK]

NORWAY (official)
[OFFENTLIG SAK]

GREENLAND
[GRØNLAND]

[See **Russia, U.S.S.R., et al** for additional stamps of Finland]

FINLAND
[SUOMI]

FINLAND (military)
[KENTTÄPOSTIA]

FINLAND (military)
[KENTTÄPOSTIA]

KARELIA
[*o/p* ITÄ-KARJALA/ Sot.hallinto]

QUICK IDENTIFIER: Western Europe

BAVARIA
[BAYERN]

BAVARIA (railway)
[o/p Bayer. Staatseisenb.]

BAVARIA (People's State)
[o/p Volksstaat Bayern]

BAVARIA (official)
[DIENSTMARKE/ BAYERN]

HAMBURG

BADEN (rural postage due)
[LAND POST/ PORTO-MARKE]

GERMANY (income tax)
[EINKOMMENSTEUER/ D- R-]

WÜRTTEMBERG (People's State)
[o/p Volksstaat Württemberg]

SCHLESWIG (plebiscite)
[PLEBISCIT/ SLESVIG]

THURN und TAXIS
(Southern District)

GERMANY (provisional)
[Deutsches Reich o/p on Bavarian stamp]

GERMANY (semi-postal)
[Deutsches Reich + o/p]

EAST GERMANY
[DEUTSCHE DEMO- REP-]

E. GERMANY (semi-postal)
[D- D- R-; o/p HELFT ÄGYPTEN + 10]

E. GERMANY (semi-postal)
[DDR]

EAST GERMANY (official)
[D- D- R-/ DIENSTMARKE]

GERMANY (semi-postal)
[Deutsches Reich + *o/p*]

WEST GERMANY
[DEUTSCHE POST]

VIENNA et al (provisional)
[Österreich *o/p on German stamp*]

GERMANY (w/ column value)
[Deutsches Reich; *Nazi swastika*]

AUSTRIA
[OESTERR.POST.]

AUSTRIA (special handling)
[*Mercury on triangular stamp*]

AUSTRIA (military)
[K-u-K MILITÄRPOST]

AUSTRIA (military)
[K-u-K FELDPOST]

AUSTRIA (newspaper)
[Zeitungsmarke]

AUSTRIA (postage due)
[Porto]

AUSTRIA (semi-postal)
[ÖSTERREICHISCHEPOST]

AUSTRIA
[ÖSTERREICHISCHEPOST]

AUSTRIA (postage due)
[*o/p* Nachmarke]

AUSTRIA (special handling)
[Österreich; *arrow & posthorn*]

AUSTRIA
[Deutschösterreich]

REPUBLIC of AUSTRIA
[REPUBLIK ÖSTERREICH]

QUICK IDENTIFIER: **Spanish-Speaking**

SPAIN (revenue)
[COMUNICACIONES]

SPAIN (telegraph)
[CORREOS Y TELEGS]

SPAIN (Red Cross)
[LA CRUZ ROJA ESPAÑOLA]

SPAIN
[ESPAÑA]

SPAIN
[ESTADO ESPAÑOL]

SPAIN (special delivery)
[CORRESPONDENCIA URGENTE]

PHILIPPINES
[FILIPINAS]

PHILIPPINES (revenue)
[DERECHOS DE FIRMA]

PHILIPPINES
[FILIPINAS]

PHILIPPINES (telegraph)
[FILIPINAS/ TELEGRAFOS]

PHILIPPINES (telegraph)
[FILIPINAS/ TELEGRAFOS]

PHILIPPINES (newspaper)
[FILIPINAS/ IMPRESOS]

COSTA RICA

VENEZUELA (postal/revenue)
[ESCUELAS]

VENEZUELA (postal/revenue)
[INSTRUCCIÓN]

VENEZUELA
[EEUU de VENEZUELA]

QUICK IDENTIFIER: Spanish-Speaking

CAPE JUBY
[CABO JUBY]

MEXICO
[SERVICIO POSTAL MEXICANO]

IFNI
(former Spanish colony)

GUATEMALA (official)
[Franqueo Oficial Guatemala]

CHILE (postage due)
[CHILE/ MULTA]

FERNANDO POO
(former Spanish province)

CUBA
[ULTRAMAR]

CUBA
[ISLA DE CUBA]

CUBA
[ULTRAMAR]

CUBA

CUBA

CUBA (newspaper)
[CUBA - IMPRESOS]

CUBA

SPAIN (postage stamp
used as currency during the
Spanish Civil War, 1936-39)

[Spanish stamp affixed to the back
of a thin cardboard disk.
Royal insignia printed on front.]

CUBA (telegraph)
[CUBA. TELÉGRAFOS]

324

QUICK IDENTIFIER: Eastern Europe

GREECE
[ΕΛΛΑΣ]

GREECE (memorial/surcharge)
[*black borders w/ 250 in circle*]

CRETE
[Π- Τ- ΗΡΑΚΛΕΙΟΥ]

ESTONIA (occup./ semi-postal)
[ESTLAND - EESTI]

LATVIA
[LATVIJA]

LATVIA
[LATWIJA]

LATVIA (surcharge)
[LATVIJA; *o/p* DIVI/ 2RUB.2]

LATVIA
[LATVIJA]

ALBANIA
[SHQIPËTARE]

ALBANIA
[P R SH]

ALBANIA
[R- P- E SHQIPERISE]

ALBANIA (King./ provisional)
[REP. SHQIPTARE *w/ circular o/p*]

ALBANIA
[Shqipëria]

ALBANIA
[R.P.E. SHQIPERISE]

ALBANIA (bogus: gov. in exile)
[SHQIPNIJA]

ALBANIA
[SHQIPERIA]

QUICK IDENTIFIER: **Eastern Europe**

BULGARIA
[БЪЛГАРСКА ПОЩА]

BULGARIA
[БЪЛГАРСКА ПОЩА]

BULGARIA
[БЪЛГАРИЯ]

BULGARIA
[15 СТОТ(инки) (*15 STOTinki*)]

BULGARIA
[БЪЛГАРИЯ]

BULGARIA
[1 СТОТИНКА (*1 STOTINKA*)]

BULGARIA (lib. of Macedonia)
[ЦАРст.БЪЛГАРИЯ]

BULGARIA
[БЪЛГАРИЯ]

BULGARIA
[ЦАРСТВО БЪЛГАРИЯ]

BULGARIA (Royal Wedding)
[БЪЛГАРИЯ]

BULGARIA
[ЦАРСТВО БЪЛГАРИЯ]

BULGARIA
[БЪЛГАРИЯ]

BULGARIA (airmail)
[Н- Р- БЪЛГАРИЯ]

BULGARIA
[Н- Р- БЪЛГАРИЯ]

BULGARIA
[БЪЛГАРИЯ]

BULGARIA
[ЦАРСТВО БЪЛГАРИЯ]

QUICK IDENTIFIER: **Eastern Europe**

BULGARIA
[N R BULGARIA]

BULGARIA [Н Р България]

BULGARIA
[Н Р БЪЛГАРИЯ]

BULGARIA
[ЦАРСТВО БЪЛГАРИЯ]

BULGARIA
[Н Р БЪЛГАРИЯ]

BULGARIA
[N R BULGARIA]

BULGARIA (official)
[БЪЛГАРИЯ/ ОБЩИНСКА ПОЩА]

BULGARIA
[БЪЛГАРИЯ]

BULGARIA (Anniversary)
[Н Р БЪЛГАРИЯ - ПОЩА]

BULGARIA
[БЪЛГАРИЯ]

BULGARIA
[N R BULGARIA]

BULGARIA
[БЪЛГАРИЯ]

BULGARIA
[ЦАРСТВО БЪЛГАРИЯ]

BULGARIA
[БЪЛГАРИЯ]

QUICK IDENTIFIER: Eastern Europe

LITHUANIA (orphans' fund)
[LIETUVA]

LITHUANIA (airmail)   [LIETUVA PAŠTAS/ ORO]

LITHUANIA (orphans' fund)
[LIETUVA]

LITHUANIA
[LIETUVA]

ROMANIA
[REPUBLICA POPULARA ROMANA]

ROMANIA
[R.P.ROMINA]

ROMANIA (tax)
[o/p SCUTIT DE TAXA POSTALA]

ROMANIA (postal tax due)
[o/p M.V.i.R. (German occupation)]

HUNGARY (Repub./ provisional)
[MAGYAR; o/p KÖZTÁRSASÁG]

HUNGARY (King./ provisional)
[MAGYAR; o/p "heads of wheat"/ 1919]

HUNGARY (King./ provisional)
[MAGYAR; o/p "heads of wheat"/ 1919]

HUNGARY (Szeged issue)
[o/p M- N- K-/ Szeged, 1919]

HUNGARY (Repub./ provisional)
[MAGYAR; o/p 1945/ 8 pengő]

HUNGARY (Repub./postage due)
[MAGYAR; o/p 1945/ 60 fillér]

W. HUNGARY (unrecognized)
[LAJTABÁNSÁG]

QUICK IDENTIFIER: Yugoslav Area

BOSNIA-HERZEG. (mil.)
[BOSNIEN HERCEGOVINA/ K-u-K]

BOSNIA & HERZEGOVINA
[o/p Босна и Херцеговина]

BOSNIA & HERZEGOVINA
[o/p Bosna i Hercegovina]

BOSNIA-HERZEG. (mil.)
[BOSNIEN HERCEGOVINA/ K-u-K]

BOSNIA-HERZEG. (mil.)
[BOSNIEN HERCEGOVINA/ K-u-K]

BOSNIA & HERZEGOVINA
[newspaper stamp if imperforate]

BOSNIA-HERZEG. (mil.)
[BOSNIEN HERCEGOVINA/ K-u-K]

SERBIA
[СРПСКА]

SERBIA (occup. postage due)
[СРБИЈА/ ПОРТО]

SERBIA
[ПАРА (PARA, the denomination)]

SERBIA
[СРБИЈА]

SERBIA (postage due)
[ПАРА/ ПОРТО МАРКА]

SERBIA (occup. semi-postal)
[СРБИЈА]

SERBIA (occup. semi-postal)
[СРБИЈА]

YUGOSLAVIA (Kingdom)
[SRBA, HRVATA I SLOVENACA]

YUGOSLAVIA (Kingdom)
[SRBA, HRVATA I SLOVENACA]

QUICK IDENTIFIER: Yugoslav Area

SLOVENIA
[*head of King Peter I*]

SLOVENIA
[KRALJEVSTVO SHS]

SLOVENIA
[*"Chain Breaker"*]

SLOVENIA (postage due)

CROATIA-SLAVONIA
[*o/p* SHS/HRVATSKA *on Hung. stamp*]

CROATIA-SLAVONIA
[*o/p* SHS/HRVATSKA *on Hung. stamp*]

CROATIA-SLAVONIA
[HRVATSKA]

CROATIA (postage due)
[*o/p* N- D- HRVATSKA + *crest*]

CROATIA (official)
[HRVATSKA/ SLUŽBENA]

CROATIA (postal tax)
[N. D. HRVATSKA]

CROATIA (postage due)
[HRVATSKA PORTO MARKA]

CROATIA (postage due)
[HRVATSKA PORTO]

CROATIA (Red Cross)
[NEZAVISNA DRŽAVA HRVATSKA]

CROATIA
[N. D. HRVATSKA]

CROATIA
[NEZAVISNA DRŽAVA HRVATSKA]

CROATIA (semi-postal)
[N. D. HRVATSKA]

QUICK IDENTIFIER: **Yugoslav Area**

YUGOSLAVIA (postage due)
[SRBA, HRVATA...; PORTO]

YUGOSLAVIA
[ЈУГОСЛАВИЈА]

LJUBLJANA [Lubiana] (occup.)
[*Ital. o/p* Co-Ci *on Yugoslav stamp*]

MONTENEGRO
[ЦР. ГОРА]

MONTENEGRO (Anniversary)
[ПОШТЕЦРНЕГОРЕ]

MONTENEGRO
[ПОШТЕЦРНЕГОРЕ]

MONTENEGRO
[ЦРНА ГОРА]

MONTENEGRO
[ПОШТЕЦРНЕГОРЕ]

MONTENEGRO
[ПОШТЕЦРНЕГОРЕ]

MONTENEGRO
[ЦРНА ГОРА]

MONTENEGRO (ack. of receipt)
[ПОШТЕ ЦР. ГОРА]

MONTENEGRO
[КРАЉ ЦРНАГОРА]

MONTENEGRO (occupation)
[*German o/p on Yugoslavian stamp*]

MONTENEGRO (occupation)
[*o/p* ЦРНА ГОРА *on Italian stamp*]

MONTENEGRO (occup. airmail)
[ЦРНА ГОРА]

MONTENEGRO (exile; unissued)
[*o/p* СЛОБОДНА ЦРНАГОРА]

QUICK IDENTIFIER: Russia, U.S.S.R., et al

RUSSIA
[ПЯТЬ КОП. (*FIVE KOP[eks]*)]

FINLAND
[5 PEN.*[nia]* (*Finnish denom.)*]

RUSSIA
[СЕМЬ КОП. (*SEVEN KOP[eks]*)]

FINLAND
[20 PEN.*[nia]* (*Finnish denom.)*]

RUSSIA
[20 КОП. (*denomination*)]

RUSSIA
[ПОЧТОВАЯ МАРКА]

FINLAND
[*deep serpentine rouletting*]

SOUTH RUSSIA
[*o/p 70 on Russian stamp*]

RUSSIA
[4 КОП. (*denomination*)]

ARMENIA
[*o/p shown above on Russian stamp*]

ARMENIA
[*o/p shown above on Russian stamp*]

RUSSIA (Offices in Turkey)
[ВОСТОЧНАЯ КОРРЕСПОНДЕНЦІЯ]

RUSSIA
[ПОЧТОВАЯ МАРКА]

RUSSIA
(Army of the North)

RUSSIA
(Army of the North)

RUSSIA
[ПОЧТОВАЯ МАРКА]

QUICK IDENTIFIER: Russia, U.S.S.R., et al

RUSSIA
[*head of Czar Peter the Great*]

RUSSIA (postage currency;
both sides shown above)

[ungummed on thin cardboard
with message printed on the back]

RUSSIA (semi-postal)
[ПОЧТА]

RUSSIA
[*design also used on postage currency*]

RUSSIA
[*bust of Czarina Katherine the Great*]

RUSSIAN WESTERN ARMY
[*occup. of Latvia; unissued*]

R.S.F.S.R. (provisional)
[*communist o/p on czarist stamp*]

RUSS. SOV. FED. SOC. REP.
[РСФСР]

RUSS. SOV. FED. SOC. REP.
[РСФСР]

RUSS. SOV. FED. SOC. REP.
[РСФСР]

RUSS. SOV. FED. SOC. REP.
[РСФСР]

RUSS. SOV. FED. SOC. REP.
[РСФСР]

RUSS. SOV. FED. SOC. REP.
[РОССIЯ]

U.S.S.R.
[CCCP]

U.S.S.R.
[CCCP]

333

QUICK IDENTIFIER: Russia, U.S.S.R., et al

U.S.S.R.
[CCCP]

U.S.S.R. (with *burélage*)
[ПОЧТА СССР]

U.S.S.R. (without *burélage*)
[ПОЧТА СССР]

U.S.S.R.
[CCCP *at the side*]

U.S.S.R. (w/ *se-tenant* label)
[ПОЧТА СССР]

U.S.S.R. (New Year's stamp) [ПОЧТА СССР]

AZERBAIJAN (semi-postal)
[ACCP]

UKRAINE (occupation of)
[*o/p* UKRAINE *on German stamp*]

UKRAINE (unissued)
[*trident-like Ukranian symbol at corners*]

UKRAINE (unissued)
[*trident-like Ukranian symbol at sides*]

UKRAINE (unissued)
[*trident-like Ukranian symbol at corners*]

UKRAINE (unissued)
[*trident-like Ukranian symbol at the top*]

UKRAINE (unissued)
[*trident-like Ukranian symbol at the top*]

[the 14 unissued stamps of the 1920
series exist perforate or imperforate]

UKRAINE (semi-postal)
[*"Death Stalking Peasants"*]

QUICK IDENTIFIER: Middle East

ISRAEL (w/ tab)
[ישראל]

ETHIOPIA

MOROCCO
(Cherifien Local Post)

MOROCCO (German Offices)
[*o/p* Marokko *on German stamp*]

UNITED ARAB REPUBLIC
(official)

BAHRAIN [*surcharged in Indian currency on U.K. stamp*]

OTTOMAN EMPIRE
[EMP. OTTOMAN]

OTTOMAN EMPIRE
[POSTES OTTOMANES]

TURKEY
[*star & crescent; toughra (top center)*]

TURKEY (official)
[RESMÎ]

TURKEY (Army in Thessaly)
[*8-sided; toughra*]

TURKEY
[TÜRKİYE]

LEBANON (French Mandate)
[*o/p* GRAND LIBAN]

LEBANON (provisional)
[*o/p* RÉPUBLIQUE LIBANAISE]

LEBANON
[GRAND LIBAN]

LEBANON
[GRAND LIBAN]

QUICK IDENTIFIER: **Middle East**

PERSIA (IRAN)
[POSTES PERSANES]

PERSIA (IRAN) (provisional)
[*o/p* PROVISOIRE]

PERSIA (IRAN)
[*handstamped overprint*]

PERSIA (IRAN)
[*silver margins*]

PERSIA (IRAN)
[POSTES PERSANES]

PERSIA (IRAN)
[POSTES PERSANES]

PERSIA (IRAN)
[POSTES PERSANES + *o/p*]

PERSIA (IRAN) (official)
[*o/p* SERVICE]

PERSIA (IRAN) (w/ surcharge)
[POSTES PERSANES]

IRAN [w/ & w/o POSTES IRANIENNES]

IRAN (provisional)
[PAHLAVI *o/p on Treasury Dept. stamp*]

PERSIA (IRAN)
[POSTES PERSANES]

PERSIA (IRAN)
[POSTES PERSANES *on ribbon*]

PERSIA (IRAN)
[50 D(*inars*)]

PERSIA (IRAN)
[75 D(*inars*)]

QUICK IDENTIFIER: Middle East

IRAN
[10 D(inars)]

IRAN (airmail; provisional)
[IRAN o/p on Persian airmail stamp]

PERSIA (IRAN) (postal tax)
[Red Lion & Sun emblem]

IRAN
[10 R(ials)]

SAUDI ARABIA
[ROYAUME DE L'ARABIE SAOUDITE]

MESOPOTAMIA (Mosul issue)
[o/p POSTAGE/ I.E.F.'D'/ 1 Anna]

MESOPOTAMIA (Mosul issue)
[o/p POSTAGE/ I.E.F.'D'/ 1/2 Anna]

IRAQ (British occupation of)
[above o/p w/ surcharges in Indian currency on Ottoman Emp. stamps]

LIBYA

IRAQ (official)
[o/p ON STATE SERVICE]

LIBYA
[TRIPOLI]

LIBYA [SOCIALIST PEOPLE'S
LIBYAN ARAB JAMAHIRIYA]

LIBYA
[LAR]

LIBYA
[LAR]

QUICK IDENTIFIER: India; Southeast Asia

INDIA (official)
[India stamp with o/p]

JIND (Indian State)
[India stamp with JIND o/p]

HYDERABAD (official)
[w/ official o/p]

CAMBODIA
(Int'l Comm. in Indo-China)

COCHIN ANCHAL

BURMA
(under Japanese occupation)

BURMA
(under Japanese occupation)

ARMENIA

THAILAND (Siam)

THAILAND (Siam)

THAILAND (Siam)

NEPAL

NEPAL
[figure of Siva Mahadeva]

NEPAL
[figure of Siva Mahadeva]

NEPAL

NEPAL

QUICK IDENTIFIER: Far East

CHINA
[face of Sun Yat-sen]

CHINA

CHINA

CHINA

CHINA

CHINA
(w/ gold yuan surcharge)

CHINA
(w/ gold yuan surcharge)

CHINA
[bust of Sun Yat-sen]

CHINA

CHINA (postage due)

CHINA (postage due)

REPUBLIC of CHINA
(w/ surcharge)

REPUBLIC of CHINA
(w/ surcharge)

REPUBLIC of CHINA
[Chinese flag]

REPUBLIC of CHINA
[map of China]

CHINA

QUICK IDENTIFIER: **Far East**

REPUBLIC of CHINA

REPUBLIC of CHINA

REPUBLIC of CHINA

REPUBLIC of CHINA
[w/ or w/o o/p for Pres. Eisenhower]

REPUBLIC of CHINA

REPUBLIC of CHINA

REPUBLIC of CHINA

P.R.C.
[insignia]

P.R.C. (provisional)
[o/p on Chinese stamp]

PEOPLE'S REPUBLIC of CHINA
[Communist Chinese flag]

P.R.C. (provisional)
[o/p on Chinese stamp]

P.R.C.

P.R.C.

MANCHUKUO
[FEN (the denomination)]

MANCHUKUO
[FEN (the denomination)]

QUICK IDENTIFIER: **Far East**

NORTH CHINA
[remittance stamp of China w/ surcharge]

NORTH CHINA

NORTH CHINA

NORTH CHINA

CENTRAL CHINA
[1949 (year of Communist takeover)]

CENTRAL CHINA
[1949 (year of Communist takeover)]

**NORTHEASTERN
PROVINCES**

NORTHEAST CHINA

EAST CHINA
[1949 (year of Communist takeover)]

EAST CHINA (provisionals) *[o/p on stamps of China;
amount of surcharge indicated in the left-hand column of o/p]*

EAST CHINA

SOUTH CHINA
[1949 (year of Communist takeover)]

KOREA
[10 Ch]

KOREA

KOREA

QUICK IDENTIFIER: Far East

KOREA

SOUTH KOREA
[REPUBLIC OF KOREA; *ying-yang in upper left-hand corner*]

SOUTH KOREA
[*ying-yang*]

KOREA (revenue)

JAPAN
[JAPANESE EMPIRE]

JAPAN
[5 SEN (*the denomination*)]

JAPAN
[3 Sⁿ; *chrysanthemum*]

JAPAN
[1/2 Sⁿ; *chrysanthemum*]

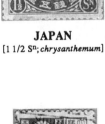

JAPAN
[1 1/2 Sⁿ; *chrysanthemum*]

JAPAN
[*chrysanthemum*]

JAPAN
[50 SEN (*the denomination*)]

JAPAN
[*chrysanthemum*]

JAPAN
[*chrysanthemum*]

JAPAN
[*chrysanthemum*]

JAPAN

QUICK IDENTIFIER: Miscellaneous

SOMALI COAST
[CÔTE FRANÇAISE DES SOMALIS]

PORTUGUESE GUINEA
[GUINÉ]

PORT. GUINEA (postage due)
[GUINÉ/ PORTEADO]

UPPER VOLTA
[RÉPUBLIQUE DE HAUTE-VOLTA]

BRAZIL
["Cat's Eye"]

BRAZIL
["Bull's Eye"]

BRAZIL
[BRASIL]

ANGRA (district of the Azores)
[ANGRA]

TANNU TUVA
[TOUVA]

TANNU TUVA
[TOUVA]

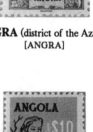

REP. of the COMOROS
[ARCHIPEL DES COMORES]

ANGOLA (postal tax)
[ANGOLA/ ASSISTÊNCIA]

CAPE VERDE ISLANDS
[CABO VERDE]

GUADELOUPE (postage due)
[GUADELOUPE/ CHIFFRE TAXE]

ST. THOMAS & PRINCE IS.
(news.) [S. THOMÉ E PRINCIPE]

MOZAMBIQUE (newspaper)
[MOÇAMBIQUE + o/p]

Multi-Language Matrix

The Multi-Language Matrix provides translations of 432 philatelically-useful terms into twenty modern languages. Included are many business and general words likely to be found in stamp catalogues and price lists, as well as the technical terminology unique to the field.

Languages are not absolute. Regional differences within the same language do exist, and not every possible translation of an English word can be incorporated into a matrix. For that reason, the translators have made every effort to include only the most universal choices when several possible translations could be given. If a translation is omitted, either the term does not exist in that language or there was no consensus among the experts.

Specifics:

—Verbs are given in their infinitive form in all languages except Hebrew. Hebrew verbs are in the *plene* form, third person singular past tense which corresponds to the three-letter root of the word.

—For gender languages (French, Russian, Spanish, etc.), adjectives are given in masculine singular form unless a different version is appropriate for that particular language.

—Words on this list are only capitalized if they are *always* capitalized, such as the names of countries and all German nouns.

—The forms of Chinese used here are the Simplified Character, the newer version preferred in the P.R.C., and the Complex Character, the version still used in Taiwan.

—Some parts of the Dutch-speaking world still retain the masculine and feminine genders of nouns, while other areas have adopted the concept of common gender. To satisfy both groups, Dutch nouns are designated *m.-c.* and *f.-c.* in this dictionary.

ENGLISH	GERMAN	FRENCH
abbreviation	Abkürzung (f.)	abréviation (f.)
accolated	vereint	accolé
account (financial or transactional)	Konto (n.)	compte (m.)
acquisition	Erwerbung (f.)	acquisition (f.)
aérogramme; air letter	Luftpostleichtbrief (m.)	aérogramme (m.)
aerophilately	Luftpostphilatelie (f.)	aérophilatélie (f.)
airmail	Luftpost (f.)	poste aérienne (f.)
air stamp; airmail stamp	Luftpostmarke (f.)	timbre pour la poste aérienne
album	Album (n.)	album (m.)
almost	fast; nahezu	presque
alter (verb)	ändern; verändern	retoucher; altérer; modifier
alteration	Änderung (f.); Veränderung (f.)	modification (f.); retouche (f.)
amount	Betrag (m.)	montant (m.)
aniline	Anilin (m.)	aniline (f.)
anomaly	Anomalie (f.)	anomalie (f.)
April	April	avril
Argentina	Argentinien	Argentine
art	Kunst (f.)	art (m.)
attribute (verb)	zuschreiben; kennzeichnen	attribuer; imputer
attribution	Zuschreibung (f.); Kennzeichnung (f.)	attribution (f.); imputation (f.)
auction	Auktion (f.); Versteigerung (f.)	vente aux enchères; à l'encan
auction catalogue	Auktionskatalog (m.)	catalogue de vente aux enchères
auction sale	Auktionsverkauf (m.)	vente aux enchères; vente à l'encan
August	August	août
Australia	Australien	Australie
Austria	Österreich	Autriche
authentic	authentisch; echt	authentique
authentication mark	Echtheitszeichen (n.)	marque d'authenticité
barred	überdruckt	barré
Belgium	Belgien	Belgique
bicolored; bicoloured	zweifarbig	bicolore
bid (noun: auction bid)	Gebot (n.)	enchère (f.); offre (f.); mise (f.)
bid (verb)	bieten	faire une offre; faire une mise
bid sheet	Angebotesetz (m.)	feuille de soumission des offres
bilingual	zweisprachig	bilingue
bisected	halbiert	coupé

PORTUGUESE	ITALIAN	SPANISH
abreviatura (*f.*)	abbreviazione (*f.*)	abreviatura (*f.*)
acolado	accollato	acolado
conta (*f.*)	conto (*m.*)	cuenta (*f.*)
aquisição (*f.*)	acquisto (*m.*)	adquisición (*f.*)
aerograma (*m.*)	aerogramma (*m.*)	aerograma (*m.*)
aerofilatélia (*f.*)	aerofilatelia (*f.*)	aerofilatelia (*f.*)
correio aéreo (*m.*); mala aérea (*f.*)	posta aerea (*f.*)	correo aéreo (*m.*)
selo de correio aéreo	francobollo di posta aerea	sello aéreo (*m.*)
álbum (*m.*)	album (*m.*)	álbum (*m.*)
quase	quasi	casi
alterar	alterare	alterar
alteração (*f.*)	alterazione (*f.*)	alteración (*f.*)
soma (*f.*)	somma (*f.*)	cantidad (*f.*); suma (*f.*)
anilina (*f.*)	anilina (*f.*)	anilina (*f.*)
anomalia (*f.*)	anomalia (*f.*)	anomalía (*f.*)
abril	aprile	abril
Argentina	Argentina	Argentina
arte (*f.*)	arte (*f.*)	arte (*m./f.*)
atribuir	attribuire	atribuir
atribuição (*f.*)	attribuzione (*f.*)	atribución (*f.*)
hasta pública (*f.*); leilão (*f.*)	asta (*f.*)	subasta (*f.*)
catálogo de leilão	catalogo d'asta (*m.*)	catálogo de subasta
venda em leilão	vendita all'asta (*f.*)	venta en subasta (*f.*)
agosto	agosto	agosto
Austrália	Australia	Australia
Áustria	Austria	Austria
autêntico	autentico	auténtico
marca de autenticação	timbro di autenticazione (*m.*)	marca de autenticación (*f.*)
com barras	sovrastampato a righe tipografiche	con barras; barrado
Bélgica	Belgio	Bélgica
bicolor	a due colori	bicolor
lanço (*m.*); oferta (*f.*)	offerta (ad un'asta) (*f.*)	oferta (*f.*); licitación (*f.*); puja (*f.*)
fazer uma oferta; lançar	fare un'offerta	ofrecer; licitar
impresso de oferta	foglio di offerta; modulo di offerta	hoja de licitación (*f.*); hoja de oferta (*f.*)
bilíngüe	bilingue	bilingüe
bisseto; bipartido	frazionato diagonalmente	biseccionado

ENGLISH	GERMAN	FRENCH
block	Markenblock (*m.*); Block (*m.*)	bloc (*m.*)
block of four	Viererblock (*m.*)	bloc de quatre
booklet (of stamps)	Heft (*n.*)	carnet (*m.*)
bottom	unten	bas (*m.*)
Brazil	Brasilien	Brésil
burélage; burelé	Unterdruck (*m.*)	burélage; burelé
buy (*verb*)	kaufen	acheter
buyer	Käufer (*m.*)	acheteur (*m.*)
cachet	Cachet (*n.*)	cachet (*m.*)
Canada	Kanada	Canada
cancel (*verb*)	abstempeln; entwerten	oblitérer; annuler
cancellation; cancelation	Abstempelung (*f.*)	oblitération (*f.*)
cancelled to order	Gefälligkeitsabstempelung (*f.*)	oblitéré de complaisance
cash (ready money)	Bargeld (*n.*)	espèces (*f.pl.*)
cash on delivery (C.O.D.)	Nachnahme (*f.*)	paiement contre remboursement
catalog; catalogue	Katalog (*m.*)	catalogue (*m.*)
catalogue value	Katalogwert (*m.*)	valeur de catalogue
censored mail	zensierte Post (*f.*)	courrier passé par la censure
centennial; centenary	Hundertjahrfeier (*f.*)	centenaire (*m.*)
centered	zentriert; mittig	centré
centering	Mittigkeit (*f.*)	centrage (*m.*)
centimeter; centimetre	Zentimeter (*m.*)	centimètre (*m.*)
chalky paper	Kreidepapier (*n.*)	papier couché (*m.*)
charity stamp	Wohlfartsmarke (*f.*)	timbre de bienfaisance
check; cheque	Scheck (*m.*)	chèque (*m.*)
China	China	Chine
classification	Klassifizierung (*f.*)	classement (*m.*)
classify (*verb*)	klassifizieren	classer
coil	Rolle (*f.*)	rouleau (*m.*)
collect (*verb*)	sammeln	collectionner
collection	Sammlung (*f.*)	collection (*f.*)
collector	Sammler (*m.*)	collectionneur (*m.*)
Colombia	Kolumbien	Colombie
color; colour	Farbe (*f.*)	couleur (*f.*)
comb perforation	Kammzähnung (*f.*)	dentelure en peigne
commemorative (*adjective*)	Gedenk-	commémoratif

PORTUGUESE	ITALIAN	SPANISH
bloco (m.)	blocco (m.)	bloque (m.)
bloco de quatro	quartina (f.)	bloque de cuatro (m.)
caderneta de selos	libretto di francobolli (m.)	cuadernillo (m.); librillo (m.)
fundo (m.); base (f.)	basso (m.)	parte inferior (f.); fondo (m.)
Brasil	Brasile	Brasil
burilagem	burelage (m.)	burelado
comprar	comprare	comprar
comprador (m.)	compratore (m.)	comprador (m.)
desenho ornamental (m.)	disegno illustrativo (m.)	cachet (m.)
Canadá	Canada	Canadá
carimbar	annullare	cancelar; anular
carimbo (m.); obliteração (f.)	annullamento (m.)	anulación (f.); matasellos (m.); cancelación (f.)
obliteração por favor	annullato di favore	cancelado a la orden
dinheiro contado (m.)	contante (m.)	dinero efectivo (m.)
reembolso postal	pagamento alla consegna	pago contra reembolso
catálogo (m.)	catalogo (m.)	catálogo (m.)
valor de catálogo	valore di catalogo (m.)	valoración de catálogo (m.)
correspondência censurada (f.)	corrispondenza censurata (f.)	correspondencia censurada (f.)
centenário (m.)	centenario (m.)	centenario (m.)
centrado	centrato	centrado
centragem (f.)	centratura (f.)	centralización (f.)
centímetro (m.)	centimetro (m.)	centímetro (m.)
papel porcelana (m.)	carta gessata (f.)	papel estucado (m.)
selo de beneficência	francobollo di beneficenza (m.)	sello de beneficencia
cheque (m.)	assegno (m.)	cheque (m.); talón (m.)
China	Cina	China
classificação (f.)	classificazione (f.)	clasificación (f.)
classificar	classificare	clasificar
rolo (de selos)	rotolo (m.); bobina (f.)	rollo (m.); bobina (f.)
colecionar	collezionare	coleccionar
coleção (f.); conjunto (m.)	collezione (f.)	colección (f.)
colecionador (m.)	collezionista (m./f.)	coleccionista (m./f.)
Colômbia	Colombia	Colombia
cor (f.)	colore (m.)	color (m.)
perfuração de pente	dentellatura a pettine	dentado de peine
comemorativo	commemorativo	conmemorativo

ENGLISH	GERMAN	FRENCH
common	gewöhnlich	courant; commun
complete	vollständig	complet
conjoined	vereint	conjugué; accolé
copy (*noun*)	Kopie (*f.*); Reproduktion (*f.*)	exemplaire (*m.*); copie (*f.*)
copy (*verb*)	kopieren; reproduzieren	copier
cover	Briefumschlag (*m.*); Umschlag (*m.*)	pli (*m.*); enveloppe (*f.*)
— on cover	auf Umschlag; auf Briefumschlag	sur enveloppe
crease (*noun*)	Falte (*f.*)	pli (*m.*)
crease (*verb*)	falten	plisser
credit	Kredit (*m.*)	crédit (*m.*)
credit card	Kreditkarte (*f.*)	carte de crédit
credit cards accepted	Kreditkarten akzeptiert	paiements par carte de crédit acceptés
crown (royal headpiece)	Krone (*f.*)	couronne (*f.*)
cruzeiro	Cruzeiro (*m.*)	cruzeiro (*m.*)
cut cancellation	Schnittentwertung (*f.*)	annulation par découpage
cut square	Vierkantausschnitt (*m.*)	coupure d'entier postal
damaged	beschädigt	endommagé
dark (*re*: color)	dunkel	foncé
date	Datum (*n.*)	date (*f.*)
December	Dezember	décembre
deep (*re*: color)	dunkel; tief	foncé
defect (*noun*)	Fehler (*m.*); Defekt (*m.*)	défaut (*m.*); imperfection (*f.*)
defective	mangelhaft	défectueux
definitive (*adjective*)	endgültig	définitif
demonetization	Demonetisierung (*f.*)	démonétisation (*f.*)
Denmark	Dänemark	Danemark
denomination	Nennwert (*m.*)	dénomination (*f.*)
deposit (of funds)	Anzahlung (*f.*)	dépôt (*m.*); acompte (*m.*)
deposit required	anzahlungspflichtig	un dépôt est requis; un acompte est requis
design (*noun*)	Entwurf (*m.*); Zeichnung (*f.*)	motif (*m.*)
devaluation	Abwertung (*f.*)	dévaluation (*f.*)
dollar	Dollar (*m.*)	dollar (*m.*)
domestic	heimisch; inländisch	intérieur
duplicate (*adjective*)	dupliziert; verdoppelt	double
duplicate (*noun*)	Duplikat (*n.*)	double (*m.*)
duplicate (*verb*)	duplizieren; verdoppeln	faire un double

PORTUGUESE	ITALIAN	SPANISH
comum; ordinário	comune	común
completo	completo	completo
acolado	accollato	acolado
cópia (f.)	copia (f.)	copia (f.); reproducción (f.)
copiar	copiare	copiar
sobrecarta (f.); envelope (m.); carta (f.)	busta (f.)	sobre postal (m.)
no envelope; sobre carta	su busta	sello pegado al sobre
ruga (f.)	piega (f.)	pliegue (m.); arruga (f.); doblez (m.)
enrugar; vincar	piegare	doblar; plegar
crédito (m.)	credito (m.)	crédito (m.)
cartão de crédito	carta di credito (f.)	tarjeta de crédito
aceitam-se cartões de crédito	sono accettate le carte di credito	se aceptan tarjetas de crédito
coroa (f.)	corona (f.)	corona (f.)
cruzeiro (m.)	cruzeiro (m.)	cruzeiro (m.)
obliteração por corte	annullo a taglio (m.)	cancelación mediante corte
cortado quadrado	ritaglio (m.)	cortado en cuadrado
danificado	danneggiato	dañado
escuro	scuro	oscuro
data (f.)	data (f.)	fecha (f.)
dezembro	dicembre	diciembre
escuro	cupo; scuro	oscuro
defeito (m.)	difetto (m.)	defecto (m.)
defectivo; defeituoso	difettoso	defectuoso
definitivo	ordinario	definitivo
desmonetização (f.)	fuori corso (m.)	desmonetización (f.)
Dinamarca	Danimarca	Dinamarca
denominação (f.)	valore (m.)	denominación (f.); valor (m.)
depósito (m.)	caparra (f.); anticipo (m.)	a cuenta; depósito (m.)
requer-se um depósito	deposito obbligatorio (m.)	se requiere un depósito
desenho (m.)	disegno (m.)	diseño (m.)
desvalorização (f.)	svalutazione (f.)	devaluación (f.)
dólar (m.)	dollaro (m.)	dólar (m.)
doméstico	interno	nacional
duplicado	doppio	duplicado
duplicado (m.); cópia (f.)	doppio (m.)	duplicado (m.)
duplicar	duplicare	duplicar

ENGLISH	GERMAN	FRENCH
eagle	Adler (*m.*)	aigle (*f.*)
East Germany (D.D.R.)	Deutsche Demokratische Republik	Allemagne de l'Est
effigy	Bildnis (*n.*)	effigie (*f.*)
eight	acht	huit
eighty	achtzig	quatre-vingts
embossing	Prägedruck (*m.*)	impression en relief
emperor	Kaiser (*m.*)	empereur (*m.*)
encased postage stamp	eingekapselte Briefmarke (*f.*)	timbre-poste enchâssé
England	England	Angleterre
engraved	eingraviert; graviert	gravé
envelope	Briefumschlag (*m.*)	enveloppe (*f.*)
error	Fehler (*m.*)	erreur (*f.*)
essay	Essay (*m./n.*); Probedruck (*m.*)	essai (*m.*); épreuve (*f.*)
exhibit (*verb*)	ausstellen	exposer
exhibition	Ausstellung (*f.*)	exposition (*f.*)
face value	Nennwert (*m.*)	valeur nominale (*f.*)
February	Februar	février
field post	Feldpost (*f.*)	poste militaire; poste de campagne
fifth (*noun*)	Fünftel (*n.*)	cinquième (*m.*)
fifty	fünfzig	cinquante
Finland	Finnland	Finlande
first day cover	Ersttagsbrief (*m.*)	enveloppe du premier jour d'émission
fiscal stamp	Gebührenmarke (*f.*)	timbre fiscal (*m.*)
five	fünf	cinq
fold (*noun*)	Falte (*f.*); Knick (*m.*); Kniff (*m.*)	pli (*m.*)
fold (*verb*)	falten; knicken	plier
foreign	ausländisch; fremd	étranger
foreign currency	Auslandswährung (*f.*); Fremdwährung (*f.*)	devise étrangère (*f.*)
forty	vierzig	quarante
four	vier	quatre
fourth (*noun*)	Viertel (*n.*)	quart (*m.*)
fraction	Bruchteil (*f.*)	fraction (*f.*)
frame	Einfassung (*f.*)	cadre (*m.*)
franc	Franc (*m.*)	franc (*m.*)
France	Frankreich	France
franchise stamp	Portofreiheitsmarke (*f.*)	timbre de franchise

PORTUGUESE	ITALIAN	SPANISH
águia (*f.*)	aquila (*f.*)	águila (*f.*)
Alemanha Oriental	Repubblica Democratica Tedesca	República Democrática de Alemania
efígie (*f.*); vulto (*m.*)	effige (*f.*)	efigie (*f.*)
oito	otto	ocho
oitenta	ottanta	ochenta
impressão em relêvo	goffratura (*f.*); impressione a rilievo (*f.*)	impresión en relieve
imperador (*m.*)	imperatore (*m.*)	emperador (*m.*)
selo encapsulado (*m.*)	francobollo circolante come moneta	sello encapsulado (*m.*)
Inglaterra	Inghilterra	Inglaterra
gravado	inciso	grabado
sobrecarta (*f.*); envelope (*m.*)	busta (*f.*)	sobre (*m.*)
erro (*m.*)	errore (*m.*)	error (*m.*); yerro (*m.*)
ensaio (*m.*)	saggio (*m.*)	ensayo (*m.*)
exibir	mettere in mostra; esporre	exponer; exhibir; presentar
exibição (*f.*); exposição (*f.*)	mostra (*f.*); esposizione (*f.*)	expositión (*f.*); exhibición (*f.*)
valor facial (*m.*)	valore nominale (*m.*)	valor facial (*m.*); valor nominal (*m.*)
fevereiro	febbraio	febrero
correio de campanha	ufficio postale militare	correo de campaña
quinto (*m.*)	quinto (*m.*)	quinto (*m.*)
cinqüenta	cinquanta	cincuenta
Finlândia	Finlandia	Finlandia
envelope de primeiro dia	busta primo giorno di emissione	sobre primer día de emisión
selo fiscal (*m.*)	francobollo fiscale (*m.*); marca da bollo	sello fiscal (*m.*)
cinco	cinque	cinco
dobra (*f.*)	piega (*f.*)	pliegue (*m.*); doblez (*m.*)
dobrar	piegare	doblar; plegar
estrangeiro	straniero	extranjero
moeda estrangeira (*f.*)	valuta straniera (*f.*)	moneda extranjera (*f.*); divisa (*f.*)
quarenta	quaranta	cuarenta
quatro	quattro	cuatro
quarto (*m.*)	quarto (*m.*)	cuarto (*m.*)
fração (*f.*)	frazione (*f.*)	fracción (*f.*)
cercadura (*f.*)	cornice (*f.*); riquadro (*m.*)	marco (*m.*)
franco (*m.*)	franco (*m.*)	franco (*m.*)
França	Francia	Francia
selo de porte franco (*m.*)	bollo di franchigia	sello de franquicia; estampilla de franquicia

ENGLISH	GERMAN	FRENCH
frank (*noun*)	Frankatur (*f.*); Maschinenfrankatur	marque d'affranchissement
frank (*verb*)	frankieren	affranchir
genuine	echt	authentique
Germany	Deutschland	Allemagne
glossy paper	Glanzpapier (*n.*)	papier brillant (*m.*); papier glacé (*m.*)
grade (*noun*)	Erhaltungsgrad (*m.*)	classement (*m.*)
grade (*verb*)	abstufen	classer
granite paper	Faserpapier (*n.*)	papier mélangé de fils de soie
Great Britain	Großbritannien	Grande Bretagne
Greece	Griechenland	Grèce
gum	Gummierung (*f.*)	gomme (*f.*)
gutter	Zwischensteg (*m.*)	interpanneau (*m.*)
half (*adjective*)	halb	demi
half (*noun*)	Hälfte (*f.*)	moitié (*f.*)
hinge	Befestigungsleiste (*f.*); Falz (*m.*)	charnière (*f.*)
hinged	gefalzt; eingefalzt	avec charnière
Holland	Holland	Pays Bas; Hollande
Hong Kong	Hongkong	Hong-kong
hundred	hundert	cent
hundredth (*noun*)	Hundertstel (*n.*)	centième (*m.*)
imperforate	ungezähnt	non dentelé
inch	Zoll (*m.*)	pouce (*m.*)
incomplete	unvollständig	incomplet
ink	Tinte (*f.*)	encre (*f.*)
inscription	Inschrift (*f.*); Beschriftung (*f.*)	inscription (*f.*); légende (*f.*)
intaglio	Heliogravüre (*f.*)	intaille (*f.*)
international	international	international
interrupted perforation	unterbrochene Lochung (*f.*)	dentelure syncopée (*f.*)
inverted	kopfstehend	renversé
Ireland	Irland	Irlande
irregular	unregelmäßig	irrégulier
Israel	Israel	Israël
issue (*noun*); issuance	Ausgabe (*f.*)	émission (*f.*)
issue (*verb*)	herausgeben	émettre
Italy	Italien	Italie
January	Januar	janvier

PORTUGUESE	ITALIAN	SPANISH
franquia postal (f.)	franchigia	franquicia postal (f.)
franquear	affrancare	franquear
genuíno; autêntico	autentico	genuino; auténtico; legítimo
Alemanha	Germania	Alemania
papel lustrado (m.); papel esmalte (m.)	carta patinata (f.)	papel brillo (m.)
grau (m.); qualidade (f.)	qualità (f.)	graduación (f.); grado de conservación
classificar	esaminare qualitativamente	graduar; clasificar
papel com fios de seda	carta con fili di seta	papel granito (m.)
Grã-Bretanha	Gran Bretagna	Gran Bretaña
Grécia	Grecia	Grecia
goma (f.)	gomma (f.)	goma (f.)
espaçamento (m.)	interspazio (m.)	medianil (m.)
meio	mezzo	medio
metade (f.)	metà (f.)	mitad (f.)
charneira (f.)	linguella (f.)	fijasello (m.); charnela (f.)
charneirado; com charneira	linguellato	con charnela; con fijasello
Holanda; Países Baixos	Olanda	Holanda; Países Bajos
Hong Kong	Hong Kong	Hong Kong
cem	cento	cien; ciento
centésimo (m.)	centesimo (m.)	centésimo (m.)
não denteado; sem denteação	non dentellato	sin dentar
polegada (f.)	pollice (m.)	pulgada (f.)
incompleto	incompleto	incompleto
tinta (f.)	inchiostro (m.)	tinta (f.)
inscrição (f.)	iscrizione (f.)	inscripción (f.)
fotogravura à entalhe (f.)	rotocalco (m.)	impresión intaglio (f.)
internacional	internazionale	internacional
denteação parcial (f.); denteação irregular (f.)	perforazione interrotta (f.)	perforación sincopada (f.)
invertido	invertito	invertido
Irlanda	Irlanda	Irlanda
irregular	irregolare	irregular
Israel	Israele	Israel
emissão (f.)	emissione (f.)	emisión (f.)
emitir	emettere	emitir
Itália	Italia	Italia
janeiro	gennaio	enero

ENGLISH	GERMAN	FRENCH
Japan	Japan	Japon
jugate	vereint	conjugué; accolé
July	Juli	juillet
June	Juni	juin
king	König (*m.*)	roi (*m.*)
laid paper	gestreiftes Papier (*n.*)	papier vergé (*m.*)
language	Sprache (*f.*)	langue (*f.*)
large	groß	grand; gros
laureate	lorbeerbekränzt	lauréat
left (direction or position)	links	gauche (*f.*)
liberty	Freiheit (*f.*)	liberté (*f.*)
light (*re*: color)	hell	clair
line perforation	Linienzähnung (*f.*)	dentelure en lignes
lithography	Lithographie (*f.*)	lithographie (*f.*)
lot (*i.e.*, auction lot)	Los (*n.*); Posten (*m.*)	lot (*m.*)
lozenge roulette	rautenförmiger Durchstich (*m.*)	percé en losanges
magnifying glass	Vergrößerungsglas (*n.*)	loupe (*f.*)
mail (*noun*)	Post (*f.*)	courrier (*m.*)
mail (*verb*)	zur Post geben	expédier
mail bid sale	Auktion per Postweg; Briefauktion (*f.*)	vente aux enchères par correspondance
mailman	Postbote (*m.*)	facteur (*m.*)
March	März	mars
mark	Mark (*f.*)	mark (*m.*)
May	Mai	mai
Mexico	Mexiko	Mexique
military postage stamp	Militärpostmarke (*f.*)	timbre-poste militaire (*m.*)
millimeter; millimetre	Millimeter (*m.*)	millimètre (*m.*)
million	Million (*f.*)	million
minimum bid	Niedrigstgebot (*f.*)	mise minimum (*f.*); offre minimum (*f.*)
monetary system	Währungssystem (*n.*)	système monétaire (*m.*)
money	Geld (*n.*)	argent (*m.*)
month	Monat (*m.*)	mois (*m.*)
multicolored; multicoloured	mehrfarbig	multicolore
national	national	national
nationality	Nationalität (*f.*)	nationalité (*f.*)
Netherlands, The	Holland	Pays Bas; Hollande

PORTUGUESE	ITALIAN	SPANISH
Japão	Giappone	Japón
acolado	accollato	acolado
julho	luglio	julio
junho	giugno	junio
rei (*m.*)	re (*m.*)	rey (*m.*)
papel enrugado (*m.*); papel avergoado (*m.*)	carta vergata (*f.*)	papel verjurado (*m.*)
língua (*f.*)	lingua (*f.*)	lengua (*f.*); idioma (*m.*)
grande	grande	grande
laureado	laureato; coronato di lauro	laureado
esquerdo	sinistra (*f.*)	izquierda (*f.*)
liberdade (*f.*)	libertà (*f.*)	libertad (*f.*)
claro	chiaro	claro
denteação em linhas	dentellatura lineare (*f.*)	dentado en línea
litografia (*f.*)	litografia (*f.*)	litografía (*f.*)
lote (*m.*)	lotto (*m.*)	lote (*m.*)
corte em linhas de losangos	foratura a losanghe	troquelado en forma de rombos
lupa (*f.*)	lente d'ingrandimento (*f.*)	lupa (*f.*); lente de aumento
correio (*m.*); mala postal (*f.*)	posta (*f.*)	correo (*m.*)
mandar pelo correio	mandare per posta	enviar por correo; echar al correo
leilão pelo correio	vendita all'asta per posta	subasta por correo
carteiro (*m.*)	postino (*m.*)	cartero (*m.*)
março	marzo	marzo
marco (*m.*)	marco (*m.*)	marco (*m.*)
maio	maggio	mayo
México	Messico	México; Méjico
selo militar	francobollo per posta militare	franquicia postal militar
milímetro (*m.*)	millimetro (*m.*)	milímetro (*m.*)
milhão	milione	millón
oferta mínima (*f.*)	offerta minima (*f.*)	licitación mínima (*f.*); oferta de salida (*f.*)
sistema monetário (*m.*)	sistema monetario (*m.*)	sistema monetario (*m.*)
dinheiro (*m.*)	denaro (*m.*)	dinero (*m.*)
mês (*m.*)	mese (*m.*)	mes (*m.*)
policromo	policromo	multicolor; policromo
nacional	nazionale	nacional
nacionalidade (*f.*)	nazionalità (*f.*)	nacionalidad (*f.*)
Holanda; Países Baixos	Olanda	Holanda; Países Bajos

ENGLISH	GERMAN	FRENCH
never hinged	nie gefalzt	neuf sans charnière
new	neu	nouveau; neuf
newspaper stamp	Zeitungsmarke (f.)	timbre pour journaux
New Zealand	Neuseeland	Nouvelle-Zélande
nine	neun	neuf
ninety	neunzig	quatre-vingt-dix
Northern Ireland	Nordirland	Irlande du Nord
Norway	Norwegen	Norvège
not issued	nicht ausgegeben	non-émis
no unlimited bids accepted	Unbegrenzte Angebote nicht angenommen	les offres sans limite ne sont pas acceptées
November	November	novembre
number	Zahl (f.)	numéro (m.)
obliteration	Tilgungsentwertung (f.)	oblitération (f.)
obsolete	veraltet	périmé
October	Oktober	octobre
offer (noun)	Angebot (n.)	offre (f.)
offer (verb)	anbieten	offrir
official	amtlich	de service
official stamp	Dienstmarke (f.)	timbre de service; timbre officiel
old	alt	vieux
on approval	zur Ansicht	pour approbation; à condition
on cover	auf Umschlag; auf Briefumschlag	sur enveloppe
one	eins	un (m.adj.); une (f.adj.)
on the back	rückseitig	au verso
order form	Bestellformular (n.)	bon de commande; bulletin de commande
original	original	original
original gum	Originalgummi (m./n.)	gomme d'origine
overprint	Überdruck (m.)	surimpression (f.)
package	Paket (n.)	colis (m.)
pair	Paar (n.)	paire (f.)
pane	Bogenblatt (n.)	panneau (m.)
paper	Papier (n.)	papier (m.)
parcel post	Paketpost (f.)	colis postal
parcel post stamp	Paketmarke (f.)	timbre pour colis postal
pedigree; provenance	Stammbaum (m.)	lignée (f.)
peel (verb)	ablösen	décoller

PORTUGUESE	ITALIAN	SPANISH
sem charneira	non linguellato	sin charnela; sin fijasello
novo	nuovo	nuevo
selo para jornais (*m.*)	francobollo per giornali	sello para periódicos; timbre para periódicos
Nova Zelândia	Nuova Zelanda	Nueva Zelandia; Nueva Zelanda
nove	nove	nueve
noventa	novanta	noventa
Irlanda do Norte	Irlanda del Nord	Irlanda del Norte
Noruega	Norvegia	Noruega
não emitido	non emesso	no emitido
não se aceitam propostas sem limites	offerte illimitate sono proibite	no se aceptan licitaciones sin límite
novembro	novembre	noviembre
número (*m.*)	numero (*m.*)	número (*m.*)
obliteração (*f.*)	annullamento (*m.*); obliterazione (*f.*)	obliteración (*f.*)
obsoleto	obsoleto	anticuado; obsoleto; en desuso
outubro	ottobre	octubre
oferta (*f.*)	offerta (*f.*)	oferta (*f.*); propuesta (*f.*)
oferecer	offrire in vendita	ofrecer
oficial	ufficiale	oficial
selo de serviço oficial (*m.*)	francobollo di servizio	sello servicio oficial
velho	vecchio	viejo
sujeito a aprovação	invio a scelta	en espera de aprobación
no envelope	su busta	sello pegado al sobre
um (*m.adj.*); uma (*f.adj.*)	uno (*m.adj.*); una (*f.adj.*)	un (*m.adj.*); uno (*m.adj.*); una (*f.adj.*)
no verso	rovescio (*m.*)	en el reverso; sobre el reverso
formulário de pedido	modulo d'ordine	pedido (*m.*); formulario de pedido (*m.*)
original	originale	original
goma original (*f.*)	gomma originale (*f.*)	goma original (*f.*)
sobreimpressão (*f.*); sobrecarga (*f.*)	sovrastampa (*f.*)	sobreimpresión (*f.*)
pacote (*m.*); embrulho (*m.*)	pacco (*m.*)	paquete (*m.*)
par (*m.*)	coppia (*f.*)	par (*m.*)
painel (*m.*)	blocco (*m.*)	hoja (*f.*)
papel (*m.*)	carta (*f.*)	papel (*m.*)
encomenda postal (*f.*)	pacchi postali	servicio de paquetes postales
selo para encomenda postal	francobollo per pacchi	sello para paquete postal
pedigree (*m.*)	elenco dei proprietari precendenti	pedigrí (*m.*); procedencia (*f.*)
descascar	staccare; pelare	despegar

ENGLISH	GERMAN	FRENCH
pen cancelled	durch Schriftzug entwertet	oblitéré à plume; oblitéré à stylo
People's Republic of China (P.R.C.)	Volksrepublik China	République Populaire de Chine
percé	Durchstich (m.)	percé
perfect	makellos; perfekt	parfait
perforated	gezähnt	dentelé
perforation	Zähnung (f.)	dentelure (f.)
Peru	Peru	Pérou
peseta	Peseta (f.)	péséta (f.)
peso	Peso (m.)	péso (m.)
philatelic	philatelistisch	philatélique
philatelist	Philatelist (m.)	philatéliste (m.)
philately	Philatelie (f.)	philatélie (f.)
phosphor	Phosphor (m.)	phosphore (m.)
phosphorescent	phosphoreszierend	phosphorescent
photogravure	Photogravüre (f.)	photogravure (f.)
pin perforation	Stichzähnung (f.)	percé en points
pope	Papst (m.)	pape (m.)
portrait	Bildnis (n.); Porträt (n.)	effigie (f.); portrait (m.)
Portugal	Portugal	Portugal
postage	Porto (n.); Briefgebühr (f.)	affranchissement (m.)
postage due	fällige Postgebühr (f.)	surtaxe (f.)
postage due stamp	Portomarke (f.)	timbre-taxe (m.)
postage stamp	Briefmarke (f.); Marke (f.)	timbre-poste (m.)
postal card	Postkarte (f.)	entier postal (m.)
postcard	Ansichtskarte (f.)	carte postale (f.)
postman	Postbote (m.)	facteur (m.)
postmark	Stempel (m.)	oblitération (f.)
post office	Postamt (n.)	bureau de poste (m.)
pound Sterling (£)	Pfund Sterling (n.)	livre sterling (f.)
precancel (noun)	Vorausentwertung (f.)	timbre préoblitéré
prepayment	Vorauszahlung (f.)	paiement d'avance (m.)
president	Präsident (m.)	président (m.)
price	Preis (m.)	prix (m.)
price list	Preisliste (f.)	liste de prix
print (verb)	drucken	imprimer
propaganda stamp	Werbemarke (f.); Propagandamarke (f.)	timbre de propagande

PORTUGUESE	ITALIAN	SPANISH
obliterado à pena	annullo a penna	cancelado a pluma
República Popular da China	Repubblica Popolare Cinese	República Popular China
percê	forato	troquelado; cortado
perfeito; impecável	perfetto	perfecto
denteado	dentellato	perforado; dentado; trepado
denteação (f.)	dentellatura (f.); perforazione (f.)	perforación (f.); dentado (m.); trepa (f.)
Peru	Perù	Perú
peseta (f.)	peseta (f.)	peseta (f.)
peso (m.)	peso (m.)	peso (m.)
filatélico	filatelico	filatélico
filatelista (m./f.)	filatelista (m./f.)	filatélico (m.); filatelista (m./f.)
filatelia (f.)	filatelia (f.)	filatelia (f.)
fósforo (m.)	fosforo (m.)	fósforo (m.)
fosforescente	fosforescente	fosforescente
fotogravura (f.)	fotoincisione (f.)	fotograbado (m.)
cortado em pontos	perforazione a punti	cortado en puntos; troquelado en puntos
papa (m.)	papa (m.)	papa (m.)
retrato (m.)	ritratto (m.)	retrato (m.)
Portugal	Portogallo	Portugal
porte (m.); franquia (f.)	spese postali (f.pl.)	franqueo (m.); porte de correos
insuficiencia de porte	segnatasse (m.)	franqueo insuficiente (m.)
selo de porteado	timbro di affrancatura insufficiente	sello de franqueo insuficiente
selo postal (m.); selo de correio (m.)	francobollo (m.); francobollo postale (m.)	sello de correo (m.); estampilla postal (f.)
bilhete postal (m.)	cartolina postale (f.)	entero postal (m.)
cartão postal (m.)	cartolina (f.)	tarjeta postal (f.)
carteiro (m.)	postino (m.)	cartero (m.)
carimbo postal (m.)	timbro postale (m.); annullo (m.)	matasellos (m.)
correio (m.); estação postal (f.);	ufficio postale (m.)	casa de correos; oficina de correos
libra esterlina (f.)	sterlina (f.)	libra esterlina (f.)
pre-obliteração (f.)	preobliterazione (f.)	precancelado
pagamento antecipado (m.)	pagamento anticipato (m.)	pago adelantado (m.)
presidente (m.)	presidente (m.)	presidente (m.)
preço (m.)	prezzo (m.)	precio (m.)
lista de preços (f.)	listino prezzi (m.)	lista de precios
imprimir	stampare	imprimir
selo de propaganda	francobollo di propaganda	sello de propaganda

ENGLISH	GERMAN	FRENCH
protective reserve bid	Reserveschutzgebot (*n.*)	mise ajoutée; mise de protection
provisional (*noun*)	Aushilfsmarke (*f.*)	provisoire; provisionnel
punch cancellation	Lochentwertung (*f.*)	oblitération au poinçon
quadrillé	Gitter (*n.*); Gittermuster (*n.*)	quadrillé
queen	Königin (*f.*)	reine (*f.*)
rare	selten	rare
rarity	Seltenheit (*f.*)	rareté (*f.*)
receipt	Quittung (*f.*)	reçu (*m.*)
rectangular	rechteckig	rectangulaire
Red Cross	Rotes Kreuz	Croix Rouge
registration stamp	Einschreibmarke (*f.*)	timbre pour lettre recommandée
regummed	nachgummiert	regommé
remainder	Restbestand (*m.*)	restant de stock; inventaire restant
repaired	repariert	réparé
reprint (*noun*)	Nachdruck (*m.*)	réimpression (*f.*)
reproduction	Faksimile (*n.*); Nachdruck (*m.*)	reproduction (*f.*)
republic	Republik (*f.*)	république (*f.*)
Republic of China (Taiwan)	Taiwan (*i.e*, Republik China)	République de Chine
right (direction or position)	rechts	droite (*f.*)
roulette	Durchstich (*m.*)	perçage (*m.*)
rouletted	durchgestochen	percé
round	rund	rond
Russia	Rußland	Russie
Saudi Arabia	Saudi-Arabien	Arabie Séoudite; Arabie Saoudite
scarce	rar; selten	rare
Scotland	Schottland	Ecosse
secret mark	Geheimzeichen (*n.*)	marque secrète (*f.*)
sell (*verb*)	verkaufen	vendre
seller	Verkäufer (*m.*)	vendeur (*m.*)
separation	Trennung (*f.*)	séparation (*f.*)
September	September	septembre
serpentine roulette	Serpentinendurchstich (*m.*)	percé en serpentin
serrated roulette	sägezahnartiger Durchstich	percé en scie
se-tenant	Zusammendruck (*m.*)	se-tenant
seven	sieben	sept
seventy	siebzig	soixante-dix

PORTUGUESE	ITALIAN	SPANISH
preço mínimo de adjudicação	offerta minima di riserva	precio de reserva
provisório (*m.*)	francobollo provvisorio	sello provisional; estampilla provisional
obliteração por perfuração	annullo a punzone	cancelación por taladro circular
quadriculado	foglio quadrettato (*m.*)	cuadriculado
rainha (*f.*)	regina (*f.*)	reina (*f.*)
raro	raro	raro
raridade (*f.*)	rarità (*f.*)	rareza (*f.*)
recibo (*m.*)	ricevuta (*f.*)	recibo (*m.*)
retangular	rettangolare	rectangular
Cruz Vermelha	Croce Rossa	Cruz Roja
selo de registrado	francobollo per raccomandate	sello de certificado
regomado	rigommato	re-engomado; engomado de nuevo
saldo (*m.*); final de estoque; sobra (*f.*)	surplus	mercancía residual (*f.*)
reparado	riparato	reparado
reimpressão (*f.*)	ristampa (*f.*)	reimpresión (*f.*)
reprodução (*f.*); réplica (*f.*)	riproduzione (*f.*)	reproducción (*f.*); copia (*f.*)
república (*f.*)	repubblica (*f.*)	república (*f.*)
República da China; Formosa	Formosa	República de China
direito	destra (*f.*)	derecha (*f.*)
corte percê	foratura (*f.*)	roleta (*f.*)
cortado em linha; percê	forato	cortado; troquelado
redondo	rotondo	redondo
Rússia	Russia	Rusia
Arábia Saudita	Arabia Saudita	Arabia Saudita; Arabia Saudí
escasso	raro	raro; escaso
Escócia	Scozia	Escocia
marca secreta (*f.*)	segno segreto (*m.*)	marca secreta (*f.*)
vender	vendere	vender
vendedor (*m.*)	venditore (*m.*)	vendedor (*m.*)
separação (*f.*)	separazione (*f.*)	separación (*f.*)
setembro	settembre	septiembre; setiembre
corte em serpentina	foratura a serpentina	cortado a serpentina
corte em serra	foratura à zigzag	cortado en zigzag
se-tenant	combinazione (*f.*)	se-tenant
sete	sette	siete
sesenta	settanta	setenta

ENGLISH	GERMAN	FRENCH
shade (*re*: color)	Tönung (*f.*); Nuance (*f.*)	nuance (*f.*)
sheet (of stamps)	Bogen (*m.*)	feuille (*f.*)
silk thread	Seidenfaden (*m.*)	fil de soie
six	sechs	six
sixty	sechzig	soixante
skinned spot	Dünnstelle (*f.*)	amincissement (*m.*)
small	klein	petit
South Africa	Südafrika	Afrique du Sud
souvenir sheet	Sondermarkenblock (*m.*)	bloc commémoratif
Soviet Union (U.S.S.R.)	Sowjetunion	Union Soviétique
Spain	Spanien	Espagne
specimen	Muster (*n.*)	spécimen (*m.*)
square (*adjective*)	quadratisch	carré
stain	Makel (*m.*); Fleck (*m.*)	tache (*f.*)
stamp (postage)	Briefmarke (*f.*); Marke (*f.*)	timbre-poste (*m.*)
star	Stern (*m.*)	étoile (*f.*)
steel engraving	Stahlstich (*m.*)	gravure sur acier
stock remainder	Restbestand (*m.*)	restant de stock; inventaire restant
strip (of stamps)	Streifen (*m.*)	bande (*f.*)
suggested bid	Bietempfehlung (*f.*)	mise suggérée (*f.*)
surcharge	Aufdruck (*m.*)	surcharge (*f.*)
surtax	Zuschlagmarke (*f.*)	surtaxe (*f.*)
Sweden	Schweden	Suède
Switzerland	Schweiz, die	Suisse
symbol	Symbol (*n.*)	symbole (*m.*)
syncopated perforation	synkopierte Lochung (*f.*)	dentelure syncopée (*f.*)
tagged stamp	markierte Briefmarke (*f.*)	timbre embouté (*m.*)
tax (*noun*)	Steuer (*f.*)	taxe (*f.*)
tear (*noun*)	Riß (*m.*)	déchirure (*f.*)
tear (*verb*)	reißen	déchirer
telegraph stamp	Telegrafenmarke (*f.*)	timbre-télégraphe
ten	zehn	dix
tenth (*noun*)	Zehntel (*n.*)	dixième (*m.*)
tête-bêche	Kehrdruck (*m.*)	tête-bêche (*f.*)
thin spot	Dünnstelle (*f.*)	amincissement (*m.*)
third (*noun*)	Drittel (*n.*)	tiers (*m.*)

PORTUGUESE	ITALIAN	SPANISH
tonalidade (*f.*)	gradazione (*f.*); sfumatura (*f.*)	gama (*f.*); tono (*m.*)
folha (*f.*)	foglio (*m.*)	hoja (*f.*)
fio de seda	filo di seta (*f.*)	hilo de seda
seis	sei	seis
sessenta	sessanta	sesenta
adelgaçamento (*m.*)	spellatura (*f.*)	punto delgado (*m.*)
pequeno	piccolo	pequeño
África do Sul	Sud Africa	África del Sur; Suráfrica; Sudáfrica
bloco comemorativo (*m.*)	foglietto (*m.*)	hoja recuerdo (*f.*)
União Soviética	Unione delle Repubbliche Socialiste Sovietiche	Unión Soviética
Espanha	Spagna	España
espécimen (*m.*)	esemplare (*m.*)	muestra (*f.*); ejemplar (*m.*)
quadrado	quadrato	cuadrado
mancha (*f.*)	macchia (*f.*)	mancha (*f.*)
selo postal (*m.*); selo de correio (*m.*)	francobollo (*m.*); francobollo postale (*m.*)	sello de correo (*m.*); estampilla postal (*f.*)
estrela (*f.*)	stella (*f.*)	estrella (*f.*)
gravura em aço	incisione su acciaio	grabado en acero (*m.*)
saldo (*m.*); sobras de «stock» (*f.pl*)	surplus	mercancía residual (*f.*)
tira (*f.*); fita (*f.*)	striscia (*f.*)	banda (*f.*)
oferta sugerida (*f.*)	offerta suggerita (*f.*)	licitación sugerida; oferta recomendada
sobretaxa (*f.*)	sovrapprezzo (*m.*); sovratassa (*f.*)	sobrecarga (*f.*); sobretasa (*f.*)
porte adicional (*m.*)	sovratassa (*f.*)	sobrecarga (*f.*)
Suécia	Svezia	Suecia
Suíça	Svizzera	Suiza
símbolo (*m.*)	simbolo (*m.*)	símbolo (*m.*)
denteação parcial (*f.*); denteação irregular (*f.*)	perforazione interrotta (*f.*)	perforación sincopada (*f.*)
selo fosforescente (*m.*)	francobollo fluorescente (*m.*)	sello luminescente; estampilla luminescente
imposto (*m.*); taxa (*f.*)	tassa (*f.*)	impuesto (*m.*)
rasgão (*f.*)	strappo (*m.*)	rasgón (*m.*); rasgadura (*f.*)
rasgar	strappare	rasgar
selo de telégrafo (*m.*)	francobollo per telegrafo (*m.*)	sello de telégrafos; estampilla de telégrafos
dez	dieci	diez
décimo (*m.*)	decimo (*m.*)	décimo (*m.*)
tête-bêche	tête-bêche; coppia invertita	tête-bêche
adelgaçamento (*m.*)	spellatura (*f.*)	punto delgado (*m.*)
têrço (*m.*)	terzo (*m.*)	tercio (*m.*)

ENGLISH	GERMAN	FRENCH
thirty	dreißig	trente
thousand	tausend	mille
three	drei	trois
tongs	Pinzette (*f.*)	pinces (*f.pl.*)
top	oben	haut (*m.*)
topical; thematic	thematisch	topique
torn	zerrissen	déchiré
trade (*verb*)	tauschen	échanger
twenty	zwanzig	vingt
two	zwei	deux
typography	Typographie (*f.*)	typographie (*f.*)
unattributed	nicht zugeschrieben	non attribué
undeliverable	unzustellbar	non livrable
ungummed	ohne Gummierung	sans gomme
unhinged	ungefalzt; uneingefalzt	sans charnière
unique	einzigartig	unique
United Kingdom (U.K.)	Vereinigtes Königreich	Royaume Uni
United States of America (U.S.A.)	Vereinigte Staaten von Amerika	États-Unis d'Amérique
unknown	unbekannt	inconnu
unofficial	nicht amtlich	non officiel
unpublished	unveröffentlicht	non publié
unsevered	ungetrennt	pas séparé
unused	unbenutzt	neuf
used	gebraucht	oblitéré
valuable	wertvoll	de valeur
value	Wert (*m.*)	valeur (*f.*)
variety	Abart (*f.*)	variété (*f.*)
Venezuela	Venezuela	Vénézuéla
Wales	Wales	Pays de Galles
watermark	Wasserzeichen (*n.*)	filigrane (*m.*)
West Germany (B.R.D.)	Bundesrepublik Deutschland	Allemagne de l'Ouest
wove paper	ungeripptes Papier (*n.*); Velinpapier (*n.*)	vélin (*m.*); papier ordinaire (*m.*)
year	Jahr (*n.*)	an (*m.*); année (*f.*)
Yugoslavia; Jugoslavia	Jugoslawien	Yougoslavie
zero	Null (*f.*)	zéro
zigzag roulette	sägezahnartiger Durchstich	percé en zigzag; percé en scie

PORTUGUESE	ITALIAN	SPANISH
trinta	trenta	treinta
mil	mille	mil
três	tre	tres
pinça (f.)	pinzette (f.pl.)	pinzas (f.pl.)
topo (m.); cimo (m.)	alto (m.)	parte superior (f.); parte de arriba (f.)
temático	tematico	temático
rasgado	strappato	rasgado
trocar	scambiare	comerciar
vinte	venti	veinte
dois (m.adj.); duas (f.adj.)	due	dos
tipografia (f.)	tipografia (f.)	tipografía (f.)
não atribuído	non attribuito	no atribuido; sin atribución
destinatário desconhecido	recapito impossibile	no entregable
sem goma	non gommato; senza gomma	sin goma
sem charneira	illinguellato	sin charnela; sin fijasello
único	unico	único
Reino Unido	Regno Unito	Reino Unido
Estados Unidos da América	Stati Uniti d'America	Estados Unidos de América
desconhecido	sconosciuto	desconocido
não oficial	ufficioso	no oficial; oficioso
não publicado	non catalogato	no publicado
não separado	non staccato; intonso	no separado
desusado; novo	nuovo	no usado; nuevo
usado	usato	usado
valioso	di gran valore	valioso; de valor
valor (m.)	valore (m.)	valor (m.)
variedade (f.)	varietà (f.)	variedad (f.)
Venezuela	Venezuela	Venezuela
País de Gales	Galles	Gales
filigrana (f.)	filigrana (f.)	filigrana (f.)
Alemanha Ocidental	Repubblica Federale Tedesca	República Federal de Alemania
papel tecido (m.)	carta unita (f.); carta liscia (f.)	papel avitelado (m.)
ano (m.)	anno (m.)	año (m.)
Iugoslávia; Jugoslávia	Jugoslavia	Yugoslavia
zero	zero	cero
corte em zigzag	foratura à zigzag	cortado en zigzag

ENGLISH	GERMAN	FRENCH
amber	bernsteingelb	ambre
azure	himmelblau	bleu azur
bister	nußbraun	bistre
black	schwarz	noir
blue	blau	bleu
bronze	bronze	bronze
brown	braun	brun
carmine	karminrot	carmin
cerise	kirschrot	cerise
cobalt	kobaltblau	cobalt
crimson	purpurrot	cramoisi
emerald	smaragdgrün	vert-émeraude
gray	grau	gris
green	grün	vert
heliotrope	heliotrop	héliotrope
indigo	indigo	indigo
lavender	lavendel	lavande
lemon	zitronengelb	jaune-citron
lilac	lila	lilas
magenta	fuchsinrot	magenta
maroon	rotbraun	bordeaux
olive	olivgrün; oliv	olive
orange	orange	orange
pink	rosa	rose
Prussian blue	preußischblau	bleu de Prusse
purple	purpur	pourpre
red	rot	rouge
royal blue	königsblau	bleu roi
sapphire	saphirblau	saphir
scarlet	scharlachrot	écarlate
turquoise	türkischblau	turquoise
ultramarine	ultramarin	outremer
vermilion	zinnoberrot	vermillon
violet	violett	violet
white	weiß	blanc
yellow	gelb	jaune

PORTUGUESE	ITALIAN	SPANISH
amarelo-âmbar	ambra	ámbar; succino
azulado	celeste	azul celeste
bistre	bistro	bistre
preto	nero	negro
azul	blu	azul
bronze	bronzo	bronce
castanho; marrom	marrone	moreno; pardo
carmim	carminio	carmín
cereja	rosso ciliegia	color cereza
cobalto	cobalto	cobalto
carmesim	cremisi	carmesí
verde esmeralda	verde smeraldo	color esmeraldo; esmeraldino
cinzento	grigio	gris
verde	verde	verde
heliotrópio; púrpura claro	eliotropio	heliotropo
índigo	indaco	añil; índigo
cor de lavanda	lavanda	azul espliego
limão	limone	color limón
lilás	lilla	lila; lilas
vermelho magenta	magenta	magenta
carmesim acastanhado	bordeaux	marrón
azeitona; verde oliva	verde oliva	oliva
cor de laranja	arancio	anaranjado
cor de rosa; rosa	rosa	rosado; rosa
azul da Prússia	blu di Prussia	azul de Prusia
púrpura	violaceo	púrpura; morado
vermelho	rosso	rojo
azul real	blu savoia	azul real
azul safira	zaffiro	zafiro; azul zafiro
escarlate	scarlatto	escarlata; encarnado
azul-turquesa	turchese	turquesa
azul ultramarino	azzurro oltremare	ultramarino; azul ultramarino
vermelhão	cinabro	bermellón; cinabrio
violeta	violetto	violeta
branco	bianco	blanco
amarelo	giallo	amarillo

ENGLISH	DUTCH	FINNISH
abbreviation	afkorting (f./c.)	lyhenne
accolated	verbonden	yhdistetty
account (financial or transactional)	rekening (f./c.)	tili
acquisition	aanschaffing (f./c.); verwerving (f./c.)	hankinta; saanti
aérogramme; air letter	luchtpostblad (n.); aërogram (n.)	ilmakirje
aerophilately	luchtpostfilatelie (f./c.); aërofilatelie (f./c.)	lentopostimerkkien keräily
airmail	luchtpost (f./c.)	lentoposti
air stamp; airmail stamp	luchtpostzegel (m./c.)	lentopostimerkki
album	album (n.)	albumi; kansio
almost	bijna	melkein
alter (verb)	vervalsen	muuttaa
alteration	vervalsing (f./c.)	muutos
amount	bedrag (n.)	summa
aniline	aniline (m./f./c.)	aniliini
anomaly	afwijking (f./c.); onregelmatigheid (f./c.)	poikkeavaisuus
April	april	huhtikuu
Argentina	Argentinië	Argentiina
art	kunst (f./c.)	taide
attribute (verb)	toeschrijven; toekennen	määrittää
attribution	toeschrijving (f./c.)	määritys
auction	veiling (f./c.)	huutokauppa
auction catalogue	veilingcatalogus (m./c.)	huutokauppaluettelo
auction sale	veilingverkoop (m./c.)	huutokauppa
August	augustus	elokuu
Australia	Australië	Australia
Austria	Oostenrijk	Itävalta
authentic	authentiek	aito
authentication mark	waarmerk (n.)	aitousmerkki
barred	met balken (overdruk)	viivattu
Belgium	België	Belgia
bicolored; bicoloured	tweekleurig	kaksivärinen
bid (noun: auction bid)	bod (n.)	tarjous
bid (verb)	bieden	tarjota
bid sheet	biedformulier (n.)	tarjouslista
bilingual	tweetalig	kaksikielinen
bisected	gehalveerd	halkaistu; kahteen leikattu

SWEDISH	DANISH	NORWEGIAN
förkortning (r.)	forkortelse (c.)	forkortelse (m.)
bredvid varandra	sammensat	forbundet; parvis sammenstilt
konto (n.)	konto (c.)	konto (m.)
förvärv (n.)	erhvervelse (c.)	akkvisisjon (m.)
aerogram (n.)	aerogram	aerogram (n.)
flygpostfilateli (n.); aerofilateli (n.)	luftpostfilateli (c.)	aerofilateli (n.)
flygpost	luftpost (c.)	luftpost (m.)
flygpostmärke (n.)	luftpostfrimærke (n.)	luftpostfrimerke (n.)
album (n.)	album (n.)	album (n.)
nästan	næsten	nesten
förändra	ændre	forandre
förändring (r.)	forandring (c.)	forandring (m.)
belopp (n.)	beløb (n.)	beløp (n.)
anilin-	anilin (c.)	anilin (m.)
oregelbundenhet (n.)	uregelmæssighed (c.)	anomali (m.)
april	april	april
Argentina	Argentina	Argentina
konst (r.)	kunst (c.)	kunst (m.)
tillskriva	henføre til	tilskrive; tillegge
bestämning (r.)	attribut (c.); kendetegn (n.)	-----
auktion (r.)	auktion (c.)	auksjon (m.)
auktionskatalog (r.)	auktionskatalog (n.)	auksjonskatalog (m.)
auktionsförsäljning (r.)	auktionssalg (n.)	auksjon (m.)
augusti	august	august
Australien	Australien	Australia
Österrike	Østrig	Østerrike
autentisk; äkta	ægte; autentisk	ekte; autentisk
expertsignatur (r.)	ægthedsbevis (n.)	legaliseringsmerke (n.)
spärrad; med balkar	overstemplet	overtrykket
Belgien	Belgien	Belgia
tvåfärgad	tofarvet	tofarget
anbud (n.)	bud (n.)	bud (n.)
bjuda	byde	by
anbudslapp (r.)	budliste (c.)	tilbudsskjema (n.)
tvåspråkig	tosproget	tospråklig
tvådelad	halveret	halvert

ENGLISH	DUTCH	FINNISH
block	blok (n.)	ryhmä
block of four	blok van vier (n.)	nelilö
booklet (of stamps)	postzegelboekje (n.)	vihko
bottom	onderkant (m./c.)	pohja; alaosa
Brazil	Brazilië	Brasilia
burélage; burelé	netwerk (n.)	taustakuviointi; pohjapainanta
buy (verb)	kopen	ostaa
buyer	koper (m./c.)	ostaja
cachet	cachet (n.)	koristeellinen kirjekuori
Canada	Canada	Kanada
cancel (verb)	afstempelen	mitätöidä
cancellation; cancelation	afstempeling (f./c.)	mitätöinti
cancelled to order	afstempeling op bestelling (f./c.)	suosioleimattu
cash (ready money)	contant (adj.); baar geld (n.)	käteinen
cash on delivery (C.O.D.)	(onder) rembours	postiennakko
catalog; catalogue	catalogus (m./c.); cataloog (m./c.)	luettelo
catalogue value	cataloguswaarde (f./c.)	luetteloarvo
censored mail	gecensureerde post (f./c.)	sensuroitu posti
centennial; centenary	honderdjarig (bestaan)	satavuotinen
centered	gecentreerd	keskitetty
centering	centrering (f./c.)	keskitys
centimeter; centimetre	centimeter (m./c.)	senttimetri
chalky paper	krijtpapier (n.)	liitupaperi
charity stamp	liefdadigheidszegel (m./c.)	hyväntekeväisyysmerkki
check; cheque	cheque (m./c.)	shekki; šekki
China	China	Kiina
classification	classificatie (f./c.)	luokitus
classify (verb)	klasseren	luokitella
coil	postzegelrol (f./c.)	rulla
collect (verb)	verzamelen	kerätä
collection	verzameling (f./c.)	kokoelma
collector	verzamelaar (m./c.)	keräilijä
Colombia	Colombia; Columbia	Kolumbia
color; colour	kleur (f./c.); tint (f./c.)	väri
comb perforation	kamperforatie (f./c.); kamtanding (f./c.)	kampahammastus
commemorative (adjective)	herdenkings-	muisto-

SWEDISH	DANISH	NORWEGIAN
block (*n.*)	blok (*c.*)	blokk (*m.*)
fyrblock (*n.*)	fireblok (*c.*)	fireblokk (*m.*)
häfte (*n.*)	frimærkehæfte (*n.*)	hefte (*n.*)
botten	bund (*c.*)	bunn (*m.*)
Brasilien	Brasilien	Brasil
undertryck; undertryckt	undertryk (*n.*)	burelering (*m.*)
köpa	købe	kjøpe
köpare (*r.*)	køber (*c.*)	kjøper (*m.*)
ickepostal sidostämpel	særpræg (*n.*)	dekorasjon (*m.*)
Kanada	Canada	Canada
makulera	stemple	annullere
makulering (*r.*)	stempling (*c.*)	annullering (*m.*)
favörstämplat; orderstämplat	annuleret efter ønske	annullert på bestilling
kontanter (*r.pl.*)	kontant	kontant
postförskott (*n.*)	pr. efterkrav	mot etterkrav
katalog (*r.*)	katalog (*n.*)	katalog (*m.*)
katalogvärde (*n.*)	katalogværdi (*c.*)	katalogverdi (*m.*)
censurerad post (*r.*)	censureret post	sensurert post (*m.*)
hundraårsjublieum (*n.*)	hundredårsdag (*c.*)	hundreårsjubileum (*n.*)
centrerad	centreret	sentralt plassert
centrering (*r.*)	centrering (*c.*)	sentering
centimeter (*r.*)	centimeter (*c.*)	centimeter (*m.*)
kritat papper (*n.*)	præpareret papir (*n.*)	kalkholdig paper (*n.*)
välgörenhetsfrimärke (*n.*)	velgørenhedsfrimærke (*n.*)	hjelpmerke (*n.*)
check (*r.*)	check (*c.*)	sjekk (*m.*)
Kina	Kina	Kina
klassificering (*r.*)	klassifikation (*c.*)	klassifikasjon (*m.*)
klassicera	klassificere	klassifisere
rulle (*r.*)	rulle (*c.*)	frimerkerull (*m.*)
samla	samle	samle
samling (*r.*)	samling (*c.*)	samling (*m.*)
samlare (*r.*)	samler (*c.*)	samler (*m.*)
Colombia	Colombia	Colombia
färg (*r.*)	farve (*c.*)	farge (*m.*)
kamtandning (*r.*)	kamtakning (*c.*)	kam-perforering (*m.*)
minnes-	særfrimærke (*n.*)	minne-

ENGLISH	DUTCH	FINNISH
common	gewoon	yleinen
complete	volledig	täydellinen
conjoined	verbonden	yhdistetty
copy (*noun*)	kopie (*f./c.*); exemplaar (*n.*)	kopio
copy (*verb*)	kopiëren	kopioida; jäljentää
cover	envelop (*f./c.*); omslag (*m./c./n.*)	kuori
— on cover	zegel op brief; op envelop; op omslag	kuorella
crease (*noun*)	vouw (*f./c.*)	taitos
crease (*verb*)	vouwen	taittaa
credit	krediet (*n.*)	luotto
credit card	creditcard (*m./c.*); kredietkaart (*f./c.*)	luottokortti
credit cards accepted	kredietkaarten worden aangenomen	luottokortit hyväksytään
crown (royal headpiece)	kroon (*f./c.*)	kruunu
cruzeiro	cruzeiro (*m./c.*)	cruzeiro
cut cancellation	postzegel-beschadigingsstempel (*n.*)	leikkaamalla mitätöity
cut square	uitgeknipt vierkant (*n.*)	ehiöleike
damaged	beschadigd	vahingoittunut
dark (*re:* color)	donker	tumma
date	datum (*m./c.*)	päivä
December	december	joulukuu
deep (*re:* color)	donker	syvä; tumma
defect (*noun*)	fout (*f./c.*)	vika
defective	foutief; met gebreken	viallinen
definitive (*adjective*)	definitieve; gewoon	lopullinen
demonetization	demonetisering (*f./c.*)	rahan poistaminen käytöstä
Denmark	Denemarken	Tanska
denomination	munteenheid (*f./c.*); waarde (*f./c.*)	nimellisarvo
deposit (of funds)	aanbetaling (*f./c.*)	talletus
deposit required	waarborgsom vereist	varausmaksu vaaditaan
design (*noun*)	ontwerp (*n.*); tekening (*m./c.*)	muotoilu
devaluation	devaluatie (*f./c.*); waardevermindering (*f./c.*)	arvonalennus; devalvaatio
dollar	dollar (*m./c.*)	dollari
domestic	binnenlands	kotimainen
duplicate (*adjective*)	dubbele	kaksois-
duplicate (*noun*)	dubbel (*n.*); duplicaat (*n.*)	kaksoiskappale
duplicate (*verb*)	verdubbelen; dupliceren	jäljentää

SWEDISH	DANISH	NORWEGIAN
vanlig	almindelig	alminnelig
fullständig	komplet	fullstendig
bredvid varandra	sammensat	forbundet; parvis sammenstilt
kopia (r.)	kopi (c.)	kopi (m.)
kopiera	kopiere	kopiere
brev (n.); försändelse (r.)	omslag (n.)	innpakning (m.)
på brev; på försändelse	på brev	på original konvolutt
veck (n.)	fold (c.)	brett (m.)
vika	folde	brette
kredit (r.)	kredit (c.)	kreditt (m.)
kreditkort (n.)	kreditkort (n.)	kredittkort (n.)
kreditkort gäller	kreditkort accepteres	kredittkort akseptert
krona (r.)	krone (c.)	krone (m.)
cruzeiro (r.)	cruzeiro (c.)	cruzeiro (m.)
utklippt stämpel (r.)	gennemstukket annulering (c.)	hullstempel (n.)
fyrkantigt utklippt	påtrykt frimærkeafklip (n.)	utklipp (n.)
skadad	beskadiget	skadet
mörk	mørk	mørk
datum (n.)	årstal (n.)	dato (m.)
december	december	desember
djup	dyb	dyp
defekt (r.)	defekt (c.)	mangel (m.)
felaktig	defekt	mangelfull
slutgiltig	daglig-	bestemmende
indragning (r.)	ugyldiggørelse (c.)	inndraging (m.)
Danmark	Danmark	Danmark
valör (r.)	møntenhed (c.)	pålydende (n.)
handpenning (r.)	depositum (n.)	depositum (n.)
handpenning erfordras	depositum nødvendigt	depositum nødvendig
design (r.)	design (n.)	utforming (m.); design (m.)
devalvering (r.)	devaluering (c.)	devaluering (m.)
dollar (r.)	dollar (c.)	dollar (m.)
inhemsk	indenlandsk	innenlandsk
dubblett-	ens	duplisert
dubblett (r.)	dublet (c.)	duplikat (n.)
duplicera	duplikere	duplisere

374

ENGLISH	DUTCH	FINNISH
eagle	adelaar (m./c.)	kotka
East Germany (D.D.R.)	Oost-Duitsland	Itä-Saksa
effigy	portret (n.); afbeelding (f./c.)	muotokuva
eight	acht	kahdeksan
eighty	tachtig	kahdeksankymmentä
embossing	reliëfdruk (m./c.)	kohopainanta
emperor	keizer (m./c.)	keisari
encased postage stamp	omhulsde postzegel (m./c.)	koteloitu postimerkki
England	Engeland	Englanti
engraved	gegraveerd	kaiverrettu
envelope	briefomslag (n.); enveloppe (f./c.)	kirjekuori
error	fout (f./c.)	virhe
essay	proef (f./c.); proefdruk (m./c.)	ehdote; koe
exhibit (verb)	tentoonstellen	asettaa näytteille
exhibition	tentoonstelling (f./c.)	näyttely
face value	nominale waarde (f./c.)	nimellisarvo
February	februari	helmikuu
field post	veldpost (kantoor) (n.)	kenttäposti
fifth (noun)	vijfde	viidesosa
fifty	vijftig	viisikymmentä
Finland	Finland	Suomi
first day cover	eerste-dagenveloppe; eerste-dagomslag	ensipäivän kuori
fiscal stamp	belastingzegel (m./c.)	veromerkki
five	vijf	viisi
fold (noun)	vouw (f./c.)	taitos; laskos
fold (verb)	vouwen	taittaa
foreign	buitenlands	ulkomainen
foreign currency	buitenlandse valuta (m./f./c.)	ulkomaan raha; valuutta
forty	veertig	neljäkymmentä
four	vier	neljä
fourth (noun)	vierde	neljäsosa
fraction	fractie (f./c.); breuk (f./c.)	murto-osa
frame	omlijsting (f./c.); kader (n.)	kehys
franc	frank (m./c.)	frangi
France	Frankrijk	Ranska
franchise stamp	portvrijdomzegel (m./c.)	postimaksuvapausmerkki

SWEDISH	DANISH	NORWEGIAN
örn (r.)	ørn (c.)	ørn (m.)
Östtyskland	Østtyskland	Øst-Tyskland
avbildning (r.)	portrætbillede (n.)	bilde (n.); portrett (n.)
åtta	otte	åtte
åttio	firs	åtti
relieftryck (n.)	ophøjet tryk (n.)	embossere
kejsare (m.)	kejser (c.)	keiser (m.)
frimärksmynt (n.)	frimærkepenge	frimerke i eske
England	England	England
graverad	graveret	gravert
kuvert (n.)	konvolut (c.)	konvolutt (m.)
fel	fejl (c.)	feil (m.)
utkast; förslagsmärke	prøvefrimærke (n.)	vraket utkast
ställa ut	udstille	utstille; stille ut
utställning (r.)	udstilling (c.)	utstilling (m.)
nominellt värde (n.)	pålydende værdi (c.)	pålydende verdi
februari	februar	februar
militärpost (r.); fältpost (r.)	feltpost (c.); soldaterfrimærker (n.)	feltpost (m.)
femtedel (r.)	femtedel (c.)	femtedel (m.)
femtio	halvtreds	femti
Finland	Finland	Finnland
förstadagsbrev (n.)	førstedagsbrev (c.)	førstedagsbrev (n.)
skattemärke (n.)	stempelmærke (n.)	skatte-frimerke (n.)
fem	fem	fem
veck (n.)	fold (c.)	brett (m.)
vika	folde	brette
utländsk	fremmed; udenlandsk	utenlandsk
utländsk valuta	udenlandsk valuta (c.)	utenlandsk mynt (m.)
fyrtio	fyrre	førti
fyra	fire	fire
fjärdedel (r.)	fjerdedel (c.)	fjerdedel (m.)
del (r.)	brøkdel (c.)	brøkdel (m.)
ram (r.)	ramme (c.)	ramme (m.)
franc (r.)	franc (c.)	franc (m.)
Frankrike	Frankrig	Frankrike
portofrihetsmärke (n.)	fri-frankering (c.)	gratis frimerke (n.)

ENGLISH	DUTCH	FINNISH
frank (*noun*)	frankeerrecht (*n.*)	frankeeraus
frank (*verb*)	frankeren	frankeerata
genuine	echt	aito
Germany	Duitsland	Saksa
glossy paper	glanzend papier (*n.*)	kiiltävä paperi
grade (*noun*)	kwaliteitsaanduiding (*f./c.*)	kuntoluokka
grade (*verb*)	klasseren	luokitella
granite paper	papier met zijdedraad	graniittipaperi
Great Britain	Groot-Brittannië	Iso-Britannia
Greece	Griekenland	Kreikka
gum	gom (*n.*)	liima
gutter	groèf (*f./c.*); goot (*f./c.*)	väliö
half (*adjective*)	half	puoli
half (*noun*)	helft (*f./c.*)	puolikas
hinge	plakker (*m./c.*)	liimake
hinged	met plakker	liimakkeellinen
Holland	Koninkrijk der Nederlanden; Nederland	Alankomaat
Hong Kong	Hong Kong	Hongkong
hundred	honderd	sata
hundredth (*noun*)	honderdste	sadasosa
imperforate	ongetand; ongeperforeerd	hammastamaton
inch	inch (*m./c.*)	tuuma
incomplete	onvolledig; niet compleet	epätäydellinen
ink	inkt (*m./c.*)	muste
inscription	inscriptie (*f.-c.*)	inskriptio; muistokirjoitus
intaglio	diepdruk (*m./c.*); intaglio druk (*m./c.*)	intaglio-painanta
international	internationaal	kansainvälinen
interrupted perforation	roltanding (*f./c.*); gesyncopeerde perforatie	mykkä hammaste
inverted	omgekeerd	ylösalaisin
Ireland	Ierland	Irlanti
irregular	onregelmatig	epäsäännöllinen
Israel	Israël	Israel
issue (*noun*); issuance	uitgave (*f./c.*)	julkaisu; painos
issue (*verb*)	uitgeven	laskea liikkeeseen; julkaista
Italy	Italië	Italia
January	januari	tammikuu

SWEDISH	DANISH	NORWEGIAN
frankering (r.)	påskrift der attesterer et brevs portofrihed	portofri (m.)
frankera	attestere (brev) som portofrit	frankere
äkta	ægte	ekte
Tyskland	Tyskland	Tyskland
glättat papper (n.)	blankt papir (n.)	glassert papir (n.)
grad (r.); klass (r.)	kvalitet (c.)	klasse (m.)
gradera	kvalitetsbedømme	klassifisere
granitpapper (n.)	papir med silketråde (n.)	papir med silketråder
Storbritannien	Storbritannien	Storbritannia
Grekland	Grækenland	Hellas
gummering (r.)	gummi (c.)	lim (n.)
vitt tandat fält mellan frimärken	marginalpapir (n.)	marg (m.)
halv	halv	halv
halva (r.)	halvdel (c.)	halvpart (m.)
fastsättare (r.)	frimærkehængsel (c.)	hengsel (n.)
ej postfrisk; med fastsättare	hængslet	hengslet
Holland	Holland	Nederland; Holland
Hong Kong	Hong Kong	Hong Kong
hundra	hundrede	hundre
hundradel (r.)	hundrededel (c.)	hundrededel (m.)
operforerad	utakket	uperforert
tum (r.)	tomme (c.)	tomme (m.)
ofullständig	ufuldstændig	ufullstendig
bläck (n.)	blæk (n.)	blekk (n.)
inskription (r.)	inskription (c.)	inskripsjon (m.)
intaglio (r.)	dybtryk	intaglio gravering (m.)
internationell	international	internasjonal
avbruten tandning (r.)	forskudt takning (c.)	avbrudt perforering (m.)
upp-och-ner vänd	omvendt	opp ned
Irland	Irland	Irland
oregelbunden; avart	uregelmæssig	irregulær
Israel	Israel	Israel
utgåva (r.)	udgivelse (c.)	utstedelse (m.)
utge	udstede; udgive	utstede
Italien	Italien	Italia
januari	januar	januar

ENGLISH	DUTCH	FINNISH
Japan	Japan	Japani
jugate	verbonden	yhdistetty
July	juli	heinäkuu
June	juni	kesäkuu
king	koning (m./c.)	kuningas
laid paper	papier vergé (n.); gestreept papier (n.)	juovikas paperi
language	taal (f./c.)	kieli
large	groot	suuri
laureate	gelauwerd; met lauwerkrans	seppelöity (laakeriseppele)
left (direction or position)	links	vasen
liberty	vrijheid (f./c.)	vapaus
light (re: color)	licht-	vaalea
line perforation	lijntanding (f./c.); lijnperforatie (f./c.)	viivahammaste
lithography	lithografie (f./c.)	litografia
lot (i.e., auction lot)	lot (n.)	kohde
lozenge roulette	ruitvormige tanding (f./c.)	ristiläviste
magnifying glass	vergrootglas (n.)	suurennuslasi
mail (noun)	post (f./c.)	posti
mail (verb)	posten	postittaa
mail bid sale	post-veiling verkoop; mail bid sale	postihuutokauppa
mailman	postbode (m./c.)	postinkantaja
March	maart	maaliskuu
mark	mark (m./c.)	markka
May	mei	toukokuu
Mexico	Mexico	Meksiko
military postage stamp	militaire postzegel (m./c.)	sotilaspostimerkki
millimeter; millimetre	millimeter (m./c.)	millimetri
million	miljoen	miljoona
minimum bid	laagste bod (n.)	pohjahinta
monetary system	monetaire stelsel (n.); muntstelsel (n.)	rahajärjestelmä
money	geld (n.)	raha
month	maand (f./c.)	kuukausi
multicolored; multicoloured	veelkleurig	monivärinen
national	nationaal	kansallinen
nationality	nationaliteit (f./c.)	kansallisuus
Netherlands, The	Koninkrijk der Nederlanden; Nederland	Alankomaat

SWEDISH	DANISH	NORWEGIAN
Japan	Japan	Japan
bredvid varandra	sammensat	forbundet; parvis sammenstilt
juli	juli	juli
juni	juni	juni
kung (*m.*)	konge (*c.*)	konge (*m.*)
randat papper (*n.*)	håndlagt papir (*n.*)	linjepapir (*n.*)
språk (*n.*)	sprog (*n.*)	språk (*n.*)
stor	stor	stor
lagerkransad	laurbærkranset	laurbærkronet
vänster	venstre	venstre
frihet (*r.*)	frihed (*c.*)	frihet (*m.*)
ljus	lys	lys
linjetandning (*r.*)	linietakning (*c.*)	linjeperforering (*m.*)
litografi (*r.*)	litografi (*c.*)	litografi (*n.*)
lot (*r.*)	auktionsnummer (*n.*)	parti (*n.*)
stortandad	rudeformet gennemstik (*n.*)	X formede kutt for separering av frimerker
förstoringsglas (*n.*)	forstørrelsesglas (*n.*)	forstørrelsesglass (*n.*)
post (*r.*)	post (*c.*)	post (*m.*)
posta	poste; sende	sende med posten
anbudsauktion (*r.*)	brevbudsauktion (*c.*)	postauksjon (*m.*)
brevbärare (*m.*)	postbud (*c.*)	postbud (*n.*)
mars	marts	mars
mark (*r.*)	mark (*c.*)	tysk mark (*m.*)
maj	maj	mai
Mexiko	Mexico	Mexico
fältpostfrimärke (*n.*); militärfrimärke (*n.*)	soldaterfrimærke (*n.*)	militært frimerke (*n.*)
millimeter (*r.*)	millimeter (*c.*)	millimeter (*m.*)
miljon	million	million (*m.*)
minimibud (*n.*)	minimumsbud (*n.*)	minstebud (*n.*)
valutasystem (*n.*)	møntsystem (*n.*)	pengesystem (*n.*)
pengar (*r.pl.*)	penge (*pl.*)	penger (*m.pl.*)
månad (*r.*)	måned (*c.*)	måned (*m.*)
flerfärgad	mangefarvet	flerfarget
nationell	national	nasjonal
nationalitet (*r.*)	nationalitet (*c.*)	nasjonalitet (*m.*)
Holland	Holland; Nederlandene	Nederland; Holland

ENGLISH	DUTCH	FINNISH
never hinged	postfris	postituore
new	nieuw	uusi
newspaper stamp	krantenzegel (m./c.)	sanomalehtipostimerkki
New Zeeland	Nieuw-Zeeland	Uusi-Seelanti
nine	negen	yhdeksän
ninety	negentig	yhdeksänkymmentä
Northern Ireland	Noord-Ierland	Pohjois-Irlanti
Norway	Noorwegen	Norja
not issued	niet uitgegeven; onuitgegeven	liikkeeseen laskematon
no unlimited bids accepted	geen ongelimiteerde biedingen geaccepteerd	rajoittamattomia tarjouksia ei hyväksytä
November	november	marraskuu
number	nummer (n.); getal (n.)	numero
obliteration	afstempeling (f./c.)	mitätöinti
obsolete	verouderd; niet langer in gebruik	käytöstä poistettu
October	oktober	lokakuu
offer (noun)	aanbieding (f./c.)	tarjous
offer (verb)	aanbieden	tarjota
official	officieel	virallinen
official stamp	officiële zegel (m./c.)	virkapostimerkki
old	oud	vanha
on approval	op zicht	hyväksyttäväksi
on cover	op envelop; op omslag	kuorella
one	één	yksi
on the back	op de achterkant; op de achterzijde	takasivulla
order form	bestelformulier (n.)	tilauslomake
original	origineel	alkuperäinen
original gum	originele gom (n.)	alkuperäinen liima
overprint	opdruk (m./c.)	lisäpainama
package	pak (n.); pakket (n.)	paketti
pair	paar (n.)	pari
pane	paneel (n.)	myyntiarkki
paper	papier (n.)	paperi
parcel post	pakketpost (m./c.)	pakettiposti
parcel post stamp	pakketpost-zegel (m./c.)	(posti)pakettimerkki
pedigree; provenance	stamboom (m./c.)	sukupuu
peel (verb)	pellen	irroittaa

SWEDISH	DANISH	NORWEGIAN
postfrisk	aldrig hængslet	postfrisk
ny	ny	ny
tidningsmärke (n.)	avisportomærke (n.)	trykksaksfrimerke (n.)
Nya Zeeland	New Zealand	New Zealand
nio	ni	ni
nittio	halvfems	nitti
Nordirland	Nordirland	Nord-Irland
Norge	Norge	Norge; Noreg
ej utgiven	ikke udgivet	ikke utgitt
olimiterade bud accepteras ej	bud uden øvre grænse accepteres ikke	kun faste bud akseptert
november	november	november
nummer (n.)	nummer (n.)	nummer (n.)
makulering (r.); stämpling (r.)	tilintetgørelse	utslettelse (n.)
föråldrad	forældet	foreldet
oktober	oktober	oktober
anbud (n.)	tilbud (n.)	tilbud (n.)
offerera	tilbyde	tilby
officiell	officiel	offisiell
tjänstefrimärke (n.)	tjenestefrimærke (n.)	frimerke for offisielt bruk
gammal	gammel	gammel
till påseende	på prøve; til gennemsyn	på prøve
på brev; på försändelse	på brev	på original konvolutt
en	en (c.); et (n.)	en
på baksidan	på bagsiden	på baksiden
beställningssedel (r.)	bestillingsblanket	ordreseddel (m.)
original	original	original
originalgummering (n.)	originalgummi (c.)	originalt lim (n.)
övertryck (n.)	overtryk (n.); påtryk (n.)	overtrykk (n.)
paket (n.)	pakke (c.)	pakke (m.)
par (n.)	par (n.)	par (n.)
ark (n.)	ark (n.)	ark (n.)
papper (n.)	papir (n.)	papir (n.)
paketpost (r.)	pakkepost (c.)	pakkepost (m.)
paketpostmärke (n.)	pakkepost mærke	pakkepostmerke (n.)
proveniens (r.)	stamtræ (n.)	liste over tidligere eiere
skala	tage af	flasse av

ENGLISH	DUTCH	FINNISH
pen cancelled	ontwaardigd met pen	mustemitätöinti
People's Republic of China (P.R.C.)	Chinese Volksrepubliek	Kiinan kansantasavalta
percé	gerouletteerd	lävistetty
perfect	volmaakt; perfect	virheetön
perforated	geperforeerd; getand	hammastettu
perforation	perforatie (f./c.); tanding (f./c.)	hammaste
Peru	Peru	Peru
peseta	peseta (m./c.)	peseta
peso	peso (m./c.)	peso
philatelic	filatelistisch	filateelinen
philatelist	filatelist (m./c.); postzegelverzamelaar (m./c.)	filatelisti
philately	filatelie (f./c.)	filatelia; postimerkkeily
phosphor	fosfor (n.)	fosfori
phosphorescent	fosforescerend	fosforihohteinen
photogravure	fotogravure (m./c.)	fotogravyyri
pin perforation	pinperforatie (f./c.)	neulahammaste
pope	paus (m./c.)	paavi
portrait	portret (n.)	muotokuva
Portugal	Portugal	Portugali
postage	porto (m./c.); posttarief (n.)	postimaksu
postage due	strafport (m./c.)	lunastus maksu
postage due stamp	strafportzegel (m./c.)	(posti)lunastusmerkki
postage stamp	postzegel (m./c.)	postimerkki
postal card	-----	ehiökortti
postcard	briefkaart (m./f./c.)	postikortti
postman	postbode (m./c.)	postinkantaja
postmark	poststempel (m./c.); postmerk (n.)	postileima
post office	postkantoor (n.)	postitoimisto
pound Sterling (£)	pond sterling (n.)	punta
precancel (noun)	voorafstempeling (f./c.)	etukäteen mitätöity
prepayment	vooruitbetaling (f./c.)	ennakkomaksu
president	president (m./c.)	presidentti; puheenjohtaja
price	prijs (m./c.)	hinta
price list	prijslijst (m./c.)	hintaluettelo; hinnasto
print (verb)	drukken	painaa
propaganda stamp	propagandazegel (m./c.)	propagandamerkki

SWEDISH	DANISH	NORWEGIAN

bläckmakulerad; bläckmakulerat
Folkrepubliken Kina
genomstucken
perfekt

penneannulering (c.)
Folkerepublikken Kina
gennemstikning (c.)
perfekt

håndannullert; blekkannullert
Folkerepublikken Kina
roulett perforering (m.)
perfekt

perforerad
perforering (r.); tandning (r.)
Peru
peseta (r.)

takket
takning (c.)
Peru
peseta (c.)

perforert
perforering
Peru
peseta (m.)

peso (r.)
filatelistisk
frimärkssamlare (m./f.); filatelist (m./f.)
filateli (r.)

peso (c.)
filatelistisk
filatelist (c.)
filateli (c.)

peso (m.)
filatelistisk
filatelist (m.)
filateli (n.)

fosfor (r.)
fosforescerande
fotogravyr (r.)
nåltandning (r.)

fosfor (n.)
fosforiserende
fotogravure (c.)
pintakning (c.)

fosforescens (n.)
fosforescende
fotogravyre (m.)
hull perforering (m.)

påve (m.)
porträtt (n.)
Portugal
porto (n.)

pave (c.)
portræt (n.)
Portugal
porto (c.)

pave (m.)
portrett (n.)
Portugal
porto (m.)

lösen
lösenmärke (n.)
frimärke (n.)
brevkort (n.)

underfrankeret
underfrankeringsstempel (n.)
frimærke (n.); postfrimærke (n.)
brevkort (n.)

skyldig porto (m.)
portomerke (n.)
frimerke (n.)
brevkort (n.)

vykort (n.)
brevbärare (m.)
poststämpel (r.)
postkontor (n.)

postkort (n.)
postbud (c.)
poststempel (n.)
posthus (n.)

postkort (n.)
postbud (n.)
poststempel (n.)
postkontor (n.)

pund sterling (n.)
förmakulera
förskottsbetalning (r.)
president (m.)

pund sterling
præannulleret
forudbetaling (c.)
præsident (c.)

pund (n.)
preannullering (n.)
forhåndsbetaling (m.)
president (m.)

pris (n.)
prislista (r.)
trycka
propagandamärke (n.)

pris (c.)
prisliste (c.)
trykke
propagandamærke (n.)

pris (m.)
prisliste (m.)
trykke
propaganda frimerke (n.)

ENGLISH	DUTCH	FINNISH
protective reserve bid	beschermend bod (n.)	pohjatarjous
provisional (noun)	tijdelijke zegel (m./c.); hulpzegel (m./c.)	tilapäisjulkaisu
punch cancellation	perforatie-afstempeling (f./c.)	reikämitätöinti
quadrillé	geruit albumblad (n.)	ruudutettu
queen	koningin (f./c.)	kuningatar
rare	zeldzaam	harvinainen
rarity	zeldzaamheid (f./c.)	harvinaisuus
receipt	ontvangstbewijs (n.)	kuitti
rectangular	rechthoekig	suorakulmainen
Red Cross	Rode Kruis	Punainen Risti
registration stamp	registratiezegel (m./c.)	kirjaamislipuke
regummed	opnieuw gegomd; hergomd	uudelleen liimoitettu
remainder	overschot (n.)	jäännösvarasto
repaired	gerepareerd	korjattu
reprint (noun)	herdruk (m./c.); nadruk (m./c.)	uusintapainos
reproduction	reproductie (f./c.)	jäljennös
republic	republiek (f./c.)	tasavalta
Republic of China (Taiwan)	Chinese Republiek	Kiinan tasavalta
right (direction or position)	rechts	oikea
roulette	roulette (m./c.); raadje (n.)	läviste
rouletted	gerouletteerd; doorstoken	lävistetty
round	rond	pyöreä
Russia	Rusland	Venäjä
Saudi Arabia	Saoedi-Arabië	Saudi-Arabia
scarce	schaars	harvinainen
Scotland	Schotland	Skotlanti
secret mark	verborgen merk (n.); geheim merk (n.)	salamerkki
sell (verb)	verkopen	myydä
seller	verkoper (m./c.)	myyjä
separation	separatie (f./c.); afscheiding (f./c.)	erottaminen
September	september	syyskuu
serpentine roulette	slangenroulette (n.)	uurrostusläviste
serrated roulette	zaagvormige roulette; zaag-tanding	kaariläviste
se-tenant	samenhangend	(seka)pari
seven	zeven	seitsemän
seventy	zeventig	seitsemänkymmentä

SWEDISH	DANISH	NORWEGIAN
bevakningspris (n.)	sælgers minimumspris	minstepris (m.)
provisorium (n.)	provisorie (n.)	provisorisk utgave (m.)
makulering med hålslag	gennemhulsannulering (c.)	hullmakulering (m.)
papper med rektangulär vattenstämpel	kvadrille (c.)	kvadrilj (m.)
drottning (f.)	dronning (c.)	dronning (m./f.)
sällsynt	sjælden	sjelden
raritet (r.)	sjældenhed (c.)	sjeldenhet (m.)
kvitto (n.)	kvittering (c.)	kvittering (m.)
rektangulär	rektangulær	rektangulær
Röda Korset	Røde Kors	Røde Kors
rekommenderingsmärke (n.)	registreringsmærke (n.)	recommandert stempel (n.)
regummerad; eftergummerad	regummieret	regummiert
restlager (n.)	restlager (n.)	lager tilåvers (n.)
lagad	repareret	reparert
nyutgåva (r.)	genoptryk (n.)	opptrykk (m.)
reproduktion (r.)	reproduktion (c.)	reproduksjon (m.)
republic (r.)	republik (c.)	republikk (m.)
Republiken Kina	Republikken Kina	Republikken Kina
höger	højre	høyre
roulett; linjetandning	gennemstikning (c.)	roulett perforering (m.)
genomstucken; linjetandad	gennemstukket	roulett-perforert
rund	rund	rund
Ryssland	Rusland	Russland
Saudiarabien	Saudi Arabien	Saudi-Arabia
sällsynt	valmindelig	sjelden
Skottland	Skotland	Skottland
hemligt märke (n.)	hemmeligt mærke (n.)	skjult merke (n.)
sälja	sælge	selge
säljare (m.)	sælger (c.)	selger (m.)
separation (r.)	afskilning (c.)	separasjon (m.)
september	september	september
linjetandad i serpentinmönster	slange gennemstik (n.)	slangetagging
linjetandad i sågtandsmönster	savtakning	sikk sakk roulett
sammantryckt; kombinationspar	sammentryk (n.)	horisontalt par AB
sju	syv	sju
sjuttio	halvfjerds	sytti

ENGLISH	DUTCH	FINNISH
shade (*re:* color)	tint (*f./c.*); nuance (*f./c.*)	vivahde
sheet (of stamps)	vel (*n.*)	painoarkki
silk thread	zijden draad (*n.*)	silkkilanka
six	zes	kuusi
sixty	zestig	kuusikymmentä
skinned spot	dunne plek (*f./c.*)	ohut kohta
small	klein	pieni
South Africa	Zuid-Afrika	Etelä-Afrikka
souvenir sheet	herdenkingsblad (*n.*)	muistoarkki
Soviet Union (U.S.S.R.)	Sovjetunie	Neuvostoliitto
Spain	Spanje	Espanja
specimen	specimen (*n.*)	näyte; mallikappale
square (*adjective*)	vierkant	nelikulmainen
stain	vlek (*f./c.*)	tahra
stamp (postage)	postzegel (*m./c.*)	postimerkki
star	ster (*m./c.*)	tähti
steel engraving	staalgravure (*f./c.*)	teräskaiverrus
stock remainder	overschot (*n.*)	jäännösvarasto
strip (of stamps)	strook (*f./c.*)	rivilö
suggested bid	voorgesteld bod (*n.*)	ehdotettu tarjous
surcharge	overdruk (*m./c.*)	lisäpainama
surtax	toeslag (*m./c.*)	lisämaksu
Sweden	Zweden	Ruotsi
Switzerland	Zwitserland	Sveitsi
symbol	symbool (*n.*)	tunnuskuva; symboli
syncopated perforation	afwijkende roltanding (*f./c.*)	mykkä hammaste
tagged stamp	luminescerende postzegel (*m./c.*)	fosforoitu merkki
tax (*noun*)	belasting (*f./c.*)	vero
tear (*noun*)	scheur (*m./c.*)	repeämä
tear (*verb*)	scheuren	repiä
telegraph stamp	telegraafzegel (*m./c.*)	lennätinmerkki
ten	tien	kymmenen
tenth (*noun*)	tiende	kymmenesosa
tête-bêche	keerdruk; tête-bêche	päikkö
thin spot	dunne plek (*f./c.*)	ohut kohta
third (*noun*)	derde	kolmasosa

SWEDISH	DANISH	NORWEGIAN
nyans (r.)	farvestyrke (c.)	nyanse (m.)
ark (n.)	ark (n.)	ark (n.)
silkestråd (r.)	silketråd (c.)	sikkerhetsfibre
sex	seks	seks
sextio	tres	seksti
tunn fläck (r.)	tynd plet	tynn flekk
liten	lille	liten
Sydafrika	Sydafrika	Syd-Afrika
miniatyrark (n.); minnesblock (n.)	souvenirark (n.)	souvenirark (n.)
Sovjetunionen	Sovjetunionen	Sovjetsamveldet
Spanien	Spanien	Spania
prov (n.)	prøveeksemplar (n.)	eksemplar (n.)
kvadratiskt	firkantet; kvadratisk	kvadratisk
fläck (r.)	plet (c.)	flekk (m.)
frimärke (n.)	frimærke (n.)	frimerke (n.)
stjärna (r.)	stjerne (c.)	stjerne (m.)
stålgravyr (r.)	stålstik; stålgravure	stålgravering (m.)
restlager (n.)	restlager (n.)	lager tilåvers (n.)
remsa (r.)	række (c.)	remse (m.)
utropspris (n.)	foreslået bud (n.)	utropspris (m.)
provision (r.)	ekstra afgift (c.)	tillegg (n.)
skatt (r.)	ekstraskat (c.)	tilleggsskatt (m.)
Sverige	Sverige	Sverige
Schweiz	Schweiz	Sveits
symbol (r.)	symbol (n.)	symbol (n.)
synkoperad tandning	forskudt takning (c.)	avbrudt perforering (m.)
fluoriscerande frimärke (n.)	fluoresceret frimærke (n.)	elektronisk merket frimerke
skatt (r.)	skat (c.)	skatt (n.)
reva (r.)	rift (c.)	rift (m.)
reva	rive	rive
telegrafmärke (n.)	telegrafmærke (n.)	telegram frimerke
tio	ti	ti
tiondel (r.)	tiendedel (c.)	tiendedel (m.)
tête-bêche	tête-bêche	tête-bêche
tunn fläck (r.)	tynd plet	tynn flekk
tredjedel (r.)	trediedel (c.)	tredjedel (m.)

ENGLISH	DUTCH	FINNISH
thirty	dertig	kolmekymmentä
thousand	duizend	tuhat
three	drie	kolme
tongs	pincet (m./c.); postzegeltang (f./c.)	atulat; pihdit
top	bovenkant (m./c.)	yläosa; huippu
topical; thematic	onderwerp	aihe-
torn	gescheurd	repeytynyt
trade (verb)	ruilen	vaihtaa; käydä kauppaa
twenty	twintig	kaksikymmentä
two	twee	kaksi
typography	typografie (f./c.)	typografia
unattributed	niet toegeschreven	määrittelemätön
undeliverable	onbestelbaar	perille toimittamaton
ungummed	ongegomd	liimaton; ilman liimaa
unhinged	zonder plakker	ilman liimaketta; postituore
unique	uniek	ainutlaatuinen; uniikki
United Kingdom (U.K.)	Verenigd Koninkrijk	Yhdistynyt kuningaskunta
United States of America (U.S.A.)	Verenigde Staten van Amerika	Amerikan Yhdysvallat
unknown	onbekend	tuntematon
unofficial	onofficieel	epävirallinen
unpublished	ongepubliceerd; niet gepubliceerd	julkaisematon
unsevered	niet afgescheurd	erottamaton
unused	ongebruikt	käyttämätön
used	gebruikt	käytetty
valuable	waardevol	arvokas
value	waarde (f./c.)	arvo
variety	variëteit (f./c.); afwijking (f./c.)	variantti
Venezuela	Venezuela	Venezuela
Wales	Wales	Wales
watermark	watermerk (n.)	vesileima
West Germany (B.R.D.)	West-Duitsland	Länsi-Saksa
wove paper	gewoon papier (n.)	tavallinen paperi
year	jaar (n.)	vuosi
Yugoslavia; Jugoslavia	Joegoslavië	Jugoslavia
zero	nul	nolla
zigzag roulette	zig-zag roulette; zaag-tanding	polvekeläviste

SWEDISH	DANISH	NORWEGIAN
trettio	tredive	tretti
tusen	tusind	tusen
tre	tre	tre
pincett (r.)	pincet (c.)	tenger
topp	top (c.)	øverst
lokal; orts-	emnespecificeret	emne
sönderriven	iturevet; revet i tu	revet
handla med; byta	bytte	handle; bytte
tjugo	tyve	tjue
två	to	to
typografi (r.)	typografi (c.)	typografi (n.)
obestämt	uidentificeret	ufullstendig identifisert
obeställbar	vanbringelig	ikke leverbar
ogummerad	ugummieret	ulimet
postfrisk	uhængslet	uhengslet
unik	unik	unik
Storbritannien	Storbritannien	Storbritannia
Amerikas Förenta Stater	Forenede Stater	Forente Stater
okänd	ukendt	ukjent
inofficiell	uofficiel	uoffisiell
opublicerat; opublicerad	upubliceret	ikke katalogført
ej skild	ubrudt	-----
oanvänd	ubrugt	ubrukt
använd	brugt	brukt
värdefull	værdifuld	verdifull
värde (n.)	værdi (c.)	verdi
variant (r.); mångfald (r.)	variant (c.)	mangfoldighet (m.)
Venezuela	Venezuela	Venezuela
Wales	Wales	Wales
vattenmärke (n.)	vandmærke (n.)	vannmerke (n.)
Västtyskland	Vesttyskland	Vest-Tyskland
vävt papper (n.)	vævet papir (n.)	vevemønstret papir (n.)
år (n.)	år (n.)	år (n.)
Jugoslavien	Jugoslavien	Jugoslavia
noll	nul	null
sicksackformat genomstick	zig-zag gennemstik (n.)	sikk sakk roulett

ENGLISH	DUTCH	FINNISH
amber	ambergeel	meripihkanvärinen
azure	azuur; hemelsblauw	taivaansininen
bister	donkerbruin	tummanruskea
black	zwart	musta
blue	blauw	sininen
bronze	brons	pronssinvärinen
brown	bruin	ruskea
carmine	karmijnrood	karmiininpunainen
cerise	kersrood	kirsikanpunainen
cobalt	kobalt(blauw)	koboltinsininen
crimson	karmozijnrood	heleänpunainen
emerald	smaragdgroen	smaragdinvihreä
gray	grijs	harmaa
green	groen	vihreä
heliotrope	heliotroop	heliotrooppi
indigo	indigo	indigosininen
lavender	lavendel(paars)	laventelinsininen
lemon	citroen(geel)	sitruunankeltainen
lilac	lila	lila; violetti
magenta	roodpaars; magenta	aniliininpunainen
maroon	kastanje(bruin)	ruosteenvärinen; ruskeanpunainen
olive	olijfgroen	oliivinvärinen
orange	oranje	oranssi
pink	rose; roze	vaaleanpunainen
Prussian blue	Berlijnsblauw	preussinsininen
purple	purper; paars	sinipunainen; purppura
red	rood	punainen
royal blue	koninklijk blauw	koboltinsininen
sapphire	saffier(blauw)	safiirinsininen
scarlet	scharlaken; vuurrood	tulipunainen
turquoise	turkoois	turkoosinsininen
ultramarine	ultramarijn(blauw)	ultramariini
vermilion	vermiljoen(rood)	sinooperinpunainen
violet	violet	sinipunainen
white	wit	valkoinen
yellow	geel	keltainen

SWEDISH	DANISH	NORWEGIAN
bärnstensfärgad	ravgul	ravfarget
himmelsblå	himmelblå	himmelblå
ljust smutsbrun	gulbrun; mørkebrun	grå-gulbrun
svart	sort	svart
blå	blå	blå
brons	bronzefarvet	bronsefarget
brun	brun	brun
karminröd	karminrød	høyrød
körsbärsröd	kirsebærrød	kirsebærfarget
kobolt	koboltblå	blågrønn
karmosinröd	karmosinrød	karmosinrød
smaragdgrön	smaragdgrøn	smaragdgrønn
grå	grå	grå
grön	grøn	grønn
heliotrop; svagt purpur	heliotropfarvet	purpur
indigoblå	indigo	indigoblå
lavendel	lavendelblå	lavenderfarget
citrongul	citron	sitrongul
lila	lilla	lilla
rödviolett	magentarød	purpurfarget
karmosinbrun	rødbrun	rødbrun
oliv	olivengrøn	olivenfarget
orange	orange	oransje
rosa	lyserød	lyserød
berlinerblå	berlinerblå	prøyssisk blå
purpur	violet	purpur
röd	rød	rød
kungsblå	kongeblå	kongeblå
safirblå	safirblå	safirblå
scharlakansröd	skarlagen	skarlagenrød
turkos	turkis	turkisfarget
ultramarin	ultramarinefarvet	ultramarinefarget
orangeröd	zinnober; zinnoberrød	sinoberød
violett	violet	fiolett
vit	hvid	hvit
gul	gul	gul

ENGLISH	POLISH	ROMANIAN
abbreviation	skrót (*m.*)	abreviere (*f.*); prescurtare (*f.*)
accolated	portret podwójny ("gemmowy")	acolat; alăturat; acostat
account (financial or transactional)	rachunek (*m.*); konto (*n.*)	cont (*n.*)
acquisition	nabycie (*n.*); zakup (*m.*)	achiziție (*f.*)
aérogramme; air letter	aerogram (*m.*); listownik lotniczy (*m.*)	aerogramă (*f.*)
aerophilately	aerofilatelistyka (*f.*)	aerofilatelie (*f.*)
airmail	poczta lotnicza (*f.*)	poștă aeriană
air stamp; airmail stamp	znaczek lotniczy (*m.*)	marcă pentru poșta aeriană (*f.*)
album	album (*m.*)	album (*n.*)
almost	prawie	aproape
alter (*verb*)	podrabiać	modifica
alteration	podrobienie (*n.*); podróbka (*f.*)	alterare (*f.*); modificare (*f.*)
amount	suma (*f.*); kwota (*f.*)	sumă (*f.*)
aniline	anilina (*f.*)	anilină (*f.*)
anomaly	anomalia (*f.*)	anomalie (*f.*)
April	kwiecień	Aprilie
Argentina	Argentyna	Argentina
art	sztuka (*f.*)	artă (*f.*)
attribute (*verb*)	przypisywać; atrybuować	atribui
attribution	atrybucja (*f.*)	atribuire (*f.*); identificare (*f.*)
auction	aukcja (*f.*)	licitație (*f.*)
auction catalogue	katalog aukcyjny (*m.*)	catalog de licitație (*n.*)
auction sale	sprzedaż aukcyjna	licitație (*f.*)
August	sierpień	August
Australia	Australia	Australia
Austria	Austria	Austria
authentic	autentyczny	autentic; veritabil
authentication mark	znak autentyczności (*m.*)	semn de autentificare
barred	z nadrukiem kasującym	barat
Belgium	Belgia	Belgia
bicolored; bicoloured	dwukolorowy	bicolor
bid (*noun:* auction bid)	cena licytowana (*f.*); oferta cenowa (*f.*)	licitare (*f.*); preț (*n.*)
bid (*verb*)	licytować (*v.*)	licita
bid sheet	zlecenie zakupu (*n.*)	ofertă de licitație (*f.*)
bilingual	dwujęzyczny	bilingv
bisected	połówkowy (znaczek)	bisectat

TURKISH	GREEK	HEBREW
kisaltma	σύντμηση (f.)	קִצּוּר (m.)
üstüste ve aynı yöne bakan	συνδεδεμένο	מְצֻמָּד
hesap	λογαριασμός (m.)	חֶשְׁבּוֹן (m.)
elde etme; kazanç	απόκτηση (f.)	רְכִישָׁה (f.)
telsiz telgraf	αεροεπιστολή (f.)	אִגֶּרֶת אֲוִיר (f.)
uçak pulu toplama	αεροφιλοτελισμός (m.)	בּוּלָאוּת-דֹּאַר אֲוִיר (f.)
uçak ile	αεροπορικόν (n.)	דֹּאַר אֲוִיר (m.)
uçak postası pulu	αεροπορικόν γραμματόσημον (n.)	בּוּל דֹּאַר-אֲוִיר (m.)
albüm	λεύκωμα (n.)	אַלְבּוֹם (m.)
hemen hemen	σχεδόν	כִּמְעַט
değiştirmek	μεταβάλλω	שִׁנָּה
değiştirme	αλλοίωση ; τροποποίηση	שִׁנּוּי (m.)
miktar	ποσόν (n.)	סְכוּם (m.)
anilin	ανιλίνη	אֲנִילִין (m.)
kural veya kaide dışı; aykırı	ανωμαλία (f.)	סְטִיָּה (f.)
Nisan	Απρίλιος	אַפְּרִיל
Arjantin	Αργεντινή	אַרְגֶּנְטִינָה
sanat	τέχνη	אָמָּנוּת (f.)
tanımlamak	αποδίδω	יִחֵס
tanımlama	αποδιδόμενο (n.)	יִחוּס (m.)
mezat; müzayede	δημοπρασία (f.)	מְכִירָה פּוּמְבִּית (f.)
mezat kataloğu	κατάλογος πλειστηριασμού (m.)	קַטָלוֹג מְכִירָה פּוּמְבִּית (m.)
artırma ile satış	πλειστηριασμός (m.)	מְכִירָה פּוּמְבִּית (f.)
Ağustos	Αύγουστος	אוֹגוּסְט
Avustralya	Αυστραλία	אוֹסְטְרַלְיָה
Avusturya	Αυστρία	אוֹסְטְרִיָה
gerçek; hakiki; otantik	γνήσιον	אֲמִתִּי
doğruluk markası	γνησιότητος σημείο (n.)	סִימָן אוֹתֶנְטִיּוּת (m.)
çizgili	καθετες ραβδώσεις	מָדְפָּס בְּפַסִּים
Belçika	Βέλγιο	בֶּלְגְּיָה
iki renkli	δίχρωμο	דּוּ-גּוֹנִי
teklif	προσφορά (f.)	הַצָּעַת מְחִיר
fiyat arttırmak; teklif vermek	προσφέρω	הִצִּיעַ מְחִיר
teklif formu	κατάλογος προσφορών	טוֹפֶס הַצָּעָה (m.)
iki lisan bilen	δίγλωσσος	דּוּ-לְשׁוֹנִי
yarıya bölünmüs	διχοτομισμένο	חָצוּי

ENGLISH	POLISH	ROMANIAN
block	blok (*m.*)	bloc (*n.*)
block of four	czworoblok znaczków (*m.*)	bloc de patru (*n.*)
booklet (of stamps)	zeszycik znaczkowy (*m.*)	carnet de mărci (*n.*)
bottom	dół (*m.*)	jos; dedesubt
Brazil	Brazylia	Brazilia
burélage; burelé	markacyjny znak drukarski (*m.*)	burelaj (*n.*)
buy (*verb*)	kupować	cumpăra
buyer	nabywca (*m.*)	cumpărător (*m.*)
cachet	stempel okolicznościowy (*m.*)	cachet
Canada	Kanada	Canada
cancel (*verb*)	skasować; ostemplować	ştampila; anula; oblitera
cancellation; cancelation	kasowanie (*n.*); ostemplowanie (*n.*)	ştampilare (*f.*); anulare (*f.*)
cancelled to order	ostemplowany dla kolekcjonerów	ştampilat de complezenţă
cash (ready money)	gotówka (*f.*)	numerar (*n.*); peşin (*n.*) (archaic)
cash on delivery (C.O.D.)	za zaliczeniem pocztowym	plata la livrare
catalog; catalogue	katalog (*m.*)	catalog (*n.*)
catalogue value	cena katalogowa	valoare de catalog (*f.*)
censored mail	przesyłka cenzurowana (*f.*)	corespondenţă cenzurată (*f.*)
centennial; centenary	stuletni (*m.*)	centenar (*n.*)
centered	wycentrowany; wyśrodkowany	centrat
centering	środkowanie (*n.*); centorwanie (*n.*)	centrare (*f.*)
centimeter; centimetre	centymetr (*m.*)	centimetru (*m.*)
chalky paper	papier kredowany (*m.*)	hârtie cretată (*f.*)
charity stamp	znaczek na cele dobroczynne (*m.*)	timbru de binefacere (*n.*)
check; cheque	czek (*m.*)	cec (*n.*)
China	Chiny	China
classification	klasyfikacja (*f.*)	clasificare (*f.*)
classify (*verb*)	klasyfikować	clasifica
coil	rolka (znaczków) (*f.*)	rolă de mărci (*f.*)
collect (*verb*)	kolekcjonować; zbierać	colecţiona
collection	kolekcja (*f.*); zbiór (*m.*)	colecţie (*f.*)
collector	kolekcjoner (*m.*); zbieracz (*m.*)	colecţionar (*m.*)
Colombia	Kolumbia	Columbia
color; colour	kolor (*m.*)	culoare (*f.*)
comb perforation	perforacja grzebieniowa (*f.*)	dantelură în pieptene (*f.*)
commemorative (*adjective*)	okolicznościowy; pamiątkowy	comemorativ

TURKISH	GREEK	HEBREW
blok	μεγάλο κομμάτι; εξάδα	צְמוּדָה (f.)
dörtlü blok	κομμάτι τῶν τεσσάρων; τετράδα	צְמוּדַת אַרְבַּע (f.)
pul defteri; pul karnesi	βιβλιαράκι (n.)	קֻנְטְרֵס (m.)
alt	κάτω; πυθμένας	תַּחְתִּית (f.)
Brezilya	Βραζιλία	בְּרָזִיל
büröle	σημείο ασφαλείας (f.)	הֶדְפֵּס רֶקַע (m.)
satın almak	αγοράζω	קָנָה
alıcı	αγοραστής	קוֹנֶה (m.)
kaşe	σφραγίς (n.)	חוֹתֶמֶת נִלְוֵית (m.) ; קִשּׁוּט (f.)
Kanada	Καναδάς	קָנַדָה
iptal etmek	ακυρώνω	הֶחְתִּים
iptal etme	ακύρωσις (n.)	הַחְתָּמָה
tedavülden kaldırılmış	ακύρωση μετά εντολής	מָחְתָּם לְפִי הַזְמָנָה
nakit; para	χρήματα (n.pl)	מְזֻמָּן (m.)
ödemeli	πληρωμή επί παραδόσεως	תַּשְׁלוּם בְּעֵת הַמְּסִירָה
katalog	κατάλογος (m.)	קָטָלוֹג (m.)
katalog değeri	τιμή καταλόγου	עֵרֶךְ קָטָלוֹגִי (m.)
sansürlü posta	λογοκριμένο ταχυδρομείο (f.)	דְּבַר דֹּאַר מְצֻנְזָר (m.)
yüzüncü yıl dönümü	εκατονταετηρίδα (f.)	חֲגִיגַת שְׁנַת הַמֵּאָה (f.)
ortalanmış	επικεντρομένο	מְמֻרְכָּז
ortalama	εκικέντρωσις (n.)	מִרְכּוּן (m.)
santimetre	εκατοστό (n.)	סֶנְטִימֶטֶר (m.)
tebeşir kağıdı	χάρτης χρώματος λευκού κιμωλίας	נְיַר גִּירִי (m.)
yardım pulu	φιλανθρωπικόν γραμματόσημον (n.)	בּוּל צְדָקָה (m.)
çek	επιταγή (f.)	הַמְחָאָה (f.)
Çin	Κίνα	סִין
sınıflama	ταξινομία (f.); κατάταξη (f.)	מִיּוּן (m.)
sınıflamak	ταξινομῶ; κατατάσσω	מִיֵּן
rulo pul	ρολό γραμματοσήμων	גְּלִיל בּוּלִים (m.)
koleksiyon yapmak	συλλέγω	אָסַף
koleksiyon	συλλογή (f.)	אֹסֶף (m.)
koleksiyoncu	συλλέκτης	אַסְפָן (m.)
Kolombiya	Κολομβία	קוֹלוֹמְבְּיָה
renk	χρώμα (n.)	צֶבַע (m.)
tarak dantel	διάτρισις κτένας	נִקְבּוּב מְסָרֵק (m.)
hatıra	αναμνηστικόν	הוֹצָאַת זִכָּרוֹן

ENGLISH	POLISH	ROMANIAN
common	pospolity	comun
complete	kompletny	complet
conjoined	portret podwójny ("gemmowy")	acolat; alăturat; acostat
copy (*noun*)	kopia (*f.*)	copie (*f.*)
copy (*verb*)	kopiować	copia
cover	koperta (*f.*); całość pocztowa (*f.*)	ambalaj (*n.*); plic (*n.*)
— on cover	całostka pocztosa	pe plic
crease (*noun*)	załamanie (*n.*); zagięcie (*n.*)	cută (*f.*); pliu (*n.*)
crease (*verb*)	załamac (*v.*)	face cută; plia
credit	kredyt (*m.*)	credit (*n.*)
credit card	karta kredytowa (*f.*)	carte de credit (*f.*)
credit cards accepted	przyjmujemy karty kredytowe	carţi de credit acceptate
crown (royal headpiece)	korona (*f.*)	coroană (*f.*)
cruzeiro	cruseiro (*n.*)	cruzeiro (*m.*)
cut cancellation	kasowanie przez nacięcie (*n.*)	anulare prin tăiere (*f.*)
cut square	wycinek (*m.*)	marcă poştală pe fragment (*f.*)
damaged	uszkodzony	deteriorat
dark (*re*: color)	ciemny	închis
date	data (*f.*)	dată (*f.*)
December	grudzień	Decembrie
deep (*re*: color)	głęboki	intens
defect (*noun*)	uszkodzenie (*n.*); defekt (*m.*)	defect (*n.*); imperfecţiune (*f.*)
defective	uszkodzony	cu defect
definitive (*adjective*)	definitywny; obiegowy	definitiv
demonetization	demonetyzacja (*f.*)	demonetizare (*f.*)
Denmark	Dania	Danemarca
denomination	nominał (*m.*)	valoare nominală (*f.*)
deposit (of funds)	wadium (*n.*); kaucja (*f.*)	acont (*n.*)
deposit required	wadium wymagane	depozit obligatoriu
design (*noun*)	wzór (*m.*)	motiv (*n.*); desen (*n.*)
devaluation	dewaluacja (*f.*)	devalorizare (*f.*)
dollar	dolar (*m.*)	dolar (*n.*)
domestic	krajowy	de uz intern
duplicate (*adjective*)	kopiować (*v.*); duplikować (*v.*)	duplicat
duplicate (*noun*)	duplikat (*m.*)	duplicat (*n.*)
duplicate (*verb*)	duplikować	duplica

TURKISH	GREEK	HEBREW
alelade	κοινός	שָׁכִיחַ
tamam	πλήρες	שָׁלֵם
üstüste ve aynı yöne bakan	συνδεδεμένο	מְצֻמָּד
kopya	αντίγραφο (n.)	עֹתֶק (m.)
kopya etmek	αντιγράφω	הַעְתֵּק
zarf	φάκελλος (m.)	מַעֲטָפָה (f.)
zarf üzerinde	επί επιστολής	מֻדְבָּק לַמַּעֲטָפָה
kat	τσάκισμα (n.)	קֶמֶט (m.)
katlanmak	τσακίζω	קָמַט (v.)
kredi	πίστωση (f.)	אַשְׁרַאי (m.)
kredi kartı	πιστωτική κάρτα (f.)	כַּרְטִיס אַשְׁרַאי (m.)
kredi kartı kabul edilir	δεχόμαστε πιστωτικές κάρτες	כְּרְטִיסֵי אַשְׁרַאי מִתְקַבְּלִים
taç	στέμμα (n.)	כֶּתֶר (m.)
kruzero	κρουζέϊρο (m.)	קְרוּזֶרוֹ (m.)
kesilerek iptal edilmiş	ακύρωση κοπής (f.)	בִּטּוּל בְּחִתּוּךְ (m.)
dörtgen kesilmiş antiyer pul fragmanı	τετραγωνική κοπή (f.)	מַלְבֵּן גָּזוּר (מְסַבִּיב לַבּוּל)
bozuk	χαλασμένο	פָּגוּם
koyu	σκοτεινός	כֵּהֶה (m.)
tarih	ημερομηνία (f.)	תַּאֲרִיךְ (m.)
Aralık	Δεκέμβριος	דֵּצֶמְבֶּר
koyu	βαθύ	עָמוֹק
kusur; defo	ελάττωμα (n.)	לִקּוּי (m.)
kusurlu	ελαττωματικό	לָקוּי
kati desenli	οριστικόν	מִן הַמִּנְיָן
tedavülden kaldırmak	απόσυρσις νομίσματος απο την κυκλοφορία	הוֹצָאָה מִתּוֹקֶף (f.)
Danimarka	Δανία	דַּנְמַרְק
bozuk para	μονάδα χρημάτων	עֵרֶךְ נָקוּב (m.)
kaparo; depozito	προκαταβολή (f.)	פִּקָּדוֹן (m.)
depozito gereklidir	προκαταβολή απαιτείται	פִּקָּדוֹן דָּרוּשׁ
desen	σχέδιο (n.)	תֶּכֶן (m.)
devalüasyon; değer düşürme	υποτίμηση (f.)	פִּחוּת (m.)
dolar	δολλάριο (n.)	דוֹלָר (m.)
yerli	οικιακός	פְּנִים
çift	διπλοτυπωμένο	כָּפוּל
çift kopya	διπλότυπον	כֶּפֶל (m.)
aynısından çoğaltmak	διπλασιάζω	שִׁכְפֵּל

ENGLISH	POLISH	ROMANIAN
eagle	orzeł (*m.*)	vultur (*m.*)
East Germany (D.D.R.)	Niemcy Wschodnie	Germania de Est
effigy	wizerunek (*m.*); postać (*f.*)	efigie (*f.*)
eight	osiem	opt
eighty	osiemdziesiąt	optzeci
embossing	sucha pieczęć (*f.*)	imprimare în relief (*f.*)
emperor	cesarz (*m.*)	împărat (*m.*)
encased postage stamp	-----	marcă îmbrăcată protectiv (folosită ca valută)
England	Anglia	Anglia
engraved	-----	gravat
envelope	koperta (*f.*)	plic (*n.*)
error	błąd (*m.*)	eroare (*f.*); greşeală (*f.*)
essay	próba (*f.*)	eseu (*n.*)
exhibit (*verb*)	wystawiać (*v.*); eksponować (*v.*)	expune
exhibition	wystawa (*f.*); ekspozycja (*f.*)	expoziţie (*f.*)
face value	wartość nominalna (*f.*)	valoare nominală (*f.*)
February	luty	Februarie
field post	poczta polowa (*f.*)	poştă militară (*f.*)
fifth (*noun*)	jedna piąta (*f.*)	cincime (*f.*)
fifty	pięćdziesiąt	cincizeci
Finland	Finlandia	Finlanda
first day cover	koperta pierwszego dnia obiegu	plic prima zi (*n.*)
fiscal stamp	znaczek skarbowy (*m.*)	timbru fiscal (*n.*)
five	pięć	cinci
fold (*noun*)	zagięcie (*n.*); zgięcie (*n.*)	îndoitură (*f.*); pliu (*n.*)
fold (*verb*)	zaginać (*v.*); zginać (*v.*)	îndoi; plia
foreign	zagraniczny; obcy	străin
foreign currency	obca waluta (*f.*); dewizy (*f.pl.*)	valută străină (*f.*)
forty	czterdzieści	patruzeci
four	cztery	patru
fourth (*noun*)	jedna czwarta (*f.*)	pătrime (*f.*)
fraction	frakcja (*v.*)	fracţiune (*f.*)
frame	ramka (*f.*)	cadru (*n.*)
franc	frank (*m.*)	franc (*m.*)
France	Francja	Franţa
franchise stamp	znaczek zwalniający od opłaty pocztowej	marcă poştală pentru scutire de porto

TURKISH	GREEK	HEBREW
kartal	αετός (m.)	נֶשֶׁר (m.)
Doğu Almanya	Ανατολική Γερμανία	גֶּרְמַנְיָה הַמִּזְרָחִית
madeni paradaki portre	ομοίωμα (n.)	דְּמוּת (f.)
sekiz	οκτώ	שְׁמוֹנָה
seksen	ογδόντα	שְׁמוֹנִים
kabartma	ανάγλυφον (n.)	פִּתּוּחַ תַּבְלִיט
imparator	αυτοκράτορας (m.)	קֵיסָר (m.)
para pulu	γραμματόσημο εσωκλειόμενο (n.)	בּוּל בְּצוּרַת נַרְתִּיק (m.)
İngiltere	Αγγλία	אַנְגְלִיָּה
nakşedilmiş	χαρακτικόν	חָרוּת
zarf	φάκελλος (m.)	מַעֲטָפָה (f.)
hata	λάθος (n.)	טָעוּת (f.)
ese	δοκίμιο	תִּכְנוּן שֶׁלֹּא יָצָא לְבִצּוּעַ (m.)
sergilemek	εκθέτω	הִצִּיג
sergi	έκθεση (f.)	תַּעֲרוּכָה (f.)
itibari değer	ονομαστική αξία (f.)	עֵרֶךְ נָקוּב (m.)
Şubat	Φεβρουάριος	פֶבְּרוּאָר
sahra postası	στρατιωτικό ταχυδρομείο (n.)	שֵׁרוּת דֹּאַר צְבָאִי (m.)
beşte bir	πέμπτον (n.)	חֲמִשִׁית (f.)
elli	πενήντα	חֲמִשִׁים
Finlandiya	Φιλανδία	פִינְלַנְד
ilkgün zarfı	φάκελλος κρώτης ημέρας κυκλοφορίας	מַעֲטֶפֶת בּוּלִים מִיּוֹם-רִאשׁוֹן הַהַנְפָּקָה
harç pulu	γραμματόσημο δημοσίου (n.)	בּוּל הַכְנָסָה (m.)
beş	πέντε	חֲמִשָּׁה
kat	πτυχή (f.)	קֶפֶל (m.)
katlamak	διπλώνω	קִפֵּל
yabancı	αλλοδαπός; ξένος	זָר
döviz; yabancı para	ξένο νόμισμα (n.)	מַטְבֵּעַ זָר
kırk	σαράντα	אַרְבָּעִים
dört	τέσσερα	אַרְבָּעָה
dörtte bir	τέταρτον (n.)	רֶבַע (m.)
parça; kesir	κλάσμα (n.)	שֶׁבֶר (m.)
çerçeve	κορνίζα (f.)	מִסְגֶּרֶת (f.)
frank	φράγκο (n.)	פְרַנְק (m.)
Fransa	Γαλλία	צָרְפַת
özel kişiler için hazırlanmış pul	-----	בּוּל פְּטוֹר (m.)

ENGLISH	POLISH	ROMANIAN
frank (*noun*)	franco (*n.*); francowanie (*n.*)	privilegiu de francare prin semnătură
frank (*verb*)	ofrankować	semna în loc de timbru
genuine	prawdziwy	autentic; veritabil
Germany	Niemcy	Germania
glossy paper	papier błyszczący (*m.*)	hârtie lucioasă (*f.*)
grade (*noun*)	stan (zachowania) (*m.*)	stare de conservare (*f.*)
grade (*verb*)	oceniać (stan zachowania) (*v.*)	califica; aprecia
granite paper	papier granitowy (*m.*)	hârtie cu fire de mătase (*f.*)
Great Britain	Wielka Brytania	Marea Britanie
Greece	Grecja	Grecia
gum	guma (*f.*)	gumă (*f.*)
gutter	margines zewnętrzny (*m.*)	bandă intermediară (*f.*)
half (*adjective*)	pół; przepołowiony	jumătate
half (*noun*)	połowa (*f.*); połówka (*f.*)	jumătate (*f.*)
hinge	podlepka (*f.*)	şarnieră (*f.*)
hinged	ślad podlepki (*m.*)	cu şarnieră
Holland	Holandia	Olanda
Hong Kong	Hong Kong	Hong Kong
hundred	sto	sută
hundredth (*noun*)	jedna setna (*f.*)	sutime (*f.*)
imperforate	nieperforowany; niezząbkowany	neperforat
inch	cal (*m.*)	inci (*m.*); ţol (*m.*) (archaic)
incomplete	niekompletny	incomplet
ink	atrament (*m.*)	cerneală (*f.*)
inscription	napis (*m.*)	inscripţie (*f.*)
intaglio	intaglio (*n.*)	intaglio (*n.*)
international	międzynarodowy	internaţional
interrupted perforation	perforacja rolkowa (*f.*)	dantelură întreruptă (*f.*)
inverted	odwrócony	inversat
Ireland	Irlandia	Irlanda
irregular	nieregularny; nietypowy	neregulat
Israel	Izrael	Israel
issue (*noun*); **issuance**	emisja (*f.*); wydanie (*n.*)	emisiune (*f.*)
issue (*verb*)	wydawać (*v.*); emitować (*v.*)	emite
Italy	Włochy	Italia
January	styczeń	Ianuarie

TURKISH	GREEK	HEBREW
imza ile damgalanmış	γραμματοσημασμένο	חוֹתֶמֶת פָּטוֹר (f.)
imza ile damgalamak	γραμματοσημασμένο μέ (adj.)	בֵּיל
hakiki	γνήσιον	אֲמִתִּי
Almanya	Γερμανία	גֶּרְמַנְיָה
parlak kâğıt; kuşe kâğıt	γιαλιστερό χαρτί (n.)	נְיָר מַבְרִיק (m.)
derece	βαθμός (m.)	מַדְרֵגָה (f.)
derecelemek	βαθμολογώ	דֵּרֵג
granit kâğıdı	χαρτί σκληρό (n.)	נְיָר עִם סִיבֵּי מֶשִׁי (לְהַגֵּן מְזִיוּף)
Büyük Britanya	Μεγάλη Βρεττανία	בְּרִיטַנְיָה הַגְּדוֹלָה
Yunanistan	Ελλάς	יָוָן
zamk	γόμμα (f.)	דֶּבֶק (m.)
köprü gutterpair; köprülü çift	περιθώριο (n.)	שׁוּלַיִם (m.)
yarım	μισό	חֲצִי
yarı	μισό (n.)	חֲצִי (m.)
şarniyer	σαρνιέρα (f.)	מַדְבֵּקָה
şarniyerli	μέ σαρνιέρα	מְמוּדְבָּק
Hollanda	Ολλανδία	הוֹלַנְד
Hong Kong	Χόγνκ Κόγνκ	הוֹנְג-קוֹנְג
yüz	εκατό	מֵאָה (f.)
yüzde bir	εκατοστόν	מֵאִית (f.)
dantelsiz	χωρίς οδόντωση	לֹא מְנֻקָּב
inç	ίντσα (f.)	אִינְץ' (m.)
eksik	ατελές	בִּלְתִּי מֻשְׁלָם
mürekkep	μελάνι (n.)	דְּיוֹ (m./f.)
yazı	επιγραφή (f.)	כְּתוֹבִית
oyma metodu ile yapılmış baskı	εγχάραξη (f.)	דְּפוּס שֶׁקַע (m.)
uluslar arası	διεθνής	בֵּין-לְאֻמִּי
aralıklı delikli dantel	διακοπτομένη διάτρησις (f.)	נָקוּב דּוֹלֵג (m.)
tersine çevrilmiş	ανεστραμμένο	מְהֻפָּךְ
İrlanda	Ιρλανδία	אִירְלַנְד
gayrı muntazam	ανώμαλος	חָרִיג (m.)
İsrail	Ισραήλ	יִשְׂרָאֵל
emisyon	έκδοση (f.)	הַנְפָּקָה
tedavüle çıkarmak	εκδίδω	הַנְפֵּק
İtalya	Ιταλία	אִיטַלְיָה (f.)
Ocak	Ιανουάριος	יַנוּאָר

ENGLISH	POLISH	ROMANIAN
Japan	Japonia	Japonia
jugate	portret podwójny ("gemmowy")	acolat; alăturat; acostat
July	lipiec	Iulie
June	czerwiec	Iunie
king	król (*m.*)	rege (*m.*)
laid paper	papier prążkowany (*m.*)	hărtie vărgată (*f.*)
language	język (*m.*)	limbă (*f.*)
large	wielki; duży	mare
laureate	uwieńczony	laureat
left (direction or position)	na lewo; lewa strona (*f.*)	stănga
liberty	wolność (*f.*)	libertate (*f.*)
light (*re:* color)	jasny	deschis
line perforation	perforacja liniowa (*f.*)	dantelură în linie (*f.*)
lithography	litografia (*f.*)	litografie (*f.*)
lot (*i.e.,* auction lot)	lot (*m.*); zestaw (*m.*)	lot (*n.*)
lozenge roulette	nacinanie krzyżowe (*n.*)	străpungere în romburi (*f.*)
magnifying glass	lupa (*f.*); szkło powiększające (*n.*)	lupă (*f.*)
mail (*noun*)	poczta (*f.*)	corespondență (*f.*)
mail (*verb*)	wysyłać pocztą (*v.*)	expedia
mail bid sale	aukcja na oferty pocztowe (*f.*)	licitație prin poștă (*f.*)
mailman	listonosz (*m.*)	poștaș (*m.*); factor poștal (*m.*)
March	marzec	Martie
mark	marka (*f.*)	marcă (*f.*)
May	maj	Mai
Mexico	Meksyk	Mexico
military postage stamp	znaczek poczty wojskowej (*m.*)	marcă a poștei militare (*f.*)
millimeter; millimetre	milimetr (*m.*)	milimetru (*m.*)
million	milion	milion
minimum bid	najniższa cena (*f.*)	ofertă minimă de licitație (*f.*)
monetary system	system monetarny (*m.*)	sistem monetar (*n.*)
money	pieniądze (*m.pl.*)	bani (*m.pl.*)
month	miesiąc (*m.*)	lună (*f.*)
multicolored; multicoloured	wielokolorowy; wielobarwny	multicolor
national	narodowy	național
nationality	narodowość (*f.*)	naționalitate (*f.*)
Netherlands, The	Holandia	Olanda

TURKISH	GREEK	HEBREW
Japonya	Ιαπωνία	יָפָן
üstüste ve aynı yöne bakan	συνδεδεμένο	מְצֻמָּד
Temmuz	Ιούλιος	יוּלִי
Haziran	Ιούνιος	יוּנִי
kral	βασιλιάς (m.)	מֶלֶךְ (m.)
ince çizgili kâğıt	χαρακωμένο χαρτί	נְיָר מְצֻלָּע (m.)
dil	γλώσσα (f.)	שָׂפָה (f.)
büyük	μεγάλο	גָּדוֹל
defne yaprağı taçlı baş	δαφνοστεφής	עֲטוּר דַּפְנָה (m.)
sol	αριστερός	שְׂמֹאל
hürriyet	ελευθερία (f.)	דְּרוֹר (m.)
açık	ανοικτόχρωμο	בָּהִיר
hat dantel	ευθεία διάτρησις (f.)	נִקְבּוּב קַו (m.)
taş basması	λιθογραφία (f.)	לִיתּוֹגְרַפְיָה (f.)
lot	λαχνός (m.)	פְּרִיט (m.)
çaprazlı dantel	ρομβοειδής τροχίσκος	נִקְבּוּב בְּצוּרַת מְעֻיָּן (m.)
büyüteç	μεγενθυτικός φακός (m.)	זְכוּכִית מַגְדֶּלֶת (f.)
posta	γράμμα (n.)	דֹּאַר (m.) ; דּוֹאַר (m.)
postalamak	ταχυδρομώ	שָׁלַח בַּדֹּאַר
mektupla müzayede	πώληση μέσω ταχυδρομείου	מְכִירָה פְּנִימִית דֶּרֶךְ הַצָּעוֹת נִשְׁלָחוֹת בַּדֹּאַר
postacı	ταχυδρόμος	דַּוָּר (m.)
Mart	Μάρτιος	מַרְס
mark	μάρκο (n.)	מַרְק (m.)
Mayıs	Μάιος	מַאי
Meksika	Μεξικό	מֶקְסִיקוֹ
askeri posta pulu	στρατιωτικά γραμματόσημα	בּוּל דֹּאַר צְבָאִי (m.)
milimetre	χιλιοστό (n.)	מִילִימֶטֶר (m.)
milyon	εκατομμύριο (n.)	מִילְיוֹן (m.)
asgarî teklif	ελάχιστη προσφορά (f.)	הַצָּעַת מְחִיר מִינִימוּם (f.)
para sistemi	νομισματικό σύστημα	מַעֲרֶכֶת הַכְּסָפִים (f.)
para	χρήματα (npl)	כֶּסֶף (m.)
ay	μήνας (m.)	חֹדֶשׁ (m.)
çok renkli	πολύχρωμο	רַבְגּוֹנִי
ulusal	εθνικός	לְאֻמִּי
milliyet	εθνικότητα (f.)	לְאוֹם (m.)
Hollanda	Ολλανδία	הוֹלַנְד

ENGLISH	POLISH	ROMANIAN
never hinged	guma idealna (*f.*)	fără semn de șarnieră
new	nowy	nou
newspaper stamp	znaczek gazetowy (*m.*)	marcă poștală (*f.*)
New Zealand	Nowa Zelandia	Noua Zeelandă
nine	dziewięć	nouă
ninety	dziewięćdziesiąt	nouăzeci
Northern Ireland	Irlandia Północna	Irlanda de Nord
Norway	Norwegia	Norvegia
not issued	nie wprowadzony do obiegu	ne-emis
no unlimited bids accepted	nie przyjmuje się zleceń bez limitu	oferte nelimitate de licitație neacceptate
November	listopad	Noiembrie
number	numer (*m.*)	număr (*n.*)
obliteration	kasowanie unieważniające (*n.*)	obliterare (*f.*)
obsolete	przestarzały	învechit
October	październik	Octombrie
offer (*noun*)	oferta (*f.*)	ofertă (*f.*)
offer (*verb*)	oferować	oferi
official	oficjalny; urzędowy	oficial
official stamp	znaczek urzędowy (*m.*)	marcă poștală oficială (*f.*)
old	stary	vechi
on approval	za zgodą	spre aprobare
on cover	całostka pocztosa	pe plic
one	jeden	unu
on the back	na odwrociu; na rewersie	pe verso
order form	formularz zamówienia (*m.*)	formular de comandă (*n.*)
original	oryginalny	original
original gum	guma oryginalna (*f.*)	gumă originală (*f.*)
overprint	nadruk (*m.*)	supratipar (*n.*)
package	paczka (*f.*); pakunek (*m.*)	colet (*n.*); pachet (*n.*)
pair	para (*f.*)	pereche (*f.*)
pane	sektor (*m.*)	bloc (*n.*); fragment de coală (*n.*)
paper	papier (*m.*)	hărtie (*f.*)
parcel post	poczta paczkowa (*f.*)	mesagerie (*f.*)
parcel post stamp	znaczek poczty paczkowej (*m.*)	marcă pentru colet poștal (*f.*)
pedigree; provenance	proweniencja (*f.*); pochodzenie (*n.*)	listă de proprietari (*f.*)
peel (*verb*)	odkleić (*v.*); usunąć (*v.*)	dezlipi

TURKISH	GREEK	HEBREW
hiç şarniyerlenmemiş	χωρίς σαρνιέρα	אַף פַּעַם לֹא מְמוּדְבָּק
yeni	καινούργιο	חָדָשׁ
gazete pulu	γραμματόσημο εφημερίδας (f.)	בּוּל לְמִשְׁלוֹחַ עִתּוֹנִים (m.)
Yeni Zelanda	Νέα Ζηλανδία	נְיוּ זִילַנְד
dokuz	εννέα	תִּשְׁעָה
doksan	ενενήντα	תִּשְׁעִים
Kuzey İrlanda	Βόρεια Ιρλανδία	אִירְלַנְד הַצְּפוֹנִית
Norveç	Νορβηγία	נוֹרְבֶּגְיָה
tedavüle çıkarılmamış	μή εκδοθέντα	שֶׁלֹּא יָצָא לְהַנְפָּקָה
-----	προσφορές άνευ ορίου δέν αποδέχονται	לֹא מִתְקַבְּלוֹת הַצָּעוֹת בִּלְתִּי מֻגְבָּלוֹת
Kasım	Νοέμβριος	נוֹבֶמְבֶּר
numara	αριθμός (m.)	מִסְפָּר
iptal; oblitere	εξαλειφόμενον (n.)	חוֹתֶמֶת פְּסִילָה (f.)
modası geçmiş	απαρχαιομένο	מָחוּץ לְמַחֲזוֹר
Ekim	Οκτώβριος	אוֹקְטוֹבֶּר
teklif	προσφορά (f.)	הַצָּעָה (f.)
teklif vermek	προσφέρω	הִצִּיעַ
resmi	επίσημος	רִשְׁמִי
resmî pul	επίσημον γραμματόσημον (n.)	בּוּל שֵׁרוּת (m.)
eski	παλιός	יָשָׁן
tasvip edilmek şartıyla	υπό εγκρίσει	לְנִסָּיוֹן
zarf üzerinde	επί επιστολής	מֻדְבָּק לַמַּעֲטָפָה
bir	ένα	אֶחָד (m.adj) ; אַחַת (f.adj)
arka yüzde	όπισθεν	עַל הַגַּב
ısmarlama formu	δελτίον παραγγελιών (n.)	טוֹפֶס הַזְמָנָה (m.)
orijinal	πρωτότυπος	מְקוֹרִי
orijinal zamk	γνήσια γόμμα (f.)	דֶּבֶק מְקוֹרִי (m.)
sürşarj	επισφράγισης (f.)	הֶדְפֵּס מֵעַל (m.)
paket	δέμα (n.)	חֲבִילָה (f.)
çift	ζευγάρι (n.)	זוּג (m.)
pano	μπλοκάκι (n.)	תַּת-גִּלָּיוֹן (m.)
kağıt	χαρτί (n.)	נְיָר (m.)
paket postası	ταχυδρομείον δεμάτων (n.)	דֹּאַר חֲבִילוֹת (m.)
paket postası pulu	γραμματόσημον για δέμα (n.)	בּוּל דֹּאַר חֲבִילוֹת (m.)
şecere	προέλευσις (f.)	מוֹצָא (m.)
çıkarmak	ξεφλουδίζω	לְקַלֵּף

ENGLISH	POLISH	ROMANIAN
pen cancelled	skasowany piórem	anulat cu cerneală
People's Republic of China (P.R.C.)	Chińska Republika Ludowa	Republica Populară Chineză
percé	nacinanie (n.)	străpuns
perfect	doskonały	perfect
perforated	perforowany; ząbkowany	perforat
perforation	perforacja (f.); ząbkowanie (n.)	dantelură (f.); perforaţie (f.)
Peru	Peru	Peru
peseta	peseta (f.)	peseta (f.)
peso	peso (n.)	peso (m.)
philatelic	filatelistyczny	filatelic
philatelist	filatelista (m.)	filatelist (m.)
philately	filatelistyka (f.)	filatelie (f.)
phosphor	fosfor (m.)	fosfor (n.)
phosphorescent	fosforyzujący	fosforescent
photogravure	fotograwiura (f.)	fotogravură (f.)
pin perforation	perforacja igłowa (f.)	perforaţie cu ace (f.)
pope	papież (m.)	papă (m.)
portrait	portret (m.)	portret (n.)
Portugal	Portugalia	Portugalia
postage	opłata pocztowa (f.)	tarif poştal (n.); taxă poştală (f.)
postage due	porto (n.); opłata pocztowa (f.)	taxă de plată (f.); porto (n.)
postage due stamp	znaczek opłaty pocztowej (m.)	marcă poştală «taxa de plată» (f.)
postage stamp	znaczek (pocztowy) (m.)	marcă poştală (f.)
postal card	karta pocztowa (f.); całostka pocztowa (f.)	carte poştală (f.)
postcard	pocztówka (f.); widokówka (f.)	ilustrată (f.); vedere (f.)
postman	listonosz (m.)	poştaş (m.); factor poştal (m.)
postmark	stempel pocztowy (m.)	ştampilă poştală (f.)
post office	poczta (f.); urząd pocztowy (m.)	poştă (f.); oficiu poştal (n.)
pound Sterling (£)	funt szterling (m.)	livră (f.)
precancel (noun)	abonament kasowany (m.)	pre-ştampilă (f.)
prepayment	przedpłata (f.)	francare (f.)
president	prezydent (m.)	preşedinte (m.)
price	cena (f.)	preţ (n.)
price list	cennik (m.)	listă de preţuri (f.)
print (verb)	drukować	tipări
propaganda stamp	znaczek propagandowy (m.)	marcă poştală de propagandă (f.)

TURKISH	GREEK	HEBREW
kalemle iptal edilmiş	σφραγισμένο με πέννα	בְּטוּל בַּעֵט
Çin Halk Cumhuriyeti	Λαϊκή Δημοκρατία τής Κίνας	הָרֶפּוּבְּלִיקָה הָעַמָמִית שֶׁל סִין
pul danteli	μέ ρουλέττα	דִקוּר (m.)
kusursuz	άψογος	מְשֻׁלָם
perfore edilmiş; dantellenmiş	οδοντομένο	מְנָקָב
dantel; perforasyon	οδόντωση (f.)	נִקְבּוּב
Peru	Περού	פֶּרוּ
peseta	πεσέτα (f.)	פֶּסֶטָה (f.)
peso	πέσο (n.)	פֶּסוֹ (m.)
pullara ait	φιλοτελικός	בּוּלָאִי
filatelist; pul meraklısı	φιλοτελιστής (m.)	בּוּלָאִי (m.)
pul koleksiyonculuğu	φιλοτελισμός (m.)	בּוּלָאוּת (f.)
fosfor	φώσφορος (m.)	זַרְחָן (m.)
fosforlu	φωσφορίζων	זַרְחוֹנִי
fotogravür	φωτογραβούρα (f.)	דְפוּס שֶׁקַע
iğne delikli dantel; perse	διάτρησις διά βελόνης	נִקְבּוּב סִיכָּה (m.)
papa	πάπας (m.)	אַפִּיפְיוֹר (m.)
portre	πορτραίτο (n.)	דִּיוֹקָן (m.)
Portekiz	Πορτογαλία	פּוֹרְטוּגַל
posta ücreti	ταχυδρομικό τέλος (n.)	דְמֵי דֹּאַר
takse	ενάριθμα	חַיָב דְמֵי-דֹּאַר
takse pulu	ενάριθμον γραμματόσημον (n.)	בּוּל דְמֵי דֹּאַר (m.)
posta pulu	γραμματόσημο (n.)	בּוּל דֹּאַר (m.)
posta kartı	ταχυδρομική κάρτα (f.)	גְלוּיַת-דֹּאַר (f.)
kart postal	ταχυδρομική κάρτα (f.)	גְלוּיָה מְצוּיֶרֶת (f.)
postacı	ταχυδρόμος (m.)	דַּוָר (m.)
posta tarihi	σφραγίδα (f.)	חוֹתֶמֶת דֹּאַר (f.)
postane	ταχυδρομείο (n.)	דֹּאַר
İngiliz lirası	λίρα (f.)	לִירָה שְׁטֶרְלִינְג (f.)
önceden iptal edilmiş	προακύρωσις (n.)	בְּטוּל מֵרֹאשׁ (m.)
ön ödeme	προπληρωμή (f.)	תַשְׁלוּם מֵרֹאשׁ (m.)
başkan	πρόεδρος	נָשִׂיא (m.)
fiyat	τιμή (f.)	מְחִיר (m.)
fiyat listesi	τιμοκατάλογος (m.)	מְחִירוֹן (m.)
basmak	τυπώνω	הַדְפֵּס
propaganda pulu	προπαγανδιστικόν γραμματόσημον (n.)	בּוּל תַעֲמוּלָה (m.)

ENGLISH	POLISH	ROMANIAN
protective reserve bid	cena zabezpieczenia (*f.*)	ofertă de rezervă (pentru protecție) (*f.*)
provisional (*noun*)	wydanie prowizoryczne (*n.*)	provizoriu (*n.*)
punch cancellation	kasowanie przez dziurkowanie (*n.*)	anulare prin găurire (*f.*)
quadrillé	pokratkowany (*adj.*)	carelatură (*f.*)
queen	królowa (*f.*)	regină (*f.*)
rare	rzadki	rar
rarity	rzadkość (*f.*)	raritate (*f.*)
receipt	pokwitowanie (*n.*)	chitanță (*f.*); recipisă (*f.*)
rectangular	prostokątny	dreptunghiular
Red Cross	Czerwony Krzyż	Crucea Roșie
registration stamp	nalepka polecenia (*f.*); "erka" (*f.*)	etichetă de recomandare (*f.*)
regummed	powtórnie gumowany	regumat
remainder	resztka (*f.*); pozostałość magazynowa (*f.*)	stoc nevîndut (*n.*)
repaired	naprawiony	reparat
reprint (*noun*)	reprint (*m.*); nowodruk (*m.*)	retipărire (*f.*)
reproduction	reprodukcja (*f.*)	reproducere (*f.*)
republic	republika (*f.*)	republică (*f.*)
Republic of China (Taiwan)	Tajwan	Republica Chineză
right (direction or position)	na prawo; prawa strona (*f.*)	dreapta
roulette	nacinanie (*n.*)	străpungere (*f.*)
rouletted	nacinany	străpuns
round	okrągły	rotund
Russia	Rosja	Rusia
Saudi Arabia	Arabia Saudyjska	Arabia Saudită
scarce	rzadki	rar
Scotland	Szkocja	Scoția
secret mark	znak sekretny (*m.*); znak gwarancyjny (*m.*)	marcaj secret (*n.*)
sell (*verb*)	sprzedawać	vinde
seller	sprzedający (*m.*)	vânzător (*m.*)
separation	oddzielanie (*n.*)	separare (*f.*)
September	wrzesień	Septembrie
serpentine roulette	nacinanie serpentynowe (*n.*)	străpungere în serpentină (*f.*)
serrated roulette	nacinanie zygzakowate (*n.*)	străpungere dințată (*f.*)
se-tenant	se-tenant	se-tenant
seven	siedem	șapte
seventy	siedemdziesiąt	șaptezeci

TURKISH	GREEK	HEBREW
minimum müzayede değeri	διαφυλασσόμενη προσφορά	הַצָעָה שְׁמוּרָה מוּגֶנֶת (f.)
geçici	προσωρινόν (n.)	בּוּל זְמַנִי (m.)
delerek iptal etmek	σφραγισμένο διά οπών (n.)	בָּטוּל בְּנָקוּב (m.)
kadrilli	μέ λεπτά τετραγωνίδια	דַּף מְרוּשָׁת שֶׁל אַלְבּוֹם
kıraliçe	βασίλισσα (f.)	מַלְכָּה (f.)
nadir; ender	σπάνιο	נָדִיר
nadirlik	σπανιότητα (f.)	נְדִירוּת (f.)
makbuz	απόδειξη (f.)	קַבָּלָה (f.)
dikdörtgen şeklinde	ορθογώνιο	מַלְבֵּנִי
Kızıl Haç	Ερυθρός Σταυρός	הַצְּלָב הָאָדוֹם (m.)
taahhütlü etiketi	συστημένο γραμματόσημον (n.)	בּוּל רָשׁוּם (m.)
yeniden zamklanmış	επαναγομμαρισμένο	דֶּבֶק מְחוּדָּשׁ
stok bakiyesi	υπόλοιμα (n.)	שְׁאֵרִית מְלַאי (f.)
tamir edilmiş	επιδιορθωμένο	מְתָקָן
yeniden basma	ανατύπωση (f.)	הַדְפָּסָה נוֹסֶפֶת (f.)
kopya	αναπαραγωγή (f.)	שַׁעַתּוּק (m.)
cumhuriyet	δημοκρατία (f.)	רֶפּוּבְּלִיקָה (f.)
Çin Cumhuriyeti	Δημοκρατία τής Κίνας	הָרֶפּוּבְּלִיקָה שֶׁל סִין (f.)
sağ	δεξιός	יָמִין
pul danteli	ρουλέττα (f.)	דִּקוּר (m.)
dantellenmiş	μέ ρουλέττα	דָּקוּר
yuvarlak	στρογγυλός	עָגֹל
Rusya	Ρωσσία	רוּסְיָה
Suudi Arabistan	Σαουδική Αραβία	עֲרָב הַסְעוּדִית
az bulunur; nadir	σπάνιον	נָדִיר
İskoçya	Σκωτία	סְקוֹטְלַנָד
gizli işaret	μυστικό σημάδι (n.)	סִימָן נִסְתָּר (m.)
satmak	πουλῶ	מָכַר
satıcı	πωλητής	מוֹכֵר (m.)
ayırma	διαχωρισμός (m.)	הַפְרָדָה (f.)
Eylül	Σεπτέμβριος	סֶפְּטֶמְבֶּר
yılankavi dantel	ρουλέττα σερπεντίνα	דִּקוּר סֶרְפֶּנְטִין (m.)
testere dişli	ρουλέττα ζιγκ-ζαγκ (f.)	דִּקוּר סִכְסָךְ (m.)
birbirine bitişik farklı pullar	σετενάντ	צֶמֶד בּוּלִים שׁוֹנִים
yedi	επτά	שִׁבְעָה
yetmiş	εβδομήντα	שִׁבְעִים

ENGLISH	POLISH	ROMANIAN
shade (*re:* color)	odcién (*m.*)	nuanţă (*f.*)
sheet (of stamps)	arkusz (*m.*)	coală (*f.*)
silk thread	jedwabna nitka (*f.*)	fir de mătase (*n.*)
six	sześć	şase
sixty	sześćdziesiąt	şaizeci
skinned spot	prześwitka (*f.*)	subţiere (*f.*); loc subţiat (*n.*)
small	mały	mic
South Africa	Afryka Południowa	Africa de Sud
souvenir sheet	arkusik okolicznościowy (*m.*)	coliţă (*f.*)
Soviet Union (U.S.S.R.)	Związek Radziecki (Z.S.R.R.)	Uniunea Sovietică
Spain	Hiszpania	Spania
specimen	specimen (*m.*)	mostră (*f.*); specimen (*n.*)
square (*adjective*)	kwadratowy	pătrat
stain	plama (*f.*)	pată (*f.*)
stamp (postage)	znaczek pocztowy (*m.*)	marcă poştală (*f.*)
star	gwiazda (*f.*)	stea (*f.*)
steel engraving	staloryt (*m.*)	gravură în oţel (*f.*)
stock remainder	resztka (*f.*); pozostałość magazynowa (*f.*)	stoc nevândut (*n.*)
strip (of stamps)	pasek (znaczkowy) (*m.*)	fragment de coală (*n.*)
suggested bid	cena szacunkowa (*f.*)	ofertă sugerată (*f.*)
surcharge	przedruk (dopłaty) (*f.*)	surşarj (*n.*)
surtax	dopłata (*f.*)	suprataxă (*f.*)
Sweden	Szwecja	Suedia
Switzerland	Szwajcaria	Elveţia
symbol	symbol (*m.*)	simbol (*n.*)
syncopated perforation	perforacja rolkowa (*f.*)	dantelură întreruptă (*f.*)
tagged stamp	znaczek luminescencyjny (*m.*)	marcă poştală luminiscentă (*f.*)
tax (*noun*)	podatek (*m.*)	taxă (*f.*)
tear (*noun*)	naderwanie (*n.*)	ruptură (*f.*)
tear (*verb*)	nadrywać (*v.*)	rupe
telegraph stamp	znaczek telegraficzny (*m.*)	timbru pentru serviciul telegrafic
ten	dziesięć	zece
tenth (*noun*)	jedna dziesiąta (*f.*)	zecime (*f.*)
tête-bêche	tête-bêche	tête bêche
thin spot	prześwitka (*f.*)	subţiere (*f.*); loc subţiat (*n.*)
third (*noun*)	jedna trzecia (*f.*)	treime (*f.*)

TURKISH	GREEK	HEBREW
renk farkı	απόχρωση (f.)	גָּוֶון (m.)
tabaka	φύλλο (n.)	גִּלָּיוֹן (m.)
ipek çizgi; ipek iplik	μεταξωτή κλωστή (f.)	חוּט מֶשִׁי
altı	έξι	שִׁשָּׁה
altmış	εξήντα	שִׁשִּׁים
kağıdın incelmiş yeri	λέπτυνση (f.)	חַלּוֹן (m.)
küçük	μικρό	קָטָן
Güney Afrika	Νότιος Αφρική	דְּרוֹם אַפְרִיקָה
hatıra tabakası; anma tabakası	αναμνηστικό φύλλο (n.); φεγιέ	גִּלְיוֹנִית זִכָּרוֹן (f.)
Sovyetler Birliği	Σοβιετική Ένωση	בְּרִית הַמּוֹעֲצוֹת
İspanya	Ισπανία	סְפָרַד
örnek	δείγμα (n.)	דֻּגְמָא (f.)
kare	τετραγωνικό	רָבוּעַ
leke	στίγμα (n.)	כֶּתֶם (m.)
posta pulu	γραμματόσημο (n.)	בּוּל דֹּאַר (m.)
yıldız	άστρο (n.)	כּוֹכָב (m.)
çelik gravür	χάραξη επί χάλυβδος	פִּתּוּחַ פְּלָדָה (m.)
stok bakiyesi	υπόλοιμα (n.)	שְׁאֵרִית מְלַאי (f.)
şerit; bant	λουρίδα (f.)	שׁוּרַת בּוּלִים (f.)
önerilen fiat	εισηγούμενη προσφορά (f.)	הַצָּעָה מֻצַּעַת (f.)
sürşarj	επισήμασμα (n.)	הֶדְפֵּס עַל (שֶׁל עֵרֶךְ)
ek vergi	επιπρόσθετος φόρος (m.)	מַס יָסֵף (m.)
İsveç	Σουηδία	שְׁוֶדְיָה
İsviçre	Ελβετία	שְׁוַיץ
imge	σύμβολο (n.)	סֶמֶל (m.)
aralıklı delikli dantel	συγκοπτομένη διάτρησις (f.)	נִקְבּוּב דּוֹלֵג (m.)
elektronik uyarıcılı pul	γραμματόσημο με προσαρτημένη ετικέττα	בּוּל מְסֻמָּן (m.)
vergi	φόρος (m.)	מַס (m.)
yırtık	σχίσιμο	קֶרַע (m.)
yırtmak	σχίζω	קָרַע
telegraf pulu	τηλεγραφικόν γραμματόσημον (n.)	בּוּל מִבְרָק (m.)
on	δέκα	עֲשָׂרָה
onda bir	δέκατον	עֲשִׂירִית
tet beş	ανεστραμμένη εκτύπωση	צֶמֶד הָפוּכִים
kağıdın incelmiş yeri	λέπτυνση (f.)	חַלּוֹן (m.)
üçte	τρίτον (n.)	שְׁלִישׁ (m.)

ENGLISH	POLISH	ROMANIAN
thirty	trzydzieści	treizeci
thousand	tysiąc	mie
three	trzy	trei
tongs	pinceta (*f.*); pęseta (*f.*)	pensetă (*f.*)
top	góra (*f.*)	parte superioară (*f.*); sus; deasupra
topical; thematic	tematyczny	tematică
torn	naderwany	rupt
trade (*verb*)	handlować (*v.*)	face comerț
twenty	dwadzieścia	douăzeci
two	dwa	doi
typography	typografia (*f.*)	tipografie (*f.*)
unattributed	nieokreślony	neatribuit; nedeterminat
undeliverable	niedoręczalny	nelivrabil
ungummed	niegumowany; bez kleju	fără gumă; negumat
unhinged	bez podlepki	fără șarnieră
unique	unikatowy	unic
United Kingdom (U.K.)	Zjednoczone Królestwo	Regatul Unit
United States of America (U.S.A.)	Stany Zjednoczone Ameryki Północnej	Statele Unite al Americii
unknown	nieznany	necunoscut
unofficial	nieoficjalny; nieurzędowy	neoficial
unpublished	niepublikowany	nepublicat
unsevered	nieoddzielony	neseparat
unused	nieużywany	neuzat; nefolosit
used	używany	folosit; uzat
valuable	wartościowy	valoros
value	wartość (*f.*)	valoare (*f.*)
variety	odmiana (*f.*); wariant (*m.*)	varietate (*f.*)
Venezuela	Wenezuela	Venezuela
Wales	Walia	Țara Galilor
watermark	znak wodny (*m.*)	filigran (*n.*)
West Germany (B.R.D.)	Niemcy Zachodnie	Germania de Vest
wove paper	papier gładki (*m.*)	hârtie velină (*f.*)
year	rok (*m.*)	an (*m.*)
Yugoslavia; Jugoslavia	Jugosławia	Iugoslavia
zero	zero	zero
zigzag roulette	nacinanie zygzakowate (*n.*)	străpungere în zig-zag (*f.*)

TURKISH	GREEK	HEBREW
otuz	τριάντα	שְׁלֹשִׁים
bin	χίλια (n.pl.)	אֶלֶף (m.)
üç	τρία	שְׁלֹשָׁה
pul maşası	τσιμπίδα (f.)	מַלְקֵט (m.)
üst	κορυφή (f.)	רֹאשׁ (m.)
konulu	ταυτόσημα	בּוּלָאוֹת שֶׁל נוֹשֵׂא מְסוּיָם
yırtık	σχισμένο	קָרוּעַ
değiş tokuş etmek	εμπόριο	סָחַר
yirmi	είκοσι	עֶשְׂרִים
iki	δύο	שְׁנַיִם
matbaacılık	τυπογραφία (f.)	טִפּוֹגְרַפְיָה (f.)
tam tanımlanmamış	μή αποδιδόμενο	בִּלְתִּי מְזוֹהֶה
teslimi imkansız	απαράδοτο	בִּלְתִּי נִתָּן לִמְסִירָה
zamksız	χωρίς γόμμα	לְלֹא דֶּבֶק
şarnıyersiz	χωρίς σαρνιέρα	בְּלִי מַדְבֵּקָה
emsalsiz	μαναδικός	יָחִיד בְּמִינוֹ
Birleşik Kırallık	Ηνωμένον Βασίλειον	מַמְלָכָה הַמְאֻחֶדֶת
Amerika Birleşik Devletleri	Ηνωμένες Πολιτείες τής Αμερικής	אַרְצוֹת הַבְּרִית
bilinmeyen	άγνωστος	בִּלְתִּי יָדוּעַ
gayrı resmi; resmi olmayan	ανεπίσημον	לֹא-רִשְׁמִי
yayınlanmamış	μή εκδοθέν	שֶׁלֹּא פּוּרְסָם
birbirinden ayrılmamış; blok	αδιαχώριστον	לֹא מְנוּתָּק
kullanılmanış	αχρησιμοποίητο	לֹא מְשׁוּמָּשׁ
kullanılmış	μεταχειρισμένο	מְשֻׁמָּשׁ
değerli	πολύτιμος	בַּעַל-עֵרֶךְ
değer	αξία (f.)	עֵרֶךְ (m.)
tür; çeşit	ποικιλία (f.)	תַּשְׁנִית (m.)
Venezüela	Βενεζουέλα	וֶנֱצוּאֵלָה
Galler	Ουαλία	וֵילְס
filigran	υδατόσημο (n.)	סִימָן מֵימִי (m.)
Batı Almanya	Δυτική Γερμανία	גֶּרְמַנְיָה הַמַּעֲרָבִית
birinci kalite kağıt	πλεκτόν (n.)	נְיָר אָחִיד (m.)
yıl	έτος (n.); χρόνος (m.)	שָׁנָה (f.)
Yugoslavya	Γιουγκοσλαβία	יוּגוֹסְלַבְיָה
sıfır	μηδέν (n.)	אֶפֶס
zik-zak dantel; yılankavi dantel	ρουλέττα ζιγκ-ζαγκ (f.)	דִּקוּר סְכָסָךְ (m.)

ENGLISH	POLISH	ROMANIAN
amber	bursztynowy	chihlimbar
azure	lazurowy	azur
bister	orzechowobrązowy	bistru; brun-gălbui
black	czarny	negru
blue	niebieski	albastru
bronze	koloru brązu	bronz
brown	brązowy	brun
carmine	karminowy	carmin
cerise	wiśniowy	roşu-deschis; roşu-cireaşă
cobalt	kobaltowy	albastru-cobalt
crimson	karmazynowy	stacojiu
emerald	szmaragdowy	verde-smarald
gray	szary	gri
green	zielony	verde
heliotrope	heliotropowy	vaniliu
indigo	indygo	indigo
lavender	lawendowy	mov-lavandă
lemon	cytrynowy	galben-lămâie
lilac	liliowy; lila	lila
magenta	magenta	roşu-lila; vişiniu-putred
maroon	kasztanowy	castaniu; maro
olive	oliwkowy	oliv
orange	pomarańczowy	oranj; portocaliu
pink	różowy	roz
Prussian blue	błękit pruski	albastru închis
purple	purpurowy	purpuriu
red	czerwony	roşu
royal blue	błękit królewski	albastru roşiatic
sapphire	szafirowy	albastru-safir
scarlet	szkarłatny	stacojiu
turquoise	turkusowy	turcoaz
ultramarine	ultramaryna	ultramarin
vermilion	cynobrowy	cinabru
violet	fioletowy	violet
white	biały	alb
yellow	żółty	galben

TURKISH	GREEK	HEBREW
kehribar rengi	κεχριμπαρένιο	עִנְבָּר
gök mavisi	κυανόν	תְּכֵלֶת
koyu kahverengi	μπρίστ	חוּם כֵּהֶה
siyah; kara	μαύρο	שָׁחוֹר
mavi	μπλέ	כָּחֹל
bronz	μπρούνζινο	צֶבַע אָרָד
kahverengi	καφέ	חוּם
kızıl	καρμινόχρωμο	כַּרְמִין
kiraz rengi	κερασί	דֻּבְדְּבָנִי
çini mavi	μπλέ	קוֹבַּלְט
koyu kırmızı	βυσσινί	דָּמִי
zümrüt yeşili	σμαραγδένιο	כְּצֶבַע בָּרֶקֶת
gri	γκρί; φαιό	אָפֹר
yeşil	πράσινο	יָרֹק
açık mor	κιτρινωπό	אַרְגָּמָן
çivit rengi	λουλάκι	אִינְדִיגוֹ
eflatun	λεβάντα	אַרְגָּמָן-כְּחַלְחַל
limon rengi	λεμονί	צֶבַע הַלִּימוֹן
leylak moru	λιλά	לִילָךְ
macenta	κοκκινόχρους	אָדֹם-אַרְגָּמָן ; מָגֶנְטָה
bordo; vişne çürüğü	ερυθροκάστανο	עַרְמוֹנִי-כֵּהֶה
zeytin yeşili	ελαιόχρουν	זַיִת
turuncu	πορτοκαλί	כָּתֹם
pembe	ρόδινο	וָרֹד
prusya mavisi	Πρώσσικο κυανούν	כָּחֹל פְּרוּסִי
mor	πορφυρούν	אַרְגָּמָן
kırmızı	κόκκινο	אָדֹם
İngiliz mavisi	μπλέ	כָּחֹל מַלְכוּתִי
safir	σαπφειρούν	תְּכֵלֶת סַפִּיר
al	κόκκινον	שָׁנִי
turkuvaz	πράσινο-μπλέ	טוּרְקִין
lacivert	κυανό	כָּחוֹל עַז
parlak kırmızı	ζωηρό κόκκινο	וֶרְמִילְיוֹן
menekşe moru	βιολέ	סָגֹל
beyaz	άσπρο	לָבָן
sarı	κίτρινο	צָהֹב

ENGLISH	RUSSIAN	SERBIAN
abbreviation	сокращение (*n.*)	скраћеница (*f.*)
accolated	соединённый; наложенный	спојен; састављен
account (financial or transactional)	счёт (*m.*)	рачун (*m.*); фактура (*f.*)
acquisition	приобретение (*n.*)	набавка (*f.*)
aérogramme; air letter	аэрограмма (*f.*)	радиограм (*m.*); брзојав (*m.*)
aerophilately	аэрофилателия (*f.*)	марке за авионску пошту
airmail	авиапочта (*f.*)	ваздушна пошта (*f.*)
air stamp; airmail stamp	марка авиапочты (*f.*)	авионска поштанска марке
album	альбом (*m.*)	албум (*m.*)
almost	почти	скоро све
alter (*verb*)	видоизменять	променити
alteration	подделка (*f.*)	промена (*f.*)
amount	сумма (*f.*)	износ (*m.*); свота (*f.*)
aniline	анилин (*m.*)	анилин (*m.*)
anomaly	аномалия (*f.*)	аномалија (*f.*)
April	апрель	април
Argentina	Аргентина	Аргентина
art	искусство (*n.*)	уметност (*f.*)
attribute (*verb*)	определять	назначити порекло
attribution	атрибуция (*f.*)	назнака
auction	аукцион (*m.*)	лицитација (*f.*)
auction catalogue	каталог аукциона (*m.*)	каталог лицитације
auction sale	аукционная продажа (*f.*)	лицитација (*f.*)
August	август	август
Australia	Австралия	Аустралија
Austria	Австрия	Аустрија
authentic	подлинный	аутентичан
authentication mark	клеймо (*n.*)	заштитни знак (*m.*); печат произвођача
barred	полосчатый	поништење косим пругама
Belgium	Бельгия	Белгија
bicolored; bicoloured	двухцветный	двобојан
bid (*noun*: auction bid)	предложение цены (*n.*)	понуда (*f.*)
bid (*verb*)	предлагать цену	понудити цену на лицитацији
bid sheet	заявка на торгах (*f.*)	пријава за учестврвање на лицитацији
bilingual	двуязычный	двојезичан
bisected	марка, разрезанная пополам	пресечен

KOREAN	JAPANESE	CHINESE [c.c.]	CHINESE [s.c.]
약자	省略	縮寫	缩写
이중타의	結合	重童的	重童的
구좌	口座	帳目	帐目
취득	取得	獲得	获得
항공서간	航空書簡;エアログラム	航空郵簡	航空邮简
항공우취	航空切手収集	航空集郵	航空集邮
항공우편	航空便	航空信	航空信
항공우표	航空切手	航空郵票	航空邮票
앨범	アルバム	相簿	相簿
거의	ほとんど	幾乎	几乎
개조하다	改変する	更改	更改
개조	改変	改造	改造
금액	金額	金額	金额
아닐린	アニリン	苯胺	苯胺
변종	変則	異常	异常
사월	四月	四月	四月
아르헨티나	アルゼンチン	阿根廷	阿根廷
예술	美術	藝術	艺术
출처를 밝히다	分類する	鑑定	鉴定
발행출처	分類	鑑定	鉴定
경매	競売	拍賣	拍卖
경매목록	競売目録	拍賣目錄	拍卖目录
경쟁입찰판매	競売	拍賣	拍卖
팔월	八月	八月	八月
호주	オーストラリア	澳洲	澳大利亚
오스트리아	オーストリア	奧國	奥地利
진짜의	本物の	真貨	真货
인증표지	認証印	可信戳	可信戳
-----	横木の加刷	打上條紋的	打上条纹的
벨기에	ベルギー	比利時	比利时
이색의	二色の	兩色的	两色的
입찰	入札	出價	出价
입찰하다	入札する	投標	投标
입찰용지	入札用紙	標價單	标价单
이개국어 병용의	二ケ国語併用（の）	雙語的	双语的
이등분한	バイセクトの	對角郵票	对角邮票

ENGLISH	RUSSIAN	SERBIAN
block	блок (*m.*)	блок марака
block of four	квартблок (*m.*)	блок са четири марке
booklet (of stamps)	книжка марок (*f.*)	брошура (*f.*)
bottom	низ (*m.*)	најнижи
Brazil	Бразилия	Бразилија
burélage; burelé	предохранительная сеть (*f.*)	мрежица (*f.*)
buy (*verb*)	покупать	купити; куповати
buyer	покупатель (*m.*)	купац (*m.*)
cachet	декоративный узор (*m.*)	жиг ваљаности
Canada	Канада	Канада
cancel (*verb*)	погашать	отказати
cancellation; cancelation	гашение (*n.*)	поништење марке
cancelled to order	гашеная (без прохождения почты)	преоптицајно поништење (*n.*)
cash (ready money)	наличные деньги (*pl.*)	готовина (*f.*)
cash on delivery (C.O.D.)	наложенный платёж	послати поузећем (*n.*)
catalog; catalogue	каталог (*m.*)	каталог (*m.*); списак (*m.*)
catalogue value	цена по каталогу (*f.*)	вредност означена у каталогу
censored mail	почта, прошедшая цензуру (*f.*)	цензурисана пошиљка (*f.*)
centennial; centenary	столетие (*n.*)	стогодишњица (*f.*)
centered	отцентрированное изображение (*n.*)	дизајн у средишту марке
centering	центровка (*f.*)	центрирање (*n.*)
centimeter; centimetre	сантиметр (*m.*)	сентиметар (*m.*)
chalky paper	меловая бумага (*f.*)	кредаст папир (*m.*)
charity stamp	благотворительная марка (*f.*)	марка у добротворне сврхе
check; cheque	чек (*m.*)	чек (*m.*)
China	Китай	Кина
classification	классификация (*f.*)	класификација (*f.*)
classify (*verb*)	классифицировать	класифицирати; разврстати
coil	рулон (*m.*)	рола (*f.*)
collect (*verb*)	коллекционировать	скупљати
collection	коллекция (*f.*)	збирка (*f.*); колекција (*f.*)
collector	коллекционер (*m.*)	колекционар (*m.*)
Colombia	Колумбия	Коломбија
color; colour	цвет (*m.*)	боја (*f.*); фарба (*f.*)
comb perforation	гребенчатая перфорация (*f.*)	чешљаста перфорација (*f.*)
commemorative (*adjective*)	памятный	комеморативан

KOREAN	JAPANESE	CHINESE [c.c.]	CHINESE [s.c.]
전 형	ブロック	連票	连票
사매군	四枚のブロック	四方運	四方连
우표첩	切手帳	小本郵票	小本邮票
밑바닥	下	下面	下面
브라질	ブラジル	巴西	巴西
-----	-----	暗紋	暗纹
사다	買う	買	买
구매자	買い手	買主	买主
까세	カシエ	裝飾圖案	裝饰图案
캐나다	カナダ	加拿大	加拿大
소인을 찍다	澗する;キャンセルする	消印	消印
소인	消印	消印	消印
주문소인	注文取り消しの	蓋銷的	盖销的
현금	現金	現金	现金
대금상환인도	料金受取人払い	貨到收現	货到收现
목록	カタログ	目錄	目录
목록가격	カタログ価格	目錄價格	目录价格
검열필 우편	検閲済み郵便物;監察済み郵便物	檢查信	检查信
백년제	百年祭	百年的	百年的
중심이 맞은	中心の	正中央的	正中央的
인면위치	センターリング	正中	正中
센티미터	センチメートル	公分	公分
백악지	-----	白垩紙	白垩纸
자선우표	慈善切手	慈善郵票	慈善邮票
수표	小切手	支票	支票
중국	中国	中國	中国
분류	種別	類別	类别
분류하다	分離する	分類	分类
코일우표	ロール切手	一筒郵票	一筒邮票
수집하다	集める	收集	收集
수집품	収集	收集物	收集物
수집가	収集家	收集者	收集者
콜롬비아	コロンビア	哥倫比亞	哥伦比亚
색	色	顏色	颜色
빗형 천공	櫛型目打	梳齒牙孔	梳齿牙孔
기념의	記念の	紀念郵票的	纪念邮票的

ENGLISH	RUSSIAN	SERBIAN
common	обыкновенный	обичан; чест
complete	полный	потпун
conjoined	соединённый; наложенный	спојен; састављен
copy (*noun*)	копия (*f.*)	копија (*f.*); отисак (*m.*)
copy (*verb*)	копировать	копирати; пресликати
cover	конверт	коверта (*f.*)
— on cover	на конверте	на коверти
crease (*noun*)	складка (*f.*)	прегиб (*m.*)
crease (*verb*)	складывать	пресавити; набрати; направити прелом
credit	кредит (*m.*)	кредит (*m.*)
credit card	кредитная карточка (*f.*)	кредитна карта (*f.*)
credit cards accepted	кредитные карточки принимаются	кредитне карте важе
crown (royal headpiece)	корона (*f.*)	круна (*f.*)
cruzeiro	крузейро (*n.*)	крузеро (*m.*)
cut cancellation	гашение надрезом (*n.*)	поништење рупицама нлн урезом
cut square	вырезка (*f.*)	квадратни исечак (*m.*)
damaged	повреждённый	оштећен
dark (*re*: color)	тёмный	мрачан; таман
date	дата (*f.*)	датум (*m.*)
December	декабрь	децембар
deep (*re*: color)	тёмный (о цвете)	интезитет боје
defect (*noun*)	дефект (*m.*)	оштећеност (*f.*); неисправност (*f.*)
defective	дефектный	дефектан; неисправан; оштећен
definitive (*adjective*)	стандартный	стални дизајн
demonetization	демонетизация (*f.*)	одузимање вредности новчићу
Denmark	Дания	Данска
denomination	номинал (*m.*)	новчана јединица (*f.*)
deposit (of funds)	задаток (*m.*)	кауција (*f.*)
deposit required	требуется задаток (*m.*)	кауција обавезна
design (*noun*)	рисунок (*m.*)	дизајн (*m.*); нацрт (*m.*)
devaluation	девальвация (*f.*)	девалвација (*f.*)
dollar	доллар (*m.*)	долар (*m.*)
domestic	отечественный	домаћи
duplicate (*adjective*)	дубликатный	умножен; прекопиран
duplicate (*noun*)	дубликат (*m.*)	дупликат (*m.*)
duplicate (*verb*)	дублировать	умножити; копирати

KOREAN	JAPANESE	CHINESE [c.c.]	CHINESE [s.c.]
흔한	一般的	普遍	普遍
완전한	完全	完整	完整
이중타의	結合	重叠的	重叠的
사본	複製	複本	复本
복사하다	複製する；コピーする	複制	复制
봉피	カバー；エンター	封袋	封袋
봉무에	封筒に貼られた	未從信件上分離的郵票	未从信件上分离的邮票
구김살	折り目	折痕	折痕
구기다	折り目をつける	打折	打折
신용	融資	信用	信用
신용카드	クレジットカード	信用卡	信用卡
신용카드 사용가능	クレジットカードを受付ける	接受信用卡支付	接受信用卡支付
왕관	王冠	皇冠	皇冠
크루제이로	クルゼイロ	巴西幣	壶司
절단소인	切り込みに依るキャンセル	割銷	割销
-----	方形に切り取ったもの(切手)	從郵簡上裁下的郵票	从邮简上裁下的邮票
손상된	傷んだ	受損的	受损的
짙은	濃い	深色	深色
날짜	日付	日期	日期
십이월	十二月	十二月	十二月
짙은	濃い	深色的	深色的
흠	欠点	缺陷	缺陷
흠이있는	欠点のある	有缺陷的	有缺陷的
보통의	普通切手の	定期出版郵圖樣的	定期出版邮图样的
통화정지	廃貨	使貨幣廢止通用	使货币废止通用
덴마크	デンマーク	丹麥	丹麦
액면단위	単位	面額	面额
예치금	頭金	定金	定金
보증금 필요	頭金を要する	要求付押金	要求付押金
도안	デザイン	圖樣	图样
평가절하	平価切り下げ	貶值	贬值
달러	ドル	元	元
국내의	国内	國內的	国内的
복사한	二重の	復制的	复制的
복사품	二重にする	復制品	复制品
복사하다	複製する	復制	复制

ENGLISH	RUSSIAN	SERBIAN
eagle	орёл (*m.*)	орао (*m.*)
East Germany (D.D.R.)	Восточная Германия	Источна Немачка
effigy	портрет (*m.*)	слика (*f.*); лик (*m.*)
eight	восемь	осам
eighty	восемьдесят	осамдесет
embossing	тиснение (*n.*)	отисак испупчењима (*n.pl.*)
emperor	император (*m.*)	цар (*m.*); император (*m.*)
encased postage stamp	зачёхленная марка (*f.*)	уоквирена поштанска марка
England	Англия	Енглеска
engraved	гравированный	угравиран
envelope	конверт (*m.*)	коверат (*m.*)
error	ошибка (*f.*)	грешка (*f.*); омашка (*f.*); погрешка (*f.*)
essay	проба (*f.*)	мустра (*f.*)
exhibit (*verb*)	выставлять	изложити; прказивати
exhibition	выставка (*f.*)	изложба (*f.*)
face value	нарицательная стоимость	номинална вредност (*f.*)
February	февраль	фебруар
field post	полевая почта (*f.*)	војна пошта
fifth (*noun*)	пятая часть (*f.*)	петина (*f.*)
fifty	пятьдесят	педесет
Finland	Финляндия	Финска
first day cover	конверт первого дня (*m.*)	коверат првог дана огтичаја
fiscal stamp	гербовая марка (*f.*)	таксена марка
five	пять	пет
fold (*noun*)	складка (*f.*)	прегиб (*m.*); савитак са бридом (*m.*)
fold (*verb*)	складывать	пресавити; набрати
foreign	иностранный	страни; инострани; туђи
foreign currency	иностранная валюта (*f.*)	страни новац (*m.*); девиза (*f.*)
forty	сорок	четрдесет
four	четыре	четири
fourth (*noun*)	четверть (*f.*)	четвртина (*f.*)
fraction	часть (*f.*)	одломак (*m.*); парче (*n.*)
frame	рамка	оквир (*m.*)
franc	франк (*m.*)	франк (*m.*)
France	Франция	Француска
franchise stamp	льготная марка (*f.*)	бесплатна марка

KOREAN	JAPANESE	CHINESE [c.c.]	CHINESE [s.c.]
독수리	鷲	鷹	鷹
동독	東ドイツ	東德	东德
초상	肖像	肖像	肖像
팔	八	八	八
팔십	八十	八十	八十
볼록형 압인인쇄	浮出し	壓紋	压纹
황제	皇帝	皇帝	皇帝
-----	切手コイン	内嵌郵票	内嵌邮票
잉글랜드	英国；イングランド	英格蘭	英格兰
조판의	凹版の	嵌版印刷的	嵌版印刷的
봉투	封筒	信封	信封
에러	間違い；エラー	錯誤	错误
채택되지않은 도안	試作	廢棄的新郵設計	废弃的新邮设计
전시하다	出品する	展出	展出
전시회	展示；博覧会	展覽	展览
액면	額面価格	面額	面额
이월	二月	二月	二月
야외 우체국	野戦郵便局	戰地郵局	战地邮局
오분의 일	五分の一	五分之一	五分之一
오십	五十	五十	五十
핀란드	フィンランド	芬蘭	芬兰
초일봉피	初日印付カバー	首日封	首日封
수입인지	収入印紙	稅收票	税收票
오	五	五	五
접은자국	折り目	折痕	折痕
접다	折る	折疊	折叠
외국의	外国の	外國的	外国的
외화	外国通貨	外幣	外币
사십	四十	四十	四十
사	四	四	四
사분의 일	四分の一	四分之一	四分之一
분수	断片	零頭	零头
블	枠	框	框
프랑	フランク	法郎	法郎
프랑스	フランス	法國	法国
무표송달우표	一手販売の切手	特許郵票	特许邮票

ENGLISH	RUSSIAN	SERBIAN
frank (*noun*)	франкировка (*f.*)	пошиљка ослобођена поштарине
frank (*verb*)	франкировать	франкирати
genuine	подлинный	прави; оригиналан; изворни
Germany	Германия	Немачка
glossy paper	глянцевая бумага (*f.*)	сјајан улаштен папир
grade (*noun*)	состояние (*n.*)	степен вредности (*m.*); оцена (*f.*)
grade (*verb*)	сортировать	оценити вредност; дати мишљење
granite paper	мраморная бумага (*f.*)	папир са утканим свиленим концем
Great Britain	Великобритания	Велика Британтја
Greece	Греция	Грчка
gum	гуммировка (*f.*)	лепило (*n.*)
gutter	полоска (*f.*)	ивичњак (*m.*)
half (*adjective*)	половинный	половичан
half (*noun*)	половина (*f.*)	половица (*f.*)
hinge	наклейка (*f.*)	петља (*f.*); врпца (*f.*)
hinged	с наклейкой	окачен
Holland	Нидерланды; Голландия	Холандија
Hong Kong	Гонконг	Хонг Конг
hundred	сто	сто
hundredth (*noun*)	сотая часть (*f.*)	стоти
imperforate	беззубцовая	неперфориран
inch	дюйм (*m.*)	инч (*m.*)
incomplete	неполный	непотпун
ink	чернила (*n.pl.*)	мастило (*n.*)
inscription	девиз (*m.*)	запис (*m.*)
intaglio	глубокая печать (*f.*)	интаглио (*m.*)
international	интернациональный	међународни
interrupted perforation	прерывистая перфорация (*f.*)	непотпуна перфорација (*f.*)
inverted	перевернутая марка	обратно окренут
Ireland	Ирландия	Ирска
irregular	необычный	нередован; неисправан
Israel	Израиль	Израел
issue (*noun*); **issuance**	выпуск (*m.*)	изливање (*n.*); издање (*n.*)
issue (*verb*)	выпускать	издати; издавати
Italy	Италия	Италија
January	январь	јануар

KOREAN	JAPANESE	CHINESE [c.c.]	CHINESE [s.c.]
무료송달서명	無料送達署名	無票信封	无票信封
무료송달서명하다	無料送達署名をする	免費遞送	免费递送
진짜의	本物の	真品	真品
독일	ドイツ	德國	德国
광택지	光沢紙	大光紙	大光纸
등급	状態	等級	等级
등급을 매기다	格付けする	評審	评审
화강암지	毛紙	花崗紙	花岗纸
영국	イギリス；英国	大英帝國	大英帝国
그리이스	ギリシャ	希臘	希腊
고무풀	のり	背膠	背胶
것터	ガッター	對連票	对连票
절반의	半	一半的	一半的
반	半分	一半	一半
힌지	ヒンジ	貼郵票透明紙	贴邮票透明纸
힌지자국이 있는	ヒンジ付	貼過郵票透明紙的	贴过邮票透明纸的
네덜란드	オランダ	荷蘭	荷兰
홍콩	香港	香港	香港
백	百	百	百
백분의 일	百分の一	百分之一	百分之一
무공의	目打ちなしの	無齒孔的	无齿孔的
인치	インチ	吋	吋
불완전한	不完全	不完整	不完整
잉크	インク	墨水	墨水
명각	銘	銘刻	铭刻
요판	凹版印刷	凹版印刷	凹版印刷
국제적인	国際	國際的	国际的
불연속 천공	中断された目打	不連續穿孔	不连续穿孔
거꾸로된	さかさまの；逆にした	顛倒的	颠倒的
아일랜드	アイルランド	愛爾蘭	爱尔兰
불규칙한	不規則な	不規則的	不规则的
이스라엘	イスラエル	以色列	以色列
발행	発行	出版物	出版物
발행하다	発行する	發行	发行
이탈리아	イタリア	意大利	意大利
일월	一月	一月	一月

ENGLISH	RUSSIAN	SERBIAN
Japan	Япония	Јапан
jugate	соединённый; наложенный	спојен; састављен
July	июль	јули
June	июнь	јуни
king	король (*m.*)	краљ (*m.*); владар (*m.*)
laid paper	бумага верже (*f.*)	папир са утканим линијама
language	язык (*m.*)	језик (*m.*)
large	большой	велики; крупан
laureate	увенчанный	овенчан; лауреат
left (direction or position)	левый	лево (*n.*)
liberty	свобода (*f.*)	слобода (*f.*)
light (*re*: color)	светлый	светао
line perforation	линейная перфорация (*f.*)	перфорација хоризонталама и вертикалама
lithography	литография (*f.*)	литографија (*f.*)
lot (*i.e.*, auction lot)	партия (*f.*)	ставка (*f.*); партија (*f.*)
lozenge roulette	ромбовидная пробивка (*f.*)	«Х» прорез (*m.*)
magnifying glass	лупа (*f.*)	лупа (*f.*)
mail (*noun*)	почта (*f.*)	пошта (*f.*)
mail (*verb*)	отправлять почтой	послати поштом
mail bid sale	распродажа по почте (*f.*)	лицитација путем поште
mailman	почтальон (*m.*)	поштар (*m.*)
March	март	март
mark	немецкая марка (*f.*)	марка (*f.*)
May	май	мај
Mexico	Мексика	Мексико
military postage stamp	марка полевой почты (*f.*)	војна марка
millimeter; millimetre	миллиметр (*m.*)	милиметар (*m.*)
million	миллион (*m.*)	милион
minimum bid	минимальное предложение цены (*n.*)	најнижа понуда
monetary system	денежная система (*f.*)	новчани систем
money	деньги (*pl*)	новац (*m.*); паре (*f.pl.*)
month	месяц (*m.*)	месец (*m.*)
multicolored; multicoloured	многоцветный	многобојан
national	национальный	национални
nationality	национальная принадлежность (*f.*)	националност
Netherlands, The	Нидерланды; Голландия	Холандија

KOREAN	JAPANESE	CHINESE [c.c.]	CHINESE [s.c.]
일본	日本	日本	日本
이중타의	-----	重疊的	重疊的
칠월	七月	七月	七月
육월	六月	六月	六月
왕	王	國王	国王
발살무늬 종이	国産木綿紙	直紋的	直纹的
언어	言語	語言	语言
큰	大きい	大	大
월계관을 쓴	月桂冠を戴いた	榮譽的	荣誉的
왼쪽	左	左	左
자유	自由	自由	自由
엷은	薄い	淡色	浅色
선공	単線目打	線形穿孔	线形穿孔
평판	リトグラフ	石版印刷術	石版印刷术
품목	ロット	堆	堆
X 자형 선공	菱形ルーレット	菱形齒孔	菱形齿孔
확대경	虫めがね	放大鏡	放大镜
우편	郵便	郵件	邮件
우송하다	郵送する；出す	郵寄	邮寄
우편경매판매	郵便入札競売	郵政投標拍賣	邮政投标拍卖
우체부	郵便配達人	郵差	邮差
삼월	三月	三月	三月
마르크	マルク	馬克	马克
오월	五月	五月	五月
멕시코	メキシコ	墨西哥	墨西哥
군용우표	征軍徽章	軍郵票	军邮票
밀리미터	ミリメートル	公釐	公厘
백만	百万	百萬	百万
최소 입찰가	最低入札値	最低標價	最低标价
통화제도	貨幣制度	貨幣制度	货币制度
돈	金	錢	钱
월	月	月	月
다색의	多色の	多色的	多色的
전국적인	国家的	國有的	国有的
국적	国籍	國籍	国籍
네덜란드	オランダ	荷蘭	荷兰

ENGLISH	RUSSIAN	SERBIAN
never hinged	без наклейки (*f.*)	нелепљена марка
new	новый	нови
newspaper stamp	газетная марка (*f.*)	марка за слање новина
New Zealand	Новая Зеландия	Нови Зеланд
nine	девять	девет
ninety	девяносто	деведесет
Northern Ireland	Северная Ирландия	Северна Ирска
Norway	Норвегия	Норвешка
not issued	неизданный	неиздат; ван оптицаја
no unlimited bids accepted	предложения цен ограниченны	ограничене понуде
November	ноябрь	новембар
number	номер (*m.*)	број (*m.*)
obliteration	замазывание (*n.*)	жигосање (*n.*)
obsolete	устаревший	застарео
October	октябрь	октобар
offer (*noun*)	предложение (*n.*)	понуда (*f.*)
offer (*verb*)	предлагать	понудити
official	официальный	службени; званичан
official stamp	марка правительственной почты (*f.*)	службена марка
old	старый	старн; давни
on approval	на оценку	на увид
on cover	на конверте	на коверти
one	один	један
on the back	на обороте	на полеђини
order form	бланк (*m.*)	наруџбеница (*f.*); фактура (*f.*)
original	оригинал	оригиналан
original gum	первый слой клея	оригинално лепило (*n.*)
overprint	надпечатка (*f.*)	штампање поврх текста
package	пакет (*m.*)	пакет (*m.*)
pair	пара (*f.*)	пар (*m.*)
pane	лист (*m.*)	плоча (*f.*)
paper	бумага (*f.*)	хартија (*f.*); папир (*m.*)
parcel post	почтовая служба (*f.*)	пакет (*m.*); пошиљка (*f.*)
parcel post stamp	почтовые марка (*f.*)	марка на пошиљци или пакету
pedigree; provenance	происхождение (*n.*)	порекло (*n.*)
peel (*verb*)	отклеивать	скинути; одлепити

KOREAN	JAPANESE	CHINESE [c.c.]	CHINESE [s.c.]
힌지자국이 없는	ヒンジのない	未貼郵票透明紙的	未貼郵票透明紙的
새로운	新しい	新的	新的
신문우표	新聞切手	報紙票	报纸票
뉴질랜드	ニュージーランド	紐西蘭	纽西兰
구	九	九	九
구십	九十	九十	九十
북아일랜드	北アイルランド	北愛爾蘭	北爱尔兰
노르웨이	ノルウェイ	挪威	挪威
미발행의	不発行	未公開發行的	未公开发行的
무제한 입찰 불가	糊なしの入札は受付けられぬ	要求自行投標	要求自行投标
십일월	十一月	十一	十一月
번호	番号	數目	数目
소인	抹殺	消値	消値
사용되지 않는	昔の	陳舊的	陈旧的
십월	十月	十月	十月
매매제의	提出	出價	出价
팔려고 내놓다	提出する	出價	出价
공식의	公務；公式の	官方的	官方的
공용우표	公用切手	公務郵票	公务邮票
오래된	古い	古老的	古老的
현물점검후 지급조건	点検売買	試用後再購貨	试用后再购货
봉투에	封筒に貼られた	未從信件上分離的郵票	未从信件上分离的邮票
일	一	一	一
뒷면에	裏側	反面	反面
주문용지	注文用紙	定購單	定购单
원래의	最初の	原版	原版
원호	製造時の糊	原始膠	原始胶
가쇄	加刷	加蓋	加盖
포장	小包み	包裹	包裹
페어	一対	雙	双
전지	切手シート	小全張	小全张
종이	紙	紙	纸
소포우편	小包郵便	包裹郵政	包裹邮政
소포우표	小包用切手	包裹票	包裹票
계도	-----	持有人家譜	持有人家谱
벗기다	はがす	撕下	撕下

ENGLISH	RUSSIAN	SERBIAN
pen cancelled	гашеный вручную	поништено руком
People's Republic of China (P.R.C.)	Китайская Народная Республика	Народна Република Кина
percé	пробивка (*f.*)	точкић са зупцима
perfect	идеальный	савршен; потпун
perforated	перфорированный	перфориран
perforation	зубцовка (*f.*)	перфорација (*f.*)
Peru	Перу	Перу
peseta	песета (*f.*)	песета (*f.*)
peso	песо (*n.*)	пезо (*m.*)
philatelic	филателистический	филателијски
philatelist	филателист (*m.*)	филателиста (*m.*)
philately	филателия (*f.*)	филателија (*f.*)
phosphor	фосфор (*m.*)	фосфор (*m.*)
phosphorescent	светящийся	фосфоресцентан
photogravure	фотогравюра (*f.*)	фотогравура (*f.*)
pin perforation	точечная перфорация (*f.*)	игласта перфорација
pope	папа (*m.*)	папа (*m.*)
portrait	портрет (*m.*)	портрет (*m.*)
Portugal	Португалия	Португалија; Португал
postage	почтовая плата (*f.*)	поштарина (*f.*)
postage due	почтовый сбор (*m.*)	неплаћена поштарина
postage due stamp	марка почтовой оплаты (*f.*)	марка за неплаћену поштарину
postage stamp	почтовая марка (*f.*)	поштанска марка (*f.*)
postal card	почтовая карточка (*f.*)	дописница (*f.*)
postcard	открытка (*f.*)	разгледница (*f.*)
postman	почтальон (*m.*)	поштар (*m.*)
postmark	почтовый штемпель (*m.*)	поштански печат (*m.*)
post office	почта (*f.*)	пошта (*f.*)
pound Sterling (£)	фунт стерлингов (*m.*)	фунта (*f.*)
precancel (*noun*)	почтовая пометка на марке доплаты	марка поништена пре употребе
prepayment	аванс (*m.*)	претплата (*f.*)
president	президент (*m.*)	председник (*m.*)
price	цена (*f.*)	цена (*f.*)
price list	прейскурант (*m.*)	ценовник (*m.*)
print (*verb*)	печатать	штампати
propaganda stamp	пропагандистская марка (*f.*)	пропагандна марка

KOREAN	JAPANESE	CHINESE [c.c.]	CHINESE [s.c.]
펜으로 말소한	ペンで抹消された	筆注銷	笔注销
중화인민공화국	中華人民共和国	中華人民共和國	中华人民共和国
선공	ルーレット	騎縫孔	骑缝孔
완전한	完全	完整	完整
천공의	目打ちのある	壓上齒孔的	压上齿孔的
천공	目打ち	齒孔	齿孔
페루	ペルー	秘魯	秘鲁
페세타	ペセタ	西班牙幣	西班牙币
페소	ペソ	披索	披索
우표수집의	切手研究の	集郵的	集邮的
우표수집가	切手収集家	集郵者	集邮者
우표수집	切手収集	集郵	集邮
형광체	燐	燐	磷
인광성의	燐光を発する	燐光的	磷光的
그라비야	フォトグラビア	凹版印刷	凹版印刷
단선 천공	ピン目打	針形牙孔	针形牙孔
그 황	ローマ法王	擂威者	权威者
초상	肖像	肖像	肖像
포르투칼	ポルトガル	葡萄牙	葡萄牙
우편요금	郵便料金	郵資	邮资
미납우편표	料金不足	欠資	欠资
미납우표	不足料金用切手	欠資郵票	欠资邮票
우표	郵便切手	郵票	邮票
우편엽서	郵便ハガキ	郵政明信片	邮政明信片
그림엽서	ハガキ;絵ハガキ	風景明信片	风景明信片
우체부	郵便配達人	郵差	邮差
소인	消印	郵戳	邮戳
우체국	郵便局	郵局	邮局
파운드	ポンド	英磅	英磅
선소인	プリキャンセル	預蓋銷票	预盖销票
선불	前払い	預支	预支
대통령	大統領	總統	总统
가격	価格	價格	价格
가격표	価格表	價目表	价目表
인쇄하다	印刷する	印刷	印刷
선전우표	宣伝用の切手	宣傳票	宣传票

ENGLISH	RUSSIAN	SERBIAN
protective reserve bid	резервная цена (*f.*)	гарантована понуда (*f.*)
provisional (*noun*)	марка доплаты (*f.*)	привремена марка
punch cancellation	гашение компостером	поништење марке рупицама
quadrillé	кляссер (*m.*)	ишпартанн лист албума
queen	королева (*f.*)	краљица (*f.*)
rare	редкий	редак; раритет
rarity	раритет (*m.*)	реткост (*f.*); раритет (*m.*)
receipt	квитанция (*f.*)	признаница (*f.*)
rectangular	прямоугольный	правоугаони
Red Cross	Красный Крест (*m.*)	Црвени Крст
registration stamp	наклейка заказной почты (*f.*)	налепница на препорученом писму
regummed	перегуммированный	поново премазан лепком
remainder	остатки (*m.pl.*)	опомена потсетник
repaired	отреставрированный	поправљен
reprint (*noun*)	перепечатка (*f.*)	ново издање (*n.*)
reproduction	репродукция (*f.*)	репродукцнја (*f.*); умножавање (*n.*)
republic	республика (*f.*)	република (*f.*)
Republic of China (Taiwan)	Республика Китай; Тайвань	Република Кина; Тајван
right (direction or position)	правый	десно
roulette	пробивка (*f.*)	точкић са зупцима
rouletted	пробитый	прећи точкићем са зупцима
round	круглый	округао; обао
Russia	Россия	Русија
Saudi Arabia	Саудовская Аравия	Саудијска Арабија
scarce	дефицитный	оскудан; редак
Scotland	Шотландия	Шкотска
secret mark	потайной знак (*m.*)	тајни знак (*m.*)
sell (*verb*)	продавать	продати; продавати
seller	продавец (*m.*)	продавац (*m.*)
separation	разделение (*n.*)	одвајање
September	сентябрь	септембар
serpentine roulette	извилистая пробивка (*f.*)	разрез у облику «s»
serrated roulette	зубчатая пробивка (*f.*)	перфорација рупицама
se-tenant	сцепка (*f.*)	скуп разноврсних марака
seven	семь	седам
seventy	семьдесят	седамдесет

KOREAN	JAPANESE	CHINESE [c.c.]	CHINESE [s.c.]
최저 응찰가	安全のための最低値	保留投標值	保留投标值
잠용우표	暫定切手	區域票	区域票
천공소인	パンチ孔	牙銷	牙销
앨범대지	格子縞	有方形標記的集郵頁	有方形标记的集邮页
여왕	女王	皇後	皇后
진기한	珍しい	少有的	少有的
진품	珍品	稀罕	稀罕
영수증	領収書	收據	收据
직사각형의	長方形の	長方形	长方形
적십자	赤十字	紅十字	红十字
등기우편 딱지	書留用切手	掛號條	挂号条
재풀칠한	再度糊付けした	重新塗膠的	重新涂胶的
재고	在庫品	逾期失值的郵票	逾期失值的邮票
수선된	直した	修好的	修好的
재쇄	再版	加印	加印
복제품	複製	復制，仿造	复制，仿造
공화국	共和国	共和的	共和的
중화민국	台湾；中華民国	中華民國	中华民国
오른쪽	右	右	右
선공	ルーレット	騎縫孔	骑缝孔
선공의	ルーレット	帶有騎縫孔的	带有骑缝孔的
둥근	丸い	圓形	圆形
러시아	ロシア	俄國	俄國
사우디아라비아	サウジアラビア	沙烏地阿拉伯	沙特阿拉伯
드문	珍しい；稀な	稀少	稀少
스코틀랜드	スコットランド	蘇格蘭	苏格兰
비문	秘符	暗標	暗标
팔다	売る	賣	卖
매도인	売り手	賣主	卖主
분리	分離	分隔	分隔
구월	九月	九月	九月
S 자형 선공	蛇紋型ルーレット	蛇狀騎縫孔	蛇狀骑缝孔
지그재그 선공	-----	鋸齒形牙孔	锯齿形牙孔
연쇄	連刷	相鄰成組的郵票	相邻成组的邮票
칠	七	七	七
칠십	七十	七十	七十

ENGLISH	RUSSIAN	SERBIAN
shade (*re*: color)	оттенок (*m.*)	нијанса (*f.*)
sheet (of stamps)	марочный лист (*m.*)	табак (*m.*)
silk thread	шёлковая нить	свилена нит (*f.*)
six	шесть	шест
sixty	шестьдесят	шездесет
skinned spot	утончение (*n.*)	мрљица (*f.*)
small	маленький	мален; ситан
South Africa	Южная Африка	Јужна Африка
souvenir sheet	сувенирный листок (*m.*)	комеморативна серија марака
Soviet Union (U.S.S.R.)	Советский Союз (С.С.С.Р.)	Совјетски Савез
Spain	Испания	Шпанија
specimen	пробный образец (*m.*)	узорак (*m.*); примерак (*m.*)
square (*adjective*)	квадратный	четвртаст
stain	пятно (*n.*)	мрља (*f.*); вар (*m.*)
stamp (postage)	почтовая марка (*f.*)	поштанска марка (*f.*)
star	звезда (*f.*)	звезда (*f.*)
steel engraving	гравирование по стали (*m.*)	гравирање руком (*f.*)
stock remainder	остатки (*m.pl.*)	залиха непродатих марака
strip (of stamps)	полоска (*f.*)	ред нераздвојених марака
suggested bid	предлагаемая цена (*f.*)	почетна понуда (*f.*)
surcharge	доплата (*f.*)	додатна цена
surtax	благотворительный налог (*m.*)	додатна цена
Sweden	Швеция	Шведска
Switzerland	Швейцария	Швајцарска
symbol	символ (*m.*)	симбол (*m.*)
syncopated perforation	прерывистая перфорация (*f.*)	непотпуна перфорација
tagged stamp	меченая марка (*f.*)	светлуцава марка
tax (*noun*)	налог (*m.*)	порез (*m.*); тарифа (*f.*)
tear (*noun*)	разрыв (*m.*)	поцепотина (*f.*)
tear (*verb*)	разрывать	цепати; поцепати
telegraph stamp	телеграфная марка (*f.*)	марка за телеграм
ten	десять	десет
tenth (*noun*)	десятая часть (*f.*)	десетина (*f.*)
tête-bêche	тет-беш (*m.*)	тет-беш
thin spot	утончение (*n.*)	мрљица (*f.*)
third (*noun*)	третья часть (*f.*)	трећина (*f.*)

KOREAN	JAPANESE	CHINESE [c.c.]	CHINESE [s.c.]
색조	色の濃淡	濃淡	浓淡
시이트	シート	全張	全张
명주실	絹糸	絲紋	丝纹
육	六	六	六
육십	六十	六十	六十
엷게된 부분	-----	郵票被撕薄處	邮票被撕薄处
적은	小さい	小	小
남아프리카	南アフリカ	南非	南非
소형시이트	小型シート	小型張	小型张
소련	ソビエト社会主義共和国連邦	蘇聯	苏联
스페인	スペイン	西班牙	西班牙
견본	見本	樣張	样张
네모난	正方形の	方形的	方形的
얼룩	汚れ；シミ	汙點	污点
우표	郵便切手	郵票	邮票
별	星	星	星
강판조각	-----	鋼蝕制版	钢蚀制版
재고	在庫品	逾期失值的郵票	逾期失值的邮票
스트립	ストリップ	一連	一连
제안 입찰가	参考値	建議投標值	建议投标值
첨쇄	特別付加料金	加蓋票	加盖票
부가금	付加税	附加税	附加税
스웨덴	スエーデン	瑞典	瑞典
스위스	スイス	瑞士	瑞士
상징	象徴；シンボル	標記	标记
불연속 천공	中断された目打	不連續牙孔	不连续牙孔
발광성 우표	-----	熒光郵票	荧光邮票
세금	税金	税	税
찢어진 틈	裂け目	撕破處	撕破处
찢다	破る	撕破	撕破
전신우표	電信切手	電報票	电报票
십	十	十	十
십분의 일	十分の一	十分之一	十分之一
도치이언	テート・ベッシュ	對倒票	对倒票
엷게된 부분	-----	郵票被撕薄處	邮票被撕薄处
삼분의 일	三分の一	三分之一	三分之一

ENGLISH	RUSSIAN	SERBIAN
thirty	тридцать	тридесет
thousand	тысяча (*f.*)	хиљада
three	три	три
tongs	пинцет (*m.*)	пинцета (*f.*)
top	верх (*m.*)	врх (*m.*)
topical; thematic	тематический	марке са истим мотивом
torn	порванный	покидан
trade (*verb*)	обмениваться	продати; трговати
twenty	двадцать	двадесет
two	два	два
typography	книгопечатание	типографија (*f.*)
unattributed	неидентифицированный	неопредељен
undeliverable	недоставляемый	неуручљиво
ungummed	без клея	без лепила
unhinged	без наклейки	одвојена марка
unique	уникальный	јединствен
United Kingdom (U.K.)	Великобритания	Уједињено Краљевство
United States of America (U.S.A.)	Соединенные Штаты Америки	Сједињене Америчке Државе
unknown	неизвестный	непознат
unofficial	неофициальный	неслужбени; незваничан
unpublished	неопубликованный	необјављен
unsevered	нерасцепленный	неодвојен
unused	неиспользованный	неупотребљаван
used	бывший в употреблении	употребљаван
valuable	ценный	скупоцен
value	ценность (*f.*)	вредност (*f.*)
variety	разновидность (*f.*)	разноликост (*f.*)
Venezuela	Венесуэла	Венецуела
Wales	Уэльс	Велс
watermark	водяной знак (*m.*)	водени жиг (*m.*)
West Germany (B.R.D.)	Западная Германия	Западни Немачка
wove paper	веленевая бумага (*f.*)	папир за штампање марака
year	год (*m.*)	година (*f.*)
Yugoslavia; Jugoslavia	Югославия	Југославија
zero	нуль (*m.*)	нула
zigzag roulette	зазубренная; зубчатая пробивка (*f.*)	прорез у облику зиг-заг

KOREAN	JAPANESE	CHINESE [c.c.]	CHINESE [s.c.]
삼십	三十	三十	三十
천	千	千	千
삼	三	三	三
우표집게	ピンセット	郵票鉗	邮票钳
정상	上	上面	上面
주제별	シリーズ切手	同類郵的	同类邮的
찢어진	裂けている	撕破的	撕破的
서로교환하다	交換する	交易	交易
이십	二十	二十	二十
이	二	二	二
요판	活版印刷	印刷式樣	造币厂记
출처불명의	分類しない	未經確定的	未经确定的
배달불능	配達不能	無法遞送的	无法递送的
풀이없는	のりなし	無背膠的	无背胶的
힌지가 안붙은	ヒンジなし	未貼過郵票透明紙的	未贴过邮票透明纸的
유일한	唯一の	唯一的	唯一的
영국	英国	英國	英国
미국	米国；アメリカ合衆国	美利堅合眾國	美利坚合众国
미지의	知られていない	不知的	不知的
비공식의	非公式の	非官方的	非官方的
미발행의	未発行の	未公開發行的	未公开发行的
붙어있는	離されていない	未經分離的	未经分离的
미사용의	未使用	新票	新票
사용제의	使用済みの	使用過的	使用过的
값진	価値のある	有價值的	有价值的
가치	価値	價值	价值
변종	バラエティー	多種	多种
베네수엘라	ベネズエラ	委内瑞拉	委内瑞拉
웨일즈	ウェールズ	威爾斯	威尔斯
투문	すかし	透明花紋	透明花纹
서독	西ドイツ	西德	西德
-----	無地紙	布紋紙	布纹纸
년	年	年	年
유고슬라비아	ユーゴスラビア	南斯拉夫	南斯拉夫
영	ゼロ	零	零
지그재그 선공	ジグザグルーレット	鋸齒形牙孔	锯齿形牙孔

ENGLISH	RUSSIAN	SERBIAN
amber	янтарный	боја ћилибара
azure	лазурный	азурно плав
bister	тёмно-коричневый	мрк
black	чёрный	црн; мрк
blue	синий	плав; плаветан
bronze	бронзовый	боја бронзе
brown	коричневый	браун
carmine	карминный	кармин
cerise	светло-вишнёвый	боја трешње
cobalt	кобальтово-синий	кобалт
crimson	малиновый	загаситоцрвен
emerald	изумрудный	смарагдни
gray	серый	сив
green	зелёный	зелен
heliotrope	тёмно-синий	хелиотропска
indigo	фиолетовый	индиго
lavender	бледно-лиловый	боја левандуле
lemon	лимонный	боја лимуна
lilac	сиреневый	боја јоргована
magenta	пурпурно-красный	пурпурноцрвен
maroon	темно-бордовый	кестењаст
olive	оливковый	маслинаст
orange	оранжевый	наранџаст
pink	розолвый	ружичаст
Prussian blue	берлинская лазурь	дубоко плав; пруско плав
purple	лиловый	љубичаст
red	красный	црвен; румен
royal blue	ярко-синий	краљевско плаво
sapphire	темно-синий	сафирно плав
scarlet	алый	скарлетан; љубичасто црвен
turquoise	бирюзовый	плава боја као драги камен
ultramarine	ультрамариновый	азуран; азурноплав
vermilion	ярко-красный	крмез; отвтрено црвена боја
violet	фиолетовый	љубичаст
white	белый	бео
yellow	жёлтый	жут

KOREAN	JAPANESE	CHINESE [c.c.]	CHINESE [s.c.]
호박색	琥珀色	琥珀色	琥珀色
담청색	空色	天藍色	天蓝色
고동색	ビスタ色	褐色	褐色
흑색	黒い	黑	黑
청색	青い	藍	蓝
청동색	ブロンズ色	青銅色	青铜色
다갈색	茶色	棕色	棕色
양홍색	カルミン色；洋紅色	洋紅色	洋红色
담홍색	さくらんぼ色	粉紅色	粉红色
암청색	コバルト色	鈷藍色	钴蓝色
심홍색	クリムゾン色；深紅色	深紅色	深红色
선녹색	エメラルド色	翡翠色	翡翠色
회색	灰色	灰色	灰色
녹색	緑	綠色	绿色
연보라색	薄紫色	淡紫色	淡紫色
남색	藍色	靛藍色	靛蓝色
연보라색	藤色	薄紫色	薄紫色
레몬색	レモン色	檸檬色	柠檬色
엷은자색	薄紫色	淡紫色	淡紫色
자홍색	マゼンタ色	紫紅色	紫红色
적갈색	えび茶色	褐紅色	褐红色
올리브색	オリーブ色	橄欖色	橄榄色
오랜지색	オレンジ	橘色	桔色
연분홍색	ピンク	粉紅色	粉红色
감청색	にぶ青色	深藍色	深蓝色
자주색	紫	紫色	紫色
적색	赤い	紅色	红色
선명한 보라색	藤紫色	紫色	紫色
청옥색	サファイヤ色	青玉色	青玉色
주홍	赤色	非紅色	非红色
청록색	青緑色	藍綠色	蓝绿色
감청색	群青色	深藍色	深蓝色
주색	朱色	朱紅色	朱红色
보라색	すみれ色	紫羅蘭色	紫罗兰色
백색	白い	白色	白色
황색	黄色	黄色	黄色

Bibliography

Amick, George *The Inverted Jenny: Mystery, Money, Mania.* Sidney, OH: Amos Press, 1986.

Barat, *Le Nouveau "Bleus de France,"* 1976.

Black, C. F. "A Quizzical Look at Canada," *Canadian Philatelist*, May-June 1983, pp. 154-5.

Boughner, Fred. "Postage due stamps oulive usefulness," *Linn's Stamp News*, August 25, 1986, p. 53.

Breen, Walter. *Complete Encyclopedia of U.S. and Colonial Coins.* New York: F.C.I. Press Inc. (Doubleday), 1988.

Brown, Cohn, & Walske, *New Studies of the Transport of Mails in Wartime France, 1870-71*, 1986.

Brown, Ruth & Gardner. *The Bordeaux Issue of 1870-1871*, published by the France & Colonies Philatelic Society.

Cabeen, Richard McP. *Standard Handbook of Stamp Collecting.* New York: Thomas Y. Crowell Company, 1965.

Carlton, R. Scott. "A Philatelic Travelogue," *Global Stamp News*, November 1990, pp. 28-31.

Catálogo de sellos— Brasil 86. São Paulo, Brazil: Editora RHM Ltda., 1986.

Catalogo Enciclopedico Italiano, section on "Fiume."

Cirlot, J. E. *A Dictionary of Symbols* (2nd Ed.). New York: Philosophical Library, 1983.

Chanaryn, V. *The Posts of France in the Franco-German War of 1870-1871,* 1976.

Cohn, *The Flight of the "Ville d'Orleans,"* 1978.

— "The 'Papillons' of Metz," *Congress Book*, No. 33, 1967.

— and Cyril Harmer. "Metz Papillons: George T. Robinson's Airmail of 1870." American Philatelic Congress. Vol. 39, September 28-30, 1973.

"Dans la Côte d'Ivoire," *L'Écho de la Timbrologie*, 30 juin 1930 (no. 828).

Dehn, Roy A. "The Postal History of Fiume" ("*Fiume Storia Postale*"), serialized in *Il Nuovo Corriere Filatelico*, Florence, Italy, 1981.

Dietz Confederate State Catalog, The Dietz Press, 1959.

Esrati, Stephen. "Spies on Stamps," *Canadian Philatelist*, January-February 1984, pp. 36-38.

"For the Record," *France & Colonies Philatelist*, whole no. 171 (vol. 34, no. 1), pp. 13-14.

Funk & Wagnalls Guide to the World of Stamp Collecting. New York: Thomas Y. Crowell, 1978.

Funk & Wagnalls New Encyclopedia, 1984.

Gabbini, Emanuele M. *Storia Postale de Zara*, Edizioni Nico.

Galicich, Anne. *Samantha Smith: A Journey for Peace.* Minneapolis, MN: Dillon Press, Inc., 1987.

Grossman, Samuel. *Stamp Collecting Handbook*. New York: Grossman Stamp Company, 1957.

Hines, Ed. "Know the lingo, and collecting gets easier." *Stamp Collector*. January 20, 1997, p. 9.

Hotchner, John M. "Modern postage due stamps very collectible," *Linn's Stamp News*, January 19, 1987, p. 6.

Hornung, Otto. *The Illustrated Encyclopedia of Stamp Collecting*. London: Hamlyn Publishing Group Limited, 1970.

"Isle of Man: Pearl Black Crown Bridges Numismatics and Philately," *The Numismatist*, October 1990, pp. 1554-6.

"The Ivory Coast 1919-20 Emergency Currency, Made from Stamps," *France & Colonies Philatelist*, whole no. 64 (vol. 11, no. 4), front page.

"Ivory Coast," *Scott's Monthly Journal*, March 1925, p. 3.

"Ivory Coast Stamp Money," *The Stamp Collectors' Fortnightly*, June 21, 1947

Janton, H. *L'Écho de la Timbrologie*, avril-mai 1974, (nos. 1443-1444).

"Jean de Sperati: Master Forger," *The Philatelic Foundations Quarterly*, Vol. 8, No. 1, January-March 1990.

Joany, Storch, Brun, & Françon, *Timbres-Poste au Type Sage*, Amiens, 1980.

John, Eric (editor). *The Popes: A Concise Biographical History*.

Kandaouroff, Prince. *Collecting Postal History*, Larousse, New York, 1973.

Kramer, *French Philatelic Facts*, 1949, (first of a series of little booklets published 1949-51; reprinted as Billig *Handbook*, Vol. 29, undated.

Kraemer, James E. "Indicator Markings on Canadian Metered Mail," *Canadian Philatelist*, May-June 1985, pp. 190-4.

Krause, Barry. "Triangles help make collecting interesting," *Stamp Collector*, April 28, 1997, p. 5.

Kylling, Preben. *Filatelistisk Fremmedordbog*. Helsingør, Denmark: Kylling & Søn, 1978.

"Les Coloniaux françaises sur papier couché," *L'Écho de la Timbrologie*, no. 735 (15 août 1926).

Lewy, Edgar. "The 1984 *Europa* Bridge Design," *American Philatelist*, April, 1985, pp. 330-356.

Lidman, David and John D. Apfelbaum. *The World of Stamps & Stamp Collecting*. New York: Charles Scribner's Sons, 1981.

Lievsay, John E. "What's In a Name?" *Opinions II*, Philatelic Foundation, 1984.

Lindholm, John. "Three Skillings— And nearly three million Swiss francs," *The Posthorn*, November 1996, pp. 147-9.

Linn's World Stamp Almanac. Sidney, OH: Amos Press, 1978.

Ludin, E. *The Zara Stamps and their Forgeries*.

Madesker, Michael. "The *Admiral* Booklets of Canada," Part 1, *Canadian Philatelist*, March-April 1985, pp. 108-124; et al.

— "The *Scroll* Booklets of Canada," *Canadian Philatelist*, January-February 1986, pp. 37-46.

Martin, Marc. "The Hulot Plates of France," *France & Colonies Philatelist*, No. 156, April 1974.

McGuire, C. R. "Canada Mourns Her Monarch," *Canadian Philatelist*, May-June 1984, pp. 215-221, and July-August 1984, pp. 278-294.

Meyer, K.F. *Disinfected Mail*.

Michon, André. "Côte d'Ivoire 1892-1944, un Demi-Siècle de Variétés," *Le Monde des Philatélistes*, #401 (Octobre 1986), pp. 76-78.

Migliavacca, Giorgio. "A Concise Introduction to the Stamps and Postal History of the Italian Post Offices in China," *Philatelic Shopper*, Vol. I, No. 1, June 1992.

— "British Virgin Islands: Stamps and Postal History of the Reign of King George VI," *Second Annual B.V.I. Philatelic Exhibition.*

— "The magic of West Indian stamps: Rarity and Beauty," *Liat Islander* (London/Antigua), #35, May 1995, pp. 27-30.

— "The plague letter plot of 1499," *Pratique*, Vol. VI, #3.

— "Russian Health Practices of Disinfecting Mail Received from Infected Zones," *Postal History Journal*, February 1975.

— *The Stamps of Somalia and their Story*, 1997.

National Postal Museum. "Mail Arrangements for Prisoners of War and Internees Held in Canada During World War II," *Canadian Philatelist*, Part 1: November-December 1982, pp. 345-356; Part 2: January-February 1983, pp. 16-21.

O'Keefe, Donna [Editor]. *Linn's Stamp Identifier*. Sidney, OH: Amos Press, 1995.

Pickering, Vernon. *Early History of the British Virgin Islands, from Columbus to Emancipation*. Milan/New York: Falcon Publications, 1983.

Purves, J. R. W. "Victoria: The 'Butterfly' and 'Barred Oval' Cancellations, 1850-1855." Royal Philatelic Society of Victoria. 1965.

Reiche, Hans. "Thoughts About a *Weeping Princess*," *Canadian Philatelist*, March-April 1985, pp. 106-7.

Robertson. "The Sperati Forgeries," *The Philatelic Foundations Quarterly*, Vol. 8, No. 1, January-March 1990.

Shenfield, Lawrence L. *Confederate States of America: The Special Routes*. The Collectors Club, 1961.

Smithsonian World: Voices of Latin America (script of television program), WETA (Washington, DC) & Smithsonian Institution, 1987.

Stone, Lauson H. "Yugoslavia Postal History During World War II," *Postal History Journal*, #81-83.

Stone, Robert G. "*Flammes Publicitaries*: Slogan and Commemorative Cancels of the French Colonies, Union, and Overseas Departments," *France & Colonies Philatelist*, whole no. 111 (vol. 20, no. 4), pp. 25-27, 32.

— "French Colonies, 1892-1910: The Allegorical Group Type (Commerce and Navigation)," *The Congress Book*, 1962.

— "Notes on the Usage of the Allegorical Group Type Stamps of French Colonies," *France & Colonies Philatelist*, whole no. 147 (vol. 28, no. 1), pp. 7-8.

— "French Colonies: The Allegorical Group Type— Some Further Notes," *France & Colonies Philatelist*, whole no. 118 (vol. 21, no. 1), pp. 2-5.

— "The Palms Stamps (*Palmiers*) of French West Africa," *France & Colonies Philatelist*, whole no. 147 (vol. 28, no. 1), pp. 5-6.

— "*Papier Couché*— The Chalky-paper Varieties of the French Colonies, 1915-24," *France & Colonies Philatelist*, whole no. 176 (vol. 35, no. 2), pp. 41-43.

Stone, Robert G. and Edward Grabowski, "Collecting the Frehcn Colonies Group Type ("Navigation & Commerce")," *American Philatelist*, June 1984, pp. 618-32.

Sutton, R. J. *The Stamp Collector's Encyclopædia*. Philosophical Library (a division of Crown Publishers, Inc.), 1964.

Valbuena Briones, Angel. *Historia de la literatura española*, Vol. V: "Literatura hispanoamericana." Barcelona, Spain: Editorial Gustava Gili, S.A., 1969.

van Doren, Charles (editor), *Webster's American Biographies*.

"Vichy Air Mails Were Postally Used in French West Africa Before 1951," *Western Stamp Collector*, June 22, 1954, pp. 3-4.

Walthouse, Richard G. *All Nations Stamp Finder and Dictonary*. Chicago, IL: Harold Cohn & Co., Inc., 1980.

Webster's New World Dictionary. 2nd Collegiate ed. Cleveland, Ohio: The World Publishing Company, 1976.

Wellsted, W. Raife; Stuart Rossiter; John Flower. *The Stamp Atlas*. New York: Facts on File Publications, 1986.

White, Duncan M. (ed.). *Caesar to Churchill: The Years of Fulfillment (1783-1965)*. New York: Roy Publishers, 1969.

Whitney, David C. (ed.). *Founders of Freedom in America*. J. G. Ferguson Publishing Company.

Williams, L. N. "The mystery of the Missing Virgin," in *Stamps*, London, August 1987, vol. 4, no. 4, pp. 37-39.

— and M. Williams. *Rare Stamps: Pleasures and Treasures*. London: Weidenfeld and Nicolson, 1967.

Wilson, John and Nancy. "United States Postage and Fractional Currency." *The Centinel*, Vol. 28, No. 3, Fall 1980, pp. 15-28.

Winick, Les. *The White Ace Postage Stamp Identifier*. Florham Park, NJ: The Washington Press, 1984.

Wood, Kenneth A. *Basic Philately*. Albany, Oregon: Van Dahl Publications, 1984.

— *This Is Philately*. Albany, Oregon: Van Dahl Publications, 1982.

Work of Jean de Sperati, The. Two volumes. British Philatelic Association, London, 1955.

Wozniak, Maurice D. "U.S. wants its inverts back," *Stamp Collector*, December 30, 1996, pp. 1 & 23.

Youngblood, Wayne L. "What new options do self-sticks offer?" *Stamp Collector*, April 21, 1997, p. 5.

Yvert. *Catalogue Specialisé des Timbres de France*, Vol. 1, 1975.

Contributing Scholars

The author wishes to express his appreciation to the following distinguished scholars for their outstanding technical assistance. Without their efforts, this encyclopædic dictionary would not have been possible.

H. L. Arnould
Princeton, New Jersey
Selected topics

Kauko I. Aro
[A.P.S. Translation Committee]
Belleville, New Jersey
Finnish language

Stewart and Marie Bailey
[American Philatelic Society]
Cincinnati, Ohio
Philatelic research

Faith H. Barnett
Ohio Dept. of Human Services
Cuyahoga Falls, Ohio
Public assistance certificates

Peter L. Bergh
[A.P.S. Translation Committee]
Colorado Springs, Colorado
Scandinavian languages

Joseph E. Boling
Federal Way, Washington
Japanese language

Mercer Bristow
American Philatelic Society
State College, Pennsylvania
Philatelic research

Hoang Bui
[Berlitz Translation Service]
San Francisco, California
Vietnamese language

Dmytro Bykovetz, Jr.
[Chairman, A.P.S. Translation Committee]
Melrose Park, Pennsylvania
Translation assistance

Achilles Cambanis
Athens, Greece
Greek language

Halbert Carmichael, Ph.D.
North Carolina State University
Raleigh, North Carolina
Chemistry

Mário de Castro Hipólito, Ph.D.
Fundação Calouste Gulbenkian
Lisbon, Portugal
Portuguese language

Lynn Chen
Colorado Springs, Colorado
Chinese language

Louise Chouinard
Queen City Coins & Stamps
Lafayette, Georgia
Research assistance

James J. Cleary, Jr.
Jersey City, New Jersey
German language

John S. Colonias, Ph.D.
[A.P.S. Translation Committee]
Jackson, Mississippi
Greek language

Richard Corwin
[American Philatelic Society]
San Diego, California
United States philately

Richard Crum, Ph.D.
Berlitz Translation Service
Woodland Hills, California
General translation services

Frank Daniëls
Managing Director, *La Poste*
Brussels, Belgium
Dutch language

Ruth Ann Davis
Hancock County Schools
Weirton, West Virginia
Latin language; biographies

Thomas "Chuck" Diezi
Harris County Engineering Department
Houston, Texas
Drawings and sketches

Susan C. Dixon
A.P.S. Library
State College, Pennsylvania
Library services

Hüseyin Doğan & Yonca Poyraz-Doğan
[Texas Tech University (Lubbock, Texas)]
Istanbul, Turkey
Turkish language

Wim Dykshoorn
[A.P.S. Translation Committee]
Beach Park, Illinois
Dutch language

Sanae Eda
[Ohio State University (Columbus, Ohio)]
Okayama, Japan
Japanese language

Diana C. Fabiano
Buffalo, New York
Serbo-Croatian language

Albert A. Feldmann
[American Translation Association]
Seattle, Washington
Hebrew language

Barbara J. Fraize
[A.P.S. Translation Committee]
Reston, Virginia
German language

Erika Garami, Ph.D.
National Bank of Hungary
Budapest, Hungary
Hungarian language

Jean Baptiste Giard
Bibliothèque Nationale
Paris, France
French language

Nick Gluschenko
Krasnodar, Russia
Russian language

John Groot
Grand Rapids, Michigan
Dutch language

Flemming L. Hansen
Gentofte, Denmark
Danish language

Greg Herbert, D.V.M.
Owings, Mills, Maryland
Selected topics

Karl Hnilicka, Ph.D.
Chicago, Illinois
German language

W. Timothy Hunter
Cincinnati, Ohio
Research assistance

Amiteshwar Jha
Indian Institute of Research
Maharashtra, India
Hindi language

Donald H. Kellander
[A.P.S. Translation Committee]
Pittsburgh, Pennsylvania
French language

Stanley S. Kim
[A.P.S. Translation Committee]
Oakland, California
Korean language

Ole-Robert Kolberg
Central Bank of Norway
Oslo, Norway
Norwegian language

William V. Kriebel
[Brazil Philatelic Association]
Philadelphia, Pennsylvania
Portuguese language

Simcha Kuritzky
[American Numismatic Association]
Silver Spring, Maryland
Judaic Studies; Hebrew language

Jan Peter Lamm
Historiska Museet
Stockholm, Sweden
Swedish language

John E. Lievsay
[American Philatelic Society]
Old Greenwich, Connecticut
Selected topics

Jacopo M. Madaro Moro, Ph.D.
[American Translation Association]
East Boston, Massachusetts
Italian language

Pamela Makricosta
Mary H. Weir Public Library
Weirton, West Virginia
Biographies

Steve Markowitz
Gamma Productions, Inc.
San Diego, California
Multi-Lingual Scholar
  word processing software

Yvon Marquis
Bic, Québec
French language

Very Rev. Dr. Mateja Matejič
Hilander Room, Ohio State University
Columbus, Ohio
Slavic languages

Robert Mattson
Postal Museum
Stockholm, Sweden
Swedish language

Marta Męclewska
Zamek Królewski w Warszawie
Warsaw, Poland
Polish language

W. E. Melberg, Ph.D., & Florence Melberg
[Scandinavian Collectors Club]
Allenton, Wisconsin
Danish language

Giorgio Migliavacca
Tortola, British Virgin Islands
Italian colonies; Italian language

Miriam S. Mirasol
[Berlitz Translation Service]
Fairfax, Virginia
Tagalog language

Eugen Nicolae
Institutul de Arheologie
Bucharest, Romania
Romanian language

Michael S. Niddam
[American Translation Association]
Washington, D.C.
French and Spanish languages

James Oliver
London, England
Selected topics

Pinar T. Ozand, M.D., Ph.D.
King Faisal Research Center
Riyadh, Saudi Arabia
Middle Eastern languages

Carita Parker
[A.P.S. Translation Committee]
Stow, Ohio
Finnish language

Robert E. Picirilli
[American Philatelic Society]
Nashville, Tennessee
French colonies

Very Rev. Slobodan Prodanovich
St. George "Lazarica" Church
Midland, Pennsylvania
Slavic languages

Consuelo Rodríguez Selles
Fábrica Nacional de Moneda y Timbre
Madrid, Spain
Spanish language

Bilha Ron
Temple Israel
Canton, Ohio
Judaic Studies; Hebrew language

Salih Sari, Ph.D.
Yarmouk University
Irbid, Jordan
Arabic language

Zvi Shimony, Ph.D.
Postal History of Eretz-Israel
Jerusalem, Israel
Hebrew language

Tuukka Talvio
National Museum of Finland
Helsinki, Finland
Finnish language

Jian Tang
[A.P.S. Translation Committee]
Chicago, Illinois
Chinese language

Jörg Tautenhahn
[A.N.A. Translation Service]
Feldberg, Germany
German language

George V. Tomashevich, Ph.D.
State University College at Buffalo
Buffalo, New York
Serbo-Croatian language

Mel Wacks
[Magnes Museum]
Torrance, California
Judaic Studies

James R. Wilson
Computer Services Associates
North Ridgeville, Ohio
Computer and word processing expertise

John and Nancy Wilson
[American Numismatic Association]
Milwaukee, Wisconsin
Postage currency

Tin Win
[Berlitz Translation Service]
Houston, Texas
Burmese language

Yakov Zeltser
Brooklyn, New York
Russian language

Martin Zwart, Ph.D.
[A.P.S. Translation Committee]
Park Forest, Illinois
Dutch language